Rule and Ruin

RULE AND RUIN

The Downfall of Moderation and the
Destruction of the Republican Party

From Eisenhower to the Tea Party

Geoffrey Kabaservice

OXFORD
UNIVERSITY PRESS

OXFORD
UNIVERSITY PRESS

Oxford University Press

Oxford University Press, Inc., publishes works that further
Oxford University's objective of excellence
in research, scholarship, and education.

Oxford New York

Auckland   Cape Town   Dar es Salaam   Hong Kong   Karachi
Kuala Lumpur   Madrid   Melbourne   Mexico City   Nairobi
New Delhi   Shanghai   Taipei   Toronto

With offices in

Argentina   Austria   Brazil   Chile   Czech Republic   France   Greece
Guatemala   Hungary   Italy   Japan   Poland   Portugal   Singapore
South Korea   Switzerland   Thailand   Turkey   Ukraine   Vietnam

Copyright © 2012 by Geoffrey Kabaservice

Published by Oxford University Press, Inc.
198 Madison Avenue, New York, NY 10016

www.oup.com

Library of Congress Cataloging-in-Publication Data
Kabaservice, Geoffrey M.
Rule and ruin : the downfall of moderation and the destruction of the Republican Party,
from Eisenhower to the Tea Party / Geoffrey Kabaservice.
p.   cm.
Includes bibliographical references and index.
ISBN 978-0-19-976840-0 (hardcover : alk. paper) 1. Republican Party (U.S. : 1854–)
2. United States—Politics and government—1945–1989.
3. United States—Politics and government—1989– I. Title.
JK2356.K33   2012
324.2734—dc22   2011016422

9 8 7 6 5 4 3 2 1

Printed in the United States of America
on acid-free paper

To my sister,
Marah Michele Kabaservice

"All things in moderation, including moderation."
—attributed to Petronius

CONTENTS

ACKNOWLEDGMENTS

Some books flow so easily from the author's mind to the page that they seem almost to write themselves. This was not one of those books. It was written under extremely trying circumstances, and every aspect of its development has been difficult. My work has not been supported or subsidized by any institution or political organization, so I have been as independent as an independent scholar can be. But this book never would have appeared if not for the assistance of many people over the past six years.

My thanks go first of all to the men and women I interviewed, including several who did not wish to be identified, whose recollections allowed me to piece together the largely unwritten history of the moderate Republican movement. I am particularly grateful to Bill Bagley, Bruce Chapman, Bill Frenzel, Howard Gillette, Lee Huebner, Steve Livengood, John McClaughry, Tanya Melich, and Mike Smith for their patience in working with me on repeated occasions to see that I got my facts straight, though of course our interpretations are bound to differ.

I greatly relied on assistance from the librarians, archivists, and staff at the dozens of libraries and historical societies I visited. I especially appreciate the help I received at the libraries of Cornell and Georgetown universities, the American Library of Paris, Yale's Manuscripts and Archives Library, and the Madison Building at the Library of Congress (despite its architectural shortcomings). I thank those who granted me access to collections not available to the general public, including John B. Anderson, Edward W. Brooke, Christopher Buckley, William F. Buckley Jr., John C. Danforth, and William A. Rusher. My thanks also to the generous people who shared privately held documents, unpublished papers, and other materials that otherwise would have been difficult or impossible to obtain, including Christopher Bayley, Jason Bezis, Don Bliss, Ron Boster, Bruce Chapman, William Coleman, Martha Grant, Bill Gradison, David Hamstra, Amo Houghton, Andrew Kilberg, Charles McC. Mathias, John McClaughry, Tanya Melich, Kevin Michel, Jim Reichley, Mike Smith, Edith Sontag, William R. Steiger, Peter Viereck, and Charles Whalen. Steve

Livengood belongs in a special category of praise for saving much of the Ripon Society's archives from destruction.

I was fortunate to be offered a visiting assistant professorship in history at Yale University in 2007–08. I am thankful to Cynthia Russett for suggesting me for the position and to my students there, who were a joy to advise and teach. Thanks as well to Pietro Nivola and Strobe Talbott of the Brookings Institution for providing access to the library and scholars of that estimable organization. Some of the biographical profiles in this book appeared in their earliest form on the website www.FrumForum.com, and I am deeply grateful to Danielle and David Frum for their interest in my work and for providing an opportunity to share it with their online audience.

I appreciate the assistance and sympathy of my agent, Michael Carlisle, and of my friend Donald Lamm, with whom I discussed this book at its earliest stages. I thank Steven Teles, the editor of this series, for his unflagging interest and support. My editor, David McBride, improved the manuscript in manifold ways and provided invaluable historical perspective. So did Sarah Hammond, whose brilliant and perceptive comments made me laugh, furrow my brow, and rethink. Jonathan Moore's suggestions on my sections dealing with George Romney were extremely helpful. Thanks also to David A. Bell for allowing me to present an early version of Chapter 2 to the Johns Hopkins University History Department, to Timothy Thurber for useful advice, and to my fellow panelists at the Policy History Conference in June 2010 for their feedback on a portion of Chapter 6.

A legion of friends helped keep me from going under throughout the grueling process of completing this manuscript. I never would have made it if not for the support of Bill Beinecke, Heather Chase, Sarah Hammond, Manfred and Andrea Huterer, Jo Miller, and Ann Mulrooney. During the past several years in the Washington, D.C. area, I have benefited mightily from the friendship and hospitality of J. J. Barkas, Linda and Simon Carney, Sarah Collins, Jackie and Tony Dobranski, Sherri and Wil Etheredge, Anais and Tim Hughes, Ann Kammerer, Gretchen and Bruce Kirby, Jennifer and Charles Kirchmaier, Christine and John Millett, and Agata and Christopher Williams. Further afield, I am most grateful to Emily Artinian and James Smith, Brian Bell, Tracy Benedict, Alicia Ching, Courtney Davis, Jake Dell, Sheila and David Fieldhouse, Marja and Fergal Gaynor, Soli and Ken Goodall, Aliina Hirschoff, Jonathan Holloway, Tim Hutton, Steve Isenberg, David Koistinen, Elizabeth and Charley Krawczyk, Elizabeth Letcher, Huiping Pang, Alisa Plant, Tina Reyes, Marco Rosenbaum, Sophie and Justin Shubow, Sebastian Sotelo, and Allan Soave. Thanks also to LCH for incentive and the Elizabethan Club for tea.

I owe everything to my parents, Marcia and Thomas Kabaservice. My sister Marah, to whom this book is dedicated, has always been my favorite conversationalist and encourager. Jesse and Ted have been a pleasure to have as brothers. Political opinions in my family run the gamut from the left to the right and points between. If we can argue politics and still remain close, perhaps there's hope that the vast, feuding family of the American people can do the same.

PREFACE

When I was doing research for this book, I spent a considerable amount of time in the Library of Congress, which is on Capitol Hill in Washington, D.C. The library actually is made up of three different structures: the Jefferson Building, constructed in the 1890s; the Adams Building, from the 1930s; and the Madison Building, from the 1970s. If a visitor from another planet who knew nothing of the United States were asked to extrapolate the country's history from these three government buildings, the alien likely would hypothesize a sad story of national decline. The Jefferson Building is a magnificent edifice, with dazzling décor and a dome to rival the Capitol's. The mosaics and paintings that adorn the interior, mostly allegories on the progress of knowledge and world culture, seem to be the product of a strong, prosperous, and confident civilization. The Adams Building, plainer and more functional, suggests a nation reduced in circumstances yet retaining some style and spirit, evident in the structure's jazzy Art Deco flourishes. But the hideous and windowless slab of the Madison Building, with its drab rooms and bleak, undecorated corridors, could only be the work of an impoverished society fallen under the yoke of a mindless and brutal dictatorship.

In reality, of course, the United States became the most powerful nation on earth over the course of the twentieth century, and remains the world's largest economy and leading military force. But as the country enters the second decade of the new millennium, there is an uneasy sense among many Americans that while their society and culture remain vibrant, their governing system has become quarrelsome, dysfunctional, and incapable of coping with serious national problems. Politics is the area where a narrative of American decline, a descent from splendor to squalor, seems most plausible. Political discourse has become vicious and even violent. The representatives of the Republican and Democratic parties appear unable to collaborate to reduce the gargantuan national debt, rebuild the country's crumbling infrastructure, cope with the rising cost of health care, or rejuvenate an educational system that increasingly lags behind the rest of the developed world. Bitter battles over partisan advantage have replaced measured consideration of the national interest. The failures of the public sector threaten to drag down the private sector as well.

During the past decade, I have spoken with a lot of ordinary citizens about U.S. politics. Most of them believe that America's government ought to reflect what they think of as our national characteristics of balance, prudence, responsibility, tolerance, wise judgment, and common sense. Why, they wonder, have the country's politics become so extreme, antagonistic, uncompromising, and ineffectual? How have politics come unmoored from what once was called the Vital Center?

While there are many possible reasons to explain the present American political dysfunction, the leading suspect is the transformation of the Republican Party over the past half-century into a monolithically conservative organization. Throughout American history, the two principal political parties—whether those parties were Federalists and Whigs or Democrats and Republicans—had been coalitions of interest rather than ideological vehicles. The Republican Party as recently as the 1960s had contained large numbers of moderate and even liberal representatives. The form of conservatism that now wholly controls the party did not even exist until the 1950s, and remained a minority faction for many years afterward.

At the present moment, when the Republican Party has adopted a near-uniform posture of opposition to the Democratic Party and its agenda, contemporary observers can be forgiven for believing that Republicanism has always been identical with conservatism. In fact, the appearance of a Republican Party almost entirely composed of ideological conservatives is a new and historically unprecedented development. It is only in the last decade or so that movement conservatism finally succeeded in silencing, co-opting, repelling, or expelling nearly every competing strain of Republicanism from the party, to the extent that the terms "liberal Republican" or "moderate Republican" have practically become oxymorons. To state this proposition is not necessarily to criticize. But the gradual elimination of the party's internal diversity is a fact that cries out for historical explanation and analysis, which most political histories have not thus far provided.

There is a fairly well developed scholarly corpus of works on the origins and growth of modern conservatism and its impact on the Republican Party.[1] But these histories do not directly address the existence, impact, and disappearance of moderate Republicanism. Nor for the most part do historians of the Democratic Party, or political historians generally, take into account the moderate Republicans' role in programs and legislation passed from the 1930s through the 1990s.[2] The underlying assumption of many analyses of the period is that for historic reasons some members of both parties found themselves ideologically misplaced, with northern liberals in the Grand Old Party and southern conservatives in the Democratic Party, but that a more natural political ordering reasserted itself in the 1960s.

In fact, moderate Republicanism was a separate political and ideological viewpoint that found adherents in all parts of the country, among members of all racial and ethnic groups, and along all points of the socioeconomic spectrum. It overlapped on some issues with liberals, on others with conservatives, and on still others with neither. Historians who overlook the often-significant role of moderate Republicans in the twentieth century are left with a misleading view of modern American political development.

Ever since the Republican Party had formed in the 1850s, it had moderate and conservative factions, and their struggles against each other as well as against the Democrats defined the internal history and evolution of the party. Prominent Eastern moderates of the mid-twentieth century, such as Massachusetts Senator Henry Cabot Lodge Jr., could make a plausible claim to be the spiritual as well as lineal heirs of the original Republican Party founders, but so too could prominent Midwestern conservatives such as Ohio Senator Robert Taft. Journalist Theodore H. White likened the moderate and conservative factions to fratricidal twins, and at times the quarrels between them were bitter indeed.[3] Still, the shared Republican heritage of leaders like Lodge and Taft had usually helped to keep the conservatives in the fold even when the moderates controlled the party, and vice versa. So too did the dictates of political pragmatism and considerable common ground on issues such as fiscal policy and pro-business sentiment.

During the 1950s, a new breed of conservatism, which became known as the New Right, developed in reaction to President Dwight Eisenhower's brand of political moderation which, at the time, appeared to dominate the GOP. Journalists for the most part failed to take these new conservatives seriously, treating them as anachronisms attempting to revive a horse-and-buggy philosophy that was laughably unsuited to the complexities of the Space Age. Beneath the level of media scrutiny, however, the New Right was changing the nature of American politics by bringing conservatives together in a political movement. The attributes of movement conservatism included the powerful sense of cause offered by Senator Joseph McCarthy's anti-Communist crusade, the collaboration of intellectuals such as William F. Buckley Jr. and Russell Kirk to redefine conservatism as a coherent ideology, the appearance of magazines such as *National Review* to provide a forum and rallying point for conservatives, and the establishment of networks and organizations at the grassroots level to recruit like-minded individuals.[4] The immediate goal of movement conservatism was to seize the GOP's presidential nomination by taking over party organizations and the forums in which national convention delegates were chosen. The longer-term goal was to transform the Republican Party into an organ of conservative ideology and purge it of all who resisted the true faith. Moderate Republicans were the primary enemies and targets of movement conservatism. The need to do battle with Democratic liberals often was only a secondary consideration.

This history of the struggles between moderates and conservatives in the Republican Party opens with the 1960 GOP national convention, which marked the first time that the New Right entered the Republican political scene in a significant way. It was also the last moment when moderates exercised anything close to dominance of the party. Eisenhower-style moderation might have held the stage if Richard Nixon had won the 1960 presidential election. As it turned out, the period from 1960 to 1964 witnessed the conservatives' capture of most of the Republican Party machinery, culminating in the nomination of Arizona Senator Barry Goldwater as the 1964 GOP presidential candidate. Goldwater and his supporters set the tone for the conservative movement ever after by mobilizing a base of right-wing populists, refusing to compromise with moderates, and pursuing a Southern strategy aimed at attracting civil rights opponents to the GOP.

In response, a new generation of Republicans attempted to create a moderate movement to counter the conservative movement as well as to provide a winning alternative to the Democrats. In the wake of Goldwater's disastrous defeat, moderate Republicans staged furious efforts to retake control of the party. Moderate intellectuals defined their ideology in magazines such as *Advance*, organized around causes such as civil rights and opposition to the war in Vietnam, and formed think tanks and pressure groups such as the Ripon Society. Volunteers and party workers promoted the presidential candidacies of moderates such as William Scranton, Nelson Rockefeller, and George Romney. Activists struggled against neofascists and dirty tricksters in the Young Republicans organization, which brought them up against budding conservative masterminds such as Lee Atwater and Karl Rove. Republican feminists contended with the likes of Phyllis Schlafly in the National Federation of Republican Women. Moderate Republican politicians attempted to coordinate their efforts and maximize their political leverage through factional efforts in Congress and in new organizations such as the Republican Governors Association. Some of their allies included young politicians who later would switch sides and become prominent conservatives, including Dick Cheney, Newt Gingrich, Mitch McConnell, and Donald Rumsfeld. Out of the bitter struggles of this era came the forces that continue to warp and distort modern politics.

The 1960s was the pivotal decade for the moderate Republican movement, and most of this book focuses on the issues, episodes, and personalities of that decade. The moderates' focus shifted to Washington after Richard Nixon's election in 1968, when many leading moderate activists entered the government. The moderate movement faltered at the end of the decade, undermined by the ambiguous successes it achieved under Nixon's presidency as well as its own internal difficulties. A critical mass of moderate Republican politicians remained in office after 1970, although their numbers dwindled, and moderate ideas continued to have some influence on the GOP's positions. In the years after Ronald Reagan's election in 1980, however, the moderates did not simply die out, but were killed off by conservative enmity from within their own party as well as Democratic opposition and their own failures. The first decade of the twenty-first century witnessed the final decline and virtual extinction of moderates' power and representation in the Republican Party.

There remain millions of voters who define themselves as moderate Republicans, and millions more who would vote for moderate Republican candidates if they could find them. But the complete domination of the conservative infrastructure in party politics, and the absence of moderate efforts to counter grassroots movements like the Tea Party, means that the GOP has for all intents and purposes become a uniformly ideological party unlike any that has ever existed in American history. It has also become a party that has cut itself off from its own history, and indeed has become antagonistic to most of its own heritage. This unprecedented transformation of one of our major parties is likely to change our entire political system in ways that ought to concern all Americans.

Conservatives used to accuse their moderate opponents of pursuing a "rule or ruin" policy in Republican politics, preferring defeat to a party controlled by conservatives. In fact, it was the conservatives who typically took a rule-or-ruin approach. Goldwater's warning to moderates at the '64 GOP national convention that they had to support "extremism in the defense of liberty" or leave the party was a classic expression of rule-or-ruin politics. So too were the conservative efforts to purge moderate Republican officeholders, even at the cost of replacing them with liberal Democrats.

The pursuit of absolute rule gave the conservatives control of the Republican Party, but it also destroyed the party's ability to govern. The result was rule *and* ruin. Admittedly, a conservative-ruled GOP took back the House in the 2010 elections and may well retake the Senate and the presidency in 2012. But conservatives had always been much better at winning elections than at making policy. Historically, moderates had provided much of the brains of the GOP and made it an effective governing party. In some cases, their ideas and influence even helped to reshape conservatism, and made it a more realistic and powerful creed. The marginalization of the moderates actually hamstrung conservatives' ability to pass conservative policies.

Most of the moderate Republicans' story has never been written. I have based my history on oral history interviews and research from over a hundred archival collections around the United States. I looked at low-level activists and organizers as well as politicians, and at conservatives as well as moderates. I had to cast my net wide because no one source, or group of sources, could reveal the totality of political events during the period. Many developments and events had to be pieced together from fragmentary information collected from scattered archives and personal recollections. Many of the documents were hard to find and difficult to use. Most of the Ripon Society's archives, for example, had sat in a basement on Capitol Hill for a quarter-century, gathering mold and beetles and possum urine. The sad state of the documents enhanced the sense that this was a political movement that history had treated unkindly. The book's chapter titles are derived from William Butler Yeats' poem "The Second Coming," which for almost a century has been the classic expression of moderate foreboding.

The moderate Republicans have to be counted among history's losers, but this is not a history without heroes. The moderates' example may prove instructive and even inspiring in an economically straitened and politically polarized era.

Rule and Ruin

CHAPTER 1

⌒∿⌒

The Widening Gyre

The Republican Party at the 1960 Convention

At 8:50 P.M. on the evening of July 28, 1960, great cascades of brightly colored balloons drifted slowly down from the ceiling of the Chicago International Amphitheatre onto the crowd assembled below for the Republican national convention.[1] The balloons landed on a Republican Party so unlike the one we have now that it may as well have been an entirely different party, a lost Republican Atlantis. The contrasting nature of the party in 1960 is not evident from old photographs and newsreels of the convention. Most of the delegates were men, although women made up one-quarter of the delegation, which was a record for any party to that point. Nearly all of the delegates were white, although a sprinkling of black faces attested to many African-Americans' longstanding loyalty toward the party that had been founded in 1854 to oppose slavery. Delegates represented every state in the union, although in reality the party had almost no representation in the South, an enduring consequence of Republican president Abraham Lincoln's defeat of the Confederacy in the Civil War. What the photographs do not capture, however, is that in 1960 moderates were still a major part of the coalition that made up the Grand Old Party. Outgoing President Dwight Eisenhower—who undoubtedly could have been reelected to a third term if it had been constitutionally permissible—was only the most prominent of the many moderate Republicans who held power in the party. Few at that time would have predicted the GOP's slow and painful transformation over the next half century into an organization entirely dominated by ideological conservatives.

The majority of the delegates happily swatting and popping balloons would have considered themselves to be Republicans plain and simple, rather than liberals or moderates or conservatives. Indeed, many Americans at that time were unsure what those terms even meant, or what relevance they had to party politics. The Democratic Party, usually considered to be the more "liberal" party, derived much of its strength from its monopoly of the racially segregated South, and Southern Democrats were the most conservative element in Congress. The Republican Party, though considered to be the party of small government, had laid the groundwork for modern society through such active-government achievements as abolishing slavery, opening up public lands in the West for settlement by homesteaders, chartering the first transcontinental railroad, and establishing a national banking system and the land-grant colleges. Republican administrations had also reformed civil service, passed the first conservation legislation, and created the rudiments of a social welfare safety net.

The 1950s had been a decade defined by broad political consensus, and most Americans' political identities were determined by factors other than ideology. Both the Republican and Democratic parties included in their ranks representatives from a wide range of viewpoints and opinions, and the important political debates played out within the parties as well as between them. Many political observers thought that American parties' existence as coalitions of interest pragmatically seeking power, rather than more ideologically pure parties like those of Europe and Latin America, had saved the United States from succumbing to extremist ideologies like Communism and Nazism or the rule of caudillos. "No America without democracy, no democracy without politics, no parties without compromise and moderation," political scientist Clinton Rossiter pronounced in the opening of his 1960 book *Parties and Politics in America*.[2] The proper functioning of American democracy, in this view, required that each political party contain a critical mass of moderates. But the clash between the moderate and conservative wings of the Republican Party had caused strife and bitterness virtually from the party's inception, and this legacy of conflict was evident even in the tribal pageantry of the 1960 convention.

The history of moderate-conservative divisions was on the minds of those gathered in the International Amphitheatre, partly because the Republican convention was being held in Chicago for the fourteenth time.[3] Chicago's Republican conventions over the previous century had featured some memorable intra-party battles. The 1960 convention was called to order with the same gavel that had been used at the 1860 convention, in a long-vanished meeting hall called The Wigwam, which nominated Abraham Lincoln for the presidency. The party had been born only six years earlier, in 1854, when the Whig and Democratic parties had split over the issue of slavery, and the new Republican Party was cobbled together from Free Soilers, Conscience Whigs, Free Democrats, and even members of the nativist and anti-Catholic Know-Nothings. The 1868 convention in Crosby's Opera House, which nominated Civil War hero Ulysses Grant, pitted Radical Republicans who demanded a thoroughgoing Reconstruction of the defeated South against Liberal Republicans who counseled a more lenient approach. By 1880, the divisions at the Chicago convention were between "Half-Breeds"—moderates who favored civil service reform—against "Stalwarts" who supported traditional machine politics. The Republican Party's growing identification with business and industrial wealth, and the accompanying corruption of the Gilded Age, led to a split at the 1884 convention in Chicago between the supporters of corruption-tainted presidential nominee James G. Blaine and the good-government reformers known as the Mugwumps; many of the latter defected to the Democrats after Blaine's nomination and helped deliver the election to Grover Cleveland.[4]

The Chicago Coliseum—still standing on Wabash Avenue in 1960—was the site of several early twentieth century Republican convention battles between conservatism and what became known as progressivism, a wide-ranging reform movement that attempted to grapple with the problems of modern industrial society. Theodore Roosevelt, the most dynamic of the Republican progressives, was the presidential nominee at the 1904 convention. Roosevelt had become president in 1901 after the assassination of William McKinley, and had already established his reputation as a trust-buster and conservationist. William Howard Taft, TR's successor as the 1908 GOP nominee, supported a more business-oriented version of progressivism. By 1912, Roosevelt and other progressive insurgents had turned against Taft and the conservative Old Guard of the party. The progressives walked out of the convention and formed the Progressive Party, popularly known as the Bull Moose Party. The Progressive nominee Roosevelt drew more votes than the Republican candidate Taft in the 1912 presidential election, but the winner was Democrat Woodrow Wilson. By the 1916 Republican convention (also in the Chicago Coliseum), Roosevelt and some of his followers had returned to the GOP fold. Many other progressives had swung over to the Democratic Party for good, however, and Wilson was reelected in large part by appealing to these disgruntled former Republicans.[5]

For the 1960 Republican conventioneers, the Bull Moose breakaway a half-century earlier was an event receding into history, as distant to them as 1960 is to Americans today. But the 1912 bolt lingered uneasily in the Republican Party's collective memory, as a reminder that the most progressive Republicans had an alternative in the Democrats and might cross parties if pushed too far. Vice President Richard Nixon, the putative Republican presidential nominee in 1960, was well aware of the GOP's troubled history of intra-party divisions, and of the continuing threat of a bolt by the party's liberals. Nixon's sensitivity to historical resonances was evident in his refusal of the suite assigned to him at Chicago's Blackstone Hotel; Suite 408–10 had been the original "smoke-filled room," in which the Republican bosses in 1920 had designated the little-known Warren G. Harding as the party's presidential nominee over the vociferous protests of the progressives.[6] Other conventioneers with long memories could recall the continuing dissent from progressives throughout the 1920s and beyond, particularly from a bloc of mainly Western Republican senators known derisively as "The Sons of the Wild Jackass." Robert LaFollette of Wisconsin and George Norris of Nebraska led the opposition to the GOP's dominant conservatives and spoke out against the power of monopoly, inherited wealth, and vested interests. In 1925, the House Republican leadership had deprived thirteen members of their committee assignments as punishment for supporting LaFollette's Progressive Party presidential bid the year before.[7]

The 1960 convention featured an address by eighty-five year-old Herbert Hoover, the Republicans' only living ex-president, who was returning to the city in which he had been renominated for the presidency at the 1932 convention. Hoover had supported the Bull Moose Party in 1912 and carried some aspects of the progressive tradition into his presidency.[8] But most Americans in 1960 knew him as the president on whose watch the country had plummeted into the miseries of the Great Depression. The Republican Party's fortunes crashed along with the economy, and the party was almost liquidated in the elections from 1930 to 1936, losing 40 Senate seats and 182 House seats. Franklin D. Roosevelt was four times elected president and formed an indomitable political coalition to support the social welfare reforms of the New Deal. For decades afterward, Democrats continued to run against the memory of Hoover's presidency and the disastrous results to which unfettered capitalism and Republican rule inevitably would lead—or so the Democrats claimed.

The convention applauded Hoover politely, but the majority of Americans did not want to return to the old Republican orthodoxy of high tariffs, low taxes, and permissive regulation for business and the wealthy, and the near-complete absence of a government social safety net. Alf Landon, the GOP's nominee in 1936, had echoed the charges of conservative groups like the American Liberty League that the New Deal, particularly in its expansion of government power and encouragement of unionization, was a tyrannical attempt to impose Communism or fascism on the country. The virulence of these charges created a backlash that handed the GOP its worst-ever defeat in both the presidential and Congressional elections, igniting a renewed moderate-conservative struggle for party leadership.

The champion of the conservatives from the mid-'30s was Ohio Senator Robert Taft, the son of President William Howard Taft and a three-time unsuccessful contestant for the Republican presidential nomination. Balding, bespectacled, mackerel-eyed, and usually clad in old-fashioned three-piece suits, Taft embodied the WASPy Midwestern conservatism of the first half of the twentieth century. He inherited the uprightness, ambition, intelligence, and belief in rugged individualism and free enterprise that had defined the Taft family since his grandfather settled in Cincinnati in 1839. Like his forebears, he was a staunch Republican regular, opposed to reform efforts within the party, and he shared the characteristic Midwestern mistrust of Easterners, foreigners, and Wall Street. Even before his Senate election, Taft was the spearhead of opposition to Franklin Roosevelt and the New Deal, which he found wrongheaded, wasteful, arbitrary, autocratic, unconstitutional, and dangerous. "If Mr. Roosevelt is not a Communist today," he warned in 1936, "he is bound to become one."[9]

Taft won election to the Senate in 1938 along with seven other Republicans, while the GOP took 81 seats in the House, a rebound made possible by a severe economic downturn and Roosevelt's overreaching attempt to dilute the Supreme Court's conservatism by enlarging its membership with liberal appointees. Taft became a leader of the so-called conservative coalition in Congress, an informal working alliance of conservative Northern Republicans and conservative Southern Democrats. The Republicans acceded to the Southerners' blockage of civil rights legislation, while the Southerners bolstered the Republicans' efforts to lower taxes, restrict unions, and reduce government spending on social needs. Throughout the '40s and into the '50s, Taft and his Democratic counterpart, Georgia's Richard Russell, controlled the Senate "with a wink and a nod," as Texas Senator Lyndon Johnson put it.[10]

Although Taft's opponents habitually portrayed him as the blackest of reactionaries, "Mr. Conservative" didn't have much in common with what has come to be the current version of conservatism. Taft was a religious man, but religion played little role in politics at that time. He shunned populism, and while he disliked liberal intellectuals he respected intellect. During one of Taft's reelection campaigns, the senator's wife was asked at a rally whether her husband was a common man. "Oh no," she is said to have retorted, "he is not that at all. He was first in his class at Yale and first in his class at Harvard Law School. I think it would be wrong to present a common man as representative of the people of Ohio." The political professionals blanched, but the crowd gave the Tafts a standing ovation.[11] Above all, while Taft had certain deeply held principles, he was not bound by ideology. When confronted with an issue, his response was not to consult polls or conservative tablet-keepers, but to study the issue, obtain as much relevant information as possible, and only then arrive at his own conclusions.

For this reason, Taft was not the uncompromising scourge of liberalism that many imagined. Taft was no laissez-faire conservative and opposed bigness in business as well as in government and labor. He recognized that parts of the New Deal were legitimate responses to real needs, and he tried to offer social welfare alternatives more in keeping with Republican ideals of small government, sound finance, and local responsibility. He supported government-funded old age pensions, medical care for the indigent, an income floor for the deserving poor, unemployment insurance, and an increased minimum wage. Because he believed that a home was necessary for a decent family life, and because the free market was not supplying low-cost housing, he advocated urban slum clearance and public housing. Because he believed that all children deserved an equal start in life, he reversed his earlier position and called for federal aid to education. Because he did *not* believe in deficit financing, he was willing to raise taxes to pay for these needed measures. As his brother Charles recalled, Taft was "an innovator of the first class in a number of welfare fields, going beyond what the Democrats had the courage to talk about in those days."[12]

In keeping with the Midwestern isolationist tradition, Taft abhorred the military draft, which he associated with totalitarianism, and was the main opponent of a wider international role for the United States. Though disdainful of Hitler and the Nazis, in 1940 and 1941 he preferred that the country stay out of World War II rather than accept the large, activist, intrusive government that total war would require. He believed that, horrible as the victory of Nazi Germany in Europe would be, the death and bankruptcy and socialism that war would bring to the United States would be worse. After the war, he supported the United Nations and the World Court though not the Nuremburg trials, which he thought violated international law. Though a firm anti-Communist, he did not believe that the effort to contain the Soviet Union required a full-fledged Cold War, which he saw as a ploy to internationalize and institutionalize the New Deal. He became sharply critical of the military buildup, increased presidential power, and overseas involvement accompanying the conflict, which to Taft smacked of imperialism. He did not adhere to bipartisanship in foreign affairs, believing that the opposition's role was to oppose. He voted against the establishment of the North Atlantic Treaty Organization (NATO) and the International Monetary Fund (IMF), tried to cut funding for the Marshall Plan for postwar European reconstruction, and blasted what he called the "tendency to interfere in the affairs of other nations, to assume that we are a kind of demi-god and Santa Claus to solve the problems of the world."[13]

Taft's quixotic critique of a U.S. global role has continued to appeal to dissenters from the bipartisan foreign policy consensus, whether New Left-ists in the 1960s or Ron Paul libertarians in the twenty-first century. But foreign policy for Taft was always a distraction from his main interest in domestic policy. His thinking on international affairs was uncharacteristi-cally muddled, contradictory, and even Oedipal, given his father's moderate internationalism and support of globalists like Henry Stimson, who was secretary of war under both the elder Taft and FDR. Much of Taft's extreme isolationism stemmed from intense partisanship as well as his reluctance to adapt to a changing world.

Taft's anti-internationalism was the primary factor in his defeat at the hands of Eastern moderate factions in the Republican presidential conven-tions in 1940, 1948, and 1952. He lost the 1940 nomination to Wendell Willkie, an Indiana-born, internationalist Wall Street maverick who was one of the darkest of dark horses ever to win a presidential nomination. Willkie died of a heart attack in 1944, and the Republican convention in Chicago that year turned to New York Governor Thomas Dewey, the short, dynamic moderate who did more than anyone else to shape the Republican response to Franklin D. Roosevelt's New Deal.

When Tom Dewey addressed the 1960 Republican convention, the loudest cheers came from the New York and Michigan delegations. Dewey first rose to prominence as an East Coast crime-fighter, serving as special prosecutor with a mandate to combat corruption in New York City, but he had been born and raised in small-town Owosso, Michigan. This hybrid background was part of his success. Dewey made national headlines with his racket-busting exploits, and his fame helped him win the New York governorship in 1942, in the process reviving a nearly moribund state Republican Party. Dewey served three terms as governor of what was then the nation's largest state, and became the rallying point for moderates in the GOP partly because he was one of the few Republicans able to win in heavily urban and historically Democratic areas. His primary appeal was to middle-class pro-fessionals attuned to the need for social reform and an internationalist for-eign policy, but who were uncomfortable with the Democratic Party's reliance on corrupt city machines and Southern racists. At the same time, Dewey's heartland background attracted many Americans who usually mis-trusted Eastern metropolitan Republicans.

Unlike the Old Guard conservatives of the Midwest and the rural and small-town districts of the East who continued to dominate what little remained of the Republican representation in Congress in the '30s and early '40s, Dewey believed that the Depression had permanently reshaped the political landscape. It was futile, he thought, for Republicans simply to denounce the New Deal and hope in vain for the eventual disappearance of the welfare state. As Dewey said in his first gubernatorial address, "There has never been a responsible government which did not have the welfare of its people at heart. . . . [A]nybody who thinks that an attack on the fundamental idea of security and welfare is appealing to people generally is living in the Middle Ages."[14] As governor, he put forward social programs that included unemployment insurance, sickness and disability benefits, old age pensions, slum clearance, state aid to education (including the creation of the State University of New York), infrastructure projects (particularly highway construction), and pathbreaking anti-discrimination legislation.

Dewey attempted to distinguish his programs from similar Democratic programs by running a government that was acknowledged to be clean, honest, and efficient. He managed to implement his social programs while cutting taxes, reducing the state debt by over $100 million, yet still achieving budget surpluses. He also argued that while Republicans and Democrats might agree on social ends, the parties would differ in their means, with moderate Republicans emphasizing individual freedom and economic incentive over centralization and collectivization. This relatively sophisticated position inevitably opened Dewey to conservative gripes that he was a "me-too" Republican, cloaking liberal programs in conservative rhetoric, and Democratic claims that he was offering a lesser version of the genuine article.

No one could credibly charge that "the Gangbuster" was a softie. The toughness and even ruthlessness that he had exhibited while prosecuting mobsters carried over into his administration and contributed greatly to his political effectiveness. Dewey also displayed a skill for organization that most moderates lacked, and he was able to use his New York business and legal connections to build an effective national network within the GOP. After his expected wartime loss to FDR in the 1944 election, Dewey's network helped him to overcome Taft on his right and Minnesota Governor Harold Stassen on his left to gain the 1948 GOP presidential nomination. Running against the lightly regarded former Vice President Harry S. Truman, who had ascended to the presidency after FDR's death in April 1945, Dewey followed his pollsters' advice by taking a high-road approach to preserve his frontrunner status. Contrary to later allegations, he did defend the record of the GOP-controlled 80th Congress, and pointed out that the Republicans whom Truman attacked as "do-nothing" had supported the president's Cold War internationalist program, including the Marshall Plan, the Truman Doctrine, and the Vandenberg Resolution that opened the way to the NATO and other regional defensive alliances. But

Dewey's failure to counter Truman's slashing attacks, or to exploit the Democrats' potential vulnerability on the issue of Communism, cost him the election. It's perhaps significant that no other presidential contender since Dewey has worn a mustache, which made him look, in Clare Boothe Luce's cruel but memorable phrase, "like the little man on top of the wedding cake."

Dewey's defeat seemingly opened the way for Taft to gain the GOP nomination at long last. The conservative position also appeared to be strengthened by the right-wing movement led by Wisconsin Senator Joseph McCarthy, who made headlines in February 1950 with a speech in Wheeling, West Virginia in which he claimed to have a list of 205 known Communists employed by the State Department. In fact, McCarthy's movement constituted a new political force within the Republican Party, one that was very different from the Old Guard faction around Taft. Anti-Communism was a common trope of all politicians in that era, but McCarthy stood out for his ends-justify-the-means crusade against alleged domestic subversion. "McCarthyism" became a shorthand description for his shameless willingness to lie and engage in character assassination, his disregard for civil liberties, his cynical manipulation of the public and the media, and his scorn for traditional standards of decent conduct.

At times, McCarthy's anti-Communism was a secondary theme to his brawling, almost anarchistic attack on established authority. His explanation for the "loss" of China to the Communists in 1949, the outbreak of the Korean War in June 1950, and other foreign policy reversals was that the United States was run by a traitorous elite: the richest, best educated, most advantaged men and women in the country, who secretly wanted the Communists to win. The epitome of these treasonous elitists was Yale-and-Harvard-educated Secretary of State Dean Acheson, whom McCarthy in his Wheeling speech called "this pompous diplomat in striped pants, with a phony British accent."[15] One of McCarthy's moderate critics observed his unerring hatred for the nation's region of oldest settlement (the East), its founding document (the Constitution), its most upper-crust religion (Episcopalianism), its most prestigious university (Harvard), its most decorated and paternal generals (particularly George Marshall), and "the oldest, most rooted, and most deeply educated patrician families."[16] Not coincidentally, McCarthy targeted the class and region that produced many prominent moderate Republicans, such as Henry Stimson and Massachusetts Senator Henry Cabot Lodge Jr. The populist, anti-intellectual, treason-seeking aspect of McCarthy's conservatism, building on longstanding resentments, proved attractive to many Americans who had historically been Democrats, particularly McCarthy's fellow Catholics and members of the white ethnic working classes. Five years after McCarthy shot to national prominence, some of his followers, led by William F. Buckley Jr. and William Rusher, founded *National Review* magazine, which became the intellectual center and rallying point for the new breed of conservatism.

McCarthy divided the Republican Party, drawing most of his Congressional backing from the Old Guard and most of his critics (notably Maine Senator Margaret Chase Smith) from the moderate wing.[17] Taft viewed McCarthy as a reckless demagogue but a useful weapon to be used against the Democrats and liberal-dominated institutions like the State Department. The chilly, colorless Taft also coveted McCarthy's grassroots support and ability to fire a crowd's emotions. One Republican moderate who stumped alongside McCarthy was taken aback by the hysterical adoration of the senator's followers, who kissed his hands in teary-eyed fervor: "no politician should ever evoke that kind of response," he thought.[18] But Taft believed that the 1952 contest would be his last shot at the presidency, and that however distasteful it might be to rely on McCarthy, the support of McCarthy's movement combined with Taft's base of loyal party professionals would give him the Republican nomination.

The moderates' only hope of beating Taft was to draft retired general Dwight David Eisenhower. "Ike," as he was universally known, had become an international hero as Allied Supreme Commander during World War II. His leadership of the D-Day landings at Normandy made him one of the few men in history, along with Julius Caesar and William the Conqueror, to direct a successful invasion across the English Channel. Since Eisenhower had never registered a party affiliation as a military officer, leading figures in both parties begged Eisenhower to seek the presidential nomination in 1948. Notwithstanding his internationalism, however, the general was conservative on many domestic issues, particularly the need for balanced federal budgets and limited government, a viewpoint that derived from his small-town Kansas boyhood and his military service. While he mistrusted what he considered to be the fiscal incontinence of Truman's Fair Deal, he also feared the isolationism of Taft and the Midwestern conservatives. Early in 1952, Eisenhower offered to remove himself from the presidential chase if Taft would endorse NATO and the principle of collective security, but Taft wouldn't agree. The moderates thus were able to persuade Eisenhower that duty demanded that he run to keep the Democrats from bankrupting the country and Taft from bringing on World War III.

Eisenhower's immense popularity and prestige, along with his generally moderate political stance, attracted huge numbers of volunteers to his campaign. Independents were particularly enthusiastic about Eisenhower, preferring him to Taft by a nearly 4-to-1 margin in a spring 1952 Gallup poll.[19] When Ike agreed to have his name placed on the ballot in the New Hampshire GOP primary in March 1952, he defeated Taft by a considerable margin. Still, Taft's command over the party apparatus seemed likely to count for more at the convention than the energy and excitement of the newcomers, or the assistance of Dewey's network of political operatives and wealthy bankrollers. Even some of Taft's admirers, however, worried that if he were the GOP nominee, media antagonism and his own lackluster campaign skills would produce a sixth consecutive presidential victory for the Democrats—an intolerable prospect.

The 1952 Republican national convention—held yet again in Chicago—was one of the most tumultuous in the party's history. Moderates and conservatives clashed over the seating of contested delegations from the South, where regulars loyal to Taft had excluded the Ike-inspired newcomers who made up the first popular Republican upsurge in the region since the Civil War. Moderates introduced a "fair play" amendment, preventing the Taft-controlled Southern delegations from voting on their own right to be seated. Taft's followers, enraged and fearful that they would be deprived of the nomination yet again, thrust forward Illinois Senator Everett Dirksen to try to shift the convention's momentum away from the moderates. Shaking a finger at Dewey, who was still identified as the leader of the moderates, the curly-haired orator threw the gathering into pandemonium by assailing the New York governor: "We followed you before and you took us down the path to defeat!" Taft's committee blasted "the same old gang of Eastern internationalists and New Dealers who ganged up to sell the Republican Party down the river in 1940, in 1944, and in 1948."[20] Nonetheless, the fair play amendment passed, costing the conservative forces the decisive margin of victory, and the "Taft can't win" argument persuaded many delegates to back the moderate candidate. Eisenhower took the nomination on the first ballot. Though Taft was gracious in defeat, many of his partisans vowed revenge on the "Eastern kingmakers" on behalf of their thrice-denied messiah.

After the high drama of the convention, the presidential election campaign was something of an anticlimax. At Dewey's suggestion, Eisenhower chose thirty-eight year-old California Senator Richard Nixon as his running mate. After Navy service in World War II and election to the House of Representatives, Nixon had established a reputation as a hardline anti-Communist with his leadership on the House Un-American Activities Committee (HUAC), particularly in his confrontations with suspected spy Alger Hiss. Nixon incurred the lifelong distaste of many liberals with his 1950 red-baiting defeat of Helen Gaghan Douglas in the California Senate race, but impressed Dewey as a centrist. "I thought he had a very fine voting record in both the House and the Senate," the moderate leader explained, "good, intelligent, middle of the road."[21] Despite Nixon's moderate credentials, his role in the campaign was principally to attack the Truman administration and Democratic presidential nominee Adlai Stevenson as soft on Communism. Nixon's mudslinging opened the high road to Ike, who pledged that he would go to Korea to inspect the military situation there, implying that he would end the increasingly unpopular war. Eisenhower won in a landslide, taking all but seven Southern states, and the Republicans gained control of both houses of Congress for the first time since the 1930 election.

The GOP in 1952 had one of the greatest campaign slogans ever: "I Like Ike." And Americans *did* like Ike, giving him an approval rating of 64 percent across his two terms.[22] Eisenhower gave Americans what the vast majority of them wanted: eight years of peace and prosperity. He visited Korea as he had promised, and determined that the terrain was unfavorable and the war essentially unwinnable unless the United States resorted to nuclear weapons. The North Koreans and Chinese Communists accepted his cease-fire offer, and the armistice remained in effect six decades later. Eisenhower refused to send troops into Vietnam to bail out the French colonial regime in their fight with the Communists under Ho Chi Minh and warned against allowing the United States to become "an occupying power in a seething Arab world," decisions that seemed prudent and even prescient in light of later U.S. foreign interventions.[23] The economy flourished under his watch, growing by 37 percent across the 1950s in real terms, with low inflation and generally low unemployment as well.[24] After the deprivation of the Depression years and the austerity of World War II, the material abundance of the decade seemed almost wondrous to many citizens. Eisenhower's carefully constructed political persona—an all-American blend of competence, warmth, reassurance, common sense, and an aura of being above politics—calmed public fears of the Communist threat and reduced the shrillness and nastiness of partisan rhetoric and debate.

Eisenhower believed that the political opinions of Americans formed a bell-shaped distribution curve, with the vast majority in the moderate middle and only a small percentage at the extremes of right and left.[25] Political scholars generally endorsed Ike's reading, and in the early 1950s they began to speak of a moderate, conformist, middle-class "consensus" that dominated the American culture. It came as no surprise, then, that the two groups that consistently criticized the Eisenhower presidency were the groups that dissented most strongly from that consensus: liberal intellectuals and the conservative movement that had coalesced around McCarthy. Liberals scorned Ike because he garbled his syntax, had boring hobbies like bridge and golf, epitomized the status quo mentality of the era, and twice defeated their witty hero Adlai Stevenson. More seriously, they charged that his disengagement allowed the continuation of McCarthy's reign of terror and the persistence of Jim Crow segregation in the South.

Eisenhower despised McCarthy, but hoped that ignoring him would deprive McCarthy of the oxygen of publicity. Behind the scenes, Eisenhower also worked to squash the renegade senator by refusing to allow him to subpoena members of the executive branch, on grounds of national security. The assertion of executive privilege set a precedent that later culminated in Nixon's Watergate debacle, but at the time it persuaded FBI head J. Edgar Hoover to stop supplying McCarthy with the clandestine documents that had been his only, flimsy supply of evidence.[26] Eisenhower's approach facilitated McCarthy's self-destruction in the Army-McCarthy hearings and subsequent Senate censure vote, without personally involving the President or tearing apart the Republican Party. McCarthy discredited the anti-Communist cause and died a broken man in 1957. Still, he remained a hero to many on the right, and his populist emphasis on internal conspiracy shaped the future development of the conservative movement.

Eisenhower's supporters argued that he did more for civil rights than liberals acknowledged. They pointed to his desegregation of Washington, D.C. and the completion of desegregation of the armed forces, his appointment of California's progressive Republican Governor Earl Warren as head of the Supreme Court, and the Court's subsequent 9–0 ruling against school desegregation in *Brown v. Board of Education*. They also cited his sponsorship of the first civil rights bill passed since Reconstruction and his deployment of the 101st Airborne to enforce school desegregation in Little Rock, Arkansas.[27] These were substantial accomplishments, but many younger moderate Republicans increasingly agreed with the liberals that Eisenhower had failed to correct a grievous national wrong by putting his power and prestige behind the civil rights cause. Eisenhower believed that he was taking the moderate course by proceeding gradually and not seeking the immediate overthrow of long-established tradition, but his inaction pointed out that sometimes moderation amounted to little more than support of the status quo, even an unjust status quo.

Eisenhower had achieved a rapprochement with Robert Taft before the 1952 election, and worked closely with the new Senate majority leader before Taft's untimely death from cancer in July 1953. Eisenhower had the support of most of Taft's Midwestern followers, but there was no such reconciliation with the conservative movement that had arisen on Taft's right. As *National Review* publisher William Rusher later reminisced to editor-in-chief William F. Buckley Jr., "modern American conservatism largely organized itself during, and in explicit opposition to, the Eisenhower Administration."[28] Conservatives had anticipated that a Republican administration would repeal New Deal programs like Social Security, slash taxes and government spending, continue to punish the Democrats for their alleged tolerance of subversives in government, repudiate the agreements FDR had reached with the Soviets at Yalta, and attempt to roll back Communist gains in Eastern Europe and Asia.

Eisenhower, however, believed that the right's agenda was impractical and irresponsible. He recognized that most Americans had come to take a limited welfare state for granted and credited some New Deal programs for the security they'd gained since the hard years of the Depression. He realized that to try to take away those gains would not be a conservative but a radical act. He warned his right-wing older brother Edgar that "Should any political party attempt to abolish social security and eliminate labor laws and farm programs, you would not hear of that party again in our political history." He added that "There is a tiny splinter group, of course, that believes that you can do these things." But "their number is negligible and they are stupid."[29] The right's ambitions in foreign policy likewise struck him as misguided and dangerous.

Eisenhower described his approach in terms such as "progressive moderation," "moderate progressivism," and "dynamic conservatism," but the description that stuck was "modern Republicanism." The phrase became popular when Arthur Larson, Eisenhower's assistant secretary of labor, published his 1956 manifesto, *A Republican Looks at His Party*. The book became a surprise bestseller, and Larson briefly served as Ike's top speechwriter. Larson positioned modern Republicanism between the ideas of 1896 (Old Guard Republican conservatism) and those of 1936 (New Deal radicalism). In Larson's view, Eisenhower was an eclectic leader who partook of the best elements of liberalism and conservatism, but came down on the center-right. Eisenhower was a genuine fiscal conservative, who balanced the budget three times in his eight years in office—the last time any president would achieve such a feat. He cut federal civilian employment by 274,000 and reduced the ratio of the national debt to the GNP, though not the absolute level of debt. He believed that economic prosperity was as important to U.S. security as its planes and weapons, and feared that unchecked deficit spending ultimately would bring an end to American democracy. Eisenhower and other modern Republicans also felt that the balance of federal-state power under Franklin Roosevelt had swung too far in the federal direction, and that decentralization rather than further centralization was both the moral and practical path.[30]

The modern Republicans considered business to be a potentially progressive force, and argued that the New Deal had been unnecessarily hostile to free enterprise. It was on this point that Larson differed most sharply with liberals such as Arthur Schlesinger Jr., who had attempted to claim the political center for the Democrats with his 1949 bestseller *The Vital Center*. Schlesinger, influenced by his reading of economic theorist Joseph Schumpeter, predicted that capitalism would commit suicide. By increasing the wealth of the rich and the poverty of the poor, monopoly capital would lay the groundwork for a socialist society. The political incompetence and short-term thinking of the business community and their Republican tools would necessitate government management of the economy.[31] Schlesinger later admitted that he had "underrated the vitality of capitalism."[32] Larson believed that the tendency of too many Democrats to win elections by attacking business disqualified that party from speaking for the American consensus.[33]

Still, the moderates' aim was to rationalize and reform the New Deal rather than repeal it. Eisenhower wrote to his first budget director that in areas such as public housing, conservation, and the extension of social security, "I should like to put ourselves clearly on the record as being forward-looking and concerned with the welfare of all our people."[34] Nor did Eisenhower believe that human needs should be sacrificed to military spending. As he said in 1953, "Every gun that is made, every warship launched, every rocket fired signifies, in the final sense, a theft from those who hunger and are not fed, those who are cold and are not clothed." A nation that diverted too much of its national income to the arms race was "spending the sweat of its laborers, the genius of its scientists, the hopes of its children."[35] Eisenhower believed that his military experience made him uniquely able to resist the armed forces' demands for ever-increasing expenditures that conveyed little additional security. While Eisenhower generally believed in lean government, his credo of fiscal responsibility also allowed for significant government investment in public programs that offered a high return for the country, most notably in education, science and engineering, and the creation of the national highway network in the late '50s.[36]

Larson depicted modern Republicanism as, in a sense, Eisenhower's personal qualities writ large. It was as much a temperament as an ideology, espousing balance, reasonableness, prudence, and common sense. Larson felt that Eisenhower and the American people shared a common instinct for the political center, and that Ike's policies were making the GOP the party of the American center. And Larson reminded his readers that "in politics—as in chess—the man who holds the center holds a position of almost unbeatable strength."[37]

Larson's critics on both the left and right denied that Eisenhower had discovered some political golden mean. Liberals attacked modern Republicanism as a flint-hearted imitation of Democratic social concern.

Conservatives saw Larson as a traitor who was legitimizing New Deal radicalism by giving it the imprimatur of the Republican Party. Right-wing
Arizona Senator Barry Goldwater sniped that Larson had not even registered to vote until 1954, and that he was one of "the political do-gooders
and opportunists who have so lately crowded under the Republican
banner." The modern Republicans, according to Goldwater, were seeking
to subvert the basic traditions of the GOP, and Larson's philosophy "in
practically every respect parrots the old and decrepit New Dealism of
Harry S. Truman."[38] Bill Buckley conceded that Larson had "verve and
spirit," though he smirked that his book "had the singular distinction of
being read by President Eisenhower."[39] But Buckley scorned bipartisanship
in foreign affairs, considered moderate Republicanism incapable of halting
the advance of the welfare state, and blamed Larson as well as liberals for
marginalizing conservative ideas in political discourse. He thought the
epitome of the moderates was Alexander Kerensky, the head of Russia's
Provisional Government in 1917, whose overthrow of the tsarist order had
inadvertently allowed the Bolsheviks to seize power. In Buckley's view,
moderate reform was the catalyst not for good government but for disaster.[40] Above all, Buckley found the moderate philosophy to be as boring as
Eisenhower himself. In a 1957 interview, Buckley described himself as "a
revolutionary against the present liberal order. An intellectual revolutionary."[41] Like the political upstarts who would spring up on the left in the
decade to come, Buckley craved madder music and stronger wine than the
'50s centrist consensus.

Larson was not the only intellectual at work in moderate Republican circles
in the 1950s. A movement known as "new conservatism" blossomed during
the Eisenhower years, although it never received much public attention. In
the wake of the 1948 elections, moderates calling themselves "new conservatives" had formed an organization called Republican Advance, which
aimed to craft a modern philosophy for the party, develop a research fa-
cility, and wrest GOP leadership from Taft and his followers.[42] Its adherents
were mainly academics and intellectuals, including McGeorge Bundy (then
a professor of government at Harvard), poet Peter Viereck, *New York Herald Tribune* editorialist August Heckscher, Cornell political scientist Clinton Rossiter, and journalist Russell Wheeler Davenport, as well as young,
moderate congressmen like Clifford Case, Jacob Javits, Kenneth Keating,
Hugh Scott, and Richard Nixon.

Republican Advance lasted for only a few years, but the "new conservative" writers gravitated toward the magazine *Confluence*, first published
in 1952 and edited by Henry Kissinger, who at the time was a graduate
student at Harvard. The moderates looked to the examples of European

conservatives such as Edmund Burke, Benjamin Disraeli, Castlereagh, and Metternich. Like the anti-Communist liberals who founded Americans for Democratic Action (ADA), they believed that the catastrophes of World War II required intellectuals to embrace a new spirit of pragmatism, realism, humility, and an ironic appreciation for human limitations, especially their own.[43] To a greater extent than the liberals, the "new conservatives" also believed in social cohesion, respect for tradition, incremental progress, and skepticism about centralized government.[44] These moderates abominated McCarthy and believed that most of what passed for American conservatism was little more than the warmed-over laissez faire doctrine of the nineteenth-century Manchester economists. Kissinger recalled that he had always "thought of myself as a Disraeli conservative. Most American conservatives are Manchester liberals, in my opinion, or populists. I don't even consider them conservatives . . . It seems to me the essence of conservatism is to have change evolve from existing structures and to avoid sudden convulsive disruption. This means that evolution should be gradual, but also that one should not be unbending."[45] Heckscher thought the modern Republicans should build on the examples of James Madison, who understood the necessity of balancing group interests under constitutional order; the Whigs, who sought to unify the nation and build the economy through government-sponsored public works including roads and canals; and the early Republicans, who used government actions such as the Homestead Act to strengthen independent, enterprising citizens on the land. He believed that the moderate Republican tradition "had a strong respect for federal power, wielded responsibly for a good end."[46]

The "new conservatives" had little impact on public debates, and fought a losing battle to keep the right from appropriating the term "conservative." But, along with Larson, they supplied intellectual respectability to Eisenhower's efforts to remake the GOP in his image.

The extent to which Eisenhower's modern Republican philosophy had permeated his party was a matter of much dispute. Paul Hoffman, who was among Eisenhower's closest political advisors, estimated in the mid-1950s that 95 percent of the Republican rank and file supported the President's program.[47] Many of the more conservative members of the party apparatus had been replaced with moderate Eisenhower supporters. Hoffman's estimation was buttressed by a contemporary survey which revealed that forty-two state Republican chairmen and two-thirds of the RNC self-identified as modern Republicans.[48] The editors of the *National Review*, when in self-pitying mode, saw conservatives as a mere "remnant," swamped by Ike-liking opportunists in the Republican Party as well as by the broader liberal-dominated, progress-loving society. To be a conservative, as Buckley put it in his opening editorial, was to be nonconformist: *National Review* "stands athwart history, yelling Stop, at a time when no one is inclined to do so, or to have much patience with those who do."[49]

On the other hand, Eisenhower had great difficulty in persuading many of his party's representatives in Congress of the wisdom of moderation and internationalism. After Taft's death deprived Eisenhower of the man who could be trusted to keep the conservatives in line, he clashed with right-wingers in the Senate over the truce in Korea, the Yalta Agreements, foreign aid, and mutual security agreements. He required heavy Democratic support to defeat the Bricker Amendment, proposed by Ohio Republican Senator John Bricker, which would have required Senate approval for all international agreements. In 1958, conservatives prevailed over moderates by running the Republican Party on an anti-labor theme and making the election a referendum on right-to-work laws, which prevented closed union shops. The election brought out enormous numbers of angry labor supporters, who in most states tossed out the proposed laws and most of the Republican candidates on the ballot as well, with conservatives losing more heavily than moderates. The GOP had already lost control of Congress in the 1954 elections and had failed to retake either house in 1956, despite Eisenhower's easy reelection. Now the Republicans suffered their worst defeat since the Depression, giving the Democrats a nearly two-to-one majority in the House and Senate and reducing the number of Republican governors to fourteen.

After his reelection, Eisenhower had declared that "Modern Republicanism has now proved itself. And America has approved Modern Republicanism."[50] But while Ike himself remained overwhelmingly popular, the same could not be said of the Republican Party. Even in 1952, when Eisenhower had real coattails, he had run nearly 16 percent ahead of his Congressional ticket.[51] The following three Congressional elections seemed to confirm that the GOP was in danger of becoming a permanent minority party.

As the 1960 elections approached, there were four principal strategies for how the party might regain the majority. The first was the conservative strategy, expounded with the greatest force by Barry Goldwater. The 1958 GOP losses had left the Arizona senator as the most prominent conservative politician still standing, and the 1960 publication of his manifesto, *The Conscience of a Conservative*, had made him a hero on the right. Goldwater and his followers believed that a "hidden" majority of Americans were conservative; the reason that Republicans usually lost elections was that they put forward moderates who were too similar to the Democrats to inspire the conservative majority to turn up at the polls. If the parties could be divided by ideology, according to this reasoning, the alleged conservative majority would produce Republican victories.

Nonsense, responded many party professionals. Dewey had long ago criticized the "impractical theorists" who wanted a neat arrangement of liberals in the Democratic Party and a purely conservative GOP. "The results would be neatly arranged, too," he warned. "The Republicans would lose every election and the Democrats would win every election."[52] Rather than attempt ideological transformation, the GOP might regain a majority simply by doing a better job at the nuts and bolts of politics: recruiting better candidates, raising more money, mobilizing more voters, and running a more effective organization than the Democrats. The party should welcome all candidates who wanted to run under its banner, since the party should reflect the ideological diversity of the country as a whole. Republicans should be allowed to represent their districts. The relation between a politician's political stance and the interests of his or her district was brought home to one House member when he went to the funeral of Wright Patman, a populist Democrat and four-decade veteran of Congress: "When I saw the First District of Texas, I had no trouble understanding Patman's animosity toward the Federal Reserve and his 'cross of gold' type of speeches about how the farmers and ranchers of America had been screwed by the bankers. It was a poor area. They had no oil, and the land looked poor, the houses looked poor, and the cows looked poor. You could see it. I really understood Patman better."[53]

Moderates believed that Eisenhower had demonstrated that the majority of Americans would vote for a moderate Republican. They felt that the party should emulate his example in standing for moderate, prudent policies that would bring "peace, prosperity, and progress," in Eisenhower's formulation. Even if the Democrats continued to hold a registration edge, Republicans could win by appealing to independents and moderate Democrats as well as to party loyalists. Others were convinced that Republican moderates had to be seen to stand for something more compelling than prudence. The GOP should even attempt to outbid the Democrats as the real progressive party, taking action on deep-rooted national problems like poverty, urban decay, and racial segregation. In this view, Eisenhower's cautious approach and his determination to balance the budget allowed the Democrats to appeal to a majority by promising to spend more on social welfare, boost the economy through Keynesian techniques, and keep pace in the Cold War arms race with the Soviets. New York Republican senator Jacob Javits was one who expressed disappointment that Eisenhower failed to bring the GOP to "a more progressive stance."[54]

As the Republicans gathered in Chicago for the 1960 convention, political observers discerned four separate factions in the party: progressives, moderates, stalwarts, and conservatives.[55] These factions roughly corresponded to the different strategies for Republican renewal. In practice, the lines between them were difficult to draw, and the first two factions were usually lumped together as "moderates" and the latter two as "conservatives." Most Republicans did eventually come to see themselves as either on the moderate or conservative side, but the different makeup and outlook of the factions in terms of regional background, economic interests, tribal loyalties, and ideology are worth emphasizing.

The faction that probably received the most media attention at the convention was the one that was often referred to as the "liberal" Republicans, though many preferred to be called "progressives" as a way of emphasizing their spiritual kinship to Theodore Roosevelt and the vibrant reform movement of the early twentieth century. Like the fiery New England abolitionists who had helped found the Republican Party, they rallied to the standard of civil rights and civil liberties; like the Bull Moose progressives, they were willing and eager to use government power to promote economic growth and social development. The faction was strongest in the Northeast, and its most prominent representative in 1960 was New York Governor Nelson Rockefeller, who had bucked the anti-Republican tide to win office in 1958 by a commanding half-million vote margin.

Progressivism was a powerful force in other parts of the country as well. Daniel Evans, a future governor of Washington who in 1960 was poised to become the leader of the Republicans in the state legislature, thought that the progressive attitude was strongest in the original areas of Yankee settlement, from New England to the Upper Midwest to California and the Northwest; the Pilgrim heritage came west in wagon trains like the one that brought his maternal grandfather from Connecticut to Wisconsin and on to Washington. Progressive ranks in the Washington GOP were greatly strengthened by the influx of returning veterans from World War II and the Korean war. "We all became activists," Evan recalled. "It was not only that we were in a hurry to create families and get on with our careers; we were impatient with and in a hurry to change everything that seemed old and outdated." The Washington GOP activists struggled to find appropriate solutions to the postwar problems of urban congestion and suburban sprawl, the pollution of Lake Washington, the absence of effective municipal government, and the need to open Seattle to international trade. Evans saw these reforms as being "in the progressive tradition. Progressives saw a problem and an effective way to handle it, and the idea of a somewhat larger government for a very limited purpose didn't frighten them."[56]

Conservatives claimed that progressives were liberal Democrats in Republican clothing, and Jacob Javits and some other progressives were never able to shake the suspicion that they became Republicans largely because the party offered an easier path to their political advancement.[57] But the progressives differed from Democrats in their pro-business attitudes, support for decentralization of government responsibility from federal to state and local levels, and moralistic suspicion of personal and group "liberation." James Reichley, who worked for several progressive Republican politicians in the early 1960s before becoming a political scientist, wrote that the progressives "remained essentially conservative in that they viewed reform as a means for preserving the underlying soundness of the existing system. . . . Like Theodore Roosevelt, looking back on his own career in 1916, they claimed that the progressive approach represented 'not wild radicalism . . . [but] the highest and wisest form of conservatism.'"[58] Jacob Riis, who had done much to spark the progressive movement with his 1890 muckraking work *How the Other Half Lives*, had described a destitute man on a corner of Fifth Avenue in Manhattan, hungry and ragged, gazing enviously at the passing parade of wealthy shoppers who would spend enough in an hour to feed the man and his children for a year. "There rose up before him the picture of these little ones crying for bread around the cold and cheerless hearth," Riis wrote, "then he sprang into the throng and slashed about him with a knife, blindly seeking to kill, to revenge."[59] Much progressive reform, particularly in urban Eastern areas, was driven by well-off Republicans who wanted to soften the hard workings of the capitalist system just enough so that they wouldn't end up on the receiving end of that knife.

The moderate faction represented the mainstream of Dewey and Eisenhower Republicans. They were descended from progressives such as Elihu Root and Henry Cabot Lodge Sr. who had chosen to remain in the GOP after the Bull Moose bolt of 1912. In the Disraelian tradition, they accepted the need to accommodate the inevitable changes that accompanied a dynamic industrial society, but moderates tended not to initiate reforms themselves. They upheld the virtues of prudence and pragmatism, and stood for good (but restrained) government and enlightened management. Their willingness to build upon some New Deal and Fair Deal reforms in the name of greater societal security separated them from small-government conservatives. So too did their internationalism, which in turn differed from the progressives' variety in its promotion of national interest rather than Wilsonian moralism. The moderates tended to be fiscally conservative but socially tolerant. Their bases were the urban corporate headquarters of the larger cities of the East, Midwest, and West. While it was an exaggeration to claim, as many Democrats and some conservatives did, that the majority of moderate Republicans hailed from Wall Street, those who worked there did tend toward moderation as a consequence of being cosmopolitan, outward looking, interested in worldwide trade and markets, and more or less comfortable with the diversity of peoples and lifestyles found in a huge global city like New York. As the party of Wall Street, the GOP under moderate control could be trusted to keep a steady hand on the economy and be responsible on foreign and domestic policy. The trouble was that this approach left the Democrats as the party of the people, which threatened to consign the Republicans to permanent minority status.

A representative moderate Republican was Paul G. Hoffman, now mostly forgotten but in 1960 one of Eisenhower's best known counselors.[60] Hoffman became famous for reviving the Studebaker Corporation, a midsized auto manufacturer, after its near bankruptcy during the Depression, and for his innovations in marketing and salesmanship. Henry Luce's *Fortune* magazine lauded him as a young, intelligent business leader bringing a reforming spirit of rational and scientific management to the auto industry. In 1942, he founded and served as first chairman of the Committee on Economic Development (CED), an organization of business leaders and academics created to prevent a postwar depression and serve as a counter to reactionary business organizations like the National Association of Manufacturers (NAM).[61] As a Republican and corporate executive, Hoffman was disturbed by the anti-business animus of the New Deal and its attempts to control prices and profits, but believed that the era of laissez faire was over and that government needed to meliorate the harsher aspects of capitalism. It was in the enlightened self-interest of business, he thought, to negotiate in good faith with labor unions and to support government social welfare programs such as unemployment insurance and the minimum wage. Robber-baron types who kept wages low and tried to squelch unions actually threatened the free enterprise system; by refusing to give workers an equitable share of capitalism's benefits, they sparked class conflict and undermined the economy by allowing potential consumers too little purchasing power. Probably only a minority of businessmen held such views, and the NAM bitterly criticized Hoffman and the CED for surrendering to socialism. But many executives during the '40s and '50s, especially the heads of large corporations, believed that they had to demonstrate social "responsibility" and win back the public confidence that was lost when the economy collapsed into the Depression.

Hoffman had grown up in the isolationist Midwest, but like his political mentor, Michigan Republican Senator Arthur Vandenberg, he became convinced that peace after World War II required American international involvement and bipartisan agreement on foreign policy. Hoffman's moderation led Harry Truman to select him as head of the Economic Cooperation Administration, the agency set up in 1948 to administer the Marshall Plan. The United States spent some $13 billion, a stupendous sum at the time, to rebuild Western Europe after the war's devastation. While Hoffman acknowledged that it was in the interest of the United States to revive overseas export markets, he stressed the program's contribution toward making Europe sufficiently strong, integrated, and prosperous that it could resist Communism's appeal and Soviet domination. Later, as U.S. delegate to the General Assembly of the United Nations and a top-ranked official in the UN Secretariat, he became the foremost American advocate of policies to help the less developed countries, both to enable them to buy U.S. exports and to advance peaceful economic development as an alternative to Communism and revolution.

Hoffman was representative of a sizable swathe of Republican business opinion that considered conservative domestic and foreign policies to be outmoded and irresponsible. Their opponents in turn regarded such businessmen as a graver threat than liberal politicians. Conservative critics of Hoffman were fond of quoting Lenin's supposed prediction that the capitalists would sell him the rope he would use to hang them.

Eisenhower admired Hoffman as a forceful executive and an equally forceful exponent of the moderate Republican position. In private, Eisenhower often cursed his supporters in Congress for lacking "guts," particularly for their unwillingness to take on Joe McCarthy. He told aides that "we really need a few good hatchet men on *our* side up there."[62] The moderate temperament sometimes manifested as a gentlemanly reluctance to engage in confrontation and real political battle. Leverett Saltonstall, a moderate Republican senator from Massachusetts who was descended from nine governors of the state, was a low-ranking member of the Senate Republican leadership in the early '60s when the death of Styles Bridges opened the possibility of his becoming chairman of the Policy Committee, a position with real power. His assistant advised him that to gain the post he would have to do some discreet campaigning for the job at Bridges' funeral. "He wouldn't do it," the assistant recalled with a wince. "His culture wouldn't permit it. People brought up the way Leverett was, people in that tradition of Yankee leadership, did not express their appreciation for the dead by politicking at a religious ceremony intended to let them rest in peace. And so Leverett lost, and that's why he lost."[63]

While most moderates were party loyalists, few were rabid partisans. The upper-class lawyers and bankers of the Eastern establishment were predominantly moderate Republicans, but they believed that the imperatives of public service obliged them to accept prominent government positions under Democratic administrations, in keeping with the bipartisan tradition represented by Henry Stimson when he agreed to become FDR's secretary of war. Moderate Republicans did not think it inconsistent to have Democratic friends or even to admire some Democratic politicians. Representative Fred Schwengel of Iowa was a moderate Republican and a proud GOP historian, but one of his favorite forms of after-dinner entertainment was listening to recordings of Adlai Stevenson's campaign speeches.[64]

The third faction in the GOP, variously described as "stalwarts" or "regulars" or "Taftites," was composed principally of the followers of the late Senator Taft, and was by far the largest faction in the party in 1960. They came mostly from the Protestant middle classes of the smaller cities and towns of the Midwest and the border states of the South, and some of the rural areas outside of the South and West. Their small-government, fiscal-discipline views would have been familiar to Midwestern Republicans in the nineteenth century. As economic conservatives, they tended to identify with small businesses rather than big corporations, Main Street rather than Wall Street. They were free marketeers but not laissez-faire purists, supporting fair trade laws and selective tariffs.

The experiences of Depression, war, and Cold War had altered some of the stalwarts' ancestral beliefs. By 1960, most of the leading members of this faction, such as Illinois Senator Everett Dirksen and Michigan Representive Gerald Ford, had abandoned the Prohibitionism and isolationism of their forebears, but retained strong moralistic views and suspicions of excessive international commitments. While they tended to identify themselves as conservatives, they remained loyal to the GOP's legacy as the Party of Lincoln. In 1960, many of them were genuinely uncertain as to whether they should continue to support the "conservative coalition" with the Southern Democrats. They were not opposed to all change and occasionally defended New Deal institutions as necessary for societal stability, but they wanted change to occur gradually and in keeping with past experience and tradition. In practice, their concern with economy in government meant that they rarely put forward any Republican alternatives to Democratic programs or approaches.

Many aspects of the moderate and progressive approaches struck the stalwarts as wrongheaded, but most were prepared to tolerate divergent views within the party in order to win elections. Robert Taft had been a consummate party professional, and the idea of purging the Republican Party of its moderates in the name of ideological purity would have struck him as absurd. Indeed, in the fullness of time many of the stalwarts would come to be regarded as moderates themselves, though others would gravitate toward the conservative ranks.

The last GOP faction was the group that Americans know as conservatives today: militant economic, social, and cultural right-wingers, anti-government in rhetoric if not always in practice, predominantly from the South and West. This was probably the smallest of the Republican factions in 1960, but much like the Bolshevik Party in revolutionary Russia they claimed to speak for a majority. They were the only Republican tribe that had a sense of themselves as an ideologically coherent group joined in a movement, and their sense of heroic embattlement was enhanced by their opponents' tendency to view them as not merely wrong but insane. The conservatives were also the sole faction calling for an ideological realignment of the American political system. They argued that converting the GOP into a party of pure conservatism would bring in some previously unrepresented groups such as white Southerners and working-class white ethnics, including many Catholics. Their positions on domestic and foreign policy put them greatly at odds with the moderates and progressives, and often the stalwarts as well. Moderates such as Hoffman believed that the conservatives were "a totally new element" in the party, dating from Joe McCarthy's rise to prominence, and had "nothing in common with rigid but honest conservatives such as Senator Robert A. Taft."[65] The conservatives in turn saw the moderates and progressives not as misguided brethren but as traitors to be destroyed; in their view even the stalwarts were appeasers. Conservatives' loyalty to their beliefs often took precedence over their loyalty to the Republican Party. Some conservatives in 1960 believed that the Democratic Party might yet make the better vehicle for their doctrine, while others advocated breaking away from the GOP to form a third, conservative party.

Conservatives considered the New Deal to be wholly alien to the American tradition and aimed to eradicate it. They objected as well to the progressive movement's earlier attempts to meliorate the rawest outcomes of industrial society. They believed (or affected to believe) that liberalism led inexorably to socialism and Communism, and that the smallest government effort to provide for the general welfare constituted the first step on "The Road to Serfdom," in the titular argument of Friedrich Hayek's 1944 bestseller. Hoffman, again, felt that the conservatives were unable to accept "the modern America with its needs of social security, or balanced labor-management relations, or government partnership or guardianship of our complex economy."[66]

Conservatives opposed federal efforts to desegregate the South, usually on constitutional grounds but in some cases because they approved of racial segregation. In 1957, *National Review*, which acted as the mouthpiece of this form of conservatism, carried an editorial by Bill Buckley asking "whether the white community in the South is entitled to take such measures as are necessary to prevail, politically and culturally . . . The so-bering answer is *Yes*—the white community is so entitled because, for the time being, it is the advanced race."[67] Buckley would try to distance the conservative movement from the overt racism and anti-Semitism that had characterized the Old Right before World War II, but conservatives had little sympathy with the civil rights movement that increasingly weighed upon the consciences of other Republicans.

Many conservatives had supported the America First Committee, the populist and nativist group that attempted to keep the United States out of World War II. By 1960, however, most on the right believed the need to combat Communism required the nation to build up a formidable military and to project power abroad. (Heavy defense spending also buoyed the economies of many Southern and Western states.) Progressives, moderates, and stalwarts were all anti-Communist, but the conservatives were more extreme, seeking to root out internal left-wing influences in the United States and roll back Communism abroad even at the risk of nuclear war; some even advocated a preemptive nuclear strike against the Soviet Union. Many of the conservatives had been McCarthy die-hards. The John Birch Society, founded in 1958, kept the McCarthyist spirit alive, attracting hundreds of thousands of Americans with its paranoid speculations about Communist treason at the highest levels of government. Anti-Communism provided a unifying cause for traditionalist conservatives and libertarians, who otherwise would have argued more over their many points of disagreement.[68]

A scenario in which the conservative faction would take over the entire party and force all Republicans to dance to their tune would have strained credibility in 1960. Nixon, nervously weighing the balance of forces in the GOP, felt no need to strike a deal with the conservatives in pursuit of his nomination at the convention. The faction that he worried most about was the progressives, and particularly Nelson Rockefeller.

Nelson Aldrich Rockefeller remains the best-known progressive Republican of recent times. Even today, anyone who diverges from the conservative line of the GOP may be referred to as a "Rockefeller Republican." As the grandson of Senate Republican chieftain Nelson Aldrich and Standard Oil magnate John D. Rockefeller, he was advantageously placed for a career in Republican politics. Forceful, magnetic, handsome in a square-headed way, and of course immensely rich—the Rockefeller family fortune was estimated at between three and six billion dollars in 1960—Nelson Rockefeller was the leading light of the GOP's progressives and one of the dominant political figures of his era.[69] He was the target of Garry Wills' famous barb that while first-generation millionaires give us libraries, succeeding generations think they should give us themselves.[70] In truth, the ultra-rich usually avoided subjecting themselves to the messy and intrusive process of elective politics. Rockefeller was an exception because he was more ambitious than most billionaires' sons. "Ever since I was a kid," he mused, he had wanted to be president. "After all, when you think of what I had, what else was there to aspire to?"[71] But most Americans would have a difficult time identifying with a man who wanted the presidency mostly because he already had everything else.

Rockefeller's first major step toward that goal came with his upset victory in the New York gubernatorial election of 1958, which immediately thrust him toward the top of political handicappers' lists for the 1960 presidential election. In addition to his money and celebrity, "Rocky," as he was known to the press and public, had considerable political resources even at that early stage of his career. He had foreign policy experience, particularly in Central and South America, from his service in the Roosevelt, Truman, and Eisenhower administrations. He had a reputation for innovative and activist government, an ability to attract the most talented advisors (such as Harvard professor Henry Kissinger), a capacity for glad-handing ("Hiya, fella!") and blintz-eating, and a sophisticated public relations operation. One young Republican remembered that when Rockefeller's delegation came to state conventions, "They would sweep in, and you just had a sense of, 'Boy, this is what power feels like.'" Rockefeller oozed power and charisma: "He was high and he was mighty, and he had his minions, and he could really make things happen."[72] Like many extremely wealthy people, however, Rockefeller also exuded an off-putting sense of entitlement, and he never bothered to cultivate the party organization and the network of low-level party officials that his predecessor, Tom Dewey, had created.

Rockefeller had sniffed out the possibility of gaining the 1960 GOP presidential nomination, and quickly discovered that Nixon had a lock on the loyalty of the party regulars, the pledges of Republican business leaders, and the votes of convention delegates. He announced in December 1959 that he would not challenge Nixon for the nomination. But the first months of 1960 brought recession, a wave of sit-in protests at segregated lunch counters in the South, and foreign policy crises in abundance, including the Soviets' shoot-down of an American U-2 spy plane and the subsequent cancellation of Eisenhower's disarmament summit with Soviet leader Nikita Khrushchev. In early June, a month and a half before the Republican convention, Rockefeller issued a statement declaring that in view of the national and international emergency, the GOP had to embrace an action program to accelerate economic growth, secure civil rights for Southern blacks, and rebuild national defense. Rockefeller may have hoped to throw the convention into sufficient turmoil that delegates might turn to him as an alternative to Nixon, or he may simply have wanted to push the GOP toward progressivism. Citizens for Rockefeller, a grassroots organization that had been created the previous summer when the governor was exploring a presidential campaign, reactivated and delivered an impressive 260,000 pieces of mail to the opening of the Chicago convention, urging delegates to heed Rockefeller's call.[73]

Nixon did not believe that Rockefeller had the slightest chance of stampeding the convention. Nonetheless, he wanted a united party behind him as he began his presidential campaign. A floor fight over what was shaping up to be a too-conservative party platform, particularly on civil rights, would do him no good. He also wanted to attract the independent voters he would need as candidate of the minority party.[74] And so Nixon, without telling several of his top aides, flew secretly to New York on July 22 and met with Rockefeller at his opulent Fifth Avenue apartment. After dinner and some dickering over the vice-presidential nomination—Rockefeller didn't want it, and Nixon later claimed he didn't offer it—the two men stayed up the rest of the night trying to reconcile Rockefeller's proposed statement of principles with the party platform that was still being hammered out in Chicago. The joint fourteen-point statement released the next morning was widely interpreted as a Nixon surrender to Rockefeller, largely because it seemed to reflect progressive views on civil rights, jobs, housing, and defense. The press dubbed it "The Compact of Fifth Avenue." Goldwater, speaking for the conservatives, deemed it a "Republican Munich," a sellout of core party principles.

    In fact, the statement represented no real concessions on Nixon's part. Nixon insisted that "it was Rockefeller who did the 'surrendering,'" on proposals for old-age health insurance financed from Social Security, compulsory arbitration in the settlement of labor disputes, and an annual economic growth rate target of 5 or 6 percent.[75] Moreover, Nixon's and Rockefeller's views on the points the governor raised were not far apart. By emphasizing his overall agreement with the progressives, Nixon was looking ahead to his battle against Democratic nominee John F. Kennedy. At their convention two weeks earlier in Los Angeles, the Democrats had passed a considerably more liberal civil rights plank than at their 1956 convention, and Kennedy had proclaimed the need to get America "moving again" after the supposed stagnation of the Eisenhower years, particularly in terms of raising the growth rate and closing the alleged "missile gap" between U.S. and Soviet defense forces. Nixon needed to stress to the platform committee conservatives the desirability of producing a positive, forward-looking platform. He also needed to subtly distance himself from Eisenhower without disavowing the administration of which he himself had been part. Nixon's agreement with Rockefeller served these useful functions.

Back in Chicago, Nixon forced the platform committee to reconsider the civil rights plank it had adopted. The Southerners on the civil rights sub-committee, led by future Texas Senator John Tower, had claimed that the sit-in demonstrations were likely to result in violence and would be taken over by Communists.[76] The original plank did not support the sit-ins or promise federal intervention to secure job equality for African-Americans— both points the Democrats had approved in Los Angeles. Nixon called in his chits to force the conservatives to back down and pass a civil rights plank that was as strong as the Democrats'. Nixon's team found face-saving language to emphasize the need for strong defense without repudiating Eisenhower's military economy, and finessed the rest of the platform language in a way that was more or less acceptable to all party factions. "In its entirety," one contemporary study concluded, "the final platform draft was a Nixon document."[77] If Nixon had won the presidential election, the platform controversy would have been seen as an indication of his control over the party and the strength of moderates in the GOP.

Rockefeller was satisfied with the civil rights plank and declined to challenge Nixon over the defense plank. Some conservatives whose enthusiasm exceeded their grasp of political reality hoped that Goldwater might somehow obtain the nomination, but the Arizonan was well aware that Nixon had it in the bag. In a speech before the convention, Goldwater withdrew his name from consideration and advised conservatives to "grow up" and vote for Nixon, but he made clear that the conservative movement intended to control the GOP: "If we want to take this Party back, and I think we can someday, let's get to work."[78] Goldwater's enthusiasts mounted an eleven-minute demonstration in support of their hero, but this paled in comparison to the pro-Stevenson revolt that had shaken the Democratic convention two weeks earlier. Nixon gained the nomination with ease and named former Massachusetts senator Henry Cabot Lodge Jr., Eisenhower's 1952 campaign manager and a leader of the moderate faction, as his vice presidential running mate. Nixon's selection of Lodge, who was then serving as U.S. ambassador to the United Nations, indicated his intention to concentrate on foreign rather than domestic policy in the campaign, and provided further confirmation of his turn to the moderate and progressive side. Overall, reporters believed that conservatives had been forced into what was described as "a virtual capitulation" to the moderates.[79]

As is well known, Kennedy narrowly defeated Nixon in the 1960 election, and may have owed his margin of victory to electoral fraud in Illinois and Texas. Nixon considered contesting the vote, but in the end decided that such a divisive course would not benefit the nation, the GOP, or his future electoral chances. Given the razor-thin outcome, every explanation for Nixon's defeat was plausible. The experts' post-mortems cited Nixon's poor performance in his first televised debate with Kennedy, his rash promise to campaign in all fifty states, Eisenhower's lukewarm endorsement, the mild recession of 1960, and Nixon's vacillating approach that attempted to please all factions of the GOP but ended up satisfying none of them. Progressives argued that if Nixon had taken a more forthright stance on civil rights, and had dared to follow Kennedy's example by telephoning Martin Luther King Jr.'s wife after the civil rights activist had been sent to prison in Georgia, he would have won the African-American vote and hence the election. Conservatives countered that Nixon lost because he ran a "me-too" campaign that failed to offer a clear alternative to the Democrats. In this interpretation, if Nixon had soft-pedaled civil rights at the convention, he would have taken a decisive margin of support from the Southern states. In the quarrels over who was responsible for Nixon's loss, Nelson Rockefeller was a figure of particular odium for conservatives. One griped that "Governor Rockefeller did nothing but sit on his hands, despite the fact that he imposed his 'liberal' credo on the Platform Committee. Had Mr. Nixon been blessed with the fortitude to ignore the ravings of the Governor and run on a Republican plank, he would today be President-elect."[80] The GOP made modest Congressional gains in 1960, but failed to make up the losses of the disastrous 1958 elections. The stage was set for civil war between the party's moderate and conservative factions.

Historians have all but unanimously concluded that the conservatives' victory in this struggle was inevitable. Indeed, one recent study declares that by December 1960, "conservatives had effectively taken control of the Republican Party."[81] But in fact, the general historical consensus around the reasons for conservatism's rise actually has little to say about the reasons for moderation's decline. It's true that the conservatives organized an impressive grassroots movement beginning in the 1950s, but moderates had also mounted triumphant citizens movements around presidential nominations, starting with the Wendell Willkie boom in 1940 and continuing through Eisenhower's victory over Robert Taft in 1952. The Dewey network, built on the Young Republicans organization, was at least as formidable as the later YR-based network mobilized by conservatives for the 1964 Goldwater campaign. The intellectuals around William F. Buckley Jr.'s conservative *National Review* magazine in the 1950s were not more impressive than the intellectuals of the moderate "new conservative" movement around Henry Kissinger's *Confluence* magazine during the same decade. Moderate Republican moneymen like Nelson and David Rockefeller, John Hay Whitney, and William Paley had considerably deeper pockets than most of their conservative counterparts. Moderates had much greater access to the media and influence within the academy and the establishment. Conservatives developed a clear alternative to what became the liberal overreach of the '60s, but so too did the moderates.

The great political mystery of the 1960s, then, may be why the conservatives prospered at the moderates' expense, despite the apparent advantages that the moderates enjoyed. A fuller understanding of the forces at work in the Republican Party after the 1960 election requires a close examination of all levels of the party, from elected politicians and party officials through intellectuals and grassroots activists, as a new political era began.

CHAPTER 2

⌀

Things Fall Apart

Advance *Magazine and the Decay of the*
Moderate Establishment, 1961–63

Three of the four candidates on the 1960 presidential ballot still present familiar images to most Americans today. John F. Kennedy's blend of glamour, rhetorical idealism, and operational pragmatism was an obvious inspiration for Barack Obama. Lyndon Johnson remains a cautionary figure for Democrats, responsible for some of liberalism's highest achievements and worst hubris. Richard Nixon is a model for Republicans both to emulate, for his eventual triumphant comeback after crushing political setbacks, and to avoid, for obvious reasons. But who was Henry Cabot Lodge Jr., Nixon's 1960 Republican running-mate? Few people nowadays can remember what he looked like or recall what he stood for. Historians mention him not for his political career but for his stint as ambassador to South Vietnam under Kennedy and Johnson, an example of the bipartisan responsibility for failure in the Vietnam war.

Lodge's obscurity reflects the fate meted out to most failed vice-presidential candidates. But Lodge has also been forgotten because the tradition of moderate Republicanism that he represented is extinct. In that sense, his unfamiliarity paradoxically does more to illuminate the bygone political environment than the more familiar figures of the 1960 race. The 1960 Republican convention was the last where the deals that mattered were cut between moderates and progressives. Nixon believed that the constituency he truly needed to shore up was the Eastern progressive wing of the GOP. He secured its support by negotiating with New York Governor

Nelson Rockefeller for a stronger civil rights plank for the party platform and naming Eastern favorite Lodge as his running mate.

Henry Cabot Lodge Jr.—known to friends as Cabot—was the descendant of one of Boston's great quasi-aristocratic families. Among his family memorabilia was a parchment commission, signed by President John Adams, making his ancestor George Cabot the first secretary of the U.S. Navy. He could count half a dozen senators among his forebears, including his grandfather and namesake, Henry Cabot Lodge Sr., who had been President Theodore Roosevelt's most trusted confidant. His heritage also included many of the leading lights of New England culture, including William and Henry James, and his parents had been close friends of writers and thinkers such as Henry Adams and Edith Wharton. Like a noble Roman of old, Lodge impressed his friends as someone conscious of the need to live up to the example set by his ancestors.

After four years in the Massachusetts legislature, Lodge defeated the rascally Governor James Michael Curley in the 1936 election to become a U.S. Senator, the only Republican to displace a Democrat that year. In 1942, when members of the Senate were prohibited from military service, he resigned to enter the Army, becoming the first U.S. Senator since the Civil War to leave the upper house to go to war. After combat duty in Italy, France, and Germany, eventually rising to the rank of brigadier general, he won reelection to the Senate in 1946.

Lodge described himself as a "practical progressive."[1] Although he had been an isolationist in his first Senate term, when it was widely noted that his grandfather had led the fight against the United States joining the League of Nations, the war's experience made him an internationalist and defender of the United Nations. He pursued a generally moderate course, supporting tax cuts and the Taft-Hartley bill that was anathema to labor, but also upholding civil rights and health care for the indigent. He became manager of Dwight Eisenhower's presidential campaign in 1952, angering conservatives when he secured the Republican nomination for his candidate over right-wing favorite Robert Taft. Conservative opposition combined with the demands of the presidential campaign led him to lose his Senate reelection bid that year to John F. Kennedy, who thereby revenged the defeat of his grandfather, John F. Fitzgerald, for the same seat in 1916 by Henry Cabot Lodge Sr. Eisenhower named Lodge the U.S. ambassador to the UN, where he became an early television star through his combative confrontations with the Soviets in one of the more public battlegrounds of the Cold War.

A September 1960 Gallup poll found that Lodge generated the highest voter enthusiasm of any of the candidates on the presidential ballot.[2] He was popular with African-American audiences, partly because of their residual loyalty to the Party of Lincoln and partly because Lodge, unlike most politicians at that time, had experience negotiating with black leaders—those from the newly emergent African states. The six-foot-two, blue-eyed Lodge also produced shrieks of female approval comparable to the concurrent hysteria over Kennedy.

While commentators lauded Lodge's intelligence, integrity, industry, and measured judgment, he was no better able than most moderates to define what Eisenhower's "modern Republicanism" meant and how it differed from Kennedy's moderate liberalism. Lodge embodied the vagueness of moderation, coming across as a collection of fine qualities in search of a personality. He was old-fashioned in many ways—often addressing reporters as "My good man" or "My dear man"—at a time when much of the nation was looking to the future. And he was too much the gentleman to play a political hatchet-man, a necessary party function that Nixon had performed for Eisenhower. Indeed, Lodge seemed overly comfortable with the GOP in the role of what he called "a truly and completely patriotic opposition" that was not seeking "partisan advantage."[3]

Lodge's variety of moderate Republicanism was the inherited creed of the Eastern ruling class, carried down from the likes of Theodore Roosevelt and adapted to changing circumstances. To many Americans in the early 1960s, both that class and creed seemed stuffy, paternalistic, and confining. In contrast to Lodge, Kennedy's barrier-breaking push to become the first Irish-American and Catholic president inspired millions of Americans who resented the dominance of the WASP establishment. This resentment was actually stronger on the right than on the left, and Lodge was second only to Nelson Rockefeller as a devil figure for right-wing, East-hating populists.[4] Lodge represented not just moderation but the old tradition of American authority with which it was associated.

The Eisenhower years had brought the country peace, strong economic growth, low inflation, low unemployment, and widespread political consensus. By the start of the 1960s, however, these achievements didn't seem to count for much. Kennedy voiced the opinion of liberals and conservatives alike that America in 1960 was characterized by boredom and anxiety. It had lost its sense of national purpose. Material abundance had translated into a bland, vapid, self-satisfied society, which lacked the moral resolve to confront domestic and world problems. Dissidents of both the left and right agreed that the authority and conformity of the Eisenhower years would have to go. They wanted the 1960s to be a romantic decade of upheaval and liberation. They would get their wish.

The moderate Republicanism represented by Eisenhower and Lodge had upheld the values of stability and deference to traditional authority. As the 1960s unrolled, young moderate activists became increasingly aware that the old model was not one that they could rely on. Moderation would have to be reinvented to meet the needs of a new society and the demands of a new generation. Moderates would also have to unite in a movement to challenge the conservative movement emerging on the right.

Oddly, the first sizeable group of Americans to get a detailed glimpse of the changing political dynamic at the level of grassroots youth activism were the teenage girls who read *Mademoiselle* magazine. In the summer of 1961, the magazine carried an unusually sophisticated and informed analysis of the wave of political activism that was rippling through the nation's colleges and universities, written by a University of Michigan junior. After the quiescence of the "silent generation," he proclaimed, a new generation had "restored action and political dialogue to the college campus."[5]

The author focused on three student organizations that had been founded in 1960. One was Students for a Democratic Society (SDS), which at that point was a small left-wing group numbering 575 members in twenty campus chapters.[6] The second was the right-wing Young Americans for Freedom (YAF), founded on William F. Buckley Jr.'s family estate by a group of Barry Goldwater's student supporters in the wake of the 1960 Republican convention. And the third was *Advance*, a progressive Republican magazine published by Harvard undergraduates.

The article's author was Thomas Hayden, whose photograph revealed him to be at that time a clean-cut young man in coat and tie and button-down shirt. Most of the ideas of what would become the New Left were already boiling inside his head. Within a year, Hayden would be elected the president of SDS, write the organization's "Port Huron Statement," grow his hair long, and become internationally notorious. By the end of the decade, SDS would emerge as America's largest radical organization and would galvanize millions of people to protest against the Vietnam war. Although left-wing protesters would define the image of youthful activism during the '60s, at the time of Hayden's article many observers thought the student movement would be led from the right. In 1961, Young Americans for Freedom was the vanguard of an alleged "conservative revolution" among youth, claiming 24,000 student members on over a hundred campuses. "YAFers" would become a major force in Goldwater's gaining the 1964 Republican presidential nomination, and the group's alumni would end up in prominent positions in conservative Republican politics.[7]

Like the activists of SDS and YAF, the members of *Advance* were young and idealistic, driven by moral urgency, mistrustful of established liberal authorities and institutions, and militant in their demands for change. They enjoyed media attention, the financial backing and encouragement of older supporters, and easy access to political figures at high levels of government.

But *Advance* was not destined to mobilize masses of young people for the middle in the way that SDS and YAF would do for the extremes of left and right. It was the magazine's fate to chronicle the conservatives' stunning seizure of power within the Republican Party between 1961 and 1964, when *Advance* collapsed along with the moderate Republicanism it had championed.

While SDS and YAF attracted international headlines and inspired a torrent of dissertations and books charting their lasting impact on American politics, *Advance* has been almost entirely forgotten. Ironically, the principal founders of *Advance* would later become prominent conservative spokesmen. But Tom Hayden's instincts in singling out the magazine were on target. In the course of defending the political center and doing battle with ideological movements left and right, *Advance* formed a clearer view of the moderate Republican establishment's vulnerabilities than the establishment had of itself.

Advance was the brainchild of Bruce K. Chapman and George F. Gilder, undergraduates in the Harvard College Class of 1962. Chapman was born in Illinois in 1940, and grew up in the small town of Monmouth, near the Iowa border. Neither of his parents, who had divorced when he was young, was a Republican. His mother, a high school teacher in Monmouth, was a liberal Democrat. His father, with whom Chapman spent his boyhood summers in Chicago, was a supporter of Henry Wallace's Progressive Party in 1948 and likely a Communist. He had opposed American entry into World War II until the Germans invaded the Soviet Union in 1941; twenty-four hours later he had become an ardent interventionist. As Chapman observed, that instant reversal "was often a reliable sign" of Communist Party membership.[8] From a very young age, Chapman accompanied his father to Popular Front rallies, Pete Seeger performances, and soapbox orations in the Chicago park nicknamed "Bughouse Square." His father also tried to educate his son about the world's inequities by taking him to see hospital wards, Skid Row vagrants, inmates in the county jail, and Democratic machine-appointed functionaries working in the county courthouse.

These experiences did not convert Chapman to Communism any more than a visit to the Chicago stockyards converted him to his father's vegetarianism. But Chapman's father did encourage his independent interest in politics, and allowed him the life-changing experience of attending the 1952 Republican convention in Chicago, where he discovered "a previously unimagined political fairyland of color, glamour and celebrity."[9] The eleven year-old Chapman roamed the convention by himself, picking up free souvenirs and Coca-Colas, listening to roving musical bands, shaking hands with celebrities like John Wayne, and sharing a sandwich with his idol,

Senator Robert Taft. Chapman was watching from the balcony through plumes of tobacco smoke when the conservative fell to Eisenhower on the first ballot. He threw Taft campaign pamphlets onto the victorious candidate's motorcade the next day as an obscure juvenile protest. He quickly learned to like Ike, however, and was a thoroughly modern Republican by the time he arrived at Harvard in the fall of 1958. By his sophomore year, he was active with the campus Young Republicans club. In 1959, he organized a group of Harvard enthusiasts for Nelson Rockefeller's incipient presidential campaign, which grew into a federation of Students for Rockefeller clubs on other campuses. Chapman's boyish looks belied a solemn bearing and intense political focus; he seemed prematurely serious to many of his contemporaries.

Chapman's backing of the New York governor's presidential ambitions brought him into contact with his classmate George Gilder, whose allegiance to Rockefeller was in some measure a family obligation. Gilder was born in New York in 1939, but was raised mainly on his stepfather's dairy farm in the Massachusetts Berkshires. Gilder's father had been killed in an Army Air Corps crash in World War II, when George was three years old. His father's Harvard roommate and best friend David Rockefeller, Nelson's youngest brother, became something like a substitute father. Gilder was the descendant of a distinguished East Coast family, whose great-grandfathers included glassmaker Louis Comfort Tiffany and Richard Watson Gilder, the renowned editor, public intellectual, and Mugwump who was close to writers such as Walt Whitman and politicians including Theodore Roosevelt. By the time George was born, however, the family's wealth had dissipated, with a large part of the family fortune spent on the endowment of the Gideon Bible Society. As Chapman wrote about his friend's upbringing, the Gilder family principles "derived from America's high WASP culture, but by the time they were taught to George, the money that once gave the ancient standards their worldly glitter was gone. There were Persian carpets on the floor, but they were threadbare."[10]

David Rockefeller paid Gilder's tuition during his restless student years at the Hamilton School (a progressive school in New York), Phillips Exeter, and Harvard. Gilder had originally enrolled at the university a year before Chapman, but flunked out, joined the Marines, and eventually was readmitted to Harvard as a member of the Class of '62. To support himself, he sold sandwiches in the corridors of the law school at night and hawked programs at football games in the fall. Gilder was celebrated in undergraduate circles for his wild absent-mindedness. Chapman recalled an occasion when his forgetful friend drove from Boston to Philadelphia to attend a track meet, then flew home and wondered what had become of his car.[11] Once when having lunch with the Rockefellers, the conversation turned to china patterns and Gilder turned his soup bowl over to look at its mark of origin, failing to notice that the bowl was full.[12]

Chapman and Gilder had arranged several rallies for Rockefeller in the fall of '59, but disbanded their federation after the governor withdrew from the presidential race in early 1960. Chapman remained in touch with the Rockefeller organization, however, which led to an invitation to work with the Rockefeller delegation at the 1960 Republican convention in Chicago. He was on the convention floor to witness Barry Goldwater's speech to his faithful, and couldn't help but notice that the most enthusiastic Goldwater partisans were young people his own age. Although most media commentators predicted that Rockefeller would be the GOP heir apparent if Nixon fell short in the presidential election, Chapman came away from the Republican convention convinced that Goldwater conservatives were likely to take over the party if nothing was done to stop them. From his involvement in YR activities and from his reading of the political temperature on campus, moreover, he believed that the political center was under attack from both left and right.

As Tom Hayden observed in his *Mademoiselle* article, most college students in the early '60s were not active or even much interested in politics, and their occasional revolts merely took the form of "riots at Fort Lauderdale, panty raids, [and] mass partying."[13] But 1960 had given rise to a strong political minority on many campuses, sparked by meetings and protests over issues ranging from ROTC and the nuclear arms race to parietal rules and fraternity control of student government. The sit-ins by Southern black undergraduates at segregated lunch counters had particular resonance for young people around the country, who were moved by the spectacle of their courageous contemporaries putting their bodies on the line for a transcendent moral cause. Chapman and Gilder formed a Republican civil rights group to set up a sympathy picket of the local branch of Woolworth's. The energy generated around specific causes spilled over into student involvement in politics more generally, and unprecedented numbers of young people turned out for rallies of both presidential candidates in the fall.

Much of the early activism came from the political left, such as the Berkeley-led protest against the House Un-American Activities Committee hearings in San Francisco in May 1960. At Harvard, Chapman noticed that Marxism was becoming trendy among undergraduates who regarded themselves as intellectually serious and politically advanced, and who stood out from the crowd by wearing overalls and growing beards. "This whole idea of Harvard students dressing in faux-worker clothes was really nonsensical to me," he remembered. "I'd had early exposure to that sort of thing with my father, and I was inoculated against the idea that Marxism was fashionable or good." Many students and professors, however, were captivated by the engagement, intellectual rigor, and moral commitment of the emerging New Left. Harvard undergraduate Todd Gitlin, who lived in the same residential hall as Chapman and Gilder, began his college career as a liberal, then moved through peace activism to strident ideological leftism, and eventually followed Tom Hayden as president of SDS.[14] Chapman and the other moderates found it increasingly difficult to communicate with Gitlin and his group: "They were developing a whole different language that we didn't like at all."[15]

While students on the left claimed most of the headlines in the early '60s, the new spirit of activism galvanized students on the right as well, to the extent that some commentators believed that a wave of conservatism was sweeping the campuses. Right-wing students had rarely participated in demonstrations in the past, but now groups formed around causes including support for nuclear testing and the loyalty oath required of students receiving financial aid. Chapters of Young Americans for Freedom cropped up at colleges and universities across the country soon after its founding. The numbers claimed for organizations such as YAF were inflated, and the clear undergraduate trend was in the direction of liberalism. But as one political scientist at Notre Dame observed in 1961, while conservatives were a minority on campus, "an increasing number of good students are now aggressive about their conservatism. As recently as six or seven years ago, you were rated slightly stupid if you took a conservative stance. Not so today."[16]

At Harvard, the YAF chapter was led by Howard Phillips, a burly native Bostonian and tireless right-wing activist, who claimed among his other accomplishments to have pulled Fidel Castro's beard when the Cuban revolutionary visited Cambridge in 1959.[17] Phillips clashed with Chapman's allies in the Harvard Young Republican Club (HYRC), although more for reasons of personality than ideology since all members of the club united around Nixon in the 1960 presidential election. While Phillips failed to gain control of the HYRC, he succeeded in becoming president of the Harvard student council. The national media proclaimed that Phillips' election showed that conservatism was sweeping the universities. In fact, it really meant that the student council was so unimportant that even a conservative could get elected as its president.[18]

The emerging New Left and New Right disagreed on nearly everything in political terms, but the spirit behind both movements was quite similar. Both left and right reacted against what they perceived to have been the boring conformity of the '50s, and the sense that an unaccountable establishment had been making the important national decisions without the input of ordinary citizens. Both rebelled against what seemed to be their liberal professors' smug assumption that all the basic questions of political and social organization had been settled, that managerial and technical expertise would see to the remaining problems, and that an "end of ideology," in the words of Daniel Bell's influential 1960 essay, had been reached. YAF no less than SDS was proud to claim the mantle of radicalism, revolution, even treason against the established order, and to embrace an ethos of freedom, individuality, and authenticity. As YAF's national chairman, Robert Schuchman, told Tom Hayden, "We do not want to be told what we must do . . . we want to be self-determined."[19] Chapman observed that conservatives who were older than the YAFers might not have known any more about the issues, "but when asked to nominate candidates or pass resolutions at a national convention, they are at least aware of the mood of the voters and the realities of 20th-century politics. For the senior party, thoughtless or extreme stands cost votes, victories and jobs." For young conservatives, however, rebelling against such practical considerations brought a sort of existential liberation, and the disapproval of their elders added to the attraction of extreme conservatism. Chapman noted that "parallel situations arise in many liberal organizations."[20]

Chapman and Gilder shared much of the younger generation's impatience and independence. They didn't need to be told that the times were a-changin'; the folk-singing political activist Joan Baez was going out with a student who lived across the hall, and when she sang in the shower they could hear her through the bathroom vents. They also knew that their opponents on both the right and left were greatly advantaged by their sense of being part of ideologically driven movements. However, they believed that moderate Republicanism could become a "fighting faith" to rally the "vital center," somewhat as their professor Arthur Schlesinger Jr. and the Americans for Democratic Action had invigorated liberal Democrats in the late 1940s.

And so in the aftermath of the November 1960 election, Chapman and Gilder and several other like-minded Harvard undergraduates created *Advance: A Journal of Political Thought.*[21] They wanted to establish a campus organization that could battle with SDS and YAF for the allegiance of the newly politicized college generation. As Chapman wrote to potential financial backers, "The political ideology that captures these students' loyalty will be the nation's guiding philosophy in years to come."[22] The group's ambition rose higher than student politics, as they hoped to provide a counterweight to conservative journals like *National Review* and *Human Events.* Chapman pointed out that at the time, "There was no moderate Republican magazine of any kind; in fact, no Republican magazine. *National Review,* nursed on conservative anger with Eisenhower, was not inclined, as we were, to announce itself plainly as Republican."[23]

Chapman and Gilder's timing was fortuitous. The need for a magazine such as *Advance* had occurred to other Republican politicians. Massachusetts district attorney Elliot Richardson wrote to Nixon after the election suggesting "a thoughtful, high-level journal of opinion," to be published under Republican auspices but without official sponsorship. It would serve as a forum for "responsible criticism, constructive alternatives to administrative proposals, new ideas, and the gradual articulation of a positive and dynamic Republican philosophy."[24] *Advance* fit closely with the lines of Richardson's proposal, and he offered useful support in getting it started.

Advance also came into being at a time when a power vacuum had opened within the Republican Party, and the GOP found itself badly in need of redefinition and revitalization. Gradually it would become clear that the forces that had sustained "modern Republicanism" in the GOP during Eisenhower's presidency were sputtering. Eisenhower himself had retired to his farmhouse in Gettysburg, Pennsylvania. While most Republicans still revered him, he was no longer able to play a determining role in the party, even if he had wanted to. Contrary to the opinion of many political observers, Ike had made a serious attempt to build up the Republican Party, and had partially succeeded; he had refilled its coffers and bolstered its organizational capacities.[25] Still, he had failed to recast the GOP in his image or to impress his moderate philosophy on the party in the way that Franklin D. Roosevelt had unified the Democratic Party around New Deal liberalism. Eisenhower deserved more credit than he received for reconciling with the conservative followers of Robert Taft; by the time he left office, the primal schism between Midwesterners and Northeasterners was largely a thing of the past. But the gap between the party's extremes was more dangerous than at any time since the 1912 Bull Moose bolt, because there were too few Ike-style moderate leaders to broker peace between the new forces on the left and right of the party.

This party split was, in a sense, the subtext of Eisenhower's famous farewell address in January 1961. The outgoing president warned against the dangers of the "military-industrial complex," and the temptations of fiscal irresponsibility and deficit spending: "plundering, for our own ease and convenience, the precious resources of tomorrow."[26] But who were the Republican leaders who would adhere to Eisenhower's stern credo of fiscal responsibility and constant pressure to hold down military costs? Nixon believed that Eisenhower's tight fiscal policy and the perceived "missile gap" had cost him the presidency. Rockefeller, in his proposed amendments to the 1960 Republican platform, had tried to pressure Nixon into outpromising the Democrats on defense spending, economic growth, and government expansion. Goldwater, like many Western and

Southern conservatives, was only a rhetorical conservative in fiscal matters, representing a region that clung to a self-image of rugged individualism while gobbling up millions of dollars of federal defense and public works spending. Arizona had become fixed in this pattern during the New Deal years, taking in $342 million in federal funds while remitting only $16 million in taxes.[27]

Like George Washington, Eisenhower left behind no political heirs. Nixon, whom Ike treated like an ugly stepchild, was a partial exception, but essentially built his own political career and network. Rockefeller had been a member of the Eisenhower administration in various capacities, but operated independently of Ike's political organization. The overwhelming majority of the people who served in the administration during the Eisenhower years left government to return to their former occupations, like so many Cincinnati returning to the plows, and made no attempt to pursue electoral politics. Stephen Hess, a speechwriter for Ike, calculated that only two of the twenty people who served in the Cabinet, and one of the 104 people on the White House staff, subsequently ran for office.[28] Eisenhower had hoped to recruit "virile, forward-looking, energetic Republican candidates as opposed to the 'party hack' type.'"[29] But one telling indication of the decrepitude of the Grand Old Party was that the average age of a Republican candidate in the 1958 Congressional elections was 60, compared to the Democratic average of 42.[30]

At the grassroots level, Ike had failed to persuade the millions of supporters who had joined the Citizens for Eisenhower groups to take an active part in Republican Party politics. Ike ruefully acknowledged that moderates' dependence on the quadrennial flood of citizen-volunteers, as opposed to longstanding party loyalists, made the GOP seem like "a kind of hibernating elephant who wakes with a mighty trumpet blast at election time and then rests calmly until the next campaign."[31] *New York Herald Tribune* publisher and party activist Walter Thayer, writing to Nixon after the 1960 election, lamented that Eisenhower's citizens organizations had been allowed to disintegrate following his victories in 1952 and 1956: "We have missed during the last eight years the greatest opportunity there ever was to build a strong party."[32] This lesson from the past was destined to go unremembered, and the volunteer organizations that were built around Nixon's 1960 campaign followed their predecessors into oblivion. Finally, although it was little noticed at the time, the national network of operatives at the grassroots level who had made up Dewey's machine, and who had been instrumental in lifting Eisenhower to victory in 1952, had been allowed to decay. By the early '60s many of those moderate precinct- or county-level leaders had died or retired. In short, the Republican Party was ripe for takeover.

Conservatives would be the ultimate beneficiaries of the party vacuum, but for a time it looked as though newly energized moderates might gain the upper hand. Republicans had gained twenty new House seats in the 1960 Congressional elections, and many of those new members were moderates. House Republicans selected Robert Stafford, the progressive former governor of Vermont, as the first chairman of the "Class of 1960." The most prominent freshman was moderate William Scranton, whose bipartisan appeal had produced a stunning victory in Democrat-dominated Pennsylvania that was already leading to talk of his presidential possibilities.

In his first month in office, Scranton defied the party leadership by joining other Republican moderates in voting to enlarge the House Rules Committee. The committee, under the iron-handed chairmanship of Virginia Democrat Howard Smith, was the keystone of the informal "conservative coalition" of right-wing Republicans and Southern Democrats that had ruled Congress since the late 1930s. Conservative dominance of the Rules Committee, which had the power to block or emasculate any domestic legislation unsatisfactory to conservatives, made it a drowning pool for civil rights initiatives in particular. House Minority Leader Charles Halleck gleefully anticipated that the Rules Committee would prevent Kennedy's domestic proposals from even coming to the House floor for a vote. He met with Smith and other Dixiecrats after the elections to consolidate working arrangements of the conservative coalition, telling reporters that they would see "eye to eye" in the new Congress.[33]

The minority leader's eagerness to do devilish deals with reactionary Democratic racists enraged seven moderate House Republicans, who issued a challenge to their party leadership in January 1961. "We repudiate any suggestion of a coalition of Southern Democrats . . . based on opposition either to civil rights or to other constructive legislation," they declared. Halleck's attempt "to narrow the base of our party, to dull its conscience, to transform it into a negative weapon of obstruction" would give the GOP "an image which has consistently been rejected by the Republican Party and by the American people."[34] Halleck shook some of his colleagues by their lapels to try to get them to fall in line, but the "Saintly Seven" persuaded other moderate and mainly Northeastern GOP representatives to vote to enlarge the Rules Committee and thereby overturn its controlling conservative majority. The twenty-two Republican dissenters provided the margin of victory in the 217–212 vote, leading the *Washington Post* to speculate that a moderate Republican bloc might hold the balance of power in the new Congress.[35]

In the wake of the Rules Committee fight, Chapman and Gilder's *Advance* magazine debuted to a blare of publicity in February 1961. The upheaval within the Republican Party resulted in more media attention and political interest than a student publication would have had any right to expect in less troubled times.[36] The novelty of college students proclaiming a passion for moderate Republicanism, which by the tail end of the Eisenhower era had a certain fuddy-duddy quality, piqued the press. So too did the incongruity of Harvard undergraduates opposing their alma mater's leading alumnus, despite Kennedy's legendary appeal to bright young people. Kennedy not only embodied the witty, cosmopolitan, pragmatic idealism that most Harvard students admired, his administration also drew upon the talents of many Harvard administrators and professors. The leading member of Kennedy's Crimson crew was McGeorge Bundy, Harvard's Dean of Faculty when Chapman and Gilder arrived on campus and a notable moderate Republican. Other Republicans in Kennedy's Cabinet included former Harvard Business School professor Robert McNamara at Defense and C. Douglas Dillon at Treasury. Columnist Walter Lippmann saw Kennedy's bipartisan appointments and the Rules Committee outcome as confirmation that "there is a consensus in the country, which may work out as a coalition in Congress, among the modern and progressive members of both parties."[37]

The *Advance* staffers recognized that JFK was essentially a centrist, and they were not immune to his allure. Chapman confessed later that "Of course, privately, we admired much of what Kennedy was and did."[38] Moderate Republicans knew that Kennedy excited young people and involved them in the Democratic Party in a way that few moderate Republicans—and only Goldwater on the GOP side—could. Over time, however, Chapman and Gilder and their fellow activists provided a coherent explanation for why they opposed both Kennedy and the Democrats on the one hand and Goldwater-style conservatives on the other. Theirs was in fact the most persuasive rationale for moderate Republicanism since Arthur Larson's 1956 bestseller *A Republican Looks at His Party*. It took a while for the editors to articulate a coherent position. Initially, *Advance* was content to assume that moderate Republicanism was defined by the politicians who claimed the label, and let the matter go at that. But the editors did eventually offer a compelling argument for why young idealists, even at Harvard during the Kennedy era, might look to the Republican Party for the fulfillment of their hopes.

"America continues in need of a new political philosophy," Chapman declared in *Advance*'s first editorial, "one that borrows freely from the best of 'conservatism' and 'liberalism' and whose essence is not mere moderation."[39] The editors were wary of being written off as "mere moderates," tied to the status quo. In one of their early promotional brochures, they dedicated their magazine to the cause of "an aggressive Republican party,

successfully applying conservative principles to meet the problems and opportunities posed by our modern age. Conservatism, to win, and to deserve
to win, must be progressive. To meet the threat of complacent liberalism,
conservatism must demonstrate its greater ability to provide for both man's
comfort and his freedom."[40] As the brochure's language suggests, the
seeming oxymoron "progressive conservative" was the magazine's favored
phrase to describe its outlook, although writers referred interchangeably to
their brand of Republicanism as liberal, progressive, moderate, "modern,"
"mainstream," and "constructive conservative" as well.

The *Advance* worldview began with the recognition that American society had, over the previous two decades, been reshaped by war, global responsibility, the baby boom, burgeoning prosperity, technological advances,
and an increasingly urban and suburban way of life. "Regional, class, religious and even racial distinctions are becoming always less important," the
editors argued. Any viable political party had to acknowledge these changes
and attempt to guide them "so as to conserve and advance the basic traditions, values and interests of the American people."[41] The editors believed
the Republican Party was best qualified to play that role, in view of its historic championship of civil rights and its claim to greater national "responsibility." But the party's failure to grapple with the complexities of modern
American political life had relegated it to the minority, with only two
Republican Congresses out of sixteen since 1930.

Republican inaction handed initiative to the Democrats by default, but
the party of the donkey was blemished in various ways that unsuited it for
leadership. Most importantly, Democratic dependence on the solid South
and long-serving Southern Democratic committee chairmen made the
party the primary obstacle to achieving civil rights for African-Americans,
despite much hypocritical liberal rhetoric. In the North, the Democrat-
controlled urban machines led to the election of precinct hacks, who were,
according to *Advance*, "as lethargic and myopic as the Southerners."[42] The
machines also spawned corruption and electoral fraud, which likely cost
Nixon the presidency in 1960, and elected mayors like New York City's
Robert Wagner who were content to preside over worsening urban decay.
When Democrats attempted to take action on pressing social problems,
they did so in a way that enlarged the federal role at the expense of state and
local government, and larded even worthwhile social programs with pork.
Advance's critique of the Democrats, like that of most moderate Republicans, tended to focus on domestic more than foreign policy. The magazine opposed ban-the-bomb activists on the left and superpatriots on the
right who were hostile to the United Nations and foreign aid and seemed
too willing to risk nuclear war. In practice, this meant that *Advance*
endorsed the bipartisan foreign policy consensus on free trade and

Communist containment, although occasionally they denounced Democratic handling of particular measures such as foreign aid bills, or issues such as civil defense.

Moderate Republicans considered Kennedy an ineffective leader, incapable of achieving significant legislation despite Democratic majorities of almost two to one in both House and Senate. To the limited extent that he tried to take action in the civil rights debate, he was stalemated by the resistance of conservative Southerners, resulting in his "cynical and cowardly abandonment of the solemn pledges of his campaign."[43] The President's good intentions were also frustrated by his party's dependence on special interests, particularly organized labor, which produced near-unanimous liberal Democratic opposition to Kennedy's bill to crack down on labor racketeering.[44] Chapman insisted that "You simply cannot blame the failures of Congress on the GOP. The Administration was and is chiefly responsible. Most of the liberal columnists and commentators agree on this point."[45]

So there was an opportunity for the GOP to take the reins of national leadership and even to promote itself as the more progressive party. In *Advance*'s view, there were two major changes the Republicans needed to make to become the party of the future. The first was the party's need to devise its own distinctive solutions to the issues of the day. The Republicans' failure to generate their own constructive and affirmative proposals was due largely to the party's negligible intellectual and policy-generating resources, reflecting the neglect of the party leadership.[46]

The other Republican imperative was to reach out to groups who had become less inclined to support Republicans, particularly minorities, intellectuals, city-dwellers, and young people. The RNC's research director William Prendergast had warned after the 1958 elections that the GOP's greatest weakness was in the metropolitan areas, and the need to reach out to urban constituencies was confirmed by the findings of an RNC committee on city politics after the 1960 elections.[47] To make this kind of outreach, the party would have to overcome the siren song of the "Southern strategy" and resist Barry Goldwater's counsel to "go hunting where the ducks are," i.e., to recruit segregationist and conservative Southern white Democrats. In fact, the major exception to *Advance*'s proposal for GOP outreach was the editors' willingness to write off the blue-collar demographic, the George Wallace voters of the future: "In the North *and* in the South, the most racially bigoted group in society is the lowest economic class, which feels the most threatened. This is also the group that nationally votes most Democratic; there is little hope for the Republicans here."[48] From its beginnings, the moderate Republican movement was antagonistic to any kind of populist appeal. But its elite approach, evident in its unwillingness to grapple with the working class, ultimately would limit its constituency and its potential as a national movement.

The editors vehemently resisted Goldwater's claim that the road to GOP success was to offer a consistent conservative ideological alternative to liberalism—"a choice not an echo," as the senator would put it. They saw Goldwater-style conservatism—or worse yet, conservatism of the radical right, John Birch Society variety—as a losing cause, morally and practically. They insisted that moderates were "the true conservatives," in a Burkean way, because they believed in devoting "judicious government attention" to problems that could spiral out of control and produce pressure for "extreme governmental action."[49] The editors agreed with Senator Clifford Case, who warned in the pages of *Advance* that dividing the parties along ideological lines might lead to division of the country along sectional, class, economic, and religious lines as well. The success of American democracy in keeping domestic order and peace in such a huge and diverse nation, Case believed, was "due in great part to the fact that the process takes place within each of our two great parties and not in conflict between parties."[50] In any case, the editors believed, a strict left-right split between parties would mean "abandonment of the center to the Democrats," leaving the GOP "a permanent and impotent minority."[51]

Such was the moderate outlook as Chapman and Gilder set out to fight opponents left and right. Their first battleground was the Young Republican National Federation. The national party had largely neglected the organization during Eisenhower's presidency, and many political observers wrote it off as unimportant since relatively few Republican politicians had participated in its activities in their younger years. However, many of those who took part in the organization went on to play less visible but significant roles in the senior party, particularly on the local level. Dewey had been active in the YR association in New York, along with Herbert Brownell and other close allies, and the national YR network had been instrumental in Dewey's campaigns for the New York governorship and the presidency, and later in Eisenhower's 1952 campaign. Dewey actually had a secret action group, known as the Mallards, made up largely of his supporters who had come up through the YR organization.[52]

While many moderates had forgotten the value of the Young Republicans, leaders of the conservative movement in the early '60s had not. For more than a decade, the YRs had been controlled by a faction known as "the Syndicate," though its members preferred to call themselves "the Hard Core" or "the Old Friends." Most members of the Syndicate were minor Republican functionaries, but the faction's leaders were two of the most important architects of the conservative movement: William A.

Rusher, the publisher of William Buckley's right-wing *National Review* magazine, and political strategist F. Clifton White. The YR organization was their primary power base, and by 1961, they had clandestinely resolved to use their control of the YRs, their network of contacts, and the Young Americans for Freedom to secure the 1964 GOP presidential nomination for Barry Goldwater.[53]

Chapman and Gilder had met Rusher shortly after they arrived at college and joined the Harvard Young Republican Club. The club had been founded in 1946 by Rusher and Charles K. McWhorter, who, like Rusher, was a returning World War II veteran and Harvard Law student. Rusher and McWhorter became allies in the national YR federation, and conspired to elect McWhorter president of the YRs in 1956. By the '60s, however, Rusher and McWhorter had ended up in antagonistic political camps. Both began as moderates and backers of Dewey and Eisenhower; Rusher had even supported progressives like Harold Stassen and Wendell Willkie while an undergraduate at Princeton.

Rusher was also, however, a committed acolyte of Senator Joseph McCarthy and other anti-Communist crusaders. When the Eisenhower administration attempted to curb McCarthy's excesses, with Nixon's mild and implicit rebuke of the senator in March 1954, Rusher was devastated. He heard the Vice President's radio address while on a car ride back to New York City after a weekend in the Hamptons, and faced "the realization that my support of Eisenhower had been a ghastly mistake . . . a whole young lifetime of uncomplicated devotion to the Republican Party was bleeding away, there in the back seat."[54] It was a sort of religious conversion. Eisenhower's sin, in Rusher's view, was that he refused to punish liberals for having "acquiesced all too easily in the presence of Communists among their colleagues" in the '30s and '40s. The point was not whether the threat of internal subversion in the '50s was real or illusory, but rather that Ike "let the liberals off altogether" and cravenly sought to restore national harmony instead of pursuing McCarthy's politics of revenge.[55] Rusher left the Republican Party in 1956 and began to describe himself as a "revolutionary" seeking to build a conservative third party.[56]

Rusher and McWhorter continued to keep in touch with their successors in the Harvard Young Republican Club, but their increasingly divergent political views made those reunions uncomfortable. McWhorter was appointed legislative assistant to Vice President Nixon in 1957, and remained an advocate of Eisenhower pragmatism and moderation. One member of the Harvard YR club recalled an awkward occasion in 1959, at the time of Soviet premier Nikita Khrushchev's state visit to New York, when Rusher screamed at McWhorter that "Your boss"—meaning Nixon—"has caused the Red Flag to hang over Fifth Avenue!"[57] Chapman remembered that he saw Rusher in those days as a hard-boiled ideologue with "a real mentality of 'you're with us or you're against us.'"[58]

Although Rusher had left the Republican Party, he still retained his backstage influence within the YRs with the assistance of his Syndicate partner "Clif" White, who had become increasingly interested in Rusher's brand of conservatism as a means for seizing power within the GOP. As a graduate student and instructor of political science at Cornell University in 1946, White had run in the Republican primary for the local Congressional seat and was trounced. He decided to enter the world of practical electoral politics "in order to find out why I had lost."[59] He became faculty advisor to the Cornell Young Republican Club, and rose rapidly through the ranks of the New York YR association and concurrently through the state Republican organization. By early 1949, he had formed a clique with Rusher and McWhorter that dominated the New York YR elections, largely by playing on the resentments of the rest of the state against Manhattan. In national YR politics, White and his clique teamed with allies in strategically selected states—usually in the South, West, and Midwest—to form the Syndicate. Their faction succeeded in placing their candidate in the top office at the 1949 national YR convention, and at the next five biennial conventions as well. White worked for Dewey's gubernatorial campaign in 1950 and Eisenhower's and Nixon's presidential campaigns, and generally toed the moderate Republican line. He was minimally rewarded for his efforts, however, because despite his mild manner and tweedy, bow-tied appearance, White was acquiring a reputation as a dangerous man.

When he had first arrived at Cornell after his war service, White had formed a chapter of the American Veterans Committee. The AVC was an idealistic but non-ideological organization of World War II veterans that agitated for jobs and housing assistance for returning servicemen, a strong United Nations, and an end to racial and ethnic discrimination. When White ran for state chairman in 1946, his candidacy was sabotaged by Communists, under orders from Moscow, who were attempting to infiltrate and take over the AVC along with many other liberal-leaning organizations. Although the Communists were greatly outnumbered, they were able to get their way through secrecy, rigid unity, manipulation of parliamentary procedure, and sheer ruthlessness. Sometimes the Communists simply demonstrated a superior grasp of organization and tactics, for example by voting as a bloc for one candidate while their opponents spread their votes across multiple candidates. At other times they would run roughshod over the democratic process, employing stalling motions to keep a meeting going all night until enough of their opponents had left in disgust, then ramming home the vote. Or they would wait until a rival candidate had built up such a majority that most serious challengers had dropped out, then destroy the front-runner through foul play and make their own candidate available as a last-minute substitute. That was the fate that befell Clif White, as he was on his way to victory in the state chairman's race, when at the eleventh hour the Communists spread a rumor that he had diverted AVC funds to an adulterous tryst with his secretary.[60]

Most of the non-Communists who witnessed these abuses of democracy were horrified; some were moved to join the CIA in order to dedicate themselves to attacking the evils of Communism around the world.[61] White, on the other hand, wanted to emulate the Communists. He saw in their example the methods by which a small, disciplined minority, uninhibited by bourgeois scruples over fair play or tradition or truth, could defeat a majority and bend an organization to its will. White used some of the tactics he learned from the Communists to score victories for the Syndicate, though success also derived from his meticulous attention to detail, mastery of parliamentary procedure, and maintenance of tight communication among his ranks.

As the '50s turned to the '60s, both White and the Syndicate turned toward conservatism. White became increasingly embittered by his lack of recognition from the moderate Republicans for whom he labored. He had received no reward for his work for Eisenhower, and though he was director of organization for the National Nixon-Lodge Volunteers in the 1960 election, Nixon snubbed him and refused to see him even when both were aboard the campaign plane. As White became disillusioned with the moderates, he became intrigued by the conservative activities supported by his friend and political ally Rusher. He had struggled to infuse his YR forces with the sense of belonging and importance that was crucial to maintaining discipline and unity. Ideologically committed groups like the Young Americans for Freedom already had that *esprit de corps*. While watching the YAF founders at work, conservative organizer and former Communist Marvin Liebman felt "nostalgic for my Young Communist League days." The young conservatives were "exactly like" the Red Guards of the '30s, "with the same anger and the same passion."[62] White saw in movement conservatism the vehicle through which to take over the Republican Party, using tactics he had learned from the Communists.

YAF members, under White's tutelage, began to put those lessons into action. Tom Hayden noticed that YAFers attending a spring 1961 meeting of a national conference on the Peace Corps "arrived unannounced and spread out in diamond formation (an old Communist trick) through the committees' discussion groups, in order to extend their influence." They also established a front group, the Committee for an Effective Peace Corps, with no mention of its YAF affiliation, which Hayden recognized as "another Party tactic."[63] And at the direction of White and Rusher and other members of the Syndicate, and with backing from a network of generous right-wing donors, the YAF cadres moved into the YR federation to build what Lieb- man called "a permanent nationwide union" of youthful conservatives.[64] Soon the New York State YR president was alerting moderates to YAF's plan "to thoroughly orient the campuses along the Goldwater line and to use the students as a vocal and militant force for Goldwater," and to infil- trate YAFers into the Young Republicans. The money being spent in this effort was "amazing," he reported. YAF had brought students from around the country and as far away as Washington State to a Goldwater rally in New York City a few days earlier; total transportation costs for the event may have run in excess of $50,000. The YR leader warned that "The senior people who are pushing this movement"—using the students to further their ends—"are being unreasonable and are quite willing to tear down the Republican Party to rebuild it along their image."[65]

The Communist-inspired maneuvers that White and his allies brought into movement conservatism provided an important reason for why the battles within the Republican Party between moderates and conservatives became so bitter. Moderates objected not only to the ideas of the right wing, but also to the movement's antidemocratic, take-no-prisoners, ends- justify-the-means approach to grassroots politics, which mixed McCarthy- ism and Communism in bizarre ways. Conservatives frequently asserted that their ideas were those of the silent American majority, but their behav- ior belied that claim. As one moderate activist commented, "We just didn't believe that the market [for the New Right] was that big. . . . Why else would the conservatives have had to resort to all the sneakiness and the bullying tactics?"[66]

The conservatives' manipulations often generated a backlash among the Republican rank and file, as happened at the YR national convention in Minneapolis in July 1961. That convention brought a heartening victory for the moderates, which Chapman was on hand to witness. Nelson Rockefell- er's operatives had recruited Leonard Nadasdy of Minnesota as a candidate for the national chairmanship "upon whom moderate forces, including the Nixon people, could probably unite," according to Rockefeller's political ad- visor George Hinman.[67] Rockefeller prevailed on Nadasdy's employer, Gen- eral Mills, to give him time off to run for the chairmanship and serve if he won, and contributed a nominal amount—around $10,000—to operations on his behalf.[68] The Syndicate was in an unusual state of disarray, having pulled their original candidate late in the game, and Rusher and White had turned over direct management of the campaign to junior lieutenants. (White was, after all, forty-three years old by this time, and no longer such a "young" Republican.) Nadasdy ran as a moderate conservative and an anti-Syndicate champion of clean government and party unity; his faction called themselves "the Gangbusters." Nadasdy won by a landslide.

The rest of the convention, however, was a defeat from the moderates' standpoint. In the race for co-chair (traditionally occupied by a woman), the Syndicate's candidate Pat Hutar won a narrow victory, while Chapman's former roommate, Tom Alberg, a moderate Nixon supporter, lost the race for the presidency of the College Republicans to an ultraconservative YAF-backed candidate. Chapman lamented that the moderates were unable to post their campaign mailings for lack of funds, and their homemade signs provided a sad contrast with the slick, professionally produced placards of the conservatives. The right's campaign was "financed by YAF and *actively* abetted by Goldwater aides." Chapman felt that "the crucial resource at the convention ultimately was not votes but money. . . . The 'Conservative Resurgence' is in truth little more than the product of well-financed activity in organization." But, he added, that was more than progressives had on the youth level nationally.[69] Overall, he concluded in a letter to New York GOP leader Judson Morhouse, "we're being out-maneuvered."[70]

After the YR convention, Rusher traveled to Washington to meet with John Ashbrook, a dedicated young conservative Syndicate member who had been elected YR chairman in 1957 and was now an Ohio representative in Congress. Both were irritated that an anti-Syndicate moderate had been elected YR chairman, and shared ideas about how they could whip their ranks back into shape. As the discussion moved to the continuing disarray of the GOP, Rusher had a brainstorm: what if a reunited group of Syndicate alumni extended their reach beyond the YR National Federation to a take-over of the Republican Party as a whole? They would constitute one of the largest factions in the party, and many of them had by now risen to positions of importance at the lower reaches of party politics. Their experience in the "black art" of winning YR conventions could easily translate to winning GOP conventions, particularly given that there hadn't been a contested nomination within the party since 1952. There was an obvious precedent in Dewey's use of his YR faction to create a political machine that took him to the top of the GOP heap. Further, as Rusher noted, most of the Syndicate's members "had, like White and myself, grown steadily more conservative" since their days as Dewey and Eisenhower supporters, although some like McWhorter had remained moderates and would have to be excluded from the conspiracy. Rusher and Ashbrook flew to New York to rendezvous with White and lay the groundwork for what became the Goldwater Draft Committee in the fall of 1961.[71]

Chapman and Gilder had high hopes that Nelson Rockefeller would provide funds for progressive Republican initiatives to counter the conservative surge within the GOP. In October, they asked the governor for $2,000 to fund a Republican Freedom Ride to Mississippi, where they intended to be arrested in solidarity with the integrated bus rides sponsored by the Congress of Racial Equality (CORE).[72] Rockefeller declined to support any such creative Republican activity. On the contrary, the correspondence of his advisor George Hinman bristled with hostility toward *Advance*. In October 1961, Hinman insisted that "It is important that we not be identified with Advance beyond what we have been thru David [Rockefeller] (which is too much). We can't be a sales org. for Advance. It will probably fail anyway + soon."[73]

The Rockefeller organization's antipathy toward *Advance* was surprising given that the magazine was enthusiastically supportive of the governor and his political positions, and Chapman was sufficiently close to be invited to dinner before Rockefeller delivered the Godkin Lectures at Harvard.[74] Nor were Rockefeller's donations to *Advance*—the largest of which was a $2,500 grant funneled through the National Committee for an Effective Congress in the spring of 1962—a drain on the governor's finances. They amounted to pocket change in comparison to the Babylonian sums he lavished on his profligate pursuit of the presidency throughout the 1960s.[75]

The main reason for Hinman's resentment of *Advance* was that he believed Rockefeller would take the GOP nomination if he could convince conservatives that he could be a party unifier, or at least if they would resign themselves to the inevitability of his nomination in '64. For that reason, Hinman was deeply opposed to moderate Republican activism of any kind. He believed that conservatives' opposition would be overcome not through confrontation but by educating them as to Rockefeller's essential soundness and appealing to their pragmatic desire to beat the Democrats. One member of Hinman's staff interviewed a YAF advisor and discerned that beneath his hostility to Rockefeller was an admiration for "many qualities about NAR, namely, his enthusiasm, energy, forthrightness and probably most important . . . his dedication to American principles and ideals." This conservative was also "a realist and quite significantly pointed out that if his views of freedom, liberty etc. were to succeed he must be with a WINNER."[76] Hinman wrote to Rockefeller complaining that progressive Republican Senator Jacob "Jack" Javits had a "penchant for attacking conservatives and conservative positions," and that this was "stupid politics. It can't do any good. The one thing that Jack does not need to prove is that he is a liberal. His problem is to win as many moderate and conservative votes as he can, and he certainly doesn't do it by this kind of talk."[77] Hinman believed that if Rockefeller acted as "a unifying and consolidating force" in the GOP, "the net effect will be to enlighten and liberalize the Party's total position."

Therefore, he believed that "it is vitally important that Nelson not get himself involved in the ideological divisions within the Party."[78]

At worst, Rockefeller and his advisors figured, conservatives could be bought off. The early 1960s intra-GOP struggle between conservatives and moderates acquired added piquancy and paranoia as each side engaged in clandestine warfare, recruiting spies and planting provocateurs in the enemy's ranks. Rockefeller maintained a network of paid and unpaid informants, whom his advisors referred to as Number 1, Number 2, and so on.[79] These men—"our conservative 'agents,'" as one Rockefeller aide called them—were well-connected figures in Republican and conservative circles, including YAF co-founder Douglas Caddy, RNC officer Ray Humphreys, and several members of Congress.[80] Chapman irritated the Rockefeller organization because he blundered across relationships that they wanted to keep secret and criticized conservatives who were in effect Rockefeller operatives, even when they appeared to be working against him. At the right moment, these conservatives would be called upon to declare themselves for Rockefeller, and strengthen his aura of inevitability. As a Rockefeller aide gloated about one of their prized spies, "No. 2 has the confidence of many of these conservative groups and has been an invaluable source of material. At the right time however, a well publicized move by No. 2 could be pretty dramatic."[81]

Hinman advised a confidant that "Bruce [Chapman] is taking some of his inspiration from people who don't have the best possible judgment about the Party's overall interest or our own."[82] One of the people Hinman had in mind was Representative Thomas B. Curtis of Missouri. Chapman and Gilder frequently were accused of being boosters for Rockefeller and New York Representative John Lindsay, but in fact the Republican politician singled out for the most frequent and lavish praise in the pages of *Advance* was Curtis, who in 1961 was fifty years old and serving in his sixth term as congressman. Although he has been almost entirely forgotten and never had a high public profile, Curtis had a substantial following within the GOP, and exerted significant influence on up-and-coming moderate politicians in the 1960s such as Donald Rumsfeld.

Curtis came from a long line of Democrats, but turned against his ancestral party to fight Democratic bossism, particularly the Kansas City Pendergast machine that had produced Harry Truman. Elected to Congress in 1950 as one of only a handful of GOP officials in Missouri, Curtis insisted on studying and deliberating issues individually, without reference to a precast ideology or opinion polls. In his view, this was "the Burkean theory of representative government" and the only possible approach for realists.[83] Curtis was a small-government conservative, but a pragmatic and flexible one. On the vexed issue of federal-state-local responsibilities, he wrote to the mayor of St. Louis: "I try to seek a balance. For the long pull, I believe it is better if people do things for themselves; the next best is for families to do things; the next best thing is for the private institutions within the community to function; the next best the local community governments; then the state governments; then the Federal government." On the other hand, he conceded that certain functions could only be well performed at the higher levels.[84] Curtis' approach typically led him to take positions that were strongly conservative on fiscal matters but moderate on social issues of the time.

Curtis campaigned for Taft in 1948 and 1952, but approved of Eisenhower's restraint with regard to fiscal matters and the power of the executive branch. He won his first election attacking Truman for his failure to seek adequate Congressional authorization for the Korean war, and later would make the same criticism of Lyndon Johnson's war in Vietnam. He believed that Eisenhower's military reputation gave him unique credibility to check the growth of the military-industrial complex. Curtis, who served in the Navy during World War II, led the effort to reduce waste within the military bureaucracy. He helped end the services' practice of running their own procurement agencies; the Navy, he discovered, tried to produce all of its own supplies, even down to the level of roasting its own coffee. Until the mid-1960s, Curtis also was one of the few Congressional opponents of the military draft.

Curtis faced repeated primary challenges from the right for his support of free trade, much resented by protectionist industries such as Monsanto in St. Louis, and civil liberties against the likes of Joe McCarthy. What particularly raised anger against him in the Jim Crow state of Missouri, however, was his unswerving advocacy of civil rights for African-Americans. Curtis' defense of civil rights was rooted partly in the Lincoln tradition of the GOP, but more simply in the belief that civil rights were at the base of the American philosophy of government and Judeo-Christian morality, and that their defense was "the most fundamental issue that confronts any government at any time."[85] Progressives did not agree with Curtis on all things, but as Chapman wrote to another moderate activist, they maintained "a friendly spirit" toward Curtis despite areas where he was more conservative than they were: "we overlook his failings and voting record (don't we?) because we properly respect his positive innovations in several other areas."[86]

Curtis was one of the prime movers in the "Young Turks" revolt of moderate Republicans in the House in the late '50s and early '60s, which included congressmen such as John Lindsay, Charles Goodell, Donald Rumsfeld, and Frederick Schwengel, with support from senators including Kenneth Keating and Hugh Scott. Rumsfeld remembered that Curtis "was kind of the intellectual leader of that group . . . a very thoughtful man, a real student, a teacher and a leader."[87] After the heavy GOP losses in the 1958 elections, the Young Turks helped to overthrow minority leader Joseph W. Martin Jr. His successor, Charles Halleck of Indiana, pledged to support the Young Turks' efforts to make the House GOP more aggressive and intellectually serious, but made no real attempt at reform.[88] Discontent with the Republican leadership continued to bubble among the Young Turks, erupting on occasions such as the vote on the Rules Committee enlargement, where Curtis was the leader of the "Saintly Seven." The Young Turks' critique found periodic expression in outlets such as Roscoe Drummond's column in the *New York Herald Tribune*.[89]

The fullest articulation of the Young Turks' argument, however, appeared in the March 1962 issue of *Advance*, in a series of articles entitled "Revise and Dissent: The Republicans on Capitol Hill." *Advance* offered a comprehensive catalogue of Republican flaws: the party's wholly negativist stance, the consequent lack of impact on legislation or the national course, the poor quality of many Republican congressmen, the "immoral" and "foolish" pursuit of the segregationist South, the neglect of black voters, and the deterioration of the minority, labor, and ethnic divisions in the RNC.

Ultimately, moderates felt, the party leaders were to blame for this state of affairs. *Advance* criticized the leadership's indulgence of Goldwater and his Southern strategizing. The moderates were unhappy with many of the attitudes and procedures of the leadership, particularly those which privileged the rural districts of the standpatters over the cities and suburbs.[90] Senate Minority Leader Everett Dirksen was only intermittently aware of the need for Republicans to offer a constructive alternative to Democratic proposals, while Halleck was intellectually lethargic. A series of press conferences with Dirksen and Halleck, dubbed "The Ev and Charlie Show," was an embarrassment, valued by the press "for little more than comic relief and quotable evidence of Republican intellectual pauperism."[91] With Eisenhower having retreated to the remoteness of Gettysburg, the absence of anything like a shadow cabinet on the British model, and Halleck and Dirksen's failure to provide effective leadership, the party was adrift.

The GOP's underdeveloped research and policy-making apparatus was both cause and consequence of the party's problems. The party required a well-researched and effectively presented program to succeed, but could not do so as long as the leadership held a basically anti-intellectual outlook and failed to address themselves to "the essential facts of modern American political life."[92] The pamphlets and papers of the House Republican Policy Committee, when occasionally produced, were "vague, unscholarly, boring, and very, very trite."[93] The Senate Republican Policy Committee was better funded but not much more productive. The leadership neglected to make use of professors and other sources of outside expertise, or to support individual congressmen who attempted to offer policy alternatives.

The leadership's most egregious failure in this regard was their acquiescence in the gross imbalance in Democratic to Republican Congressional staff workers—researchers, writers, counsels, and clerks. While the ratio of Democrats to Republicans in the House was approximately six to four, the ratio of Democratic to Republican staff employees on key committees ranged from seven to one (Public Works) up to thirty-two to one (Interstate and Foreign Commerce), with some committees having no Republican staffers at all. A similar imbalance prevailed in the Senate. As a result, the Republicans lacked the capacity to find the flaws in Democratic bills or to craft constructive alternative legislation. *Advance* characterized the imbalance as "a threat to the very concept of two-party government."[94]

"Revise and Dissent" was a highly public airing of the Republican Party's dirty laundry. The issue received wide media attention and plaudits from moderates like Nixon and Keating. Goldwater also offered backhanded praise, pointing out that he too had "prepared a number of position papers for the Republican Party, none of which has received too much attention from what we call the leadership here."[95] Goldwater's response highlighted the fact that both moderate and conservative activists opposed the GOP's stalwart leadership, although both groups obviously wanted to take the party in different directions. In addition, not all conservatives were as exercised as Goldwater about the staffing imbalance since, as *Advance* pointed out, "The dominant group in the constituencies of the right-wingers demands only opposition to the Kennedy Administration," not new Republican proposals.[96] Their rigid ideology largely spared conservatives the need to consider each separate issue on the evidence and its merits, which was no small advantage in their battles with moderates.

Advance's criticisms did not provoke any serious response from the party leadership, although the staffing imbalance in particular would continue to agitate the Young Turks. Nonetheless, it was an impressive effort for a magazine headed by two college seniors, although by this point a number of older contributors, including MIT junior professor John S. Saloma III and Harvard law student Emil Frankel, had joined the staff. After Chapman and Gilder graduated in 1962 and moved *Advance* to Washington, Saloma and Frankel would create the Ripon Society to carry the banner of moderate Republican activism in the Northeast.

Shortly after "Revise and Dissent" appeared, *Advance*'s benefactor Walter Thayer wrote to Chapman to say that Dwight Eisenhower had read the issue and wanted to be put on the mailing list.[97] The extent to which the former president was a fan was not clear to Chapman, however, until he sat under a candy-striped tent on Eisenhower's farm and heard Ike praising him before an assemblage of Republican bigwigs. The occasion was the All-Republican Conference (ARC) that *Advance* had pushed for since its first issue, and which finally took place on June 29–30, 1962. In attendance at the founding meeting of the new ARC organization were about a hundred members, ranging from Eisenhower and Nixon through YR president Leonard Nadasdy and a sprinkling of Republican professors and intellectuals. On the second day of the gathering, Eisenhower recommended *Advance* "very highly," and advised all those present to take out subscriptions.[98]

New York Senator Kenneth Keating was the prime mover behind the All-Republican Conference, which he described as an effort "to develop a newer and stronger base of Republican power," and to serve "as a top-level Party public relations and advisory body." Keating envisioned the ARC as a means of overcoming the huge Democratic advantage in power and public relations by providing "a ringing new voice to clarify, dramatize and publicize affirmative Republican positions and to challenge the opposition."[99] As Chapman and Gilder later characterized it, the ARC was to be "a grand Sanhedrin for the Grand Old Party."[100]

The same Gettysburg conclave also witnessed the announcement of a new National Republican Citizens Committee (NRCC), with an interlocking directorate with the ARC.[101] *New York Herald Tribune* publisher Walter Thayer had proposed it as a means of addressing the GOP's failure to harness the energies of the grassroots citizens' organizations that had sprouted and then been allowed to wither after the presidential elections from 1952 to 1960. The NRCC would be a permanent organization to bring in persuadable Democrats, independents, and Republicans who for whatever reason were not taking part in the regular party organization, such as the businessmen and professionals who joined the Republican Associates in California and similar volunteer organizations in Illinois and Pennsylvania.[102]

Both the ARC and the NRCC were attempts to respond to what Eisenhower and his associates—and also the editors of *Advance*—saw as systemic weaknesses of the Republican Party. Ike naturally felt that the Republicans' ideals and principles were those of the American majority and that his administration's record of solid accomplishments was superior to Kennedy's, but that the Democrats had done a better job of salesmanship. Kennedy was a media supernova and appealed to the public's emotions and instincts where Republicans offered only logic and statistics. At the same time, the GOP had not made sufficient efforts to reach out beyond its typical old, rich, and Caucasian clientele. Earlier that month, Ike had sent around a quote from a letter he'd received from former RNC chairman

Leonard Hall: "I was struck by the type of people we always have at Republican gatherings. I get the impression that we are still trying to elect candidates with descendants of the people who came over on the Mayflower. That boat was just not big enough! We never seem to have Italian-Americans, Polish-Americans, Negroes or many Catholics and Jews at such gatherings. This is one of the reasons why most of these groups do not feel at home with the Republican Party. It is also, in my opinion, one of the reasons why these groups do not feel that the Party is concerned with their problems."[103] Both the ARC and the NRCC would be means of improving the GOP's popular appeal, broadening its base, strengthening its showing among young and urban voters, sharpening its critical faculties, and improving its capabilities for fundraising and candidate recruitment. Ike praised the formation of these groups as "the most progressive steps our Party as such has taken in many years."[104]

Whatever hopes the ARC and NRCC inspired in Chapman and Gilder at the time, ultimately they came to see the Gettysburg conference and its aftermath as a case study in moderate failure. RNC chairman William Miller sabotaged the conference by opening it to the press (ensuring that no controversial issue would be discussed) and assembling a long line of speakers, who "unwittingly served to filibuster the conference to death with the same anti-Kennedy wisecracks and turgid clichés one could find in any day's *Congressional Record*."[105] The Gettysburg assembly was the first "quarterly" meeting of the ARC. "Unhappily it was left to Miller to call the second, which he never has," Chapman observed much later.[106] The ARC never met again. The NRCC lasted for several years, and succeeded in putting out some competent publications through its Critical Issues Committee, headed by Ike's brother, Johns Hopkins University president Milton Eisenhower. But like the ARC, the NRCC was undone by a combination of conservative opposition and moderate inertia.

Neither Goldwater nor Rockefeller attended the Gettysburg meeting. Both were suspicious of the Dewey/Eisenhower moderates and believed that the new citizens organization would be a stalking horse for a rival presidential hopeful like Michigan gubernatorial candidate George Romney. Shortly after the gathering, Goldwater blasted the conference and its organizers, especially Eisenhower. "These are the same people who have caused most of our present Party troubles," he wrote to Miller. "It is unthinkable that they should be given another opportunity to lead us down the path to political destruction." While this was a peculiar way to characterize the first Republican president to serve two terms since Ulysses Grant, Goldwater defiantly asserted that the creation of the ARC and NRCC "ran counter to the traditional principles of the Republican Party and the counsel of regular Party leaders."[107] He questioned whether the organizers were real Republicans, and criticized the new organizations as "splinter groups" detracting from the regular party organization. Goldwater added that "anyone who thinks that a group acting in such a capacity doesn't have designs on the formulation of policy or the selection of candidates is politically naïve."

Goldwater claimed that "no one [has worked] any harder than I have to create unity within this party," but he ultimately would countenance Clif White's decidedly unofficial conspiracy, already under way, to build a conservative counter-organization, mount a sort of *coup d'etat* against the party, and seize the nomination for Goldwater himself in 1964.[108] He would also give his blessing to the growth of a veritable infrastructure of conservative "splinter groups," many of which would be actively hostile to the official Republican Party organization. The best that can be said is that he genuinely seemed to believe that such conservative activism was ultimately party-strengthening, while the moderates' efforts were divisive and weakening. Likewise, he never understood that his stand against civil rights would sunder the party.

The moderates, for their part, were naïve for not understanding Goldwater and the conservatives. Keating had taken care to include within the ARC the twelve-man Congressional team, headed by Representative Melvin Laird, that had produced a "declaration of principles" on which all Republicans in 1962 supposedly could agree. But Goldwater's approval of such a vague statement of principles, in place of a strong and detailed platform, should have been a tip-off to the moderates that their aspirations for party unity were hopelessly misplaced. Instead of an issue-oriented platform, Goldwater would suggest "a simple statement like, 'We believe in the freedom of the individual.' All right. Senator Javits can take that in New York and apply it to civil rights, the Negro question and everything else. I can take it and apply it to 'right to work.' I can apply it to states' rights."[109] In other words, moderates were free to interpret the Republican "declaration of principles" as supporting integration, while Goldwater and his followers would interpret it as a defense of segregation. There could be no real party unity on these terms.

Nonetheless, the moderates would do their best to placate the implacable. Privately, Ike fumed about Goldwater after his post-Gettysburg outburst: "I am getting awfully sick of him." He was convinced that Goldwater was seeking the presidential nomination, although "he has no illusions he could be elected. . . . [W]hat is really annoying is that he wants to set himself up as the single authority and guiding voice for the Republican Party."[110] But in the name of "unity," the moderates would ask arch-conservatives to join the NRCC executive committee, thereby neutralizing its potential as a renovating force in the factional struggle that increasingly consumed the party.

Most analysts predicted that the party in power would lose seats in the 1962 off-year contests, but those expectations were confounded by the Cuban Missile Crisis which unfolded shortly before the elections. For several weeks before the crisis, Republicans had been pressing Kennedy with regard to potential Soviet aggression in Cuba. On October 10, Keating made a dramatic statement from the Senate floor that Cuba now possessed Soviet intermediate-range nuclear missiles capable of striking the American heartland. The administration dismissed Keating's claims, but they were confirmed three days later when a U-2 mission provided photographic evidence of Soviet nuclear missile sites in western Cuba. Kennedy thought the crisis would bring electoral disaster upon the Democrats in November. "Ken Keating will probably be the next president," he told an assistant when he showed him the U-2 photographs.[111] Instead, the successful resolution of the crisis, the inevitable rally-'round-the-flag effect, and the public perception that Kennedy had faced down the Soviets and forced the withdrawal of the missiles without making concessions lifted the Democrats.

Ted Kennedy's victory over Henry Cabot Lodge's son George in the Massachusetts Senate race was particularly galling to *Advance*'s staff, who had gone out of their way to describe the President's brother as someone who "has yet to distinguish himself in any commendable way" and was running on "a record of international sightseeing and an academic career highlighted by expulsion from college for cheating and dropping a pass in the Yale game."[112] The Republicans did elect some promising moderate governors, including George Romney in Michigan, William Scranton in Pennsylvania, Mark Hatfield in Oregon, and John Chafee in Rhode Island, while Nelson Rockefeller won reelection in New York. But the GOP gained only two seats in the House and lost four seats in the Senate. Vermont elected its first Democratic governor in 108 years.

Richard Nixon not only lost the gubernatorial race in California, but his famous farewell blast at reporters—"You won't have Nixon to kick around any more"—seemed to end his political career.[113] *Advance* had confidently predicted a Nixon victory and asserted that almost all those Republicans who had backed Joe Shell, Nixon's conservative primary challenger, were now behind the former Vice President, "except for a handful of what the Californians call 'Kooks.'"[114] But most observers felt that Shell's right-wing supporters had sat on their hands rather than vote for Nixon, costing him the election. Indeed, one Rockefeller contact had reported as early as March that "The John Birch Society cannot be underrated in Southern California. . . . They are young, emotional and well-financed. They see in Nixon's defeat a way to show their own strength."[115]

More alarming than the electoral defeats were the lessons the party leadership appeared to be drawing from its campaigns in the South. *Advance* had criticized the leadership's "suicidal" decision to allow Barry Goldwater to be chairman of the Republican Senate Campaign Committee and reorient it toward his non-mainstream conservatism, and had applauded the effort of Jacob Javits to remove Goldwater from that sensitive post.[116] The moderate position seemingly was vindicated by the overall failure of the Republican Senate campaign. But instead Goldwater and I. Lee Potter of the RNC's Operation Dixie were publicly exulting over the Southern "accomplishments," and urging even greater outreach to conservative and segregationist Southern whites. If their interpretation prevailed, moderates were sure, the '64 election would be a catastrophe.[117]

Moderates had long argued that the South was being transformed by industrialization and in-migration from other parts of the country, and that the GOP could form a winning coalition in the region built on the white middle class and the increasing numbers of registered black voters.[118] Support for racist GOP candidates would scupper this approach and would damage northern Republican candidates, such as Romney, Rockefeller, Javits, Scranton, and the new Ohio Governor James Rhodes, who had all garnered respectable percentages of African-American votes in the 1962 election. Lack of Republican participation in voting drives to enfranchise Southern blacks risked turning African-Americans into a Democratic voting bloc by default. The GOP had a chance to regain blacks' traditional loyalty to the party, however, by actions such as publicizing the victory of Edward Brooke, an African-American Republican who had just been elected Massachusetts Attorney General.

Advance confidently predicted that the GOP would become a force for integration in the South. They reported that the Republican Party in Georgia was "fully integrated" and had an African-American as vice-chairman of the state organization, and the North Carolina GOP had "welcomed Negroes and, to an extent, championed their needs." Many Republican candidates actively sought black votes in Georgia and the border states, while the race issue was avoided in Virginia and Florida. The editors predicted that some Southern Republicans would be "sufficiently far-sighted to seek Negro support," while "others, such as Senator [John] Tower of Texas, will be enough aware of the course of history to pose as slightly more moderate than their Dixiecrat opponents." But the editors continued to worry, with good reason, that Southern segregationists would be welcomed into the GOP and their views written into the next party platform.[119] William Rusher would soon pen his enormously influential *National Review* article "Crossroads for the GOP," which argued that the GOP *ought* to have Southern segregationists within its ranks to be a truly national party, and that further only a conservative like Barry Goldwater could win the South and therefore the presidency.[120]

Moderates' fortunes rose in January 1963, with the latest coup of the Young Turks in electing Gerald Ford as chairman of the House Republican Conference.[121] *Advance* also landed back in the headlines with an inside scoop of the Goldwater draft movement. An *Advance* informant had infiltrated the meeting in early December 1962 called by Clif White at the Essex Motor Inn outside Chicago. Although the spy had leaked the outlines of the meeting to the media shortly after the meeting, *Advance*'s version was the first full account, complete with verbatim quotes. The story described the persons in attendance at the meeting, the budgetary goals of the draft group, its organizational structure, its geographic strategy, and the roles of particular individuals such as William Rusher, who was to be "liaison with the 'nuts'—in charge of keeping the lunatic fringe helping without stigmatizing the Goldwater effort." The scoop also revealed the organization's plan to seize control of the Republican Party through a takeover of the National Federation of Republican Women and the Young Republicans, the recruitment of delegates to the 1964 GOP national convention, and the election of conservatives in mayoral and special elections.[122] A contrite White wrote to Goldwater that "The article which appeared in Republican Advance shocked and disturbed me greatly, as I am sure it did you. . . . I have now fairly reliably established that someone at the Chicago meeting must have had one of the small, secret tape recorders."[123]

Rockefeller's lieutenants had already been negotiating with the Syndicate on a peace settlement for the YR national chairmanship race. Rockefeller did not insist on a progressive as chairman, but merely hoped that the chairman would concentrate on building up Republican support across the board, as the moderate outgoing chairman Nadasdy had done, and not take sides in the '64 presidential election. All participants agreed that the GOP would be hurt if there was an embarrassing row at the upcoming YR convention. However, the Draft Goldwater forces had already been advancing funds and support for their designated candidate Donald "Buz" Lukens, as well as Nadasdy's disloyal co-chair Pat Hutar, for several months. Lukens was committed to breaking precedent and campaigning openly for Goldwater if elected. Rockefeller suggested Charles McDevitt, an Idaho conservative, as a compromise candidate. McDevitt had, however, acted as Nadasdy's campaign manager in 1960, which for Clif White was enough to classify McDevitt as a "liberal," though by this point White defined liberalism as any opposition to Clif White and his works.[124] So the Syndicate decided that it would be war at the San Francisco convention after all, and the Republican Party image be damned.

Soon thereafter, Rockefeller was informed that a John Birch Society member, Robert Gaston, had been elected as chairman of California's Young Republicans. Former Congressman John Rousselot, now a paid

Birch Society representative, had organized the Gaston campaign, paid for his delegate costs (including rental of over a hundred hotel rooms), and spent untold sums establishing "paper" clubs to provide enough votes to swing the convention.[125] "There is a definite, well-organized, well-financed program spearheaded by Rousselot to repeat this California situation in state after state," Rockefeller's source warned. "I cannot overestimate the importance that this group gives to controlling the young voter. . . . This California loss will make our task in San Francisco much more difficult." He added that "This situation is one we cannot walk away from without creating a void that could cause great embarrassment in 1964."[126] Chapman also insisted that Rockefeller faced a similar threat from the College YRs, and "that NAR is involved in this fight whether we like it or not and whether we invest a penny or not."[127] But Rockefeller did nothing. Columnist Robert Novak reported that when Chapman showed Hinman proof that Goldwaterite Young Republicans had locked up twelve states, and asked him for $50,000 to forestall a conservative takeover, Hinman flatly refused; Rockefeller was still trying to seduce the conservatives, after all.[128]

The 1963 YR convention proved to be a triumph for the Syndicate, a disaster for the moderates, and an embarrassment for the Republican Party. Chapman characterized it as "a rightist putsch."[129] Nadasdy remembered bitterly that "we were not facing the usual Syndicate operation at the Young Republican convention in San Francisco in 1963. Clif White was there, and he called all the shots. We had no preparation for the amount of time they spent on this operation, the money they threw into it, and the tactics that they used."[130] White and Rusher, leaving nothing to chance this time, directed the action from backstage and unleashed their full panoply of techniques. The Syndicate's forces kept Nadasdy in the speaker's chair for a solid twenty-two hours, preventing the convention from accomplishing any business by lodging an unending series of roll calls on abstruse parliamentary points. The Syndicate bought off California's Birch-controlled delegation by promising a patronage job to Gaston's wife. Syndicate bully-boys reduced the proceedings to chaos with constant noise and clamor, fistfights, thrown chairs, and a flying-wedge effort to physically force Nadasdy off the podium. Robert Novak found it revolting to watch "these hard-faced, implacable young men with crew cuts and buttoned-down collars, shrieking into floor microphones and chanting and stamping their feet in union in a systematic effort to disrupt the convention."

A report on the convention by the Delaware YR delegation complained of the "people who came with the openly admitted purpose of disrupting the proceedings, so that the convention could be prolonged to the point where many delegates would be forced to return home, leaving the convention in the hands of the few who remained behind." They believed that the

Syndicate's tactics showed "their utter contempt for their fellow delegates and for the parliamentary institutions which undergird the practice of freedom." A South Dakota delegate added that "We thought we knew what it meant to be conservatives until we saw these people. . . . [S]uddenly we found ourselves—mostly pro-Goldwater—becoming 'middle-of-the-road-ers' in comparison with the extremists."[131] The Syndicate may actually have lost the chairman's election; the chaos made a true count impossible, and when conflicting tallies at 5:15 in the morning showed McDevitt either winning or losing by two ballots, he opted to throw in the towel.

Although Lukens was declared the winner, he wasn't able to savor his victory. The Syndicate had picked him for his tractability and had forced him to agree that all his campaign decisions would be made by the Syndicate, and that they likewise would make all appointments subsequent to his election and could veto any promises he made during the campaign. As Edward Failor, one of Lukens' masters, reminded him, "The above agreements were specifically reviewed by you and myself . . . and you reaffirmed them. Pursuant to these promises we produced your election overcoming large odds." Failor listed dozens of appointments that Lukens was now obligated to make, including committee chairmanships and spots on coveted European jaunts. "These appointments were promised by Pat [Hutar] and/or myself for the sole purpose of securing your election," he insisted. "While we are pleased with most of them—because they will support you—they are *your* appointments resulting from *your* election."[132] Lukens had made his Faustian pact, and the devil demanded his due.

The Syndicate's victory pointed the way toward a similar right-wing takeover of the GOP national convention in 1964. Nadasdy told reporters that the YR convention was "a word of warning that the national convention in San Francisco next year is going to be one of the toughest ones the party's ever had. Far-righters spent much time and money to elect their man to head the Young Republicans, and they'll spend ten times as much to take over the senior party."[133] The right gained control of a significant piece of the party organization and never relinquished it. The convention's platform endorsement of abolition of federal income tax, U.S. withdrawal from the United Nations, the creation of a "Court of the Union" over and above the Supreme Court, and continuation of Southern segregation indicated how radical the organization had become. In their enthusiastic pursuit of victory through chaos, despite the national embarrassment to the GOP, the right demonstrated that they placed a much higher value on conservatism than the Republican Party. Lukens' endorsement of Goldwater and the direct participation of congressmen and Syndicate elders in the convention proceedings, all in violation of precedent and the organization's by-laws, showed that the right was prepared to cast aside rules and tradition in pursuit of its ends. And the ferocious post-convention propaganda offensive by Ashbrook and others—claiming that it was really Nadasdy and his allies who were responsible for chaos, that the right was only seeking to counter Rockefeller money and dirty tricks, that moderate Republicans were pursuing a "rule or ruin" strategy—met no real response on the moderate side.[134] The lone exception was Rockefeller's July 14 blast at the GOP's "subversion by a radical, well-financed, and highly disciplined minority."[135] But Rockefeller's statement was used to paint him as a "divider" by Goldwater and others, and it was too little, too late.

Further, Rockefeller's viability as a presidential candidate had been destroyed by his remarriage to Margaretta "Happy" Murphy that spring. Rockefeller's separation from his wife of thirty-two years, Mary Todhunter Clark, had produced only a temporary dip in his poll ratings; the American public had become more tolerant of divorce.[136] But Happy Murphy was almost two decades younger than the governor, and was the mother of four children ranging from three to twelve years old. She divorced her husband and signed over custody of the children to him only a month before she married Rockefeller. To much of the American public, Rockefeller's casting off his wife for a younger woman, and Murphy's abandonment of her young children, were truly scandalous. Women were particularly offended. The political reaction against Rockefeller was instant and adverse, with most commentators agreeing that he had committed political suicide.[137] His poll numbers plummeted, with the Gallup poll finding that while 43 percent of Republicans had preferred him for the presidential nomination the week before, now only 30 percent did; Goldwater, meanwhile, jumped from 26 to 35 percent.[138] The governor's aides were soon reporting the defections of many previous supporters. One described the reaction of former GOP nominee Alf Landon, who "thinks NAR is dead politically. He said he was very unhappy about the new situation and that before it happened he was for him, but that now he and his wife—especially his wife—wouldn't be able to support him."[139] Former Minnesota Governor Elmer Andersen told Chapman he had "the deepest admiration for NAR but . . . he probably has cooked his political goose."[140]

After the YR convention and Rockefeller's nosedive, Chapman and other moderate activists devoted most of their efforts to the civil rights fight. Meg Greenfield, who later became managing editor of the *Washington Post*, first arrived as a reporter in the nation's capital in the early '60s and gradually discovered that in terms of the political forces at work opposing and defending segregation, "I seemed to have the lineup of players just about completely wrong." With the Democratic Party heavily dependent on its Southern wing, even the northern liberal Democrats who were most vociferous in their denunciations of Jim Crow were mainly posturing. At that moment, she recalled, "the principal force truly committed to taking immediate action against the kinds of crude racial repression still officially in place seemed to be, of all things, a bunch of Republicans, many of them unknown." Some were Californians like Senator Thomas Kuchel or Northeasterners with urban constituencies like Javits and Case, but the most active organizers were "a few generally conservative midwestern House members," notably Thomas Curtis of Missouri and William McCulloch of Ohio. And the staffers within "this unexpected, loosely organized little community of conviction" were "young men who were subsequently to take off in wildly different ideological directions and make their own names in public affairs and Republican politics [including] Bruce Chapman . . . and George Gilder. But back then they were kids with a cause." Greenfield remembered that she was "utterly unprepared for the existence of such a group and felt as if I had happened upon some political Brigadoon." But she credited them with keeping the pressure on the civil rights issue and shaming their Democratic colleagues. When the events of Birmingham shone a national spotlight on the civil rights movement, "they were there and ready."[141]

By the summer of 1963, *Advance*'s editors were insisting that the civil rights struggle had become "the nation's most important domestic issue." The editors repeated their familiar criticism of Democratic hypocrisy and inaction, reserving particular scorn for Attorney General Robert Kennedy, who had not even bothered to read the muscular public accommodations bill introduced by thirty House Republicans. But the editors also slammed the Republican leadership, which had made no organized effort to expose Kennedy's failures or publicize the GOP's superior legislation and accomplishments. The RNC's summer meeting in Denver was lily-white and "deliberately contrived to give an impression of indifference to the Negro drive." The operating assumption of "Operation Dixie" was that the party had to organize itself around extremist candidates in the South before turning to racial moderation, whereas "The way to demonstrate the true Republican position would be to oppose racist Democrats with moderate Republicans." Halleck's reported view that "we don't have the Negro vote, we don't need the Negro vote, and we won't get the Negro vote" was self-fulfilling defeatism. On the positive side of the ledger, *Advance* singled out Michigan Governor George Romney's "exemplary" leadership of a protest march against housing discrimination in a fashionable Detroit suburb, adding that "it was noticed by Negroes across the country, and prominently reported in the Negro press. The party needs to break out of its political prudery on this issue."[142]

Advance's analysis of the Southern situation rested on the assumption that there were moderates in the region who would support civil rights.

This assumption was half correct. In many Southern communities, the terms of debate over integration were set by the business leaders and members of the local establishment, few of whom were fire-breathing racists. Indeed, they counted themselves, in the context of the time and place, as racial moderates. Their rallying cry was not "Segregation forever" but "Integration—someday." But these moderates were actually segregation's most effective defenders.

Rev. Martin Luther King Jr.'s 1963 "Letter from a Birmingham Jail" is best remembered for its searing descriptions of racist oppression and the famous statement "Injustice anywhere is a threat to justice everywhere," but essentially the letter is an attack on Southern white moderates who criticized King's tactics of nonviolent civil disobedience. King suggested that "the Negro's great stumbling block in his stride toward freedom is not the White Citizen's Councilor or the Ku Klux Klanner, but the white moderate, who is more devoted to 'order' than justice." The white moderates disdained the vigilante violence of the Klan, but equally deplored the civil rights movement's direct-action protests. They abhorred crude racism but had little interest in meaningful integration, particularly if it would disturb the status quo. They failed to comprehend the moral enormity of segregation and the moral necessity of breaking unjust laws. They advised activists like King to wait for such a time when the white Southern establishment would voluntarily grant African-Americans their constitutional rights, but King understood that "This 'Wait' has almost always meant 'Never.'"[143]

The civil rights movement made little headway in Southern towns where the white moderates were in charge. A yearlong campaign in Albany, Georgia failed because police chief Laurie Pritchett exercised moderation and restraint in handling demonstrators, often praying with them before arresting them, thereby depriving the movement of publicity and leaving the city's segregationist system entirely unchanged. The movement succeeded where blatant racists, such as police commissioner Eugene "Bull" Connor in Birmingham, Alabama, were in control. Connor and other reactionaries could be counted on to act brutally toward nonviolent black protestors, creating a televised spectacle of redemptive suffering that would horrify viewers and move the national conscience.[144] If all Southern communities had been led by moderates like Pritchett, the South might have remained segregated for years to come.

At the same time that *Advance* was scaling new heights of political visibility and influence, it was running out of money. *National Review* maliciously speculated that "evidently the economics of publishing (or a cramp in David Rockefeller's writing hand) have caught up with *Advance*."[145] The magazine boasted reasonably impressive distribution figures as well as increasing advertising revenue, but it was not enough. By August, the magazine was thousands of dollars in arrears for printing charges, salaries, and tax, with only $50 in the bank and insufficient funds to post renewal requests.[146] Hinman reported to Rockefeller that *Advance* had to come up with $7,000 or fold, and recommended letting the magazine die: "I think we could use our funds to better advantage and with better control of the results." Hinman conceded that "these fellows are dedicated and the only progressive voice that's being raised in the Party today, but I still think we shouldn't help them."[147]

Advance's creditors held off for the time being, and their printer agreed to publish their autumn issue despite the magazine's outstanding bills. In a desperate gamble that *Advance* would either become a national publication or fold, Chapman arranged to print an enormous run of 70,000 copies to promote the magazine in new markets. Then President Kennedy was assassinated in Dallas, devastating the nation and rearranging the electoral outlook for 1964. *Advance*'s cover featured a cartoon of an unhappy Kennedy under the headline "Can the GOP Beat JFK?," and was slated for mass distribution on November 22. The issue was immediately rendered unsalable and had to be pulped.[148] "[S]ending it out would have shown disrespect to the memory of the late President," Chapman and Gilder felt.[149]

The fall 1963 issue turned out to be the final appearance of the magazine, making *Advance* almost exactly coterminous with Kennedy's presidency. The assassination did not change Chapman's view of Kennedy's record as president: "history is not going to accord JFK with the laurels of greatness. He served through three relatively uneventful years, and made relatively few momentous decisions. He might well have achieved greatness if he had lived, but he did not."[150] The successes Kennedy did have were mainly symbolic, such as the Peace Corps and the nuclear test ban treaty, which were "commendable, but small and relatively unimportant," although both had been "inflated to epochal proportions."[151] Like most Republicans, Chapman and Gilder rejected Kennedy's proposed federal tax cuts—later enacted under Lyndon Johnson—as fiscally imprudent. Fiscal conservatives then believed that while lower taxes were desirable, to cut taxes at a time when the federal government was running a deficit would spur inflation and drown the economy in red ink. The notion that taxes should never, ever be raised would have struck them as grossly irresponsible.

Over the next several months of desperate and largely fruitless pleas for funds, Chapman and Gilder managed to produce and mail a number of short political analyses. *Advance* had concluded in its final issue that Goldwater could not beat Kennedy in the '64 elections, and that the conservative claim that he could was based on historical revisionism (i.e., the claim that Nixon lost the 1960 election because he was too moderate) and a host of faulty assumptions. "On issue after issue," the editors wrote, Goldwater "stands completely outside the mainstream of American political thought. Yet it is within that mainstream that a winning political campaign must be conducted. . . . [I]f led by Goldwater, the GOP will receive the enthusiastic kiss of death from the Radical Right."[152] The case against Goldwater had only strengthened now that Johnson would be the nominee, since Kennedy's assassination had produced a revulsion against extremes of both right and left, and "the candidacy of the first Southern President in this century undercuts hopes for a massive shift to the GOP in the South and gains from the alleged 'white revolt' in the North."

Chapman warned that "you moderates will be cruelly disillusioned if you think that just because a Goldwater candidacy is absurd it won't happen." And for Goldwater's backers, the delivery of the Republican Party machinery into the hands of the right wing was as desirable as victory in the presidential campaign. But the moderates remained oblivious: "Eisenhower and a number of other moderates have failed to see the extent of the right wing takeover since 1960, and to see as well that it is a far less respectable movement than that which he faced in 1952." Moderates were failing to become active or to match the hardball tactics of the right. They were making self-defeating compromises with conservatives, particularly in the composition of state delegations for the 1964 presidential convention. "The moderate leaders will discover too late that they should have fought things out ahead of time," Chapman foretold with Cassandra-like accuracy.[153]

When *Advance*'s creditors finally pulled the plug, Chapman and Gilder sent a bittersweet farewell letter to the magazine's friends and supporters, in which they were pitilessly pessimistic about the prospects for progressive Republicanism. At the root of the moderates' plight, as they saw it, was their "lack of self-conscious identity . . . like it or not, there is a body of thought, an outlook and a political strategy that is progressive Republican. . . . To deny it, to pretend that you're not a part of it when by your views you are, is to ask for political extermination by your less naïve opponents." Moderate Republicanism, considered as a long-range political movement, was "in terrible shape." It lacked articulate spokesmen, movement-conscious intelligentsia, action organizations, financial backers, and coordination. "The present deplorable situation," the editors concluded, was "the result of the progressives' failure to institutionalize their movement during the Eisenhower years. Now we do not even have the presidency to rally around. Individual candidates feel helpless against the right wing juggernaut, which began its mobilization even before 1960."[154] But they vowed to continue the fight.

Critics of moderate Republicanism have identified its crucial shortcoming as the lack of a national grassroots organization.[155] Chapman and

Gilder had earlier addressed this criticism when they rejected calls that they develop such a national action organization. "*Advance* exists to stimulate thought and provide information, not to elect office-holders, win convention delegates, canvass precincts, or picket meetings of SANE," the magazine informed its readers. "Such activities rightfully belong to the regular organization, to the Women's Federation, the Young Republicans, and to each state, county, ward and precinct organization." Yet these were precisely the venues in which the conservatives effected their takeover of the Republican Party in the 1960–64 period.

After his magazine's collapse, Chapman gave no encouragement to the groups of young people who came to him with plans for national moderate youth organizations and a revival of *Advance*. "I have told everyone discussing these matters that in my opinion any 'grass roots' movement of progressives has little hope of success," he wrote to George Hinman. If there was to be a national moderate movement, Nelson Rockefeller would have to create it. "Unless the governor, or someone like him (and there are very few 'like' him) does serve as a prime mover for a coordinated series of projects, all the advantage of the present and immediate future will be dissipated."[156] But by this point, Chapman no longer harbored much hope that Rockefeller would take action.

Advance bore witness to the collapse of the moderate Republican establishment during the short, thousand-day span of its existence. The full extent of the devastation, however, would not become clear until the party's nomination fell to Barry Goldwater and the conservative movement.

CHAPTER 3

✧

The Center Cannot Hold

The Republican Primaries of 1964

On the afternoon of November 22, 1963, a handful of young men were having a late lunch in the austere Bauhaus-style dining room of Harvard's graduate center. Most were members of the Ripon Society, a new and little-known organization of moderate Republicans. It seemed appropriate, as they sat underneath murals by modernist icons such as Joan Miró and Jean Arp, that they were planning a campaign trip on behalf of Nelson Rockefeller, a politician who was also a famous patron of modern art. Rockefeller, New York's progressive Republican governor, had two weeks earlier become the first GOP candidate to declare that he would enter the New Hampshire primary for the 1964 presidential race. As the lunch ended, the students gathered their Rockefeller posters and brochures and prepared to drive up to New Hampshire. Suddenly word crackled through the dining hall that President John F. Kennedy had been shot in Dallas. "All of us were stunned," one of the group recalled.[1] Although they were Republicans, JFK had been their political inspiration. When the news confirmed that Kennedy had been killed, they were caught between grief for their fallen hero and fear of Lyndon Johnson, who succeeded to the presidency; Dwight Eisenhower was hardly the only Republican who considered Johnson "an unprincipled political animal."[2]

Their visit to New Hampshire abandoned, the members of the Ripon Society gathered to discuss how the political situation had changed and what they should do next. Over the next several weeks, they hammered out a manifesto, "A Call to Excellence in Leadership: An Open Letter to the New Generation of Republicans." The Ripon declaration made headlines around the country, was reprinted in full in newspapers such as the *New York Herald Tribune*, and catapulted the group into the leading ranks of moderate Republican activists. The open letter was intended to be the moderates' "call to arms" against the increasing momentum of the conservative campaign for Barry Goldwater.[3]

The Ripon Society grew out of Bruce Chapman's and George Gilder's *Advance* magazine, and in time would replace *Advance* as the most visible moderate Republican activist organization. Its *raison d'etre* was an article published in *Advance* in March 1962 by Emil Frankel, a Harvard law student who had spent the previous year studying in England on a Fulbright scholarship. While in Britain, Frankel had met several members of the Bow Group, a research organization founded in 1951 by bright young university graduates dissatisfied with the Conservatives' image as "the Stupid Party."[4] He was impressed with the way those young men and women would conduct an in-depth study of a problem such as tax policy, make themselves experts in the subject, and then, taking into account the Conservative tradition and the current political situation, state what they believed the Tory position ought to be. Although the Bow Group was not at that time directly tied to the party leadership, Frankel pointed out in his *Advance* article that "its sheer intellectual power and vigor brings it considerable influence."[5] Several Bow Group chairmen went on to Tory cabinets, including Geoffrey Howe, Norman Lamont, and Michael Howard. The group did not have a set political stance, but its insistence on considering issues without prejudging the conclusions, its reliance on research, and its freedom from ideological conformity inclined it toward moderation.

Frankel became an editor at *Advance*, as did John S. Saloma III, a charismatic young professor at the Massachusetts Institute of Technology. Like Frankel, "Jack" Saloma had studied in England as a Fulbright scholar and had crossed paths with some members of the Bow Group. As a graduate student in government and political economy at Harvard, Saloma interned for Massachusetts Senator Leverett Saltonstall and Missouri Representative Thomas B. Curtis, both moderate Republicans. He considered running for Congress from his home district in Weymouth, Massachusetts—he was attractive, well-connected, and a forceful speaker—but grew disillusioned with party politics in the Bay State and instead tried to advance the moderate position in the GOP from behind the scenes. He served as a consultant to moderate Republicans in Congress and wrote papers for the American Enterprise Institute, a fledgling conservative think tank. Saloma later speculated that since AEI was under investigation by the Internal Revenue Service at the time, the organization "must have found it advantageous to have a visibly liberal Republican among its authors."[6]

Frankel and Saloma continued on as *Advance* editors after the magazine relocated to Washington in the fall of 1962, but they felt that moderate Republican energies in the Boston area needed a new organizational focus. The Bow Group model of a research organization appealed to young, educated Republican moderates who were annoyed by liberal condescension at places like Harvard and by the anti-intellectualism of many regulars in the Grand Old Party. In the words of one of those moderates, "we were tired of apologizing to the world of ideas for being Republicans, and to fellow Republicans for being interested in ideas."[7] And so in December 1962, Frankel and Saloma circulated a confidential "Proposal for an American Bow Group." They observed that the same conditions that led to the Bow Group's formation in Britain now bedeviled the Republican Party in the United States. The GOP offered few opportunities for young professional people in the 20–35 age range, who were turned off by "the popular image of the Republican Party as a party of obstruction and negativism." They worried that the party might not survive if ideological conservatives succeeded in forcing a break with its progressive tradition, and they saw an opportunity for a research group to support moderate Republicans and to form a bridge between the academic community and the GOP. If such an organization were to succeed on the scale of the Bow Group, they concluded, "it can play a crucial role in reshaping the Republican Party and its image."[8]

Saloma served as chairman of the group that became the Ripon Society from its first meeting in December 1962. The organization evolved slowly over the next year. It took its name from Ripon, Wisconsin, the birthplace of the Republican Party. (The town's claim was disputed by Jackson, Michigan, but a Republican organization was unlikely to name itself the Jackson Society.) The Society's meetings took place every month or so at locations around Harvard. Some sixty individuals attended at least one Ripon meeting during its first year, and about half became active members. Most were graduate or professional students and young professors from Harvard, M.I.T., and the Fletcher School of Diplomacy at Tufts. All were men; it would take several years before Ripon included significant numbers of women. Although conservatives liked to pretend that progressive, East Coast Republicans were all top-hatted aristocrats, the members of the Ripon Society were mainly middle-class, and a preponderance of them were from the Midwest. A representative member was Lee Huebner, who emerged as the organization's lead writer. He grew up in a middle-class Lutheran family in Sheboygan, Wisconsin, where both his parents were high school teachers, and attended Northwestern University before going to Harvard to pursue a Ph.D. in history.

The group decided at its first meeting not to become an expansive grassroots organization, since its members lacked the time, money, and bureaucratic talent to form a moderate counterpart to conservative activist outfits such as Young Americans for Freedom. They resolved to educate themselves politically through systematic study of policy problems, supplemented by discussion meetings with guest speakers. They hoped to influence Republican party policy through research and publication, redefine the range of political debate "to favor the expression of a progressive or constructive Republican point of view," and change the image of the GOP "from one of reaction to one of action, to that of a party capable of providing mature and responsible leadership in and solving the problems of the twentieth century." While the idea of a "Third Way" was not yet current, Saloma did ask the group to think about "the emerging or still virgin political issues where we can assert a Republican position of our liking, pre-empting both the Republican old guard and the Democratic liberals."[9]

Like other political organizations of young people during the 1960s, including Students for a Democratic Society (SDS) and Young Americans for Freedom (YAF), Ripon spent a great deal of energy and effort on internal disputes over the correct course of action. Saloma spoke for one faction that emphasized practical commitment to moderate politicians, political campaigns, and work in the Republican Party machinery. He believed that the organization's main function was to recruit and train a "cadre" of intelligent and energetic young people who could advance the moderate position in the GOP as party workers or candidates. These recruits would fan out across the country to involve themselves directly on behalf of moderate Republican politicians and form an idea- and information-sharing network while reporting back to a central office in Cambridge. An early study of the organization asserted that "Saloma envisioned the Ripon Society as a machine to wage war against the conservatives, in order to return the Republican party to the path of sanity."[10] Another faction was more interested in research and intellectual theorizing, more academic in approach, and less consistently critical of conservatism and conservatives. In contrast to SDS and YAF, however, most of Ripon's members were moderates temperamentally as well as politically, and debates within the Society rarely became personal or inflammatory.

Whatever their tactical views, the Riponers unanimously agreed that the civil rights struggle was the most important challenge facing the GOP. One member, Eugene Marans, went to Washington to work with his old college roommates Chapman and Gilder to assist Republican congressmen in preparing civil rights proposals and pressuring the Kennedy administration to take action against Jim Crow. The moderates' stance naturally opposed them to the ideological conservatives who were willing to sacrifice civil rights in order to recruit Southern segregationists to the GOP ranks. The civil rights struggle aside, however, most of Ripon's members initially confined their activities to research and study, with only a few taking a direct part in political activities, such as Rockefeller's nascent campaign. Saloma in hindsight faulted Ripon for "remain[ing] quiescent" at a moment when "conservatives were quietly mobilizing the Draft Goldwater movement, taking over one state organization after another."[11]

Kennedy's assassination galvanized the Ripon Society to activism. The Society's "Call to Excellence" manifesto, issued a little more than a month after Kennedy's death, displayed a certain appreciative ambivalence toward the late president. It echoed the Republican charge that Kennedy's policies were too much style and not enough substance. But it insisted that the Republican Party "seek in its future leadership those qualities of vision, intellectual force, humaneness and courage that Americans saw and admired in Kennedy."[12] An early article on the Society commented that "When they dream, Ripon members like to think of themselves as heirs of Kennedy, not Eisenhower."[13] The open letter further observed that while Kennedy "moved with shrewd political understanding to preempt the political center," Republican moderates for the most part remained silent. The GOP would have had great difficulty in reclaiming the center from Kennedy if he had lived, but his passing meant that "the center is once again contestable"—unless the party was foolish enough to select a divisive conservative like Goldwater as its presidential nominee. The "Call to Excellence" urgently warned against a Southern strategy that would align the small-population states of the South and West against more urbanized parts of the country, "or any similar realignment that would pit American against American on the basis of distrust or suspicion." Ripon was optimistic about the possibility of building a coalition around a moderate consensus, adding to the traditional Republican base the new, suburban middle classes of North and West, recent college graduates, young professional men and women, and "the moderates of the New South."

The open letter made an eloquent plea for moderation, conceding that it was not "a full-blown philosophy proclaiming the answers to all our problems" but rather "a point of view, a plea for political sophistication, for a certain skepticism to total solutions. The moderate has the audacity to be adaptable." While a Republican moderate would approach problems from a more conservative perspective, and a Democratic moderate from a more liberal one, "The fact that we may meet on common ground is not 'me-tooism.' It is time to put away the tired old notion that to be 'real Republicans' we must be as different as possible from our opponents!"[14]

At the same time, Ripon's members were well aware that conservatives had a strong rhetorical point in arguing that moderates lacked conviction, and that this argument had some basis in fact. Saloma had seen at first hand, during his internships in Congress, how moderates often failed to muster sufficient passion for battling their conservative opponents. "Many of the moderates owed their success to candidate organizations and media campaigns directed by political consultants," he observed. "They disliked the tough infighting of Republican national politics. Conservatives in Congress privately referred to the [moderates] as 'the soft slipper boys.'"[15] Two of Ripon's members pointed out that the "Call to Excellence" grew out of long internal debates "as to whether political centrists were inherently at a disadvantage in competition with ultra-rightists or extremists of the left. Could one see both sides of an issue and yet hold strong views about it? Was it possible to be a compromiser and to retain the conviction and authority to lead?"[16]

Accordingly, the open letter called for moderates to take on "the image of conviction and dedication" that hitherto had been the attraction of extremists throughout history. "We must show our world that our emotion can be aroused by a purpose more noble and a challenge more universal than the cries of an irresponsible extremism.... We must learn to be as excited about openmindedness as we once were about final answers." While retaining an "honest uncertainty," moderates should not be afraid to embark upon crusades, particularly when a moral issue such as civil rights was at stake. In ringing tones, the letter concluded: "The question has often been asked, 'Where does one find "fiery moderates"'? Recent events show only too clearly how much we need such men. If we cannot find them, let us become them."[17]

The extensive media attention given to the "Call to Excellence" thrust Ripon onto the national stage. The *Washington Star* was one of the many papers that editorially hailed the Society as "a new voice in the land . . . a voice that ought to be heeded."[18] Lee Huebner recalled that "The wide response reinforced members' conviction that one could contribute to the American dialogue by saying the right thing at the right time."[19] The group stepped into the vacuum created by the silence of moderate Republicans nationally and the bankruptcy of *Advance* magazine after Kennedy's assassination. And as the editors of *Advance* had already discovered, the controversy sparked by Republicans criticizing their own party made good copy.

For all its eloquence, however, the "Call to Excellence" raised questions about moderates' identity that the organization would wrestle with for years to come. The leader of the Trumbull Society of New York, a moderate Republican organization at Columbia University, congratulated Frankel on Ripon's achievement: "For the first time Republicans of our generation have had something intelligent and perceptive to say.... It is time to dispel the common misconception that the Democrats have a monopoly on progressive thought and action." Still, Frankel's correspondent was bothered by "the problem of identification. What is a progressive Republican? How does he differ from a moderate Democrat? And if he does not differ, why be a progressive Republican?"[20]

Another interested reader of the letter was former president Eisenhower, who wrote to *New York Herald Tribune* publisher Walter Thayer to convey "my delight that an obviously intelligent group of people has taken the trouble to voice its concensus [*sic*] on this important subject, and also to express my basic agreement in the mainstream of its thinking." Eisenhower somewhat petulantly refused to concede that Kennedy had been a centrist, although he did agree that the Republican Party had been "too slow—and possibly too complacent—to recognize the value of and need for adopting a doctrine of the center."[21] Ripon would encounter difficulties in working with Eisenhower-generation moderate organizations such as the National Republican Citizens' Committee, and its members did not see themselves as "modern Republicans" in the 1950s mold. Younger activists such as Saloma and Chapman frequently expressed impatience with the lingering influence and cautious approach of Ike-style moderates within the GOP.[22] But Ripon's members did see Eisenhower as "the beginning of our modern political story," and his early endorsement of the group's first statement was helpful.[23]

The figure from the Eisenhower era who retained the most appeal for many in Ripon was former Vice President Richard Nixon. Shortly after Kennedy's assassination, by which point Nixon had relocated to New York in the wake of his defeat and disgrace in the California gubernatorial election, several Ripon members met with Nixon at the Recess Club on Wall Street. Nixon mesmerized the group with his signature *tour d'horizon* presentation of foreign policy issues. Huebner marveled that "He knew more about the inside politics and policy considerations in every country he ever visited than most political observers even within those countries."[24] Even these relatively unsophisticated young men could tell that Nixon was stiff, shy, and evidently uncomfortable with small talk. But they were favorably impressed and flattered when he asked for their help in preparing memoranda on the moderate position in the 1964 campaign.

When the GOP presidential contenders resumed their activities after the month-long hiatus following Kennedy's death, Ripon members traveled from Boston to New Hampshire to work for moderates, including Rockefeller and other declared or undeclared candidates such as Pennsylvania Governor William Scranton, Michigan Governor George Romney, and Maine Senator Margaret Chase Smith, the first woman ever to run for president. Others focused on stalling Barry Goldwater's candidacy. A Ripon group of Harvard Law School students, dubbed "the Truth Squad" by the press, followed the Arizona senator around the Granite State asking loaded questions. "We want to make him express his sillier views," one student told a reporter, with the goal of tripping him up so that attention might turn to "more meaningful consideration of other candidates."[25] On the stump, Goldwater proved gratifyingly inarticulate, ill-prepared for the question-and-answer format of New Hampshire campaigning, and prone to shoot from the hip. Goldwater protested that the press distorted his positions, but in fact most movement conservatives agreed with the views that he blurted out under questioning, including the advisability of invading Cuba, making Social Security voluntary, establishing a national "right-to-work" law, giving control of nuclear weapons to battlefield commanders, and pulling the United States out of the United Nations if Red China were admitted. Such radicalism went over poorly with New Hampshire Republicans, who believed in low taxes and penny-pinching government but were not prepared to overturn the New Deal's achievements or risk nuclear war. Goldwater was accustomed to addressing audiences that shared his ideological assumptions, but his first sortie outside the bubble of movement conservatism revealed that the articles of faith in its catechism sounded strange and downright dangerous to many Americans.

While Goldwater alarmed voters in the political middle, moderate Republicans couldn't unite around one person to oppose him. Rockefeller was the obvious challenger, but his controversial remarriage had soured his prospects, particularly with the prim New Hampshire electorate. As the state's leading newspaper, the *Manchester Union-Leader*, daily denounced the governor as a "wife-swapper," Rockefeller regretted that he had passed up a chance in 1948 to wrest the paper from its ultra-conservative publisher, William Loeb.[26] Polls showed that neither Goldwater nor Rockefeller attracted a majority of the state's Republicans, just as both failed to excite most rank-and-file Republicans nationwide.

Henry Cabot Lodge Jr., the 1960 GOP vice presidential candidate, emerged as the first in a succession of alternatives to Rockefeller upon whom moderates pinned their hopes. A group of four young Bostonians who had campaigned for Lodge's son George in his quixotic 1962 senatorial race against Teddy Kennedy put together a draft movement for the elder Lodge, who by that time was the U.S. ambassador to South Vietnam. George wrote to his father to tell him about the brewing campaign, "and he wrote me back a very fuzzy letter about how Foreign Service regulations prevented him from taking part in politics. But I could tell that he was delighted."[27] The Rockefeller and Lodge families had long been entwined in various ways, and the two candidates' grandfathers had been political allies. Rockefeller warned his friend "Cabot" that "any fragmentation of the moderate effort could be dangerous," and extracted from him a promise not to authorize a campaign on his behalf.[28] Lodge would not set foot in New

Hampshire during the primary season, but neither would he repudiate the draft movement. His supporters denied that they were splitting the moderate ranks, given the low enthusiasm for Rockefeller as well as other moderate candidates on the ballot such as Harold Stassen and Margaret Chase Smith: "The need for an alternative was clear and it was on that basis that we offered Lodge."[29]

The Lodge campaign had a flavor of kids putting on a show. Most of the participants were political amateurs and unpaid volunteers. While Rockefeller and Goldwater forces spent hundreds of thousands of dollars on the race, the Lodge campaign stayed within a $25,000 limit, most of it raised locally. The group mailed letters to all 96,000 registered Republicans in New Hampshire, and received back an astonishingly high number of postcards pledging support for Lodge as a write-in candidate. The remainder of the budget went toward television ads recycled from the 1960 campaign showing Lodge as a World War II hero and popular anti-Communist battler at the United Nations.[30] When the votes were counted on March 10, Lodge won an upset victory with 35 percent of the vote to Goldwater's 22 percent and Rockefeller's 21 percent, with 17 percent for Nixon as a write-in candidate. Lodge also collected all of the state's delegates, although most of New Hampshire's leading Republicans were candidates pledged to Goldwater.

Lodge's defeat of Goldwater in New Hampshire demonstrated that hardcore ideological conservatism was a turnoff for many Republicans. So too did a less-heralded contest in Maryland's Sixth Congressional District in the spring of 1964. The incumbent Representative Charles McC. Mathias faced a primary challenge from L. Brent Bozell Jr., brother-in-law and political soul mate of William F. Buckley Jr. Although little recognized at the time, this was one of the first elections pitting an ideological champion of the New Right against a moderate Republican.

Bozell was one of the golden boys of the conservative movement. He had co-authored a book with Buckley defending Joseph McCarthy and had served as a speechwriter for the senator. He had been a founding editor of *National Review,* and for many years Buckley's will stipulated that in the event of his death sole control of the magazine would pass to Bozell.[31] He was a powerful writer and debater who had catapulted Barry Goldwater into his position atop the conservative movement by ghostwriting his 1960 bestseller *The Conscience of a Conservative.* Bozell was not only an intellectual but a compelling personality and a plausible political figure in his own right; many believed he might become president someday.[32] His goal in entering the Maryland primary, however, was not to win office so much as to push the GOP to the right. He acknowledged that it was practically impossible to elect a conservative Republican in a district with a three-to-two

Democratic registration edge, but believed Mathias was too liberal to be allowed to represent the Republican Party.

In fact, "Mac" Mathias embodied Eisenhower's saying that a man might be conservative in some areas and liberal in others. He came from an old and wealthy Maryland family, long active in politics. His great-grandfather had helped to found the state's Republican Party, his grandfather was a state senator who had campaigned with Theodore Roosevelt, and his father took him to the White House to meet presidents Coolidge and Hoover. As a Congressman, he was an ardent anti-Communist and a fiscal conservative who voted repeatedly against agricultural subsidies, increases in the national debt, and government competition with privately owned utilities. The Republican Policy Committee determined that he had supported party positions 83 percent of the time, and even the conservative Americans for Constitutional Action gave him a 50 percent rating.

At the same time, Mathias believed that legislators were obliged to be open-minded, to consider the issues unemotionally, and to follow the dictates of conscience. He felt that the GOP could not "continue to be a truly national party unless we have the benefit of the views of those who are conservative, those who are moderates, and those who are liberals," much as the party had to balance the views of rural and urban interests, labor and management, industry and agriculture.[33] His service in World War II, when he was among the first Americans to inspect the smoking ruins of Hiroshima and Nagasaki, made him skeptical about the use of nuclear weapons. Marriage to the daughter of a Republican governor of Massachusetts broadened his political network. The pollution of his beloved Chesapeake Bay turned him into a pioneering environmentalist.

Mathias was vulnerable to a conservative challenge, however, principally because he was one of the few Southerners in Congress to stand publicly against segregation. As he saw it, opposition to oppression had defined Republicans since his great-grandfather ran for office in 1860 on the same anti-slavery ticket as Abraham Lincoln. As city attorney of Frederick in the 1950s, Mathias abolished segregated seating in the town opera house and other public facilities. He voted to enlarge the House Rules Committee in 1961, and he was one of the three Republican members of the Judiciary Committee who, in January 1963, submitted the first civil rights bill to integrate public accommodations. This was a courageous stance in a state that regularly provoked diplomatic incidents when ambassadors from newly independent African nations were thrown out of segregated restaurants only a few miles away from the U.S. Capitol.[34]

Bozell attacked Mathias' support for civil rights legislation, which he luridly predicted would lead to "compulsory integration" at bayonet-point. He claimed that Mathias was soft on Communism and favored foreign aid "give-aways" and "Big Government" programs. He also proved decades ahead of his time in attacking his opponent's religion, insinuating that Mathias was an atheist since he had given only lukewarm support to a Constitutional amendment authorizing prayer in public schools. (Mathias was actually a devout Episcopalian who supported voluntary school prayer but agreed with the Supreme Court's rulings prohibiting compulsory prayer.) Bozell emphasized that he would be "A Republican Who Will VOTE REPUBLICAN."[35]

The claim that he was not a "real" Republican stung Mathias, whose party loyalty was bred deep in his bones. He asked the Ripon Society to research Bozell's philosophy in depth to find material that could be used against him. This was not hard to do, since Bozell had detonated one inflammatory statement after another in his roles as editor and movement activist. Lee Huebner pored through a stack of *National Reviews*, chuckling and gasping at "all of these outrageous things that Bozell had written."[36] As Goldwater's ghostwriter, Bozell had affected a generally libertarian stance. Shortly after finishing *Conscience of a Conservative* in 1960, however, he had moved his family to Spain, where he was impressed by the Catholic domination of society enforced by the dictator Francisco Franco. His wife rhapsodized over the medieval poverty and piety of Spain, so unlike modern materialistic America: "No machines—and no drabness; no television—so they have their feast days which *they* make fine by their spirit and laughter; no social security—so they take care of their own."[37]

Bozell returned to the United States inspired to use government power to inhibit citizens' freedom and enforce their virtue. This was in keeping with the American tradition, he believed, since the Founding Fathers' writings contained "not a hint of the ideology of freedom . . . not a word suggesting that freedom is the goal of the commonwealth."[38] As Huebner summed up Bozell's position: "His ideology eschews the usual values of individualism; he openly courts a totalitarian-authoritarian way of thinking."[39] As it happened, Huebner's verdict was shared even within *National Review*. Buckley's protégé Garry Wills warned that Bozell, by editorializing against freedom, was "taking an authoritarian course that can do NR no good, I am afraid. Franco may be good for Spain, but transferred to America his kind of rule goes down hard. . . . I know the stock cry of fascism shouldn't keep the Right from sticking to its principles; but Brent's piece is the first that gives that accusation some philosophic grounds in NR."[40]

Mathias selected a few choice offerings from the smorgasbord of Bozell's extremist views for ridicule, including demands for a U.S. invasion of Cuba, demolition of the Berlin Wall, a revival of McCarthyism, and legislative defiance of court orders. He deplored Bozell's "demagoguery" on civil rights, foreign affairs, and especially religion and the manner in which Bozell used it "to play upon the emotions of many devout citizens."[41] Bozell, in Mathias' view, was a "radical" seeking to impose an "alien doctrine" on the GOP.[42]

Mathias focused his attack on what he called the conservative movement's "subversion of the Republican Party."[43] He pointed to Bozell's 1961 *National Review* editorial calling for conservative "infiltration" of the GOP, with the caveat that the movement "preserve its freedom of action" by ensuring that "its ties with the Republican organization will be, as a practical matter, severable—ideally at a moment's notice."[44] The contest in the primary election, in Mathias' view, was not between conservative and liberal points of view. Rather it was "between those who have given their whole loyalty to the Party of their choice and those who acknowledge a superior allegiance that permits them to use the Republican Party at their will and to discard it when it has served their purposes."[45] Bozell protested that this was in effect red-baiting, substituting "conservative" for "Communist," but his own McCarthyist background limited sympathy for this claim.

Despite Bozell's high-profile endorsements from Goldwater and other conservative heroes, and considerable out-of-state money and volunteer assistance, Mathias swamped him in the primary election.[46] Mathias observed that he was not the only moderate under attack: "These people are trying to tear the Republican Party apart all over the country," he wrote after the election. In Ohio, "the same gang" ran against Robert Taft Jr., claiming that he was a "left-wing liberal," and even minority leader Charles Halleck faced a right-wing primary challenge. "But the regular Republicans stood together and held the party together."[47] "Conservatives often claim that if the voters are given a genuine choice between conservatism and liberalism, conservatism will prevail," one Maryland paper editorialized after Mathias' election. "It would appear that a conservative myth has been exploded, at least temporarily."[48] Mathias' victory suggested that moderates could prevail against the right-wing minority if they had attractive candidates and refused to concede that movement conservatism was the most authentic form of Republicanism.

In the wake of his triumph in New Hampshire, Henry Cabot Lodge would go on to win (still in absentia) on a write-in vote in the New Jersey and Massachusetts primaries. A Gallup poll in April suggested that Lodge was the choice of 46 percent of Republican voters, with Nixon trailing at 17 percent, Goldwater at 14 percent, and Rockefeller at 13 percent. But since he continued to refuse to put himself forward as a candidate, his success suggested that the voters' real preference was for "none of the above." Meanwhile, although Goldwater proved unable to win a contested primary throughout the early months of 1964, Clif White's clandestine mobilization of volunteers to take over county and state organizations continued to pick up convention delegates. White's erstwhile ally, Charles McWhorter, recognized the Syndicate's tactics at work and was among the first to realize that Goldwater's delegate totals would be insurmountable unless he was stopped in the California primary in June.[49] Unfortunately, the only candidate who was in a position to oppose him there was Nelson Rockefeller, the candidate from the moderate/progressive wing who stood the least chance of winning.

No less an authority than Robert F. Kennedy believed that if Rockefeller had been the Republican presidential candidate in 1960, he would have won the election.[50] Rockefeller might well have attained the Oval Office after 1960 had it not been for his divorce and remarriage, and even more importantly for the fact that he was Public Enemy Number One for GOP conservatives. "Every movement needs a villain," conservative strategist William Rusher once reflected. "For the GOP Right, Nelson Rockefeller was it."[51] Rockefeller even provoked the creation of the Conservative Party of New York State in 1962 to mount candidates against the governor and his Republican allies. Some of the reasons for that enmity reflect well on Rockefeller, such as his fervent advocacy of civil rights and criticism of far-right kookery. More broadly, some of the hatred reflected an angry and enduring American populism that abominated the Rockefellers along with the East Coast, bankers, cities, Jews, immigrants, cosmopolitanism, modernism, ethnic diversity, and other perceived alien forces.

But not all the criticism was unmerited. Rockefeller represented a commingling of financial and political power that worried many liberals as well as conservatives, and much of the banking and insurance legislation he advanced as New York's governor was highly beneficial to his family's interests. Rockefeller presented himself as a hard-liner in foreign policy, taking a firm stand against Communism and in favor of the growing American involvement in the Vietnam war. In other respects, however, he was hard to tell apart from many liberal Democrats. He dispensed patronage on a scale that would have impressed Boss Tweed. He would attempt to out-do Lyndon Johnson's Great Society in producing vast numbers of government programs at correspondingly vast expense.[52] The Brasilia-style plaza and architectural complex that he had built behind the state capitol in Albany, at a budget-busting cost of $2 billion, is a modernist ode to big government in marble and concrete: gargantuan, sterile, inefficient, and utterly lacking in human scale. Rockefeller did not share most moderate Republicans' preference for decentralization and skepticism regarding government's limitations. And while he liked to say that he was an economic conservative since "No one has as much to conserve as I do," he was already showing a willingness to jettison his early claim of fiscal restraint. Eventually he would make end runs around the state constitution and engage in financial chicanery that helped bring on New York's near-bankruptcy in the mid-'70s.

Rockefeller never understood the extent to which he was anathema to the GOP's right wing, and he followed an inconsistent strategy of alternately attacking and then abasing himself before the conservatives. At times he showed a willingness to match the intraparty trickery of the right, for example by maintaining a spy network within conservative circles. But he failed to do for Republican moderates and progressives what a few wealthy individuals were doing at that time for the conservatives: building an enduring political infrastructure of opinion journals, think tanks, donor networks, and grassroots organizational support. Because he proved incapable of recruiting and raising up his own delegates to the GOP national conventions, he was forced to accommodate himself to the delegates who had already been chosen, usually by conservatives. Despite his assets and abilities, Rockefeller did not produce a lasting political legacy. Ultimately his failures dragged down the moderate Republican cause.

By the spring of 1964, after his poor showing in the early primaries, it was evident that Rockefeller had little chance to secure the nomination. He stayed in the race largely in the hope of spoiling Goldwater's bid and opening the way for a moderate nominee at the convention. The California primary would bring both his formidable advantages and even more formidable drawbacks to the fore.

Rockefeller's road to California led through the Oregon primary in mid-May. With his back against the wall, Rockefeller mounted an unusually emotional campaign against Goldwater, whom he declared to be out of the "mainstream" of the Republican Party and American life in general. Oregon was a state with a significant number of moderate Republicans, who were in fighting fettle after a right-wing coup seized the party machinery in Multnomah County, home to Portland and the state's most populous county. Other voters were drawn by the campaign's inspired slogan, "He Cared Enough to Come," which highlighted the absence of Lodge as well as Goldwater.[53] Rockefeller won a surprise victory, the Lodge campaign collapsed, and the Republican primary campaign boiled down to the California race between Rockefeller and Goldwater.

It was fitting that California should be the stage for a duel to the death between the left and right factions of the Republican Party. That clash had been playing out in the state since the early twentieth century, when California's politics had been decisively influenced by the progressive movement. Though there is little agreement on what the movement was, or even whether it existed at all, in California progressivism was defined by Republican Governor Hiram Johnson's campaign against the Southern Pacific Railroad's virtual ownership of the Republican Party and the state's government. Johnson led a middle-class, moral reform movement that stood for clean government, an active and educated citizenry, weak political parties, and an absence of machine bosses.[54] A key progressive reform was the practice of cross-filing, which allowed candidates to compete in any party primary regardless of party affiliation. Cross-filing favored moderates with wide appeal such as Earl Warren, who in the 1946 gubernatorial primaries won the nominations of both the Democratic and Republican parties. California's nonpartisan political culture tended to force successful officeholders to base policies on factual analysis and justify them with concrete results. Lacking the safety net of ideology and party support, politicians were obliged to negotiate with constituencies outside the usual party interests. This meant that Democrats had to broker compromises acceptable to management as well as labor, and Republicans had to act to improve social welfare.[55]

In practice, cross-filing favored the Republicans, as up until the late 1950s the Democrats elected only one governor in the twentieth century and commanded both houses of the state legislature for only one term. As California expanded, tripling its population from under 6 million in 1930 to 18 million by 1964, the dominant Republican pragmatists began to struggle with a harder-edged and more ideological form of conservatism. The source of this new conservatism continues to be the subject of much speculation, but many political observers at the time believed it to be related to the dislocating effects of rapid growth and population influx, particularly in southern California, and the heavy presence of military installations and defense contracting corporations.[56] The new conservative movement first flexed its strength in 1958, when it overcame moderate opposition to put an anti-union "right-to-work" law on the ballot, with disastrous results. The party lost its registration edge, control of the legislature, and the contests for governor and senator. The Democrats promptly abolished cross-filing and reapportioned the state's legislative districts to entrench their dominance.

The right wing was energized rather than discouraged by these GOP setbacks, and conservatives mounted a takeover of the party's grassroots organizations such as the Young Republicans and the California Republican Assembly (CRA), the state's largest and most influential party-affiliated volunteer organization. In 1963, when the CRA was still operating under the banner of "Reasonable Responsible Republicanism," rightists created a rival organization, United Republicans of California, whose abbreviation (UROC) was meant to evoke the mythical roc, a bird big enough to carry off an elephant.[57] At the chaotic March 1964 CRA convention, conservatives used tactics from Clif White's playbook to complete their takeover of the last remaining moderate-controlled organization. The conservative leaders of these groups included a large number of members of the extreme right-wing John Birch Society. Former Republican Congressman John Rousselot, now the Birch Society's spokesman on the West Coast, was pleased to tell reporters that the platforms and resolutions passed by the conservative-dominated Young Republicans, UROC, and CRA were "similar to John Birch Society positions" in their opposition to civil rights and the United Nations, and their support for the Liberty Amendment to abolish federal taxes.

The defeated moderate candidate for the CRA presidency charged that while some Goldwater supporters were sincere and dedicated Republicans, their victory at the convention "would not have been possible but for the active help of John Birch Society members and those who are in close sympathy with them. Goldwater should certainly repudiate this support—but he has to date refused to do so."[58] Goldwater was indeed reluctant to repudiate the JBS members, partly because one of the lessons of Nixon's 1962 gubernatorial primary campaign against right-wing challenger Joe Shell seemed to be that many California Republican voters would interpret criticism of the Birchers as an attack on all conservatives. And, as one internal Goldwater campaign memorandum admitted, "Fortunately or unfortunately, the Birchers are contributing a substantial portion of our workers and some of our leaders in many important areas and can be expected to be increasingly in evidence as the campaign progresses."[59]

The Goldwater campaign was a vehicle through which the right wing sought to gain control of the GOP volunteer organizations and the state Republican Party itself. Dr. Bernard M. Tully, head of the Citizens Committee of California, claimed to have raised $500,000 to put a conservative on the ballot for every office in the state.[60] The *Los Angeles Times* observed that "From one end of California to the other, bitter campaigns are under way for posts on GOP county central committees that in most election years are coveted by few Republicans." Conservatives reportedly spent $25,000 in Orange County alone to boost their candidates in races for unpaid party posts. The right wing mounted primary challenges to moderate Republicans running for Congress and the state legislature. Houston Flournoy, a moderate from Sacramento running for reelection to the Assembly, faced off against a John Birch Society member who was endorsed by the YRs and supported by an army of volunteers from UROC. Flournoy's opponent had little chance of winning in the general election, but this was beside the point for the conservatives. Since all of the candidates for the 139 Congressional and state offices on the June 2 ballot would have one vote apiece in writing the party platform at the state GOP convention in August, performance in the November general elections was a secondary concern.

The main goal was the promotion of the conservative cause, which could be achieved with or without Republican electoral victories. As conservative strategist William Rusher emphasized, even if Goldwater lost in California, he should stay in the race to make the best possible bargain for conservatives on the candidate, platform, and control of the party machinery. If he won in California but dragged the GOP down to disastrous defeat in November, his candidacy would still have had numerous "compensating advantages." Conservative Republican candidates from the South and West would fare better under Goldwater than under any other candidate, "and those elected would in turn affect the complexion of the Republican delegations in state legislatures and in the Congress." Conservatives would retain many party offices to which they had been promoted during the campaign. "Above all, a genuinely conservative campaign is the only method by which the conservative cause can be reintroduced into what is now called 'the mainstream of American life'—and this would occur whether our defeat was disastrous or not."[61] For moderates like Flournoy, this sort of gamesmanship that privileged the conservative movement over the Republican Party carried horrible risks. He warned that Republicans had to decide "whether or not the Republican Party is going to retain a position of power and elect candidates or whether it will turn into an ideological sect." Victory for the conservatives would "destroy the party as a competitive force on the California scene.... They're more interested in their own little game than in the party."[62]

The leaders of the state party—mostly moderates—seconded Flournoy's criticism of the right-wing push. The most dynamic Republicans in the Assembly, a group known as the Young Turks (which included Flournoy, William Bagley, Robert Monagan, and John Veneman), were all moderates and critics of "extremism" at the local level. Senator Thomas Kuchel, a protégé of Earl Warren, blasted "the odious techniques of subversion and intrigue" that were being used by a "well-disciplined few to capture and control our party." State GOP chair Caspar Weinberger, an enemy of the right since he had endorsed Nixon over Shell in 1962, decried the efforts of "a small, narrowly based and heavily financed group ... whose real aim is the destruction of the Republican Party."[63] Weinberger felt in hindsight that the conservative movement had much in common with the confrontation policies of the left a few years later in the '60s: "[I]f you weren't with me, you were against me. And if you were against me, you had to be crushed.... It was totally antithetical to anything that might have been described as a way to win. It wasn't a winning strategy—it wasn't designed to be."[64] However, the California progressive tradition had reduced the ability of party authorities to check insurgence at the grassroots. For the conservative rebels, the opposition of the party establishment only increased their sense of righteousness.

The thrill of defying moderate elites was central to the appeal of the Goldwater campaign. The single piece of campaign literature that best captured the anti-establishment, anti-moderate mentality of Goldwater conservatism was the short book *A Choice Not an Echo*, self-published by conservative activist Phyllis Schlafly in April 1964. Goldwater volunteers in California distributed half a million copies of the book during the primary campaign.[65] In Schlafly's conspiratorial view, America's so-called democracy was controlled by "secret kingmakers," a shadowy group mostly made up of internationalist New York investment bankers. These bankers dominated the media and drew other elites into their cabal through conclaves such as the Bilderberg Meetings, a series of conferences sponsored by the royal family of the Netherlands to discuss matters of common European-American concern. The kingmakers operated through "their most trusted agents," men like Nelson Rockefeller, Henry Cabot Lodge Jr., and Robert McNamara, who had served in high-ranking government positions during both Democratic and Republican administrations. Bipartisanship of this sort was not praiseworthy but rather was "destructive of the two-party system. The voters expect Republicans to be Republicans, and Democrats to be Democrats. Trading in and out of both parties confuses the issues and especially the responsibility" for policy-making.[66]

According to Schlafly, the nefarious kingmakers endeavored to select the presidential nominees of both parties, determine the outcome of elections through "brainwashing and propaganda blitzes," and "work toward 'convergence' between the Republican and Democratic parties so as to preserve their America Last foreign policy and eliminate foreign policy from political campaigns."[67] They had manipulated every Republican national convention from 1936 to 1960, purposely selecting "me-too" moderates who would lose elections rather than risk the nomination of an uncontrollable conservative such as Robert Taft who would have campaigned "on the issues" and won.[68] They had drawn the United States into World War II "to get the American taxpayers to protect the kingmakers' heavy investments in England and Western Europe," and they propped up Communist regimes so that they could engorge themselves on foreign aid programs. They profited from the welfare state and deficit spending, and "Since the New York kingmakers dominate the consortium which fixes the interest rate the Government has to pay on its obligations, they have no incentive to see deficit financing stop."[69] Moderate Republicans, in short, were dupes of the bankers, for whom the moderate wing of the GOP was their political instrument. The kingmakers could be thwarted only by the people's nomination of a presidential candidate who would stand up to them—namely Barry Goldwater, who had called for the GOP to offer "a choice not an echo" in his nominating speech.

Consciously or not, Schlafly evoked a centuries-long tradition of rage against treasonous elites in secret control of the world; in that sense,

A Choice Not an Echo bore some uncomfortable similarities to the conspiratorial explanations of the "Protocols of the Elders of Zion" as well as anti-Masonic and Know-Nothing tracts. Her pamphlet essentially restated the Birch Society's fulmination against "the Establishment that has been running the Roosevelt-Truman-Eisenhower-Kennedy Administration . . . those tremendous forces which, throughout all of this one continuous administration under different names and fronts, have been striving 'so to change the economic and political structure of the United States so that it can be comfortably merged with Soviet Russia in a one-world socialist government.'"[70] Indeed, the Society's founder Robert Welch referred to Schlafly as "one of our most loyal members." Many California Republicans found the paranoia of the Schlafly-Birch outlook repulsive. But for the persuadable, *A Choice Not an Echo* offered an all-encompassing explanation of political reality and a powerful stimulus for action.

Even conservatives who were not Birchers and did not believe that political outcomes were dictated by all-powerful string-pullers were galvanized by Schlafly's call for resistance against Eastern elites. Resentment of the East and its financial establishment had long been a theme of Southern and Western populism, although Schlafly was standing the nineteenth-century radical tradition on its head by rallying the grassroots to defend free-market capitalism and antistatist policies.[71] Schlafly also articulated a key article of conservative faith, which was that a "hidden" majority of Americans were conservative but rarely participated in elections since there was so little to choose from between the two parties. If the moderates could be thwarted and a true conservative like Goldwater could gain the Republican presidential nomination, the parties at last would divide along ideological lines, and a newly energized conservative majority would sweep the Republicans to victory.

On the surface, most of the advantages in the California contest between Goldwater and Rockefeller seemed to belong to the Arizona senator. For conservatives, the opportunity to oppose Rockefeller—the rich, arrogant, liberal libertine, whose family and state had long occupied honored spots in populist demonology—was as rewarding as the opportunity to support Goldwater. UROC's president declared that Rockefeller was "socialist, monopolist, internationalist, pro-communist . . . he is a *licentious* person politically and economically—*not fit for any political office.*"[72] Others on the far right accused Rockefeller and his family of controlling the media, dictating the content of public education, attempting to deprive citizens of their right to vote, and seeking to allow the World Court to declare the U.S. Constitution and Bill of Rights illegal.[73] In the face of this apocalyptic threat, the ideological zeal and total certainty of the Goldwater volunteers propelled them to tireless efforts on behalf of the campaign, to the point that many of them neglected their careers and families. One conservative activist remembered that the Goldwater workers "felt so strongly about the issues in that campaign that they were willing to lose tremendous amounts of money, to lose their business. Many of them, really, almost destroyed themselves."[74]

Rockefeller began with virtually no presence at the grassroots level. The very concepts of precinct organization and door-to-door campaigning—the areas where Clif White and other conservative tacticians excelled—were foreign to him. Rockefeller was able to line up an impressive array of California's establishment on his delegate slate, headed by Kuchel and including some of the state's most prominent industrial, financial, civic, and citizen leaders, with a sprinkling of artists, scientists, architects, and doctors thrown in for good measure. But the theory that voters would line up behind the "natural leaders" of the community no longer held in the increasingly anti-establishment climate of the 1960s. Indeed, one leader of the anti-Rockefeller Conservative Party of New York thought the greatest appeal of the Goldwater campaign was its revolt against "the good, the wellborn, and the able."[75]

Doug Bailey, one of the founding members of the Ripon Society, had worked for Rockefeller since 1960, and by 1964 was the number-two person on Rockefeller's foreign policy staff behind Henry Kissinger. Bailey recalled that "there was a mentality in [Rockefeller's] campaign staff (although they'd never admit to it or recognize it) that, 'Look, we've got all this money. We should be able to buy the people necessary to get this done. And you buy from the top down.' . . . I don't believe that the Rockefeller people ever understood that the best and most effective political organizations flow from the bottom up and involve the people in a genuine sense." Bailey also recognized, however, the considerable difficulty of attempting to rally moderates at the grassroots level: "Moderates are moderates. Raising the sword of moderation and marching down a street is a contradiction in terms. . . . With people who feel passionately about something and are certain that they are right, it's easier to get them to organize and march and do the things necessary to be sure that their position prevails—because they have no doubt. On the other hand, if you're moderate, it basically means you have some doubts. You're not as certain of your beliefs, and they may not dominate every moment of your existence. And therefore it's not likely that you're going to make the commitment of time, energy, money, resources, and passion to try to turn your beliefs into reality."[76]

The Rockefeller effort suffered from this lack of moderate passion and involvement. Rockefeller was forced to hire commercial organizations to secure the necessary 13,702 signatures to place him on ballot, an effort which required a month and considerable expense. Goldwater volunteers collected 50,000 signatures in a few hours.[77] While Goldwater was setting records for contributions received, mostly in the form of small donations from ordinary citizens, Rockefeller found it nearly impossible to get anyone in California to contribute to his campaign, and thereby become personally invested in it in the most literal sense. People laughed at the very idea that they would be asked to give money to the son of a billionaire. Rockefeller also began the race at a severe deficit in the polls, with one survey showing him running more than thirty percentage points behind Goldwater.[78]

But the Rockefeller approach, which was the opposite of Goldwater's in nearly every way, had a number of advantages as well. Rockefeller's emissary George Hinman had made a lot of friends in his travels, and as one observer recalled, "Many, many people in the country were for Rockefeller because George Hinman wanted them to be, and they didn't want to offend George Hinman."[79] One of Goldwater's fundraisers in northern California found that Hinman and other Rockefeller representatives had previously met with bankers and business leaders and succeeded in winning them over: "As a result when I tried to find prominent northern Californians to join the Goldwater movement I found that I had been pretty well foreclosed from getting support from any of the normal sources of funds. . . . [Rockefeller] was able to seal off a large portion of community leaders from supporting Goldwater even though they were in favor of the philosophy Goldwater advocated."[80] The Young Turks in the California legislature, who were deeply alarmed by the right-wing insurgency, enlisted in the Rockefeller effort. Assemblyman Bill Bagley remembered that from March to June they flew all over the state on chartered airplanes to meet with reporters, press representatives from outside California, and nearly every editorial board in the state.[81] Rockefeller would enjoy almost unanimous endorsement from California's newspapers.

Rockefeller also possessed the funds and savvy to hire Stuart Spencer and William Roberts, two young men who would help create the field of professional campaign management. Both were moderates who had fought conservatives in the Los Angeles County YRs and had helped to create the Republican Alliance, an organization that sought to interest young executives in party politics through research and educational activities, along lines similar to the Ripon Society.[82] When the Spencer-Roberts organization was created in 1960, there were only two other such firms in existence. Doug Bailey, who was another pioneering political consultant of that era, emphasized that at the time he first became involved in politics, with George Lodge's Senate race in 1962, "most campaigns were awful—just awful!" They tended to be run by amateurs on a part-time basis, and "Quite aside from whether the candidate was good or bad, whether the people involved were good or bad, or whether the philosophy of the campaign was good or bad . . . there was no organization, structure, strategy, or game plan."[83] Spencer and Roberts were the proverbial one-eyed men in the land of the blind, and they infused the Rockefeller campaign with an order, discipline, and consistency of message that was conspicuously lacking in Goldwater's campaign.

Although the Spencer-Roberts team would go on to many future triumphs, including Ronald Reagan's gubernatorial and presidential victories, William Roberts felt in hindsight that Rockefeller's 1964 effort was "the best campaign that we *ever* ran." Because of the problems that Rockefeller faced—including his inability to raise money in California, his lack of grassroots support, the continuing fallout from his divorce and remarriage, and the fact that the state GOP organizations like the CRA were overwhelmingly for Goldwater—his managers were forced into bold and successful innovation. They devised operations that "went around the party apparatus," according to Roberts, to appeal directly to "the general voter in the Republican Party."[84] They held receptions featuring Rockefeller and prominent supporters such as Senator Kuchel that drew up to 15,000 people. They created their own organization, and mounted a massive publicity effort that included television, radio, billboards, advertisements, and direct mailings to every registered Republican in the state.

Rockefeller made a special effort to appeal to minorities, who were particularly apprehensive at the prospect of a Goldwater victory. The campaign's outreach to blacks and Hispanics was its most successful grassroots mobilization. Stuart Spencer estimated that the campaign succeeded in registering some 50,000 African-Americans as Republicans so that they could vote in the primary. He believed that Rockefeller's outspoken advocacy of civil rights, and the Rockefeller family's longstanding support for the historically black colleges in the South, inspired an outpouring of African-American volunteers—particularly middle-income and college-educated black people—into the campaign: "We didn't know where they were coming from."[85]

Above all, the Rockefeller campaign hammered at Goldwater's philosophy, depicting him not as a conservative but as a radical reactionary, backed by extremists, who would abolish Social Security, renounce civil rights and the United Nations, and pursue dangerous foreign policies. Goldwater reinforced his Dr. Strangelove image in late May when he called for the use of low-yield nuclear weapons in Vietnam to defoliate Communist supply lines.[86] Two million Californians received a Spencer-Roberts mailer asking whether they would prefer to have Rockefeller or Goldwater in the room with the H-Bomb. Voting for Rockefeller, the brochure emphasized, would "insure a responsible Republican Party—a Party guaranteeing a safe and sane America," a message that carried the strong implication that Goldwater and his followers were not responsible or safe, and perhaps not even sane.[87]

Rockefeller stressed that his rival was not only outside the mainstream of American opinion, he was also a loner within the Republican Party, antagonistic to the party consensus as expressed in the platforms of 1952, 1956, and 1960. In a widely publicized memorandum, Kuchel's assistant Stephen Horn documented that Goldwater had opposed every one of the twenty-five major issues specifically favored by the 1960 platform, while Kuchel had supported all of them and the majority of Senate Republicans had supported 23 of 25. Indeed, Horn concluded, "if the Republican National Platform of 1960 means anything at all, Barry Goldwater is not even a Republican."[88] *New York Herald Tribune* publisher Walter Thayer prevailed upon Dwight Eisenhower to write a statement describing, without naming any names, the kind of candidate whom the Republicans ought to nominate. The attributes listed by Ike—including protection of civil rights, backing for programs addressing domestic needs, "loyal support for the United Nations," and prudence in foreign policy—implicitly disqualified Goldwater, although the former president unconvincingly claimed that he had no intention to "read Goldwater out of the party."[89]

Rockefeller offered little by way of a distinctive philosophy of his own, but he successfully accentuated Goldwater's negatives and began to close the gap in the polls. At the same time, the scorched-earth approach of both sides made it increasingly unlikely that a moderate Republican would consider supporting a conservative in the general election, and vice versa. Goldwater was driven to distraction by what seemed to him the grossly distorted caricature of his views. "Rockefeller will never quit until he has destroyed me politically," he raged to Bill Buckley. "I have never been so downright disappointed in any man in my life as I have this fellow. His disregard for truth and his personal ambitions are appalling beyond belief."[90] Goldwater's supporters retaliated by harassing Rockefeller forces with obscene phone calls, vandalism, bomb threats, and other unpalatable actions that confirmed moderates' belief that ideological conservatives were beyond the pale.[91] The moderate Republican *New York Herald Tribune* portrayed conservatives as angry adolescents, unfit for political responsibility. The paper editorialized that the Goldwater movement was "powered and driven by those in revolt—in revolt against the Eisenhower record, against the maddening subtleties and frustrating necessities of a troubled and troublesome world." The conservatives were drunk with rebellion, but ignorant of "the simple truth that national policies require a national consensus, and that the limits of this consensus set the limits of the politically possible."[92]

Rockefeller and Goldwater each believed himself to be advocating unity in the face of party-wrecking polarization from the other side, and each man believed that he had in fact exercised statesmanlike restraint over advisors who had urged more divisive action. Much as Goldwater would later veto as racist the Clif White–produced film *Choice*, which contrasted Goldwater's traditional rectitude with the race riots and moral licentiousness permitted by his opponents, Rockefeller quashed *The Extremists*, a documentary produced by Spencer-Roberts on radical right fanatics in California. The film featured blood-boiling interviews with one man whose civil rights meeting in a Los Angeles suburb was invaded by right-wing haters, another whose CRA chapter was taken over by a mob of Birchers, and a Lutheran minister whose house was bombed while he participated in a panel discussion on "Is the Radical Right a Threat to Democracy?" Rockefeller refused to allow it to be aired, believing that it was "McCarthyism-in-reverse" in connecting Goldwater with the Birchers and other extremists.[93]

Nonetheless, divisions within the party hardened, and as the June 2 election drew near Rockefeller and Goldwater appeared to be deadlocked. The number of undecided voters increased, however—an indication that neither candidate was winning new converts.[94] A reporter interviewing a San Francisco–area widow who planned to vote for Rockefeller asked her why she liked the New York governor. "I don't like him," she snapped. "I dislike Goldwater more." Another Californian ventured that "I don't care for how Rockefeller behaves but Goldwater is too dangerous."[95] In the end, most inside observers believed that what tipped the race was the accident of Happy Rockefeller giving birth to Nelson Jr. a few days before the election. According to Roberts, "I think that the baby's birth served to bring out again, to the women's attention especially, the problem that we dealt with during the whole campaign—that he was a wife-stealer and that she was a home-wrecker."[96] Rockefeller won all of California's counties except Los Angeles, Orange, and San Diego, but lost the state by a margin of 59,000 votes out of more than two million cast.[97]

The California primary was a tale full of sound and fury signifying . . . what exactly? Goldwater had won his first contested primary and, in the eyes of his backers, established his electability. But he had barely eked out a victory against the deeply flawed Nelson Rockefeller. How would he have fared against a more moderate and attractive opponent such as Scranton or Romney? Moreover, his campaign had relied on a sort of class warfare strategy within the Republican Party, pitting the conservative grassroots against the trunk of moderate voters and the crown of party leadership. The enmities stirred by the struggle, as well as moderates' dismay over Goldwater's positions, made it extremely likely that some large portion of the million voters who had supported Rockefeller would turn to the Democrats, which in a state with a three to two Democratic registration edge would lead to a Republican wipeout of epic proportions. As GOP party professionals around the country began to realize that this dynamic was likely to play out in their states as well, now that Goldwater had all but secured the nomination, they began to panic. The pragmatists had finally heeded the moderate activists' warnings, but too late. The conservatives were in the driver's seat and were speeding toward the nearest cliff.

CHAPTER 4

The Blood-Dimmed Tide Is Loosed

The GOP and the Goldwater Campaign, 1964

As Republican moderates and pragmatists desperately cast about for someone to rescue them from the impending electoral disaster of 1964, their savior seemed likeliest to emerge from the ranks of the GOP governors. The Republican governors historically had constituted the core of moderate power in the party. Most Republican governors tended to be moderates, for several reasons. They were typically the products of political organizations rather than ideological movements, and usually had long experience in practical politics. They had to win over a majority of the voters of an entire state, not just a safe conservative district, which meant that they had to appeal to at least some Democrats and independents as well as Republicans. Once in office, they had to take account of the demands of labor as well as business, and the cities and suburbs as well as conservative rural areas. One Republican governor believed that most of his colleagues were moderate because "the governors are on the line dealing every day with real problems that they've got to resolve," while the GOP members of Congress were "one step removed from all of that, dealing with issues that somebody else has to resolve."[1] Republican governors had to negotiate with Democrats and seek compromise if they were to balance their budgets and take action on unavoidable issues like education, transportation, and sanitation. Ideology was a luxury that few of them could afford.

When Nelson Rockefeller dropped out of the 1964 presidential race, leaving Barry Goldwater in possession of an apparently insurmountable delegate lead, Republican moderates debated whether they should continue to fight the Arizonan and his movement. They looked for direction to the Republican governors, who assembled at the annual Governor's Conference in Cleveland from June 7–10. In 1952, when twenty-five governors were Republican, Thomas Dewey of New York had rallied them behind Dwight Eisenhower's candidacy and helped to shift the party convention toward the forces of moderation. Perhaps the Republican governors of 1964, though reduced to fifteen in number, could do the same.

Jack Saloma and Eugene Marans of the Ripon Society went to Cleveland hoping to witness the birth of an anti-Goldwater front, but found the moderates in disarray. While some like Michigan governor George Romney pledged to fight for a progressive platform, others like Oregon's Mark Hatfield resigned themselves to Goldwater's nomination and hoped that he could be influenced to adjust some of his stands. The moderates ardently aspired to have someone oppose the conservative wing, but none were eager to take on that role themselves. By the end of the convention, Saloma and Marans complained, "NO ONE but Governor Rockefeller was willing to challenge Senator Goldwater frontally. No effective lines of communication had been established between the various centers of persisting resistance to his candidacy." There was "no convincing evidence that the moderates would be able to field an effective team in a platform contest. 'Despondency' was perhaps the most appropriate description of the Governors as they dispersed."[2]

For most moderates, the possibility of cooperating with Goldwater disintegrated on June 10, when Goldwater returned to the Senate and was one of only six Republicans to join segregationist Democrats in voting against ending the Southern filibuster over the Civil Rights Act of 1964. The Senate overcame the opposition of Goldwater and the Southerners by voting for cloture, 71–29—the first time in history that the Senate had mustered the necessary two-thirds vote to shut off a filibuster on a civil rights bill. Nine days later, Goldwater again was one of six Republicans to vote against the bill itself, which passed 73–27.[3] In opposing the Civil Rights Act, Goldwater was setting his standard against not only one of the most significant pieces of Congressional legislation in the twentieth century, but also one of the greatest achievements of the Republican Party.

The Civil Rights Act of 1964 was as much a Republican accomplishment as a Democratic one. What was likely its earliest version had been written in the office of Missouri Republican Representative Thomas Curtis in October 1962 and introduced by the Republican members of the House Judiciary Committee and other GOP colleagues in January 1963.[4] It incorporated the 1960 Republican Party platform positions on civil rights and a more robust proposal on nondiscrimination in public accommodations.[5] It preceded Kennedy's first civil rights message, and his June 1963 civil rights bill, by several months. Curtis emphasized that "One reason [Kennedy's] message came up was that there was some heat on him, because of the bill introduced by the Republicans in January."[6] The minority members on Judiciary were attempting to force the President's civil rights bill out of the committee, where it had been bottled up by Democratic chairman Emmanuel Celler. After Kennedy's assassination, the political calculus changed drastically. Lyndon Johnson resolved to make passage of the civil rights bill a monument to the fallen president, overriding the Southerners who made up a third or more of the Democrats' Congressional delegation. Even so, the bill had no chance of becoming law without overwhelming Republican support.

Republican champions of the civil rights bill in the House included many Northeastern urban and suburban progressives such as John Lindsay of Manhattan and Ogden Reid of Westchester. The Republican leader of the legislative effort, however, was a Midwestern stalwart: William M. McCulloch, the ranking member of the House Judiciary Committee.

McCulloch was a farm boy turned country lawyer from the small town of Piqua, Ohio. He seemed a figure out of the nineteenth century when he would campaign, snowy-haired and in red suspenders, at county fairs and on courthouse steps. He was a typical rural Midwestern conservative in most respects: in favor of school prayer and gun ownership; opposed to foreign aid, federal involvement in education, Johnson's poverty program, and the Supreme Court's "one man, one vote" rulings that cut back the overrepresentation of rural areas in state governments. He was an annual recipient of the "Golden Watchdog of the Treasury" award, and took pride in returning to the government a portion of his Congressional office allowance every year. He rarely attempted to secure federal assistance for his district. He often proclaimed that he was "proud of western Ohio, where there is so little pressure by hard-working, frugal, energetic, ambitious citizens for 'pork.'"[7]

And yet McCulloch was a hero to Republican moderates and progressives because he had always been one of the most determined Congressional activists for civil rights. Although African-Americans represented only 2.7 percent of his constituents, McCulloch believed deeply in equality of opportunity and the obligation of Congress to intervene when individuals or government authorities discriminated against minorities. "To do less," in McCulloch's view, "would be to shirk our responsibility as national legislators, and as human beings who honor the principles of liberty and justice."[8]

McCulloch negotiated with Judiciary chairman Celler and both the Kennedy and Johnson administrations to shape a strong civil rights bill. The bill would outlaw segregation in public facilities and racial discrimination in education and employment, but would command support sufficiently broad to be enacted. As the co-sponsor of the bill, McCulloch came under intense criticism from Democratic liberals who wanted it to include measures that struck him as unconstitutional or overreaching, including the elimination of racial imbalance in education, federal controls on banks and mortgage companies, and racial quotas for employers. McCulloch also altered the bill's original plan to give statutory authority to a fair employment practices commission with oversight over government contracts, an innovation that Republicans had opposed for decades as an excessive federal and bureaucratic intrusion into private enterprise. The new commission, under McCulloch's revision, would be limited to investigatory and conciliatory functions.[9] Some Republicans lobbied to retain the bill's original objectionable features in his rewriting of the measure, hoping that they would poison the bill and deprive the Johnson administration of a legislative triumph in an election year.[10] McCulloch beat back the pressures from all sides and in January 1964 succeeded in presenting the House with a bill that he described as "comprehensive in scope, yet moderate in application."[11] According to Meg Greenfield, then a Washington reporter, the morning after McCulloch had succeeded in sending the bill to the House floor for action, he and his Republican supporters arrived in the chamber to find tightly furled umbrellas lying across their desks, which were meant to cast McCulloch and his colleagues as "Neville Chamberlains, weaklings and betrayers of their own." She recalled later that "The stunt sounds silly now, but it had an eerie, sinister feel to it at the time." She was struck by how much more McCulloch had paid for his efforts than had "all those congressmen from districts where, unlike his, it was to their political advantage to support the bill and who, having acquiesced in no action for all that time, were now sighing, 'At last!' and pretending it was their handiwork."[12]

Eighty percent of House Republicans supported the bill, as opposed to sixty percent of House Democrats. The measure went to the Senate, where it was filibustered by Southern Democrats and championed by liberals of both parties, with Thomas Kuchel, Jacob Javits, Kenneth Keating, and Clifford Case as the GOP representatives on the steering committee for the bill. The pivotal figure, however, was another Midwestern stalwart, minority leader Everett Dirksen. Since no civil rights legislation could escape from the Judiciary Committee chaired by Mississippi Senator James Eastland, Dirksen's negotiations with Lyndon Johnson and his designated allies in effect took the place of committee action. The venerable Illinois orator initially protested against what he considered the big-government intrusiveness of aspects of Title 2, to outlaw segregation in public facilities, and Title 7, to outlaw employment discrimination. But Dirksen also recognized that Southern segregation shamed the nation and that the tide of public opinion, influenced by the moral force and epic drama of the civil rights movement, had turned decisively in favor of reform.[13]

Dirksen allowed himself to be wooed by Johnson and Senator Hubert Humphrey, the bill's Democratic floor leader, and negotiated bipartisan compromises on provisions that he thought members of his party would find most objectionable. He faced down opposition within his ranks and dramatically expressed the need for action with a paraphrase of Victor Hugo: "No army can withstand the strength of an idea whose time has come."[14] When twenty-seven of the Senate's thirty-three Republican members voted with Dirksen to end the filibuster on June 10, it was "the most meaningful triumph of his career," according to his biographer.[15] As with the House vote, a greater proportion of Senate Republicans than Democrats voted for cloture and passage of the bill: more than four-fifths of the Republicans but only some two-thirds of the Democrats.[16] Although the bill's passage did not end segregation overnight, and enforcement turned out to be a long and arduous process, it was the most significant piece of federal legislation on behalf of equal rights for African-Americans since the Reconstruction era.

But the credit—even the glory—that the Republican Party should have enjoyed for its support for the Civil Rights Act of 1964 was effectively negated when its presumptive presidential nominee voted against the measure. As his defenders have tirelessly explained, Goldwater was not personally a racist. He had supported the Arizona NAACP, helped to desegregate the Arizona National Guard, and so forth. In giving aid and comfort to Southern segregationists, however, Goldwater was certainly a fellow traveler of racists. In his 1960 manifesto, *Conscience of a Conservative*, Goldwater had declared (or allowed his ghostwriter Brent Bozell to declare on his behalf) that he was "not impressed by the claim that the Supreme Court's decision on school integration is the law of the land."[17] He added that the federal government had no role to play in enforcing the rights of blacks living under Jim Crow, which was exactly what white supremacists in the South wanted to hear. Southern race relations, Goldwater added, were "best handled by the people directly concerned."[18] Since the white power structure in the South had no intention of moving toward integration unless compelled, Goldwater's approach in effect would mean, in Alabama Governor George Wallace's famous phrase, "segregation forever."

In voting against the Civil Rights Act, Goldwater claimed that it was an unconstitutional infringement on the rights of private property, particularly in its sections on public accommodations and the establishment of a fair employment practices commission, despite the restrictions of the McCulloch compromise. Its enforcement would require "the creation of a federal police state of mammoth proportions" and encourage citizens to spy on and turn in their neighbors, fellow workers, and business competitors who were not in compliance with the law. "These, the federal police force and an 'informer' psychology," he concluded, "are the hallmarks of the police state and landmarks in the destruction of a free society."[19] As the NAACP's executive secretary Roy Wilkins pointed out, Goldwater was unable "to recognize a genuine police state like Mississippi, already alive and in being in our midst."[20]

Goldwater thereby put his stamp—and, by association, that of the Republican Party—on the side of Southern resistance to what was now the law of the land. His perfervid claims were distressingly similar to those of the Birchers and other right-wing extremists. "The 'Civil Rights' Bill is a misnamed, unconstitutional horror" that would "impose slavery on Americans," alleged one Bircher. It would "destroy the American way of life, free enterprise, property rights, individual freedom and reduce our dynamic, competitive and cultural life to a single common denominator: Statism."[21] Goldwater's vote also made clear that his campaign would depend on a strategy appealing to segregationists in the South—three Southern Democratic senators crossed the aisle to congratulate him after his vote.[22] It would also depend on white backlash in the North, which had given George Wallace his unexpected success in the 1964 Democratic primaries in states like Wisconsin, Maryland, and Indiana.[23] While Goldwater did not stoop to Wallace's explicitly racist appeals, his comments that the poor were stupid and lazy and his equation of civil rights protests with street crime stoked many of the same resentments. The NAACP, breaking a long tradition of neutrality in elections, denounced Goldwater for using "fear bigotry" to promote his campaign.[24]

Goldwater's inflammatory charges about the Civil Rights Act had already been answered by McCulloch when he had introduced the bill in the House. He noted that thirty-two states had already enacted public accommodations laws, often broader in scope than the civil rights bill, and that twenty-five states had passed fair employment legislation. These laws had been in operation for almost two decades in some cases, and no unconstitutional invasions of privacy, personal property, or personal liberties had been observed. On the other hand, it was patently obvious that blacks in the South were denied equal opportunity by the discrimination of private establishments. That discrimination was enforced—and often mandated— by state and local governments, and it would be impossible to right this egregious wrong without the help of the federal government.[25] Goldwater and his legal advisors, William Rehnquist and Robert Bork—both destined to play significant roles in conservative politics—were narrowly correct in pointing out that the Civil Rights Act would entail an expansion of federal power to regulate private enterprise that was not contemplated by the Founding Fathers. But only the sophistry of doctrinaire conservative ideology could produce the conclusion that the cause of freedom was best served by maintenance of the South's apartheid regime.

In the wake of Goldwater's vote, a spate of opinion pieces appeared comparing the Arizonan unfavorably to the late Senator Robert Taft, his predecessor as the standard-bearer of Republican conservatism. Writers such as Walter Lippmann and Richard Rovere, who now wrote in praise of Taft, had not in fact been great fans of him while he was alive.[26] However, the debate over the civil rights bill had illuminated a key difference between the Midwestern stalwart conservatives and the new conservatives in the Goldwater mold: the Taft tradition was supportive of civil rights in a way that ideological conservatism was not.

NAACP counsel Clarence Mitchell spoke in Ohio shortly after the passage of the Civil Rights Act. He praised McCulloch and his fellow Ohio Republican Representative Clarence Brown, emphasizing that "it is no exaggeration to say that this bill would not have become law without them."[27] Brown, like McCulloch, was another stalwart follower of Taft, and had generally voted in coalition with conservative Southern Democrats on fiscal and social issues. Unlike the Southerners, however, he was influenced by the Midwestern Republican heritage of abolitionism and Unionism in the Civil War. Clarence Brown Jr., who inherited his father's House seat, was proud to point out that the main line of the Underground Railroad, the network through which Southern slaves escaped to freedom in Canada, ran directly through the district that the Browns represented.[28] As the ranking minority member of the Rules Committee, the senior Brown had threatened to wrest control of the committee from chairman Howard Smith, the Virginia segregationist Democrat, if Smith refused to hold hearings on the civil rights bill. Brown's threat had worked, and Smith had been forced to consent to the bill's passage out of the committee in February 1964.

Mitchell observed that both of the senators and twenty-three of the twenty-four representatives from Taft's home state of Ohio had voted in favor of the civil rights bill. The lone holdout was John Ashbrook, the former Young Republicans chairman, a key member of Clif White's Syndicate and a dedicated Goldwater supporter. Mitchell acidly remarked that Ashbrook showed that "while we customarily think of Mississippi as the nation's chief trouble spot, actually there is a little bit of Mississippi everywhere—even in Ohio."[29] Ashbrook's vote provided further confirmation that Goldwater conservatism was inimical to civil rights in a way that traditional Midwestern Republicanism was not. It also indicated, as alert political observers were realizing, that the new conservatism was in many ways different from and even hostile to the old Taft-style stalwart Republicanism.

A number of political scientists and historians have concluded that by the early 1960s, America's two major parties had "essentially switched positions on civil rights issues," with the Democrats embracing racial liberalism and the Republican Party espousing the cause of racial conservatism.[30] This interpretation greatly exaggerates the spread of the new conservatism in the GOP at that time and ignores the genuine Republican civil rights idealism that influenced even Midwestern stalwarts like McCulloch, Dirksen, and Brown. These scholars are thus unable to understand why Republicans overwhelmingly supported the Civil Rights Act of 1964, or even to explain how the bill passed at all.

It's true that for many Republicans, the civil rights movement was a somewhat abstract proposition. Democratic Party activists and politicians, particularly in the northern cities, were more likely than Republicans to include African-Americans in their coalitions and to have direct contact with them. The massive national attention and sympathy directed toward the civil rights movement in the early '60s, however, forced Republicans as well as Democrats to think about racial issues that they had never previously considered. While some reacted negatively to these new issues, the majority of Republicans supported the civil rights movement despite the change it boded. For example, while many academics have assumed that the free-market, anti-regulatory ideology of big business must have made it hostile to civil rights policies, in fact at the time the civil rights bill was being debated, journalists noticed that "Significantly missing from the list of active opponents were major business groups."[31]

One Republican businessman who was mulling over the meaning of civil rights was William S. Beinecke, the president of the Sperry and Hutchinson Company, the maker of S&H Green Stamps. Like many other wealthy New York Republicans in his circle, Beinecke had little interaction with minorities: "The only contact I had with black people," he recalled, "was when a porter would carry my bags." Although he did not participate in the civil rights movement, he couldn't help but follow it in the news, which eventually led him to wonder why all of his employees were white. As he observed later, "That was the benefit of the protest movements of that era; they pointed out that most people took the status quo for granted and never questioned it." Looking into the matter with his personnel executive, he discovered that S&H's employment agency would automatically screen out all black applicants for open positions. This discrimination offended his free-market instincts: "I just thought, Here we are in a city with two million potential black employees, and this whole vast section of the labor market is being denied to us." And so Beinecke's company began to hire black people, "not for humanitarian reasons but because it seemed to be a more realistic and hard-headed capitalist way to go about business."[32] Beinecke himself became one of the many businessmen, predominantly Republican, who established such civil rights programs as A Better Chance, Inc., which sought out talented young minorities and paid for them to attend some of the best preparatory schools in the nation. Beinecke and his associates also supported the Opportunities Industrialization Centers started by the Reverend Leon H. Sullivan, which provided training for disadvantaged minority job-seekers and worked with industry to place them in secure employment. These pro-civil rights Republican businessmen did typically object to big-government remedies such as the fair employment practices commission, but to characterize them as opponents of civil rights for this reason is highly misleading.

Goldwater's vote against the Civil Rights Act enraged millions of moderate Republicans who saw it as a betrayal of the party's heritage. One of those in a position to do something about it was Pennsylvania's governor, William Warren Scranton. Moderates had looked yearningly toward Scranton at the start of the 1964 presidential race. The media was drawn to him mainly because he seemed like a Republican version of John F. Kennedy: born within two months of JFK, slim and handsome, and projecting a Kennedyesque image of charm, cool, urbanity, and elegance. Scranton was the scion of a family whose American roots traced back to the 1630s. His industrialist forebears had helped found the Republican Party and the city of Scranton, Pennsylvania, which was named in their honor. He learned politics from his mother, who was the Republican national committeewoman from Pennsylvania from 1928 to 1951, and attended his first GOP convention with her when he was eleven. Educated at fancy preparatory schools and Yale, he moved comfortably in establishment circles; his law school eating club, before his education was interrupted by service in World War II, had included future Supreme Court justices Potter Stewart and Byron White as well as future president Gerald Ford. His media profile was not harmed in the least by the marriage of one of his sisters to James A. Linen III, president of the Time-Life publishing empire.

But there were more substantive reasons why many moderates saw Scranton as their leader. He had experience in business and civic leadership, having begun his public career as the head of a citizens committee trying to cope with the decay of his hometown brought on by the mining industry's collapse. He was well versed in foreign relations through his work as a special assistant to Secretaries of State John Foster Dulles and Christian Herter. Elected to Congress in 1960, he was an independent-minded supporter of foreign aid, the Peace Corps, civil rights, and the Kennedy administration's stimulus plan for private businesses in depressed urban and rural areas. He described himself as "a liberal on civil rights, a conservative on fiscal policy, and an internationalist on foreign affairs."[33] When the Pennsylvania GOP's moderate and conservative factions threatened a party-splitting primary in the 1962 gubernatorial race, all sixty-seven county chairmen endorsed Scranton as the "harmony" candidate. Though his Democratic opponent mocked him as "Little Lord Fauntleroy," he proved a surprisingly tough campaigner and won the race by half a million votes.

Scranton became an effective governor, whose early efforts blended cost-cutting and economic development initiatives with good-government reforms of civil service and state administration and the neglected education sector. He succeeded in getting a one-cent sales tax increase through the legislature, which wiped out the substantial deficit he inherited from the previous administration. His consistent drive to attract new industry to the state took some liberal forms, such as more money for schools and roads, and some conservative ones, such as unemployment compensation reform that unions bitterly opposed. By the end of his first year, Scranton had cut unemployment by almost a third, moved 56,000 people off the welfare rolls, boosted business activity, and secured promises of 700 new factories and plant expansions.[34] Contrary to many early predictions, he also brought peace to the turbulent state GOP. He worked as well with Old Guard pols like Harvey Taylor, the octogenarian leader of the Pennsylvania legislature, as he did with reformers like Senator Hugh Scott, the pipe-smoking, intellectual dean of the Senate's moderate Republicans.

The problem for moderates who hoped Scranton would oppose Goldwater for the presidential nomination was that he didn't particularly want to become president.[35] As journalist Theodore H. White perceived, Scranton was "a man interested in government—not politics. He lacks the raw appetite for power of more elemental men."[36] A more skeptical commentator speculated that "Republicans, especially moderate Republicans, tend to be a little over-bred, like Scranton. I guess that by the time you get to be a big Republican you've spent so much time trying to be a member of some club or other, have everyone like you and think you're safe, that you've lost an edge, become timid and restrained."[37] Aides noticed that although Scranton spoke well in public, he was uncomfortable with the travel demands of campaigning and was vulnerable to asthmatic episodes in times of stress.[38] For all these reasons, Scranton resisted the efforts of his assistants and admirers to push him into the presidential campaign, and removed his name from the New Hampshire primary rolls.

Two principal factors changed Scranton's mind about running. The first was Goldwater's indication that he would vote against cloture in the civil rights debate and against the bill itself. Scranton told Eisenhower that Goldwater's opposition to civil rights made him sick. "How can you be against civil rights in the year 1964?" he wondered.[39] The second was that Scranton was deluged with pleas to run from Republican politicians who, after the California primary, were awakening to the reality that Goldwater's nomination would cost them their political lives. Pennsylvania Senator Hugh Scott, who had created a Congressional Committee to Elect Bill Scranton, advised the governor that the Republicans could lose thirty seats in the House.[40] The Ripon Society, in a confidential analysis leaked to the New York Times, projected that Goldwater would lose every state outside the South and that a Goldwater ticket would devastate hundreds of local Republican organizations and candidates. They admonished the GOP leadership: "Ours is a generation which in a decade will inherit the Republican Party. We hope that there is something left to inherit."[41] Columnist Roscoe Drummond counseled moderates who were reluctant to rock the boat of party unity that "it is one thing to be willing to accept a party nominee of divergent opinion and quite another to accept the prospect of such a grievous decimating of the party at every level of government."[42] On June 11, the day after Goldwater voted against cloture, Scranton called a meeting of his principal advisors at the governor's mansion in Indiantown Gap, and after lengthy debate resolved to enter the race. "We must do it," he concluded, "because it is right."[43]

Announcing his candidacy the next day, Scranton warned Republicans not to turn their backs on "the century-old progressive history of our party," lest the GOP follow the Federalists and Whigs into extinction. While he did not mention his opponent by name, he denounced the ultra-conservative position as "a cause which has no roots in American history" and a "weird parody" of traditional Republican beliefs. He also sounded the alarm about the Republican losses that were sure to follow "if we let an exclusion-minded minority dominate our platform and choose our candidates." Scranton emphasized the inclusivity of his own moderate position: "I need the help of every Republican. We are reading no one out of our party."[44]

Few political observers thought that, with only a month to go before the party convention, Scranton had any realistic chance of defeating Goldwater. Scranton himself knew that he faced extremely long odds, since his campaign had launched too late and Goldwater already had a majority of the delegates locked up. But moderates believed that his candidacy was a necessary moral protest against the conservative takeover, and might increase the number of moderate delegates fighting over the platform at the convention. A Scranton candidacy would also reassure the nation that not all Republicans had given in to extremism. Scranton's resistance, they hoped, would inspire moderates battling to take back the party after Goldwater's inevitable defeat. As Kentucky's moderate Senator John Sherman Cooper said in urging Scranton to run, "It is not a question of stopping Senator Goldwater. It is a question of the Republican delegates from all over the country deciding the position of the Party on the issues before the country—foreign policy, civil rights, and a responsible fiscal policy with concern for the less fortunate. . . . Those responsible positions should not be abandoned to suit the whim and interest of a single candidate."[45]

The members of the Ripon Society welcomed Scranton's candidacy as a godsend, and the Society's president, Jack Saloma, immediately joined the campaign as a speechwriter. Ripon's members were horrified by Goldwater's vote against the Civil Rights Act and his tirade against its enforcement, particularly given their awareness of the moral significance of the civil rights movement for the younger generation and the vicarious sense of participation it inspired. At the same time, they hoped that Goldwater's stand against the Lincoln tradition might, paradoxically, shake moderates out of their moderation and fill them with the passion and commitment that were usually found only in their opponents. One Ripon member wrote to Saloma that Goldwater's opposition to civil rights "has given us something we lacked before—a potent emotional and moral issue, of meaning and force to Republicans. . . . I believe this line of attack should be used by all of us— from Scranton down to us . . . until we have won the Party back."[46]

On the fourth of July, 1964, Saloma and four other Ripon members traveled to the small white schoolhouse in Ripon, Wisconsin, where the Republican Party was founded in 1854. From the party's birthplace they issued a "Declaration of Conscience," evoking the GOP's founding spirit, which they described as the "moral force of free men seeking moderate solutions to great crises." Just as the nation now faced another moral struggle in the civil rights saga, so too the Republican Party faced "its greatest internal crisis since its founding. . . . It must choose within the next two weeks whether or not it will embrace a candidate who has by his actions in the Congress and by his silence in the face of national crisis disqualified himself to be the leader of the party of Lincoln." They condemned the Goldwater strategy "that must inevitably exploit the 'white backlash' to the civil rights movement," and asked rhetorically, "Can the Republican party turn its back on the principles and ideals which gave it birth?" The declaration denied that conservatism was the party's founding tradition, and lamented the stillness and silence within Republican ranks as "a great political party" prepared "to violate its own moral basis."[47]

"I have felt the remarkable stillness of which you speak," Dwight Eisenhower wrote to Saloma a few days later, "and I have been disappointed at its persistence." While Eisenhower could not bring himself to mention Goldwater by name, he regretted the party's failure over the previous year to build a public consensus around "its convictions and its responsibilities and opportunities," and professed to be "delighted that the Ripon Society is doing its best to concentrate some attention on those concepts that are truly the foundation of our Party."[48] By this time, however, Eisenhower had vacillated over Goldwater to such an extent that moderates had given up on persuading him to speak out on the conservative peril. A psychiatrist commissioned by Nelson Rockefeller to analyze the former president's behavior concluded that Eisenhower was in such poor health that he would agree with whatever his visitors wanted to hear in order to make them go away.[49]

Moderates and progressives rallied to Scranton's eleventh-hour candidacy. Rockefeller officially ended his campaign on June 15, and not only endorsed his fellow governor but loaned him his research unit and nationwide professional organization for the balance of the campaign, all at Rockefeller's expense. "The hour is late," Rockefeller announced, "but if all leaders in the moderate mainstream of the Republican Party will unite upon a platform and upon Governor Scranton as the candidate, the moderate cause can still be won."[50] Eight days later, Henry Cabot Lodge Jr. resigned as U.S. ambassador to South Vietnam and returned to the States to campaign for Scranton. Lodge believed it was his duty to the Republican Party to forestall Goldwater's nomination. "There is a threshold below which no party should go," he told reporters. "[B]oth parties should always nominate men who are prudent, men who are not impulsive in the conduct of foreign affairs."[51]

Scranton's campaign picked up where Lodge's and Rockefeller's had left off, contrasting Goldwater's defects with Scranton's admirable characteristics rather than defining the moderate political position. Scranton attacked the "small but vocal minority (that) too often has made our party sound naïve, irresponsible, reactionary and heartless."[52] His campaign lambasted Goldwater's calls to make Social Security voluntary, drop atomic bombs in Asia, break diplomatic relations with the Soviet Union, and repeal the income tax laws. Scranton's natural base was in the moderate Northeast, and he made much of Goldwater's famous statement that the East Coast ought to be sawed off from the rest of the country and allowed to drift out to sea. Still, Scranton also drew enthusiastic crowds in Atlanta, where he declared that the Republican Party and "the new South—all citizens of the new South—belong together." While he predicted that Republican senators and representatives would someday dominate every state of the Old Confederacy, he added that "that day will not be brought closer by those who would cynically exploit the problems of the South—by those who would reopen old wounds by phony invocation of the Constitution or by comparison of the Federal Government of the United States with a police state dictatorship."[53] Scranton's advocates represented the Pennsylvanian as the true conservative and Goldwater as the wild-eyed radical. "Barry Goldwater is *not* a true conservative," insisted one of Scranton's advertisements, "*he is an extremist*. He has no positive program."[54] The Scranton national committee proclaimed that "Goldwater is outside the Taft tradition . . . outside the Lincoln tradition . . . outside the Eisenhower tradition . . . outside the Republican tradition! Bill Scranton is the true heir of Bob Taft in the Republican Party of 1964. He stands for reasoned conservatism—for responsible conservatism—against radicalism of every kind!"[55]

Goldwater's followers complained that Scranton and his backers, by hammering away so enthusiastically at the Arizonan, were seeking "to ruin what they cannot rule."[56] Phyllis Schlafly updated *A Choice Not an Echo* to portray Scranton as the tool of the Eastern kingmakers, while a pamphlet put out by segregationist conservatives portrayed him as "an ardent Leftwinger with a record of actions which prove his softness-on-Communism."[57] A *Cincinnati Enquirer* editorial against Scranton sneered that for a man to be a moderate, "he must be faceless . . . gutless . . . devoid of a good sense of history and judgment . . . and not too far to the right of the Communist [leader], Gus Hall. He must be a man who mouths words without meaning; who cheerfully embraces coexistence with the devil himself; who shrinks from any hazard. This 'moderate' is the most dangerous figure in American politics."[58]

Despite the amateurish and haphazard nature of his campaign, Scranton's poll numbers bounced sharply upward. The June 28 Gallup Poll showed that the Pennsylvania governor had overtaken Goldwater as the choice of Republican voters, with 55 percent for Scranton as opposed to only 34 percent for Goldwater and 11 percent undecided. Independents were almost three times as likely to vote for Scranton as for Goldwater.[59] These glad tidings made Scranton's advisors dream that he could attract enough delegates to deny Goldwater a first-ballot victory at the convention, opening the door to his nomination. James Reichley, Scranton's legislative assistant and speechwriter, recalled that the delegates from the Midwest who were contacted by the campaign were very different from the Goldwater conservatives. Most were conservatives in the Taft tradition: moralistic, small-town, small-business types who were still basically isolationist. They feared Goldwater's call for anti-Communist rollback as well the extremism of his followers, "and the Taftites were worried sick about Goldwater's impact on their local races. There were enough of them, and if we could have swung a hundred of those delegates, we could have done it."[60]

But it was too late. Goldwater's delegates from the South and West and even some northern states were a new breed in GOP politics, totally ideologically committed and immune to the arguments about the greater party good that had swayed delegates of past conventions to the moderate side. Goldwater boasted that his "hard-core" of some 425 delegates "will stay right to the end and march out the back of this convention if they don't get what they want. This is how hard these people are."[61] Many of the Goldwater delegates from states like California, Illinois, New Jersey, Michigan, and Oregon were at war with the moderate leadership of their state parties. Trying to persuade them that a Goldwater candidacy would destroy the GOP was as futile as arguing the perils of nuclear war with cockroaches. The Midwestern stalwarts were uneasy about Goldwater, but nonetheless resented the long dominance of Eastern moderates and their past sins against the sainted Taft. They were not going to rally around an Eastern establishment figure like Scranton. And even moderates who might have supported Scranton if he had been in the race from the beginning, particularly party professionals like former RNC chairmen Leonard Hall and Meade Alcorn, kept their distance from what they saw as Scranton's quixotic adventure.

And so the miserably divided Republican Party lurched into its 1964 convention at the Cow Palace in San Francisco. The first indication of the kind of gathering it would be came with the pre-convention negotiations over the party platform. Moderates and liberals assumed that the platform that would result would be a consensus document much like the 1960 platform. They thought that Representative Melvin Laird of Wisconsin, the platform committee chairman and a stalwart in the Taft tradition, would broker a compromise, although Laird warned Scranton's advisors that two-thirds of the committee members were pro-Goldwater and half of those were "of the unreasoning variety."[62] This accorded with most observers' calculation that one-third of the delegates were moderates and liberals, another third Goldwater-leaning party regulars, and another third committed Goldwaterites. Still, most newspapers initially reported that conservatives felt so secure of victory that they would allow progressives and moderates to dominate the platform.[63] And, as an aide to California Senator Thomas Kuchel believed, the conservatives would be concerned to "minimize defections and keep overall party strength as broad as possible. The simple fact is that the party ticket will inevitably benefit from the strength of the moderates."[64] As it turned out, none of these assumptions were true.

In fact, the conservative mission in the platform sessions was to crush the moderates and produce an ideological statement of uncompromising purity. In part this reflected the accurate perception of Clif White, the mastermind of the Goldwater forces, that Scranton's only hope of victory lay in provoking an incident of some kind that would disrupt the convention.

White's strategy, which he had learned from his 1940s battles with Communists, was to deny the Scranton camp any opening by rejecting their every proposal, even if they advocated motherhood and apple pie. Further, many hardline conservatives also wished to rid the party of all who disagreed with them and to redefine Republicanism in their own image.

Senator Hugh Scott, who was both Pennsylvania's representative on the platform committee and Scranton's floor manager, hadn't expected the Goldwater people to yield much, but "I could hardly believe the degree of inflexibility I had encountered."[65] Scott quickly realized that Clif White's organizational efforts had extended to the platform committee, which automatically voted down every issue raised by the moderates. Texas Senator John Tower torpedoed a plank committing the party to "enforcement" of the Civil Rights Act on the grounds that the word "enforcement" had negative implications in the South.[66] A debate over immigration reform nearly came to blows when one mossback insulted Italians, provoking a heated response from Massachusetts moderate Representative Silvio Conte. Laird insisted that the committee deliver a document suited to Goldwater's preferences and positions, resulting in a platform that was the Republicans' most conservative since 1936. Scott, looking back on the fight more than a dozen years later, believed that the platform committee was "the most knot-headed aggregation, I suppose, that had ever assembled under one roof. It was never as bad before, and it's never been as bad since. But these people were filled with this Puritan, almost religious fervor, that they were in sole possession of the truth, that anyone else was an infidel."[67]

After the platform was reported out of the committee, the Scranton forces decided, after many sleepless strategy sessions, to bring to the floor three substitute planks. One would repudiate extremist groups, specifically including the Communist Party on the left and the John Birch Society and Ku Klux Klan on the right. Another would support full "enforcement" of the Civil Rights Act and the "constitutional responsibility" of the federal government to assure the right to vote for all Americans. The third would affirm the exclusive authority of the president over the use of nuclear weapons. The floor fight around these planks might boost Scranton's chances, but in any case Scott believed it was important to the party's survival that traditional Republicans publicly dramatize their losing battle in the platform committee "to show that there was less than monolithic support" for the conservative positions.[68]

Scranton's position weakened considerably, however, when his young aide William Keisling sent Goldwater an intemperate challenge in the candidate's name. The letter accused Scranton's opponent of buying delegate support, allowing himself to be used by extremists, casually prescribing nuclear war, and a host of other crimes. "Goldwaterism," it charged, "has come

to stand for a whole crazy-quilt collection of absurd and dangerous positions that would be soundly repudiated by the American people in November."[69] Goldwater was rightfully outraged and sent a copy of the letter to all
the convention delegates, calling it "an insult to every Republican in San
Francisco."[70] Scranton was forced to admit that he had neither signed nor
seen the letter, a public confession of incompetence that his assistant Reichley felt "hurt his national standing . . . it was a terrible mistake."[71] The letter
further blighted relations between the Scranton and Goldwater camps.

Goldwater's supporters trounced the moderates on the convention floor
in the Cow Palace, rejecting the civil rights plank by an 897–409 vote and
the others by even more lopsided margins.[72] The bitterness of the split
within the Republican ranks was most evident when Nelson Rockefeller
attempted to speak in favor of the plank on extremism. The assembled conservatives, confronted with the leader of the despised progressive wing of
the party, responded as Rockefeller no doubt expected they would, con-
firming his point about the infiltration of Know-Nothings into the GOP.
Rockefeller's recounting of his firsthand experiences with the Birch Society's unacceptable methods, including hate literature, goon tactics, and
bombings, brought a storm of boos, chants, jeers, hisses, and catcalls that
made it impossible for him to be heard no matter how hard convention
chair Senator Thruston Morton attempted to gavel the hall into silence.
Rockefeller almost gleefully defied the angry crowd. "It is still a free country," the governor called out over the roar. "Some of you don't like to hear it,
ladies and gentlemen, but it is the truth."[73]

Most of the howling came from the galleries, as Clif White attempted
to restore order on the floor, but the official delegations were part of the
uproar. Doug Bailey was at the convention, and he was sure that the clamor
"wasn't just the galleries. It was the floor, it was the hall. The venom of the
booing and the hatred in people's eyes really was quite stunning. I remember I was standing next to an officer from the San Mateo County Sheriff's
Office, who was there to keep the peace, and there he was, with his pistol
unsheathed, booing along with everyone else."[74] Tanya Melich, the political research director for ABC News at the convention and a moderate
involved with the New York YRs, remembered that the anger directed at
Rockefeller was "horrible. I felt like I was in Nazi Germany. It was really
scary."[75] Dwight Eisenhower found the tumult "unpardonable—and a
complete negation of the spirit of democracy. I was bitterly ashamed."[76]
Ike later claimed that his young niece had been "molested" by Goldwater thugs
on the convention floor.[77]

The rejection of Rockefeller, like the convention's repeated eruptions of
anger toward the media, stemmed from the long-simmering revolt of the
party's out-groups against its in-groups, and the rest of the country against

the Eastern establishment. As journalist Murray Kempton shrewdly observed, "This convention is historic because it is the emancipation of the serfs. . . . The serfs have seized the estate of their masters."[78] Many Americans— and even many Goldwater supporters—had expected that the Dewey-Eisenhower forces would somehow derail the conservative triumph. But the convention revealed to the public that the once-masterful Eastern elites of the earlier era had passed from the political scene.

More broadly, the East no longer held the preponderance of economic and cultural power in American society that had undergirded its political dominance in the Republican Party. Many of the industries that created the Eastern aristocracy were in decline, like the coal, iron, and steel businesses that had provided the Scranton family fortune. Others, like textiles and defense contracting, were moving to the South and West. The Northeast was losing population to what came to be called the Sunbelt, and the country's economic power was decentralizing. By 1964, California was the nation's largest state. San Francisco was home to the world's largest bank, the Bank of America, and the nation's second-largest aluminum company, Kaiser Aluminum. Pacific Gas & Electric was almost ten times larger than any other U.S. utility. Columnist Drew Pearson observed that "No longer can a Wall Street bank phone a Western bank and threaten to cut off deposits if the GOP delegates don't switch from Goldwater to Scranton. It was done on behalf of Mr. Eisenhower. But it can't be done any more."[79] On a less tangible level, the Eastern WASP model of gentlemanly behavior, of decorum and prudence and restraint, was also losing popular sway.[80]

One wall poster at the convention exulted that the events at the Cow Palace marked "the end of a long chapter in political history—when the East finally loses its conclusive power in American Republican politics. . . . [T]he Eastern leadership has got inbred, stuffy, jaded, exhausted—but still it resents the prospect of losing effective power. And so they come in here and make cracks about 'California extremists.'"[81] In its way, the crudity of Rockefeller's hecklers was a rebellion against the prim and proper mores of the East.

If the East no longer dominated the country as it once had, however, realistic conservatives understood that they could not write off its money, ignore its influence, and alienate its voters and still have any chance of winning the presidential election. Every rule of political logic should have compelled Goldwater to make peace with the moderates and offer them some gesture of conciliation. This Goldwater resolutely refused to do, for reasons that remain mysterious. He had long stated his reverence for party unity and acceptance of ideological diversity, at least in the abstract. After he won the California primary, he had attempted to be magnanimous and inclusive. The GOP "is a conservative party, and the liberals are only a minority in it," he had claimed. "But they belong in the party, and they're good for it."[82]

There had even been a moment in the early 1960s when Goldwater had issued a manifesto suggesting that his brand of conservatism could be infused with a pragmatic acceptance of government and stripped of dogmatism in an effort to broaden its appeal. Goldwater had aides draft conservative alternatives to Democratic initiatives that would have provided for federal aid to education, assistance to depressed areas, a minimum wage, and medical care for the aged. The greening of Goldwater was a short-lived phenomenon, however, and he quickly backed away from his nascent proposals and returned to tried-and-true ideological crusading.[83]

Goldwater was unusually thin-skinned for a politician, and shared his followers' fury over what he perceived as his unfair treatment at the hands of Scranton, the media, party professionals, and the Eastern establishment. But he was also in many ways the prisoner of the movement he led. The historian Robert Alan Goldberg has aptly termed the 1964 San Francisco convention "the conservatives' Woodstock," and many ideologically intoxicated Goldwaterites were as resistant to the counsels of realism as the flower children of the late '60s.[84] In the golden summer of '64, Gerhart Niemeyer, a Notre Dame professor and ordinarily a sober Catholic intellectual, was one of the many Goldwater supporters who turned into a utopian dreamer. Niemeyer hailed a coming Aquarian Age of conservatism: "Goldwater will win the election. . . . I anticipate that the feeling that Goldwater means a new departure, a new era, will spread among the people, and many will be seized by it without knowing why. They will see in him a new kind of man who has been absent from American politics for too long. They will sense a kind of liberation from the humdrum of American routine. They will experience a hunch that all things have become possible."[85] Goldwater himself had a much clearer-eyed understanding of his limitations, and those of the conservative movement, than most of his devotees. But as many a countercultural hero was to discover later in the decade, his appeal to his true believers rested on what they perceived as his moral and existential authenticity. Any move toward greater electability or compromise with moderates would be denounced as sellout, heresy, and betrayal.

And so Goldwater gave the moderates no quarter. He did not allow them any half-victories in the platform debates. When it came time to choose a new RNC chair, he bypassed prominent pragmatic professionals—even Clif White, who had contributed so much to his movement's success—to give the post to Dean Burch, an archconservative but politically inexperienced member of the "Arizona Mafia." While Goldwater had once favored Scranton as his vice-presidential candidate, he now gave the nod to former RNC chair William Miller, a crusty conservative with no appeal to moderates. And his acceptance speech would amount to a veritable sentence of excommunication for his intra-party enemies.

As expected, Goldwater cruised to an easy 883–214 victory over Scranton to gain the nomination. When the vote was in, Scranton gracefully moved to make the first ballot unanimous, pledging that he would "work for and fully support the ticket chosen by this convention."[86] Goldwater's acceptance speech eloquently invoked freedom and morality, and raised issues on which he might have secured a considerable degree of party unity, including anti-Communism, fiscal responsibility, the threat of rising crime, the problem of government corruption, and the danger of rampant materialism. But instead he offered an unmistakable warning to the moderates that they would be part of the Goldwater Republican Party on his terms or not at all: "Anyone who joins us in all sincerity, we welcome. Those who do not care for our cause, we don't expect to enter our ranks in any case. And let our Republicanism, so focused and so dedicated, not be made fuzzy and futile by unthinking and stupid labels." Then Goldwater let loose with the ringing, too-memorable pronouncement that threw the convention into pandemonium: "I would remind you that extremism in the defense of liberty is no vice. And let me remind you also that moderation in the pursuit of justice is no virtue." While Goldwater's speechwriters could claim respectable Ciceronian origins for their phrases, given the circumstances of the convention the first sentence could only be interpreted as a taunting dismissal of the moderates' concerns about the John Birch Society and other right-wing extremists in the GOP. The second sentence expressed contempt for moderates and moderation itself. Goldwater had not only failed to bind up the party's wounds, he had "opened new wounds and then rubbed salt in them," as Richard Nixon put it.[87] He had also handed the Democrats all the evidence they would need to paint him as a self-admitted extremist in the fall campaign.

Goldwater's famous quote was intended to polarize, and it did. Upon hearing those words, New York Senator Kenneth Keating, a moderate who faced long odds in his reelection bid against Democratic challenger Robert Kennedy, stalked out of the convention. Rockefeller castigated Goldwater with a statement that "To extol extremism—whether 'in defense of liberty' or in 'pursuit of justice'–is dangerous, irresponsible, and frightening."[88] "If Barry Goldwater wants war with the moderates in his own party," the *New York Herald Tribune* rumbled, "he can have it." The paper's editorial page summarized the speech as "an arrogant declaration that Republicanism is now Goldwaterism." Whatever Goldwater meant by his comment on extremism, the editors noted, "it came at the end of a week of wrangling over Birchism and Ku-Kluxism—and in that context it rang out as a rallying cry to the simple-minded zealots to whom the 'defense of liberty'—their own—excuses any militancy, any tactics."[89] Close to a dozen members of the Ripon Society had attended the convention, most of them as members of the Rockefeller and Scranton staffs, and they came away in a daze. "None of us who participated in the events of these days," Saloma wrote shortly after the convention ended, "will ever be quite the same again. None of us will ever be able to take the meaning of our being Republican again in the way we did before San Francisco. . . . I think we all have to take a new look at what price we are willing to pay individually as Republicans and as Americans to fight Goldwaterism to the bitter end."[90]

The message that Goldwater's followers took from his address became clear the day after the convention when California's Republican delegates met in the party's convention "office," a trailer next to the Cow Palace. The Young Turks, who had supported Rockefeller in the California GOP primary, issued a statement in which they hoped that bygones could be bygones and declared their willingness to get behind the nominee and work for a Goldwater victory in November. Former Senator William Knowland, the titular head of the GOP in California, read aloud the statement and the list of signers to the gathering. Then he tore it up and threw the pieces on the floor, to wild applause. "The conservatives had no interest in cooperating with the moderates," Assemblyman William Bagley remembered, "even when it would have been in their best interests."[91] Even moderates who wanted to participate in the Goldwater campaign would be excluded. A similar scenario followed in other states and on the Republican National Committee, where Goldwater's allies purged many of the party professionals whom they thought were insufficiently committed to the conservative cause, replacing them with inexperienced ideologues.[92] Goldwater himself proceeded to conduct a campaign that combined remarkable ineptitude with an unbending refusal to alter his conservative stance in any way.

Many progressive and moderate Republicans did not want to participate in the Goldwater campaign in any way, shape, or form. The party's African-American supporters were a special case in point. The Republican Party was founded largely out of opposition to slavery, and for many decades afterwards black voters were uniformly Republicans. The New Deal did not immediately or completely dissolve the longstanding loyalty of African-American voters to the "Party of Lincoln." Dwight Eisenhower received 39 percent of the black vote in 1956, and Richard Nixon 32 percent in 1960. But Goldwater's vote against the Civil Rights Bill, his campaign's Southern strategy, and the events of the Republican convention made certain that black support for the GOP ticket would drop precipitously. Not only had the convention's platform committee squelched the moderates' resolutions favoring enforcement of the civil rights laws, but the credentials committee had denied New York progressive John Lindsay's motion to prohibit racial discrimination in choosing delegates. At the same time, the committee admitted delegations from Southern states that had long been integrated but had recently forced out their black delegates.

African-Americans comprised only one percent of delegates and alternates at the convention, a record low. Even so, there were some ugly incidents when Southern whites baited the blacks with insults and racial epithets and, in one case, deliberately burned a black delegate's suit jacket with cigarettes.[93] When New York's delegation was asked to change its vote in order to cast a unanimous ballot for Goldwater, black delegate Harold C. Burton retorted, "I'd rather be lynched than vote for this guy."[94] Former baseball star Jackie Robinson, one of the most prominent African-American Republicans in the convention audience, felt that he was witnessing white supremacy in action: "I now believe I know how it felt to be a Jew in Hitler's Germany."[95] Many of the black delegates and alternates walked out of the convention. Those who stayed did so mostly out of determination not to give satisfaction to their enemies.[96]

Many of these delegates and other longtime black Republicans formed the National Negro Republican Assembly to combat conservatives, whom George Fleming, the organization's first president, characterized as "those who have infiltrated the party and are seeking to drive the Negro out."[97] They resolved to oppose Goldwater but to support and endorse pro-civil rights Republicans and to create "a new atmosphere within the Republican Party that will make it unmistakably clear that the Negro is needed, wanted, and welcome."[98] But their position in the GOP became ever more untenable as Goldwater and his allies dissolved the Minorities Division of the RNC, welcomed segregationist senator Strom Thurmond when he switched parties, and allowed him to keep his old committee slots without loss of seniority.[99] Moderates at the conservative-dominated California Republican state convention, held after the national convention, barely managed to block a resolution to the state party platform to "send Negroes back to Africa."[100] Segregationist Democrat George Wallace dropped out of the presidential race, declaring that now that the GOP had become a conservative party, racially and otherwise, "My mission has been accomplished."[101]

Outside the South, however, voters recoiled from the spectacle of this new and frightening GOP. Johnson and the Democrats ran a brutal and effective campaign depicting Goldwater as a dangerous radical threatening America's domestic and foreign security. The Democrats' lead widened with every passing week. Around the country, Republican politicians became aware of growing defections from rank-and-file party members. An organization called Republicans & Independents for Johnson began urging Republicans to "Split Your Ticket . . . Not Your Country." One Maryland couple threatened Representative Charles Mathias: "If you do not publicly and emphatically renounce the Goldwater-Miller ticket, and run as an independent Republican, we shall vote for anyone on the Democratic ticket who is running against you."[102] Another of Mathias' constituents wrote that while he had always supported Republicans, he would now help the party learn from "bitter experience": "A smashing defeat at the national level will not destroy the Republican party or the two-party system. It will merely discredit those who think they can win by exploiting the forces of reaction. Those of us who are voting Democratic will return to the fold in coming years, when responsible Republicanism has reassumed party leadership."[103] Republicans' campaigns suffered not only by association with Goldwater and his positions, but also because they encountered difficulty raising funds from traditional sources, particularly businesses. At the same time, conservatives set up watchdog outfits to pressure Republican candidates who did not endorse the party's nominee or his agenda. Mathias' former opponent Brent Bozell used direct mail to emphasize that candidates who were unwilling to support Goldwater "are not entitled to the support of the Republican Party."[104] The RNC in many cases withheld financial and logistical support from candidates whom they deemed too moderate or too distant from Goldwater's positions.

Republicans facing elections in the fall were caught between these upper and nether millstones. Some Northeastern progressives, faced with the prospect that Goldwater might lose their state by a million voters or more, simply disavowed Goldwater. New York Senator Kenneth Keating stipulated that he was not bolting the GOP: "The Republican party is bigger than one man or one Convention. . . . In the past, Republicanism has been almost synonymous with moderation. Senator Goldwater cannot expect to win the support of a broad cross-section of Republicans by his attacks on moderation and his defense of extremism, whether in our foreign or domestic policies."[105] Other moderates such as Mathias and Scott endorsed Goldwater after being threatened with loss of party endorsements and funds if they refused, but continued to emphasize their disagreements with Goldwater and the 1964 platform.[106]

Still others had to decide what distance they would try to put between themselves and their toxic nominee. In Tennessee, promising young senatorial candidate Howard Baker invited Goldwater to the state to speak on his behalf, then listened in stunned disbelief as the conservative called for the government to sell off the immensely popular Tennessee Valley Authority. As Baker sat on the platform, "I could see my prospects going right down the drain," he recalled.[107] In Washington State, the RNC notified moderate gubernatorial candidate Dan Evans that Goldwater planned to make a one-day speaking appearance in Spokane. Evans' advisor Slade Gorton, the future senator, knew that Goldwater was going to be "slaughtered" in the state, but in the end the campaign team decided that Evans had to appear with Goldwater at the GOP rally: "there just wasn't any way that he couldn't do that and still be a part of the party." The campaign instructed a bulky farmer, the aptly named Don Moos, to stand between Evans and the press and television cameras at all times when Evans was close to Goldwater. Moos succeeded in his assignment, Gorton was amused to recall, "and the Democrats couldn't get the picture of Goldwater with Evans that they wanted to put on television. I'll tell you, this was a major planning operation in the Evans campaign! But it wasn't because we hated Goldwater, it was just that he was poison."[108]

In another dire indication for the Goldwater campaign, traditionally Republican newspapers began giving their editorial support to Johnson. The *Kansas City Star* endorsed a Democrat for the first time since 1892, worrying about Goldwater's nuclear irresponsibility. The *Saturday Evening Post* endorsed a Democrat for the first time in the twentieth century, grumbling that "Barry Goldwater's tongue is like quicksilver; his mind like quicksand." Two Vermont newspapers supported their first Democratic candidate since 1864, while New York's *Binghamton Sun-Bulletin* gave its first nod to a Democrat since 1856, calling Goldwater "temperamentally unfit for the Presidency."[109] The *New York Herald Tribune*, which advertised itself as "Republican before there was a Republican Party," endorsed a Democratic presidential candidate for the first time in its history. The paper repeated its criticism of Goldwater's "simplistic" views of world affairs, his Southern strategy, and his appeal to "ugly racial passions." They blamed Goldwater and his backers for attempting "to convert a great national party into a narrow ideological faction," and thereby destroying the balance of political power in the country. The paper denied that the "mass defection" from the Goldwater ticket could be attributed to sour grapes on the part of the losing moderates: "It's a nationwide, grass-roots defection, a mass exodus based on a lack of confidence and respect. Senator Goldwater could have made it possible for many, even most, of these people to support him; instead he made it extraordinarily difficult, if not impossible."[110]

Throughout the autumn, the Ripon Society had been gathering information on national and local campaigns for a project that would provide rapid analysis and evaluation of the election. The Society's executive committee believed that such an analysis would provide ammunition for moderates after the anticipated Goldwater defeat: "Progressive Republicans must have information to refute any unreal claims on behalf of the Southern strategy or allegations against progressive Republicans. We must be able to know and document whether the national ticket helped or hurt local tickets."[111] On election night, as horror-stricken Republicans across the land watched the returns, some thirty Ripon members and their spouses

set up an elaborate communications center and monitored calls from contacts in thirty-one states.

The picture was grim indeed for Republicans. As anticipated, Goldwater
was buried in a Johnson landslide, carrying only five of the Deep South
states and his home state of Arizona. He trailed Johnson by sixteen million
votes, and the twenty-seven million votes he received were almost seven
million fewer than Nixon had received four years before.[112] The scale of the
disaster was evident in the fact that Goldwater carried only sixteen Congressional districts outside the South; six of those were in Southern California, which cast doubt upon how representative a victory he had won there
in the June primary. The Republicans shed two seats in the Senate—fewer
than anticipated—but the real carnage was further down the ticket. The
party dropped thirty-eight seats in the House, reducing Republican representation to its lowest level since the 1936 election. The Ripon Society calculated that in the state legislatures the party lost some ninety members of
the upper houses and almost four hundred and fifty members of the lower
houses, again reducing Republican numbers to levels they had not touched
since the Depression.[113] It was difficult to tally how many Republicans had
been ousted from other local offices, but columnists Evans and Novak
pointed out that in Nassau County on Long Island, controlled top to
bottom by Republicans prior to the election, the posts of county clerk,
county comptroller, and county sheriff, which provided more than two
hundred patronage jobs, fell to the Democrats. The election had "dried up
the party in its grass roots where the political thrust and energy for victory
at the top are generated."[114] Commentators seriously debated whether the
Republicans might follow the Whigs into extinction.

The Ripon Society rapidly compiled a detailed picture of the GOP disaster and two days later issued a much-publicized nine-page statement asking
Goldwater to drop his party leadership role.[115] "The claims of the Goldwater party have met a crushing vote of no confidence from the American
people," the report declared. Ripon pointed to widespread evidence of a
"reverse coat-tail" effect on Republican candidates, the failure of the Southern strategy, and the reverses among minority and suburban voters. They
also criticized the strategy and conduct of "one of the most inept and un-
professional campaigns in American political history," its failure to accommodate moderates in any way, and the "oppressive exclusiveness" of the
Goldwater leadership, which "put loyalty to a small cabal ahead of loyalty to
the Republican Party."[116]

Over time a mythology has grown up among conservatives that the
Goldwater loss was not the debacle for the Republican Party that it appeared
at the time. Indeed, given that Ronald Reagan ran a successful presidential
campaign along allegedly similar conservative lines in 1980, many on the

right have come to agree with columnist George Will's witticism that Goldwater did win the 1964 election, it just took sixteen years to count all the votes.[117] It's true that Goldwater's campaign gave the GOP what would prove to be an enduring foothold among Southern white voters, and pioneered strategies playing upon anti-government sentiments, racial resentments, and resistance to social and cultural change that would pay off for conservative Republicans in the future.[118] The conservative movement that coalesced around Goldwater had a lasting impact on American politics, and Reagan's much-ballyhooed televised campaign speech on Goldwater's behalf, "A Time for Choosing," was instrumental in his political rise.

But in fact the Goldwater campaign was every bit the catastrophe it seemed, and one that echoed across the American political scene for decades. By dragging so many Republican candidates down to defeat, Goldwater ensured that Lyndon Johnson would have a liberal supermajority in Congress that Democrats had not enjoyed since the high tide of Franklin Roosevelt's presidency. Emancipated from the restraint of conservative Southern Democrats, Johnson would have free rein to pass what amounted to a second New Deal.

The magnitude of Goldwater's defeat chastened the conservative movement. Politicians like Reagan and intellectuals like William F. Buckley Jr. eventually came to realize that the *enragé* quality of the Goldwater campaign—its embrace of extremism and unpopular positions, its nihilistic antagonism toward potential allies—was a formula for defeat. They would modulate conservatism and make it a more inclusive, realistic, and successful political force. It would be forty years before a Republican presidential nominee would again be so dismissive of moderates. From the moderate standpoint, the Goldwater experience shocked moderates out of their naïveté about the dangers posed by the conservative movement. Still, many realized that they would have to reach some kind of accommodation with their intra-party rivals to prevent the Republican Party from being marginalized or even eliminated from American politics.

In the immediate aftermath of the 1964 election, however, Republicans had not yet learned wisdom from their painful defeat. In the meantime, there were scores to be settled and more blood to be spilled.

CHAPTER 5

❧

The Ceremony of Innocence
Is Drowned

Moderates Attempt to Regain Control
of the GOP, 1965

In the wake of the 1964 election, the surviving Republicans took stock of the disaster, like shivering survivors of a flood surveying the hideous transformation of a once-familiar landscape. GOP representation in the new Congress was reduced to levels unseen since FDR's heyday. Democrats outnumbered Republicans 68 to 32 in the Senate and 295 to 140 in the House. Outside of the Deep South, the most conservative Republicans had incurred the most casualties, suffering disproportionately from voter disapproval of Barry Goldwater.[1] The elections marginally strengthened the relative position of moderates and progressives within the GOP; they made up more than a third of the party delegation in the House and nearly two-fifths in the Senate.[2] But this still left moderates as a minority within a minority.

The remaining progressive and moderate GOP members of Congress gathered in Washington for an all-day meeting that was part therapy session, part war council. New York progressive John Lindsay, speaking for the group, announced that they would "have to rebuild the Republican party out of the ashes. We hope we can work with other moderate groups throughout the country to return the party to the tradition of Lincoln."[3] Most moderates were convinced that the conservative supporters of presidential nominee Barry Goldwater, who had led Republicans to defeat, would have to yield back leadership of the party. But those on the right were equally determined not to relinquish their newly won control, and to press on with their mission of converting the GOP into an instrument of ideological conservatism.

The moderates believed that the election debacle had vindicated their criticism of Goldwater. They had predicted that his uncompromising conservatism, flying in the face of the national consensus on both domestic and foreign policy, would alienate the American electorate and drag down the rest of the Republican ticket. "I do not want to be in a position of saying 'I told you so,'" wrote Kentucky Senator John Sherman Cooper, "but it is true that those of us who had served with Senator Goldwater and knew his views could foresee some of the problems we had during the election."[4] Cooper made clear that he and his fellow senators liked Goldwater as a man, but they "had listened to his extreme views for many years and did not believe that he could win." Goldwater's extreme conservativism allowed Johnson to get away with portraying the Democratic Party as a force for reasonable moderation rather than the ambitious liberalism that most Republican professionals believed it stood for. Now, thanks to Goldwater, "Democrats control the Congress over two to one and can do practically what they want to. This is bad for the two party system and bad for the country."[5]

Moderates and progressives believed that the election results proved that the "Southern strategy" was not only immoral but politically stupid as well. Conservatives' betrayal of the Republican civil rights heritage had won the votes of the Deep South states but lost every other state in the country, aside from Goldwater's home state of Arizona. Even in the South, Goldwater lost states such as Florida, North Carolina, Kentucky, and Texas that had voted for Eisenhower and Nixon. The anti-civil rights strategy had merely traded the urban and industrialized parts of the South for its most rural and segregationist regions. Meanwhile, all twelve southern and border state Democrats who had voted for the Civil Rights Act won reelection.[6] The Republican Party was in particular trouble with black voters. While the Republican ticket lost ground among almost every conceivable group outside the Deep South, from urbanites to suburbanites, northern Protestants to Midwestern farmers, the GOP suffered its most dramatic plunge in support from African-Americans. Nixon had received thirty-two percent of the black vote in 1960, but only six percent of blacks voted for the Republican presidential candidate in 1964, which constituted the largest percentage loss among any group of voters.

Black voters provided the margin that defeated Republicans not only in northern cities but also in elections across the South. Charles Percy, for whom lack of black support had been a critical factor in his losing the Illinois governor's race, insisted that Republicans must "take this party away from being a sort of Anglo-Saxon, white Protestant party . . . if we are to go forward in the future."[7] In the North Carolina governor's race, approximately 97 percent of black voters preferred segregationist Democrat Dan K. Moore to his integrationist Republican opponent, Robert L. Gavin. As Gavin explained, "This I believe was because of the determination of the Negro race to defeat our national ticket."[8] Further, the number of Southern black voters was bound to grow if the civil rights movement succeeded in overcoming Jim Crow restrictions on black enfranchisement. As civil rights leader Martin Luther King Jr. pointed out to President Lyndon Johnson, all of the Black Belt states that Goldwater carried had near-majorities of African-American residents who were not allowed to vote.[9] For moderate and progressive Republicans, it was imperative that the party reach out to blacks and other minorities as well as to other groups who had become less inclined to support Republicans, particularly intellectuals, city-dwellers, blue-collar workers, and young people.

The conservative strategists' unwillingness to broaden their base and their exclusion of all but right-wing true believers from Republican campaigns seemed suicidal to most observers. One of the few apparent conservative victories in 1964, former song-and-dance man George Murphy's defeat of Democratic incumbent Pierre Salinger in the Senate race in California, actually relied on heavy moderate and progressive participation. Columnists Evans and Novak reported that California's veteran Republican activists, "[s]hut out by the Goldwater militants" in the 1964 presidential campaign, threw their energies into the Murphy effort.[10] One longtime party worker recalled that "The Murphy campaign was a combination of Kuchel people, Rockefeller people, Nixon people... The moderates weren't wanted [in the Goldwater campaign]. They had no place to go. Here this was their vehicle."[11] With Nixon advisor Robert Finch masterminding his campaign, Murphy toned down his right-wing views, kept his distance from Goldwater, assembled a wide range of Republican support, and surged to victory while running eleven percent ahead of the national ticket.[12]

The claim that a "hidden" conservative majority would materialize at the polls if offered a sharp ideological choice between parties had proven to be false. So had the theory that a Southern strategy, combined with an appeal to a putative white backlash against civil rights in the North, would allow the GOP to win without carrying big states like New York or California. As one Republican analyst concluded, Goldwater's vote against the Civil Rights Act of 1964 "set in motion the most passionate bloc voting in history" against the candidate and Republicans generally.[13] Moderates denied that the twenty-seven million voters who cast their ballots for Goldwater were all conservatives. Pollster Louis Harris concluded that only about six million of those who voted for the Arizonan could be considered "hard-core, down-the-line Goldwater supporters," along with three million voters (two-thirds of them Southern Democrats) motivated mainly by racial issues. The remaining eighteen million voted for the Republican candidate "primarily because of party loyalty" while expressing reservations about his policies.[14]

Goldwater loyalists unsurprisingly had a different view of the lessons to be drawn from the election. Goldwater believed that he lost because "I wasn't dishonest enough to win." He blamed the "sad, sorry mess" of columnists and opinion-makers, who had allegedly indulged in character assassination and given credence to phony Democratic claims that he was a warmonger who wanted to abolish Social Security.[15] He faulted Lyndon Johnson, who he claimed had used the presidency's power to threaten recipients of federal largesse that "if you do not go along with LBJ, then something is going to happen to you."[16] Goldwater also blamed progressive and moderate Republicans who had not voted or worked for him.[17] He refused to acknowledge that the conservative cause had in any way been tarnished by the magnitude of his defeat, and insisted that he and his followers ought to remain in control of the GOP.

Goldwater's hand-picked Republican National Committee chairman, Dean Burch, added that the Republican loss had been foreordained because of public reverence for the fallen John F. Kennedy and "massive sympathy for the whole Kennedy-Johnson era." He also cited the defections of businessmen and the delusions of black voters, who had almost unanimously supported the Democrats merely because of "one vote" by Goldwater— which happened to be against the Civil Rights Act of 1964. He claimed that the election had been a victory of sorts for the GOP, since it brought an army of dedicated conservative activists into politics and achieved breakthroughs in the South "which will last long after the current civil rights turmoil is past." Above all, he felt, the GOP would achieve future victories only if it remained a conservative party, since polls showed that "A healthy majority of the American people, a plurality even among Democrats, consider *themselves* to be conservatives."[18] There was also a widespread sense among conservatives that they deserved the party leadership because they made up a disproportionate share of the party's grassroots activists. One of those activists contended that "To the extent that dedicated volunteer workers are anywhere, most of them inhabit the conservative camp; furthermore, working between elections with no candidate in sight requires a dedication to principles rather than a loyalty to personalities." Conservatives, he felt, had the necessary dedication to ideals, "while most liberals are candidate-oriented, and require a visible candidate (preferably with a catchy slogan) before they can become motivated to do any work."[19]

Within both the conservative and moderate camps, many called for full-fledged fratricide against their party opponents. Prominent Goldwater supporter Ronald Reagan, speaking before the Los Angeles County Young Republicans after the election, charged that the conservative nominee might well have triumphed if not for the "worst campaign of vilification and the worst betrayal of those who should have given us their trust"—that is, the party's progressives and moderates. He did not allow the inconvenient fact that purge-minded conservatives had excluded these Republicans from the campaign to interfere with this stab-in-the-back explanation for Goldwater's defeat. Reagan stoked the bloodlust of the YRs with his insistence that conservatives must not "turn the Republican Party over to the traitors in the battle just ended."[20] One vengeful conservative activist wrote to Goldwater that he was forming a local group "to eradicate from our county Republican organization all the 'moderates' & 'liberals' who refused to work for you, and tried to destroy our efforts."[21] Others insisted that they would leave the party, or perhaps attempt to form a third party, if GOP control reverted to the moderates. Conservatives created new national organizations such as the American Conservative Union and the Free Society Association to build upon the Goldwater movement and continue their battles against liberal Democrats and moderate Republicans alike.

Many moderates likewise itched to go to war against their conservative rivals. Maryland Representative Charles Mathias had warned long before the 1964 election that moderates should never allow the GOP to put forward a reactionary presidential candidate. Even if the nomination resulted in the party's decimation, "the irrationality of the Right" meant that conservatives would never "accept the verdict of the polls as final. There would always be one more rationalization."[22] For this reason it was imperative that moderates destroy the conservatives before the conservatives could destroy the party again. The most detailed moderate battle plan came from Doug Bailey, a Ripon Society founder and Rockefeller aide, and David Goldberg, a Boston attorney and one of the originators of the draft movement that had won the 1964 New Hampshire GOP primary for Henry Cabot Lodge Jr. Both had attended the 1964 Republican convention in San Francisco, and were sufficiently horrified that they drew up an analysis of what would be required to reverse the conservative takeover.

The Bailey-Goldberg plan called for a widespread moderate effort to replicate F. Clifton White's seizure of the party machinery at the grassroots level, building a moderate counterpart to the conservative political infrastructure that had sprung up in the previous decade. They laid out the necessary steps to develop the staff, financing, and popular support that would enable moderates to seize control of the regular Republican Party structure. Their plan would require a separate organization parallel to the official Republican organization, which would include a finance committee, a research division, a communications arm, and a political organization network. It would entail political field workers, a Congressional study group, a speaker's bureau, an information clearinghouse, and a magazine to counter conservative publications like *National Review* and *Human Events*. The annual budget would be a minimum of $400,000.

Bailey and Goldberg believed that the battle would have to be fought in official and unofficial Republican bodies at all levels: city and town committees, state committees, the national committee, elective offices, state delegate-selecting conventions, the YRs and Republican women's organizations. They also insisted that moderates would have to generate clearly defined policy proposals and an inspiring ideology that they had so far lacked. The right-wing ideology, in their view, was the source of the conservative movement's greatest appeal. Though it may have been self-contradictory, anachronistic, and wrong, it was also "loud and bold and exciting." It allowed conservatives to "provide answers to questions which bother people. They may not be good answers but they are the only ones available within today's Republican Party, and they hypnotize their believers, raise money for their candidates, and unite their movement."[23]

"We sent the proposal far and wide," Bailey remembered ruefully, "and it was ignored far and wide. . . . No moderates ever mounted that kind of grassroots effort, so far as I'm aware, despite the obvious need."[24] One or another candidate or organization tackled elements of the plan, but moderates never came close to matching the overall scale, unity, and coordination of the conservative effort.

Nonetheless, negative reaction to the Goldwater campaign had stimulated the development of existing moderate Republican organizations and given birth to several new ones. A number of these groups met together in New York City after the election to form an umbrella association called the Council of Republican Organizations (CRO).[25] The Ripon Society, already the leading moderate intellectual outfit, sent its president Jack Saloma. Charles P. Taft, brother of the late Midwestern conservative icon Robert Taft, was present in his capacity as the head of the Committee to Support Moderate Republicans, an organization he had created in the fall of '64 to channel funds to moderate GOP candidates such as Hugh Scott, John Lindsay, and his nephew Robert Taft Jr.[26] The National Negro Republican Assembly, formed in the wake of the San Francisco convention, sent a representative, as did the Committee of '68, a carryover of the Citizens for Scranton group. Other organizations present included the Committee for Forward-Looking Republicans, the National Council for Civil Responsibility, the National Council of Republican Workshops, and the California Republican Action Committee.[27] When the press reported on the CRO's first meetings, some attendees, including former Minnesota Governor Elmer Andersen, had to make clear that the groups were loyal to the Republican

Party though antagonistic to conservative control.[28] Columnist Roscoe Drummond wrote that their main purpose was "to return the moderates to maximum influence in the Republican party and to persuade elected Republican officials to support moderate rather than far-Right policies. . . . These groups felt they had to work outside the Republican National Committee, since at San Francisco and after the moderates had been sentenced to some Republican Siberia."[29]

The Republican governors were also active in the wake of the election. Pennsylvania Governor William Scranton pointed out to his fellow moderate governors that "This is the only body in which we have a majority of the members, and therefore it should be the first to operate effectively."[30] The Ripon Society applauded Scranton's initiative and called for the governors to become a "Third Force" in the Republican Party, breaking free of the conservatives in the Republican National Committee and playing a direct role in party affairs and legislation.[31] Saloma attended the first meeting of the new organization, the Republican Governors Association (RGA), in Denver in early December. The governors agreed to establish an office and staff for the RGA in Washington and embark on a comprehensive research program.[32] Michigan Governor George Romney encouraged moderates' hopes that the governors might play a leading role in taking back the party, touting the RGA as "particularly qualified to develop the greater grass-roots participation which is needed."[33] The governors issued a pointed statement emphasizing that the GOP needed to become inclusive rather than exclusive: "We need to win elections and serve America as a great broad-based political party, far greater and far more effective than any narrow, exclusive political clique can ever hope to become."[34] They demanded that the Republican Party oppose racial discrimination, eschew all forms of political radicalism, and recommit to the use of government to address human needs, although preferably at the state and local levels. Without mentioning Dean Burch by name, they strongly implied that he had to go if the RNC was to move beyond the purge-minded mentality that had characterized the leadership in the election campaigns.

The Republican governors' statement sparked an extraordinary exchange between Goldwater and Romney, who had refused to endorse Goldwater in the election. Obviously wounded by Romney's betrayal, as he saw it, Goldwater claimed to be "confused" by the moderate governors' charge that the GOP under his direction had become ideologically exclusive. Who, he asked Romney rhetorically, had pleaded with all Republicans at the 1960 convention to set aside philosophical differences and work together to elect Richard Nixon as president? "If you don't remember, it was me. Now let's get to 1964 and ask ourselves who it was in the Party who said, in effect, if I can't have my way I'm not going to play? One of those men happens to be you." Goldwater believed that it was the governors who were being exclusive, demanding that he compromise his principles to meet moderates' standards or suffer expulsion. This struck him as terribly unfair, since he shared the moderates' opposition to centralized government power and discrimination against minorities. He even agreed with the governors' "long-overdue" explanation of why exactly they objected to extremism. "Frankly," he concluded, "I don't understand what principles of mine you disagree with."[35]

Romney responded with a twelve-page, single-spaced missive, much of which rehashed the events of the San Francisco convention and Goldwater's failure to restore party unity. He pointed out that the two men differed on the desirability of realigning the Republican and Democratic parties into "conservative" and "liberal" parties along the European model: "Dogmatic ideological parties tend to splinter the political and social fabric of a nation, lead to governmental crises and deadlocks, and stymie the compromises so often necessary to preserve freedom and achieve progress." But the most profound difference between them was Goldwater's vote against the Civil Rights Act and his willingness to countenance a campaign geared toward Southern white segregationists and the white backlash in the North. "I cannot accept the blame for the divisiveness in the party," Romney insisted, "when you, your representatives, and your campaign strategy refused to encompass those of us who had reservations based on basic American and Republican principles." Romney supported Goldwater's ideals of Americanism and strong constitutional government, "but I know they cannot be realized if foundation principles of American freedom are compromised."[36] Because civil rights constituted such a moral blind spot for the Arizonan, Goldwater found Romney's reservations incomprehensible; he protested that the Michigan governor "didn't explain anything."[37]

Also present at the Denver meeting of the Republican governors were observers from the House Wednesday Group, another potential force for moderation within the party.[38] The group had begun to coalesce in the spring of 1961 as an informal association of several pro-civil rights Republicans who had bucked the party line to vote for enlargement of the House Rules Committee. It was formally organized in the fall of that year. One of its original members, Maryland's Charles Mathias, described it as "an association of thoughtful Republicans who could exchange legislative information and work together in developing sound constructive Republican positions on some of the complicated problems which face the nation."[39] It was similar to other Congressional fraternities such as the SOS, the Acorns, and the Chowder and Marching Club, but while those societies tended to be mainly social, the Wednesday Group was intended to be more analytical and willing to explore alternatives to the party line.[40] Its membership was mostly made up of moderates and progressives such as Mathias, John Lindsay and Ogden Reid of New York, Silvio Conte of Massachusetts, Alphonzo Bell of California, and Robert Stafford of Vermont, but also included some congressmen in the Taft tradition, such as Herman Schneebli of Pennsylvania and Robert Ellsworth of Kansas.[41]

Although *National Review* suspected that the leader of the House Wednesday Group was their archenemy Lindsay, in fact the founder and driving force was Brad Morse, a little-known moderate from Massachusetts.[42] One account described Morse as looking "like a rumpled bureaucrat in the second or third tier of, say, the Department of Agriculture," but behind his unprepossessing exterior was one of the sharpest minds and fastest tongues in Congress. He was a fiscal conservative and an internationalist, and came from one of the most diverse and Democratic districts represented by a Republican. He was a master of backstage maneuvering but, unlike many better known Congressional operators, enjoyed both the flesh-pressing aspect of politics and the intricate details of policy-making. One of his colleagues marveled that Morse "can go to a Polish picnic in his district, drink beer and dance, then catch a plane for Washington, sit down with a dozen Ph.D.'s at Brookings Institution for a discussion of world problems, and put on a display of intellect and knowledge that grabs you."[43] In December 1964, Morse hired Doug Bailey as the staff director for the Wednesday Group, with funds supplied by Charles Taft's group Republicans for Progress.[44] On the first day Bailey came to work, Morse advised him that "There's no limit to what you can get done if you don't care who gets the credit." Bailey believed that "a great many of the good ideas that other people became famous for" resulted from Morse's efforts.[45]

By late 1964, the Republican side of the House was a place of swirling intrigue and long knives, with moves afoot to overthrow the minority leader Charles Halleck and others in the leadership who had contributed to the electoral calamity. The lead actors in the plot were not the members of the Wednesday Group but the moderately conservative and mostly Midwestern "Young Turks" who had been trying to reform the House and the GOP for several years.[46] Their sachem was Thomas Curtis of Missouri, the leader in the coup that had replaced previous minority leader Joseph Martin with Halleck back in 1959. The moving force in this revolt, however, was Donald Rumsfeld, who had represented Chicago's wealthy northern suburbs since he was first elected to the House two years earlier at age thirty. He appeared to one observer in late 1964 to be "brash, ambitious, somewhat arrogant," like Young Republicans leader Buz Lukens "with a few more years of polish."[47] Rumsfeld, for all his arrogance, was most deferential toward his mentor Tom Curtis, whom he admired for his "knowledge of government, intelligence, integrity, courage and understanding of the country."[48] Rumsfeld sat next to Curtis on the floor of the House to listen and learn from him.

After the Goldwater defeat, Curtis and Rumsfeld discussed how the Republicans should respond. "I don't want to continue to be a member of the minority party," Rumsfeld said at the time. He believed that the House members needed to respond to defeat by making the GOP "a reasonable, constructive, and effective force."[49] In consultation with Rumsfeld, Curtis sent a letter to all his party colleagues urging them to call a meeting of the House Republican Conference before the end of the session in order to address long-unresolved problems that made the Republicans ineffective even as an opposition.[50] At the meeting, duly held in mid-December, Halleck proved indifferent to the need for change, brushing off criticisms by reminding the group that he had been in the House in 1936 when the Republicans were reduced to a mere 88 members. Moderate discontent boiled over into rebellion. The Young Turks originally proposed Melvin Laird as a candidate to replace Halleck, but the Wednesday Group, with still-painful memories of Laird's willingness to do Goldwater's bidding as chairman of the Platform Committee at the San Francisco convention, vetoed his nomination. The compromise choice of both groups was Gerald Ford, a personable Michigan stalwart who, after Goldwater's defeat, had written an article for *Fortune* magazine calling for the GOP to reclaim "the high middle road of moderation" and resist takeover by "any elements that are not interested in building a party, but only in advancing their own narrow views."[51] Rumsfeld, Curtis, and New York's Charles Goodell took the lead in managing Ford's campaign.[52]

When the Republican Conference convened on January 4, 1965, the opening day of the 89th Congress, Ford won a narrow 73 to 67 victory and replaced Halleck as House Republican Leader.[53] Illinois Representative John B. Anderson, one of the Young Turks, pointed out that Ford's triumph was made possible by the election defeats of "some of the older mossbacks" and "young fogies" like ultra-conservative Bruce Alger from Texas, who would have supported Halleck if they had still been in office.[54] Although Ford's voting record to that point was similar to Halleck's, his election represented a Republican move toward the center. Ford was more willing and able than Halleck had been to work with the reformers, adopt an inclusive style of leadership, and present a more vigorous and forward-looking image of the party. He also was less inclined to try to revive the old conservative coalition with Southern Democrats, partly because he wanted to make an aggressive effort to elect Republicans in the South.[55] After his election, Ford wrote to his colleagues that he considered it of prime importance that they be associated with "a program of positive and constructive legislation. We are all aware of the handicap which Republican candidates have because of the widespread, but erroneous, impression that Republicans have no constructive ideas."[56]

The next scene of battle loomed at the January 21–22 meeting of the Republican National Committee in Chicago. RNC chair Dean Burch did not want to step down, threatening that if he were to be removed because he was a symbol of the Goldwater movement, millions of conservatives might bolt the party.[57] Barry Goldwater insisted that he would interpret Burch's removal as a repudiation of his leadership, and that the GOP would become "meaningless" if it abandoned his conservative cause to chase "the vanity of today's popularity."[58] He snarled to William F. Buckley Jr. that the anti-Burch drive by the party's "idiot fringe" was "a personal attack on me and I intend to treat it as such. We may lose, but if we do it will be after a fight and not after a compromise."[59] Certainly George Romney was in full pursuit of Burch, writing to Eisenhower that Goldwater's appointee "lacks the background and understanding required to bring people together rather than to continue a program that tends to drive people apart."[60]

It became increasingly apparent, however, that the call to remove Burch was coming from conservatives as well as moderates and progressives. At a secret meeting of Midwestern RNC members in Chicago, Don Ross of Nebraska was one of several former Goldwater supporters arguing that the party needed a broader approach than Burch could provide.[61] Columnists Evans and Novak interviewed Texas Republican leaders and found widespread disillusionment with Goldwater. One of his Texan supporters acknowledged that Goldwater's presence atop the ticket was the main reason that Republicans got "clobbered" in the state on November 3: "With almost anybody else running for President—Romney, Scranton, even Lodge—it wouldn't have been so bad." The conservative faction of the party in Texas successfully fended off the moderate faction's bid for control, but even the conservatives agreed that the party would have to pursue a more moderate course and appeal to new constituencies such as "blue collar workers and Latin Americans," as Evans and Novak put it. While the "rank-and-file zealots" insisted that Burch be kept on at the RNC, "many party leaders believe privately that Burch must go. Nor are they the slightest bit interested in retaining the Goldwaterites at the National Committee. Indeed, many are quite willing to let the Eastern moderates have a crack at the Presidency in 1968."[62] Like morning-after partygoers wrestling with painful hangovers, defeat had forced Texan conservative leaders into coldwater pragmatism.

The leading Republican exponent of this sort of sober campaign realism was Ohio's GOP chairman Ray Bliss, the man widely favored to replace

Burch as head of the RNC. A short, bespectacled insurance broker from Akron, Bliss had entered party politics in 1932 as a precinct committeeman and worked his way up the ladder, becoming the leader of the state party in 1949. Although he was a poor speaker who was uncomfortable at large social affairs, he became one of the party's most successful organizers through his emphasis on discipline, detail, party unity, and the "nuts and bolts" of politics. When he was first named chairman, he obtained the membership rosters of Republican-leaning groups such as the Rotarians, chambers of commerce, and country clubs, then cross-checked them against county registration lists. When he spoke at Republican forums around the state, he shamed these groups into greater political participation by producing evidence that fewer than two-thirds of the men were registered voters and fewer than half of their wives had ever voted.[63] Bliss despised ideology of any sort, and had made a national reputation for himself in 1958 by warning the Ohio business elite that their crusade for a "right to work" law would lead to Republicans losing elections across the board, as indeed happened.[64] His prescriptions for a broader GOP outreach effort, codified in his 1962 RNC report on capturing the big-city vote, were exactly in line with the wishes of the party's left wing. Progressives, however, distrusted Bliss as much as conservatives did. Both groups resisted being yoked into his harness of party unity. Bliss' repression of primary challenges and his agnostic willingness to campaign with equal vigor for conservatives and progressives alike, if he thought they could win, struck them as undemocratic and cynical. For Republicans who had tired of ideological adventures and losing campaigns, however, the technician's approach epitomized by Bliss pointed the way toward party recovery.

Faced with the certainty of a no-confidence vote, Burch quit and Bliss became the new chairman. Burch complained to the RNC meeting in Chicago that "obviously this is more or less a forced resignation," but given the dire election results summarized at the meeting, he had little choice.[65] Bliss emphasized that while the '64 results had been dreadful for the Republicans, in the longer view the party's decline had been ongoing since the 1930s, with the GOP controlling Congress for only four of the previous thirty-five years. The Republicans were actually stronger than the Democrats organizationally and financially, which meant, in Bliss' view, that the real problem was the GOP's lack of popular appeal. Further, "one of the reasons we don't have any appeal for people is all we do is fight each other. Until such time as we learn how to run a party, we aren't going to be able to run the United States." The Republicans could not afford any more splits, and would have to adopt a moderate posture: "We have been shoved out onto the curb by the broad hips of Lyndon Johnson, and we have got to get back into the middle of the road where the Republican Party traditionally has been." The committee members endorsed Bliss' unity call. Louisiana committeeman Tom Stagg, who only a few months earlier had rejoiced that moderates were forced to "walk the plank" at the San Francisco convention, now stated that "if Adam Clayton Powell can vote in the same party as Richard Russell, I can vote in the same party with Jacob Javits."[66] Even Burch, in his final report as RNC chairman, emphasized the unity theme: "This Party needs *two* wings, two wings *and* a center, or I fear it may never fly again."[67]

The creation of the Republican Governors Association, Gerald Ford's election as House Republican Leader, and the selection of Bliss as RNC chairman meant that "Goldwater is out," according to columnist Roscoe Drummond. "The moderate Republicans are back in control. . . . Thus ends the Republican party's experiment with extreme conservatism."[68] This was not a completely accurate assessment. The hard right still commanded the grassroots and organizations such as the Young Republicans. Conservatism was destined to grow in popular appeal later in the decade, though this would have seemed scarcely imaginable in early 1965. Even progressives now recognized that conservatives were a more important bloc of the party than they had seemed in 1960, when Nixon had taken conservative support for granted while taking pains to shore up liberal support through his platform agreement with Rockefeller and his selection of Lodge as his running mate. Still, all sides had reached a party consensus on the need for balance and some degree of unity between conservatives, moderates, and progressives, and it would last for years to come. Nixon, always attuned to the party's shifting center of gravity, proclaimed in 1965 that "The Conservatives can't live without the Liberals and the Liberals can't live without the Conservatives. I want them both wherever we can get them."[69]

Conservative intellectuals and activists, unlike conservative politicians, generally refused to sign onto this new consensus. Even in the councils of *National Review*, however, there was grudging recognition that the magnitude of the Republican defeat required a certain rethinking. The magazine devoted most of its post-election issue to the question of what went wrong and what conservatism's prospects were for the future. Frank Meyer, one of the magazine's hardest-line supporters of the Goldwater candidacy, claimed that nothing in the campaign "demonstrated anything wrong or weak—morally or philosophically or logically—in the conservative position." But he conceded that conservatives could no longer openly seek to repeal the New Deal, as they had done since the 1930s. For good or ill, most Americans would now interpret a move to abolish or weaken programs like Social Security as "a radical tearing down of established institutions. . . . There is no question but that conservatism is arrayed against the basic development since FDR; but it has to be made very clear that conservatives by their nature proceed in all changes with caution."[70] James Burnham believed that the future of conservatism would rest on the proposition that modern liberalism was incapable of solving the challenges that "threaten the survival of our country and civilization—none of them partisan problems." At a moment of relative international tranquility and domestic prosperity, however, "the American conservative movement was not ready in 1964, in program or in leadership, to run the country. The Goldwater candidacy, from conservative perspective, was premature."[71]

National Review's forum included Ronald Reagan, who repeated his demand that conservatives not allow command of the party to return to the hands of "traitors." But it also included moderates such as Connecticut's John Davis Lodge, who criticized Goldwater supporters who were "unconciliatory in their attitude towards other Republicans," and George H. W. Bush of Texas, who called on the party to "welcome all who want to be Republicans."[72] Bush's inclusion sparked an angry response from a Texan critic who charged that Bush was not a conservative and furthermore had avoided so much as mentioning Goldwater in his failed senatorial campaign. "I think it behooves all conservatives to reserve easy judgment on George Bush," Bill Buckley responded, "for he is unquestionably an attractive, articulate campaigner and a man of personal integrity." Buckley added that "the Republican Presidential campaign was not of such a nature as to persuade ambitious young candidates to align themselves with it."[73]

Buckley's toleration toward moderates had been growing for some time. He had proposed Dwight Eisenhower, his old nemesis, as Goldwater's vice-presidential running mate in order to balance the ticket and "bind up the wounds of the Party."[74] But he remained firmly opposed to Republican progressives such as Charles P. Taft, who raised money for and lent the Taft imprimatur to "Republicans whose voting records are indistinguishable from Democrats," as Buckley saw it. "[H]e seeks to make Republicanism a perfectly meaningless symbol. As such, in my judgment, he does much more damage than any dozen Democrats."[75] Buckley had also, in the '64 election, donated to the campaign of the Democratic challenger of Connecticut progressive Republican Representative Abner Sibal, one of the founders of the House Wednesday Group, despite the fact that the Democrat was by far the more liberal candidate.[76] When one of Buckley's associates was asked why he was opposing Sibal, he replied, "In a contest between a liberal Democrat and a liberal Republican, we'll back the Democrat." Columnists Evans and Novak denounced this attitude as "calculated sabotage of the Republican center" and "political cannibalism."[77]

Conservatives who objected to progressive Republican officeholders had, over the years, asked themselves how far they were prepared to go to rid themselves of their intra-party rivals. In the case of California's senator Thomas Kuchel, the answer was: very far indeed. Kuchel, who had been raised up by his mentor Earl Warren, was among the last of the California progressives. He served in state elective and appointive office from 1937 until 1953, when Warren appointed him to the U.S. Senate to replace newly elected Vice President Richard Nixon. He won election to the Senate in his own right in 1954, and was reelected in 1956 and 1962, when he became the last U.S. Senate nominee to win all of California's 58 counties. He was a highly effective lawmaker who was also popular with his Senate Republican colleagues, serving a record five terms as minority whip.[78] Kuchel was a strong advocate of fiscal discipline, outspoken in his opposition to what he considered the irresponsible and inflationary back-door spending of Congress on public programs, and a staunch anti-Communist. But he raised conservative hackles by supporting Democrat-sponsored measures such as the atomic test ban treaty, co-managing the Civil Rights Act of 1964, and bringing into politics young progressives such as Leon Panetta, a legislative assistant to Kuchel who later would become a Democratic politician and Barack Obama's head of the CIA and secretary of defense.[79]

What cinched the conservative case against Kuchel, however, was his fierce criticism of the John Birch Society, which was a formidable grassroots force in California Republican politics in the early 1960s; by 1965, a Ripon Society correspondent in the state judged that "the grass-roots party out here is roughly 90% 'kook' at the moment."[80] Kuchel's office received thousands of form letters from Birchers demanding that he take action against rumored threats to the nation: a plot by Chinese Communists to invade the United States via Mexico, another plot by a "1313" committee of University of Chicago eggheads to deprive Americans of their rights to vote and hold property, and still another by the United Nations to train barefoot African cannibals in Georgia for yet another takeover of the United States. When Kuchel responded that there was no evidence for any of these outlandish claims, the Birchers labeled him a "Comsymp" who by professing ignorance of these conspiracies proved he was guilty of treason. "Treason!" Kuchel exclaimed on the Senate floor. "I still cannot believe my eyes when I stare at the ugliest word in the American lexicon tossed about in a letter as casually as the 'Dear Senator' or 'Dear Congressman' salutation." Referring to the Birchers' efforts to impeach Supreme Court Justice Warren, and their leader Robert Welch's claim that Dwight Eisenhower was a Communist agent, Kuchel raged that "The big lie, the smear and witch hunts are not the hallmarks of conservatism, but are the trademarks of communism and fascism."[81]

In late 1964, Kuchel learned that his enemies had produced an affidavit, signed by a former Los Angeles police officer, alleging that he had been arrested in 1949 for committing homosexual offenses. Right-wing groups around the country secretly circulated the affidavit and made it available to the public at Birch Society bookstores. The Senate Internal Security subcommittee also obtained a copy. The Senator, who was a married man with a daughter, knew that this was a ruinous rumor but that the publicity that would ensue from fighting it could be equally ruinous. He chose to proceed with a libel action nonetheless, which resulted in a no-contest plea from four perpetrators. One was a top assistant for public relations to Patrick Frawley Jr., a leading California conservative moneyman, who admitted to the police that "We did it to get rid of Kuchel."[82] This caused considerable speculation among political observers as to whether Frawley was directly involved in the plot and, if so, what his motives were. Frawley, the entrepreneur behind Paper Mate pens and Schick stainless steel razors, was an obsessive anti-Communist and the nation's leading donor to right-wing causes, channeling an average $1 million a year to conservative politicians and outfits such as the Christian Anti-Communism Crusade. Polls predicted that Kuchel was the Republican best able to defeat Democratic incumbent Governor Pat Brown in the 1966 California gubernatorial election, but conservatives including Frawley already were plumping for right-wing favorite Ronald Reagan to enter the race. Was the smear an attempt to besmirch Kuchel's reputation in order to clear the way for Reagan?[83] Newspapers around the country hailed Kuchel in the early months of 1965 as a man who had courageously defied his defamers, but the smear undoubtedly took a toll on his political viability.[84]

At the same time that Kuchel was coping with his libel action, he was negotiating with the Johnson administration, along with other members of the Republican leadership, over the next phase of the civil rights revolution. The Civil Rights Act of 1964, like the acts of 1957 and 1960, had done little to address the denial of voting rights to African-Americans in the South. Johnson had proposed in his January inaugural address that some kind of federal legislation be passed to redress the massive disenfranchisement of Southern blacks, but he was in no hurry to make this happen, fearing that a divisive debate would damage his other legislative priorities. The Justice Department had proposed a constitutional amendment to address the problem, but that process would take years to complete.

Martin Luther King Jr. and other civil rights leaders had placed a tacit moratorium on demonstrations during the fall of 1964 to deny the Goldwater campaign the benefits of backlash, but now they sought a confrontation that would accelerate the passage of voting rights protections. They found their venue in Selma, Alabama, chosen both for its blatant discrimination— of the city's 15,000 blacks of voting age, only 355 were registered to vote— and for its pigheaded police chief, Sheriff Jim Clark. He could be depended on to lose his cool and produce a televised tableau of violent oppression that would dramatize the voting rights issue. Sure enough, Clark and his deputies overreacted to a series of voting rights demonstrations, culminating in "Bloody Sunday" on March 7, 1965, when police used appalling force to disperse a civil rights march, beating and whipping and gassing the nonviolent demonstrators like so many Nazi storm troopers. When the horrific scenes played and replayed on television, the storm of outrage all but forced Congress and the President to take action. Johnson addressed a joint session of Congress on March 15, in a moving speech in which he insisted that the civil rights cause must be embraced not just by blacks but by "all of us who must overcome the crippling legacy of bigotry and injustice. And we shall overcome." Congress took up consideration of a voting rights bill two days later. "The long, sordid history of unconstitutional denial of the right of the franchise must now come to a halt," Kuchel told reporters after Johnson's address. "The President's recommendation to Congress is urgent. I shall support him."[85]

For some time, a group of progressive Republicans had been trying to pressure the administration into taking action on voting rights, with little success. Three members of the House Wednesday Group—Mathias, Morse, and Reid—had traveled to Selma the previous month at their own expense, along with a dozen Democratic members of Congress, to witness the unfolding demonstrations and lend their support to the imprisoned Martin Luther King. All were revolted by the brutal conduct of the jailors, who forced the demonstrators to stand on tiptoes and shocked them with electric cattle prods if they failed to comply.[86] In an attempt to dampen the Republican progressives' criticism of Johnson, Democrats included them in secret negotiations with Attorney General Nicholas Katzenbach over the particulars of a voting rights bill.[87] Lindsay and other Wednesday Group members introduced a bill to speed up registration in the South, and later twenty-six Republican members of Congress and five Republican governors issued a statement calling for the administration to stop stalling. "Despite abuse, threats and beatings, Dr. King and his people walk the streets of Selma in protest," the statement read. "Republicans march with them. Their cause is just. The Administration must move and move promptly to remove the cause of their protests."[88] Katzenbach, however, more or less ignored the Republican progressives in favor of negotiations with the more conservative Senate minority leader Everett Dirksen, whom he regarded as the key to bringing along Midwestern stalwarts and overcoming a Southern filibuster.

After "Bloody Sunday" and Johnson's "We Shall Overcome" address, Congressional Republicans were almost unanimous in their advocacy of voting rights legislation. Not all party members, to be sure, supported such a measure. Barry Goldwater, no longer in the Senate, fulminated that the bill would mean the "end of democratic processes and the republican form of government we have so long enjoyed."[89] An Indianapolis judge spoke for many conservative Republicans who believed that it would be impossible to "out-promise" Democrats on rights and benefits for minorities, and that therefore "the more of these people who are pressured into registering and voting, the greater our party will suffer."[90] Wirt Yerger Jr., head of the Mississippi Republican Party and of the Southern Association of Republican Chairmen, warned that the pending legislation, "conceived in an atmosphere of hysteria and malice with a view to crucifying certain states," would be harmful to party-building in the South. He predicted that demagogues in the region would "have a field day if large numbers of ignorant, illiterate persons are suddenly given the vote."[91] But the Republican Coordinating Committee, a new GOP group aimed at fixing an official party consensus on major issues, spoke with one voice in expressing outrage at the disenfranchisement of Southern blacks, and put the party on record as urgently favoring federal action to assure equal voting rights.[92]

Elliot Richardson, the lieutenant governor of Massachusetts, was one of several Republicans who traveled to Selma to take part in the memorial service for Rev. James Reeb, a white Episcopal minister who was killed there by segregationist goons after attending a civil rights rally. The gathering in Brown's Chapel was an expression of national unity around the Southern civil rights cause, bringing together Republicans and Democrats, blacks and whites, youthful protestors and establishment patricians, and representatives of nearly every religious denomination in America. Swaying in his pew as he sang "We Shall Overcome," grasping the hand of a black Methodist bishop on his right and a Greek Orthodox priest on his left, Richardson felt that "In that small enclosed space the voices were strong, ringing—full of promise."[93] It was, in hindsight, the high tide of bipartisan, biracial togetherness in the civil rights movement.

The voting rights bill presented Republicans with an opportunity to "reestablish our communication with the Negro community," as Senator Thruston Morton had put it in his address to the RNC at the beginning of 1965. Morton estimated that Republicans would need at least twenty percent of the black vote to be viable in races in both the South and northern cities, yet the party would also have to crack the Democratic "solid South" if it ever was to be a majority party. The solution to this conundrum, as Morton saw it, was to overturn segregation with as much bipartisan support as possible, thereby removing the issue from the national agenda. African-Americans presumably would appreciate the GOP's overwhelming support of civil rights, while white Southerners would be equally unhappy with both parties. As segregation receded, however, the Southerners would find that the GOP "offers a better political vehicle, a more attractive political home to the Southerner than does the Democratic Party of today. We are indeed closer to the Party of Jefferson than is the Democratic Party today." Morton believed that in the South, particularly outside the Black Belt, there was a "sound foundation for Republicanism not based on racism."[94] While the GOP could not compromise on civil rights, then, it ought to treat the South as equitably as possible.

This approach informed the House Republican alternative to the administration's voting rights bill, put forward by minority leader Gerald Ford and the GOP's longtime civil rights conscience William McCulloch. While the administration's bill applied only to the Deep South states, and more specifically to counties in those states that employed literacy tests and where less than half of the voting-age population had registered to vote, the Ford-McCulloch bill applied to the whole country. It therefore had potentially broader scope than the administration's bill, since it would have applied to states without literacy tests, including Florida, Tennessee, and Texas. It also would have applied to areas where black citizens were denied the franchise yet sufficient numbers of whites were registered to vote to meet the fifty-percent cutoff. The Republican bill authorized the appointment of a federal examiner for any district where the attorney general received twenty-five or more voting rights complaints, and the provision of as many federal registrars as necessary to register voters in those districts where discrimination occurred. Although the Republican bill waived literacy requirements for citizens with a sixth-grade education, and banned poll taxes that had discriminatory impact, it honored "the rights of the States to fix and enforce nondiscriminatory voter qualifications."[95]

The Ford-McCulloch bill was distinctively Republican in its preference for a more limited federal role and the preservation of certain states' rights, its application to a wide range of corrupt voting practices, and its concern that the South be judged on the same standard as all other regions of the country. The Republicans intended it to be a stronger bill than the administration's version, but it lacked an automatic trigger and raised fears that blacks might be intimidated out of making the complaints that would lead to an examination of a district's voting practices.[96] For that reason, liberals and civil rights groups attacked the bill out of all proportion to its presumed drawbacks, with Martin Luther King Jr. and other civil rights leaders mounting a major publicity initiative to derail it. Lyndon Johnson chortled to King that the bill showed that "the Republicans are . . . going to quit the Negroes. They will not let the Negro vote for them. Every time they get a chance to help out a little, they'll blow it."[97] Embarrassed by Southern Democrats' embrace of the Ford-McCulloch bill as the least stringent alternative, Republicans dropped the measure and backed the administration's version. Despite the criticism, the Ford-McCulloch bill marked the beginning of a moderate Republican Southern strategy that was pro-civil rights yet calculated to appeal to Southern sensibilities.

A greater percentage of Republicans than Democrats supported the Voting Rights Act of 1965, as had been the case with the 1964 Civil Rights Act. In the Senate, Everett Dirksen secured a compromise with the administration, eliminating a measure to ban all state poll taxes, which in turn produced sufficient Republican support to end a Southern filibuster. One-third of the Senate's Democrats voted against the bill, but only two Republicans, John Tower of Texas and Strom Thurmond of South Carolina. In the House, 82 percent of Republicans voted for the bill, compared to 72 percent of Democrats.[98] After the bill became law, NAACP counsel Clarence Mitchell wrote to McCulloch expressing his gratitude for "keeping the issue of civil rights a bi-partisan matter."[99]

But how much credit did accrue to the GOP for the party's role in passing the Voting Rights Act and other major initiatives of Lyndon Johnson's Great Society program? Most moderate Republicans believed that the President's measures were in the national interest. Many moderates had long advocated the causes that were embodied in the Great Society legislation, including voting rights for black citizens, some form of government medical care for the aged, help for those in poverty, federal aid to education, environmental protection, and reform of immigration laws. But the party's negligible numbers meant that when these issues came to a vote in the first half of 1965, Congressional Republicans faced the stark choice of supporting or opposing Johnson's program as he presented it to them, with little opportunity to advance their own alternatives or modify aspects of the legislation that they found objectionable. And when the major components of the Great Society passed, the public and the media hailed them as victories for Johnson and the Democratic Party regardless of how much Republican support they received.

At the start of the legislative session, Ohio Representative Frank Bow had warned his Republican colleagues that "Unless something is done in the immediate future, the Democratic party will soon be pointing with pride to a new program of hospital care for the aged and the Republican party once again will be cast in the role of the blind, reactionary opposition, being pulled kicking and screaming across the threshold of a new era."[100] For years, Bow had championed the cause of federally assisted elder medical care, particularly for "men and women of modest means whose resources can be wiped out by a major illness." Johnson embraced the same goal with his proposal for Medicare, which would create compulsory hospitalization insurance for nearly all Americans sixty-five or more years of age, subsidized by Social Security tax increases. Bow believed his alternative to

Medicare would in certain respects provide superior benefits while avoiding the problems of what he called "socialized medicine" and federal regulation inherent in the Democratic approach. Bow proposed a voluntary system of private health insurance for the elderly, with tax credit incentives for those who could underwrite all or part of the cost of their medical expenses and outright government assistance for those who could not, to be paid for through higher income taxes if necessary.[101]

The House came close to passing a Medicare alternative bill along Bow's lines, but the measure failed thanks largely to the liberal Democratic freshman class, which opposed it 58 to 7. It's interesting but pointless to speculate whether the Republican formula might have proven better able to contain the galloping medical costs that the Democratic program predictably unleashed. In the event, nearly all of the House Republicans—128 of 140—voted to kill Medicare by recommitting the administration's Health Care Act of 1965 to the Ways and Means Committee with instructions to strike the section on Medicare. When this failed, however, Republicans confronted an omnibus bill that included three components that they favored—eldercare, aid to the needy in cooperation with the states, and amendments to the Social Security Act—along with Medicare. Freed from party discipline, a bare majority of House Republicans voted for the legislation.[102] More than half of Republican senators opposed the measure, but GOP whip Kuchel was the spokesman for the "baker's dozen" of Republican senators who "provided the necessary margin for passage," as he recalled. He defended his vote in later years by arguing that "If it weren't for Medicare today, there would be tens of thousands of Americans living in the poorhouse, with no care."[103] Even so, as Frank Bow had predicted, the media heralded the measure as a Democratic triumph.

When Republicans favored administration measures, they got little credit for it. Such was the case with the issue of immigration reform, for example, even though the most dramatic Senate hearings pitted New York Republican Jacob Javits' heated defense of immigrants' contributions against North Carolina Democrat Sam Ervin's insistence that white Anglo-Saxon Protestants were "the people who made America great."[104] Conversely, when Republicans opposed administration bills, they were either too divided or too few in number to make a difference. Republican moderates and even progressives found many reasons to criticize Johnson's anti-poverty program, which they thought gave too little weight to private enterprise and too much to centralized government. Eisenhower told audiences that the program was an effort "to establish instant paradise," while Senator Hugh Scott castigated the poverty program for corruption and its diversion of funds into Democratic patronage jobs.[105] But these criticisms did not add up to a coherent critique of Johnsonian liberalism, which most Americans appeared to support.

The irrelevance of Republicans to the legislative proceedings paradoxically stimulated the moderate reformers' efforts to make the party more creative and forward-looking. In some cases this led Republicans to offer social measures more generous than what the Democrats proposed. Young Turks Charles Goodell and Thomas Curtis introduced an innovative House Republican plan for federal aid to education that the *Wall Street Journal* estimated would cost $5 billion yearly compared to the administration bill's $1.5 billion annual outlay. Since the Republican initiative had no chance of passing, however, its importance lay in demonstrating that the GOP could devise a coherent and appealing plan consistent with Republican principles, in this case by seeking to stimulate school support at the local level as opposed to the administration's Washington-centric approach. "The only way we're going to get back on top as a party," as one Young Turk put it, "is to get completely away from our stereotype as 'aginners' and 'me-tooers.' And that means showing the public that Republicans can produce distinct and meaningful solutions to the nation's problems." The *Journal* emphasized that the Young Turks were able to make a strong public case for their initiatives, since they "probably know as much about making news and projecting images as any group in Washington."[106] Minority leader Ford was able to sell Republican initiatives with bravura during his frequent television and news conferences, and the GOP leadership made a particular effort to be more accessible to the press than their Democratic counterparts.

The Republican Governors Association made its own leap into policy innovation with "Government for Tomorrow," a report jointly written with the Ripon Society calling for unconditional sharing of federal tax revenues with state and local governments. The plan proposed that Washington would return to the states a flat percentage of the federal tax dollars raised in each state. In place of federal categorical grants-in-aid, which invariably came with rigid specifications on how the money could be spent, the states and localities would use the revenues to provide services as they saw fit. The authors admitted that the idea was independently conceived by Republican Representative Melvin Laird and Walter Heller, Johnson's chief economic advisor, and that both Republican and Democratic platforms had endorsed the concept in 1964. But "Government for Tomorrow" was a concise and forceful brief for federal revenue-sharing. It argued that state and local governments had taken on much greater responsibilities while relying on an outdated and inadequate financial base, and that revenue sharing was a fair and effective approach to solving problems that transcended party politics in areas such as education, fire and police protection, health and sanitation, water resources, welfare, and transportation. At the same time, the concept of revenue sharing offered an example of a positive, Republican program that was not simple "me-too" liberalism, and which put some flesh on the idea of "creative federalism." The report forcefully defended the virtues of decentralized government, the potential of small-scale government to innovate and experiment (as in the Progressive Era), the greater flexibility and appropriateness of decisions made closer to the source, and the potential for increased citizen participation and reduced political alienation. Not least, the report noted that state and local governments could provide a power base on which Republicans could build a new consensus, perhaps as a counter to the labor union pressure that had led Johnson to drag his feet on revenue sharing.[107] The paper enjoyed a splash of nationwide media publicity, and several Republican members of Congress introduced revenue-sharing legislation along the lines of the Ripon-RGA recommendation.[108]

There was one area where the Republicans might have chosen to draw a vivid contrast with the Democratic administration: the U.S. military involvement in Vietnam. John F. Kennedy had sent an increasing number of American military advisors to South Vietnam to train and assist the country's armed forces in their war against the Communist forces of North Vietnam and the National Liberation Front, or Vietcong, in South Vietnam. Lyndon Johnson plunged the United States into direct and large-scale military confrontation through a series of incremental steps: securing open-ended Congressional approval for intervention through the Gulf of Tonkin Resolution in August 1964, initiating a bombing campaign against North Vietnam in February 1965, landing the Marines at Da Nang in March, and granting General William Westmoreland authorization to commit troops to combat in whatever ways he felt necessary. In a little-publicized announcement in July, the administration increased the number of U.S. troops in Vietnam to 125,000. Soon nightly news watchers became familiar with terms like "search and destroy" missions and progress measured by kill ratios.[109]

During the 1950s, Eisenhower had resisted military entanglement in Vietnam after the fall of the French colonial regime, in sharp distinction to the decisions made by two successive Democratic administrations. By the mid-1960s, however, the Republican strategy was not to oppose the descent into the quagmire of Vietnam, or to call for diplomatic negotiations to seek a way out, but to ardently support Johnson's escalation. Agreement on the need to confront Communism in Vietnam transcended the party's internal divisions and partisan politics. Goldwater had refrained from making Vietnam into a campaign issue, pledging his full support of the administration's policies. Eisenhower and Senate minority leader Everett Dirksen backed Johnson to the hilt. Young Turk Representative Charles Goodell stressed that "stopping Communist aggression and safeguarding the freedom and independence of South Vietnam is the duty of all responsible people."[110] The Ripon Society's faculty advisor, Harvard international relations professor Morton Halperin, informed the group that Vietnam was a key area where Red China was testing American will, and that U.S. forces needed to be more aggressive in carrying the conflict into enemy territory.[111] Elliot Richardson also told the Riponers that "the Republican party can offer no meaningful alternative to the administration's foreign policy."[112]

Johnson's Vietnam decisions were dictated not only by the logic of Cold War anti-Communist containment but by his conviction that South Vietnam's collapse would reproduce the political dynamic of the late '40s and early '50s, when China's fall to the Communists led to Congress and the presidency falling to the Republicans. Congressional Republicans, while overtly supportive of Johnson, made plain that they would make the administration pay for any slackening of support for South Vietnam. They were quick to charge that the handful of Democrats who favored negotiation with the Communists were guilty of defeatism, retreatism, and "running up the white flag."[113] And yet many Republicans, as well as Johnson himself, privately doubted whether propping up the tottering South Vietnamese regime was worth the huge cost in U.S. blood and treasure. "I am frankly delighted that you are 4F," Bill Buckley wrote to a young friend in February 1965, "inasmuch as I cannot see any purpose in joining the American Army at this moment. Some other war, perhaps."[114] But Johnson made no effort to convince Republicans or the country at large that an alternative course ought to be followed in Vietnam.

Some of the remaining isolationist Republicans spoke out against the administration's Vietnam policy. In the spring of 1965, former Congressman Hamilton Fish Jr., who had been a prominent critic of U.S. participation in World War II prior to Pearl Harbor, called for neutralizing South Vietnam. "Every time the people elect a Democratic President," Fish complained, "he seems to believe he has a mandate to involve the United States in foreign wars." Fish reminded his fellow citizens that it was easy to provoke foreign wars but difficult to disengage from them. He invoked Robert Taft's warning against sending a single American soldier to Southeast Asia, where in the long run the United States could not win. "What the United States needs," according to Fish, "is an immediate agonizing reappraisal of our whole misguided, outmoded and ruinous foreign policy which has been based on 100 percent internationalism. We should stop interfering in every other nation's business."[115] Another crusty old follower of Taft, Kentucky Representative Eugene Siler, cast the lone Republican vote against the Gulf of Tonkin Resolution.[116]

By 1965, however, Goldwater-style interventionism had largely displaced the Taft tradition of conservative isolationism, and even those Republicans who were skeptical of the direction of Vietnam policy for the most part limited themselves to an oblique expression of concerns. The House Wednesday Group called for the administration to provide more information to Congress and the public about the situation in Vietnam, and suggested that military escalation be accompanied by "an equally intensive diplomatic offensive" to assure other countries that the United States would accept a negotiated settlement.[117] Moderates acquiesced to the Johnson policy largely because the President shrewdly presented it as a middle way between the unacceptable extremes of unlimited military intervention, which risked nuclear war with China and the Soviet Union, and ignominious withdrawal, which allegedly would damage U.S. credibility around the world.

What little open Republican Congressional opposition there was to Vietnam initially came from the few who had cultivated reputations as independents or mavericks. These included senators John Sherman Cooper of Kentucky and George Aiken of Vermont, who only half-jokingly suggested that the United States should simply declare victory and leave. Representative John Lindsay of New York, though he had voted for the Tonkin Gulf Resolution, became one of the sharpest critics of the U.S. intervention in Vietnam once the Rolling Thunder bombing campaign began. He found it evident that the administration had "no clear policy except an aimless patchwork of scotch tape and bailing wire that becomes more confused every day." He anticipated an escalating round of strikes and counterstrikes "until the little remaining cover is totally stripped away and the involvement that is euphemistically known as military support becomes a naked U.S. war that has neither front lines nor back lines, nor beginning nor ending, nor commitment by the very people we seek to defend."[118] However, Lindsay abandoned plans to develop a Republican alternative to the administration's Vietnam policies in May 1965, when he announced that he would run for mayor of New York City.

Even John Vliet Lindsay's worst enemies would admit that he was one of the best-looking politicians ever to mount the hustings: six feet three inches tall, with chiseled features, blue eyes, and wavy blond hair.[119] His glamour led people to overestimate him in other ways. One New Yorker remembered that when he was first introduced to Lindsay, resplendent in a sky-blue sports coat, "I thought he was the richest man in the world."[120] But although Lindsay had been expensively educated at private schools, Yale College, and Yale Law School, and belonged to the Social Register and an assortment of top-drawer WASPy clubs and associations, he was not particularly rich. Neither was he as intellectual as his supporters liked to believe, although John F. Kennedy's admirers had overestimated him in the same way and for much the same reasons. And, as would become evident over the next several years, it was beyond Lindsay's powers to restore the peaceful and prosperous New York City of bygone decades. But for a shining moment in the mid-1960s, Lindsay struck conservative and progressive Republicans alike as a man intended by destiny to become president someday, though the progressives were determined to assist his ascent and the conservatives to resist it.

Conservatives affected to believe that Lindsay was merely a liberal Democrat masquerading as a Republican, but in fact he was a pure product of the New York Republican establishment. He got his start in politics in the late '40s as a leader of the faction in the New York Young Republicans Club opposed by the faction led by two of the most important architects of the conservative movement, William Rusher and F. Clifton White, though at that time the members of the two factions disliked each other for personal rather than political reasons. He became a protégé of Thomas Dewey's campaign strategist Herbert Brownell, and was one of the eleven founders of the Youth for Eisenhower movement in 1951. When Brownell became Ike's attorney general, Lindsay followed him to Washington to serve as his executive assistant. He returned to New York in 1957, and the next year ran for Congress in the "Silk Stocking" District, which encompassed Manhattan's East Side from Harlem in the north to Greenwich Village in the south. Despite his district's heavy Democratic registration edge, he triumphed over the Democratic-Liberal candidate in the election, enjoying the support of blue-collar workers and Wall Street bankers, the tabloids and the *New York Times* and *New York Herald Tribune.* He won subsequent elections by ever-increasing margins.

Over the course of his seven years in the House, Lindsay became known as an incorruptible "Mr. Clean" and the despair of Republican leaders who tried to get him to toe the party line. While Lindsay was a leader in the House Wednesday Group, he conceded that he had many admirers but few followers in Congress, since "I'm sufficiently independent to have come close to the edge of being ineffective."[121] But Lindsay maintained that his progressive stands were deeply in the Republican tradition, particularly his support of civil rights and civil liberties, and that his adamant defense of these values made him obnoxious to the Democrats as well as to his own party's leadership.

In the early 1960s, Lindsay stood up almost single-handedly to Attorney General Robert F. Kennedy. Lindsay considered him a partisan threat to national freedoms, more loyal to his brother and the Democratic Party than to the Constitution and Bill of Rights. Lindsay was not alone in this assessment: one of the men who worked for Kennedy claimed that he "used his office as if he were the Godfather getting even with the enemies of the Family."[122] New York Republican Senator Kenneth Keating, convinced that RFK was bugging his offices, held important conferences in the corridors of Capitol Hill buildings.[123] In 1963, Bobby Kennedy sought to expand the Sedition Act of 1918 to prohibit Americans anywhere in the world from writing or speaking anything deemed disloyal, profane, scurrilous, or abusive about the United States government. Lindsay protested on the House floor that "The abuses to free speech in this bill are so great that even a congressman possibly could be cited and prosecuted for verbal attacks on United States policies and action."

Lindsay also battled Representative Francis Walter, Democratic chairman of the House Un-American Activities Committee, whose proposed industrial security bill would permit any of the five million private sector employees working on defense contracts or related research to be fired if suspected of ill-defined security risks. The people who lost their jobs would be unable to confront their accusers or to examine the alleged evidence against them, nor would they be allowed to appeal to the courts. Lindsay mounted a Horatio-at-the-bridge defense against this abuse of civil liberties, and eventually rounded up enough allies to scotch the bill, which fell only six votes short of passage. It was the first time that HUAC was defeated on the House floor.[124] The episode served as a reminder that McCarthyism remained an active force in American life long after McCarthy himself had died, and moderate and progressive Republicans were among the few defenders of traditional liberties.

Lindsay counted himself a Republican in part because he opposed the corruption and decay that accompanied urban Democratic machines. He told a youth group that he was by nature "a bit of a rebel" and had learned his politics from Fiorello LaGuardia, the progressive Republican mayor of New York City: "He was a good guy fighting the bad guys, and the bad guys were the Tammany Hall bosses."[125] The good-government position implied not only that government should be honest but that it could do good, and Lindsay believed that Republicans were as much obligated as Democrats to wrestle with the problems of the day. Though the New York City mayoralty seemed an unlikely launching pad for Lindsay's presidential hopes, pundits frequently referred to the office as "the second toughest job in America," and it was the cockpit of the nation's engagement with the "urban crisis." The cities were the venues where moderate and progressive Republicans' concerns over good government, race relations, education, prosperity, and social harmony played out.

Lindsay took his rationale for running for mayor from a series of articles entitled "City in Crisis" in the leading moderate Republican newspaper, the

New York Herald Tribune. The series catalogued the ills that plagued New York, including rising crime, poverty, drug addiction, and pollution, an exodus of businesses and middle-class whites, sclerotic bureaucracy, impending financial catastrophe, and the inability of corrupt one-party government to cope with these problems. The paper, all but pleading for Lindsay to stand for office, editorialized that the city desperately needed "the excitement and ferment of a new administration, tied neither to the mistakes of the past nor to a self-perpetuating organization too long in power," as well as "the kind of political challenge only a revitalized Republican party, behind a clearly outstanding candidate, can provide."[126]

Lindsay relished the challenge, and his backers hoped that his campaign would improve the image of the GOP in the big cities where voters had turned away from the party in the previous two presidential elections. The ideas that Lindsay's campaign put forward to address the urban challenge differed from those of liberal Democrats, Tammany Democrats, and conservative Republicans. They revolved around distinctively moderate Republican concepts such as meritocracy, good government, modernization, racial neutralism, and decentralization. It remained to be seen how some of these ideas would translate into practical policies, but the idealistic moderates who worked up the "white papers" of campaign proposals hoped to bring government closer to the people, break up centralized bureaucracies, bring to heel the unaccountable and racially exclusive unions, and end the tradition of ethnic and racial fiefdoms in city government.

Lindsay ran on a fusion ticket with the Liberal Party of New York. He assiduously avoided the Republican label, even to the extent of asking prominent Republicans not to make campaign appearances on his behalf. It made sense for Lindsay to downplay his Republican affiliation in a city where Democrats outnumbered Republicans seven to two. But like LaGuardia before him, he distanced himself from his party in the distinctively Republican tradition of progressivism, which carried a number of liabilities for a politician who wanted to be successful. Progressives tended to be hostile to political parties, believing (like the Founding Fathers) that factionalism worked against the public good. Their watchword was bipartisanship, or nonpartisanship. Progressivism also blended the seemingly contradictory impulses of elitism and populism. On the one hand, progressives upheld the importance of disinterested, technocratic experts, who could make difficult decisions with a view to the long term, insulated from the selfishness and short-sightedness of the masses. On the other, progressives also espoused a faith in the wisdom of the voters and their ability to make their own decisions and spurn the call of demagogues. The ideal progressive leader was one with a foot in both the elitist and populist camps:

independent (or rich) enough to be incorruptible, charismatic enough to be the popular choice and the people's tribune.

But Lindsay's campaign image as a hero riding to the rescue on a white horse raised unrealistic expectations and pointed to future problems. One of Lindsay's most astute biographers, Nat Hentoff, observed that the mayoral candidate had written his undergraduate thesis on Oliver Cromwell, in which he quoted a Puritan preacher informing Parliament about "two fundamental demands common to all Puritan sects: liberty of conscience, and reform—of the universities, the countries, the cities."[127] Though Lindsay was wary of Cromwell's extremism, he undoubtedly saw himself as a reformer in the Puritan mold. In minimizing the value of longstanding institutions and popular folkways, however, he underestimated the resistance he would encounter in his effort to modernize the city and its administration. At the same time, he overestimated his ability to effect change without the backing of interest groups and the structure provided by a party organization.

The Conservative Party of New York had vowed to run a candidate against Lindsay in an election for any office he sought, as revenge for his support of Democratic measures in the House and his refusal to endorse Goldwater in 1964. It was a tribute to the danger Lindsay presented that the CPNY's candidate to oppose him was William F. Buckley Jr., the nation's best known conservative aside from Barry Goldwater. An impudent wit who admitted that he was running "half in fun," Buckley and his unique blend of hauteur and camp made great copy for the New York media. Journalist Murray Kempton likened Buckley's supercilious manner at his first press conference in late June 1965 to that of "an Edwardian resident commissioner reading aloud the 39 articles of the Anglican establishment to a conscript assemblage of Zulus."[128] When asked how many votes he expected to get, conservatively speaking, Buckley replied, "Conservatively speaking, one," and later quipped that if he was elected he would "Demand a recount."[129]

Beneath the froth, however, Buckley grimly intended to pull enough votes away from Lindsay to elect his Democratic opponent, who at that point he anticipated would be incumbent mayor Robert Wagner. Buckley's determination to undermine Lindsay was consistent with the continuing conservative drive to purge the Republican Party of its progressives. As Goldwater wrote to one of his allies, Lindsay "presents no more a Republican candidate to me than would Mayor Wagner. While I know New York needs better government, if I were living there and wanted a New Dealer, a spendthrift, an unconstitutionalist, I would pick Wagner because he has the greatest experience in the field."[130] Beyond the election, Buckley hoped to derail Lindsay's political career. Conservative moles intercepted a Lindsay campaign memo contending that Buckley was not driven by personal animus but rather sought "to eliminate from elective office a moderate Republican who would, if elected, become a threat—within the Republican Party—to the Goldwater extremists, of whom WFB is one." Buckley, in reprinting the memo, thought this analysis "Quite correct."[131]

Buckley had intended to run on a program of fiscal stringency, but ended up as the voice of the white backlash. He abandoned his original approach when he found that Manhattan's affluent, WASPy Republican minority, to whom he aimed his pocketbook appeal, mistrusted his social conservatism. The great discovery of the Buckley campaign was that the people who were most excited by his expansive anti-liberalism were outer-borough working class and lower middle-class voters, predominantly from Irish, Italian, and Eastern European ethnic backgrounds. These were not people with whom Buckley had any real familiarity. He initially resisted any ethnic outreach efforts on the grounds that to do so would be to treat individuals as Democrats did: as members of monolithic interest groups. But he soon found that his base of support was the white ethnics, who had become sufficiently prosperous since the Depression that they were abandoning their old New Deal loyalties. By 1965, they were less worried about unemployment than high taxes, welfare costs, and crime. They agreed with Buckley that these unsavory developments were due to the city's rapidly expanding African-American and Puerto Rican populations, abetted by what one of Lindsay's later opponents would refer to as "limousine liberals."

The conservative movement owed much of its later success, ironically, to the passage of the Civil Rights Act of 1964 and the Voting Rights Act of 1965. Like most conservatives, Buckley had failed to comprehend the Southern civil rights movement, and only gradually acknowledged its moral and practical necessity. Other conservatives did not reach this level of hindsight, but simply had to resign themselves to the end of legally sanctioned racial segregation as an accomplished fact. Either way, the civil rights acts freed conservatives from the need to defend the most morally objectionable and politically radioactive aspect of their philosophy. The resentments provoked by the northward turn of the civil rights movement after Selma, and its new focus on structural discrimination and racially unequal outcomes and living standards, offered an opportunity for conservatives to make a case against the movement without being forced to support Jim Crow segregation.

Buckley's 1965 mayoral run was the first conservative campaign to feature this shift of direction. The conservative did not argue against equality of opportunity for racial minorities, but rather against the presumption that social arrangements needed to be altered to produce racial equality. If New York's black population did not achieve levels of education, employment, and earnings comparable to those of other races and ethnicities, Buckley insisted, this was due to their individual failings, reflected in greater levels of welfare dependence, family instability, and criminality. He dismissed black resentments of police brutality and minimized the obstacles presented by segregated housing, schools, and job markets. Arguing in a similar vein, conservative economist and later Nobel Prize winner George Stigler claimed that the basic problem of the black American was that "on average he lacks a desire to improve himself, and lacks a willingness to discipline himself to this end." The African-American male's lack of employment owed not to discrimination but to "his own inferiority as a worker." Residential segregation existed because "the Negro family is, on average, a loose, morally lax group, and brings with its presence a rapid rise in crime and vandalism." Equality for African-Americans would arrive only when they imitated the virtues of an earlier generation of Jewish immigrants: "a veneration and irrepressible desire for learning; frugality; and respect for the civilization of the western world."[132]

Most liberals reflexively dismissed all such contentions as mere bigotry, though Buckley angrily denied that he was a racist. NAACP leader Roy Wilkins, in a more subtle analysis, viewed Buckley's cultivation of the white backlash as "yet another stand of the Haves against the increasingly frequent and increasingly diversified sallies of the Have Nots," made more effective by the blackness and brownness of the Have Nots. Wilkins mockingly suggested to Buckley that he had been forced to take up the cause of backlash because of the exhaustion of the conservative bogeyman, "dat ole debbil Communism."[133] The Buckley campaign did attract a number of self-professed racists, mainly young white men who trailed Lindsay to insult him as a "pinko" and "nigger-lover."[134] But the conservative argument appealed to many ordinary white New Yorkers because neither Lindsay nor his eventual Democratic opponent, city comptroller Abraham Beame, dared to address the racial dimensions of urban problems. To do so would have invited the furious attacks that liberals and civil rights groups made on White House advisor Daniel Patrick Moynihan after the August release of his famous report, "The Negro Family: A Case for Action." Because Moynihan pinpointed rising illegitimacy rates in lower-class black areas as the root cause of welfare dependency, school failure, and youth crime, liberals savaged him for "blaming the victim." And yet few could deny that crime was on the rise, at a rate estimated to be five times that of population growth. Also evident to anyone reading a newspaper, in the days before news reports suppressed mention of criminals' racial identities, was that blacks committed a disproportionate amount of urban crime.[135] The spreading fear of crime, more than any other factor, worked to undermine the sense of social solidarity and trust between fellow citizens on which public support of welfare and other liberal programs depended.[136]

The unease that many whites felt over racial issues was compounded by the six-day riot in August in the predominantly black Los Angeles neighborhood of Watts, which left thirty-four dead, reduced hundreds of buildings to charred rubble, and required 15,000 law enforcement officers to bring under control. It was the worst race riot of the century to that point, and an ominous harbinger of "long hot summers" to come. It occurred not in the South but in Los Angeles, which the respected journalist Theodore H. White had judged to be "that city of the United States where the Negro probably receives the most decent treatment and has the best opportunity for decent housing."[137] And the riot erupted five days after the signing of the Voting Rights Act of 1965, which suggested that the successes of the civil rights movement and liberal anti-poverty programs had done little to assuage the frustrations in the black ghettos around the country. Watts reflected and stimulated divisions within the civil rights movement. The liberal coalition continued to break apart as younger and angrier activists rejected integration, incrementalism, and non-violence.

Republican responses to the riots generally followed the divisions within the party. Conservatives such as Buckley, Ronald Reagan, and California Senator George Murphy blamed the civil rights movement, the courts, and the swelling student protest movement for creating a culture of lawlessness. Murphy believed that the riots had nothing to do with ghetto conditions, but resulted from "growing disrespect for law and order."[138] Moderates such as Gerald Ford condemned the violence but conceded that "certain things must be done to give jobs, to give education to those in the Negro race who need them."[139] Progressives in the Ripon Society insisted that the GOP not succumb to the temptation to use white backlash as a political strategy, but instead seize upon African-American disaffection with the Democrats and the Johnson administration's vulnerability on civil rights issues. They proposed that Republicans in Congress study "the condition of Negro life in this country," with special attention to issues like police brutality and the root causes of racial unrest.[140]

Lindsay, in responding to the problems presented by racial disturbances and other issues, neglected numerous opportunities to stake out a distinctive Republican position. While the ideas that fueled his campaign were quite different from those of liberal Democrats, he presented himself as the only liberal in the race and made no real effort to refute Buckley's claim that his ideas were indistinguishable from those of Lyndon Johnson. He continued to run away from the Republican label, feuded openly with his fellow GOP progressive Nelson Rockefeller, and had to rely on Senator Jacob Javits to shore up his eroding party support.[141] He castigated Buckley as a right-wing extremist at the very moment when Buckley, in his capacity as editor of *National Review*, was opening the way for moderate-conservative rapprochement by reading the John Birch Society out of the conservative movement. In passionately identifying himself with the cause of black equality, Lindsay downplayed his previous opposition to racial quotas and ethnic tokenism. He was happy to have the New York NAACP convention blast Buckley as a racist demagogue, but did not criticize the organization's claim that it was racist for employers to question potential hires about their arrest records.[142]

Nonetheless, Lindsay's campaign successfully blended liberals' fear of Buckley and reformers' disdain for the machine Democrat Beame, and garnered further appeal from celebrity endorsements, the youthful idealism of an army of storefront headquarter volunteers, and Lindsay's formidable charisma. On election night, Lindsay emerged the victor with 43.3 percent of the vote, making him what *Newsweek* called "the most exciting political property on the national stage since America glimpsed stardust on John F. Kennedy."[143] Beame pulled 39.5 percent of the vote and Buckley 12.9 percent.

Republicans argued over the significance of Lindsay's victory. As far as Goldwater was concerned, there were no lessons for the party, since Lindsay "ran as an out-and-out liberal and disassociating himself from the Republican party."[144] Ray Bliss contended that "He ran on the Republican ticket, he's a Republican and everybody knows he's a Republican." Nixon believed that Lindsay had won a personal rather than a party victory, but "Had he run as an old-line Republican regular, he wouldn't be mayor today."[145]

Lindsay's victory appeared to show that moderate and progressive Republicans could regain the votes of minorities and urbanites that had disappeared in 1964. He received 42 percent of the black vote—a vast improvement over Goldwater's performance—and 43 percent of the traditionally Democratic Jewish vote, while retaining the votes of three-quarters of the city's Republicans. Most commentators concluded that the election results demonstrated anew the public's distaste for conservatism and the corresponding necessity for Republican moderation. Buckley had received the same percentage of the vote as Lawrence Gerosima, a right-wing, anti-tax, third-party candidate who had run for the mayoralty in 1961. Buckley's poor showing, according to one op-ed writer, "confirmed most Republican professionals in their judgment that the salvation of the GOP lies in modernizing the party's basic concepts Lindsayward regardless of the wails this would evoke from the 13 percent fringe."[146] One of Charles Percy's advisors deduced from Lindsay's election that "Clearly, it is the 'swing' vote in the middle which determines elections these days; much more than the old dichotomy of Republicans and Democrats."[147]

To Buckley, the new conventional wisdom purveyed in the press was that "the GOP absolutely must without fail assuredly in 1966 and 1968 and forever after nominate Lindsay and Lindsayites and Lindsayoids—but I wax lyric."[148] Needless to say, he did not agree. He had expected to get 100,000 more votes than the 341,000 he received, and he was haunted by the thought that he may have drained off conservative Democratic votes in sufficient numbers to have permitted Lindsay to slip through. Still, he believed that his campaign had educated the public and succeeded in its basic aim of tarnishing Lindsay's image: "I do not doubt at all that there will be those who will try to propel him towards the presidency. If they do, they will find it hard, I think, thanks to the record I tried hard to publicize in the course of the campaign."[149]

The historical significance of the Buckley candidacy, however, was its unanticipated success in attracting white ethnic voters discontented with liberalism and the emerging multicultural social order. Buckley's campaign also stands out in hindsight for the underappreciated creativity and unorthodoxy of some of his policy proposals. Liberals were repulsed by Buckley's plan to relocate incorrigible welfare recipients to camps on the city's outskirts. They also pointed out that other elements in his platform displayed a lack of concern for political or financial realities, such as his suggestions that drugs be legalized and that the city's sales taxes be cut without finding replacement revenues. But his proposal for an elevated commuter bicycle path was decades ahead of its time, as was his idea to impose daily fees on out-of-town cars and trucks.[150] As the high priest of conservatism, Buckley was secure enough in his beliefs and his position that he could indulge in a little heresy now and then without worrying overmuch about his acceptability to other conservatives. This gave him more common ground with forward-thinking Republican moderates and progressives than most people suspected. One member of the Ripon Society wrote to him that "your campaign proved—among other things—that there are no uniquely Republican ways to cure the ills of a city. There was, to us, no special Republican or even conservative flavor to your proposals—other than the fact that they came from a conservative source."[151]

While Lindsay's was the highest-profile election victory in 1965, the Ripon Society was actually more enthusiastic about Arlen Specter's election as Philadelphia's district attorney. Specter at the time was an ambitious thirty-four year-old who had won a reputation—as a Democrat—as a vigorous but fair assistant district attorney in Philadelphia. He became known (not for the last time) as "Benedict Arlen" and "Specter the Defector" when, without even waiting to change his party registration, he stood as the Republican Party's challenger to the incumbent district attorney James Crumlish, who happened to be Specter's boss. It would be foolish to deny that Specter's personal ambitions were responsible for his party jump, but it would be equally foolish to deny that his real personal convictions also played a role. The Philadelphia Democratic machine, known locally as "the Octopus of Walnut Street," was deeply corrupt. Its tentacular stranglehold meant expensive, inefficient, and ineffective city government at a time of worsening crime and urban decay. Specter was offended by this state of affairs and attracted to the Republican good-government tradition.

Several senior Republican leaders, particularly Pennsylvania Governor William Scranton and Senator Hugh Scott, personally convinced Specter that he could be the octopus-slayer the city needed. Scranton and Scott were able to persuade conservative Republicans to accept a defecting Democrat and a moderate campaign geared to win over Democratic voters. They argued that this was a practical necessity in the City of Brotherly Love, where Democrats held a nearly two-to-one registration advantage. Goldwater had lost Philadelphia by 441,000 votes in 1964, and the GOP had not won a municipal office in a dozen years.

Specter ran as a reformer and problem-solver, a man of integrity with no ties to any political machine. Modeling his campaign after Lindsay's, Specter advanced a series of well thought-out position papers on Philadelphia's social and economic problems. He also presented himself as the more youthful, harder-working candidate, putting in twenty-hour days fueled by a diet of raw meat and megavitamins. Specter proved difficult to fit into the received political categories. Democratic boss Frank Smith sent thousands of letters to the city's Republican employees charging that Specter was the "puppet" of the liberal Americans for Democratic Action, which was supporting Specter over his Democratic opponent. While many Republican regulars worked hard on Specter's behalf, many also questioned whether he was a Republican in a meaningful sense. When Specter won the election by 36,000 votes, a reporter overheard one of his Republican campaign workers mock-exult, "Hooray, we've elected a Democrat."[152] Scranton, however, credited the victory to "a miracle of hard work," and rejoiced that "the old adage that Republicans cannot win in cities is now out the window."[153]

Specter believed that "the Republican Party must win over Democrats if the Republican Party is to become the dominant party," but that the GOP could do so in a constructive way while remaining true to the example of Theodore Roosevelt, who "first protected the average citizen from the trusts and abuses of big business."[154] Specter also put himself forward as the more fiscally conservative candidate, and attacked Democratic Mayor James Tate's ill-timed mid-campaign proposal to boost taxes. He invoked the Republican heritage of civil rights and succeeded in garnering the support of a sizable fraction of Philadelphia's growing minority population. This was of particular significance in a racially tense city that had experienced a major riot the year before, resulting in no deaths but hundreds of injured, including 66 policemen, and hundreds of stores looted and burned. Specter opposed the heavy-handed tactics of Democratic police commissioner and later mayor Frank Rizzo, proposing instead to elevate the lot of Philadelphia's African-Americans through a program of jobs, educational improvements, and cracking open the city's racist construction unions. At the same time, Specter presented himself as a hardliner on crime, with one of his television commercials presenting a woman fleeing down a dark street pursued by the heavier footfalls of a shadowy rapist. The result was that Specter received the votes both of racial liberals and of backlash voters, particularly in areas where blacks were moving into previously Jewish neighborhoods such as Mount Airy and Germantown.[155]

The Lindsay and Specter wins suggested that the old urban Democratic coalition was breaking up and could be remolded along moderate Republican lines. In a year when African-American voters changed election outcomes across the nation, moderates saw positive portents in the election results in Louisville, Kentucky. The GOP had won the mayor's office in 1961, after twenty-eight years in the cold, and had passed the South's first public accommodations law. Outgoing Republican Mayor William Cowger explained that he had integrated the city because "times change, and I knew that they were changing pretty fast, and I knew I was going to have my back against the wall. And anyway, lately, I felt Louisville was ready for it."[156] The black vote in 1965 helped the Republicans elect a moderate mayor and the first African-American ever to serve as prosecutor of the city police court.[157]

Many other black voters, however, had yet to forgive the party's turn toward the segregationists the previous year. Clarence Townes, a member of the National Negro Republican Assembly and an unsuccessful candidate for the Virginia legislature in the 1965 elections, lamented that "This Goldwater thing was just too much for us. It's a helluva thing to overcome." Virginia's Republican gubernatorial candidate Linwood Holton, a racial moderate, also failed to defeat his Democratic opponent, Mills Godwin. Holton had been among the few prominent Virginians who had campaigned to keep public schools open after the Supreme Court's *Brown* decision, while Godwin had been a "Massive Resister" who had insisted on closing any white public school that admitted a black child. Holton pledged to recruit blacks for appointment to high office and campaigned against the poll tax, both issues on which Godwin equivocated. Nonetheless, labor leaders and even civil rights groups threw themselves behind the partially reformed segregationist Democrat. Although Richmond's predominantly black First Precinct had supported the Republican candidate by a ten-to-one margin in 1961, in 1965 it voted five-to-one for the Democratic candidate.[158] Such was the lingering impact of Goldwater as well as the positive appeal of Johnson's Great Society.

William Story, a die-hard segregationist and John Birch Society member, also led a right-wing third party effort to oppose Holton, prompting the Ripon Society to complain that although conservatives had attacked moderates who disassociated themselves from Goldwater in 1964, they now "showed their true colors . . . as spoilers and self-servers."[159] Story received approximately 13 percent of the vote, which, as the *Washington Star* pointed out, was about what Buckley had received in New York City.[160] One percent of the state's voters supported George Lincoln Rockwell of the American Nazi Party. Nonetheless, Holton won more votes than any GOP nominee for state office since Reconstruction, benefited from a rare campaign appearance from Eisenhower, and laid the groundwork for a successful moderate Republican Party in Virginia.[161]

Wayne Dumont's disastrous campaign for the New Jersey governorship reinforced moderates' conviction that the conservative approach was electoral poison. A small-town lawyer and state senator, Dumont had a reputation as a moderate, and asked Al Abrahams, the executive director of Republicans for Progress, to manage his campaign. Dumont began his gubernatorial race by endorsing the self-help center for Newark ghetto residents that was set up by the Committee of '68, a moderate Republican activist organization; the center offered free services and counseling by lawyers, businessmen, social workers, and teachers, and was a comparatively rare case of a Republican direct-action anti-poverty project.[162] But increasingly Dumont came under the influence of members of his staff who were associated with Young Americans for Freedom and the right-wing faction of the state Young Republicans. They convinced him that his best bet to unseat the incumbent Democrat Richard Hughes, in heavily Republican New Jersey, was to excite the allegedly conservative "base" of the party with the red-meat issues of Communism and the Vietnam war.

Dumont dropped his pragmatic reform agenda for the state's underfunded public highways, hospitals, and colleges, and focused his campaign around Eugene Genovese, a Marxist professor of history at Rutgers who had expressed sympathy for the Vietcong. Dumont demanded that Hughes fire Genovese from the state university; the governor refused, protesting that all cases of academic freedom had to be decided by Rutgers's board of governors.[163] Richard Nixon, reverting to red-baiting form in support of Dumont, declared that there was no such thing as free speech in wartime, since if the Communists won in Vietnam, "the right of free speech will be extinguished throughout the world."[164] Out the window went Dumont's hoped-for endorsement by the *New York Times*, which sniffed that "McCarthyism is a dead horse. If Mr. Dumont does not climb off it and start riding some live issues, his campaign will be a waste of time."[165] Abrahams resigned from the campaign.[166] New Jersey voters wanted their politicians to act on the state's real and pressing problems, and had no wish to revive bygone witch-hunting rituals. They punished Dumont, who went down by a record margin, and the Republicans as well, who lost control of both houses of the state legislature for the first time since 1912.[167]

In the year after the Goldwater election disaster, the moderates' morale had revived along with their electoral hopes. Some conservative groups persisted in their campaign to take over the GOP from within, but others moved toward some kind of accommodation with party moderates. Bill Buckley, speaking a few days after the elections at the tenth anniversary dinner of *National Review*, inclined toward pessimism about conservatism's prospects: "The joys of warmaking presuppose the eventual stillness of victory; and that, so far as I can see, is beyond our reach."[168] Progressives meanwhile experienced some of the same intoxication that had earlier seized the Goldwaterites, amid predictions that "liberal Republicanism combined with Negro unrest is the one hope of Republican revival, and the one explosive combination that can bring down an entrenched Democratic regime."[169] Neither the conservative pessimism nor the progressive optimism would be fully warranted, but the fortunes of the Republican Party as a whole clearly were on the upswing.

CHAPTER 6

Full of Passionate Intensity

From Rat Finks to Reagan, 1966

In late January 1966, American newspaper readers made the acquaintance of the Rat Finks, the conservative faction of the New Jersey Young Republicans. Stories revealed that the self-styled Rat Finks had enlivened YR gatherings throughout the previous year with renditions from their songbook, which gave lyric form to the youthful conservative worldview. One song advocated hanging moderate Republicans such as William Scranton, Nelson Rockefeller, and New Jersey Senator Clifford Case from a sour apple tree. One mock-lamented, in thick minstrel dialect, the killings of civil rights workers in Alabama, while another extolled the joys of "Riding through the Reich/In my Mercedes-Benz/Shooting all the kikes . . ." Still another, sung to the tune of "Where Have All the Flowers Gone?," inquired: "Where has all the money gone? Gone to taxes./Where have all the taxes gone? Gone to welfare./Where has all the welfare gone? Gone to niggers."[1] The ensuing controversy over racism and anti-Semitism in the YRs was a setback for Republican National Committee chairman Ray Bliss' efforts to restore party harmony and regain the sympathies of African-Americans and urban voters. The scandal also made clear that right-wing extremists continued to burrow into the GOP, and that some parts of the Republican Party apparatus were still in the control of Goldwater partisans. The battles between moderates and conservatives raged on at the grassroots even while a spirit of grudging accommodation was taking hold at the national level.

The Young Republicans had been an obstacle to Bliss' plans for party renewal during his first year in office. The GOP had experienced a significant decline in young voters' support for its presidential candidates. 57 percent of the 21-to-29 year-old age group had voted for Eisenhower in 1956, 46 percent for Nixon in 1960, but only 36 percent for Goldwater in 1964. College students' support for the Republicans also dropped, particularly at the nation's most prominent colleges and universities.[2] The party's reputation for negativism and its perceived unwillingness to grapple with the problems of the age partly accounted for its poor showing among youth, but the failure of the Young Republicans organization and its College Service Committee were also to blame. The tendency of YR members toward militant and uncompromising conservative ideology had been on display at the 1965 YR national convention in Miami, where the newly elected chairman, Kansas state senator Tom Van Sickle, felt moved to attack the Civil Rights Act of 1964 and boast of his support from South Carolina segregationist Senator Strom Thurmond.[3] This did not broaden the Young Republicans' appeal with most politically active young people in the baby boom generation, for whom the civil rights movement remained a transcendent moral cause. The GOP's public image also suffered negative publicity from the conservative drive to oust moderate-dominated YR chapters from college campuses and replace them with units of the right-wing group Young Americans for Freedom.[4] As columnists Evans and Novak observed, the YR mission had changed from youth outreach and promotion of Republicanism to "training conservatives for intra-party warfare."[5]

Van Sickle was the candidate of the Syndicate, the political machine within the YRs overseen by conservative movement elders including *National Review* publisher William Rusher and political consultant Clif White. The Syndicate had maintained its hold over the national federation after reasserting control at the chaotic 1963 YR convention in San Francisco. Its members were all conservative, but the cabal's primary concern was not so much ideology as self-perpetuation, exercised through a wide range of tactics including the creation of paper organizations, manipulation of voting procedures, dissolution of unmanageable chapters, and financial subvention underwritten by donations from conservative supporters. At the 1965 YR convention, for example, the Syndicate provided certain delegates with plane tickets to Miami, but they received their tickets home only after voting in the proper way.[6] The Syndicate also countenanced outright violence when deemed organizationally necessary. When insurgents in the Washington, D.C. YR chapter narrowly won the chairmanship on a platform of political outreach to the District's urban minorities, a conservative mob invaded the next meeting, forced the new leader from the podium, and declared his election null and void. Police had to be summoned to restore order.[7] The constant infighting and righter-than-thou ideological warfare opened the way for extremist infiltration. California's state YR organization included three admitted John Birch Society members as top officers, and the Long Beach chapter elected as its president a member of the American Nazi Party.[8]

The combination of Syndicate control, ideological fanaticism, and extremist penetration repelled even those young people who were interested in the Republican Party. A case in point was the experience of Christie Todd, who later, as Christine Todd Whitman, became the first woman elected governor of New Jersey. As the daughter of two prominent New Jersey Republican leaders, she naturally was attracted to the YR organization. When she attended a YR meeting in her home county, however, she found that the group had been taken over by Rat Finks, many of whom were tied to the John Birch Society. She was taken aback when one of the Rat Finks "stood up and, looking straight at me, warned that the club had to watch out for 'communist-fascists' who were trying to infiltrate the organization."[9] Another woman in the New Jersey YRs was subjected to physical harassment "bordering on terrorism," including one incident in which her car was forced off the road and rocked violently by Rat Finks screaming insults and threats. Some opponents of the Rat Finks, calling themselves the Exterminators, disaffiliated their chapters from the New Jersey state federation. Many others simply left the YR organization in disgust, including the entire membership of a predominantly African-American club in Newark.[10] And, as the *New York Herald Tribune* editorialized, the "bigotry, paranoia and anti-intellectualism of the [YR] extremists . . . 'throws out' countless potential Republicans before they consider joining."[11] Because the Rat Finks were allied with the Syndicate, however, state and national YR leaders refused to rein in their excesses.

RNC chair Ray Bliss initially hoped to settle the Rat Fink scandal quietly and "within the lodge," as he put it, so as not to disrupt party unity.[12] It proved impossible, however, to ignore the widespread condemnation from editorialists, civil rights organizations, and religious groups such as the Episcopal Church, which threatened to excommunicate any of its members who were found to have produced or distributed the Rat Fink songs.[13] Moderate and progressive Republicans would not allow Bliss to sweep the matter under the rug, because they genuinely believed that the YRs had become a disgrace to the party and also because they saw an opportunity to claw back control from the conservatives. Nelson Rockefeller's advisor George Hinman warned Bliss that the National Committee must not "continue to tolerate and finance a Young Republican apparatus that is in the hands of a faction which is using it to advance its own narrow interests and to divide and embarrass the senior party."[14] Pennsylvania moderate Senator Hugh Scott spoke before the Washington, D.C. chapter of the YRs and argued that the organization's ideologues were undercutting Republicans' efforts to repair the damage of 1964, particularly in regaining the African-American vote. In his view, these initiatives were doomed by YR members' support of the Rat Finks and the white racist regime in Rhodesia. Nor did it help that the D.C. chapter's newsletter, under the editorship of a Birch Society member, had termed the Civil Rights Act of 1964 a Communist plot. He pleaded with the YRs to stop alienating potential voters and to put aside the Syndicate's Leninist tactics and win-at-all-costs mentality. He reminded them that "power comes from public opinion and public backing and not from backroom intrigues and petty trickery." The YR members would not make a positive contribution to public life, he predicted, if they were unwilling to compromise or to adhere to "the basic American standards of fair play," but instead spent all of their time "trying to figure out how to put the shaft to somebody else."[15]

Ray Bliss also recognized that movement conservatives, in the Young Republicans and elsewhere, were the primary obstacle to the party unity that he sought. The Los Angeles County YRs passed a resolution declaring Senator Thomas Kuchel "a Republican in name only," years before that particular epithet gained common currency. The YRs demanded that Kuchel switch parties and resolved to oppose his candidacy at all times regardless of party label.[16] Bliss had a researcher investigate one of his conservative critics, Young Americans for Freedom national chairman Robert Bauman, who had claimed that Bliss was attempting to destroy the YR National Federation "because of its conservative influence."[17] Bliss found that Bauman had been given GOP patronage employment as a telephone page in the House of Representatives, but took no part in any party activities in his home state or county. His principal contribution to party affairs had come in 1964 when he had singlehandedly held up the election of Milton Eisenhower, a well-known moderate and brother of the former president, to the Maryland national GOP convention delegation; Barry Goldwater was forced to intervene to prevent what would have been an embarrassing incident. Bauman was also secretary of the American Conservative Union (ACU), a splinter group that vied with Goldwater's Free Society Association for leadership of the conservative movement. One of the goals of the ACU, as founding member William Rusher put it, was to divert conservatives' campaign contributions away from the RNC and other party organizations that might support moderate candidates.[18]

Bliss found it necessary, therefore, to use the Rat Fink episode as a way of putting a leash on the Young Republicans and by extension the movement conservatives working against party unity. The RNC called YR president Van Sickle on the carpet at its annual midyear meeting. Bliss remonstrated with the young conservative for allowing the YRs to become "too ideology oriented," and complained that "Rightly or wrongly, the implication has developed that the National Federation is trying to protect so-called 'Rat Fink' groups," imperiling the GOP's chances in the fall elections. Van Sickle insolently defied the party leaders, but ultimately they forced him to agree to changes that restricted his organization's ability to act as a party within a party. At one point, Van Sickle had a tense exchange with RNC vice chairman Don Ross, a Nebraska conservative, over the National Federation's refusal to remove Richard Plechner, the New Jersey YR state chairman and head of the Rat Finks. "You are telling us to do something impossible under the circumstances," Van Sickle protested to Ross, who shot back: "I am not sure that it is impossible for you. I think maybe if you came between a choice between Mr. Plechner and financing of the National Federation, I would say you would choose financing." Drake Edens, a South Carolina conservative, was equally insistent that "I am not ready to let the state of New Jersey strangle the Republican Party."[19] The RNC unanimously passed a resolution emphasizing that the GOP opposed all forms of bigotry. The Committee ordered that Rat Finks be removed from their positions in the YR national leadership, and curtailed the autonomy of the YRs by designating RNC members Ross and Connecticut moderate Tina Harrower as observers at all National Federation executive committee meetings. According to Evans and Novak, the moves signified that "the restoration of the party machinery to post-Goldwater normality, which should have begun 18 months ago, is underway."[20]

Moderates did not savor their victory, however, since the Rat Fink saga unfolded against the collapse of the *New York Herald Tribune*, the daily newspaper that historically had defined moderate, Eastern Republicanism. The *Tribune* had long been the only real rival to the *New York Times* as the nation's paper of note, although after World War II the *Times* began to pull ahead decisively in terms of reputation and profitability. Increasingly, the *Tribune* fell prey to inexorable forces that would winnow the number of New York newspapers from twenty-five in 1900 to three by the end of the 1960s.[21] These forces included competition from radio and television broadcasting, and the rise of morning tabloids and suburban papers such as Long Island's *Newsday*. The *Tribune* also suffered from erratic management and the departure of large numbers of white, middle-class Republicans from the city to the suburbs and beyond. Above all, *Trib* insiders blamed the paper's demise on an unsustainable increase in costs brought about by intransigent labor unions, abetted by the overly generous concessions of the *Times* to many of the same unions.

In 1958, the Reid family, which had owned the paper since 1872, had been forced by the relentless rise of red ink to cede control to multimillionaire John Hay Whitney, who was then Eisenhower's ambassador to Great

Britain, and his principal business advisor, Walter Thayer. By 1966, Thayer had concluded that the paper, which was losing money at a pace of $5 million a year, was not financially viable.[22] Whitney and Thayer agreed to merge the *Herald Tribune* with two other declining New York papers, the *Journal-American* and the *World-Telegram & Sun*, to form the *World Journal Tribune*, with the *Tribune* continuing to appear as a separate morning paper. The *Tribune's* last issue appeared on April 23, 1966. The press unions mounted a 114-day strike rather than permit any automation or employment reductions. By August, most of the paper's staff had left for other positions, and Whitney and his partners agreed not to resume publication of the *Tribune*. "It is a very bitter blow to have finally had to abandon the Herald Tribune," Whitney wrote to Eisenhower. "Labor is directly to blame, of course, but the leadership in labor relations exercised by the New York Times and the Daily News over the past fifteen years has been so weak that the blame is there, too. It seems almost to have been designed to accomplish what has just happened. Quien sabe?!"[23] Chief editorial writer Raymond Price took down the editorial room's portrait of Horace Greeley, who had founded the paper in 1841, and kept it as a melancholy souvenir. The *Tribune* building's demolition soon followed the paper's dissolution. The *World Journal Tribune*, commonly known as "the Widget," lasted less than eight months.

Most of the memorials for the *Tribune* mourned the disappearance of its lively stable of writers, which had included such luminaries as Walter Lippmann, Marguerite Higgins, Homer Bigart, Art Buchwald, Red Smith, Walter Kerr, Jimmy Breslin, and Dick Schaap. In its last years, the *Tribune* had even pioneered what became known as the New Journalism, in the form of Tom Wolfe's supercharged, free-form reportage in the Sunday *New York* magazine section. For an establishment publication, the *Tribune* was surprisingly attuned to the cultural avant-garde. For Ray Price, the collision between the several worlds of the *Tribune* was encapsulated one New Year's Eve when he brought Beat writer Jack Kerouac, garbed in an orange sweatshirt and dirty jeans, to a black-tie party on the Upper East Side.[24]

Price believed that what the nation truly lost with the *Tribune's* disappearance was the distinctive voice of moderate Republicanism. The *Tribune's* version of Republicanism hewed to the political center, "but it was different from a centrist Democratic version, like that of the *New York Times*. We believed more firmly than the Democrats did in the rewards and disciplines of a capitalist system and free enterprise." While the *Tribune* acknowledged the need for the federal government and its regulatory powers, it took greater pains than liberal papers to analyze whether the desirable ends of government were supported by what Price called "means that are appropriate to a civilized democratic society."[25] When the editors determined that those means were ineffective or inappropriate, they often took some strongly libertarian positions. Confronted with the seemingly anodyne issue of the Surgeon General's advisory warning on the health risks of smoking, the *Tribune* blasted "the concept of the Coddled American, who has to be protected against himself at every turn, who can't be trusted to manage his own affairs or make his own decisions, or provide for his own welfare, or to buy a pack of cigarettes without being warned, These May Kill You."[26] Unlike most conservative papers, however, the *Tribune* had a cosmopolitan worldview, partly because it published a Paris-based international edition of the paper, which was what Jean Seberg's character sold on Parisian boulevards at the beginning of Jean-Luc Godard's 1960 film *Breathless*. "When you wrote editorials," Price pointed out, "you had both audiences in mind. That helped make us internationalist, and that was part of the DNA of the paper."[27] The Paris edition outlasted its parent; renamed the *International Herald Tribune*, it became a joint venture owned by the Whitney Communications Corporation, the *New York Times*, and the *Washington Post*.

The *Tribune* epitomized the values of the WASPy establishment whose political, economic, and cultural power was eroding under the tidal pressures of the 1960s. Like that establishment, it paid little attention to the country beyond the Eastern seaboard and took a fundamentally elitist perspective, tending to view challenges to the established order as impractical and irresponsible. It dismissed the New Right as immature zealots, the New Left as bearded fools, Democrats as spendthrift Tammanyites, and labor unions as impudent conspiracies against the public interest. Its position on Vietnam was blinkered and dogmatic, and it wrote off Martin Luther King's thoughtful comparisons of the war with social injustice at home as an attempt "to see analogies where none exist."[28] While it consistently supported civil rights, the paper took a jaundiced view of what one editorial termed the "out-migration of the prosperous middle and upper-middle classes to the suburbs, and the massive in-migration of the poor, the ignorant, the crime-prone." But the same editorial discerned that the situation of urban minorities was the consequence of "generations of national neglect," and that decades of effort and vast expense would be required to make these citizens into "productive, responsible members of a society too many of them regard as the enemy."[29] If the *Tribune* was slow to recognize the emerging multicultural society, it clung steadfastly to a colorblind vision of merit and was free of the sentimental egalitarianism that had begun to infect liberalism, particularly where racial issues were concerned.

The *Tribune*'s memorialists, looking back through the sepia scrim of nostalgia, believed that the paper's old-fashioned credo of duty, decency, and intellectual honesty would be sorely missed in American politics in years to come. Unquestionably the GOP would miss the enlivening effect of the

paper's encouragement of forward-looking Republican ideas. In more practical terms, moderates lost one of their most significant, durable, and influential institutions. Nothing could replace the *Tribune*'s importance as a
publicist for moderate Republican politicians, a mouthpiece for moderate
values, and an outlet for some of the faction's best writers and intellectuals.
While John Hay Whitney made a strictly dollars-and-cents decision to fold
up his investment, many conservative businessmen who were nowhere
near as rich as Whitney would endure far greater losses to support conservative papers and magazines. The *Tribune*'s disappearance was further testimony that moderates were simply less willing than conservatives to suffer
and sacrifice for their cause.

Another blow for moderates in mid-1966 was that the circumstances that
had allowed Goldwater and the conservatives to take power appeared to be
repeating themselves in California. Ever since Goldwater's defeat, the
Ripon Society had been sounding an alarm about "creeping Reaganism":
the danger that California's 1966 gubernatorial election might provide a
launching pad for Ronald Reagan, the genial right-wing actor and corporate
pitchman. Political talent scouts had picked Reagan as a likely candidate
ever since his televised speech "A Time for Choosing" had electrified conservatives in the waning days of the Goldwater campaign. In June 1965,
Ripon had warned that "Moderates, who waited too long before taking the
rise of Goldwater seriously, are now faced with a possible repetition of that
story. If Reagan is to be stopped before he becomes the focus of another
national wave of right-wing emotion, he should be stopped now."[30]
The Democrats' candidate would be the two-term incumbent Governor
Edmund G. "Pat" Brown, who epitomized the expansive liberalism of the
early '60s. Many of the reforms he brought to California were models for
Great Society legislation. He had passed a Fair Employment Practices Act
to guard against discrimination in employment, created a consumer protection agency and an economic development agency, and reorganized state
government and made it more efficient. In his role as the state's master
builder, he pushed through massive infrastructural improvements, providing for the construction of highways, byways, freeways, bridges, tunnels,
rail systems, waterways, and schools. His most important achievements included a $2 billion water project and the Master Plan of Higher Education,
which created three new campuses in the University of California system
and raised the system as a whole to levels of excellence unsurpassed by any
public education system anywhere in the world. By 1966, however, Brown
and the liberalism that he represented had been shaken by the Watts riots,
rising crime rates, the Free Speech Movement and other disorderly protests
at the University of California at Berkeley, and an emerging counterculture

that flouted American values and traditional morality. Brown also suffered from the public discontent that accompanied nearly a decade of Democratic domination of the state government. California voters had grown tired of Brown and he would be vulnerable to almost any candidate the Republicans were likely to put forward.

The moderates' best chance of preventing Reagan's rise was to have Senator Thomas Kuchel, the most popular politician in California, enter the governor's race. In fact, Kuchel's legislative assistant Stephen Horn had as early as June 1964 worked out a detailed plan for a Kuchel gubernatorial drive, building on Nelson Rockefeller's presidential primary campaign organization in order to revive moderate Republican forces across the state.[31] But Kuchel had been badly hurt by his enemies' attempts to ruin him with a homosexual smear accusation, and he lacked the stomach for an Armageddon-style battle against the conservatives. After many months of indecision he declared that he would not campaign for the governorship. In his announcement he blasted the "fanatical neo-fascist political cult" of right-wingers within the California GOP, a group driven by "a strange mixture of corrosive hatred and sickening fear" that was "recklessly determined to control our party or destroy it."[32] A disappointed Steve Horn decamped for the Brookings Institution, while Democrats crowed that Brown's reelection to a third term was all but assured.[33]

The moderates' second-choice candidate to oppose Reagan was George Christopher, the former Republican mayor of San Francisco. Christopher had lived the American dream, coming to the United States as the son of penniless Greek immigrants and working his way up in business and politics. He was a dynamic and successful two-term mayor of San Francisco, a builder and a coalition-maker, who had brought order and efficiency to the municipal administration's endemic corruption and disarray. While he had a reputation as a humanitarian who had good relations with urban minority communities, no less a conservative than Herbert Hoover had called him "the best mayor of any large city with which I am acquainted."[34] Christopher's supporters claimed that Reagan, who lacked any exposure to legislative or administrative government, was unqualified for the job. The former mayor sternly emphasized that the governorship was "not a toy, not a plaything. It is a vast responsibility. There is no such thing as instant education or instant experience."[35] Christopher also trumpeted his abhorrence of the John Birch Society, which Reagan had refused to repudiate. He argued that Republicans would lose with a conservative candidate in '66 just as they had two years earlier, and that only a moderate could defeat Brown.

The outcome of the GOP primary was shaped behind the scenes by the actions of a small handful of political decision makers. Two of the most significant were Stuart Spencer and William Roberts, who had vaulted to the top rank of political consultants with their management of Nelson Rockefeller's campaign against Goldwater in the California '64 presidential primary. Christopher wanted Spencer-Roberts to run his campaign, but surprisingly so too did Reagan. Spencer-Roberts had mainly backed moderate Republicans to that point, including the likes of Rockefeller and Kuchel, whom Reagan had attacked as "traitors" after the '64 election.[36] But evidently Reagan had come to appreciate that neither his career nor the GOP would prosper if the party remained divided. Spencer and Roberts, who had believed that right-wingers were political losers, realized after meeting Reagan that he was moderate in temperament if not philosophy, and that he could be persuaded to distance himself from the Birchers and reach out to the moderates. The two political operatives came to the cold and clinical decision that although Christopher was closer to their political outlook, the advantages were all on Reagan's side. Reagan was from southern California, where the bulk of the Republican vote and financial base was located, and he was a fresh face who could give the party a new image. Spencer and Roberts felt that Reagan would be better able than Christopher to unify the party after the primary election, and had a better chance of beating Brown in the fall elections. Reagan was also "the first master of the electronic media the state of California ever had," Spencer believed, while in the final analysis, "time had passed George by."[37]

Spencer-Roberts signed on with Reagan, much to the chagrin of their erstwhile moderate allies. They helped Reagan do an artful job of separating himself from the moderate-repelling elements of his right-wing base while retaining overall conservative loyalty. For example, Reagan stated that while he found Birch Society head Robert Welch's slanders against Eisenhower "utterly reprehensible," he would welcome support from all individuals including Birchers "by persuading them to accept my philosophy, not by my accepting theirs."[38] Spencer-Roberts led a successful effort "to keep what we called the right-wing nuts out of running the campaign," according to one Reagan operative.[39] Reagan himself came to feel that many conservative activists were not to be trusted, particularly former leader Joe Shell; Nancy Reagan complained to Bill Buckley that Shell had grown jealous of her husband and was "busy telling everyone Ronnie is an admitted Communist!"[40] Reporter Mary McGrory noticed that during the primary campaign, Reagan "tailored his candidate script for the moderates" and consciously held back from sounding the pure chords of conservatism that had filled Goldwater's followers with quasi-religious fervor. The conservative true believers would vote for Reagan, McGrory predicted, "but they may not die for him."[41] It was a new indication of conservative sophistication. By lowering the ideological temperature of his campaign, Reagan made himself less threatening to moderates.

Gaylord Parkinson, the chairman of the California Republican Party, also boosted Reagan's chances in the GOP primary by articulating his so-called Eleventh Commandment: "Thou shalt not speak ill of any fellow Republican."[42] Parkinson sincerely sought to heal the divisions in the California GOP that had resulted in the defeats of Nixon in the 1962 gubernatorial race, when conservatives had sat out the election, and Goldwater in the 1964 presidential race, when moderates and progressives had bolted to the Democrats. Parkinson presented himself as a neutral figure above factional warfare, and the Eleventh Commandment was a means of calling a ceasefire in the battles of moderates against conservatives, and the northern part of the state against the south. William Roberts emphasized that the 1964 GOP presidential primary in California had been "a blood bath" that no one wanted to repeat.[43] Nonetheless, as Reagan's press secretary Franklyn "Lyn" Nofziger admitted, "The purpose of the 'Eleventh Commandment' was to keep the other side in the primary from attacking Reagan, because we felt clearly that Reagan was ahead. Therefore, if we could keep these people from going on the attack, you could render them impotent." With his issuance of the Eleventh Commandment, "Parkinson pretty much helped assure a Reagan victory."[44] Parkinson also helped the Reagan campaign by shutting up the state's Young Republicans, who had reached such a toxic level of ideological extremism that any public statement of theirs was bound to generate adverse publicity for conservative candidates.[45]

Many moderates saw the Eleventh Commandment as a sort of Trojan horse enabling a right-wing takeover of the GOP under cover of "unity" statements. It seemed to them that moderates were being asked to placate conservatives despite the lack of conservative reciprocity; Bill Buckley had not cared overmuch about "unity" in seeking to knock off John Lindsay in New York City the year before. The Ripon Society blasted the naïveté of Christopher's forces for accepting "the fatal admonitions of the party chairman," which prevented moderates from hammering at Reagan's political vulnerabilities such as his continuing support from the Birch Society, his lack of administrative experience, and his "checkered and unstable ideological career."[46] Many moderates and progressives outside the state refused to accede to Reagan's ascent or to abide by the Eleventh Commandment. Nelson Rockefeller made a sizable grant to Christopher's campaign, and John Lindsay sent a key aide to run a research operation aimed at collecting incriminating statements from Reagan.[47]

Still, the Eleventh Commandment came at a moment when all the California GOP's factions had grown weary of the infighting that seemingly condemned the party to permanent defeat. "This is a horrible admission," one prominent California moderate confessed, "but . . . I'm beginning to hear the siren call for unity behind our ex-movie actor, Ronald Reagan. I'm not sure George Christopher, our liberal Republican friend, could squeak through the primary with enough gas left over after the dog fight with the conservatives to win in the final election. I'm tired of this self-destructive fratricide in California. I am thinking that perhaps we ought to infiltrate Reagan."[48] In the long run, the Eleventh Commandment benefited moderates as well. Reagan would make Parkinson's commandment his own and would seek to build a "big tent" Republican Party, albeit one dominated by conservatives.[49]

The Christopher campaign performed well through the spring of 1966. Various polls conducted in May showed Christopher running only two percentage points behind Reagan, with 18 percent of the electorate still undecided.[50] A group of progressive Republican members of the state Assembly cited another poll projecting that Christopher would defeat Brown while Reagan would lose, and asked the conservative to "withdraw from the Gubernatorial race and from this point forward devote all of your talent, energy and financial resources to the Christopher campaign."[51] The moderate candidate also began to pick up some conservative support, including an endorsement from the Los Angeles County Taxpayers League, which approved of Christopher's performance as San Francisco mayor in holding down the city's tax structure.[52]

Then newspaper columnist Drew Pearson dredged up Christopher's 1940 arrest when, as head of a dairy business, he had been charged with buying and selling milk at prices below the state's legal limit. Brown and his aides had fed the story to Pearson, convinced that they had to "screw" the formidable moderate Christopher in order to ensure that the governor's Republican opponent would be the weaker "fringe" candidate, Reagan.[53] Pearson's column was a hatchet job; Christopher had committed no real crime. All of California's dairy industries had fought the state's price-fixing law, whose constitutionality was under question, and Christopher had been exonerated of any serious wrongdoing. But according to Michael Chabot Smith, a Ripon Society member who served on Christopher's research staff, the Pearson column "put Christopher on the defensive. He was a terribly underwhelming candidate to begin with, but his attempt to respond to the smear revealed him to be hopelessly inarticulate; he never got his story straight. It was awful. The charges distracted the campaign off its moorings, and they revealed the candidate's weakness, so from then on we were dead men walking."[54]

Reagan took the June 8 primary in a landslide, winning 77 percent of the vote. In stark contrast to the gloating and purging that Goldwater's conservatives had indulged in two years earlier, Reagan's team made peace with the defeated moderates and asked them to join a unity ticket. Many of Christopher's top supporters and financial backers were given high positions on the Reagan team, Christopher's workers were absorbed into the Reagan campaign, and Reagan actively reached out to calm intra-party quarrels and bring moderates on board. Nofziger remembered it as "the smoothest putting together of two campaigns I've ever seen ... People really put aside differences."[55] Many conservatives smarted over Reagan's solicitude toward their enemies, but the right's desire to see their hero take office meant that they were willing to sacrifice some ideological purity in the name of political pragmatism.[56] Moderate and progressive Republicans also wanted to defeat Brown, and embraced the opportunity offered by the Reagan campaign to demonstrate their party loyalty. Assemblyman Bill Bagley testified that he and other progressive Republicans who became honorary chairmen in the Reagan campaign were "trying to show that we weren't as bad as the far right, who would *not* participate when they lost."[57]

Reagan's positions were also not so extreme as to alienate the moderates. Christopher had emphasized many of the same themes as the Reagan campaign, including the need for fiscal austerity, the threat to individual liberty from centralized government control, the virtues of private enterprise, the parasitism of welfare, and the dangers of crime, social disorder, and waning traditional morality. It was Christopher who had characterized the student demonstrations at Berkeley as an "atrocity," and warned that "The Carthaginian and Roman empires decayed from within. We must restore our moral and spiritual precepts."[58] Former CIA director John McCone had donated to both Christopher's and Reagan's campaigns because he thought there was "no real basic difference between the two men with respect to the principles of the Republican Party."[59] Reagan for his part insisted that conservatives "must recognize we have to convert those people of a more liberal view. We don't win elections by destroying them or making them disappear." To suggest that a unity ticket amounted to a sellout of conservative principles was "foolishness."[60] While the moderate and conservative positions were hardly interchangeable, the factions of the party were willing— temporarily, at least—to minimize their differences and maximize their common ground.

Outside of California, relations between moderates and conservatives were not all sweetness and light. In many states, the conservative movement continued to work for itself rather than the Republican Party as a whole. Goldwater forces refused RNC chair Ray Bliss' request that the Goldwater-Miller Citizens Committee turn over to the party the $300,000 that they had saved from the '64 election; those funds would go exclusively toward conservative candidates.[61] In Ohio, Birch Society member William Flax challenged Robert Taft Jr., seeking to keep the moderate son of "Mr. Conservative" out of Congress. Young Americans for Freedom provided the money and manpower behind Flax's primary campaign. Though Taft won the primary by a four to one margin, he refused the endorsement of his defeated opponent, and his supporters worried that the divisions caused by the election could damage his chances in November.[62] In Pennsylvania, YAF and other conservative groups set up a front organization, "Committee for the Commonwealth," to purge moderate Republican congressmen in the primary elections. One of those targeted, Representative Richard S. Schweiker, was a prototypical middle-roader, rated 44 percent conservative by Americans for Constitutional Action and 47 percent liberal by Americans for Democratic Action. His offense, in the eyes of rightists, had been to vote for the repeal of Section 14-B of the Taft-Hartley Act, which permitted states to pass "right-to-work" laws. Since union-heavy Pennsylvania would never implement such a right-to-work law, Schweiker's vote was a symbolic gesture intended to make the state GOP more attractive to labor, but for the right wing it was a betrayal requiring Schweiker's political extermination.[63]

The right won a number of victories in primary battles against moderates and the party establishment, knocking off prominent moderates such as Idaho Governor Robert Smylie, who had led the Republican Governors Association. A sizable donation from Citizens for Goldwater-Miller helped push Donald "Buz" Lukens, the former chairman of the Young Republicans, to victory over the moderate candidate preferred by the Ohio GOP organization.[64] A *Congressional Quarterly* survey claimed that conservatives emerged triumphant in virtually every primary contest in which they were opposed by moderate or progressive Republicans, a testimony to their superior resources and organizational energies.[65] This was an overstatement. Taft, Schweiker, and many other moderates were able to fend off their right-wing challengers, and the losses of moderate incumbents were balanced by the victories of moderate challengers over more conservative officeholders. In Massachusetts, for example, moderate Margaret "Peggy" Heckler, a housewife and party volunteer, defeated Representative Joseph W. Martin Jr., who had previously been Speaker of the House and had first been elected to Congress six years before Heckler was born.[66]

Moderate and conservative activist groups continued to lob salvoes at each other. In April, the Ripon Society received widespread media attention for "China Today—Containment and Contact," a white paper calling for the GOP to lead a "searching re-examination" of U.S. policy toward Peking. Ripon recommended a halt to U.S. efforts to ban Red China from United Nations membership and a "rethinking" of the position "which considers Taiwan the only 'legitimate' government of all China."[67] To conservatives like Bill Buckley, who had worked hand in glove with The Committee of One Million and other pro-Taiwan outfits, this was anathema. Magazines like *National Review* and *Human Events* sounded the alarm that leaders of "the ultra-liberal splinter group" were "worming their way into several campaigns throughout the country."[68] The American Conservative Union piled on with a study characterizing Ripon as "progressive Republicanism's intellectual elite." The ACU charged that Ripon believed "that there must be a two-party system divided only on the question of who can manage the Great Society programs more efficiently."[69] This criticism seemed unfair to one of Ripon's principal theorists, Lee Auspitz: "If you looked at the policies that Ripon advocated, they were not open to the charge of me-tooism. We really did try to locate a third way between conservative Republicans and liberal Democrats. The early policy papers were quite consistently based on a different notion of government than New Deal government."[70] But conservative attacks on Ripon sharpened as the Society's media profile grew.

Overall, however, the tone of the '66 Republican effort was set by Richard Nixon, who continued to pursue his political revival by undertaking the sweaty work of campaigning for all party candidates regardless of their ideological positions. "The effective control of both Houses of Congress does not depend upon the members' ideological convictions but upon their political affiliation," he lectured a conservative who protested Nixon's work on behalf of moderates and progressives. "Both our parties are broadly based as I believe they should be, and while the one party generally emphasizes one set of principles before another, the overlap between the two is enormous. To say that one cannot support a party that entertains men of varying views in this country is tantamount to saying that one cannot remain within a party that has a chance of national success."[71] Wherever he went, Nixon brought at least a temporary truce to the party's warring factions. One reporter pointed out that "Nixon was perhaps the one national Republican speaker out on the circuit about whom local 'liberals' and 'conservatives' could unite for an evening without having to surrender their mutual contempt of one another."[72] Nixon continued to cultivate bright young progressive members of the Ripon Society, but also courted conservatives such as Tom Charles Huston, leader of Young Americans for Freedom.[73] He maintained a studied ambiguity with regard to divisive issues such as Vietnam and the "white backlash."

The white backlash was a phenomenon that had been analyzed *ad nauseam* in the media ever since the campaigns of George Wallace and Barry Goldwater in 1964. The backlash allegedly revealed itself in California's 1964 vote to repeal the state's fair-housing laws, and popular resistance to the proposal to establish a Civilian Complaint Review Board for the New York City police department. In the summer of '66, pundits discerned a growing white resentment of the civil rights movement, government assistance for blacks, and black people in general. The causes of the back-lash were thought to include the rise of Black Power militancy, the shift of emphasis in the civil rights movement from equality of opportunity to equality of outcome, rioting in minority neighborhoods in Baltimore, Chicago, Cleveland, Atlanta, San Francisco, and other cities, and growing rates of minority crime, welfare dependency, and familial disintegration in the nation's urban ghettos.[74] The extent of the white backlash, however, was a matter of speculation. So too was the question of whether it would benefit the Republican Party.

Conservative Republicans and African-Americans continued to have little use for each other. "Negroes have come to equate Racism and Bigotry with Conservatism," black GOP leader Grant Reynolds told an audience of Young Republicans. "On every issue vital to their progress, their welfare, and in some instances their very existence, there are *Conservatives* in vociferous opposition."[75] Reagan made minimal effort to attract black voters, believing them to be irretrievably tied to the Democrats, though he hotly denied insinuations that he was a racist and insisted that he was not trying to cultivate the white backlash.

The Republican Party as a whole, however, remained very much committed to reaching out to minorities. Ray Bliss had driven home to the Republican National Committee that the party didn't need a majority of black votes to win, "but we must have larger percentages than six percent"—Goldwater's percentage of the black vote in 1964.[76] Bliss met with black leaders and appointed Clarence Townes, of the National Negro Republican Assembly, to head a revived Minorities Division within the RNC. He also offered financial and logistical support to Republicans who tried to attract minority votes, including a small number of black GOP candidates.

Charles Percy's Senate race in Illinois illustrated some of the complexities of the Republican effort to bring in minority votes while still attracting the white majority. Percy had long been a moderate Republican favorite. He had risen to national prominence in 1949 as the thirty year-old CEO of the Bell & Howell Corporation, a camera manufacturer, and oversaw its booming growth over the next decade. Unlike many corporate chieftains, he had known real hardship during the Depression, when his family was forced to rely on welfare assistance. President Dwight Eisenhower admired Percy's entrepreneurial drive and clean-living Christian Science faith, and appointed him head of the Presidential Commission on National Goals as preparation for his chairmanship of the 1960 Republican Platform Committee. Percy was the GOP's candidate for the Illinois governor's race in 1964, but lost in part because he was tied to the unpopular Goldwater and neglected to take a forthright stand in favor of civil rights.

Partly as an act of penance, Percy created the New Illinois Committee (NIC) after his defeat. The committee offered a way to put into practice Percy's call for private sector assistance for the ghetto. Funded by Percy and his corporate allies, the NIC conducted literacy classes, posted job openings, offered legal aid and day care, and connected local minority-owned businesses with Republican executives who offered advice and assistance. The NIC's highest-profile operation was its "Call for Action," a telephone help line that inner-city residents could call with complaints about absentee landlords, ineffective city departments, and chiseling merchants. The NIC had no patronage power, but did succeed in helping its minority clientele with issues like trash removal, welfare-check processing, and rat control. It also succeeded in its goal of familiarizing ghetto voters with Percy and giving him credibility as a Republican who cared about inner-city African-Americans and their concerns.[77]

In preparation for his 1966 Senate run, Percy hired a young southern Illinois native named John McClaughry as his research director. McClaughry, a nuclear engineer turned political scientist, was a libertarian who prided himself on being hard to categorize politically, describing himself as "a Jeffersonian distributist, decentralist, Western progressive, Locofoco, Tertium quid Reaganaut."[78] Nonetheless, in the early 1960s he had fought in the trenches for moderate Republican causes and candidates, beginning his political career as an assistant to Vermont Senator Winston Prouty and as an associate editor of *Advance* magazine with Bruce Chapman and George Gilder. McClaughry became deeply involved in the civil rights movement, and was part of the Republican staff group on Capitol Hill that coordinated GOP civil rights efforts with members of Congress. He sought out many African-American leaders and became a friend and admirer of Dr. Nathan Wright Jr., who by 1966 was emerging as a spokesman for the moderate wing of the Black Power movement. One member of the Ripon Society who worked for Percy remembered that "Black Power was a respectable term in John McClaughry's office, even at a time when it terrified more conventional thinkers."[79]

Black Power was a protean phrase, which had polarized Americans since it was coined by Stokely Carmichael, the controversial head of the Student Nonviolent Coordinating Committee. Depending on the speaker and the context, Black Power could mean intellectual rediscovery of Afro-American history and culture, or black economic self-sufficiency, or a bloody-minded rejection of the civil rights movement's faith in integration and nonviolence. McClaughry defined his understanding of Black Power, in a letter he wrote to an African-American associate, as a quest for "*the power* and *the means* to build the kind of community your people want and deserve to have, and the sole right to benefit from the profits that result. You not only should want better homes, but also to own those homes. You not only should want decent food in the supermarket, but ownership of that supermarket. You should want not only a respectful audience from Congress, but the clout to make Congress move."[80]

McClaughry prepared Percy's most significant campaign proposal: the promotion of home ownership by the urban poor as an incentive to move away from permanent welfare dependency. The "New Dawn for Our Cities" plan would address riots and urban decay by mounting a national effort to rebuild declining neighborhoods and permit their inhabitants to become homeowners. It stood in stark contrast to Johnson's strategy for the inner cities, which McClaughry characterized as "urban renewal on a grand scale, bulldozing entire neighborhoods, and using big contractors and thousands of unionized construction workers to put up new buildings." The Percy strategy, by contrast, aimed "to find neighborhoods that had some prospects, if everybody worked together, and rehabilitate them from the ground up."[81] The model was the Bicentennial Civic Improvement Corporation of St. Louis, where residents in the shadows of the ghastly Pruitt-Igoe public housing complex worked with local institutions, including the gas company and the Catholic church, to renew their neighborhood. The strategy relied on a mix of public and private programs combined with local leadership to create jobs, offer job training, improve public education and municipal services, and encourage mutual self-help efforts. It envisioned using small-scale, minority-owned contractors to rehabilitate the existing housing stock. The goal was a critical mass of home ownership by neighborhood residents.[82] The neighborhood strategy would not work in every area and would not provide for new units on the massive scale of Johnson's programs, but it potentially had more to offer black urban areas like Chicago's South Side, which was home to most of the minority voters Percy sought to attract.

The South Side made up most of Illinois' First Congressional District, which had been gerrymandered to include a majority of Chicago's African-Americans. The district had been represented since 1943 by William L. Dawson, a former Republican who had shifted to the Democrats along with most of Chicago's black voters during the New Deal as Chicago became a one-party city. Dawson became in effect the lifetime boss of black Chicago, first as a cog in the Kelly-Nash machine, then as part of Mayor Richard Daley's operation. But because the Democratic vote of the First District was never in doubt, the low-level patronage that Dawson gained in exchange for his obedience did little to offset the gathering misery, joblessness, and deterioration of the city's black ghettos—despite Dawson's claim that "I've done more for my people than any man in America."[83] During his long service in Congress, Dawson did not initiate any significant legislation.

He rarely responded to constituent mail, did not issue a congressional newsletter, and didn't even maintain an office in his district. He usually didn't bother to campaign for reelection, which was assured thanks to one-party control augmented by threats to potential rivals, harassment of dissident businesses and landlords, and cash payments to precinct captains. He was widely rumored to be tied into slum housing and policy rackets. When Martin Luther King Jr. brought the civil rights movement north in the mid-1960s to protest against poverty, slums, and residential segregation in Chicago, Dawson and the Daley machine helped to thwart his efforts.

Many of Chicago's black residents, especially the more ambitious among them, had become increasingly unhappy with Dawson, whom they referred to as "the Old Man" and "Super Tom."[84] In 1964, black South Side residents created an idealistic reform organization called the New Breed Committee. By 1966, most of the several hundred members were in their late twenties or early thirties. The group was predominantly college-educated and included a number of returned Vietnam war veterans. The New Breed led protests against substandard housing, education, and employment conditions in the First District. Mayor Daley met with members of the group but dismissed them with a rhetorical question: "If your people are so dissatisfied, why do they vote for me?"[85] In response, the Committee began to move toward political opposition to the Daley machine. In the spring of 1966, Dawson faced a Democratic primary challenge, for the first time in decades, from a New Breed-affiliated activist, social worker Fred Hubbard. Dawson resorted to expedients like offering an all-expenses paid extravaganza at an amusement park to 50,000 of his constituents. One night while Hubbard worked late in his campaign office, he was shot in the shoulder by a never-identified gunman. Even with a skeleton operation, however, Hubbard was able to take 38 percent of the vote.[86] At that point, Percy and McClaughry encouraged New Breed Committee president David R. Reed to run against Dawson as a Republican.

Dave Reed was a twenty-five year-old sales representative with a local power company who also owned and operated a karate school on the South Side. He had attended Drake University on a basketball scholarship, majored in political science, and returned to his native district to raise a family. He was six feet four inches tall, a teetotaler, and was described by one Republican National Committee observer as "a man of unusual intelligence, personal integrity, and levelheadedness. He has a consuming desire to achieve real social, economic, and political progress and evidences no trace of a desire for personal power."[87] Like other members of the New Breed Committee, Reed was an angry dissident Democrat but required considerable persuasion before he would agree to run under the banner of the party that had put forward Barry Goldwater two years earlier.

Percy was able to win him over in large part because he could point to his work with the New Illinois Committee and his vocal support for fair-housing laws.

McClaughry made the case to Reed that the South Side would continue to suffer until genuine political competition posed a challenge to boss rule. Reed was still suspicious of the conservative influence, but was persuaded that "if the Republican Party could learn to translate its high principles into language relevant to people here, in practical terms and in a completely sincere manner, two-party politics could be returned to this island of despair."[88] Or as he said in a campaign speech, "One-party rule means corruption and contempt for the people. Effective two-party rule means competition and concern for the people."[89] Percy temporarily loaned McClaughry to the Reed campaign and provided money to support storefront campaign headquarters and other expenses.

Reed and the New Breed of course were using their new Republican Party affiliation for the resources and possibilities it offered more than they were making any changes to their own beliefs. But the Reed campaign was consistent with efforts under way within the GOP to rehabilitate the party in the eyes of black voters. Moderate and progressive Republicans were trying to translate party principles into programs that could benefit black people and the inner city in a distinctively Republican way, different from Dawson-style patronage or Lyndon Johnson's War on Poverty. And these moderate Republican ideas were largely compatible with the idealistic, grassroots Black Power ethos of the New Breed.

Moderate Republicans generally disliked bigness and bureaucracy, and preferred to devolve power and responsibility as close to the people as was practically possible. This fit nicely with the New Breed's desire for local and responsive leadership, and emancipation from what Reed called "Mayor Daley's plantation."[90] But the preference for decentralization also made allies of Reed and Republicans in criticizing Johnson's War on Poverty. Reed denounced the program before a House Republican task force for not fulfilling its requirement of Maximum Feasible Participation of the poor. Instead Daley ran the program with what Reed called "iron-fisted control," with millions spent on subsidizing "future assistant Democratic precinct workers" and very few poverty funds trickling down to benefit the poor for whom they were intended.[91]

On the same principle of decentralization, Reed opposed busing to remedy racial imbalance in the schools, instead insisting that schools in the black community get the same amounts of government assistance that he proved statistically went to predominantly white schools in Chicago.[92] School decentralization, the breakup of a centralized Board of Education, and the concept of local control of schools were ideas that were gaining traction in John Lindsay's New York City at the same time; they all fit with what were considered to be traditional Republican preferences.[93]

Moderate Republicans tended to favor, where practicable, private sector over government solutions, self-help efforts over welfare, and incremental reform over sweeping change. These too were ideas that Reed and the New Breed found sympathetic. Reed endorsed the moderate Republican idea of a guaranteed minimum income to replace the welfare bureaucracy, an idea that would later find expression as Nixon's Family Assistance Plan. Reed favored welfare reform not only because he opposed welfare's disincentives to work and family stability, but also because Dawson's henchmen used threats of welfare cutoffs to keep the poor in line. Reed and Percy put out joint flyers opposing centralized, high-rise public housing, which destroyed any sense of neighborhood community and allowed criminals to operate with impunity. They proposed that the high-rises be replaced with scatter-site public housing units no more than three stories high. Reed also backed Percy's plan for urban home ownership, and his related proposal that public housing tenants be able to purchase their apartments.[94]

Reed in his turn carried the Republican Party into some strange new territory, particularly when he introduced McClaughry and other Percy assistants to the 3,000-member Blackstone Rangers, Chicago's most powerful and feared black street gang.[95] Reed's work with young people brought him into contact with some of the Rangers. Members of the New Breed approached the gang to try to get them not to harm Reed's workers in the district, particularly white volunteers and people on loan from the Percy campaign. Some members of the New Breed believed that the Rangers could provide access to voters in the housing projects, while others hoped to channel the gang's energies away from violence and into political activism.[96] Reed became a liaison between the gang and the Republicans working for his campaign, which led to meetings with the gang's charismatic kingpin, Jeff Fort, and late-night basketball games with gang members. For a while, McClaughry was optimistic about a possible Republican-Ranger entente. "There is no doubt in my mind at all that Jeff [Fort] could go to City Council or even further, with his ability and magnetic leadership," he wrote to Reed. "If the Rangers get the message, there could really be a peaceful revolution *within people,* as well as within the district."[97] McClaughry recalled later that "The Blackstone Rangers were at war with City Hall and the Democratic power structure, and so were the Republicans, so there was some interest in this group. The Republicans put out a tentative feeler, because if these guys actually voted, or if they intimidated whole neighborhoods into voting, they could be a powerful voting bloc. But this was risky business, since the Rangers were criminals."[98]

In the end, the Republicans decided that the risks of working with the Rangers outweighed the benefits. The Rangers would in fact form a grass-roots political organization and would receive a million-dollar Office of Economic Opportunity grant from the Johnson administration. At the same time, Fort and the Rangers expanded into increasingly ambitious criminal enterprises. Fort's path would take him not to City Hall but to a life sentence in a supermax prison on charges of drug trafficking, murder, and terrorism.[99] But the Blackstone Rangers episode was an example of how Republicans as well as Democrats were grappling with the complexities of the inner cities during the mid-1960s.

The columnists Evans and Novak reported that Chicago's Republican money men had "no interest in developing a Negro political base" and seemed "dismayed and somewhat confused by the Republican variety of black power" on display in Reed's organization.[100] But the Republican National Committee conducted a political workshop in the district on Reed's behalf and sponsored a fundraiser for him on Capitol Hill. Richard Nixon gave a speech for Reed in Chicago, and Percy made frequent campaign appearances in the ghetto with Reed at his side. Percy also used similar themes in his pamphlets distributed to First District voters, one of which asked: "Had enough? Tired of empty promises? Tired of One Party Domination? Tired of being taken for granted?"[101] The *Chicago Sun-Times* endorsed Reed alongside a moderate Republican from the North Shore, resulting in what would later seem the improbable headline: "For Reed and Rumsfeld."[102]

The highest-profile black candidate for higher office in 1966 was another Republican, Massachusetts' Edward W. Brooke, who was seeking to become the first African-American elected to the U.S. Senate by popular vote. Unlike Reed's electoral effort, race was a minor theme in Brooke's campaign, though an inescapable element in his biography. Brooke had grown up in Washington, D.C. at a time when the nation's capital was still highly segregated. He attended all-black schools, graduated from Howard University, fought in Italy with a segregated infantry unit in World War II, and returned to the States to earn a law degree from Boston University. Entering state politics in Massachusetts in the 1950s, Brooke ran as a Republican because of his family tradition, and because he admired the Republican virtues of duty, self-help, thrift, and free enterprise. He distrusted big government and agreed with Lincoln that "government should do for the people only that which they cannot do for themselves."[103] While the Massachusetts Democratic Party was corrupt and mean-spirited, launching McCarthyite attacks on Harvard and resisting antidiscrimination laws, the state's moderate-dominated Republican Party upheld civil rights and civil liberties. And while the Democrats were largely controlled by Irish-Americans who neglected blacks, the Republican Party had realized that it needed to expand beyond its traditional base of upper-class WASPs and had assembled diverse tickets including "swamp Yankees" (from the hinterlands beyond Boston), Irish, Italians, Jews, and African-Americans.

Brooke worked his way up the political ranks, losing several races for state office before winning election as Massachusetts attorney general in 1962. He had to overcome covert and dirty Democratic efforts to play the race card, which included sending a car "filled with flamboyantly dressed, half drunk, cursing blacks into fashionable suburbs, boisterously inquiring about houses for sale. They loudly and obscenely told realtors that they'd been sent to find a suitable house for Ed Brooke, the next attorney general."[104] His victory made him the nation's highest African-American elected official. Brooke blazed the trail for future generations of black candidates, and began to get calls from minorities around the country who were thinking of running for public office.[105] He became a media magnet and valuable political property for Republican Party moderates, who tapped him to deliver the nominating speech for William Scranton at the 1964 GOP national convention. Brooke was an existential refutation of the Goldwater campaign's anti-civil rights strategy, and he refused to endorse the conservative presidential nominee. While he believed that his stand against Goldwater "haunted me for the rest of my political career," in his reelection campaign he amassed the largest plurality achieved by any Republican nationwide in 1964.[106] Brooke ruffled some feathers in the Massachusetts GOP when, after only three years in office, he announced that he would campaign to succeed retiring Senator Leverett Saltonstall in the 1966 elections, bypassing more senior and established party figures. But he was among the strongest vote-getters in the party, and the election in which Brooke would oppose Democratic nominee Endicott "Chub" Peabody—the grandson of slaves running against the grandson of the founding headmaster of the Groton School—would be an irresistible national story.

Brooke sympathized with the civil rights movement but did not want to be a civil rights leader, or to be limited or defined by his race. Moderation as he conceived it was about understanding different points of view. Political necessity as well as conviction required him to take a broad and inclusive approach as a Republican in overwhelmingly Democratic Massachusetts, a Protestant in a predominantly Catholic region, and a black candidate in a state where blacks comprised only some two percent of the electorate. He ran on his record as a vigorous prosecutor of organized crime and a tribune of anti-corruption who had indicted high government officials, including the state chief of police and the speaker of the House of Representatives. He also upheld the ideal of racial neutralism, ruling against the black parents who proposed a boycott to protest racial segregation in Boston's public schools, which led some angry activists to insult him as an "Uncle Tom."[107] He believed that blacks should not allow themselves to be taken for granted by the Democrats, and that minority groups "must win allies, not conquer adversaries."[108]

Brooke was far ahead of his time in envisioning a post-racial America. He lamented that "Like a life form trapped in amber, I was forever categorized in terms of race."[109] He wanted to prove that an African-American could impartially represent people of all races, and that "white voters would vote for qualified Negro candidates, just as Negroes had voted for qualified white candidates."[110] At a time of Black Power separatism and rising black-white antagonism, Brooke associated the Republicans with a more hopeful vision of race relations. His candidacy implied that equal opportunity for blacks was possible both within the GOP and under the American system, and his victory would suggest that the majority of voters were fair-minded despite all the talk of white backlash. It didn't hurt, of course, that Brooke was extremely attractive in a way that was not threatening to white people: blue-eyed, mocha-skinned, with high cheekbones suggesting his partial Cherokee ancestry. But for those who believed that African-American progress would come only through angry and uncompromising protest, Brooke was literally and figuratively "not black enough."

In place of radical rhetoric, Brooke offered a bold and progressive alternative to Lyndon Johnson's War on Poverty, which would benefit lower-income Americans of all races. Brooke's proposals reflected the thinking of the Ripon Society, whose president Brooke hired as his first research director and whose members produced white papers and statements for the campaign.[111] Brooke called for the construction of affordable housing, an increase in the minimum wage, the extension of Medicare to children, and massive investment in subpar urban schools. He attacked welfare, arguing that "If you give a man a handout you establish a chain of dependence and lack of self-respect that won't be broken easily."[112] He claimed that while the Democrats benefited from keeping impoverished minorities in a perpetual state of dependence, Republicans sought to improve their skills, ambitions, aspirations, and self-respect.

Brooke endorsed the Ripon Society's proposal for a negative income tax: the replacement of welfare with a guaranteed annual minimum income for all Americans below the poverty line, combined with various incentives to encourage the poor to seek employment. While the rebate from the government would be cut if the family breadwinner earned a raise or found a better-paying job, low-income workers would still have an earning incentive that was lacking in then-current welfare arrangements. As matters stood, when welfare recipients took a part-time or seasonal job, their benefits were correspondingly reduced, making them subject in effect to a 100 percent marginal tax rate. The negative income tax would, in Ripon's view, help the poor while avoiding the undesirable social side effects of welfare. It would create incentives to work where welfare destroyed them, helping the poor to help themselves. It would overthrow the philosophy of paternalism encouraged by the welfare bureaucracy and end the demeaning policing of welfare recipients' lives, which at that point still entailed midnight raids to find whether female recipients were living with husbands or boyfriends. It would eliminate inequitable differences in standards and programs from state to state. It would break up the urban political machines that held welfare recipients in check, such as William Dawson's outfit in Chicago. And it would give expression to the Republican belief that individuals usually make more efficient economic decisions than government agencies. By eliminating most of the welfare bureaucracy, the negative income tax would save money as well as reducing federal intervention in the economy.

The negative income tax reflected the conservatism of one of its original proponents, Milton Friedman, who believed that such a program would "help people as people, not as members of particular occupational groups or age groups or wage-rate groups or labor organizations or industries."[113] At the same time, the proposal was consistent with liberal beliefs that a minimum income would give poor people sufficient means to resist the temptations of crime, and that working people wouldn't resent the idea of nonworking people getting "something for nothing." Ripon argued that poverty in America was largely "an inherited malady" rather than a result of individual choices, and that "Society must accept the responsibility of assisting those whose major reason for not finding a job is the accident of their birth and upbringing."[114]

Brooke's progressivism provoked the expected response from the right. A conservative youth group, the Massachusetts Committee to Preserve the Two-Party System, picketed his speeches. J. Alan McKay, vice president of Young Americans for Freedom, challenged him at the Massachusetts GOP's preprimary convention. Brooke disposed of the conservative handily, in a 1,485 to 215 vote, and paid little heed to right-wing criticism of his positions on social issues. Nonetheless, Brooke stepped gingerly around the issue of Vietnam. With the assistance of Harvard professor Henry Kissinger, he made an amorphous critique of the political conduct of the war while supporting the principle of defending South Vietnam against Communist incursion.[115]

One of the only candidates, Republican or Democrat, who dissented from the Vietnam consensus was Oregon's GOP Senate nominee, two-term

Governor Mark Hatfield, and his criticism of the war was widely believed to have put his candidacy in jeopardy. Hatfield was one of the most openly religious men in American politics at that time, but unlike most other evangelical Baptists, his faith led him toward a generally progressive philosophy. During his Navy service in World War II, he had been among the first Americans to visit Hiroshima after the atomic bombing, and the scenes of devastation that he witnessed profoundly affected his political outlook. Shortly afterward he visited what would later become Vietnam, and was dismayed by the racism and neglect of the French colonial regime. Beginning in the Kennedy administration, he was among the earliest critics of the U.S. intervention in South Vietnam, which seemed to him to be simply picking up where the French left off. He saw the Vietnam conflict as a civil war in which nationalism rather than Communism was the key factor. He could see no clearly defined objectives in the administration's war effort, and doubted that the United States could "win" in any meaningful sense. At the National Governors' Conferences in 1965 and 1966, he stood alone in refusing to endorse Johnson's Vietnam policy. The American bombing of North Vietnam struck him as especially immoral. "Terroristic or indiscriminate bombing must involve the deaths of non-combatant men, women, and children and merits the general condemnation of humanity," he insisted. "It cannot be justified as an instrument for the fulfillment of United States foreign policy."[116]

Most of Hatfield's fellow governors believed that he was committing political suicide by opposing the Vietnam intervention. Hatfield was aware that 76 percent of Oregonians supported the war, but maintained that "Modifying my convictions just wasn't possible."[117] Offsetting his unpopular stand on Vietnam were his accomplishments as governor, including an ambitious effort to attract new industry, foster high-tech businesses in the state's so-called Silicon Forest, promote exports, and expand trade with Asia. During his tenure, Oregon's per capita income had risen from the lowest of the states on the Pacific coast to the highest, while unemployment all but disappeared. Hatfield was a hero to management, yet also was one of the few Republicans endorsed by the AFL-CIO. While progressive Republicans admired his leadership on issues of education, civil rights, and welfare, conservatives liked him personally—he exuded "an aura of old-fashioned goodness as palpable as pine soap," according to writer Louise Sweeney—and respected his party loyalty.[118] In 1964, Hatfield had achieved the rare distinction of becoming the first keynote speaker to be booed at a Republican national convention, when he condemned the Birch Society and other extremist groups. Nonetheless, he devoted unstinting efforts to Goldwater and the rest of the GOP ticket in the fall elections. As Goldwater attested, "Hatfield is a man Republicans can buy . . . He didn't agree with the platform completely, but, by God, he got out and worked."[119] Hatfield's campaign managers hoped that his positive image and achievements would outweigh his stubborn refusal to bend on Vietnam.

Election Day 1966 began especially early in Chicago. Dave Reed and Tom Roeser, one of Charles Percy's assistants, drove around the South Side hours before the polls opened at six A.M. Roeser remembered looking through the storefront windows of the polling places to see William Dawson's Democratic precinct captains "standing at the machines before opening of the polls, casting votes repeatedly with the curtains flying open and flying shut over and over and over again."[120] John McClaughry, serving as a poll watcher in a predominantly African-American ward, was appalled to see Democratic poll watchers accompanying voters into the booths to "help" them fill out their ballots properly, a practice known in Chicago as "four-legged voting." When he protested, police arrived to throw him out. "The voting was so fraudulent that it was comical," he recalled.[121] A member of Reed's New Breed Committee was arrested on election day, held until the election was over, then released without being charged.[122] When a genuinely outraged Percy went over to Dawson's headquarters to complain about the rampant vote fraud, the octogenarian congressman placidly accused the Republican senatorial candidate of grandstanding in order to show the suburbs that "you can take care of us thieves."[123] Reed probably would not have won in a fair election, but Dawson's machine ensured that he lost resoundingly.

For most Republican candidates, however, the elections brought many happy returns. Percy defeated his former economics professor, the veteran Senator Paul Douglas, immediately provoking speculation about his possibilities as a dark-horse candidate for the 1968 presidential race. Democrats claimed that Percy, notwithstanding his numerous campaign appearances in the ghetto alongside Dave Reed and his vociferous support for human rights, had benefited from the white backlash.[124] If so, he went about cultivating it in a most peculiar way. A contemporary analysis of election returns suggested that Percy won a popular victory that cut across party and ethnic lines, and compared to his 1964 gubernatorial race had made greater gains in the black wards of Chicago than in the city as a whole.[125] His campaign manager believed that the most important issues working in Percy's favor included public unease over Vietnam (Douglas was a hardline hawk), inflation, Democratic domination of Washington, and the age difference between forty-seven year-old Percy and seventy-four year-old Douglas.[126] Percy had also received an outpouring of public sympathy after the bizarre, never-solved murder of his young daughter Valerie.

In Massachusetts, Ed Brooke made history as the first African-American elected senator by the popular vote of an overwhelmingly white electorate. Though Brooke had slipped in the polls against his Democratic opponent after several racial riots that summer, he ended up with a convincing 61 percent of the vote.[127] Ronald Reagan wrote to congratulate him on what he considered to be "a victory not only over bigotry but also for all of us Americans who believe that under our system a man can rise as far as his talents and abilities will take him. Your victory does more than any other this year to re-establish the Republican Party in the minds of the people as a party of all the people."[128]

Brooke's victory suggested that talk of the white backlash, and its identification with the Republican Party, was overblown. So too did Howard Baker's victory in the Tennessee senatorial race. Many observers viewed Baker as a conservative, and he did advocate some conservative measures such as his father-in-law Everett Dirksen's school prayer amendment. Baker considered himself a moderate, and overcame a more conservative opponent to win the Republican nomination. His moderate identification stemmed from his repudiation of the Birch Society, his advocacy of positive Republican solutions to social problems, his championing of federal revenue sharing and other decentralizing measures, and above all his vigorous campaign for African-American support. Baker opened headquarters in the black areas of the state's major cities, hired black assistants, announced his support of the principle of open housing, and encouraged African-Americans to resist being taken for granted by any party.[129] Baker won some 15 to 20 percent of the black vote—up from virtually nothing in his 1964 race—and defeated his Democratic opponent by nearly 100,000 votes, becoming Tennessee's first popularly elected Republican senator.[130] His victory suggested that moderate Republicans could take the South away from the Democrats without resorting to segregationist appeals.

The GOP captured three Democratic seats and retained all of their own, improving the Senate ratio to a still-lopsided margin of 64 Democrats to 36 Republicans. With Mark Hatfield eking out a narrow victory in Oregon and Clifford Hansen winning the Wyoming senatorial election, the Republicans sent five new senators to Washington in the 1966 elections, including two progressives (Brooke and Hatfield) and two moderates (Percy and Baker). The Ripon Society enthused that the election had brought "the brightest single infusion of Republican talent into the United States Senate in half a century."[131] Incumbent Senate moderates such as New Jersey's Clifford Case and Maine's Margaret Chase Smith in Maine were returned with unexpectedly large margins, while right-wing campaigns failed in New Hampshire, Montana, and Alabama. Even victorious conservatives such as

Paul Laxalt of Nevada and John Tower of Texas won by de-emphasizing their right-wing views and appealing to moderates and independents.

Of course, conservatives rejoiced that Ronald Reagan triumphed in the California gubernatorial election by a million-vote margin, thereby succeeding Goldwater as the *de facto* leader and presidential hopeful of the conservative movement. Historians such as Matthew Dallek have professed to see the 1966 elections as "the decisive turning point in American politics," largely because Reagan won and in so doing taught conservatives "how to push the right buttons on key issues, from race and riots to war and crime."[132] At the time, however, moderates had become increasingly comfortable with Reagan, whose positions in the election were for the most part reassuringly non-ideological. Dwight Eisenhower wrote to an associate that he had corresponded with Reagan and had several "satisfying" conversations with him over the previous year, and "I have come to the conclusion that he is *not* the 'darling of the far right.' He seems to me to represent a common sense and progressive philosophy of government and an individual's relationship to his government. This I believe in spite of the fact that in the past he has made a few statements that seem to imply that he was somewhat more reactionary than Mark Hanna."[133] Reagan went so far as to identify himself with the California progressive tradition going back to Hiram Johnson, and expressed "great pride" in the years when the state was governed by Republican progressives Earl Warren and Goodwin Knight.[134]

Reagan even tried to bury the hatchet with progressive Republican Senator Thomas Kuchel. Reagan swore to Kuchel's friend John McCone that he had not actively campaigned against the senator in past party primaries and that he had not participated in "the despicable acts to blacken his name." Reagan maintained that he had arrived at an acceptable position on the Birch question, and believed that he and Kuchel could find common ground on issues including conservation, since "I am an outdoorsman and bleed a little whenever a highway cuts through any of our scenery."[135] Kuchel obdurately refused to endorse Reagan, however. McCone lamented to Eisenhower that he had believed that Ike's unity pleas to Kuchel, "along with Mr. Reagan's moderate statements and some violent arm twisting on my part, would bring Tommy around; however, in the final analysis, I failed."[136] Still, Reagan had succeeded in demonstrating his inclusive spirit and magnanimous leadership to moderates like Eisenhower and McCone.

Reagan also demonstrated that a key to his success was his rare ability to appeal to moderate and even progressive voters while retaining the trust of his conservative base. Although right-wing organizations such as Young Americans for Freedom furiously attempted to purge moderates, like Pennsylvania's Richard Schweiker, who did not support right-to-work laws, they worshipped Reagan despite his unequivocal opposition to such laws.

Indeed, Reagan played up his six terms as president of the Screen Actors Guild and boasted that "I also was a leader of our Guild in the fight in 1958 against the right-to-work bill. I am still opposed to right-to-work."[137] Conservative groups gave Reagan a pass on what they considered impermissible heresy for moderates. This allowed his campaign managers to create a Labor for Reagan Committee touting his success as a strike leader and urging workers to "Vote for a Card Carrying Union Man."[138] Union members who were persuaded that Reagan was not out to "bust the union" gave him a hearing, despite a huge AFL-CIO effort against him, and many liked what he was saying about lower taxes and less intrusive government.[139] California party chairman Caspar Weinberger determined that Reagan had received more than 40 percent of union labor votes and almost half of the votes of union men's wives because Reagan successfully appealed to them "as people who had family responsibilities."[140]

Moderates who continued to distrust Reagan were heartened by the fact that he was not the highest vote-getter in the California election. That honor was reserved for the Republican candidate for lieutenant governor, Robert H. Finch, a pragmatic moderate who outpolled Reagan by some 230,000 votes and compiled the greatest popular margin since Earl Warren's 1950 gubernatorial victory. Finch was an experienced politician and one of Nixon's closest friends. He had managed Nixon's 1960 presidential race and George Murphy's 1964 senatorial race. An intelligent, workaholic, hard-driving former Marine, his only eccentricity was a penchant for wearing electric blue-green suits. Finch echoed the familiar moderate refrain on the need to take positive action against societal problems, but attracted conservatives with his message that solutions would emerge not so much from the federal government as from the private sector and "the world of responsible individuals voluntarily assuming the mantle of social participation."[141]

For Republicans who wanted to work for the party yet didn't want to get caught in the battles between moderates and conservatives, involvement in the Finch campaign provided what one party member called "the greatest air raid shelter in the state."[142] Finch's popular acclaim proved something of a drawback for his long-term prospects in California politics, since many in the Reagan camp, including Nancy Reagan, felt that his superior margins outshone the man atop the ticket. Reagan himself acquired a sort of resentful respect for his running mate; one of Reagan's advisors remembered that "the only way you could get his attention on political matters was to start off the conversation with, 'Let me tell you what Bob Finch is up to.'"[143]

Reagan's victory aside, moderates cheered a bumper crop of Republican victories in the governors' races around the country, which boosted the

Republican number of governorships to twenty-five. Nelson Rockefeller upset pollsters' predictions to win a come-from-behind victory in New York, thereby becoming the nation's senior governor. He achieved his comeback largely through massive expenditures on television advertising, which at that point was still a relatively new form of campaigning. He retained his White House possibilities along with his office, though he disingenuously proclaimed that he would not be a candidate in the 1968 presidential race. New York Mayor John Lindsay was conspicuous by his absence in Rockefeller's campaign, an early indication of the feud developing between the two progressives. Massachusetts' John Volpe and Rhode Island's John Chafee, both promising young moderates, won impressive victories to become second-term governors, as did Michigan's George Romney, who boosted his presidential chances by pulling Robert Griffin to victory in the state's Senatorial race along with five new moderate GOP congressmen.

Moderates also applauded gubernatorial winners such as John Love in Colorado and Raymond Shafer (a Scranton protégé) in Pennsylvania. Winthrop Rockefeller, Nelson's younger brother, defeated a segregationist Democrat to take the governorship of Arkansas. The winner of the Nebraska governor's race was Norbert Tiemann, the most progressive Republican to hold office in that conservative-dominated state since the maverick Senator George Norris. In Maryland, Spiro Agnew beat Democrat George P. Mahoney, whose campaign was based on his opposition to open-housing laws, summarized by the slogan "Your House Is Your Castle—Protect It!" Despite his later reputation as a hero of the right, in 1966 Agnew styled himself a progressive. He called for a modernized state government and increased funding for education, and promised the Ripon Society that if elected "I shall attempt to make Maryland a showcase of what progressive Republicanism can do to cope with the problems that are facing all states floundering with the results of significant population and social changes."[144] Agnew called the civil rights movement "one of the greatest moral issues of our times," and won an astonishing 70 percent of the black vote.[145]

Republicans enjoyed a forty-seven seat pickup in the House, improving their position to 187 seats against the Democrats' 248. Both conservatives and moderates claimed victory in the House gains. Conservatives reveled in the reelection of former Young Republicans leader John Ashbrook and the election of Buz Lukens in Ohio, while moderates welcomed the victories of George H. W. Bush in Texas and William Steiger in Wisconsin. Conservative groups like the ACU and moderate-progressive groups like the Ripon Society and Republicans for Progress endorsed many of the same Republican candidates, which suggested that most candidates were taking an eclectic approach and avoiding extremes of

Goldwater conservatism or Rockefeller progressivism. Both the ACU and Ripon welcomed the victories of hardline Democratic segregationists in Congressional races in the South, although for radically different reasons: the ACU hoped that the Democrats would combine with Republicans to revive the old "conservative coalition," while Ripon believed that the results demonstrated that Southern Republicans could not "out-seg" the Democrats and would have to pursue the racially inclusive approaches of winning candidates like Agnew and Winthrop Rockefeller.[146]

One of the election's biggest winners was RNC chairman Ray Bliss, who claimed vindication for his even-handed approach toward the party's factions. Republicans had vastly improved their performance since the 1964 debacle in winning a greater share of urban voters, minority voters, and labor voters. Bliss successfully squashed extremist-related controversies such as the Rat Fink scandal, and created the "Opportunities Unlimited" program as a way of reaching out to young people while bypassing the dysfunctional Young Republicans.[147] Rhode Island Governor John Chafee believed that Bliss' approach accelerated the breakup of the Democrats' New Deal coalition: "the American voter is becoming increasingly independent. No longer can he be led down the path by either political party. He'll vote for the man he chooses and isn't going to be guided by ethnic, religious or other considerations such as the AFL-CIO or anybody else."[148]

Another winner in 1966 was Richard Nixon, who had ecumenically supported conservatives, moderates, and progressives alike. He brought in money and publicity for the campaigns he visited, and—surprisingly for a man with a reputation as a two-time political loser—seemed to bestow a tangible aura of success upon the candidates he supported. The *New York Times'* Warren Weaver calculated that GOP House candidates for whom Nixon did not campaign had only a 45 percent chance of winning, while those who shared the platform with Nixon stood a 67 percent chance. "It is hard to knock a coach who raises the team average that much," Weaver concluded.[149] Nixon preached not only the catechism of Republican unity but a gospel around which a majority of the faithful could rally. Despite the well-known slipperiness of his views, he emphatically declared that the GOP must not attempt to compete with Southern Democrats for "the fool's gold of racist votes." Republicans had to repudiate both black and white racism; Nixon stingingly described George Wallace as "the Stokely Carmichael of the South."[150] Above all, the GOP had to offer a positive alternative to the Great Society, in the form of what Nixon and other Republicans were beginning to call the New Federalism.

The most eloquent and even poetic description of the New Federalism came from the Ripon Society's Lee Huebner, Nixon's once and future employee. Huebner editorialized that the ever-increasing government

centralization of the Great Society was not only burdensome and inefficient, it was coming to feel empty, "rich in statistics of progress but devoid
of the satisfactions of meaningful public action." If all the political initiative
continued to flow from Washington to the rest of the country, rather than in
the other direction, the need to compromise and persuade would atrophy
as people of opposing views would abandon "conversation with each other
in favor of shrill, extortionist harangues directed toward the center of national power." The Democrats might build a society that was "merely large,
rich and egalitarian," but moderate Republicans could create one that was
also "creative, self-respecting and just." The New Federalism would mean
"the involvement of citizens in political activity on a scale never seen before.
It means the infusion of social debate into the lowest levels of government,
into business corporations, into school systems, mental institutions, mass
media, prisons, slums, into problems of housing design, transportation,
conservation, and leisure time. It means the development of new techniques for democratic participation, new safeguards for individual rights,
and new processes for correcting bureaucratic abuse. It means that politics
must become more than a spectator sport."[151]

The struggles between moderate and conservative activists would continue. Nonetheless, the Ripon Society spoke for a majority of the GOP in
declaring that after the 1966 elections, "Republicans across the country
share a new sense of excitement and optimism for the party's future. Once
again it is 'fun' to be a Republican."[152] The party enjoyed a degree of unity,
moderate orientation, and optimism about the future that would have
seemed impossible to imagine after the disastrous elections of only two
years earlier.

CHAPTER 7

ᴄᴡᴈ

The Best Lack All Conviction

Moderation's Zenith and George Romney's Rise and Fall, 1967

For Bruce Chapman and George Gilder, the mid-1960s were years of reevaluation. The two young men had been in their early twenties when *Advance* magazine, their mutual creation and the leading progressive Republican publication of its time, went bust in 1964. They spent the next several years continuing to work for the causes and candidates they had championed at *Advance*. From their standpoint, however, the struggles between moderates and conservatives no longer burned with the intensity and animosity of the first half of the decade, when Goldwater conservatives and the extreme right were seizing power within the GOP. Their perceptions mirrored those of many other Republican moderates, who found that some of the divisions within the party no longer cut as deeply, and also found themselves drawing closer to many conservatives in response to the turmoil and dislocations of the 1960s. The conservatives no longer appeared as threatening because moderation apparently had been restored as the dominant force in the Republican coalition. The moderates had the confidence, the candidates, and the intellectual élan. In hindsight, it was the high tide of moderate fortunes in the post-Eisenhower GOP.

After *Advance*'s collapse, Gilder worked as a speechwriter for Nelson Rockefeller before taking a junior fellowship at the Council on Foreign Relations. He moved to New York's East Village, where he began dabbling in bohemianism: sleeping during the day, writing into the small hours in the Slugs jazz club and, in the first blush of the sexual revolution of the 1960s, obsessively pursuing women. Gilder later looked back with disdain on his younger self in those years as "a typical 20th century blade, a secular, liberal, priapic, poseur poetic, guilt ridden Wasp, infatuated with blacks in jazz and 'soul' and blues, sweating to suck up their swashbuckling manhood, sure that the world's greatest writers were Norman Mailer and Joan Didion and Robert Lowell . . ."[1] He retained certain Beats-style influences in his prose, particularly a tendency toward ecstatic run-on sentences. At the same time, his work as an associate editor at the anti-Communist left magazine *The New Leader* moved him rightward by exposing him to the first generation of neoconservatives: the Democratic liberals—many of them former Marxists—who were reconsidering the limits of liberalism and government planning amid the social dislocations of the 1960s and the overreach of the Great Society. Gilder was particularly influenced by Daniel Patrick Moynihan's diagnosis of welfare's pernicious effects on black family stability and Theodore Draper's dissection of Fidel Castro's ruthless regime, at a time when many young intellectuals romantically idealized the Cuban revolution.

Gilder and Chapman continued their writing partnership, co-authoring *The Party That Lost Its Head*, one of the best-informed analyses of the GOP's seizure by the right and the resulting disastrous election of 1964. They wrote most of the book months before the election, certain that Goldwater was going to lose. Its publication was delayed until 1966 after Gilder characteristically lost half of the manuscript.[2] Chapman and Gilder damned the short-sighted zealotry of the Goldwater forces, but they had come to realize that the different wings of the party would have to reach some kind of rapprochement. They argued that it was impossible and undesirable for moderates to try to "transform the party into a vehicle of centralist liberalism." Rather, they believed, "the objective of the progressive Republican should be to transform the Republican party into a responsible and effective conservative party and thus unify it."[3]

William F. Buckley Jr. disagreed with Chapman and Gilder about many things, but as Buckley entered his forties and continued to move away from his youthful revolutionary stance, the notion of a "responsible and effective conservative" GOP seemed more in line with his own outlook. He was also on the lookout for talented young writers on the Republican side, even if he didn't agree with them, and *The Party That Lost Its Head* impressed him as "a scorching, and readable, denunciation" of the Goldwater movement. So, only a few months after the book appeared, Buckley agreed to cooperate with a profile Gilder was writing about him for *Playboy* magazine. Buckley remembered that the twenty-seven year-old freelancer always seemed "slightly unfocused, dressed as if on his way to graduate school, shirt collar footloose, briefcase teeming with journalism and with a paperback classic or two."[4] Gilder's wayward appearance belied a sharp mind and talented pen. Because he worked at an agonizingly slow pace, he interviewed the conservative writer and budding television star a dozen times over the following three months, both at the New York offices of *National Review* and at Buckley's Connecticut home. "Have you found out anything interesting about my sex life?" Buckley teased Gilder during the long and drawn-out process. "Do let me know."[5]

In February 1967, Buckley invited Gilder to accompany him on a trip to Phoenix, and both stayed for a weekend at Barry Goldwater's home. Goldwater shrugged off the withering criticism Gilder had subjected him to in *The Party That Lost Its Head*. He was an affable and magnanimous host, flying Buckley and Gilder over the Grand Canyon in his private plane and allowing the young man to tag along at a dinner with Time-Life publisher Henry Luce and his wife, Clare Boothe Luce. Gilder later told Buckley that he was glad that he hadn't known Goldwater before he wrote his book because it would have blunted most of his critical edge. Gilder's experience, in Buckley's view, reflected how "Goldwater's charm had a way of imposing itself even on those who were organizationally inclined to resist it."[6]

The encounter also showed that at least some individuals in the GOP's moderate and conservative wings were rethinking their old enmities. Goldwater maintained that he would have agreed to the moderates' proposed anti-extremism plank in the '64 platform if it had been properly explained to him at the time. By the mid-1960s, his conservative-dominated home-state GOP organization was having the instructive experience of fending off a far-right takeover attempt mounted by the United Republicans of Arizona, which was largely a front group for the John Birch Society. This gave him a better appreciation of why the moderates had objected to extremist penetration of the GOP.[7] Goldwater had also taken to heart the moderates' criticism that conservatives were mere obstructionists uninterested in addressing the problems of the day. As he mused to Buckley, "The charge has often been leveled at the Republican Party that in the public mind we do not offer positive action, only negative. I feel that there is validity to this."[8] In correspondence with Chapman, however, Goldwater nonetheless insisted that the real effort of unity must come from the liberal side of the party.[9] His head may have told him that the party-splitters were on his right, but in his heart he still believed they were on his left.

Buckley for his part conceded the main argument of Gilder and Chapman that the conservative movement had erred in allowing itself to be tied to the Birch Society as well as to segregationists in the South. Buckley had gradually anathematized the Birchers and denied them legitimacy within the conservative movement, at considerable cost to *National Review*'s bottom line.[10] Chapman felt that "Buckley and his circle eventually understood much of our critique and accepted it. They knew that the extremism on the right was embarrassing to conservatism; they just got that. They bristled when people railed against Goldwater's statement that 'extremism in the defense of liberty is no vice,' but they knew that statement had been a mistake."[11] Buckley also eventually came to regret his position on segregation. As he put it, "I once believed we could evolve our way up from Jim Crow. I was wrong: federal intervention was necessary."[12] Although it took Buckley a long time to reach this view, by the latter half of the 1960s he was backing away from his earlier enthusiasm for George Wallace. Indeed, he had come to despise Wallace's combination of economic populism and thinly veiled racism, delivered with what Buckley called "uncouthness" and "abandoned coarseness." He worried that conservatives would be seduced by the Alabama governor's snarling defiance of the establishment and would prefer him to a Republican in the '68 presidential race. "I do wish I could think of a way of handling the son of a bitch," Buckley wrote to an associate. "That, you know, is what he is."[13]

While Buckley made his name by attacking the moderate establishment, he wanted his movement to be seen as respectable, and this too worked in favor of moderate-conservative rapprochement. As a founder of the conservative movement, Buckley had the latitude to make occasional departures from orthodoxy that boosted his standing with moderates and progressives without jeopardizing his conservative bona fides. The modulation of his philosophy, however, owed more to his struggles against right-wing extremists than to any desire for establishment approval. Buckley's fights against far rightists, and their bulging-eyed accusations that he had betrayed his own principles, had taught him the value of toleration among rational conservatives, and even a certain kind of moderation. "I have recently had to negotiate with my 15 year-old son," he reflected, "concerning whom, I suppose, I possess weapons as definitive as any at the disposal of the nuclearists in the Pentagon. But I found myself— not temporizing, that's the bad word. But calculating, figuring, reckoning. I do believe that it is part of the conservative function to do that. I don't think that to say so is to engage in betrayal. Betrayal, in any case, is a very ugly word, a Birchite word."[14]

In their turn, Gilder and Chapman were reconsidering their opposition to thoughtful conservatives like Buckley and Goldwater. As Chapman later wrote, "To be a 'moderate Republican' after the early Sixties, and not to keep redefining one's views in response to the changing fashions, necessarily meant finding oneself further and further to the right."[15] Both Chapman and Gilder were bothered by the growing radicalism of the antiwar movement, the posturing of Black Power extremists, and what seemed to them the grasping hubris of Great Society planners and the accompanying explosion in government spending and taxation. With conservatives less inclined to defend extremism and Southern segregation, the most serious differences between moderates and conservatives had been removed, or at least downplayed. It thus seemed more plausible for moderates and conservatives to make common cause against shared enemies. A few months after Gilder's visit to Arizona, Chapman reported that he and his writing partner "no longer thought of ourselves as 'Goldwater foes.'"[16]

After the 1964 collapse of *Advance*, Chapman had remained in the Washington, D.C. area and continued to work for Nelson Rockefeller, preparing Platform Committee testimony for the governor's use at the San Francisco convention.[17] He completed his service in the Air Force Reserves and was hired as the youngest editorial writer at the moderate Republicans' leading newspaper, the *New York Herald Tribune*. Before taking up his new job, he spent the summer and fall of 1965 on a world tour of two dozen countries, a trip he later discovered was partly underwritten by a CIA front group that paid his airfare to youth conferences in Berlin and Algiers. Armed with *Herald Tribune* press credentials, Chapman was able to interview government leaders, talk about politics and world affairs with other youngsters, and meet people from many different walks of life. In South Vietnam, he accompanied the *Herald Tribune's* Saigon bureau chief to see at first hand the growing buildup of U.S. troops and war materiel. While only a few months earlier Chapman had been "Airman Last Class" in the Reserves, he remembered, "In Vietnam I had generals and colonels flying me around the country and asking me my opinion. That was quite a shock." Visiting the Pleiku barracks whose shelling had sparked the direct U.S. intervention, he found it disorienting to "go from getting shot at in helicopters during the day to dinners at night that included steaks and ice cream and brandy and cigars, and tiger skins on the wall. . . . It was a strange juxtaposition of experiences."[18]

Upon returning to the States, Chapman joined Gilder in New York and began work at the *Tribune*. In what would prove to be the newspaper's last days, editorialists enjoyed remarkable freedom. Chapman recalled that "though I was sometimes disputed, no one ever instructed me in an editorial stand, let alone censored me, even though my opinions were speaking officially for the paper."[19] He was also given the opportunity to research and write about the military draft, a topic he had begun to take notes on while still in the Air Force Reserves. His interest in the subject traced back to Missouri Representative Tom Curtis' article in *Advance* magazine calling for the draft's abolition.[20] When the *Herald Tribune* was shut down by what would prove to be its fatal strike, Chapman continued to draw a salary from the paper and used the sabbatical opportunity to write a Ripon Society white paper proposing the creation of an all-volunteer military. As the paper grew longer and longer, he realized that he had actually written a book, soon published as *The Wrong Man in Uniform: Our Unfair and Obsolete Draft and How We Can Replace It*. A shorter version of the book appeared in December 1966 in the *Ripon Forum* (the Society's monthly publication) as an article entitled "Politics and Conscription: A Ripon Proposal to Replace the Draft."

Chapman called for eliminating the draft completely, rather than amending it with half-measures such as a lottery or alternative national service, and improving the salary, incentives, and prestige of the military in order to establish a 2.7 million man volunteer army. His proposal was detailed, ambitious, and thoroughly in keeping with Republican preferences for voluntarism and individual choice over coercion and government control. It was also ahead of its time in discerning the high costs of turnover to the military and the gender inequities inherent in proposed alternatives to the draft. Chapman had effectively responded to his own call for Republicans to address social needs through constructive, conservative programs. Richard Rovere, writing in the *New Yorker*, gave a lengthy and respectful critique of Chapman's draft proposal, calling it "a report that is not only bold, partisan, and specific in its recommendations but at the same time uncommonly lucid and vigorous." Rovere found Chapman's moral argument against the draft unpersuasive, since he pointed out that many institutions in a democracy relied upon compulsion—the income tax for example. But he agreed that the draft's sacrifices were unevenly shared, which made it "if not immoral in principle, grossly and indefensibly inequitable in practice." He concurred with Chapman that the country and even the armed services would be better off if the draft were abolished.[21]

Chapman's proposal appealed to a wide political spectrum, ranging from Young Americans for Freedom on the right to the Students for a Democratic Society on the left. Buckley demonstrated his continued receptivity by publishing Chapman's paper in *National Review*. The right tended to support Chapman's proposal because the draft, as the ultimate symbol of government restriction of individual liberty, had long been objectionable to many conservatives; Robert Taft had campaigned for its abolition. Opposition to the draft did not necessarily require opposition to the Vietnam war, which most conservatives still supported. As it happened, though, Chapman had moved from being a Vietnam enthusiast to a skeptic by 1967. "Certain GOP principles are found in both the traditions of Taft and Eisenhower," he wrote to a fellow member of the Ripon Society. "The one that I see as the most important in the present instance is that American involvement in any foreign affair should be proportionate to our engaged national interest (as, for example, Vietnam is not)."[22]

Despite his private reservations about the war, Chapman was temperamentally and politically opposed to the radicalism of antiwar organizations such as Students for a Democratic Society. In the many public discussions of conscription in which he appeared, he represented a moderate position between angry draft card–burners and the likes of General Lewis Hershey, the head of the Selective Service System, whom Chapman debated in an NBC televised event. Chapman recalled that in such debates, "There were always these radical leftists who were just anti-military. . . . And then there were people like Hershey saying that the Selective Service system needed to be defended. My reply to both positions was, 'We don't need a Selective Service system, and we can get rid of the draft, but we have to have a military. Here's how to do it.' They were fighting with each other, and I would sort of skate through the middle."[23] From the standpoint of partisan politics, it was helpful to Chapman that one of the most stubborn defenders of conscription was Democratic Senator Ted Kennedy, who made the demonstrably false claim that an all-volunteer military would be made up entirely of disadvantaged minorities. At one national conference on the draft at which Kennedy appeared, Chapman and Representative Donald Rumsfeld were able to undercut the Massachusetts liberal by persuading the participants to sign a statement supporting consideration of an all-volunteer military. While Congressional Democrats predictably stymied Republican proposals to abolish the draft, Chapman had helped inject another creative and constructive idea into the GOP political bloodstream.

Besides trying to find common ground with conservatives over the draft, Chapman thought about what other perspectives moderates might share with the conservatives they had opposed so vigorously during the *Advance* years. Chapman was intrigued by Ronald Reagan and some of his early free market–oriented proposals as California governor, including Reagan's view that students at the University of California would value their education more highly if it were not absolutely free. Even if most progressives thought Reagan was a scoundrel, Chapman asked a Ripon associate, "must everything he does be wrong? . . . Can we note, as happens to be my opinion, that he's absolutely right in demanding students pay tuition? . . . Are we to encourage East-West détente as an international policy and be hardliners on inter-factional party policy?"[24]

In an unsigned editorial in the *Ripon Forum*, Chapman pointed out that the principal divisive issues of the '64 convention no longer preoccupied Republicans in 1967. While divisions remained on issues such as open housing, affirmative action, and a Southern strategy, these were not so obviously matters of fundamental human rights as the earlier civil rights measures had been. The question of nuclear irresponsibility was not an issue either, although there was a deep division regarding Vietnam between advocates of military intervention versus advocates of détente and negotiations. In domestic affairs, Chapman identified many areas where "wide ranging Republican agreement seems to be developing," including opposition to the conduct and administration of Lyndon Johnson's poverty programs, support for expanding home ownership among the poor, enthusiasm for federal revenue sharing and welfare reform, advocacy of an all-volunteer army, and encouragement of voluntary, "independent sector" efforts to complement or replace government services. In all of these areas, there was both agreement among Republicans and a distinct difference from the programs advocated by the Democrats, who remained attached to Great Society planning efforts despite increasing questions about their effectiveness. Even one of the most progressive House Republicans, Ohio's Charles Whalen, assailed Johnson's domestic programs for their administrative obesity, corruption, inflexibility, and inefficiency. He pointed out that the administration had no way of determining if its efforts were succeeding or not, and that indeed no one knew for certain how many federal domestic programs actually existed.[25]

The real split among Republicans, as Chapman saw it, was not between moderates and conservatives, but between "those who want to use principles to solve public problems and those who do not. The rightist obstructionists and moderate do-nothings are together in the latter camp and their number is legion." The Ripon Society's ideological premises "may not be those of a libertarian-conservative like Milton Friedman, let alone a traditionalist-conservative like William Buckley (and it's time we learned to distinguish the two varieties), but we can at least grant that some intellectuals on the right are thinking."[26]

In retrospect, it was easier to make the case for moderate-conservative reconciliation because many issues that later would prove highly divisive were not so at the time. When Colorado passed a liberalized abortion bill, for example, most of GOP Governor John Love's opposition came from Catholic Democrats. No less a conservative than Reagan would sign the nation's most liberal abortion bill into law in June.[27] Nearly all factions in the party pledged at least token allegiance to the Equal Rights Amendment for women, which had been included in party platforms since 1940. Chapman's view of the Republican situation rested on a belief that "both parties are essentially coalitions," hence "What the [Republican] party needs today is a quest for ideological consensus based on a common search by all segments for new and bold programs."[28] Of course, most conservatives still held that the parties should be sharply divided by ideology. The idea of a coalition or program-based consensus, or even increased respect of each side for the views of the other, was not what they had in mind. But the GOP's decimation in 1964 had forced them to adopt a big-tent approach.

In the wake of the restorative 1966 elections, conservatives conceded that some of the party's most appealing figures and most forceful ideas were on the moderate side.

1967 was the high point of moderate fortunes in the Republican Party in the half-century following Eisenhower's presidency, a moment when it seemed to Chapman that moderates were "in better shape—*up and down the line*—than at any other time" since he had become active in politics.[29] The Ripon Society's Lee Huebner, looking back nostalgically only a year later, recalled that in 1967 "the future seemed to belong to the Republican Party. It had the leaders and the momentum." The big Republican wins in the '66 elections pointed to public impatience with big-government liberalism, inflation, mismanagement and waste in the poverty program, and lack of progress in the Vietnam war. Democrats defended the status quo while the GOP buzzed with powerful ideas. A dynamic group of Republican governors, for whom there were few Democratic equivalents, seemed poised to reach out to new constituencies and win them over. Huebner pointed out that "An unpopular President and his unpopular foreign policy seemed to give Republicans access to the urban voter, the black community, and intellectuals—groups with which it could build a new political coalition which would become the leading force in American politics in the last third of the twentieth century."[30]

Most of the top Republican politicians presented themselves as can-do reformers willing to take on the big problems in society. With the exception of Reagan, the likely Republican candidates for the presidency in 1968 were all moderates or progressives, including Richard Nixon, George Romney, Nelson Rockefeller, Charles Percy, and John Lindsay. Even the dark-horse contenders, favorite sons, and likely vice-presidential candidates were mostly moderates.[31] Connoisseurs of political horseflesh observed that these men made the GOP seem young, intelligent, and attractive. Journalist Mike Royko commented that "The modern Republican party is probably the handsomest political party in American history."[32]

Moderates appeared to be on the rise within the GOP, taking on leadership roles, introducing innovative programs, and winning votes in Congress. William Cowger, a moderate former mayor of Louisville, defeated conservative "Buz" Lukens to become president of the entering Republican class in the House, with moderates Margaret Heckler of Massachusetts and William Steiger of Wisconsin also gaining leadership posts.[33] The Republican Governors Association finally opened its long-planned Washington, D.C. office, which moderates hoped would boost the influence of the predominantly centrist group within the party.[34] Freshman Senator Charles Percy introduced his plan for a National Home Ownership Foundation, aimed at restoring stability to urban minority communities by supporting widespread home ownership and neighborhood revitalization in the ghettos. It became the first bill of "real substance," in the opinion of long-time senator Thruston Morton, to gain unanimous Republican backing in the Senate in half a century.[35]

Morton himself led Senate moderates to victory in the battle to ratify a treaty permitting the United States and Soviet Union to establish consulates on each other's territory for the first time since 1948. In consultation with former president Eisenhower, Morton preempted the opposition of minority leader Everett Dirksen with a powerful speech in favor of the consular treaty, pointing out that Eisenhower had first proposed it and that a lessening of Cold War tensions would be in the United States' long-term best interests.[36] Morton further observed that while his mail was running 100 to one against ratification, "there can be no doubt that this avalanche is largely the result of a carefully planned and well financed 'big lie' operation designed by the paranoids and fear mongers."[37] Over the screeches of the Birch Society and other anti-Communist groups, the Republicans voted 23 to 13 in favor of the treaty, permitting its passage through the Senate by the necessary two-thirds margin.[38]

Despite inevitable conflicts over issues such as the consular treaty, it appeared that better relations might prevail between moderates and conservatives in the GOP. Illinois Congressman Paul Findley, recipient of a 90 percent rating from the conservative group Americans for Constitutional Action, nonetheless chose a Ripon Society audience to become one of the first Republicans to call for establishing diplomatic relations with China.[39] Ripon members, in turn, suggested that they might make fewer attacks on conservative Republicans in the future, conceding that "perhaps the society had been overly caustic at times in its political commentary."[40]

Most remarkably, all factions of the GOP united to deny Phyllis Schlafly the presidency of the National Federation of Republican Women (NFRW) at the organization's June 1967 convention. Schlafly had long been a prominent right-wing activist, best known for her paranoiac 1964 tract *A Choice Not an Echo*, which had promoted Goldwater's candidacy while reviling moderates as Democrats in disguise. She had been elected president of the Illinois Federation of Republican Women in 1960 and a vice president of the NFRW in 1964. Schlafly was a highly polarizing personality. She was a heroine to followers who thrilled to her slashing McCarthyite attacks on alleged Communist infiltration of government and her proto-feminist demand that conservative women have more influence in GOP leadership circles. Moderate and progressive Republicans, of course, considered her to be a dangerous and irresponsible radical. But she made even many conservatives uneasy with her commissar-style rhetoric, her seeming disregard for truth or traditional standards of fair play, and her ties to extremist groups like the John Birch Society. Schlafly provided the model for conservative celebrity-activists for decades to come.

Although conservatives like Buckley and Goldwater had tried to read the Birch Society out of the GOP, throughout the 1960s the grassroots radicals continued their efforts to infiltrate and control local branches of the Republican Party. In Tennessee, for example, *Farm and Ranch* magazine publisher Thomas J. Anderson of Nashville, who was also a national councilman of the Birch Society, led a successful Birch effort in 1966 to take over the Davidson County GOP. A number of county officials resigned in protest, one telling the press that "I am a Republican first, but with this group controlling the party, it is no longer the Republican party."[41] Such reactions didn't bother Anderson, who vowed "I'm for making the Republican party conservative or making it die."[42] Anderson's wife, who had accused none other than Buckley of treason, led a parallel mission to take over the local Women's Republican Club on behalf of Schlafly's candidacy.[43] One of the club's officers reported that Anderson and her followers "arrive in great numbers and can out-scream and out-shout the devil himself. . . . There is no doubt this is a 100% Birch group. These groups are forming all over the country and seeking charters for the purpose of electing Phyllis Schlafly Federation President."[44] When the Birch group failed to take over the Nashville club, they started a rival organization called the Robert Taft Women's Republican Club, a name that provoked a protest from Taft's brother Charles, the head of Republicans for Progress.[45] The Tennessee GOP, led by Senatorial candidate Howard Baker, vowed to resist the radical rightists. The state Federation of Republican Women denied a charter to the Robert Taft Women's Club, and the national Federation rejected its petition appeal. Nonetheless, the group's 100 or so members resolved to attend the NFRW convention, where they hoped to unseat the regular club and vote Schlafly into power.[46]

Schlafly's Birchite support, in addition to her intolerance of moderates and her penchant for controversy, made the GOP leadership unwilling to see her elected president of the women's auxiliary. Republican National Committee chairman Ray Bliss and the potential Republican presidential candidates believed that 1968 would be their year of opportunity. They did not want to allow the media to resurrect the extremist issue or to risk compromising the political effectiveness of the women's group, whose 500,000 volunteers provided the underpinnings of many Republican election campaigns. Longtime Nixon associate and NFRW activist Patricia Reilly Hitt remembered that "there wasn't anyone in the Nixon campaign . . . that wanted to have the problem of Phyllis Schlafly as the National Federation of Republican Women president in a presidential campaign year. No way."[47] George Romney's ally Elly Peterson also took an active role in combating Schlafly's candidacy, partly by recruiting black women to the Michigan GOP women's federation.[48]

The NFRW nominating committee instead proposed Gladys O'Donnell of California for the presidency. O'Donnell, a past president of the California women's federation, had been a famous stunt pilot in the pioneering days of aviation. She was deeply conservative, having been an early supporter of Goldwater in '64 and Reagan in '66, but as a loyal Republican she had protested against the extremist organization Let Freedom Ring after hearing a recorded telephone message calling Eisenhower an "ersatz Communist with the pro-Communist record" and Earl Warren a "pro-Communist toady."[49] True to form, Schlafly claimed that this made O'Donnell a "liberal," and that her candidacy therefore constituted "another attempt by the New York liberals to purge from office those who whole-heartedly supported Senator Barry Goldwater in 1964."[50] She refused to address concerns over Birch Society penetration, maintaining without explanation that the issue was "as phony as a $3 bill."[51] Schlafly announced her opposition candidacy in April 1967.

Schlafly did her best to profess that she was the victim of a liberal purge attempt, but like most of her supporters she was well aware that she faced the united opposition of the entire Republican Party leadership. Indeed, her anti-establishment appeal was one of her most powerful assets. Also to her advantage was the convention's location in Washington, D.C.; though Schlafly complained bitterly about the decision to hold the convention on the East Coast, it worked to her benefit by making it difficult for O'Donnell's California supporters to attend, while large numbers of dedicated Schlafly supporters from the South packed the galleries. Schlafly was also able to gather substantial campaign funds from right-wing supporters such as New Hampshire newspaper publisher William Loeb.[52] Almost all of the other advantages belonged to her opponents, however. The RNC's Ray Bliss reached out to moderate activists like Charles Taft to raise additional money to combat the Schlafly insurgency, and the national committee lent fifteen of its members to staff the convention.[53] O'Donnell's supporters included all of the state federation presidents, most of the state officers, and most of the RNC's national committeewomen. Nelson Rockefeller and other wealthy donors assisted with O'Donnell delegates' transportation, and moderate congressmen such as George H. W. Bush offered them meals and lodging in their homes.[54] While some prominent conservatives such as Strom Thurmond campaigned for Schlafly, National Review declared itself neutral.

For those in the know, the most astonishing aspect of the convention was that the Syndicate—Clif White's conservative machine that had controlled the Young Republicans since the early 1950s—worked against Schlafly. The Syndicate's Pat Hutar, *femme fatale* for a generation of YR moderates, co-chaired O'Donnell's campaign. Bill Timmons, one of White's ablest protégés, advised O'Donnell's forces and oversaw the convention's technical details including scheduling, delegation seating, badge control, and communications. Having perpetrated so many organizational takeovers on behalf of conservatives in years past, the battle-hardened Syndicate veterans were well prepared to resist a takeover attempt from the far right. Convention officials denied credentials to Birch-sponsored delegations lacking official standing, such as the Robert Taft Women's Republican Club, despite their vociferous protests. A professional parliamentarian, without ties to any faction, ruled against right-wing attempts to hijack the convention. Hutar arranged to cut off an attempt to prolong the convention, which might have thinned the ranks of O'Donnell supporters who needed to return to their homes.

While O'Donnell's forces were careful to operate according to Federation rules so as to forestall Schlafly's post-convention legal challenges, both sides engaged in considerable skullduggery, including pass-stealing and locking delegates in their rooms. In Patricia Hitt's recollection, however, the behavior of Schlafly's delegates and supporters at the convention "was the turning point and assured Gladys the victory, because it turned people off so. . . . My God, I saw women fling their shoulder bags and hit other women over the head in the gallery. It was an incredible performance. It just got hysterical. I saw women spit on other women. And these were not young, these were middle-aged women. I'm sure under normal circumstances they would never have behaved that way."[55]

O'Donnell beat Schlafly by a vote of 1,910 to 1,494. O'Donnell told the RNC that the convention's drama made her "agree with Margaret Mead the anthropologist: Women should not be drafted for combat, they are too fierce."[56] Schlafly refused to accept the verdict of the convention and claimed ever after that she had been robbed. After her challenges to the election were rejected, she presented herself as a conservative Joan of Arc put to the torch by the GOP establishment because, as she wrote in an account of her martyrdom, "In Phyllis, they recognized one who could not be neutralized or silenced."[57] She maintained that her defeat proved that "the liberals are not willing for our side to have anything at all—not even the crumb of a non-paid woman's position with practically no power."[58] She began issuing *The Phyllis Schlafly Report* as a monthly newsletter to keep her followers in a continuing state of agitation and aggrievement. The first issue featured doggerel by Schlafly's sixteen year-old son John that set to verse his mother's resentments against O'Donnell's "ignorant dames," while Schlafly encouraged her adherents to perform a "humorous skit" entitled *Kapsule Kangaroo Konvention* ("Lots of fun guaranteed!").[59] Many of Schlafly's followers withdrew from the NFRW and created their own clubs, which formed the nucleus of Schlafly's later crusade against the Equal Rights Amendment.

Most observers considered the NFRW convention outcome to have been a victory for conservatives, since O'Donnell after all was a conservative, although not as far to the right as Schlafly. David Broder, the reporter who paid closest attention to the internal politics of the Young Republicans and the NFRW, thought that the Syndicate's performance at the convention allowed Clif White, *National Review* publisher William Rusher, and Texas Senator John Tower to burnish their reputation for "working diligently to divorce 'responsible conservatism' from the taint of amateurism and emotional extremism that it acquired in the Goldwater campaign," which in turn augmented their likely influence at the 1968 GOP convention.[60] Some right-wingers like former American Conservative Union president Donald Bruce savaged the "self-styled band of conservative 'purists' [who] linked arms with the Rockefeller-Romneyites" to deny Schlafly the victory, but the Syndicate's actions flew under the radar screen of most activists in the conservative movement.[61] On the other hand, Bruce Chapman felt that O'Donnell's election was "with qualifications, a victory for the moderates." First, it kept Schlafly out of power ("a big plus in itself"). Second, experience had shown that "past intra-party elections wherein a conservative is accused by a far-right opponent of being a secret 'liberal' has often had the psychological effect on the conservative—if he or she wins—of making him more moderate *afterwards*. Largely it's an emotional reaction, for the conservative often recognizes for the first time just how real the extremist problem is."[62] Schlafly's attacks did seem to have that effect on O'Donnell, who took increasingly moderate positions during her tenure as NFRW president.

The fact that all of the GOP's factions had cooperated in the NFRW election did not at all mean that moderates, liberals, and conservatives agreed on who the party's presidential nominee should be for 1968. Nixon retained the loyalty of many rank-and-file party leaders for his years of toil on their behalf. Progressives continued to pine for Rockefeller, despite his claim of non-candidacy. Supporters of potential candidates such as Charles Percy and John Lindsay spun scenarios in which their man could ride to the rescue of a divided convention and seize the nomination, just as Wendell Willkie had in 1940. On the right, Ronald Reagan appeared an increasingly plausible candidate. Oregon's governor Tom McCall was a Rockefeller supporter, but he was dazzled by Reagan's arrival at the Republican Governors

Association conference in the summer of 1967 "like a white knight on a charger. It was like an operetta. There's plain old governors and there's Reagan." McCall felt that Reagan was "rising faster as a national figure than any office-holder in either party at any level."[63] At the Young Republicans' national convention in Omaha, Nebraska, where the Syndicate once again crushed its opponents, the YRs demonstrated openly and ardently for Reagan, leading the Ripon Society to speculate that the organization had become "the advance guard of the Reagan presidential candidacy."[64]

Moderates were determined not to repeat the mistake of 1964 by waiting too long to unite behind a candidate, and by far their most likely contender in the wake of the 1966 elections was Michigan Governor George Romney. He seemed the moderates' best bet for any number of reasons. For one thing, he *looked* presidential: broad-shouldered, vigorous, and lantern-jawed. Several reporters pointed out that his sleek, well-tended hair, swept back from his face and graying at the temples, made him appear rather like the American national bird, the bald eagle. He had presidential qualities in abundance: charisma, sincerity, strength of purpose, and an unshakeable sense of moral principles. One of his assistants remembered that Romney "was a hell of a good guy. It's a terrible thing that in our political system the word 'integrity' has become so abused that it barely has any meaning anymore, but Romney had a lot of integrity. He was an honest, straightforward character. It was clear to those working in his campaign that we were to be straight arrows."[65] Alf Landon, the GOP's 1936 presidential nominee, wrote to Romney that "You fit what I think is the growing demand for a new sense of ethics and public and private morality, as a result of the lack of credibility in what Johnson says and does here at home and abroad."[66] This was no small advantage given that one of the other leading Republican candidates was famously nicknamed "Tricky Dick."

Romney had enjoyed a spectacular business career as CEO of the American Motors Corporation, which he had rescued from near-bankruptcy by convincing consumers to purchase smaller and more fuel-efficient cars. He brought his dynamic salesmanship and powers of persuasion to government, starting with his leadership of nonpartisan citizens groups that improved public schools and modernized Michigan's outdated constitution. He ran for governor in 1962 as an independent-minded reformer, defending the individual against the power of Big Labor, Big Industry, and Big Government. He won the 1962 race, and increased his margins of victory in his reelection campaigns in 1964 and 1966, despite his odd-bedfellows opposition of labor union bosses and conservatives in his own party.

Most of Michigan's conservatives grudgingly acknowledged that Romney was the first GOP politician in a decade to break the dominance of the Democratic Party and its powerful labor union allies. Nonetheless, they fought his drive for civil rights laws and a state income tax, which he believed was necessary to achieve a balanced budget. The size of state government grew significantly during Romney's governorship, from $684 million in 1964 to $1.3 billion in 1968. Romney doubled the state education budget during his first five years in office, offered generous social welfare benefits to the poor and unemployed, and increased support for local governments. Thanks to the passage of the income tax and generally prosperous conditions in Michigan, Romney was able to erase the considerable budget deficit he had inherited from his predecessor. He also succeeded in attracting businesses to the state and cutting unemployment to below the national average. Although he'd had a lone-wolf reputation at the start of his political career, Romney proved that his brand of moderate Republicanism had sufficiently broad appeal to elect a slate of GOP candidates in the 1966 Michigan elections, under the motto "The Action Team for the Action State."[67] Republicans under Romney made significant inroads among normally Democratic-leaning groups such as African-Americans, unionized labor, and young people.[68]

Romney's advisors, in pushing him forward for the presidency, made the case that the Michigan governor was a seasoned executive, while "Nixon never ran anything and thus tends to mush around hard decisions, or merely pander to public opinion." They also claimed that Romney was acceptable to all factions of the GOP, while Rockefeller "cannot be nominated without great internal upheaval" and Reagan "is hopelessly extreme right and will be rejected."[69] Many conservatives did not like Romney, and Barry Goldwater continued to resent his non-support in the 1964 election. Still, conservatives found the Midwesterner more acceptable than an Eastern progressive, especially if the alternative was Rockefeller. *National Review* publisher William Rusher appreciated that Romney possessed certain appealing qualities "which make him an unlikely Liberal hero in the long run: an idiosyncratic stubbornness, a noisy religiosity, and a businessman's contempt for politics and politicians."[70] Rusher's Syndicate comrade Clif White even negotiated with Romney's political strategist, former RNC chairman Leonard Hall, over the 200 or so delegates he might deliver to the campaign.[71]

Two weeks after the 1966 election, Romney topped Lyndon Johnson 54 to 46 percent in the Harris poll of presidential preferences; no other Republican even came close.[72] Nelson Rockefeller and former governor William Scranton lined up behind Romney's presidential drive, making it likely that he would enter the GOP convention with the formidable delegate totals of New York, Pennsylvania, and Michigan in his column. Romney assembled some of the best policymaking and speechwriting talent the party had to offer. Rockefeller funded much of the campaign and lent Romney's assistants the use of his research arsenal and the counsel of his foreign policy advisor, Henry Kissinger. (Romney's awed staffers compiled lengthy notes on the Harvard professor's *realpolitik* views, including his hard-boiled aphorism that "The issue in a Vietnamese election is who supervises the fraud, not who can serve the people best."[73]) Bruce Chapman and George Gilder joined the campaign, Chapman as a speechwriter and Gilder as a ghostwriter of a book in which Romney would outline his economic and urban policy. Gilder remained in fine eccentric form, arriving in Lansing in the dead of winter without a coat and loping around outside in frigid temperatures with only a scarf to keep him warm; he explained to Romney's staffers that he had once owned several winter coats but lost them all. Gilder continued his habit of working at night and sleeping all day. The car he left in front of Romney's headquarters acquired so many parking tickets that police issued a warrant for the arrest of its registered owner, David Rockefeller, and dispatched officers to Rockefeller Center in Manhattan to apprehend the miscreant.[74]

Despite Romney's merits as a candidate, his organizational advantages, and his lead in the polls, moderates did not come together in support of his presidential bid even though they were aware of the strategic necessity of backing a single candidate. Some observers blamed internal tensions in Romney's organization for the dissipation of the consensus around his candidacy.[75] Others blamed his uninspiring speaking style, particularly when he appeared with a scene-stealer like Reagan. A Ripon Society member watching Romney at a press conference alongside Reagan noticed that the Michigan governor's inability to "deal with complex issues in a simple manner" meant that he faced "tough and even bitter press grilling," while Reagan enjoyed "a gentlemanly exchange of jokes and pleasantries."[76] Former president Dwight Eisenhower also commented on Romney's tendency to create "doubt and bewilderment" among his audiences.[77] Critics claimed that Romney was unable to grapple with tangled foreign policy issues such as Vietnam, although the same criticism rarely attached to Nixon, who avoided discussing the war except in generalities, or Ronald Reagan, who simplistically called for the United States to "win or get out." Romney's candidacy also suffered from the widespread belief that he was merely a stalking horse for Nelson Rockefeller, despite the New York governor's insistence that "if we moderates want to preserve any chance of nominating a candidate who can win, we'd better stay united behind George Romney."[78]

The rising chorus of criticisms caused Romney to lose ground to Nixon in polls of the party rank and file, while liberals, intellectuals, and Easterners longed for a more exciting and sophisticated nominee such as Rockefeller or Percy.[79] Senator Thruston Morton, convinced that Romney was stumbling, implored former Pennsylvania Governor William Scranton to throw his hat in the ring; Scranton reminded Morton that the moderates needed to avoid the proliferation of candidates that led to disaster in 1964.[80] At the Republican Governors Association conference in the summer of '67, half a dozen moderate governors retreated from their previous support of Romney, while Maryland's governor Spiro Agnew called a news conference at which he all but begged Rockefeller to enter the race.[81] Instead of rallying behind Romney, the moderate governors planned to request that their delegations to the '68 convention remain uncommitted or rally behind favorite-son candidates. Their strategy, such as it was, rested on the forlorn hope that the convention would nominate the candidate most likely to win— presumably a moderate—or "broker" its way to a compromise.

Lee Huebner, the newly elected president of the Ripon Society, had serious doubts about the moderates' approach. At the Young Republicans' convention in Omaha, he had witnessed anew the conservatives' organizational and ideological strengths. The moderates, by contrast, remained the only major factional group in American politics without experienced political organizers, a national mailing list, or a widely circulated publication. Republicans for Progress, the leading fundraising organization for moderate Republicans, had teetered on the verge of insolvency for several years and finally went broke in the fall of 1967.[82] Most moderates, Huebner thought, had been "too busy, too tired, or just plain too moderate" to replicate the conservatives' organizational successes within the GOP. And their pragmatic philosophy "has often meant no philosophy at all. To generate emotion they have often relied on a handsome face or ready smile." While conservatives like Reagan understood how to make winning emotional appeals, the centrist governors failed to appreciate how difficult it was to fire up voters with worthy but abstract qualities such as "a respect for complexity, or open-mindedness, or sound judgment or restraint." If the moderates were to succeed, Huebner believed, they "must somehow inspire men and women to be more than moderate in their commitment."[83] Romney presented the moderate governors with what turned out to be their last opportunity to unite around one of their own, and to build a passionate national movement around a leader and a well-defined program. They let it pass by. Rhode Island Governor John Chafee believed that the moderate governors may simply have been too isolated and egotistical to subordinate their ambitions: "None of these guys wants to be the first one to pick up the telephone."[84]

Unfortunately for Romney's presidential ambitions, much of the criticism he received stemmed from liabilities that he couldn't overcome because they were in the nature of who he was. The most important of these was that he was a devout Mormon. "I am completely the product of the Church of

Jesus Christ of the Latter-Day Saints," Romney told reporters.[85] He was born in 1907 in a Mormon settlement near Chihuahua, Mexico, where his grandfathers had fled after federal agents chased them out of the Utah Territory for refusing to abandon their polygamous ways. Romney was one of 207 grandchildren, and by the time he became Michigan's governor, he calculated that he had 237 living first cousins and some 2,000 to 3,000 other relatives scattered across the globe.[86] Romney's parents were not polygamous, and when George was five years old they returned destitute to the United States after their settlement was expelled from Mexico by Pancho Villa's rebels. Romney later said that his people were "the first displaced persons of the twentieth century."[87] Romney grew up in poverty in California, Idaho, and Utah, did Mormon missionary work for two years in England and Scotland, studied for a semester at George Washington University, and began his business career as a lobbyist in Washington, D.C. Throughout his life, Mormonism was his most important influence, with its emphasis on family, morality, community, and hard work, and its proscriptions against alcohol, tobacco, caffeine, and profanity. Romney-watchers saw his Mormonism reflected in his politics, particularly in his evangelical zeal for causes such as civil rights, his blend of conservative and progressive views, and his total moral self-assurance.

As the first Latter-Day Saint to run for president since the religion's founder, Joseph Smith, Romney attracted the enthusiastic support of his co-religionists in Western states like Utah, Arizona, and California. But many other Americans found Romney's personal history and his idiosyncratic religion to be off-putting. His foreign birth raised the question—never definitively answered—of whether he was "a natural born Citizen," in the words of the U.S. Constitution, and therefore eligible for the presidency. While some conservative Protestants, particularly in the South, denied Mormonism's claim to be a Christian faith, most of the suspicion of Romney's religion in the 1960s came from liberals. Some doubted that Mormons adhered to the principle of separation of church and state, while others pointed to the involvement of many Mormon officials in far-right superpatriot organizations such as the John Birch Society.

The most significant criticism of Mormonism that Romney encountered from liberals concerned his church's refusal to admit persons of African descent to its priesthood, the inner organization of laymen who ran the churches and would ascend to the higher reaches of heaven. According to one of Joseph Smith's revelations, black people bore the mark of Cain and were descended from Ham, the son of Noah cursed by God, and therefore were barred from equal status among the Saints. American Nazi Party leader George Lincoln Rockwell told his audiences that Romney was a hypocrite for supporting civil rights despite his church's stand "that

Negroes are like animals."[88] While the Mormon Church denied it was institutionally biased against black people, one of the church's top leaders warned Romney that the 1964 Civil Rights Bill was "vicious legislation" in contradiction to God's "curse upon the Negro," and that civil rights advocates likely would meet divine punishment, as presidents Lincoln and Kennedy had.[89] Romney could only argue in his defense that he had been among the GOP's most consistent supporters of civil rights ever since he had led the drive to desegregate Detroit's public housing after the city's 1943 race riots, and that "While my religion superficially appears to be otherwise, it is not racist."[90]

Romney's religiosity puzzled two other groups who would have significant influence on his quest for the presidency: journalists and rank-and-file Republicans. John McClaughry had helped Romney write a speech he delivered at the National Press Club in Washington, D.C. midway through his first term as governor, when it appeared that he might be an alternative to Goldwater as the 1964 presidential nominee. It was Romney's first introduction to the national media, and while he spoke feelingly and showed great presence, McClaughry could tell in looking around the room that the speech was not going well. McClaughry had attempted to secularize the speech as much as Romney would let him, but "The main message the press would have taken away was that God has a plan for humanity and He has chosen the American people to lead the way." This was not the right message for the members of the Washington press, whom McClaughry characterized as "a bunch of cynical, hard-drinking, gossip-mongering people eager to get a story and beat the competition. They had great doubts about divinity in the first place and George Romney in the second, and they panned him terribly for this speech."[91] Reporters joked that Romney wanted the presidency as a stepping stone to higher office.

At a Lincoln Day speech in Boston in 1966, Romney described the Declaration of Independence and the Constitution as "divinely-inspired documents, written by men especially raised up by their Creator for that purpose." In later years, after the GOP had become thoroughly infused with the language of religious fundamentalism, particularly of the Southern Protestant variety, Romney's speech would seem wholly unremarkable. At the time, however, it was described as "exotic fare for the average Republican contributor, who has come to expect nothing more exalted with his roast beef than an attack on the Democrats and their evil works."[92] Romney's candidacy had the potential to bridge the gap between a political establishment that had become thoroughly secularized and the large segment of the American population that remained strongly religious. Perhaps Romney might also have helped to channel American religious sentiment away from the influence of right-wing evangelical preachers such as Billy James

Hargis, who appeared on hundreds of radio and television stations in the late 1960s and reached an audience in the millions.[93] In the run-up to the 1968 election, however, Romney's faith led many of his fellow Republicans to regard him as a sanctimonious killjoy while journalists caricatured him as an old-fashioned square and a dullard.

Romney's strong moral orientation was a little-recognized aspect of his connection with black audiences, who shared and appreciated his view of politics through the lens of sin and redemption. Romney's interest in drawing black voters to the Republican Party led Michigan GOP chair Elly Peterson to set up the Detroit Action Center in 1967 as a means of inner-city outreach. Peterson, who once was awkwardly introduced at a Michigan Republican convention as "one of the finest women who has ever walked the streets," was a longtime party activist and advocate of Republican efforts to broaden the party's base beyond the affluent suburbs.[94] She had been inspired by Charles Percy's New Illinois Committee, and set up a similar ombudsman operation in Detroit's downtrodden 13th Congressional District. Residents of the predominantly black and Democratic district brought problems and complaints to the Action Center, which put them in touch with potential employers, municipal agencies, legal aid services, and helpful Republican officials. While the center produced little in the way of immediate Republican electoral gains among inner-city African-Americans, Romney and Peterson believed the effort would pay long-term dividends for the GOP.[95]

Three months after the Republicans created the Action Center, Detroit exploded in the worst urban riot the country had experienced since the Civil War. The riot began at four A.M. on a Sunday morning in July when police arrested eighty African-Americans in a raid on a "blind pig," an illegal after-hours drinking club, where they had gathered to celebrate the return of several servicemen from Vietnam. A crowd gathered, rumors of police brutality spread, and someone threw a bottle through the rear window of a police car. The crowd began smashing windows, looting stores, and setting fires. Within hours, flames blazed across Detroit. The violence would spread across fourteen square miles of ghetto and leave 43 people dead, 1,300 buildings destroyed, and 2,700 businesses ransacked. Romney flew over the riot area in a helicopter and thought "It looked like the city had been bombed."[96] He realized that city police and the Michigan National Guard could not restore order, and he conducted tense negotiations with Lyndon Johnson, the man he sought to replace in the presidency, to persuade him to order federal troops into Detroit. Johnson did so with great reluctance and attempted to place political responsibility for the riots on Romney, referring seven times in a nationally televised statement to the governor's inability to control his own state.[97]

In the long run, the Detroit riot, along with the massive riot in Newark, New Jersey two weeks earlier, amplified the growing white backlash against social welfare programs aimed at improving the situations of minority inner-city residents. Eventually this would damage the moderates, whom angry backlash voters would judge to have too much in common with liberals. The response of many Michigan Republicans at the time of the riots, however, was considerably different from what might have been expected. Elly Peterson contacted all the Republican county chairmen in a 150-mile radius of Detroit. Each of them converted their party headquarters into a collection center for emergency food supplies, and went on the radio to ask party members for donations. Party members responded with crate loads of canned goods, although Peterson recalled that in Lansing "a little old lady showed up with a plate of brownies."[98] Republicans sent four trucks full of food into the hardest-hit riot areas twelve hours after the violence broke out, and Republican volunteers helped to distribute the emergency aid through local churches. Republicans donated a total of eighty tons of food along with clothes and other supplies for people made homeless by the riots. John Marttila, a civil rights worker who had set up the Detroit Action Center, braved a sniper zone to deliver medical assistance to a black woman who was trapped in her home.[99]

Some Republicans tried to gain partisan advantage from the riots. The Republican Coordinating Committee blamed Johnson and the poverty program for the outbreaks of anarchy. Other right-leaning Republicans faulted the federal judiciary, the media, civil rights leaders such as Martin Luther King Jr., and black people in general. Reagan called the rioters "mad dogs."[100] Conservative ideologues claimed that the riots resulted from Communist conspiracies and had nothing to do with racial inequities or conditions within the inner cities. According to Phyllis Schlafly, "Riots don't 'just happen'—they are organized by outside agitators and armed guerrillas, by various civil rights and New Left groups saturated with Communists and pro-Communists . . . and by Federally-financed poverty workers and assorted do-gooders who think that the only way to solve the problems of the 'ghetto' is to burn it down."[101]

Romney spoke for many moderates in deploring the violence and lack of respect for law and order while also underlining the role that social and economic forces played in creating the conditions from which the riots erupted. Testifying before the hastily assembled National Advisory Commission on Civil Disorders, he maintained that his administration had been aware that racial discrimination, lack of opportunity for minorities, and the deterioration of the urban neighborhoods could create "conditions which would overwhelm our cities with conflict and violence if we did not act fast enough." He defended the progress his administration had made in improving education, establishing job training programs, and enforcing civil rights, but acknowledged that "obviously we were not moving far enough fast enough."[102] In an address to a national convention of county officials a week after the Detroit riots, he tried to rein in conservative reaction with his insistence that Americans "must recognize that the drive for human justice has gained ground during the past few years. All our efforts have not been wasted, all our programs designed to bring about equal opportunity are not now valueless. We must not permit a backlash to weaken the valuable programs and policies designed to bring about first-class status for all citizens." At the same time, he distanced himself from liberalism by emphasizing the role that private enterprise and voluntary citizen action, rather than big government programs, could play in addressing the problems of employment, welfare, housing, and race relations. He also struck a distinctively conservative note in arguing that urban violence came from "the declining moral atmosphere in our country," citing a growing disdain for authority, lack of personal responsibility, "the aura of permissiveness our society encourages," and "our reverence for gold instead of God."[103]

It was traditional for presidential candidates to embark on overseas trips to bolster their foreign policy credentials, but Romney broke the pattern by first making a tour of America's troubled cities. "I think it is important," he declared, "for public officials—and through their eyes all citizens—to see . . . the horrible conditions which breed frustration, hatred and revolt."[104] One of his advisors had cautioned that Romney should avoid meeting with black militant organizations since "The conservative wing of the Republican Party and the white middle class in general will not understand any personal visits that would tend to indicate the Negro militant represents an important viewpoint that must be listened to."[105] Romney defiantly sought out just such leaders. In Washington, D.C., he traded views with Marion Barry, the future mayor of the city, who warned him that "significant numbers" of African-Americans had given up on America, the Constitution, and hopes for peaceful progress.[106] In Rochester, New York, he ventured into the black ghetto to meet with a group that had been formed by radical organizer Saul Alinsky to pressure the Eastman Kodak Company into hiring more minorities. In the group's shabby storefront headquarters, decorated with portraits of Malcolm X and Stokely Carmichael, Romney compared notes with Alinsky and listened intently as dozens of agitated adults and teenagers aired their grievances. He approved of the group's cooperative efforts with businesses to win more jobs for blacks, but told them that they should put similar pressure on largely segregated labor unions. Romney also wagged an admonishing finger at one militant who professed his willingness to die for his beliefs: "If that's the way you try to get what you want, you'll have anarchy and chaos—the law of the jungle."[107] The group responded to Romney with both skepticism and applause. "At least he's here and that is something," one militant commented. "It seems to show he's really concerned. We haven't seen any of those other guys down here in the streets."[108]

Romney's 10,000-mile, coast-to-coast tour took him to seventeen cities over three weeks. He met with a wide range of people involved with the urban situation, including the head of Chicago's police department, public school superintendents, social workers placing unemployed Appalachian whites in jobs, the members of Atlanta's crime commission, religious service organizations, voluntary citizen action groups in Indianapolis, grassroots workers struggling to rebuild the Watts ghetto, and tenants of the infamous Pruitt-Igoe public housing development in St. Louis.[109] He came away convinced that black militancy could be diverted into constructive outlets and that independent citizens groups and local private-sector institutions could make a greater impact than federal programs in improving life in the slums. But, he warned, "I am more convinced than ever before that unless we reverse our course, [and] build a new America, the old America will be destroyed."[110] He called for a "drastic revision" of budgetary priorities, and insisted that the "human, social and economic problems of our own people" should be the top national objective. "We must arouse ourselves from our comfort, pleasure, and preoccupations and listen to the voices from the ghetto," he urged.[111]

Romney's call for a reorientation of the nation's priorities implied a reduced commitment to the bloody and seemingly endless war in Vietnam. Other moderate Republicans were calling for a similar reevaluation, including Senator Charles Percy. "If we continue to spend $66 million a day trying to save the people of South Vietnam," Percy argued, "while leaving the plight of the twenty million poor in our own country unresolved, then I think we have our priorities confused."[112] Freshman Congressman Charles Whalen, an Ohio Republican, was among the sharpest critics of the Johnson administration's policies in Vietnam from a strictly economic standpoint. In his most prominent first-year speech, he attacked Lyndon Johnson's proposal for a ten-percent surtax, on the grounds that this "would weaken further an already slack economy."[113] He further noted that the Vietnam war, and the administration's refusal to offer a full accounting of its tremendous costs, stood at the back of the tax proposal. "Had the Administration curbed its 'guns and butter' policy beginning 18 months ago," he pointed out, "this tax increase would not be before the Congress now."[114] Whalen, a former businessman and college economics professor, informed his constituents that "the Vietnam war permeated virtually everything that happened in Washington" in

1967, and that due to the war's expense, "domestic needs suffered and relatively few new programs were created."[115] Percy and Whalen, appearing together in a television interview, agreed that the bombing of North Vietnam had been ineffective, that the conflict was political rather than a straightforward military conflict, and that a diplomatic solution should be reached through a conference involving all the Asian nations. Even so, Percy felt obliged to endorse the basic aims of the administration's policies, and emphasized that members of both parties "unite on the fact that we would be opposed to unilateral withdrawal and we are all going to stand firm against communist aggression in Southeast Asia."[116]

The only Republican candidate to campaign resolutely against the Vietnam war was Paul N. "Pete" McCloskey, who made national headlines by running in a special election for a northern California Congressional seat against, among other opponents, the former child movie star Shirley Temple Black. McCloskey was a Marine Corps veteran of the Korean war, in which he had been awarded a Silver Star, the Navy Cross, and two Purple Hearts. He was well aware that his war hero status and the fact that he was carrying Russian-made shrapnel in his right leg "gave me the chance to speak out against the Vietnam war, where a liberal college president would have been called a traitor."[117] McCloskey had once been a gung-ho supporter of the American intervention in Vietnam, and had even volunteered for active duty there. But the U.S. position appeared less tenable as the number of combat deaths in Vietnam metastasized. Eighteen-hundred U.S. troops were killed in Vietnam in 1965, more than 6,000 in 1966, and more than 11,000 in 1967. Despite the military's endless flow of good news, in terms of the numbers of enemy killed and captured and weapons recovered, the public began to sense that the war was going to be long and bloody rather than the quick and relatively pain-free conflict that Johnson had advertised. McCloskey, in researching the history of America's involvement in the conflict and talking to returned veterans, concluded that the United States was not only failing to win the war, but the war was in fact unwinnable.

In September 1967, McCloskey composed a long and scholarly position paper stressing that "Vietnam is one country, not two," and that the regime in South Vietnam had no chance of attracting the vote of a majority of the Vietnamese people in a free election, as provided for in the 1954 Geneva Accords. Contrary to the rhetoric of his election opponents, all of whom took a hawkish view of America's obligation to defend free nations from Communist takeovers, McCloskey emphasized that "we are not aiding an established government which has asked our help to put down an insurrection as in Lebanon [in 1958]; we are aiding a government of a *portion* of a country which we ourselves helped to create, and which, from its inception, would have been unable to sustain itself in its own country *without* our support."[118] McCloskey recommended that the United States terminate its military commitment in Vietnam, though he counseled a gradual disengagement over two years rather than a precipitate withdrawal. He called for the United States to agree to the unification of Vietnam under a single government, recognizing that an election might well result in a Communist government.

John McClaughry, who had been an advisor to both George Romney and Charles Percy, recalled that when Richard Nixon had met with some of Percy's fundraisers and supporters during the Illinois Senatorial campaign, "One of the guys asked him, 'Mr. Nixon, what should Chuck Percy say about Vietnam?' Nixon turned to him and very earnestly said, 'Here are my four points,' and he went through them from one to four. There was a short pause, and the guy asked, 'Do you think that will really work?' Nixon said, 'No, but it will get you through the election.'"[119] Romney was constitutionally incapable of such cynicism, but neither could he bring himself, despite his growing doubts about the viability of the U.S. intervention in Vietnam, to echo McCloskey's call for withdrawal. Romney's principal foreign policy advisor was Jonathan Moore, who had been recommended by Henry Kissinger. Moore observed that Romney had "a sharp, strong mind," but that he was "at his best dealing with issues that he could comprehend in a proximate manner. When he was governor, dealing with the problems of Michigan, the issues were within his grasp—very practical, very operational. It was why he had been a success in the automotive business." But in dealing with the more abstract terrain of foreign policy, "He had a hard time working conceptually and analytically with those [issues] . . . In those situations, he would try to apply some arbitrary rules and principles, relying more on his Mormon certainties than anything else." The main flaw of Romney's shifting perspectives on Vietnam, in the view of the press, was not that he didn't have a solution to the conflict, but that he was not politically sophisticated enough to pretend that he did.

Romney and Moore did, however, eventually succeed in evolving a coherent Vietnam strategy, in consultation with Kissinger and other advisors. Moore recalled that "When we were developing this new policy, we were working very closely with Romney, because he was very hands-on and you couldn't just give him a speech and have him OK it. We had a lot of sessions."[120] Romney emphasized that a purely military victory over North Vietnam was essentially unachievable. He called for a new emphasis on a negotiated settlement to the conflict, a halt to the bombing of North Vietnam outside of the supply lines where the Communists infiltrated men and materiel into South Vietnam, and a de-Americanization of the war effort that would transfer more of the military burden to the South Vietnamese.

Without endorsing the politically unacceptable option of U.S. withdrawal, he left the door open for such action if the South Vietnamese government proved unwilling or unable to combat the Vietcong and institute the necessary reforms to win the loyalty of the South Vietnamese people.[121]

Romney's part-dove, part-hawk approach was probably the most deeply considered Vietnam strategy of any presidential candidate at that time, and was broadly similar to the strategy Nixon eventually would pursue. In the context of his overall Vietnam strategy, Romney even pointed the way toward one of Nixon's future policy breakthroughs with his call for a flexible position on the admission of Communist China to the United Nations. Romney believed that "it would be in the common interest for mainland China to enter into the community of nations and accept the responsibilities which that entails."[122]

By August 1967, Romney's attacks on Johnson's Vietnam policy had become resolute and hard-hitting. Speaking off the cuff to reporters, he said that America's involvement in Vietnam was a "tragic mistake" and that "it would have been better if we had never been involved."[123] Breaking with the notion that Johnson's Vietnam policies deserved bipartisan support, Romney predicted that the Republicans would campaign as the peace party in 1968.[124] Romney's campaign rebounded as Johnson's popularity fell and more Americans turned against the war. While Romney had trailed the President by five points in the mid-June Gallup Poll, by mid-August respondents favored Romney over Johnson 49–41, with ten percent undecided.

Romney's new position received positive notice from many newspapers that had previously been opposed to him. "Romney Starts to Emerge From the Vietnam Tangle" read the headline of a full-page editorial in the *Detroit Free Press* on August 28, 1967. The paper had long been critical of Romney's views on Vietnam, but now contrasted his "growing sure-footedness" on the issue with the "simplistic" logic and escalatory policies of Johnson. It had taken Romney a long time and many missteps to arrive at his position, but the paper praised the governor's hard work in understanding what was happening in Vietnam and his "more mature, refined thinking" on the subject. While the editorial raised the possibility that Romney's transition from hawk to dove over the previous two years was an opportunistic response to the falloff in popular support for the war, the paper offered a more charitable explanation for the governor's original position: "He appeared to be brain-washed by the military during his 1965 trip to the front."[125]

Two days later, Romney appeared on "Hot Seat," a Detroit television program hosted by Lou Gordon, in a late-night interview conducted after a long day of campaigning. How, Gordon inquired, could Romney explain the inconsistency between his approval of the war effort in 1965, when he had toured South Vietnam with other governors, and his new position? "Well," Romney replied, no doubt thinking back to the wording of the *Detroit Free Press* editorial, "you know when I came back from Vietnam, I just had the greatest brainwashing that anyone can get when you go over to Vietnam." "By the generals?" Gordon interjected. "Not only by the generals," Romney continued, "but also by the diplomatic corps over there, and they do a very thorough job. And since returning from Vietnam, I've gone into the history of Vietnam, all the way back into World War II and before. And, as a result, I have changed my mind. . . . I no longer believe that it was necessary for us to get involved in South Vietnam to stop Communist aggression."[126]

Romney's offhand remark about brainwashing was a colossal political misstep, and the national response was mocking and merciless. Countless cartoonists sketched the governor's frothing cranium. Democratic Senator Eugene McCarthy jested that in Romney's case, "a light rinse" would have sufficed.[127] Editorials lambasted Romney for his apparent admission that he lacked the necessary mental fortitude to be president. The previously supportive *Detroit News* called for him to quit the race in favor of Nelson Rockefeller, "who knows what he believes."[128] Romney was victimized in part by the changing meaning of the word "brainwashing." Most of his critics had in mind the Communist efforts to propagandize and program captive soldiers in the Korean war, though Romney obviously meant only that he had been fed misleading impressions and information by his briefers in Vietnam. "I wasn't talking about Russian-type brainwashing," Romney explained, "I was talking about LBJ brainwashing."[129]

Romney stonily insisted that he didn't regret his brainwashing remark and didn't believe he'd been hurt by having said it. When he was asked to clarify what he had meant, he told reporters that when he had visited the war zone in 1965, he had received "a systematic presentation of the idea" that U.S. forces were merely there to advise and counsel the South Vietnamese, who were making the basic military decisions: "This was the viewpoint that was expressed by military personnel all the way down the line." In light of subsequent developments, Romney felt that the assurances he received were "clearly not in accord with the direction in which we were moving, which was to take over the military conflict and Americanize it."[130] The military and the Johnson administration did in fact systematically mislead the media and the public about the scope and extent of American military involvement in Vietnam, and Romney's charges of information manipulation would soon become the conventional wisdom. In late '67, however, the brainwashing brouhaha obscured Romney's forcible dissent against the rationale for U.S. intervention. The controversy also had the practical effect of ensuring that the GOP as a whole would not take a stand against the war, although discerning observers noticed that Pete McCloskey triumphed in his antiwar campaign against Shirley Temple Black and other hawks in the fall '67 election. McCloskey's win seemed more an aberration than a harbinger, though, since much of his support came from crossover Democratic voters, particularly Stanford University students. "I wouldn't have won a Republican primary," McCloskey admitted. "I won because it was a special election and was open to voters of both parties."[131]

Regardless of the validity behind Romney's brainwashing charge, the gaffe torpedoed his campaign. He dropped sixteen percentage points in the Harris poll immediately after his fateful interview, and never regained public support. In October 1967, Bruce Chapman told a Ripon friend that Romney's campaign was in freefall: "Even as he prepares to announce his candidacy, the operating budget of the organization is being cut in *half*. Gilder says virtually everybody there is writing self-vindicating memoranda on the reasons for collapse, and few expect to be around by winter's end."[132] Romney soldiered on, announcing his candidacy in November, making the obligatory foreign tour, and crisscrossing New Hampshire in the wintry months before the GOP primary, but clearly his chances had gone glimmering. He was not helped by the frequent broadsides against him from the state's largest paper, the conservative *Manchester Union-Leader*, which labeled him "Chihuahua George" in a mocking reminder of his foreign origins. Finally in late February 1968, with his campaign poll showing him losing to Nixon five-to-one in New Hampshire and even running behind an unofficial Rockefeller write-in vote, Romney gave up. He admitted that he had not "won the wide acceptance with rank and file Republicans that I had hoped to achieve."[133]

Few moderate Republicans outside of Michigan shed tears when Romney ended his candidacy. Many progressive Republicans were ecstatic, since Romney's departure from the race seemed to assure Nelson Rockefeller's entrance. When news of Romney's exit reached the members of the Ripon Society executive board, the meeting minutes recorded that "a general feeling of excitement prevailed and the general feeling was that Rockefeller would be helped immensely by the Romney decision."[134] Rockefeller in 1968, however, would be the same flawed and difficult-to-nominate candidate that he had been in 1964. The other most viable candidate of the center, Richard Nixon, was acceptable to moderates but didn't really share their passions, particularly on civil rights. The difference between Nixon and Romney was succinctly expressed by a middle-aged Atlanta Republican who saw both of them campaign in the South. "Dick Nixon comes down South and talks hard on civil rights," the Atlanta man allowed, "but you know he has to say what he does, for the northern press." When Romney spoke, however, it was worryingly obvious that "This fellow really means it."[135]

In hindsight, Romney was the GOP moderates' last and best chance to elect one of their own to the presidency, which in turn would have preserved the long-term viability of the moderate movement. No other Republican candidate in the 1968 election—or for the next four decades, for that matter—could match the Eisenhower-like poll numbers Romney received at his zenith. None would combine his appeal to morality-minded Americans as well as secular moderates, his heartfelt support of civil rights, his potential to attract non-traditional Republican constituencies, his Midwestern and Western backing, and his willingness to challenge the Vietnam war and other Cold War shibboleths. Nor would any other moderate candidate be able to leverage the political potential of the moderate-dominated group of Republican governors, who were then at their peak of strength. The moderates would continue to exercise an influence within the party, but they would never again have the opportunity to build a national movement in the way that a successful Romney presidential candidacy, let alone a Romney presidency, could have afforded. When Romney's candidacy sank, so did the moderates' likelihood of leaving a lasting imprint on the Republican Party. For moderates, the path ahead would lead continuously downward.

CHAPTER 8

☙

Mere Anarchy

Moderate Half-Victories and the Agonies of 1968

1 968 stands out in popular memory as "The Year That Rocked the World," a time of headlong change and shattering events.[1] In the circumscribed world of Republican political journals from 1968, however, whether the *Ripon Forum* on the left or *Human Events* and *National Review* on the right, there is surprisingly little mention of many of the defining movements and moments of that year: the countercultural ferment, the campus upheavals at Wisconsin and Columbia and other universities, the flourishing of the women's movement, the strikes in Paris and riots in Mexico City, and the repression of the Prague Spring and other Eastern European rebellions. Most Republican activists were narrowly focused on the elections of 1968, especially the presidential contest, and the continuing maneuvers for intra-party advantage between moderates and conservatives. Beyond the political jockeying, however, Republican moderates responded to the rush of events that preceded the elections in ways that revealed both the strengths and weaknesses of moderates in immoderate times.

George Romney's withdrawal from the presidential race before the March 1968 New Hampshire primary briefly appeared to offer an opening to another Midwestern moderate, Illinois freshman senator Charles H. Percy. A year before the 1968 GOP convention, Donald Rumsfeld, who was then a moderate representative from Chicago's northern suburbs and one of Percy's closest Congressional allies, put together a secret group to plot Percy's presidential nomination. Rumsfeld ran the group with the brusqueness for which he would later become famous; in one memo he stipulated that

"Meetings should not include a meal—time is wasted and pleasantries rather than business result."[2] Despite the unsociable atmosphere of the Working Group for Percy, Rumsfeld and his team produced a clear-eyed analysis of the difficulties and opportunities moderates confronted in the '68 campaign. All those involved knew that Percy faced long odds, but as his Senatorial campaign manager Thomas Houser pointed out, "The national picture is as fluid as it has ever been in our memories," and a deadlocked convention might well turn to a compromise candidate like Percy.[3]

As early as July 1967, Rumsfeld had concluded that "Romney is going down and likely will not get the nomination."[4] Rockefeller, in the opinion of Rumsfeld and other members of his group, could win over a majority of the public and would be a good president, but couldn't get the GOP nomination even if he sought it. The convention delegates would be in unshakeable agreement on the "total unacceptability" of Rockefeller, for reasons relating to the New York governor's perceived spoiler role in Goldwater's 1964 campaign, Rockefeller's "personal and family problems," and his totemic status as a devil figure for the right wing. Nixon was the clear favorite of the Republican establishment—a May 1967 Gallup poll showed that he had the support of 57 percent of Republican county chairmen—and could be nominated, but likely would lose the election to Johnson.[5] Reagan too could be nominated, but was too far to the right to be viable in a general election; his candidacy would lead to a disastrous reprise of 1964. Rumsfeld's verdict was that Reagan was "on the rise," but he "could not get elected, would divide the party, and very likely would be a poor President."[6]

In the view of Rumsfeld and his conspirators, Percy was "the only major national figure with broad acceptance in the moderate and Eastern Republican power structure who can be perceived as an acceptable, winning candidate in a national election."[7] Percy appealed to moderates and progressives because of his manifest concern for civil rights, his progressive thinking on domestic issues such as home ownership for ghetto residents, his internationalism, and his willingness to criticize the conduct of the Vietnam war. In some circles, the excitement in 1968 surrounding Percy's candidacy was comparable to the buzz over another first-term Illinois senator forty years later. Conservatives were willing at least to tolerate Percy on account of his support for the Goldwater ticket in 1964, his business executive's background, his preference for private sector initiatives over the inefficiencies of government bureaucracy, and his push for the devolution of government responsibility to state and local levels. Goldwater declared Percy the only potential presidential candidate who would be acceptable to a majority of the Republican Party.[8] William F. Buckley's hopes for the '68 election rested on "the desirability of conservatizing Percy. That, I think, would be ideal. Ronald [Reagan] just isn't plausible at the moment."[9]

Percy's liabilities were also substantial. He was unknown to much of the public, and lacked the organizational advantages of other candidates: Rockefeller's money, Nixon's network of lower-level Republican operatives, and Reagan's standing in the conservative movement. Percy did not even control his own state delegation, as many of Illinois' Republican activists were right-wing followers of Phyllis Schlafly, while the state's GOP leadership consisted mainly of conservatives who were, in the words of Percy's campaign manager, "disenchanted with CHP's [Percy's] position on public issues" such as the Soviet consular treaty and open housing. "To date, these people have found it extremely difficult to relate to CHP."[10] Percy was also an ineffective public speaker. "[Y]ou have a tendency when you are talking to a Republican partisan audience to lift your voice and shout," one of his advisors chastised him, "and it sounds bad. When you do this, the voice takes on a displeasing, harsh quality and sort of 'honks.' . . . You split uncounted infinitives. You repeat yourself too much."[11]

Percy struck some of the people who worked with him as an ineffective legislator, marshmallowy and yielding in the way of many moderate politicians. "He was too well-meaning," his aide John McClaughry felt. "We called him 'Charles the Good.' . . . I rolled my eyes a dozen times listening to Chuck talk kindly about the people who were out to stick knives in his back." McClaughry became disillusioned as Percy proved unable to stand up against even the most fiscally irresponsible proposals or to master the legislative process. He watched in dismay as Senator Walter Mondale, a skilled Democratic operator acting as Lyndon Johnson's cat's-paw, eviscerated Percy's prized housing proposal without Percy even catching on to what was happening. During a negotiating session on the Housing Act of 1968, Mondale persuaded Percy to drop nearly everything of value in his original proposal and left him feeling that he had achieved some sort of compromise. "Mondale systematically removed Chuck's shirt, pants, socks, shoes, and hat during the negotiation," McClaughry sighed. "At one point, after Mondale had picked Percy's spectacles and wedding ring, I looked over at Mondale and he looked at me and winked. He knew that I knew, but he knew that I couldn't explain it to Percy."[12]

The greatest threat to Percy's presidential possibilities, however, was Nelson Rockefeller. During the time that Rockefeller was supporting Romney's campaign, Percy had to refrain from an open declaration of his own candidacy, for fear of splitting moderate strength and incurring Rocky's wrath. If he hoped to receive the New York governor's nod (and funds) if Romney faltered, Percy's advisors warned, he even had to "avoid lavish public displays of respect and friendship for [New York] Mayor [John] Lindsay," with whom Rockefeller feuded despite their near-identical views on most domestic issues. As one of Rumsfeld's associates advised him, Rockefeller held "unusually strong prejudice against intra-party adversaries even of similar philosophical orientation."[13] All of the Working Group's calculations depended on Rockefeller staying out of the race. If Rockefeller held back, perhaps Reagan and Nixon would divide the conservative vote at the convention, giving Percy the votes of the plurality of delegates who considered Reagan unelectable and Nixon untrustworthy. If Rockefeller entered, however, the dynamic would be that of the California '64 GOP primary, with the left and right wings of the party battling each other to the death, except that this time Nixon would be able to present himself as the moderate bringer of peace and consensus. In that case, one member of the Working Group predicted, "Unable to draw from the right (Reagan), the center (Nixon), or the left (Rockefeller), the Senator will have virtually no financial or organizational reserve."[14]

Nelson Rockefeller's assistant Joseph Persico believed that his employer's fever for the presidency was genuinely in remission in early 1968. Rockefeller was pleased to learn that prominent national columnists like James Reston and Walter Lippmann touted him as the best possible GOP nominee, "But this time he was not going to be swayed by ambitious staffers and political savants who believed that only Nelson Rockefeller could stop Richard Nixon's nomination. The bruises were barely healed from his last two presidential disasters."[15] Nonetheless, a subterranean Rockefeller campaign was already under way. Rockefeller's underlings had set up a delegate intelligence unit, with their master's awareness but without his active involvement. Several members of the Ripon Society's New York chapter came aboard, as did future Massachusetts governor William Weld, who had recently graduated from Harvard and was working as an investment banker. Ripon's John R. Price headed the operation, which had its inception at a meeting in New York's posh Links Club in the fall of 1967.

Former *New York Herald Tribune* owner John Hay "Jock" Whitney had become frustrated that "his party was no longer the party that was running the Republicans," as Price put it.[16] Whitney, his right-hand man Walter Thayer, and Whitney's brother-in-law, CBS head William Paley, began to host a series of fund-raising dinners for the Ripon Society at "Greentree," Whitney's Long Island mansion. The young men of Ripon were awed by the formal setting and Whitney's stunning collection of paintings. Lee Huebner recalled being "very conscious of trying not to spill my wine" at those dinners. "I almost said to Whitney, when I saw one of his Picassos, 'Oh, I have a print of that painting too,' but I stopped myself in time."[17] Lee Auspitz remembered that at one of the dinners, "The triumvirate had invited a guy from St. Louis named George Herbert Walker, whom they assumed was from the well-heeled Walker-Bush clan. He came and he sat quietly through the dinner, and when he left, he said to Jock Whitney, 'You know, I'm the wrong George Walker, but I really enjoyed the paintings.'"[18]

Whitney and Thayer invited Ripon's leadership to the Links Club to discuss how responsible, business-oriented Eastern moderates could regain some of their lost influence. Thomas "Tim" Petri, Ripon's executive director, made a case for systematically leveraging the Whitney and Rockefeller networks for political effect. Instead of sighing for bygone glories like despairing fourth-century Roman patricians, the Eastern bankers and philanthropists and social luminaries could direct their money and connections toward a delegate-hunting effort for Rockefeller that would resemble the successful Eastern establishment operation of Thomas Dewey. Price remembered that after Whitney heard Petri's presentation, the elderly multimillionaire drew himself up to his full height and declared, "Well, if we're going to be criticized for being the establishment"—he threw both hands in the air—"let's *be* the establishment!"[19]

Whitney and Thayer put Ripon's young activists in touch with J. Irwin Miller, the CEO of the Cummins Engine Company and a prominent venture capitalist, philanthropist, and progressive Republican. Miller headed up fundraising efforts for what was still a hypothetical Rockefeller presidential race, and liaised with governors like Rhode Island's John Chafee and Maryland's Spiro Agnew, who were pursuing a Rockefeller draft. Price led the operation to gather information on the 1,333 delegates to the 1968 Republican convention, under the guidance of Rockefeller's research coordinator John Deardourff. Price's team and his contacts working around the country built up dossiers on the delegates to delineate their personal networks and business relationships, in order to find out whether they had any connections that might influence them toward Rockefeller. The intelligence operation also attempted to learn about the substantive interests of the delegates, and whether Rockefeller could appeal to them on the basis of their concerns about foreign policy, the economy, defense, or other issues.

Price and the other Ripon members soon discovered that the Rockefeller political operation was not the formidable, well-oiled machine it appeared to be from outside. The Manhattan headquarters on West 55th Street was seedy, indifferently decorated and shabbily furnished.[20] Price found that George Hinman's famed "talent file," which supposedly comprehended every person of interest in Republican circles, was obsolete.[21] Many of the individuals listed in the file were dead or out of politics, and the contact information for the remainder was outdated. The research collection at Rockefeller's West 55th Street townhouses contained a vast repository of survey data and position papers that an army of experts had produced on every national issue imaginable. But when Rockefeller had granted access to the archives to staffers from campaigns he supported—William Scranton's in

1964, George Romney's in 1967–68—they invariably found the collection unwieldy, and little of the information could be used effectively. For Peter Wallison, a Ripon member who worked for Rockefeller, the cumbersome research assembly reflected the jumbled mindset of the man at the top. The governor seemed to think "that data was like a shoe store," he recalled, "with these racks and racks and racks of shoes, and you would just pull the data that you wanted off the rack. There was no sense of relevancy." For a politician to make effective use of research, Wallison believed, "You had to start off with an idea or a hypothesis for what it was you wanted to show, and collect the data that would enable you to test that hypothesis. Rockefeller didn't seem to have that idea. He just wanted people to go out and collect data."[22]

The dysfunction in the Rockefeller organization extended to the personnel. Where the Nixon '68 campaign had an ultimate arbiter in John Mitchell, the Rockefeller campaign had jerry-built, parallel structures of authority. Hinman and his assistant Robert Douglass sat atop one chain of command, and speechwriter Emmett Hughes atop another. Kissinger and the foreign policy apparatus operated in a separate sphere of authority, as did administrative guru William Ronan. John Deardourff and the research operation fought for direct access to Rockefeller. Irwin Miller and Jock Whitney functioned as outriders. Price recalled that "if someone got a 'no' from one chain of command, he'd simply start up the next one. It was totally disorganized and inefficient."[23] Rockefeller's supreme self-assurance, combined with his lordly inclination to treat his employees as chattel, turned his advisors into sycophants. "The people Nelson gathered around him were forceful figures in their own spheres, but something went out of them in his presence," Persico noticed. "Never in eleven years did I witness a staff member take him head on. No one ever said flatly, 'I disagree.' 'That's wrong, Governor.' 'That's a bad idea.'"[24] Jonathan Moore, who worked in the Rockefeller campaign after George Romney folded his tent, felt strongly that "Rockefeller was not as impressive as Romney, and the people who were running his campaign weren't anywhere near as good as Romney's people. Rockefeller's people didn't have half the passion, the integrity, the seriousness, and the commitment that the Romney people did."[25]

Even so, Rockefeller and other moderates became ever more tempted to enter the race as they perceived a vacuum at the center of the GOP field and witnessed the galloping disintegration of the Democratic Party. A boomlet for General James Gavin briefly captured some moderates' imaginations, while others speculated on the dark-horse possibilities of Ohio's flamboyant governor James Rhodes. *New York Times* columnist James Reston touted Lyndon Johnson's Republican HEW secretary John Gardner, one of the few people in either party to have evolved "a new philosophy for the present age."[26] Ripon members negotiated with a wealthy Democrat who wanted to spend up to $3 million to secure the Republican nomination for Gardner.[27]

The disorienting events of 1968 figured prominently in moderates' shifting calculations. In late January, the North Vietnamese and the Vietcong launched the Tet Offensive, a massive assault on every major city in South Vietnam. A failure as a military operation, the Tet Offensive nonetheless destroyed the Johnson administration's credibility with the American public. In mid-March, Nixon's essentially uncontested victory in the New Hampshire GOP primary was overshadowed by antiwar candidate Eugene McCarthy's stunning near-upset of Johnson in the state's Democratic primary. The South Dakota senator won 42 percent of the vote and more delegates than Johnson, which for a more-or-less unknown politician challenging a standing president was a stupendous achievement. McCarthy's candidacy relied on a motley army of young volunteers, who got "Clean for Gene" in order to convince the good people of New Hampshire to vote for their candidate. Sensing the momentum within the party, Senator Robert F. Kennedy entered the presidential race on March 16, and Lyndon Johnson left it on March 31.

In strategic terms, Republicans found Johnson's withdrawal more a problem than an opportunity. Public dissatisfaction with Johnson was so high that one fall 1967 poll gave him only a two percent lead over quadrennial loser Harold Stassen.[28] Many moderate Republicans nonetheless rejoiced at Johnson's departure. "What a great event for the country," one Ripon Society member enthused. "LBJ's decision not to run will do a lot to help this country re-evaluate both foreign and domestic affairs. It's now up to the GOP to get someone other than Dick Nixon in the race. I would hate to see Nixon become LBJ's advocate while the Democrats cleaned house and launched bold new approaches under Gene [McCarthy] or RFK. That really would be a tragic irony."[29] But this was the scenario that began to present itself. "Republicans for McCarthy" organizations sprang up around the country. One GOP member who enlisted under that banner wrote to Ripon's Tim Petri that "we feel that by working as Republicans for McCarthy we are demonstrating, in the only manner open to us, that a segment of our party demands progressive, concerned government."[30] The soundings from Ripon's younger correspondents were even more alarming. Yale undergraduate Charles Pillsbury, immortalized as Mike Doonesbury in his prep school roommate Garry Trudeau's comic strip, was one of those youths who had gone "Clean for Gene," despite the fact that his father was a Republican state senator in Minnesota and he himself was a scion of a wealthy and deep-dyed Republican family. He wrote to a Ripon officer that "I am a nominal Republican because both my parents are Republicans and in the past I have worked for the Republican party, yet how can one support a party that nominated Goldwater in '64 and *will* nominate Nixon in '68."[31]

The significance of the upwelling for McCarthy, from the GOP perspective, was that it took away the energies and constituencies that moderate Republicans had hoped to make their own. A Republican peace candidate might have attracted the idealistic students and young professionals concerned about the war, but with Romney withdrawing from the presidential campaign and Vietnam skeptics like Mark Hatfield unwilling to enter, the antiwar movement played out almost entirely within the Democratic Party. As a result, the GOP seemed increasingly irrelevant to most young people concerned about the war. In the spring of 1967, James Reston had noticed that the war was pushing undergraduates like Yale's campus newspaper editor Strobe Talbott away from the moderate consensus: "The Strobe Talbotts at Yale, serious, patriotic, progressive Republican types, might be the first to be expected to respond to General Westmoreland's noble appeal, but they don't. They are not marching in anti-Vietnam parades, but they are dissenting, and the dissent of this clean-cut, solemn, middle-class crowd of campus leaders may be much more significant than the sign-carrying protesters on the front pages."[32] By the fall, Talbott was part of the "Dump Johnson" movement that segued into McCarthy's candidacy, and he no longer was a Republican; eventually he would become deputy secretary of state under Bill Clinton. The political columnist E. J. Dionne later pointed out that McCarthy's campaign "created a whole new generation of young-professional Democrats. McCarthy's low-key cerebral style, his opposition to a strong presidency, and his ironic approach to government had an unusual appeal to liberal Republicans."[33] That appeal extended to Dionne himself, a longtime Republican who had applied for membership in the Ripon Society in the spring of 1968 as a precocious high school student, but found himself increasingly drawn to the Democrats.[34]

For many people, the extreme events of the times demanded extreme responses, and this was not a dynamic that favored moderates. One Young Republican remembered that he and his YR friends "supported Eugene McCarthy in '68 for the same reasons that we had supported Goldwater in '64." Both candidates were activists and principled "conviction politicians," who were "standing up to the establishment, whoever or whatever the establishment was."[35] In the eyes of many Americans, moderate Republicans and Democrats *were* the establishment. Ripon president Lee Huebner rued that after the moderates' peak of optimism in '67, "history began to move and it passed the Republican Party by. A whimsical Minnesota Senator who did not worship the false god of 'party unity' and who was willing to take a wild political gamble emerged and led a crusade which has toppled an administration and revolutionized American politics." If the Republican Party was to avoid becoming further isolated from a changing electorate and the new generation, he thought, "it must learn to speak to the new forces that are moving in American life. Unfortunately, such language does not come naturally to most political moderates. For they have learned too well to live by a code of safety and sensibility, playing percentages and balancing values. They will change only slowly; they do not like conflict. They will not rock the boat."[36]

New York's Republican mayor John Lindsay was a natural boat-rocker, and his supporters believed that he would be the progressive, antiwar presidential candidate the Republicans needed. One of his finest moments as mayor occurred on April 4, 1968, the day that the Reverend Martin Luther King Jr. was assassinated in Memphis. Black neighborhoods in cities across the country exploded in riots and violent protests. When news of King's assassination reached New York's black neighborhoods, "things almost blew clear across the city," Lindsay's police chief remembered.[37] The mayor went to 125th Street in Harlem and plunged directly into the anguished black crowd that had gathered, offering sorrow and sympathy. His media consultant David Garth, who accompanied him, remembered thinking, "My life is over."[38] Lindsay's rapport with minorities, the programs he had set up to deal with urban issues, the contacts his administration had maintained with black communities, and his policy of police restraint all helped to keep the city from going up in flames.

Lindsay had experienced a turbulent mayoralty, starting with the twelve-day transit strike on his inauguration day that brought New York to its knees and resulted in a series of ruinous contracts with the city's municipal labor unions. He had attracted a host of bright young people to his administration, created many innovative programs, and helped to set the urban agenda for the nation. But his efforts were proving unable to slow the city's sky-rocketing budget and short-term debt, to arrest the spiking crime rates, or to stem the outflow of citizens and industry. Barry Goldwater, for one, had no fear of the mayor running for president, since he believed that Lindsay had "pretty well shot his wad" in taking on the "impossible" task of trying to run New York. Lindsay "should never have taken that job," Goldwater felt, although he conceded that "I don't think anybody else could do the job as well."[39] Conservatives continued to fear Lindsay's charisma, but even moderates had mixed opinions about his positions and performance.

The Ripon Society, for example, experienced serious internal division over the Report of the National Advisory Commission on Civil Disorders, also known as the Kerner Report after its nominal chairman, Illinois' Democratic governor Otto Kerner. The moving force behind the Commission, though, was John Lindsay, and the group included other moderate Republicans who were prominent civil rights supporters, particularly Massachusetts Senator Edward Brooke and Ohio Representative William McCulloch. The report made international headlines with its ringing central statement that "Our nation is moving toward two societies, one black, one white—separate and unequal. . . . What white Americans have never fully understood—but what the Negro can never forget—is that white society is deeply implicated in the ghetto. White institutions created it, white institutions maintain it, and white society condones it."[40] The commission advised spending $30 billion on programs to improve the cities and disperse the ghettos.

Robert W. Gordon, reviewing the report in the *Ripon Forum*, felt that its aim was to establish a consensus for massive urban investment by forcing white people to guiltily confront their own racism. Gordon criticized this tactic on the grounds that many whites would resent being labeled as racists, and he felt that the report emphasized the gulf between blacks and whites instead of trying to close it. He rejected the argument that white hatred made blacks poor, as well as the idea that riots were essentially political protests.[41] Eugene Marans and Peter Wallison, in a much more positive review of the report, felt that it "champion[ed] many of the GOP's most progressive ideas," particularly in its recommendations for developing private-sector alternatives to federal welfare programs and in its emphasis on state and local government responsibility for urban issues. They also pointed to the Republican origin of many proposals endorsed by the report, including a federal job development and placement corporation, business tax credits for hiring the hardcore unemployed, investment incentive zones, and neighborhood action task forces. They noted the support for its recommendations from progressive and moderate Republicans such as Jacob Javits, Charles Percy, William Cowger (head of an Urban Affairs Task Force newly appointed by the Republican Conference of the House of Representatives), and Rockefeller. Nixon, however, had criticized the report on the grounds that it in effect blamed everybody for the riots except the rioters.[42]

Ripon's New York chapter, which was thick with Lindsay supporters, wrote a scathing response to Gordon's criticism. They found his analysis "carping, disingenuous, and destructive," and his rejection of its indictment of white racism "offensive." They emphasized that preeminent among the causes of the riots that the Commission had uncovered were "persistent housing discrimination, verbal abuse by police and an indifference by white society to the legitimate rights of ghetto dwellers." The chapter concluded by noting that "Martin Luther King thought the greatest stumbling block to Negro rights was not white racism itself, but the white 'liberal' establishment which condoned racism in the almighty name of societal order."[43] Ripon ought not to associate itself with such an attitude, the chapter insisted.

Martin Luther King's assassination intensified disagreements of this sort as well as adding urgency and anger to debates over urban and racial problems. Christopher DeMuth, secretary of Ripon's Cambridge chapter, attended King's funeral in Atlanta in early April. He reported on the services at Ebenezer Baptist Church and the final memorial service at Morehouse College, noting that among the scores of celebrities present, "Wilt Chamberlain stood out because of his height and [Republican] Congressman Don Riegle because of his blondness." Other Republicans in attendance included Lindsay, Brooke, Nixon, Rockefeller, Romney, and Javits.[44] A *Ripon Forum* editorial noted with dismay Nixon's initial hesitancy about attending the King funeral, as he waited to clear the trip with Alabama's John Grenier, the architect of Goldwater's Southern strategy. "Such unsolicited solicitude for Southern racial feelings spells danger for the GOP this year," the editorial warned.[45]

Some Republicans responded to King's assassination with alacrity. Ohio's moderate Congressmen William McCulloch, Robert Taft Jr., and Charles Whalen joined eighteen GOP colleagues in a letter urging every House member to vote for an unamended version of the Civil Rights Act recently passed by the Senate.[46] Other Republicans including Taft, Charles Goodell, and Thomas Curtis formed alliances with Black Power advocates to pass legislation creating community development corporations and community development banks in poor communities.[47] But the dominant theme was continued Republican foot-dragging on civil rights; for example, the GOP lagged behind the Democrats in committing to have only integrated delegations at their 1968 nominating convention.

Ripon president Huebner commented that the turbulence of 1968 had revealed the "incapacity of the so-called moderate or progressive wing of the Republican Party to respond meaningfully to the sudden acceleration of events." John Lindsay distinguished himself from the blur because of his honesty and courage, but Huebner worried that Lindsay was heading toward cynicism. The New York mayor snapped during King's funeral march that government should "do something realistic"—like implement the recommendations of the Kerner Report—instead of putting on "a one-day show of conscience. But nothing'll happen. Did it ever?" Huebner believed that moderates' judgment was needed more than ever in a time of rapid change, but that their inbred caution worked against their ability to act as compelling leaders, "willing to take risks, to experiment boldly and disagree incisively." Still, the year's traumatic events did bring out that kind of leadership in unexpected people, including Illinois Republican Congressman John B. Anderson, hitherto considered a conservative. After King's death, Anderson dramatically reversed his previous position to support open housing, in what one civil rights leader called "The best speech

I've ever heard on the floor of the House." Anderson's young daughter, listening in the gallery, told a reporter, "That man's not my daddy. That man's angry." Huebner concluded that at this moment of crisis, the moderate wing of the GOP "badly needs some men who are angry."[48]

Richard Nixon was a wellspring of anger on many subjects, but few people thought that urban affairs might be one of them. Throughout the spring of '68, however, Nixon and his staff had been meeting with and listening to disaffected groups and coming up with some creative programs. John McClaughry, a special assistant to Nixon for community affairs during the campaign, remembered that the candidate was characteristically awkward in his interactions with CORE's Floyd McKissick and Roy Innis, leaders in the Black Power movement: "Nixon was determined to show that he and Floyd McKissick were cut from the same cloth, because he had been a law student at Duke in the late '40s at the same time that McKissick had been a busboy in Durham."[49] Nonetheless, after the meeting, Nixon put forward an innovative plan to promote a new "black capitalism," to give blacks "a piece of the action" in the "exciting adventures of private enterprise." Nixon felt that "What most of the militants are asking is not separation, but to be included in—not as supplicants, but as owners, as entrepreneurs . . ." He predicted that more widespread black capital ownership would lead to "black pride, black jobs, black opportunity and yes, black power, in the best, the constructive sense of that often misapplied term."[50] Nixon backed up his rhetoric with specific plans for black home ownership, and tax incentives and capital for black-owned business and industry, as well as appealing for a "new alignment" in American politics that would include, among others, black militants and "new liberals."

The prime movers behind these proposals were Nixon aides Ray Price, the former chief editorial writer of the *New York Herald Tribune*, and McClaughry, who had advanced similar programs for Charles Percy. In the Ripon Society's view, Nixon's speeches on black enterprise "gave the former Vice President's campaign the intellectual spark and the appearance of social concern that it had sorely lacked."[51] A later analysis judged that the "cumulative impact" of these speeches was "enormous" and "brought praise from even the most hostile Nixonophobes. It may well have been the most successful single move in the entire Nixon effort."[52] Nixon's play for the black militant vote did not translate into widespread black support, although he was able to line up some influential African-American supporters such as Innis and the Reverend Leon Sullivan, founder of the Opportunities Industrialization Centers (OIC). Still, Nixon's efforts did give him an advantage in his contest with Rockefeller. Ripon's Howard Gillette, who was working for the Rockefeller campaign, recalled: "Nixon was triangulating Rockefeller by appropriating some of his language and some of his issues, even while he was already beginning to talk law and order. . . . It was a smart move on Nixon's part to talk about black enterprise, because . . . it wasn't going to alienate his business base and could also appeal to moderates. So in many ways, he was undercutting Rockefeller in terms of news media, and Rockefeller's advisors were standing back and wondering, 'How can this be happening? How can Nixon be doing this?'"[53]

Rockefeller's unacknowledged campaign had gathered steam throughout the first months of 1968. Romney's withdrawal, Robert Kennedy's entrance, and Johnson's sagging poll numbers all argued for Rockefeller to throw his hat in the ring. But just as Rockefeller had made up his mind to announce his candidacy, he met with Republican leaders and consultants who apparently convinced him that he was ill-prepared to compete in the primaries and would serve mainly as a foil for Nixon. At a March 21 news conference, the day before the deadline for permitting his name to remain on the Oregon primary ballot, Rockefeller surprised the media and disappointed his supporters by declaring that he would not "campaign directly or indirectly" for the 1968 presidential race. Rockefeller had not given any advance notice to his backers and champions, most notably Maryland governor Spiro Agnew. The leader of the "draft Rocky" effort had invited statehouse reporters into his Annapolis office to watch the news conference on television, and Agnew was severely embarrassed by Rockefeller's unexpected pullout. He immediately threw his support to Nixon, as did many other moderate Republicans who had previously supported Rockefeller, including Representative Brad Morse, the intellectual leader of the House Wednesday Group. "With the removal of Rockefeller from the race I feel somewhat like a dog without a kennel," lamented one moderate Republican to another.[54] For the Ripon members who had been working for Rockefeller, the impact was more immediate. When Rockefeller made his withdrawal announcement, Tanya Melich recalled, "We had already been hired! We'd been out calling people—I had the western states—and getting pledges of support. And then we had to call them back and say, 'I'm sorry, the Governor's not running.'"[55] Melich and other Ripon members left the abortive campaign.

On April 30, Rockefeller announced that he would make a bid for the presidency after all. He explained that "the unprecedented events of the past weeks"—Johnson's withdrawal and King's assassination—had compelled his reversal.[56] Some of his previous followers and volunteers returned to his campaign, but in the interim, Nixon had been able to corral delegates and support that otherwise would have gone to the governor. Nixon was also able to steal a march on his rival with his creative speeches and proposals on urban problems and racial issues, which took the initiative in those areas away from Rockefeller when he rejoined the contest.

On June 4, Robert Kennedy defeated Eugene McCarthy in California's Democratic primary, and then was assassinated moments after his victory statement. The prospect of RFK's nomination had been one of the best arguments for putting forward Rockefeller to counterbalance Kennedy's glamour, wealth, liberalism, and concern for minorities and civil rights. Kennedy's assassination demolished the case for Rockefeller's nomination. The Ripon Society further observed that Kennedy had paid a backhanded compliment to moderate Republicans by appropriating many of their programs and issues, including tax reform and private sector investment in the ghetto, and used them to peel off Republican support in metropolitan areas. "So long as Kennedy was around," they perceived, "Republicans had to make good their rhetoric about decentralization, private initiative, fiscal responsibility, and law and order. With his murder, the pressures for renewal in the two-party system are weaker."[57] James Reston concluded that the great irony of Kennedy's death was that "it virtually assures the nomination of Hubert Humphrey and Richard Nixon, the Old Guard Kennedy came into the presidential election to defeat."[58]

Shocked Americans largely overlooked the news that, on the same night as Kennedy's assassination, California's conservatives took another moderate Republican scalp. Max Rafferty, the right-wing State Superintendent of Public Instruction, defeated Thomas Kuchel in the GOP senatorial primary. Rafferty was a florid public speaker and aspiring demagogue who emerged from what even a conservative like William Rusher described as "the fever swamp of rightist kookery in southern California."[59] Rafferty had gained election to his post in 1962 by mixing a back-to-basics program for education with fire-breathing rants against liberalism in public schools, which he claimed produced "leather-jacketed slobs, whose favorite sport is ravishing little girls and stomping polio victims to death."[60] Much like George Wallace, Rafferty crafted a conservative populism that exuded overtones of religious revivalism as well as ultra-nationalism, antagonism toward minorities, and resistance to any form of social and cultural change. The protesting students at the University of California at Berkeley became a favorite Rafferty target. "Who pays the freight for their four-year course in sex, drugs and treason?" he asked his audiences. "You do."[61] Rafferty enjoyed the backing of the John Birch Society, grassroots conservative organizations like the California Republican Assembly, and deep-pocketed, revenge-minded funders like Patrick Frawley who had long attempted to bring down Kuchel.

Kuchel probably would have won if he had not grown overconfident of his standing as California's top vote-getter and the next-in-line for leadership of the Senate's Republicans. Rafferty no doubt was correct to say that "Seniority doesn't mean a hoot in hell to the average voter."[62] Kuchel also underestimated the damage he had suffered from the false accusations of homosexuality made against him three years earlier, conservatives' strength in the GOP primary, and the force of their anger against him. The claim that Kuchel was "a Republican in name only" was an exaggerated charge to make against a hawkish, fiscally conservative moderate who had a record of voting with a majority of the GOP on 78 percent of all roll call votes, essentially the same percentage as the Senate Republican leader Everett Dirksen.[63] Still, Kuchel had angered even rank-and-file California Republicans with his obstinate refusal to endorse Nixon in 1962, George Murphy in 1964, and Ronald Reagan in 1966. He also ran a lazy campaign, spurning the distasteful chore of fundraising and ignoring many of the conservative-leaning rural northern counties he had previously carried. He lost by only 69,632 votes out of more than two million cast.[64]

In his farewell speech to the Senate, Kuchel noted that he had been an author of every civil rights bill that had become law in the twentieth century. "Some of the votes I have cast I know have been very costly to me politically," he told his colleagues. But he believed that the greatest satisfaction of being a legislator "comes at the time he tallies the votes which he believed in his own mind were right, just and appropriate," even if public opinion was against him. He thought it "not only permissible but, indeed, vital that the Senate of the United States lead public opinion instead of following it. That is the difficult path but the only one to tread if our republic is to remain."[65] Despite his accomplishments and his noble Roman qualities, the Republican Party would treat Kuchel as a pariah for the rest of his life. Instead of being regarded as an effective and pragmatic lawmaker or honored as an elder statesman, he was held up as an example of the fate that would befall any Republican who acquired too much of a reputation for standing up against the far right.[66]

The right wing had won another Pyrrhic victory. Rafferty turned off much of the public with the violence and exaggeration of his rhetoric, and united Democrats against the GOP where Kuchel had divided them. Rafferty's Democratic opponent was Alan Cranston, who had lost his two previous bids for public office and was universally regarded as a no-hope candidate when Kuchel was still the anticipated GOP nominee. Cranston reported a typical exchange with a law partner at a prestigious Los Angeles firm, a Democrat whom Cranston sought to enlist in his campaign. The lawyer told him, "Kuchel's a good senator. I intend to support him in the general election." Cranston predicted that his opponent would not be Kuchel but the ranting Rafferty. In that case, the lawyer responded, "I'll take a leave of absence and devote full time to your campaign!"[67] Cranston was an antiwar liberal and the first president of the left-leaning California Democratic Council, which was a bogeyman for the right comparable to the John Birch Society for the left. A Rafferty fundraiser described Cranston, with some justice, as "one of the most liberal Democrats ever nominated for the Senate," and one California conservative warned that "should Cranston win, he will make Kuchel look by comparison like Francisco Franco."[68] Rafferty charged that Cranston's advocacy of a bombing halt in Vietnam was "perilously close to treason," but such claims no longer panicked the public, particularly after reporters revealed that the super-patriot Rafferty had dodged service in World War II by seeking a 4F exemption for flat feet.[69] Rafferty would have made an issue of Cranston's membership in the American Veterans Committee, an organization of World War II vets that had been penetrated by Communists, if not for the inconvenient fact that California governor Reagan had also been a member.[70] Cranston would win a narrow victory and remain in office for almost a quarter-century. Liberal Democrats had reason to be grateful for the inadvertent assistance of the Republican right.

Ronald Reagan had steered clear of the primary fight between Kuchel and Rafferty. Since taking office in January 1967, he had both confirmed and confounded expectations of how a conservative would govern. Ever since Reagan's first appearance on the national stage, the Ripon Society had worried that he would be a more effective successor to Barry Goldwater as the standard-bearer of the right wing. The group sent Michael Chabot Smith, the secretary of Ripon's national governing board, to California for several months to research how Reagan had performed in the governorship, with an eye toward alerting moderates on the danger of his covert bid for the presidency in 1968. "In a lot of ways I was surprised by what I found," Smith remembered. "I thought Reagan was going to be more of a hard-line ideologue than he was. I had assumed he wasn't very bright, but I concluded that he was."[71]

Evidence abounded of Reagan's conservative inclinations and approaches. Smith highlighted the Governor's lack of interest in governing, his inability to bring his bureaucracies under control, his simplistic views of social problems, and his tendency (more pronounced in his early months as governor) to view his opponents as evil forces with whom compromise was impossible. Smith's article criticized Reagan's ham-fisted proposal for ten percent, across-the-board cuts from all state agencies and departments, and the cutbacks he imposed in areas such as mental health that often cost more than the savings they generated. Smith noted Reagan's animus against welfare and poverty programs, as shown in his vetoes of Office of Economic Opportunity grants—more than any other governor in the country, possibly excepting Alabama's Lurleen Wallace. He compared Reagan's militant approach toward law enforcement, and his lack of interest in the conditions that bred crime and riots, to his simplistic view of Vietnam and his "dangerous faith in military solutions and in the absolute wisdom of military leadership." Smith was especially critical of Reagan's distaste for antiwar dissent, which Reagan claimed "might give aid and comfort to the enemy," and disruptive students. "Reagan stresses repression of any disturbance," he charged, "without treating the underlying causes—and often without even discussing the real grievances of students, faculty, and administration."[72] Reagan continued to view the bureaucracy and the state legislature with genuine suspicion. "I've spent the last ten years talking about the threat of big government," he said not long after taking office. "Now that I'm on the inside, I'm not going to switch over and say, 'goody-goody, let government do it.' Government is still the greatest threat to freedom in our lives."[73]

Smith conceded Reagan's smoothness and plausibility, his ability to make even hard-line positions sound reasonable, and his ability to dazzle the press and to keep his cool before hostile audiences. At Reagan's December 1967 visit to Yale University, for example, a barrage of aggressive and embarrassing questions failed to unsettle him. Smith noted that the one occasion on that visit when Reagan was wrong-footed came outside the public spotlight when a student asked him quietly about civil rights: "The student observed that whenever the Governor was asked about his position on civil rights, he would respond with stories about Jackie Robinson and Willie Mays, or about Negroes he had appointed to certain boards. But what substantive program, the student asked, did the Governor recommend as a solution? Reagan's silence in response gave listeners the impression he really hadn't given that too much thought."[74] The editors of the *Ripon Forum* concluded that Reagan lacked the managerial skills to "control, guide and limit effectively a large governmental bureaucracy," was ill-equipped to handle foreign policy, and held "doctrinaire prejudices" and a "simplistic philosophy" that showed through his polished presentations. For these reasons, the editors found Reagan unsuited for the presidency, and poured cold water on ideas of a Nixon-Reagan or Rockefeller-Reagan ticket. "If Reagan is unqualified to be President," they emphasized, "he is unqualified to be vice-president."[75]

Even hostile observers had to admit, however, that Reagan had a strong pragmatic streak that most of his critics had not anticipated. Only two months into his term, he proposed the largest tax hike ever put forward by any governor of any state, with a final price tag of approximately one billion dollars. Reagan's biographer Lou Cannon concluded that the tax bill and accompanying property tax relief measures "changed California's revenue-raising structure from a regressive one that took little account of ability to pay into a reasonably progressive system."[76] Reagan also successfully placed the blame for the tax increase on the mismanagement of his Democratic predecessor, Pat Brown. Reagan's fellow Republican governor, Dan Evans of Washington, recalled that "I didn't view Reagan as being truly devoted to the hard work of being governor, but I realized that he was pretty damn smart when you got down to it." After running on a platform of no new taxes, Reagan raised taxes "enough that he was able to lower taxes in each of his next seven years in office. In reality, he wasn't really lowering taxes; he was just cutting pieces out of what he had already raised. Nonetheless, he got the reputation as a tax-cutter."[77] Reagan further surprised moderates by proposing strong conservationist measures and reversing a campaign promise to repeal the state's fair-housing law. Reagan continued to abide by the "Eleventh Commandment" ("Thou shalt not speak ill of any fellow Republican"), and lectured the conservative-dominated California Republican Assembly against trying to convert the GOP into "a narrow sectarian party" that would soon disappear "in a blaze of glorious defeat." He commanded the Republican volunteer organization "not to further divide but to lead the way to unity. It is not your duty, responsibility or privilege to tear down or to attempt to destroy others in the tent."[78]

The members of the Ripon Society received an inside glimpse of Reagan's presidential strategy in what seems to have been a remarkably candid exchange with William Rusher, publisher of *National Review*. Rusher and his Syndicate comrade Clif White aimed to secure the presidency for Reagan at the GOP convention by forging a tacit alliance with Rockefeller's supporters to stop Nixon on the first and second ballots. "At the third ballot," according to the notes of one Ripon member at the meeting with Rusher, "Rockefeller and Nixon forces part company. Reagan, with Clif White as broker, aims at Reagan-Percy ticket with Nixon as Secretary of State and Rockefeller (with a sneer from Rusher) as 'the man who put it all together.' If Percy wouldn't take the vice-presidency, they would look for another moderate. 'If I could be convinced that Ed Brooke could deliver a portion of the Negro vote, we would take him.'" Rusher felt that the California governor would have no chance if he were perceived as the 1968 version of Goldwater, so at Miami he would "do everything possible to appear moderate, humane, and compassionate. . . . He must start appearing progressive, responsible and ecumenical in a hurry."

The Reagan-Rockefeller marriage at the convention would be strictly one of convenience. Rusher admitted that if Rockefeller actually received the GOP nomination, he would bolt to form a new party.[79] Rockefeller was still anathema to conservatives, while Reagan was almost as unacceptable to GOP progressives as Goldwater had been in 1964.

The implausibility of this left-right coalition left Richard Nixon in the center, exactly where he wanted to be. Nonetheless, Rockefeller and Reagan supporters believed that they were tantalizingly close to blocking Nixon when the GOP convention opened in Miami Beach in early August. "The Rockefeller people actually had Nixon stopped on the first ballot," Ripon's Lee Auspitz maintained. "I know this because it was Ripon people who were on the delegate count operation at the Rockefeller headquarters in Miami Beach."[80] Clif White and the Reagan team relied on Rockefeller to withhold 400 first-ballot votes from Nixon. Rockefeller more than met that target, with in excess of 250 votes of his own and about 150 favorite-son votes in his column. Reagan had to hold back another 250 votes if Nixon was to be stopped.[81] Much of the excitement centered around the delegations from Florida and Mississippi, both of which operated under the "unit rule," which awarded the entire delegation to the candidate of a majority of delegates. If Nixon failed to secure those states, he would lose 54 crucial votes.

The Rockefeller forces had little foothold in the Nixon-committed, Reagan-leaning Southern delegations. The sole presence the New Yorker maintained in the region was the New Orleans Rockefeller for President group, led by a Tulane University history graduate student named Newt Gingrich. Ripon's Tanya Melich thanked Gingrich profusely for his help: "we here in the delegate operation feel your little New Orleans group was the only really viable Rockefeller southern support that we had."[82] Rockefeller's team hoped that White's operation could cut into Nixon's strength in the South in general and Florida and Mississippi in particular. But Rockefeller's supporters had overestimated Clif White. He failed to persuade Goldwater loyalists such as Mississippi's Clarke Reed, Louisiana's Tom Stagg, and South Carolina's Roger Milliken and Strom Thurmond to cross over to the Reagan camp. White recalled that when he confronted Thurmond and asked why he was supporting Nixon instead of Reagan, Thurmond replied that if the South didn't back Nixon, Rockefeller might gain the nomination instead. White protested that the delegates would back Reagan on a second ballot. "Well, you may be right, son," Thurmond drawled, "but we just cain't take that chance and let Rockefeller slip in."[83]

Part of White's problem was that the Reagan operation had begun too late. "They couldn't transfer over what was left of their YR strength," according to Melich, "because the YR machine they had assembled had gone off into different directions," and many of the Syndicate alumni were already working for Nixon. White also erred by failing to poll the Florida delegation, which could have allowed its members to break free and vote for Reagan.[84] "It is still a great mystery to me why the Florida delegation was not polled," Melich wrote to a colleague a few days after the convention. "If

Reagan had broken open the South, we would have stopped Nixon on the first ballot and then could have gone on to victory ourselves."[85] She wrote to another correspondent that "We had a large number of second and third ballot votes, and even if California had broken open and given some votes to Nixon, we could have won."[86] As it happened, however, White was halted a few votes short of turning the South around.[87] "We were out-psyched by our syndicate psychosis," Melich lamented. "I'll never again believe in the omnipotence of your friend and mine, F. Clifton White."[88] The moderates' old enemy had let them down.

Several Ripon members had a front seat at the Rockefeller camp's subsequent loss of the nomination. Despite White's failure to muster the South, the Rockefeller forces believed that they had actually halted Nixon short of the total he needed for nomination on the first ballot. As Auspitz remembered the sequence of events: "A New Jersey millionaire breezes into Miami from Nassau or wherever he's been vacationing, gets his nose under the tent of the delegate count operation, and learns that the Rockefeller people have Nixon stopped by ten votes or however many it was. So, since he's from New Jersey, he shares this exciting news with Nelson Gross, who's the chairman of Bergen County. And then Gross suddenly realizes: 'I could shift this to Nixon!'" The Bergen County delegation split off from the state's slate, which was pledged to favorite son Clifford Case, and announced that it would vote for Nixon, "and then everybody knew— that was it."[89]

Rockefeller's supporters were fooling themselves, however, if they thought that their man had a realistic chance of becoming the convention's nominee. He was still completely unacceptable to the predominantly conservative delegates in 1968, even if they treated him more politely than Goldwater's zealots had at the 1964 convention. If Nixon had been stopped on the first or subsequent ballots, it is highly unlikely that Rockefeller would have been the beneficiary. As Kentucky Governor Louis Nunn told a reporter in Miami, "our delegates know that if they voted for Rockefeller down here they wouldn't be allowed off the plane back home."[90] A later Ripon Society analysis implicitly acknowledged that moderates and progressives had been mistaken in pinning their hopes on Rockefeller. He had failed to gain the nomination not only because of conservative antipathy but because of his indecision in announcing his candidacy, his inattention to the grassroots, and his withdrawal from intraparty activity: "The tedious but important work of cultivating political friendships, performed so assiduously during his 1964 campaign, was ignored. The network of allies around the country fell into decay."[91] The major lesson from the Rockefeller dalliance was that "Republican moderates cannot afford to let go their grasp of local party machinery, wherever they have obtained it. They must vigilantly apply themselves to the daily business of politics, working always to expand the Republican appeal beyond its minority base."[92]

Many moderates were upset and even disgusted by the events of the convention. Not only had Rockefeller failed, but Nixon gave the strong impression that he had cut a deal with Thurmond and his allies with regard to selecting Maryland Governor Spiro Agnew as his running mate and promising Southern influence in a Nixon presidency. At the time, Agnew's selection appeared to be a brilliant, Machiavellian maneuver by Nixon to play the different GOP factions against each other. To the extent that political observers outside Maryland knew who Agnew was, they placed him on the left end of the Republican spectrum. He had called for Thomas Kuchel to be the GOP presidential nominee in 1964, and led the Draft Rockefeller movement in 1967–68.[93] The *Ripon Forum*'s Maryland correspondent believed that Agnew had "unquestionably been a progressive governor in almost all ways," elected with the overwhelming support of the state's black voters and committed to a program of urban improvement and civic reform.[94] Former Pennsylvania Governor William Scranton recalled that Agnew "did a very good job with education and other fields that we 'liberal' Republicans felt were important."[95]

After the April 1968 riots following Martin Luther King's assassination, however, Agnew had summoned a group of black civil rights and community leaders in Baltimore and denounced them for failing to condemn "the treason and hate" of Black Power advocates like Stokely Carmichael and Rap Brown, the "twin priests of violence" whom he regarded as the real cause of the riots. Agnew speculated that civil rights activists' alleged silence was due to "a perverted concept of race loyalty" and a secret agreement not to openly criticize any black spokesman, however radical. The ministers and social workers, who had worked around the clock to keep the riots from spreading, became understandably indignant and many stormed out of the meeting. Backlash-minded whites were gratified by the symbolism of a white leader putting down blacks and standing up to their supposed demands for what Agnew termed "instantaneous economic equality." His performance doubtless explained why Strom Thurmond communicated to Nixon that he found the Maryland governor an acceptable vice presidential candidate. Even as he had played to the backlash, though, Agnew maintained that it was "a sign of the sickness in our society that the lunatic fringes of the black and white communities speak with wide publicity while we, the moderates, remain continuously mute."[96] At the GOP convention, many moderates and even some progressives downplayed Agnew's post-riot outburst in view of his previous record as a moderate. Of course no one yet knew about his history of bribe-taking and corruption.

Still, even those moderates who were willing to give Agnew the benefit of the doubt were angry that the likes of Lindsay, Percy, and Hatfield had been passed over. The uncoordinated moderates characteristically botched an attempt to nominate Lindsay as Vice President from the convention floor; Lindsay instead ended up giving a nominating speech for Agnew. One Ripon Society member who attended the convention pronounced that "The moderates are dead, with no effective beachhead in any part of the party including the governors." Another sighed that the outcome revealed the defects of "moderates who, like myself, are somewhat disdainful of getting down and grubbing for the precinct level control of the party."[97]

There was considerable disagreement among moderate Republicans as to whether they ought to support the Nixon-Agnew ticket. At one end of the debate was Ripon's Richard Zimmer, a future member of Congress from New Jersey, who left the convention with "the smell of decomposing pachyderm" lingering in his nostrils. Zimmer believed that the moderates' efforts had "merely cosmetized an essentially reactionary group of politicians. Our failure has reconfirmed the fact that the name of the game in American politics is power and the route to power is money, organization, and a salable candidate. To change the party in any substantive way, we must create an organization equipped to take power." He recommended that moderates should wait for Nixon's defeat, and then work to create "a national organization of politicians" that would "strive to nominate John Lindsay in 1972 by taking over the party from the precinct-level up."[98] A post-convention poll of Ripon's membership revealed that 82 percent of respondents had supported Rockefeller, versus only 12 percent for Nixon, and that only a third of the Rockefeller supporters indicated that they would definitely support Nixon-Agnew, even with reservations.[99]

Moderates had never really mustered any enthusiasm for Nixon, despite considerable evidence that he would govern from the center. He did have a few strong advocates within moderate ranks. Dwight Eisenhower, for one, wrote that he was "puzzled" by the "implication that Nixon is *not* a moderate. Certainly I always believed him to be one."[100] One Ripon Society member went so far as to argue that "Richard Nixon is a progressive," and pointed to his long support of black civil rights and even incipient affirmative action, his "clear and original domestic program," his call for a total reexamination of traditional collective security arrangements, and his freedom from ties to failed policies in Vietnam.[101] Moderates approved of Nixon's thoughtful campaign positions on domestic policy: black community self-control, tax incentives for business investment in the ghettos, a volunteer army, creation of a nationwide job bank, and a new student-teacher corps. There was even at that time reason to think that Nixon would be receptive to the Ripon Society's argument, in response to the USSR's invasion of Czechoslovakia in August, that U.S. recognition of Red China could undercut the Soviets.[102] Nixon's foreign policy memo delivered to the convention's Platform Committee recognized that Vietnam was a political rather than military struggle, and suggested that the NLF would have to be party to peace negotiations, all of which supported the view of a "new" Nixon.

While most moderates acknowledged Nixon's advocacy of policies they favored, they never saw him as one of their own—or trusted him. On Vietnam, for example, Nixon's post-convention emphasis on the military aspects of the war, and his refusal to utter the words of his platform memo in public, bolstered what the *Ripon Forum* called "the suspicion that Mr. Nixon's written statement to the platform committee was only a tactical move to head off a threatened floor fight by George Romney and other critics of the war."[103] The *Forum* was also one of the few media outlets to observe and criticize "Mr. Nixon's habit of acquiescing when his managers schedule campaign dinners in country clubs that exclude minority groups."[104] Nixon's late-campaign silence on most issues and particularly Vietnam, which one moderate called a "deodorized strategy of wooden aloofness," provoked suspicions that Nixon would lean conservative, particularly in the hopes of heading off George Wallace's independent challenge from the right.[105] Nixon had always acted as the bubble in the plumber's level, seeking the dead center of the GOP, rather than as a participant in the moderate movement with its distinctive passions and convictions. Now in a time of turmoil and backlash, "The nation is drifting to the right, carrying the center with it," one observer lamented, and Nixon seemed bound to follow that rightward drift.[106] Ripon's research director fretted that "The results of this election may be even more damaging to the morale of progressive Republicans than the Goldwater takeover four years ago."[107]

The consensus view within the Ripon leadership, however, was that the moderates should fight for power in the campaign and then, if fortune so decreed, in a Nixon presidency, which seemed even likelier after the disruption of the Democratic Party convention in Chicago by Mayor Daley's violent police repression of antiwar protests. The *Forum* endorsed Nixon, although in lukewarm tones: "Frankly, Nixon-Agnew was not our dream ticket," began the cover editorial. The Ripon editors discerned that the lesson of Nixon's success for progressives and conservatives alike was the necessity of working within the party rather than relying on attractive candidates or ideological appeals. All factions would now "participate in [Nixon's] campaign to advance their own style of Republicanism. If Nixon wins, the fight for influence will be carried on within his administration. . . . Progressives can maximize their long-term influence by working for the Party this year and supporting its national candidates."[108] Indeed, by late September, Ripon's president Huebner, governing board chairman John R. Price, and longtime member George Gilder were working full time on the Nixon for President national staff—Huebner and Gilder as speech-writers, and Price as assistant to Leonard Garment, Nixon's staff man handling advertising. The Nixon Citizens Committee gave a dinner for Ripon and enlisted their help in drafting a proposal for a national voluntary service foundation.[109]

The election was so close that Nixon didn't declare victory until the following morning. Ripon's Lee Huebner and Tim Petri had a first-hand view of the President-elect's victory celebrations, as they wangled their way into the small group of Nixon intimates gathered in his suite in New York's Waldorf-Astoria Hotel. "I remember shaking Nixon's hand and congratulating him," Huebner recalled, "and he said, 'Yes, but we didn't carry the Congress, and the press is going to be against us.' He was so negative . . . As Bill Safire said of Nixon, he was a good loser but a poor winner. I think it was partly that he defined his whole life against his enemies, and when he triumphed it took him a while to get his bearings."[110]

Nixon had in fact become the first newly elected president since Zachary Taylor in 1848 to fail to carry at least one house of Congress. Because of Wallace's strong showing in the South, Nixon received only 43 percent of the popular vote. Despite the unified state of the Republicans and the disarray of the Democrats, the anticipated GOP surge in the House did not materialize, although Republicans did gain in the Senate and to some extent on the state level. Moderates argued that Nixon had undermined the GOP by failing to campaign as the "new, mellowed, responsible centrist Nixon" he had been in the primaries. Nixon's avoidance of issues in the fall, combined with his appeal to the backlash vote through his lukewarm support of racial integration, his pandering on militarism and law and order, and his clumsy "old Nixon" attack on Humphrey's position on Vietnam, cost him the votes of progressive Republicans and moderate Democrats. He tumbled from a two-to-one edge among educated suburbanites in September to a two-to-one deficit by November. The Nixon campaign had underperformed generally in the Northeast and in large cities—Murray Kempton claimed there were no GOP victories in any city "large enough to have a bookstore"—and among suburbanites, blacks, and the young, who comprised the fastest-growing groups in the electorate. Not only had Nixon failed to shatter the New Deal coalition, he had strengthened it outside the South.

Looking to the future, members of the Ripon Society warned against trying to add George Wallace's supporters to the Republican coalition. They denied that the Republican cause in the 1970 elections would be aided by a Southern strategy, especially since the marginal districts in the House and Senate would continue to be located primarily in the more liberal parts of the country.[111] Ripon's Christopher Beal took particular pains to debunk the "myth" that Wallace had disrupted normal patterns of state-by-state party voting, or that his supporters could be won over to a more conservative Republican Party. Nixon won in states where Republicans had done well in the 1966 elections, and lost where the GOP did badly; outside the South, Wallace drew evenly from the two major parties. Beal was probably correct to suggest that in states like California, where Wallace garnered 7 percent of the vote, most of his support came from the die-hard conservatives who had supported Joe Shell against Nixon in 1962, and that Nixon could not woo these supporters without losing more numerous moderate voters.[112] Beal concluded that "We hear proposals that all liberals join together in one party, and all conservatives in another; but at no time has the division been remotely as clearcut. And nobody should expect it to be now."[113]

Nixon had retained some moderate and progressive support as well as attracting some Democrats and independents; an estimated one-fourth of his vote came from 1964 Johnson voters. The Ripon Society editorialized that Nixon had "both the capacity and the desire to be an effective President," and hoped that he would become a "healing statesman" by returning to his springtime role as the man who spoke with eloquence and understanding of "the alienated citizen" and of the possibility of new political alignments that would include black militants as well as the silent center. Ripon predicted that the new President could "expect strong support in both Houses of Congress for progressive initiatives," particularly with regard to making an early and honorable settlement of the Vietnam war.[114]

The Ripon Society's longtime antagonist Kevin Phillips, who had helped advance the Southern strategy from his position on John Mitchell's campaign staff, would shortly advance an interpretation of the election, and the likely conservative direction of the Republican Party, that would contradict nearly all of the moderates' hopeful conclusions. Most observers in 1968, however, felt that the results supported the perception of a factionally balanced GOP. Walter Thayer, writing to Dwight Eisenhower after the election, rejoiced that "The Republicans do seem to be united and there appears to be none of the division we experienced in 1964. Even the Ripons gave Dick their full support in the campaign and, as you will remember, that group of youngsters are the extreme moderates of our Party."[115]

But what was an "extreme moderate"? Was it even possible for moderates to respond effectively to the desperate needs of the times, or to remain moderate after having made the attempt? Moderates were stung by Eugene McCarthy's witticism that a moderate Republican was someone who, seeing a man drowning thirty feet offshore, would throw him a twenty-foot rope and feel that he had gone more than halfway. For the Ripon Society's Michael Chabot Smith, who described himself as "a fairly fervent moderate Republican," the events of 1968 destroyed moderate hopes and illusions. Smith had joined Ripon at Yale Law School, after an upbringing in heavily Republican Fairfield County, Connecticut and college at Princeton. He campaigned for John Lindsay, worked for moderate organizations like Ripon and Republicans for Progress, and became a staffer for politicians such as Charles Percy and Michigan Senator Robert Griffin. In his view, the GOP, as the "out" party, was likelier than the entrenched, hidebound Democratic Party to work for a more just and fair political system.

In January 1968, Smith joined the domestic version of the Peace Corps, a Great Society creation called Volunteers in Service to America, or VISTA. Soon he was living in New York City public housing, and then in even worse accommodations in the slums, trying to facilitate community self-improvement efforts. The two dozen or so volunteers in his training group were, in his recollection, "virtually all white, mostly naïve but well-intentioned young people from fairly privileged backgrounds," the sort of liberals who had been inspired by the Urban Coalition posters urging Americans to "Give a damn." The VISTA experience was not liberalizing but radicalizing. The volunteers found it difficult and frustrating to try to organize wary tenants to make collective demands on absentee landlords or public authorities, through rent strikes or other actions. The welfare rights movement with which VISTA's volunteers became embroiled placed unsupportable demands on New York's budget. During a sit-in against the city welfare administration that was organized by the VISTA workers, Smith realized that the main reason the community members were taking part in the protest "was that they believed *we* could deliver the goods—when in fact our mission was supposed to be to empower *them* to organize and make decisions for themselves."[116] The enormous gap between the needs of urban minorities and the nation's willingness to meet them led increasing numbers of VISTA's young workers to view the program as "a hypocritical and fraudulent holding action to avoid explosions in the ghettos," as Smith wrote at the time.[117]

Smith's VISTA involvement unrolled against the cataclysmic events of 1968, from the Tet Offensive through the Columbia University protests, the King and Kennedy assassinations, and the dreary, mud-smeared futility of the Poor People's Campaign in a shantytown on the Mall in Washington,

D.C. By the time of the fall '68 elections, he recalled, "I had come to the terribly sad conclusion that my former heroes like Mayor Lindsay either did not comprehend or refused to do what was necessary to deal with reality as it existed on the streets of the South Bronx and other communities like it." As a result, "I experienced such a shift in perspective that the differences between the parties appeared miniscule. By the time of the '68 presidential election, I thought all I wanted to do was 'smash capitalism,' and I saw my main philosophical challenge as the question of whether I should vote for Eldridge Cleaver or Dick Gregory as a write-in."[118] The African-American comedian Gregory campaigned for the presidency mostly as a stunt, but he was in deadly earnest in trying to persuade young white liberals like Smith that their faith in traditional American institutions and processes was misguided. In a much-publicized address, Gregory told the Yale senior class that the Ford Motor Company had hired 6,000 black people, without forcing them to pass burdensome qualifications tests, in the wake of the Detroit riots. "Why do you think they hired them?" he asked rhetorically. "Because of non-violence? You damn right know it wasn't that. The fire got too close to the Ford plant, baby. Don't scorch the Mustangs, baby. You-all, running around talking about how riots hurt, do you realize how long it would have taken us through peaceful channels to get 6,000 black folks hired and through those tests?"[119]

Smith's radicalism eventually burned out, and he became involved with the Ripon Society again through his antiwar efforts. By that point, however, he was no longer interested in the moderate, incremental programs and the forward-looking yet prudent politicians he had once supported. "I got out of liberal Republican politics when I became radicalized in '68," he remembered. "And by the time I came back into the 'system,' I just didn't believe in it anymore."[120]

While some of the young progressives in the Ripon Society thought of themselves as the right flank of the New Left, most considered themselves to be loyal members of a Republican Party that still held a place of honor for them. Ripon ended the year with a gala sixth anniversary dinner on December 15 at New York City's Plaza Hotel. Over 400 guests attended, and the event was hosted by some of the Society's moderate heroes and deep-pocketed sponsors, including Henry Kissinger (soon to be named Nixon's national security advisor), J. Irwin Miller, David Rockefeller, William Scranton, Walter Thayer, Henry Wallich, and John Hay Whitney. William Rusher, the moderates' genial foe, was among the black-tied guests and admitted that the Riponers were "lovely people—not the overload of scratchy nuts one finds in more extreme contexts."[121] Rusher's enemy John Lindsay addressed the gathering and lauded Ripon for seeking "to apply Republican principles to the most urgent national dilemmas" and fighting "the danger of confining our party's base to the privileged and secure." Curiously, the bulk of Lindsay's address saluted "the dissidents—the 'radicals' if you will," who had been the first to take direct action against discrimination in the South, poverty in the North, and the war in Vietnam. Radicals of this sort were not greatly represented among Republicans, and as Mike Smith's example showed, they did not long remain in the party once they had become radicalized. But Lindsay also suggested that an "era of greatness" might be at hand in Nixon's presidency.[122] Moderates had grounds for cautious optimism as they awaited the inauguration of the first professional Republican politician to be elected president in forty years.

CHAPTER 9

✧

Some Revelation Is at Hand

Richard Nixon's First Year in Office, 1969

During his long political career, Richard Nixon inspired countless attempts to determine his ideological and psychological identity. Was Nixon a liberal, a conservative, a moderate, or none—or all—of those things? Were there discernable principles and ideals at his core, or an echoing void, or a writhing mass of darkness? There can be no definitive answer to the quest for the "real" Nixon, but perhaps the best one-word description of him is: Republican. No one better personified the party's varied elements, its internal struggles and contradictions, its noble ideals and sordid impulses, its bright hopes and bitter resentments. For many of the delegates at the 1968 GOP convention, it was Nixon's emphasis on party unity, and his ecumenical willingness to campaign for Republicans of every stripe over the course of two decades of party service, that made him the logical choice as the presidential nominee. As a campaigner, Nixon was uniquely able to straddle the moderate and conservative factions within the GOP, and as President he would continue to offer something to each group. While moderates and progressives would enjoy only partial successes during his presidency, Nixon made sure that they had what he characteristically referred to as "a piece of the action." At the same time, Nixon both deliberately and inadvertently laid the groundwork for the decline of the Republicans' moderate wing.

Moderates applauded many of Nixon's early appointments. The Ripon Society saluted Nixon's choice of White House advisors, particularly his designation of longtime Rockefeller associate Henry Kissinger as national security advisor and Kissinger's Harvard colleague, Daniel Patrick Moynihan, a Democrat who had served in Lyndon Johnson's administration, as urban affairs counselor. Ripon predicted that Moynihan would have "the critical creative functions" in the administration and would be a bridge to the "new liberals," i.e., the neoconservative Democrats whom moderate Republicans generally viewed as allies. Ripon anticipated that centrists Melvin Laird at Defense and Robert Finch at HEW, the two youngest members of the cabinet, were also "likely to be the two most powerful" and might vie to succeed Nixon in 1976.[1] Secretary of State William Rogers was a respected moderate who had served in the Eisenhower administration; the same description fit Nixon's advisor for Congressional relations, Bryce Harlow, and the new assistant secretary of state, Elliot Richardson. Curiously, quite a few moderates were suspicious of John Volpe at Transportation and Walter Hickel at Interior. Though both men had a reputation as moderate governors of Massachusetts and Alaska, respectively, many feared that Volpe, a building contractor by trade, would swathe the American landscape in concrete while frontiersman Hickel would turn over public lands to private profiteers.[2] Ripon hoped that the third governor in the cabinet, George Romney, would "turn out to be the most interesting appointment of all, for he is the most outspoken member of the cabinet, the one least likely to play the team game at all costs."[3]

James Farmer's appointment as assistant secretary of HEW and Arthur Fletcher's as assistant secretary of labor opened the door to reconciliation with African-Americans, a high priority since no president in recent history had been elected with as little black support as Nixon.[4] Civil rights advocates hailed James Allen's designation as commissioner of education, since as New York's commissioner of education he had been strongly associated with school desegregation. Moderates regarded Donald Rumsfeld, the new head of the Office of Economic Opportunity, as a bright hope. Moderates also occupied other important though less visible positions. John Veneman, a leader of the moderate Young Turks in the California legislature, became HEW undersecretary, and in turn made Leon Panetta, a former legislative assistant to Senator Thomas Kuchel, the department's Director of Civil Rights. Rhode Island Governor John Chafee became secretary of the Navy. A large number of moderates served as Nixon's assistants, including former Congressmen Robert Ellsworth of Kansas and (somewhat later) Clark MacGregor of Minnesota.

In an ominous early indication of Nixon's need to punish his enemies, the President forced Ray Bliss out of the chairmanship of the Republican National Committee. In the 1966 elections, Bliss had caved in to Nelson Rockefeller's demands that the RNC stop funding Nixon's campaign travels; Rockefeller knew that Nixon's efforts on behalf of Republican candidates across the land would be a great help in his winning the '68 presidential nomination. Nixon took his revenge by firing Bliss, although both men maintained the fiction that Bliss had quit in order to return to his first love, accounting.[5] Still, Bliss' nuts-and-bolts approach and his even-handed management of the factional battles within the GOP remained RNC policy. Bliss' successor, Maryland Congressman Rogers C. B. Morton, was the younger brother of moderate hero Senator Thruston Morton of Kentucky, who had also been an RNC chairman during the Eisenhower presidency. The younger Morton reassured moderates that "a basic mission of the Party is to be open to free expression of individual points of view" and that "both major parties are forums for converging and diverging philosophies.... Our internal struggles are proof of our own individuality and vitality."[6]

The Ripon Society's president, Lee Huebner, became a White House staff assistant with particular responsibilities for speechwriting. He joined a writing team that included Pat Buchanan on the right, former *New York Herald Tribune* editorialist Ray Price in the center, and William Safire, whose position Huebner described as "somewhere between Buchanan and Price." Huebner believed that the diversity of Republican voices on the speechwriting team reflected the strength and eclecticism of the Nixon administration at its best. In practice, however, he felt that a speechwriter's political coloration made little difference in the finished product, since the issues that a writer took on had more to do with his writing style than his political outlook: "If the occasion called for a tough, political, hard-hitting, street-corner rousing speech, Pat Buchanan might be assigned to do that. If it was a speech that had to be more entertaining and lively and colorful, Safire might draw that. Ray Price provided lift and inspiration on things like the inaugural addresses."[7] Huebner thought that divisions in the administration were less along liberal-conservative lines than between issue-oriented types and process-oriented types, whose ranks included the advance men and operatives.

Contrary to nearly every contemporary journalistic description of the Nixon administration, Huebner found that the most influential moderate in the White House was John Ehrlichman, the President's senior staff member for domestic policy development. Though outsiders saw Ehrlichman and staff chief H. R. Haldeman as the intransigent gatekeepers atop the Nixon hierarchy—both were collectively described as "the Germans" or "the Berlin Wall"—moderates viewed Ehrlichman as a counter to Haldeman's conservative inclinations. His fellow Seattle lawyers considered Ehrlichman a moderate with a strong interest in environmental conservation, and one of his closest friends was progressive Republican Congressman Pete McCloskey.[8] For Huebner, "Ehrlichman was really my hero within the administration, right up until Watergate. He was the person in the administration who I felt was really sympathetic to the moderates . . . not just on the substantive issues, but also in matters of style and symbolism." While most observers gave Moynihan credit for the Nixon administration's progressive agenda on domestic issues, "Ehrlichman was advocating for the domestic agenda more effectively from a more influential position."[9]

More than a dozen other Ripon Society members received White House appointments. John R. Price, the Society's chairman, and four other colleagues went to work for Moynihan's newly created Urban Affairs Council. Others served as White House fellows, aides to Ehrlichman and other moderates, and members of assorted councils and commissions. Some commentators saw these appointments as reflections of "Nixon's attempt to achieve an ideological Balkanization of the government—conservatives to Justice and Defense, liberals in urban affairs."[10] But the leaders of Ripon, who had done some discreet promotion for the appointments, welcomed the visibility and influence they brought.[11] Bruce Chapman rejoiced that "At last we have a chance to have our people in government, actually making some of the decisions we've been advocating, or at least advising the decision makers. Our presence in the Administration actually enhances their receptivity to our ideas."[12] All of those Ripon members who joined the new administration resigned their staff or elective positions in the Society, though most continued to keep in close touch with the organization.

David Broder, who was keenly attuned to moderate-conservative tensions within the GOP, found it significant that Nixon's White House appointments drew on members of both the Ripon Society and the conservative Syndicate, which he described as "an informal caucus of congressional staffers, lawyers, and businessmen operating within the Young Republican National Federation." Both outfits had become important talent factories for the GOP, and opposed each other not only ideologically but in their approach to politics. Ripon provided a bridge to the intellectual community and produced innovative and practical reform proposals in the Republican tradition, calling for the abolition of the military draft, federal revenue sharing, the negative income tax, and diplomatic opening to China. Many of these proposals were taken up by the Nixon administration, and influenced even conservative consideration of the issues. The Syndicate had made the YRs into what Broder called "a reliable bastion of conservatism." It provided grassroots workers and organizational talent not only for the Goldwater and Nixon presidential campaigns but for dozens of state and Congressional contests in which the Syndicate's leaders, Clif White and William Rusher, had an interest. The Syndicate also launched many of its members into elective politics. By 1969, Syndicate alumni John Ashbrook, William Brock, and Buz Lukens were members of the House of Representatives.

While Ripon placed more of its members in the Nixon White House, none held a post as significant as the Syndicate's William Timmons, who worked with Bryce Harlow as presidential assistant for Congressional relations and succeeded him a year into the administration. Broder saw the dynamic between Ripon and the Syndicate as a "struggle between men of ideas and men of action."[13] Ripon was deficient in the area of practical politics, while the Syndicate lacked the ability to conceive and sell exciting policy ideas.

Nixon recognized the characteristic strengths and weaknesses of both the moderates and conservatives in his administration, and welcomed the frequently adversarial relations between them as beneficial to policy formation. They were in a sense the projection of the duality of his own nature, his ingrained habit of "on the one hand, on the other hand" thinking. White House counsel Leonard Garment, a self-described "birthright Democrat," saw his role as the opposite number of presidential assistant Harry Dent, former assistant to Strom Thurmond and a leading advocate and executor of the Southern strategy. "I eventually became Harry's informal counterpart, proponent of the Nixon 'northern strategy,'" Garment recalled. "Nixon's idea was that Harry and I would battle out issues of politics and race hand to hand, by fair means and foul, thereby miraculously achieving a functional balance that would be tolerable to southern conservatives and northern liberals."[14]

Nixon believed that he could succeed where Eisenhower failed in creating a durable, substantive, and popular "modern Republicanism," which would infuse the liberal desire for strong, activist government with conservative principles. Moynihan and other moderates advised Nixon that many Americans had embraced the security offered by Great Society programs such as Medicare and Medicaid. Many of those programs, Moynihan argued, had become part of the status quo, and to abolish them would be a dangerously radical rather than conservative act. This was the identical argument that the modern Republicans had made to Eisenhower in persuading him to build upon rather than repudiate the major accomplishments of the New Deal. Moynihan encouraged Nixon to see himself as an ideologically eclectic leader in the tradition of mid-nineteenth century British Prime Minister Benjamin Disraeli. Moynihan persuaded the President to read Robert Blake's biography of the creator of the modern Conservative Party, which emphasized Disraeli's ability to win working class support for the Tories by implementing the best liberal ideas, which the Liberal Party had been unable to get past the conservative opposition. Nixon endorsed the notion that it was "Tory men with liberal policies" who had really changed the world.[15] The idea of Nixon as a Disraeli figure had occurred to his conservative supporter Ralph De Toledano as early as the 1950s.[16] The

Ripon Society also speculated that "As Disraeli, hero of the rotten boroughs, brought electoral reform and gave it a conservative stamp, Nixon, the darling of the small towns who didn't carry a major urban center, may yet save the cities."[17]

While moderates generally approved of Nixon's willingness to blend liberal and conservative initiatives, they were troubled by another of his dualities. Ray Price described it as the difference between Nixon's "light side" and "dark side." Nixon could be wise, caring, generous, and idealistic, but also angry, dictatorial, vindictive, and hateful. This duality had political as well as psychological implications. It would be a gross exaggeration to wholly identify Nixon's dark side with his conservatism. The people who brought out Nixon's best qualities included conservatives like Arthur Burns and John Mitchell as well as moderates like Robert Finch and William Rogers. Price thought presidential assistant Charles "Chuck" Colson personified Nixon's dark side; he recalled asking Mitchell just what Colson's constituency was, to which Mitchell growled in reply, "The President's worst instincts." And yet Colson's mentors and supporters had been exemplary Massachusetts moderates like Leverett Saltonstall, Elliot Richardson, and Brad Morse. Even Price thought that to some extent the darkness in Nixon made him a more effective leader than if he had possessed a moderate and temperate personality: "a measure of scheming and duplicity are necessary in the real world of power politics."[18] For moderate activists who had been on the receiving end of the amoral, undemocratic, and occasionally violent tactics of right-wing groups, however, it seemed logical to conclude that Nixon's dark side reflected a brutish aspect of conservatism. It was no surprise to them when it was revealed that Nixon, seeking a plan to conduct illegal surveillance and harassment of antiwar activists, had turned to his assistant Tom Charles Huston, who had been national chair of Young Americans for Freedom.

Lee Huebner believed that Nixon's mixed feelings about the moderates in his party reflected his dual nature. On the one hand, Nixon "regarded the moderate Republicans with disdain and a little contempt; it was the hard, practical politician putting down the softness of the moderates." On the other hand, "he had enormous respect for intellect and ability, and had real admiration for some moderate Republicans, almost independent of their politics. But that was the good Nixon, and the two Nixons were always in tension."[19] Nixon's belief in the need for toughness, even ruthlessness, in the conduct of government eventually won out, leading him to despise most moderate Republicans as pious weaklings. But it was precisely his growing estrangement from moderate restraints and principles that eventually destroyed him.

In the early days of the Nixon administration, of course, that outcome was unimaginable. Huebner, when he was interviewed in the first months of 1969, said that while his side had lost the battle with conservatives over the tone and content of Nixon's campaign, "Now we've got to win the struggle over his Presidential policies, and judging from his early appointments and actions, I think we're doing all right."[20] Nixon's inaugural address sounded mostly moderate themes. The new president emphasized that "we are approaching the limits of what government alone can do," and echoed Eisenhower in calling on Americans to lower their voices and cool their rhetoric. But he also sought to convince dissenters that his administration would listen to them, and to reassure African-Americans that he would build upon rather than reverse progress in civil rights and anti-poverty efforts. He pledged that peacemaking would be his highest priority, and that internationally he would seek to move from confrontation to negotiation, in Vietnam and the Cold War generally. Nixon gratified good-government advocates by eliminating the patronage appointments of postmasters; henceforth, they would be chosen on merit through the competitive civil service. He pursued a middle course with regard to the Office of Economic Opportunity, refusing conservative demands to abolish the anti-poverty agency but angering liberals by shifting some of its operations to cabinet departments. In keeping with his campaign pledge, he created the Office of Minority Business Enterprise in the Commerce Department, to help the business efforts of blacks and other minorities. By April 1969, New York Mayor John Lindsay judged that Nixon was "performing as a centrist, as I thought he would."[21]

Nixon's Democratic critics unfavorably compared his accomplishments during his first hundred days in office to the rush of programs passed over the same span during the administrations of Franklin Roosevelt, John F. Kennedy, and Lyndon Johnson. But Ray Price argued in a memo to Nixon that Republicans of all stripes agreed that "the nation has suffered grievously from past Democratic administrations' grandstanding, their fascination with quantitative measurements, their frenzies of activity for activity's sake, their extravagant rhetoric, their 'wars' on every real or imagined social ill, their piling of promise on over-promise, their rush of half-baked legislative proposals, their substitution of emotion for reason, their basic premise that to pass a law means to solve a problem."[22] The Ripon Society, evaluating Nixon's first hundred days, felt that Nixon hadn't made a case to justify continuation of Johnson's anti-ballistic missile (ABM) system or offered grounds for optimism about an imminent negotiated settlement in Southeast Asia. But the Society praised Nixon's plans for revenue sharing and welfare overhaul, which if successful would "far surpass in their impact the contributions of the War on Poverty, with its grandiose claims and meager achievements." The cities would also benefit from revenue sharing and the administration's commitment to rebuild riot-torn areas. Ripon noted the undramatic but important work of administrative restructuring in the establishment of the Urban Affairs Council, the revival of the National Security Council, the reorganization of departments including Labor and HEW, and the establishment of common regional boundaries and headquarters for the field operations of five federal agencies.[23]

Other developments in the Republican Party in early 1969 also cheered moderates. In the Senate, Pennsylvania moderate Hugh Scott won election as minority whip over Everett Dirksen's preferred conservative candidate, Roman Hruska. In the House GOP elections, Illinois moderate John B. Anderson was voted in as Republican Conference chairman, and Robert Taft Jr. became chair of the Republican Committee on Planning and Research. Moderates failed to unseat the conservative Les Arends as whip, however, and Donald Rumsfeld's loss to Taft in the election for the Planning and Research chair likely precipitated his decision to leave Congress by accepting Nixon's offer to head the OEO.

Rumsfeld had been a leader of reform-minded Republicans in the House at least from the time of the 1965 coup that elevated Gerald Ford to minority leader. In 1968, he had rallied a baker's dozen of Republicans, who became known as "Rumsfeld's Raiders," to push the House to modernize its operations and democratize its rules and procedures. The group was mostly moderate, and included representatives such as Rumsfeld's mentor, Tom Curtis of Missouri, New Yorkers Charles Goodell and Barber Conable, Robert Taft Jr. and Charles Whalen of Ohio, and George H. W. Bush of Texas. Rumsfeld and his allies called for improved minority staff ratios on committees, greater use of oversight organizations such as the General Accounting Office to evaluate and track the costs of legislative programs, a rational division of committee jurisdictions, and restraints on the power of committee chairmen and their monopolization of information and policy decisions.[24] Rumsfeld's Raiders found the closed-door deal-making of the Democratic committee chairmen to be particularly obnoxious. "Legislative hearings should be open so people can see just how badly some of these programs have been mismanaged," Curtis complained. "Congressional secrecy is a scandal."[25]

Unfortunately for the Republican reformers, the media did not agree that the Democrats' institutional mismanagement of the House constituted a problem worthy of serious investigation. When reporter David Broder met with Rumsfeld in his office on Capitol Hill, the Congressman presented him with a huge pile of newspaper clippings on Representative Adam Clayton Powell Jr., the controversial Harlem congressman who was chairman of the Education and Labor Committee, and two or three brief stories on the reform efforts of Rumsfeld and his group. Why, Rumsfeld demanded, were Powell's shenanigans worthy of so much attention when Republican reform efforts received so little? "You're not as sexy as he is," Broder joked weakly. Broder agreed that reporters weren't paying heed to the system that allowed Powell and other chairmen to abuse power and damage the country's interests. But he felt that "nothing was going to come of Rumsfeld's crusade"—the Democratic chairmen were too powerful and entrenched—and that the whole issue of Republican marginalization "put you to sleep before you got to the typewriter." The media view that complexity was boring proved fatal to moderate reform efforts. Broder later conceded that cowardice was also a factor in the media's focus on colorful individuals' misdeeds rather than institutional failings. Systemic reform of the type Rumsfeld was proposing could lead to real shifts in power, which would disturb comfortable relationships between the media and the Democrats.[26]

In the wake of the 1968 elections, Rumsfeld brooded over the fact that the Republicans had once again failed to retake the House, and that in the previous forty years the GOP had won a majority of seats only twice (in 1946 and 1952). "Obviously, something is wrong," he concluded. "[I]t can't all be blamed on someone else—GOP Presidential candidates, philosophical splits in the party, the press, the Governors, etc. Part of the responsibility has to be with House Republicans." Rumsfeld wanted the Republicans to take on the mantle of reform because he thought it was only by dramatizing the negative effects of Democratic control that the GOP might regain a majority: "Voters must be given reasons to vote against an able, honest Democrat. . . . Partisan politics and day-to-day tactical positions are not enough."[27] His decision to leave Congress for the OEO deprived the moderate Republicans of one of their ablest leaders and the opportunity to create a national majority around a Republican reform agenda. Future leaders of GOP efforts to change the nation's political paradigm would look to the transformative power of ideological conservatism, not moderate reform.

Most moderate Republicans resisted the idea that the GOP needed to turn conservative to win a national majority. Even before the 1968 elections, members of the Ripon Society had dismissed the theory that votes for Nixon and Wallace would indicate that "the key to winning elections in the future is the support of the 'Backlash-majority.'"[28] This argument was at the crux of a debate between William F. Buckley Jr. and two officers of the Ripon Society, Tim Petri and Lee Auspitz. Petri, described by the *Boston Globe* as "a tall, blond, sunburned young man who looks as though he might have spent the spring rowing on the Charles with the Harvard crew," was the Society's most promising candidate for political office; Auspitz, who had succeeded Lee Huebner as president of Ripon, was the group's deepest thinker on political philosophy.[29] The two young moderates appeared on Buckley's television program *Firing Line* in early 1969.

Buckley referred to an article characterizing Ripon as "the ADA of the GOP" and provocatively asked his guests whether there was any difference at all between Ripon and the liberal Americans for Democratic Action. Plenty, they protested. "The Ripon Society philosophically really does reject some of the major premises of New Deal liberalism," Auspitz said, "which are the major premises in turn of ADA. We believe that this is a time when notions of decentralization, of self-help, of voluntarism are coming to the fore in American society. In addition, we are a Republican group and we seek to take these sorts of Republican notions and put them to work in the Republican Party." Petri added that Ripon's members were of a different generation than the World War II veterans who had made up most of the ADA's founders and who reflexively turned to government to solve perceived societal ills: "We've felt that the role of government should be to enlighten self-interest in the society, to be a systems manager for the people of the country rather than trying to do everything itself." For this reason, Ripon identified with the New Federalist themes emerging from the Nixon White House. Auspitz acknowledged that the conservative political network entrenched in the GOP was likely to be as permanent as the labor network in the Democratic Party, but added that Ripon would continue to support the Republicans because many conservative tenets, such as decentralization and individual freedom, were in the country's best interests, so long as they were advanced responsibly.

Buckley found it hard to argue with Ripon's call for decentralization, but charged that Republican moderates and progressives were too hospitable to "people who are sort of old-time centralizers—Rockefeller types." In fact, Buckley went on, "The Ripon Society certainly seems to me to have affected most people as an organization that is industriously engaged in trying to persuade the Republican Party to be like the Democratic Party." "No," Auspitz objected, "it's engaged in persuading the Republican Party to do those things that will enable it to compete with the Democratic Party in states where the Democratic Party is strong. That's a bit different. We try to take Republican ideas and formulate them so that they can embrace the necessary role of government in the last few decades of this century."[30] This was an effective point to make to an increasingly pragmatic Buckley, whose well-known formula regarding elections was to support "the most right, viable candidate who could win."[31]

Petri mentioned that one of Ripon's functions was to prod the GOP, as the party out of power, to do a better job of developing ideas that the party in power didn't have time to develop. "Usually when a new idea comes along," he observed, "it doesn't initially enter the political dialogue as a conservative idea or a liberal idea; it's just a new idea, and then it takes on this coloration in terms of the groups that coalesce behind it." The moderates' willingness to think deeply and originally about policy was one of their advantages over the conservatives. Auspitz observed that while the *Ripon Forum* was "perhaps too fond of proposals," the only position paper he had seen in *National Review* was a pie-in-the-sky summons for the U.S. to preemptively bomb China in order to eliminate its nuclear capability.

Ripon's members and supporters were mainly educated professionals in cities and affluent suburbs. Nixon had lost their vote in key states in the election, including California, Pennsylvania, Massachusetts, Oregon, and Wisconsin. Auspitz assumed that Nixon would have to win them back, since they were "the educated constituency that any government needs to have a governing coalition as well as an electoral coalition." The Ripon leaders heatedly opposed Buckley's contention that Nixon would have won "triumphantly" if he had more ardently courted the Wallace voters. Buckley argued that the country was becoming more conservative—or, as he more eloquently phrased it, there was "a rediscovery of realism" afoot, and "there are forces loose in America which I understand to be conservatively bent, whose natural vehicle is the Republican Party." Auspitz countered that if the GOP did stake its future on a conservative coalition, it might follow the Whigs into oblivion.

There was little in the televised conversation that alluded to the nation's upheaval and cultural ferment circa 1969, other than Petri's polka-dot tie and panelist Jeff Greenfield's period sideburns. Buckley was his usual engaging television presence, complete with darting eyebrows and purred observations. He couldn't resist taking a feline swipe at his onetime electoral opponent: "Mr. Greenfield takes a moral position against Republicans— that's why he associates with Mayor Lindsay." But the conservative icon seemed to get along well with his Ripon guests, who generally held their own in the debate. At one point Petri referred to an argument he said that Buckley had been "trying to make" earlier. The host shot back: "I don't 'try to make' arguments—I make them." "Unpersuasively in a few instances," Petri riposted.[32] Even that exchange was quite genial, though, and the civil tone of the discussion suggested that moderates and conservatives could compose at least some of their differences under the banner of Republican unity.[33]

Buckley's severest criticism of Ripon was that it failed to take a "paradigmatic" view like *National Review*. Moderate Republicans therefore were tinkering with the liberal order at its edges rather than trying to replace it—a criticism Buckley lodged against the Nixon administration as well. He believed that Ripon's calls for the GOP to end the war and desegregate Southern schools were minority positions, at odds with the Society's professed support for Republican electoral victories: "On the one hand you say that you're interested in political success; on the other you're interested in success only because you want to nourish certain idealisms. But, now, these idealisms and this success don't necessarily go hand in hand."[34] Buckley's critique could be applied to both conservative and moderate activist groups in the GOP: to what extent were they prepared to alter their views in order to win elections?

Auspitz and Petri were in their mid-twenties at the time of their appearance with Buckley, and to some degree presented themselves as spokesmen for Youth, the capital-letter subject of much angry debate in the late 1960s. Discussions of youth issues in the spring of '69 took place amid some of the worst disruptions in the history of American higher education, notably a race-related student strike at San Francisco State College, the takeover of the student union building by armed black undergraduates at Cornell University, and the Harvard University "bust," when police clubbed and beat students and onlookers in the course of breaking up a radical-led building occupation. Earlier that spring, California Governor Ronald Reagan had proclaimed a "state of emergency" in response to a series of strikes, arson, and rock-throwing protests at the University of California at Berkeley. On May 15, the Berkeley violence culminated in clashes between rioters and sheriff's deputies, in which dozens of people were injured and one killed, after radicals occupied university-owned land to create a "People's Park." Reagan sent in the National Guard to restore order and enforce martial law.

Public anger over student unrest had been a winning issue for conservatives ever since Reagan campaigned against the Berkeley protests in his 1966 California gubernatorial race. Semantics professor S. I. Hayakawa, whom Reagan appointed as San Francisco State president in late 1968, took a hard-line stance against student strikers and became a conservative folk hero; later he would ride a wave of anti-liberal, anti-youth backlash into the Senate. By the spring of '69, conservative Republicans were making Senator Claghorn–style threats to prosecute and punish rebellious students and their colleges and universities. But many moderate Republicans, and even some conservatives, felt that students had real grievances that authorities needed to take seriously. Wisconsin Representative William Steiger believed that "Much as we might be appalled by the methods of the radicals, the point remains that many of their criticisms are valid. All is not well with the educational system or with the nation, and a policy, however well-intended, which suppressed the expression of that criticism or ignored it could only have a detrimental impact upon the future of the nation."[35]

Steiger was a political prodigy who attained his first government position when he was sixteen, became national chairman of the College Republicans when he was twenty, and was elected to the Wisconsin State Assembly at twenty-two. When he was elected to Congress in 1966, at age twenty-eight, he was the youngest member of the House. Diabetic and blade-thin, he looked even younger than his age, and frequently was mistaken for a page. Steiger had started out in politics as a supporter of his state's junior senator, Joseph McCarthy, whose anti-Communist crusade divided the GOP as well as the nation. Over time, however, Steiger came to believe that Republicans had to do more to respond to the real needs of most Americans, and that programs had to be judged on their efficacy rather than on ideological criteria. As a state legislator, he sponsored Wisconsin's first open-housing law and provided summer schools for the children of migrant laborers. In his first years in the House of Representatives, he joined Rumsfeld's Raiders and urged the GOP to address the causes of urban problems, to modernize government machinery on all levels, and to enlist the brainpower of the academic community.[36]

Steiger was among the two dozen Republican congressmen who made informal, unpublicized visits to college and university campuses in the spring of 1969 to try to understand the causes and remedies of the student unrest. The visits were the idea of Representative William Brock of Tennessee, who was usually considered a conservative. Nonetheless, Brock was convinced that while only a handful of radicals were responsible for lawless actions, "there is an undeniably growing wave of rank and file discontent among students." He worried that the proposed legislation to punish the protesting campuses would lead to "greater federal domination of our universities" and would "drive student moderates into the arms of the extremists."[37] In early May, he met with Steiger, George H. W. Bush, Donald Riegle, Lou Frey, and Pete Biester to propose an unofficial Task Force on Academic Reform. Each member would select a team of three other young, articulate Republican congressmen, most in their first or second terms. They would tour several colleges and universities, at their own expense, and hold direct and informal conversations with students, faculty, and administrators. The Task Force recruited additional members and set out for the universities. "This is not a narrow, partisan political issue," the group resolved, "and there are no rigid political 'sides' involved in the issue." Their goal was "to learn about the new problems and challenges" confronting the universities, "and to do everything we can to come to grips with them in a positive manner." They also hoped to show the students by example "that progress comes through cooperation, not conflict."[38]

Steiger's assistant Richard "Dick" Cheney, a young graduate student in political science at the University of Wisconsin, served as his liaison to the troubled campuses. The Dick Cheney who wrote memos to Steiger in the spring of 1969 bore little resemblance to his future incarnation as a hard-right Wyoming congressman and Vice President under George W. Bush. The twenty-eight year-old Cheney was thoughtful, open-minded, and distinctly moderate. He had many liberal friends and even some friends on the radical fringes of Students for a Democratic Society (SDS).

Steiger and Cheney visited the University of Wisconsin at Madison in late May and met with a variety of participants in the campus drama, including a leader of the Black Student Council, city aldermen, Young Republicans, and students from differing political outlooks. They found that a wide range of grievances drove student protests, including the ongoing war in Vietnam, the campus connection to the war in the form of ROTC and military research programs, the university administration's unresponsiveness to student concerns, government and societal indifference to minorities and the poor, and the particular problems faced by black students on a predominantly white campus. The state National Guard had occupied Madison in February in response to disorder caused by a black student strike. Cheney's memos presented a sympathetic view of the black students, whose initial request that the university consider the creation of a black studies department had met with what he called "bureaucratic shuffling of responsibilities" and administrators' unwillingness to make decisions.[39] Cheney noted that "The February crisis was precipitated only after careful planning by the students. They were highly organized and very sophisticated in their choice of tactics and they had specific goals in mind when they embarked upon their course of action." The black students' goal "was not disruption for the sake of disruption but a carefully planned course of action designed to move what appeared to them to be an unresponsive university." Unlike white SDS students for whom issues were secondary to the revolutionary cause, he thought, "The black students seem to be much more concerned with getting a piece of the action, with obtaining an education in a university which is responsive to them."[40]

Representative Thomas Railsback of Illinois, who was part of another Task Force section that met with Black Power and radical student groups in the Boston area, also felt that "the black radicals were much more impressive than the white radicals. Frankly, I thought some of the SDS members were spoiled rich kids."[41] Cheney found it significant that Black Panthers leader Fred Hampton, whose rally in Madison he attended with Steiger, had been invited by SDS rather than black students. Hampton entertained the gathering with tales of how the Panthers' free breakfast programs for children had won over community support, so that "when whitey came around to bust the Panthers the little old ladies would tell the motherfuckers not to mess over the Panthers," according to Cheney's notes. Cheney concluded that "Hampton is a first rate demagogue, with probably a second rate intellect," and found it amazing that his rabble-rousing met with a rapturous reception from "what is supposedly a highly sophisticated, intelligent and critical audience."[42]

However unimpressive the radicals appeared, Cheney, Steiger, and the members of the Task Force came to believe that authorities confronted with extremist provocations should not allow themselves to be goaded into heavy-handed reactions that would alienate moderates and liberals. Cheney cautioned Steiger that a conservative proposal to transform the University of Wisconsin's campus security into a state police force would be a godsend for radicals: "Given the fact that the sole purpose of many SDS operations is to get the police on campus, why would anyone want them there on a permanent basis?"[43] Railsback learned that moderate students at Harvard who had opposed SDS had become radicalized in response to the excessive force of the police.[44] John Danforth, the newly elected moderate Republican attorney general of Missouri, emphasized that "we should all realize that the tactic of these militants is to get us to over-react to their activities."[45]

Steiger initially had supported a House bill to cut federal funds to protesting campuses, but his talks with students changed his mind.[46] Members of the Task Force asked their colleagues to vote against such legislation, which embraced the dangerous concept of collective guilt and would be used as a weapon by radical students: "Legislation which treats innocent and guilty alike inadvertently confirms extremist charges that the 'establishment' is repressive and indifferent to citizen needs and concerns."

The Task Force met with Nixon and other members of the administration to present their findings. The group rejected the widespread conservative belief that student protest was the work of monolithic leadership or Communist plotting, instead finding that it typically arose from students' genuine concern over what they felt to be the difference between American promise and performance. They warned that while the vast majority of students were not revolutionary, "many students can be radicalized when violence or confrontation on campus occurs. Also disillusionment in our system can grow, even without violence, if we place one label on all students and fail to understand that they raise many areas of legitimate concern." They advised against any "repressive legislation" aimed at students, and recommended that the Nixon administration establish a presidential commission on higher education and expand its lines of communication with the university community. The Task Force also believed that campus tensions would be reduced by lowering the voting age from twenty-one to eighteen, reforming the draft, encouraging student participation in politics, and expanding young people's involvement in community service, including programs that would allow students to teach at inner-city public schools.[47]

Nixon received the Task Force members and their report politely but coolly. As Cheney had warned Steiger before the meeting, adoption of the report's call for "greater understanding and moderation in responding to student concerns and disorders" would require a significant shift in the public position of Nixon, Agnew, Attorney General Mitchell, and other key members of the administration. Cheney predicted that Robert Finch would be the only administration member present at the meeting with Nixon who would be openly receptive to the group's recommendations, and so it proved.[48]

From Nixon's standpoint, a moderate and understanding approach toward the students who hated him would win him no votes, but stoking the silent majority's anger against radical students and the permissive elites who allegedly encouraged them offered rich political rewards. He unleashed Agnew to beat the populist drum against the students and their adult sympathizers. When the Vice President spoke at Ohio State University's graduation ceremonies, he made the inflammatory charge that "a society which comes to fear its children is effete. A sniveling, hand-wringing power structure deserves the violent rebellion it encourages."[49] The administration's deliberate decision to polarize public opinion around student protest, rather than calling a halt to intemperate rhetoric as Nixon had promised in his inaugural address, divided Republicans as well as Democrats. The Task Force's recommendation for a presidential commission on higher education would be ignored until students died in protests at Kent State and Jackson State a year later.

One result of Nixon's polarizing approach was that Republicanism, even of the moderate variety, would become increasingly unattractive to students, especially at the nation's most prestigious colleges and universities, and to the young professionals who had graduated from such institutions. A symbolic indication of youthful disaffection with moderate Republicanism occurred when Massachusetts Senator Edward Brooke addressed the Wellesley College commencement in late May 1969. Brooke, one of the Senate's most progressive Republicans as well as its lone African-American, tried to persuade his restive audience that change within the system was still possible, as demonstrated by the poverty rate's having fallen from 22 percent of Americans in 1959 to 13.3 percent in 1967. Brooke was followed on the speaker's platform by the student government president, Hillary Rodham, who was the first student ever permitted to address a Wellesley graduation ceremony. The future New York senator, then a slight blonde in Coke-bottle glasses, departed from her prepared text to tear into Brooke for his alleged indifference to poverty. "What does it mean that 13.3 percent of Americans are poor?" she demanded. "How about talking about the humans, not the statistics?" Her classmates predictably gave her a standing ovation.

Brooke was convinced that his young antagonist hijacked the occasion for her own purposes, and would have attacked any other commencement speaker: "I was there representing authority, and she was representing the frustrations of her own generation, which she did most effectively."[50] But Hillary Rodham's political trajectory suggested a broader generational significance as well. A dedicated Illinois Republican for most of the 1960s, she had been a Goldwater Girl in 1964, interned for Melvin Laird, campaigned for Brooke in 1966, and assisted the Ripon Society with an antiwar symposium in 1967.[51] By the spring of 1969, however, even a progressive Republican like Brooke appeared hopelessly reactionary to her, and she left the GOP to support the New Politics wing of the Democratic Party.

Close observers of the Nixon administration judged it to be rhetorically conservative but operationally progressive; John Mitchell had early on tipped off reporters to "Watch what we do, not what we say."[52] Nixon promoted a far-reaching and forward-looking domestic reform program in areas including civil rights and desegregation, welfare, environmental policy, and government reorganization. Nixon took care to camouflage many of his domestic accomplishments, however, by allowing Agnew and other administration spokesmen to make bellicose pronouncements against the forces of change, including students, civil rights activists, and the media. This meant that moderates as well as liberals often had trouble differentiating between the administration's conservative propaganda and its progressive substance.

Moderates, taking their lead from civil rights activists, were almost uniformly critical of the Nixon administration's early record on racial issues. During Nixon's first months in office, civil rights supporters erupted in outrage over the administration's foot-dragging in cutting off funds to segregated Southern schools, Mitchell's apparent effort to water down the Voting Rights Act of 1965, and Nixon's request that Congress reduce funding for enforcement of fair housing laws.[53] However, the early image of Nixon as a Southern-leaning conservative indifferent to civil rights led many to overlook the administration's bold action for racial equality in the form of the Philadelphia Plan, devised by Secretary of Labor George Shultz and assistant secretary Arthur Fletcher, one of the administration's highest-ranking African-Americans.

The Philadelphia Plan required construction unions, if they undertook projects financed wholly or partly through federal funds, to hire a fixed number of minority workers and apprentices and to admit them to the unions. The unions at that time were virtually all-white, and Democratic administrations had been unable to persuade them to allow blacks to compete for the kinds of jobs that had permitted previous generations of immigrants to enter the middle class. The Philadelphia Plan, as Nixon biographer Tom Wicker discerned, was "perhaps the first *real* success of any president in affirmative action."[54] It epitomized the administration's search for middle ground: the NAACP wanted much tougher action against the unions, but AFL-CIO head George Meany resisted any action at all. Later, Nixon would push through an executive order extending the Philadelphia Plan to other cities, and he got the House to squash a bill, which union-backed Democrats had forced through the Senate, that would have outlawed the measure. Nixon, in this case as in others, was a more aggressive supporter of civil rights than the Democrats could have been. Although the Democrats relied heavily on the black vote, they were even more dependent on the unions. Nixon surely appreciated the potential the Philadelphia Plan offered to aggravate divisions within Democratic ranks.[55] At the same time, he seems to have genuinely believed in equality of opportunity for all citizens, and hoped that his actions and concern would attract black support for the Republican Party.[56]

In other actions favorable to minorities and the cause of civil rights, Nixon became the first president to issue an executive order, in his first year in office, that federal agencies establish affirmative action programs for equal employment opportunities for all employees, including women as well as minorities. He expanded federal procurement from minority-owned firms and directed aid to predominantly black colleges and universities.[57] He launched the administration's program to promote black capital ownership with an executive order creating the Office of Minority Business Enterprise, which according to Commerce Secretary Maurice Stans was intended to "draw together resources of government and the private sector to provide the opportunities, funds, know-how, and business orders for promising minority businesses to begin and grow."[58]

Civil rights activists gave Nixon little credit for his actions. In part this was because the major civil rights groups had long since become wedded to the Democratic coalition, and would support even segregated unions in the larger, long-term interest of defending the coalition. In the mid-1960s, conservative Texas Senator John Tower had proposed an amendment prohibiting any labor union certified under the National Labor Relations Act from discriminating in their membership; like the Philadelphia Plan, the goal was to embarrass labor but also to advance the cause of desegregation. Republican activist John McClaughry recalled asking the NAACP's counsel Clarence Mitchell if his organization would support the Tower amendment: "He looked at me with contempt and said, 'No. We know who our friends are.'"[59] Liberals reflexively dismissed progressive Republican initiatives, reasoning that the party could never have a sincere interest in reform that would benefit anyone other than the rich. "There are no strong lobbies within the GOP for draft reform, or public housing, or aid to black businesses, or pro-labor legislation," according to one liberal critic, "simply because the groups that seek these kinds of programs—the young, the poor, the blacks—do so within the Democratic party."[60]

Nixon complained that his progressive accomplishments often met with indifference from people who would have viewed the same actions as stunning achievements if they had been carried out by a Democratic administration. This was largely his own fault, however, since he sought to achieve many goals favored by moderates, foremost among them the ending of the segregated school system in the South, while at the same time distancing his administration from those very initiatives in order to win over Southern white voters. It was Nixon's judgment that Southern desegregation was a moral and practical necessity, and yet "we will get no credit from the Blacks for doing this desegregation and a lot of heat from many of our supporters. The best approach then is quietly to do our job without press conferences or announcements of what our plans are."[61] Nixon believed that his was a "middle course" between the extremes of "instant integration" and "segregation forever," and that his approach suited the white majority's recognition that integration needed to happen, along with the hope that it would not happen too fast.[62]

The end result was that Nixon achieved many of the goals that moderates had sought for the previous decade, but without the connection to the civil rights cause, the spirit of tolerance and inclusion, and the reformist mindset that had been at the heart of the moderate Republican movement. Nixon was a centrist but not a moderate. Moderates did not identify with him despite his accomplishments. It was hardly surprising that many moderates came to mistrust an administration that didn't seem to share their core beliefs.

Nixon's deviousness and apparent lack of a fixed political identity meant that he couldn't count on the loyalties of members of his party in Congress, few of whom identified themselves as "Nixon Republicans." Over time, Nixon would have more problems with the increasingly rebellious conservatives, but the first significant opposition to a Nixon proposal came from moderates over the proposed Safeguard anti-ballistic missile system. The debate acquired huge symbolic significance as a clash over military spending versus domestic needs and the escalation of the Cold War nuclear arms race. Many Republicans believed that their opposition to the ABM was consistent with Eisenhower's warning about the military-industrial complex and GOP opposition to its growth during the Johnson administration.

The anti-ABM Senate Republican ranks could not easily be dismissed as disloyal liberals, since they included moderates like William Saxbe and Marlow Cook, as well as fiscal conservatives opposed to wasteful spending. The administration's position on the ABM reinforced moderates' suspicions of its intentions elsewhere—suspicions which seemed to be confirmed by the administration's intervention on behalf of thirty-three segregated Mississippi school districts in order to pacify Democrat John Stennis, leader of the ABM floor fight in the Senate. The administration's position prevailed by a single vote, but as Charles Percy wrote to Edward Brooke, "we established the principle that the Senate is no longer willing to accept without question the judgment of the military that a particular weapons system is vital to national survival."[63]

The ABM fight unfolded against the travails of one of the principal progressive Republican heroes, John Lindsay. The New York City mayor's image had suffered greatly from a racially charged donnybrook over school decentralization, a chaotic garbage strike, the city's inability to clear the streets after a monster snowstorm, and the general worsening of New York's quality of life. The mayor's troubles had only sharpened conservative hatred against him, and *National Review* publisher William Rusher mustered conservative forces to oppose Lindsay in the Republican primary. When a moderate asked Rusher why he continued to make Lindsay a target, now that the beleaguered mayor no longer had immediate presidential prospects, Rusher replied, "It's my hobby."[64] More to the point, however, Rusher believed that New York ought to be controlled by Democrats: "not because they are capable administrators (let alone honest ones), but because they know where the power levers are (the labor unions, the mobs, the pressure groups), and thus have a better chance of forestalling trouble than any Republican—able or otherwise."[65] For conservatives like Rusher, Republicans therefore could not be permitted to win in the big cities. By April, Lindsay was running behind John Marchi as a candidate on both the Republican and Conservative Party lines. Ripon denounced "the death-wish branch of the GOP in New York," the conservatives who were "angered at any Republican like Lindsay committing an unnatural act like winning." Lindsay was not a miracle worker, the group conceded, "but he is the highest quality mayor New York is likely to get. . . . He is also the best hope for the Republican party."[66]

New York Senator Charles Goodell, speaking at an anti-ABM press conference, made headlines with his statement that he would back Lindsay whether or not he won the Republican primary.[67] The media was particularly attuned to this controversy since Nelson Rockefeller had given notice that he would support the Republican in the fall mayoral elections, even if Lindsay was then running as a third-party candidate on the Liberal Party line.[68] Goodell wrote later that his endorsement of Lindsay had "cost me considerable support in certain segments of the Republican Party. I weighed the risks, and after doing so, I felt that [the] cause of progressive Republicanism can only be served through coming all out, all the way for Mayor Lindsay." If the Republican Party was to survive, it "must demonstrate constructive leadership in cities like New York."[69]

Conservatives rejoiced when Lindsay lost the Republican primary on June 11, receiving some 107,000 votes to Marchi's 113,000. Rusher gloated that Lindsay "may indeed win in November (though that is by no means certain) but his national ambitions have been dealt a ghastly blow."[70] The *National Review* editorialized that with Lindsay's defeat, there was "no place for him in the national Republican Party of the 1970's. . . . Whatever happens to him in November, Lindsay has been consigned to the Republican equivalent of Elba," an exile which they anticipated would be meted out to progressive Republicans generally.[71] Pat Buchanan wrote to Nixon that Marchi's victory was "a permanent defeat to the Dewey-Rockefeller, Eastern Liberal Establishment coalition." He predicted that, absent the need to placate Republican constituents and patrons, "Lindsay's advisors and the mayor himself are now *unleashed* to go where their predilections would lead them—and that is to the left, to attempt to assume leadership within New York of the anti-ABM, anti-Vietnam, McCarthy-Kennedy-Lindsay, Ripon Republican and DSG [Democratic Study Group] Democratic forces."[72]

Nixon couldn't be faulted for Lindsay's loss, however, since his administration had made clear through many actions, ranging from the rapid public transfer of the Brooklyn Navy Yard to the generous funding of the Summer Youth Corps program, that it would support a Republican mayor in New York. The Ripon Society laid much more blame for Lindsay's defeat at the door of Nelson Rockefeller, whose actions in the primary "looked suspiciously like an effort to buy Conservative Party acquiescence to his candidacy in 1970." Ripon asserted that "Unthinking application of the principle of party loyalty to the New York election simply yields absurd results," and suggested that disgruntled Republicans and Democrats repair to a new "Urban Party."[73] Backlash-driven conservative victories in GOP primary elections elsewhere confirmed Ripon's belief "that some Republican leaders still can't get over the thrill of picking inferior candidates and losing elections."[74]

The high point of Nixon's relations with GOP moderates came with his New Federalism speech in August 1969. At the heart of the domestic initiative Nixon proposed were federal-state revenue sharing and the Family Assistance Plan (FAP), a negative income tax for the working poor. Both were programs long favored by moderates, and represented attempts to achieve progressive ends through conservative means. Lee Huebner, who was the principal author of the message on revenue sharing, described it as "a very convenient issue for many people to agree on. In some ways, revenue sharing was progressive—it was spending to meet social needs. But in another way it was conservative—it was cutting back the size of the federal bureaucracy and liberal control."[75] Moderates and conservatives alike applauded when Nixon declared that "After a third of a century of power flowing from the people and the States to Washington it is time for a New Federalism in which power, funds, and responsibility will flow from Washington to the States and to the people."[76] The negative income tax was more difficult to present as a conservative measure, though one of its original advocates had been Milton Friedman, but it nodded in the conservative direction with its work requirement for welfare recipients and its aspiration to abolish the cumbersome and intrusive welfare bureaucracy.

The Ripon Society believed that "only a Republican administration could have broken this ground," since the Republicans were unburdened by "the free-spending image of the Great Society" and organized labor's opposition to government decentralization.[77] A later Ripon analysis found Nixon's detailed exposition of his reform program to the National Governors Association "an upbeat speech, full of idealism and vision, based on traditional Republican values: efficient and responsible government delivering to its constituents in a quiet but effective manner. It was a set of coherent projected accomplishments that might well have characterized the first Nixon term."[78]

Despite Nixon's New Federalist proposals, moderates continued to fear that the Nixon administration would move in a more conservative direction. These apprehensions were crystallized in the summer of 1969 by the nomination of South Carolina judge Clement Haynsworth to replace Abe Fortas on the Supreme Court, and the publication of *The Emerging Republican Majority* by John Mitchell's aide Kevin Phillips, which called for the GOP to pursue a Southern strategy. Phillips' analysis presented the most direct threat to the moderate worldview and hopes for the future direction of the Republican Party.

Phillips was a contemporary of many of the Ripon Society's leadership—he was still under thirty when *The Emerging Republican Majority* was published—and had been in contact with the Society while at the Harvard Law School and later, when he was administrative assistant to Congressman Paul A. Fino, the Republican representative from the upper Bronx. Phillips himself was native to the Bronx, the borough of many of the Irish and Italian Catholic church-goers and homeowners who had become hostile to John Lindsay. His experience of Democratic-leaning, socially conservative, working-class suburbia led him to draw considerably different political conclusions than moderate Republicans who looked to the affluent suburbs inhabited by well-educated professionals.[79]

Essentially, *The Emerging Republican Majority* did what Ripon had warned against: it took the 1968 election tallies and added Nixon's 43.5 percent to Wallace's 13.5 percent and posited a 57 percent conservative electorate. It was Phillips's thesis that the Republicans could build an enduring majority by corralling voters troubled by "the Negro Problem" and drawing in elements that had not traditionally been part of the Republican Party: conservatives from the South and West, an area for which Phillips coined the term "the Sunbelt." He believed that the Democrats' downfall was decreed when liberals shifted their support from programs that taxed the few on behalf of the many, as in the New Deal, to programs that taxed the many on behalf of the few, as in the Great Society. The few who benefited from these programs, in Phillips' view, were mainly African-Americans: "The principal force which broke up the Democratic (New Deal) coalition is the Negro socio-economic revolution." In Ripon's view, the black-white division was what Phillips saw as "the major cleavage in American politics, not North-South, East-West, urban-rural, or rich-poor, although all these divisions reinforce it."[80]

Although racial concerns had been at the heart of earlier Republican Southern strategies, Phillips' version was not a mere repetition of Goldwater's in 1964. For example, he insisted that Republicans encourage black voting in the former Confederate states—so that blacks would join the Democratic Party and thereby drive white Southerners into the GOP. He told Garry Wills during the '68 campaign that "white Democrats will desert their party in droves the minute it becomes a black party. When white Southerners move, they move fast." The secret of politics, he added, was "knowing who hates who."[81] Phillips also recommended that the GOP draw in those millions who had voted for Wallace in the North, many of them white ethnics and union rank-and-file. In reorienting itself toward these upper working-class and lower middle-class voters, the Republican Party could forget about attracting most professionals. The GOP should also ignore certain urbanized states and those areas where "Democratic trends correlate with stability and decay (New England, New York City, Michigan, West Virginia and San Francisco-Berkeley)."[82] Phillips hoped that the Republican Party would embrace populism, but a new kind of populism: "The clamor in the past has been from the urban or rural proletariat. But now 'populism' is of the middle class, which feels exploited by the Establishment. . . . This is not a movement in favor of laissez faire or any other ideology; it is opposed to welfare and the Establishment."[83] The GOP should also be more welcoming to Catholics, and should play for their votes by taking more culturally conservative positions.

Phillips was not the first to make this argument. William Rusher had offered a similar prescription in his 1963 article "Crossroads for the GOP"; he wrote an admiring letter to Phillips predicting that his book would "do for conservative Republicanism what 'Uncle Tom's Cabin' did for the cause of abolitionism."[84] Earlier in 1969, M. Stanton Evans, the principal author of the Young Americans for Freedom's 1960 Sharon Statement, had presented a similar though less sophisticated thesis in his book *The Future of Conservatism*. Evans likewise had viewed Nixon's victory as a harbinger of demographic and electoral realignment. He saw the growing middle class, increasing suburbanization, and population shift to South and West as forces pointing toward a new conservative electorate. Evans was an ideologue and a muddled thinker, which made his book easier to dismiss. So too did his belief that the GOP must abandon "the constructive approach" and embrace "the power of negative thinking." A Ripon reviewer of Evans' book noted that Nixon was "moving in a moderately progressive direction, even to the point of contradicting his own campaign statements," and huffed that "negativism is still no program for a President."[85]

The Emerging Republican Majority became one of the best-selling and most influential works of political science ever published. Ripon sniffily observed that the book was "[q]uoted by almost everyone and read by almost no one," but argued that its real significance was its apparent status as "the official outline of a new conservative Republican strategy."[86] While the book was a direct refutation of Ripon's thesis and boded ill for moderates in the GOP, it provided an opportunity for searching public debate over the future of the party. Lee Huebner debated Phillips on television, and Ripon received widespread media attention for its dispute with Phillips.

Ripon griped that Phillips had lifted one of the Society's charts without attribution, that his argument was overly dependent on political scientist Samuel Lubell's methodology, and that the book failed to mention important factors such as the Vietnam war and the McCarthy candidacy. More seriously, the Society found Phillips' analysis to be simplistic, false, racist, and dangerous for the Republican Party. For starters, Ripon claimed that it was a gross exaggeration to say that all voters could be divided into "liberal" and "conservative" camps. The moderates argued that conservatism and populism as Phillips defined them were broader phenomena than mere "opposition to black social and economic advances," and doubted that it was possible to build a populist movement shorn of the economic liberalism that was a key component of Wallace's appeal. Ripon also denied that the country was going conservative: Phillips' contention that the Catholic labor force in the North was "trending" conservative could be supported "only by blatant manipulation of isolated data."[87]

Ripon agreed that the Sunbelt was growing in population and importance, and that Republicans should make efforts to win over the South—but what kind of efforts? Two Ripon officers wrote to the *New York Times* that "Both political parties should have a 'Southern Strategy,' and neither one should have a racist one."[88] It was easy to point to the success of individual conservative and racist politicians in the Sunbelt, but was the region as a whole becoming more conservative? Many of the Sunbelt Republican victors in what Phillips called "the epochal conservative triumphs of 1966" were actually moderates, such as Jim Collins in Texas and David Cargo in New Mexico. Moderates argued that the Sunbelt cities were not necessarily conservative, and were likely to become even less so as people from other parts of the country migrated there. A recent city election in Atlanta had seemed to disprove Phillips' thesis: a liberal Jewish Democrat and a moderate Republican had led the mayoral voting, while a black Democrat had defeated a white conservative for vice mayor.

Moderates felt that it also required "a touching sort of faith" to count the Deep South states in the GOP column. Ripon believed that "Southern whites are not yet ready to let go of the Democratic Party," and that in any case "there are not enough Negroes of voting age in any Southern state—except possibly Mississippi—to force whites out of anything."[89] The Wallaceites would not settle for anything less than a total pullback on federal civil rights policy, which of course would alienate the rest of the country just as Goldwater had.[90] Ripon argued that the Southern strategy Phillips was advocating had not been effective even in the South; many of the top GOP office-holders in that region—including Winthrop Rockefeller, Howard Baker, George H. W. Bush, and John Tower—had won precisely by appealing to minorities. And, of course, Phillips' proposed course was morally inadequate, "a cynical and racially divisive path that can only end in tragedy."[91]

Even if Phillips' strategy did succeed in converting the Sunbelt to Republicanism, Ripon argued, the result would be too narrow a popular and Electoral College majority, while the Republicans would have sacrificed those states where moderate Republicans had succeeded by taking up the causes of civil rights, urban revival, and military de-emphasis.[92] Further, the actual course of the '68 campaign did not justify Phillips' projections of a conservative majority. The Democrats had what Ripon called "a number of non-recurring liabilities" that militated against the ticket, including Johnson's unprecedented unpopularity, Robert Kennedy's assassination, and the shambles of the Chicago convention.[93] Ripon's authors also noted that during the campaign, "Phillips waved his statistical tables, graphs and maps in support of his Southern strategy. Now—after Nixon refused to seek the support of disillusioned McCarthyites, blew what everyone saw as a gigantic lead, and barely limped in with a minority of the popular vote and no clear mandate—Phillips tries to pass off his handiwork as inevitable and just a matter of voting trends." Ripon concluded that "The Phillips strategy is not a Republican strategy; it is a conservative strategy, which calls upon the party to renounce its historical commitment to human rights, forfeit much of its present strength, and jeopardize its ability to govern effectively."[94]

Andrew Hacker, a professor of government at Cornell, weighed in on the Ripon-Phillips debate. He conceded that the Ripon prescription for Republican outreach to blacks, union members, and "enlightened suburbanites" had sometimes succeeded on the state level, with the election of senators such as "Mac" Mathias (Maryland), William B. Saxbe (Ohio), and Robert Packwood (Oregon). However, he essentially dismissed the Ripon approach as impractical given the composition of the GOP: "the sorts of people chosen as Republican delegates simply will not settle for a candidate to the Left of Nixon."

Hacker clearly found Phillips' diagnosis of the electorate more convincing, and saw New York's Conservative Party as the forerunner of a new, conservative GOP, rooted in the lower middle class, that would include Catholics as well as Protestants. He considered "the Ripon-Rockefeller notion that the GOP can gain black votes" to be "political science-fiction." Hacker agreed that Phillips was essentially correct in his implicit message that a majority of voting Americans could be mobilized "by approaching them in terms of their lowest common denominator: white fear of the black presence." Indeed, Hacker thought white fear of blacks had "good statistical foundation" in the disproportionate levels of criminality and drug addiction among blacks, though to polarize the electorate along racial lines would require "making use of anxieties that more gentlemanly generations thought best to ignore." Fortunately, perhaps, Republicans lacked charismatic candidates to lead this sort of white populist movement, with the exception of Ronald Reagan—but he would be well into his sixties by the 1976 election, "and there is no one else remotely like him on the Republican horizon." The GOP under Nixon instead would have to resort to "populism via bureaucratic procedures" such as postponing desegregation suits and indicting activists, as Mitchell was doing at the Department of Justice.[95]

Ripon's president, Lee Auspitz, argued with Hacker over a number of points, but emphasized that "the question is not one of irreversible voting 'trends' . . . but of conscious decisions by the national party and its nominee to write off the black vote in 1964 and 1968."[96] This was the crux of the debate: was *The Emerging Republican Majority* merely a thesis, as Phillips claimed, or a strategy, as Ripon maintained? If it was a thesis, then while the moderate arguments seemed to have logic and history on their side, they made poor prophecy. In claiming that the South was unlikely to turn Republican, for example, the authors of Ripon's critique pointed out that states like Arkansas, North Carolina, and Texas had rarely (or in Arkansas' case never) voted for the GOP in a presidential election. As it turned out, Texas would vote Republican in nine of the next ten elections, with Arkansas and North Carolina not far behind. But if Phillips' argument was the Republican strategy, then in hindsight his analysis was more of a self-fulfilling prophecy.

Ripon was prescient in discerning that a Sunbelt-centered Republican party would have an enormous appetite for federal subsidies in the form of defense spending, oil allowances, and agricultural supports. The Southern demand for federal subsidies implied "conservatism" of a very different sort than the traditional, Midwestern stalwart variety. Ripon was also correct to point out that Phillips' strategy ignored party-building activity at the state and local level, but neither Ripon nor Phillips anticipated the rise of evangelical Christians to fulfill this role in the South.

The debate over Phillips' book played out against a swelling tide of antiwar activism. While the moderate and progressive Republicans who were involved in the movement to bring the Vietnam war to an end did not see themselves as disloyal Republicans, they found themselves more and more at odds with the administration.

By the summer of 1969, Ripon's Michael Chabot Smith had returned from radicalism to the world of conventional politics, and was drawn into New York Senator Charles Goodell's efforts to curtail the Vietnam war. As the senator appointed to fill the seat of the slain Robert Kennedy, Goodell had been under intense pressure to take a stand against the war. Earlier that spring, in response to the disruptions at Cornell, Goodell had said that he would give Nixon a fixed period of time to make good on his "secret plan" to end the war. Over the next several months, he came to the realization that Nixon's strategy in Vietnam was simply to eliminate the draft, gradually withdraw American troops, escalate the bombing, and "burn the place out," as he put it.[97]

In September, Smith attended a New York City meeting with the senator that was attended by about a dozen student leaders and activists from antiwar groups such as the Vietnam Moratorium Committee and Vietnam Veterans Against the War. While the activists were pushing Goodell to co-sponsor a Sense of the Senate resolution calling for immediate withdrawal from Vietnam, Smith had another idea in mind. He had spoken the night before with Harvard Law professor Roger Fisher, an expert in negotiations whose recent book, *International Conflict for Beginners*, focused on the "yesable proposition," i.e., an offer presented with sufficient clarity to a single decision-maker "for which the answer 'yes' is all that is needed to set the plan in motion."[98] Fisher suggested that Smith ask Goodell to sponsor legislation using the Congressional power of the purse to require a 50 percent reduction of the armed forces deployed in Vietnam within one year. "That would undercut the argument that 'immediate' withdrawal was impossible," Smith thought, "and it would allow time to organize, and it would give every organizer in the community a yesable proposition to put to his or her Congressperson. The organizers would ask, 'Senator, will you vote for Senate Bill X?'—not 'Senator, are you in favor of peace?'"[99]

When Smith offered this proposal at the New York meeting, "Goodell amazed me. He said, 'Why not *complete* withdrawal in one year using the power of the purse?' And he made a commitment at that meeting that he was going to introduce legislation to cut off funding for any military presence in Vietnam one year hence." Goodell's proposal unnerved many of the attendees, some criticizing it for falling short of immediate withdrawal and others secretly fearing it would strengthen Goodell's chances against a Democrat in his Senate election campaign the next year.[100] Smith was convinced, though, and moved to Washington to set up a small office and raise money to support the initiative. Goodell introduced his bill on October 7 as Senate Bill 3000, known informally as the Vietnam Disengagement Act of 1969. Goodell failed to secure even a single co-sponsor, though he received vague encouragement from senators Mark Hatfield and George McGovern.[101] Smith's small operation was then dubbed "Citizens for S. 3000."

Goodell's bill would be one of the initiatives supported by the Moratorium to End the War in Vietnam, a large nationwide demonstration on October 15. Republicans as well as Democrats helped organize the demonstration, which they intended to show that not only students and the young but the mainstream of Americans wanted a rapid settlement of the Vietnam conflict. The organizers also sought to bolster antiwar legislative efforts of both parties. On the Republican side, these included Goodell's bill, the measure to repeal the Gulf of Tonkin Resolution sponsored by Representatives Donald Riegle and Pete McCloskey, and Paul Findley's resolution supporting Nixon's withdrawal of 60,000 troops and encouraging him to bring the remainder home at the earliest possible date. Moderates argued that the legislation and the Moratorium would provide Nixon with essential leverage in his negotiations with Saigon.[102]

Nixon, however, made it publicly known that he had watched football on television rather than pay attention to the Moratorium demonstrations, which drew crowds of up to 100,000 in cities around the country. On October 20, Spiro Agnew, who to that point had continued to present himself largely as a moderate, attacked the Moratorium leadership as "an effete corps of impudent snobs who characterize themselves as intellectuals." The Vice President commenced a conservative and consonantal crusade, lambasting liberals, castigating critics, and pursuing a pugnacious policy of "positive polarization." On November 3, Nixon announced his program of "Vietnamization," scaling back the American presence while building up the South Vietnamese army. Twenty percent of American troops would be home by the middle of December, he said, and troop withdrawal would continue steadily, though without a fixed timetable. But Nixon threw off the conciliatory posture he had taken towards antiwar critics and instead called for "the great silent majority" of Americans to resist the "vocal minority" who would try to impose their views on the nation through demonstrations. "North Vietnam cannot defeat or humiliate the U.S.," Nixon rumbled. "Only Americans can do that."[103]

Moderates criticized the President's speech on both operational and strategic levels. The Ripon Society warned that attacking the moderate peace movement would only strengthen the dead hand of bureaucratic momentum and prolong the war. The vast majority of demonstrators, they believed, wanted the U.S. to leave Vietnam "not because they want a Hanoi victory nor because they like violent confrontation. They simply think that America's moral and political interests no longer justify our presence there." Ripon also criticized Nixon's speech for "perpetuat[ing] the tragic fiction that Vietnam is the linchpin of American foreign policy for the next generation." As a candidate, Nixon had privately reassured Republican leaders and newspaper editors that conditions had changed since the U.S. sent ground forces to Vietnam, that the domino theory no longer held, and that Vietnam could be "detached" from other American interests. Ripon concluded that "Since some kind of warfare is likely to continue in Indochina throughout the next decade regardless of what America does, Mr. Nixon would do well to detach his rhetoric about it from U.S. commitments in strategically more important parts of the world."[104]

Mike Smith remembered that for those involved in the antiwar movement, the fall of 1969 was "a dizzy time." Nixon's announcement of Vietnamization "started to take some of the wind out the movement," but the March on Washington in November, which drew half a million protestors, was "thrilling. It was the first time I'd ever been part of a mass march on that scale."[105] In the week before the march, Ripon's Mike Brewer had worked with the march's leaders in Washington to prepare marshals (including several Ripon members) who would help maintain a peaceful demonstration. The November march, unlike the October demonstrations, was co-sponsored by the New Mobilization Committee to End the War in Vietnam as well as the Vietnam Moratorium Committee. The "New Mobe," as it was called, was a coalition of groups which included some who lacked the Moratorium's commitment to non-violence. Smith recalled that the New Mobe leadership "was decidedly more radical than the moderate 'Moratorium' leadership, and there was much rivalry and mutual distrust between the two groups. . . . [T]hey took a dim view of the 'liberal reformers' leading the Moratorium effort."[106]

Ripon conceded that the march would include some people seeking violent confrontation, and also that the event's leaders had in fact "made common cause with some far-out elements." The Society wanted to keep the demonstrations nonviolent in order to deny Agnew and Mitchell an opportunity "to smear the moderate peace movement and isolate it from the main body of public opinion." Ripon suggested that Agnew sought polarization in order to create a political base that would keep him from being dumped from the GOP ticket in 1972, while Mitchell was willing "to use any opportunity which will attract authoritarian Democrats to the Republican Party."[107] Mike Smith, who served as a marshal along with Mike Brewer, confirmed that "We knew that there were elements of the Mobe coalition that might try to ignite some police over-reactions, and segments of the White House who were just hoping for a chance to 'crack down' on these lawless demonstrators, all of which could turn it into a Chicago-convention type war zone instead of a massive, peaceful march." However, there were also elements within the Nixon administration who shared Ripon's view. Thanks to Leonard Garment's office in the White House, Brewer and Smith were equipped with walkie-talkies and dispatched to critical locations to establish a back-channel communication link with the White House, as well as to provide "rumor control and other bits of intel to avoid toxic misunderstandings" between police and marchers.[108]

Ripon member Howard Gillette pointed out that the Society's participation in the Moratorium was not necessarily a partisan action: "Across the board, there was a reaction to what was happening in terms of how the war was being executed, and the antagonism that created with young people. Everyone was against the war, conservatives as well as liberals." Ripon's members didn't participate in confrontations with the law, and "none of us felt that we were going to break the establishment. What we were trying to do was turn the direction of the Republican Party toward an embrace of a different agenda than the one that was being pushed on it by the right."[109] Not everyone agreed that this was the proper course of action. A few days after the Washington march, the New York Ripon chapter met with writer Jack Newfield, who insisted that the best way for progressive Republicans to influence national policy was to quit the Nixon administration.[110] But Gillette felt that "Ripon still was in the mainstream of the Republican Party at that time. And that's to a certain extent where the battle was."[111]

Some accounts have suggested that the off-year election results of 1969 proved the success of Nixon's conservative, "silent majority" approach. His-torical writer Rick Perlstein deemed that the returns showed "The White House had the better of the argument" against its New Politics critics: "Vir-ginia elected its first Republican governor since reconstruction. In New Jer-sey, a Republican won the statehouse for the first time in sixteen years, having campaigned against pornography and for government aid to paro-chial schools, and did best in areas of strong Wallace support."[112] Both of those victories, however, were won by moderates not conservatives.

Linwood Holton, Virginia's winner, was a Roanoke lawyer who had helped revive the state GOP in the early '50s, and a racial liberal who had opposed "Massive Resistance" and the closure of Virginia's public schools to prevent integration. He campaigned against the "Byrd Machine," Demo-cratic Senator Harry Flood Byrd's racist political organization that had held the state in thrall since the early '20s. Although the Byrd Machine's policy of small state government and low taxes seemed like a conservative ideal, Holton pointed out that the state's refusal to adequately fund public schools and support economic development kept Virginia poor. Local governments were forced to issue bonds to support essential government services, which—because the bonds lacked the full faith and credit of the state—ultimately resulted in higher costs to taxpayers. Holton received the en-dorsement of the Crusade for Voters, the state's largest black political organization, and the state AFL-CIO. He won the governorship with over 30 percent of the black vote, receiving up to 50 percent in Richmond, and outperformed previous Republican candidates' showings in the suburbs and central cities.[113] In his inauguration, he declared that "the era of defiance is behind us" and pledged to make Virginia "a model in race relations."[114] Soon he would provide an indelible image of Southern racial progress by escorting his smiling teenage daughter to her first day of school at a newly integrated, previously all-black high school, giving the force of personal ex-ample to his call for peaceful race relations.

William Cahill of New Jersey had narrowly won the state's GOP guber-natorial primary, defeating a conservative who had run primarily on a no-tax platform spiced with denunciation of student disorders and urban riots.[115] Cahill had been endorsed by progressive Republican Senator Clif-ford Case, and his campaign was run by moderate GOP state chairman Nelson Gross and Campaign Systems, Inc., the consulting firm of former Rockefeller aides Doug Bailey and John Deardourff. In the general election, Cahill brought in nearly every national party figure across the Republican spectrum, from Ronald Reagan to Robert Finch, to campaign on his behalf. He was elected by half a million votes, the greatest margin ever given to any governor in that state, while Republicans achieved a three-to-one majority in both the state Senate and Assembly.[116] Cahill carried every racial and ethnic group except African-Americans, but like Holton he managed to receive 30 percent of the black vote; the Republican National Committee observed that in both states the GOP had not previously captured more than 10 percent of the black vote and that usually "the percentages have been less than half of that."[117]

One particular element in the election that reinforced moderates' belief that the GOP could attract black voters if it tried was the Action Now project of the Republican National Committee. The project had been pioneered by GOP national vice-chair Elly Peterson, former chair of the Michigan Republican Party, who opened the first Action Center to reach out to black voters in Detroit's inner city in 1967. The national program was co-sponsored by Connecticut State Committeewoman Tina Harrower and the RNC's John Marttila, the first director of the Detroit Action Center. By the summer of '69, the RNC was attempting to create other such centers in traditionally Democratic ghetto neighborhoods across the country, including Newark and Wilmington.[118]

Marttila also brought his GOP outreach effort to the black community in New Haven, Connecticut, where Ripon Society member Paul Capra was attempting to become the first Republican mayor since 1953. His nomination drew wails of a "New Left" takeover from his party opponents, since his program called for deemphasizing commercial redevelopment and highway building and increasing commitment to housing, education, and neighborhood activism. Capra was Italian but supported "black self-determination," which made his candidacy plausible for black voters at a time when the Democrats were fracturing on racial lines.[119] The Republicans ended up losing the election, for the ninth straight time, though Capra trailed the Democratic victor by a narrow margin. Still, he amassed a surprising 40 percent of the black vote, in a sharp break with the tradition of near-unanimous black support for Democrats.[120] One observer concluded that the lesson of his campaign was that "where blacks are numerous enough to take over Democratic city machines, the older ethnic groups will flee to the Republican party (as in Cleveland). Where whites maintain tight control of machines (as in New Haven, New York, Louisville, and Philadelphia), the black vote may be pried loose by Republican candidates."[121]

John Lindsay, running as the Liberal candidate against Democrat Mario Procaccino and Republican (Conservative) John Marchi in the New York mayoral race, won a personal triumph in his reelection bid. In so doing, he emerged as what supporters called "the only leader of national stature with unsullied appeal to the educated young *and* to the blacks *and* to the leadership of the urban coalition *and* to the frontlash voters who supported Rockefeller and McCarthy in 1968." It remained unclear whether Lindsay would return to the Republican fold, or whether his unusual coalition of the alienated and the established could be replicated by other GOP candidates.

The Ripon Society concluded that the GOP candidates who succeeded in the 1969 elections were those who avoided polarization along racial and ideological lines, such as Holton in Virginia, Cahill in New Jersey, and the team of Arlen Specter and Tom Gola for district attorney and comptroller in Philadelphia, who ran under the slogan, "They are young, they are tough, and nobody owns them." The candidates who failed were the likes of John Marchi in New York and Alfreda Slominski in Buffalo, who resorted to backlash appeals and conservative dogmatism on Vietnam. The electorate "chose Republican candidates whose actions repudiate the posturing rhetoric of Vice-President Agnew," in Ripon's view. Moderates saw signs of Republican resurgence in urban areas, with impressive gains registered over previous GOP performances in cities such as Pittsburgh and New Haven and a significant proportion of the black vote going to Republicans. Ripon believed that the election results in the South, with the success of Holton and the defeat of conservatives in Kentucky, "repudiate the thesis of Kevin Phillips." Ripon also foresaw a brewing civil war in the Democratic Party, with New Politics groups contending with "the coalition of big city machines, reactionary labor leadership and southern courthouses."[122]

The GOP, by contrast, was still relatively united and its factions were finding some common ground. At the November 17–18 Governor's Conference on the Changing Environment, Walter Hickel and John Ehrlichman from the Nixon administration joined Republican officeholders in calling for a cleanup of environmental damage and future monitoring of the environmental impact of government and private business actions. One of those leading the chorus was Governor Ronald Reagan, the conference's sponsor. Despite his conservative reputation, Reagan's administration had compiled a respectable environmental record in protecting the Redwoods National Park, creating the Bi-State Council to plan for Lake Tahoe, and blocking the Dos Rios Dam project.[123]

There were other less auspicious straws in the wind for moderate Republicans in the fall of '69, however, particularly the victory of ultra-conservative Philip Crane in the suburban Chicago election to succeed Donald Rumsfeld. Illinois' 13th District was characterized as the safest Republican district in the country, as well as one of the most affluent and highly educated.[124] Rumsfeld's last poll revealed that half of his district favored gradual withdrawal from Vietnam.[125] In short, the district was the antithesis of the "backlash" constituency, yet it elected one of the most hawkish and right-wing representatives in Congress, who would go on to be the longest-serving Republican member of the House before he was defeated in 2004. On the other hand, the moderates had succeeded in the fall of 1969 in electing Pennsylvania's Hugh Scott as Senate Minority Leader, following Dirksen's final illness. Michigan's Robert Griffin, another moderate, was elected whip. For the first time in a quarter-century, the moderates commanded the GOP leadership in the upper house.[126]

The members of the Ripon Society remained optimistic about moderate prospects under Nixon because they ended 1969 with a terrific coup: six Ripon representatives met with the President on December 16 to discuss the youth report the Society had recently submitted to the White House. "It is heartening that the President is taking a personal interest in the problems of the generation gap," Bruce Chapman stated in a press release. "We wrote our report in the belief that it is still possible to work for change within the system and Mr. Nixon's desire to discuss the report confirms that faith."[127] Chapman was the senior editor of the report, but among the Ripon members who helped to write and edit the manuscript were George Gilder and Harvard undergraduate Frank Raines, who later went on to become a Rhodes Scholar and director of the Office of Management and Budget under Bill Clinton; as the controversy-steeped head of Fannie Mae, he was the first black CEO of a Fortune 500 company.

Ripon's December 16 meeting with Nixon—which was scheduled for fifteen minutes but extended to nearly an hour—was arranged by Senator Howard Baker, who also participated in the White House discussion. Chapman remembered having had an easy conversation with Nixon ten years earlier, but was deeply impressed by the experience of being in the Oval Office and the aura of the presidency: "The President is awesome. The atmosphere around him exhilarates. . . . The presidential presence can make one tipsy." Chapman was also taken with the Oval Office itself: "The gold and blue furnishings are crisply new, yet comfortable; logs crackle in the fireplace and the French doors display the Rose Garden's tranquility outside. Only the stunning color photograph of the earth as seen from the moon hints that this is not a fashionable country manor."[128]

Nixon discussed some of the youth report's specific recommendations with Chapman, and expressed agreement with his program for a volunteer army, which he said had influenced his own thinking on the matter. Ripon president Lee Auspitz told Nixon that he had "a two-way communication problem with young people." Youth didn't know about presidential programs that would appeal to them (including a UN-sponsored voluntary action corps and an extension of the White House fellows program to state and local government). At the same time, Nixon wasn't living up to his campaign pledge of an open presidency that would welcome young critics.[129]

Nixon engaged the group in a freewheeling discussion of education and the ineffectiveness of most programs to improve it. Students were bored and estranged by the substance of their education, he thought, and devoting more money to the educational process seemed unlikely to solve the problem. One major obstacle to improvement was that education was run by what he called "a hidebound educational establishment" that impeded innovation. This was an area where some young, moderate Nixon aides such as Chester "Checker" Finn were involved. Nixon also felt that the problem of bigness mentioned in Ripon's report was at the root of the youth revolt. Vietnam and the race issue, according to Nixon, were symptoms rather than a cause of youth unrest. Youthful unrest, he said, existed in all highly developed societies. He attributed it in part to the problem of modern bureaucracy—not only in government, but in the private and volunteer sectors. Young people came into organizations "bright-eyed and bushy-tailed" and eager to serve, but in a few years they became frustrated and demoralized.[130] Nixon flattered his youthful audience by asking them to propose means for sharing power more widely in universities, businesses, unions, and government at all levels. "Most people seem to lack a religion these days," Nixon concluded, "and there's no unifying ideal in the country any more. What is there to rally around?"[131]

Although many accounts of Nixon's presidency emphasized that the administration's incipient Southern strategy and the continuation of the war in Vietnam had turned the President toward the conservatives, in fact Nixon continued to try to keep the moderates on board. Sometimes this was through largely symbolic actions—such as meeting with the Ripon Society—but other Nixon actions were not only symbolic. Three weeks before Ripon's meeting with the President, for example, the Society sent him a congratulatory letter praising his executive order halting production of biological weapons. They believed that, like his proposals for welfare reform, Nixon's decision on germ warfare demonstrated his "willingness and ability to examine all the facts in a controversial situation and to develop fundamental reforms."[132]

By the same token, conservatives were unaware of the supposed triumph of their ideology within the administration. As 1969 came to a close, the editor of the conservative magazine *Human Events* complained to Nixon's assistant Harry Dent that "The last few weeks have been a disaster so far as the Administration's conservative image is concerned—viz. Finch's action on the Whitten Amendment [which would have barred HEW from withholding funds to segregated school districts], the doubling of money to the arts, the continuation of the poverty program, the furthering of trade with Communist China, the drastic cuts in the military. . . . Damn it, we can't sell this nonsense to our readers."[133]

Moderates and Nixon continued to hold a mistrustful respect and mutual dependence for each other. Even one of Nixon's sharpest critics in moderate Republican circles conceded that the President "did run with a number of the ideas we had. One of the reasons Nixon had to be so schizo-phrenic in his first term was that he still had to accommodate the moderate wing of his party, and he did that in a number of ways that irritated the far right. So it kept us in a situation of imbalance sometimes, too."[134]

CHAPTER 10

❧

The Rough Beast

Nixon and the Breakup of the Moderate
Republican Movement, 1970

T he world as it existed in the mind of Richard Nixon was an exceedingly hard place. Hatred was the normal condition of international
relations. Nations hated their neighbors and different races and ethnic
groups itched to exterminate one another. And the same antipathies and
divisions, the same vicious struggle of all against all, operated in the so-
called United States as the country moved into the 1970s. "Hell, the young
don't like the old—they never have," Nixon told his White House cronies.
"And the women don't like the men, generally. The men don't like the
women. They live together because of reasons that have nothing to do with
love." Liberals were afflicted by what he called "this muddleheaded, soft-
headed philosophy that if only people know each other and can sit down
and converse, their problems will evaporate and they're all going to love
each other."[1] This meant that liberals were unable to maintain peace internationally or stability domestically. At the same time, conservatives tended
to be in the grip of their own ideological illusions, and could not be trusted
to act pragmatically, to handle complexity, or to negotiate difficult, emo-
tionally unsatisfying compromises among antagonistic nations and social
groups. The responsibility of governance therefore had to rest with tough,
unsentimental men of the center.

Given Nixon's mindset, both his antagonism toward liberals and his
break with the conservative movement were completely foreseeable. But
his bleak worldview also made it inevitable that the self-proclaimed centrist

Nixon would part ways with the moderate Republican movement. The goals of the moderate movement by 1970 included the furtherance of civil rights and a quick end to the Vietnam war, causes toward which Nixon was increasingly hostile. The moderates wanted Nixon to reach out to groups such as minorities, youth, intellectuals, and professionals that he had come to regard as enemies. They wanted Nixon to embody leadership qualities of balance, toleration, and magnanimity that were not in his nature. And most moderate Republicans, in Nixon's view, were part of the establishment that he wanted to destroy. The Nixon administration continued to include many moderates in its ranks and gave them many programs and accomplishments they had long sought. But Nixon's turn against the moderate Republican movement in 1970 ultimately ended it as a viable political force.

The Nixon administration's uneasy relations with the moderate Republican movement were vividly displayed at the Ripon Society's seventh anniversary banquet at Washington D.C.'s Statler Hilton Hotel in mid-January 1970. The organization had recently released the January issue of its publication, the *Ripon Forum*, with an unflattering caricature of Attorney General John Mitchell on the cover and a lead article which accused the attorney general of playing politics with civil rights and crime control policies. The January 17 CBS Evening News broadcast included footage of correspondent David Schoumacher asking Mitchell, "What about this Ripon Society charge that you have permitted politics to play a part in your operation of the Justice Department?" "As far as those little juvenile delinquents are concerned," Mitchell snapped, "I don't think I have any comment about them."[2] The Mitchell insult, coming just hours before the banquet, gave the event "an edge of danger and excitement," according to columnist Mary McGrory. "All the speakers at the gathering referred jocosely to the attorney general's wrath."

Mitchell's attack brought the Society national media attention, including CBS and NBC television interviews at Ripon's headquarters and political director Mike Brewer's appearance on CBS national news. The Mitchell flap produced numerous media plaudits for the Society; McGrory, for example, wrote that "Ripon in fact is to Nixon what Harvard was to John Kennedy—a talent bank and an idea factory."[3] The attention also sharpened the anti-Ripon grievances of many right-wingers, including several in the administration. But Ripon's defenders included the President himself. Among the congratulatory telegrams received at the banquet was one from Nixon, which held up the Society as proof that young people could have an impact on American politics. "As you may have noticed from time to time," the telegram read, "your conclusions usually arouse opposition as well as support. But that is not a bad thing, for intellectual controversy is essential for social progress.... [T]he party and the government welcome Ripon's impatience with the tired approaches of the past and its readiness to explore ideas 'whose time is coming.'"[4]

The Mitchell-Ripon controversy highlighted the fact that neither moderates nor conservatives knew quite what to make of the Nixon administration twelve months into its first term. On the one hand, there was ample evidence that moderates continued to have real influence on Nixon's policies. Ripon's president Lee Auspitz pointed out to McGrory that Ripon's recommendations on issues such as the draft, negative income tax, revenue sharing, de-escalation of the war, and relations with China were being implemented by the administration.[5] Ripon's alumni in the White House continued to work to good effect; twenty-three year-old Christopher DeMuth, for example, headed the team that prepared Nixon's environment message to Congress in early 1970 and laid the groundwork for the establishment of the Council on Environmental Quality.[6]

Nixon's advocacy of black capitalism was more promise than performance, but the President had recently ordered federal agencies to increase the involvement of minority group contractors in federal purchasing, and the Small Business Administration had doubled the dollar amount of loans to minority businesses since the previous year.[7] The administration also held a conference with elected black officials at the White House, at which the group issued a statement commending Nixon's record of appointing African-Americans. This included sixteen presidential appointments (versus nine in the Johnson administration), six ambassadors, five federal judges, and presidential assistant Robert Brown.[8] Ripon believed that the administration had "acted courageously" in promoting Labor Secretary George Shultz's Philadelphia Plan, and that Nixon would open up "new avenues for social equality, notably in the economic realm."[9] Ripon continued to collaborate with Nixon on the youth outreach efforts they had proposed to him in December. Auspitz urged the President not to give up on young people: "The current young generation is this nation's most politicized since the early years of the Republic; they ought not to be allowed to become its most radicalized."[10]

On the other hand, moderates' mistrust of conservative tendencies in the Nixon administration was evident in their reaction against Mitchell and his perceived Southern strategy. The Ripon Society could hardly contain its frustration over Mitchell's drive to make the Justice Department into a political instrument, which reached "into virtually every area of law enforcement" and was "unparalleled in recent history." Mitchell's pursuit of white Southern votes had produced delays and even reversals of black progress in the South, although evidence suggested that white Southerners were becoming more accepting of integration than they had been. At the same time, Mitchell's approach to law and order dealt with "surface tensions" rather than basic problems, and threatened to reduce personal liberties more than reform "the serious institutional inadequacies of our criminal justice system, which impede the effective prevention, detection, and prosecution of crime."[11] The *Forum* puckishly suggested that if Mitchell was unable to keep politics out of law enforcement, he should resign "or assume the more traditional political position of Postmaster General."[12]

While Ripon did not directly attack Nixon, the question of whether the President's heart was with Mitchell or the administration's moderates continued to vex. As *New York Post* columnist Jimmy Wechsler noted, New York Mayor John Lindsay had "long defended his continued Republican registration in terms of an obligation to young Riponites who, like himself, believed that the GOP could be transformed into the party of progressivism," but Nixon's support of Mitchell cast doubt on that belief.[13] Representative Stanley Tupper, a Republican from Maine, wrote to Auspitz that "strategists within the Administration closest to the President's ear do not believe they need the votes of liberals of either Party to win in 1972. . . . Republican liberalism is at its lowest ebb."[14]

Moderates and conservatives alike mistrusted Nixon, although for opposite reasons. Where moderates decried Mitchell's attempts to appease racist Southerners, for example, the conservatives denounced the efforts of Robert Finch, Jack Veneman, and Leon Panetta at HEW to desegregate Southern schools. A typical Southern complaint, from a Louisianan who had cast his first Republican vote in 1968, was that "I thought I was voting [*sic*] for the President Mr. Nixon, I most surely was not voteing [*sic*] for this South hater Robert Finch."[15] Right-wingers acknowledged that Spiro Agnew was on their side and cultivated his support, with *National Review* publisher William Rusher flattering the Vice President in early 1970 that "Your voice . . . is increasingly the voice of the vast majority of the American people."[16] But conservatives claimed that they were outnumbered by progressives in the Nixon administration, with a particular danger coming from the large number of Ripon appointees. In the wake of Nixon's White House meeting with Ripon and his congratulatory telegram to the Society, conservatives renewed their attack on Ripon as a proxy for the progressive tendencies of the administration. The right wing roared with anger when Ripon alumnus John R. Price succeeded Daniel Patrick Moynihan as a Special Assistant to the President and executive secretary of the Urban and Rural Affairs Council in December 1969.[17]

Much of the right-wing antagonism toward creeping Riponism in the Nixon administration was overblown. The claim that moderates were undermining Nixon while the conservatives were loyal to him was also a gross exaggeration. Former Ripon Society president Lee Huebner, who served as one of Nixon's speechwriters, remembered that "Certainly the moderates (or most of them) were still on board in the Republican Party during the Nixon administration. If anything, it was the conservatives who were threatening to secede and form a third party."[18] Leading conservatives had already become disillusioned with the President by the beginning of 1970. "I don't doubt that we can get such a communication from Nixon as the Ripon people got," *National Review*'s William F. Buckley Jr. wrote to Rusher. "We should however ask ourselves searchingly whether we want it."[19]

In January 1970, Nixon's assistant Bryce Harlow made the case that the administration was squarely in the center of American public opinion, but faced the rule-or-ruin opposition of both progressive and conservative Republicans in Congress. When he went to the Senate with a proposal pleasing to conservatives, such as the ABM or the Haynsworth nomination, "I will ordinarily lose twelve to seventeen liberal-type Republicans," mainly the members of Senate Wednesday Club, a moderate association set up along the lines of the House Wednesday Group. But on liberal proposals such as the Family Assistance Plan, "my precious 43 [votes] shrinks by ten or fifteen as the Thurmonds, Towers, Goldwaters and such grumpily turn away." Harlow observed that Americans for Democratic Action "has studied us carefully and finds us reactionary," while the American Conservative Union "has done likewise and finds us left-wing. Maybe that suggests we're not doing too bad for mainstream America."[20] One observer noted that Nixon and his chief lieutenants thought of themselves as reformers, but within a limited sphere of operation: "Their reforms are largely aimed at improving the machinery of government and decentralizing politics and the economy rather than changing the American social fabric." At the same time, Nixon appealed to the white, middle-class majority of Americans by taking a hard line on "law and order" and social upheaval. Even on the war, where he was reversing the escalatory policies of his two Democratic predecessors, Nixon had to present Vietnamization as a contrast to the straw man of immediate withdrawal: "His intention, evidently, was to cloak what he feels is a liberal policy in conservative rhetoric."[21]

Whatever kind of affinity there ought to have been between moderates and the Nixon administration was overshadowed by high-profile conflicts such as moderate Republican opposition to Nixon's nomination of G. Harrold Carswell of Florida as a candidate for the Supreme Court, following the Senate's rejection of Clement Haynsworth, another Southern nominee, the previous year. As early as January 1970, the Ripon Society made public its view that, if Nixon wanted to appoint a justice from the South, there were better alternatives to Carswell, including the well-respected Judge Minor Wisdom of Louisiana and Virginia Representative Richard Poff.[22] In early March, Ripon teamed with Law Students Concerned for the Court to issue a statement that, based on a review of his record of reversals compared to national averages, "Judge Carswell exhibits serious symptoms of judicial incapacity. . . [H]e is one of the least qualified Supreme Court nominees in this century."[23] Ripon figured prominently in a meeting that put 250 Republicans under age forty on record against the nomination.[24] A Ripon white paper, "The Case Against Carswell," was the first to document that Carswell, compared to the average for federal district judges, had been reversed more than twice as often, had been cited far less in court opinions, and had written much shorter and less documented opinions. While other organizations had already cited Carswell's past support of white supremacy and evidence of his judicial biases, Ripon asserted that "the most manifest reason for refusing confirmation to this nomination is the undeniable legal inadequacy of Judge Carswell."[25]

Ripon's report was a damning indictment, which helped persuade a number of moderate Republican senators to vote against Carswell. Harlow reported to Nixon that loyal Republicans were refusing to support Carswell because "They think he's a boob, a dummy. And what counter is there to that? He is."[26] The most memorable defense of Carswell came from conservative Nebraska Senator Roman Hruska, who protested that "There are a lot of mediocre judges and people and lawyers. They are entitled to a little representation, aren't they, and a little chance?" Hruska's quote was widely mocked, but revealed the underlying truth that many populist-leaning conservatives cared little about the quality of government, and indeed found able public servants more threatening than inept ones. Populist anti-elitism often carried a tinge of anti-Semitism, as with Hruska's follow-up comment that "We can't have all Brandeises and Cardozos and Frankfurters and all stuff like that there."[27]

One of the distinguishing characteristics of Republican moderates was that while they wanted to limit government's reach, they also wanted government to perform well in the areas in which it operated. Senator Marlow Cook, a Kentucky moderate, had come under intense pressure from Nixon to support Carswell and was on the verge of voting for confirmation despite his reservations about the Florida judge's background and abilities. Then, on the day before the vote, Cook attended a ceremony at which the President presented Medals of Honor—all posthumous—to Vietnam heroes, praising their efficiency and excellence. Cook recalled that he "thought to myself, what we are saying here is that these boys gave their lives—and we sitting up here are going to put on the Supreme Court someone from whom we don't demand a high degree of efficiency and excellence. It may sound corny, but that's what happened."[28] The Senate voted 51 to 45 to reject Carswell. As with the Haynsworth vote the previous fall, moderate and progressive Republican opposition tipped the balance against the support of conservative Republicans and Southern Democrats.

In the wake of Carswell's rejection, Nixon fumed that both Haynsworth and Carswell had been the victims of "regional discrimination" against the South. The reactionary *Indianapolis News*, noting that Democratic Senator Birch Bayh had inserted Ripon's report into the *Congressional Record* and based his arguments against Carswell on the report, concluded that Nixon should purge his administration of all Ripon members: "[S]o far as the White House is concerned, the enemy is within the gates. It seems doubtful the President is going to be able to deal successfully with liberal types like Bayh on Capitol Hill until he has ousted Bayh's Republican 'soul brothers' from their positions of influence at 1600 Pennsylvania Avenue."[29] Ripon's vice president Howard Gillette remembered that the Society's efforts against Carswell's nomination were conducted "by phone, by building a formidable case and putting it out, and by just hammering away with the press at the inconsistencies in [Carswell's] record." Compared to the later battles over Robert Bork's nomination to the Court, "This was kid stuff. We were babes in the woods. But if someone like Attorney General John Mitchell was angry at us, he had damned good reason to be angry, because we took him on." Nixon also shared Mitchell's wrath over Ripon's obstruction, and the group heard that Mitchell put pressure on their sponsors. One of their largest donors, CBS head William Paley, "curtailed his giving around that time," Gillette pointed out, "possibly under threat of losing licenses."[30]

In the White House, conservative speechwriter Pat Buchanan made a play to get Ripon's alumni fired from their positions. Huebner remembered that in the wake of the flap over Mitchell and Carswell, Buchanan "decided that Ripon people in the White House had to denounce the Society, and that if we didn't come out against Ripon then we would have to go." The moderates countered that if they had to renounce Ripon, then all of the White House members of conservative organizations like Young Americans for Freedom, which had issued scathing denunciations of Nixon's proposed welfare reforms and Southern integration plans, had to break with their groups as well. At that point, chief of staff H. R. Haldeman told both sides to cease and desist. Huebner remembered that "Pat and I ran into each other in the hallway outside our offices not long afterwards, and he grinned broadly at me and said, 'Touché!' That was the end of that."[31] Nonetheless, tensions between moderate and conservative activists would persist.

During Nixon's first year and a half in office, his administration had attempted to support one of the moderate movement's principal goals by reaching out to African-Americans. The Republican National Committee was one of the primary vehicles for the outreach effort. Nixon, relaying his orders through assistant Harry Dent, had directed the new RNC chairman Rogers Morton to appeal to both black and white Southerners. Dent had instructed Morton to "intensify [the RNC's] efforts to enlist Negro leaders and, in fact, develop Negro leaders to work for our Party." The RNC hired part-time workers to recruit Southern black voters, particularly in areas where Dent believed that "the attainment of 10 to 20% of the Negro vote would mean victory."[32] Morton also doubled the budget for RNC co-chair Elly Peterson's Action Now program, which created neighborhood service centers to enlist citizen participation in the solution of local problems. The emphases of the Action Centers differed by state and locality—an Action Center set up in Connecticut in early 1970 focused on citizen responses to drug abuse and pollution—but the major thrust of the program was on inner-city minority communities.[33] Peterson remembered that one planned Action Center in Miami was thwarted by a prominent local Republican on the grounds that "After all, you know, we don't really want to get involved with Negroes."[34] Nixon, however, approved of Peterson's efforts to involve blacks with the Republican Party through the Action Centers and the Women's Advisory Council on Black Involvement, another Peterson creation.[35] Peterson recalled that at a White House meeting with Nixon, the President strongly encouraged her to continue her work with African-Americans: "They should be made to understand what our party can do for them and will do for them," he told her. "This is the group where we can make the greatest impact, and I hope you will continue this with all you have."[36]

In another initiative aimed at black voters, Morton hired Christie Todd, the future New Jersey Governor Christine Todd Whitman, to head up the RNC's Listening Program, which sounded out the political opinions of African-American voters around the country, along with parallel efforts aimed at young people and senior citizens. Todd led an RNC delegation to sixteen cities in the winter and spring of 1970, talking to several hundred people in informal group discussions. She found that blacks expressed muted enthusiasm for Nixon's call for increased black capital ownership and wanted both parties to compete for black votes. However, she believed that while the black citizens she spoke with had not completely rejected the Republican Party, "they feel that Republicans don't care about them and it is getting too late for just lip service." There was little awareness of Nixon's minority appointments and initiatives, and much resentment of what one voter called Agnew's attempt "to make whites think it's open season on Negroes." Few had any feeling for Nixon as an individual or any sense of his views on minorities. As one Atlanta resident put it, "The guy who is in the

White House now is basically a stranger to most black people and most people in general."[37]

In mid-1970, the Nixon administration reversed its previous support for Republican outreach efforts to African-Americans. Two scholars who closely examined the historical record determined that the administration began "moving away from blacks and black interests on a national scale," and indeed expressed "regret that attempts were ever made to support 'black' policies."[38] Nixon's reaction was partly a response to what he perceived as the ingratitude of black leaders and voters to his efforts on their behalf. As antiwar protest, and the reaction against it, built to a climax after the Cambodian invasion of May 1970, Nixon also decided that the civil rights movement, the student movement, and the antiwar movement were inextricably linked—a backhanded endorsement of the argument that Martin Luther King Jr. had been roundly criticized for making several years earlier. He further believed that the "silent majority" of Americans were turning away from the Democrats and liberalism in general because they were so upset by the disruption that accompanied the movements. Republican attempts to appeal to blacks thus were costing the party support from the far more numerous white swing voters, particularly Southern whites and Northern blue-collar workers. A president who considered himself the leader of the entire nation might have tried to alter this dynamic by persuading Americans that every advance made by black people was not a loss for white people and vice versa, but Richard Nixon was not that sort of president.

Nixon's understanding of the political situation was greatly influenced by the 1970 publication of Richard Scammon and Ben Wattenberg's *The Real Majority*. The authors, both neoconservative Democrats, advised their party that the majority of American voters were "unyoung, unpoor, and unblack," and that their major concern was "the Social Issue": the reaction against growing crime, disruptive social change, and eroding moral values. The authors encouraged the Democrats to win over the moderate majority of Americans by emphasizing economic issues, minimizing the impact of the social issue, and pitching their campaign to the typical voter, whom they defined as a forty-seven year-old machinist's wife from Dayton, Ohio.[39] Nixon, however, agreed with his conservative advisor Pat Buchanan that the Scammon-Wattenberg analysis meant that Republicans could counterattack by playing up social issues on which Democrats were vulnerable, including welfare, busing, crime, student radicalism, and drug abuse. In his memoirs, Nixon recalled that he resolved that "We should aim our strategy primarily at disaffected Democrats, and blue collar workers, and at working class white ethnics. We should set out to capture the vote of the forty-seven-year-old Dayton housewife."[40]

Curiously, no one thought to ask who actually won the vote of that Dayton housewife. For most of the 1960s and 1970s, it was Congressman Charles W. Whalen Jr., who was considered to be one of the most progressive Republicans in the House. Whalen was perhaps the GOP's most successful vote-getter, racking up margins of over 70 percent in most of his elections and once running unopposed, despite representing a district with a two-to-one Democratic registration edge. He was also among the leading antiwar, pro-civil rights Republicans of his era. Whalen provided a significant complication to the argument that Republicans in the early 1970s had to remake themselves as the party of social conservatism in order to succeed at the polls.

From the time of his first Congressional victory in 1966, Whalen became a leader in the moderate-leaning House Wednesday Group and a thorn in the side of the GOP leadership, invariably voting his conscience rather than the party line. It was easy to make the case that Whalen was a liberal. As a member of the Ohio state legislature from 1954 to 1966, he had been an outspoken supporter of civil rights and author of the state's first fair housing law. In Congress, he called for a reordering of national priorities to address issues such as air and water pollution, education, urban decay, and hunger and malnutrition. He opposed most new weapons systems, including the Nixon administration's proposal for an anti-ballistic missile (ABM) defense.

Whalen himself did not agree that he was a liberal. He disliked political labels and preferred to refer to himself, when pressed, as an "orthodox realist." He felt that his advocacy of civil rights, education, and the environment was well within the Republican progressive tradition. His representation of a mostly urban district influenced his belief that government needed to address social problems. He believed that conservative criticism of government efforts toward social reform often sprang "not so much from hostility or opposition but simply from lack of contact" with urban problems.[41] As Whalen wrote to one of his Dayton correspondents, he had to address himself to the needs of 75,000 blacks in the western part of his district, and the 72,000 white Appalachian migrants in East Dayton. These citizens lived in poor and effectively segregated communities subject to high levels of unemployment, crime, inadequate housing, disease, and substandard education, and "It is in reaction to these serious problems that I have supported legislation designed to cope with them." Not all of these governmental approaches had worked out as hoped, but he pointed out that ignoring the cancerous situation of the urban centers "in the long run may well adversely affect the entire community, including the business sector."[42] At the same time, Whalen's conviction that the cost of government services had to be kept low set him apart from liberals who seemed to believe, as he saw it, "that government services don't have to be paid for."[43]

As a former businessman and economics professor, Whalen balanced his social liberalism with a deep fiscal conservatism. His earliest battles with the protectionist-minded GOP leadership came because of his opposition to tariffs, and indeed he proposed a world free trade association that would have eliminated trade barriers entirely.[44] He was a severe critic of Lyndon Johnson's War on Poverty, which he found inefficient, corrupt, and overly centralized, and he pioneered the idea of a negative income tax to replace the costly and paternal welfare bureaucracy. He cast particular aspersions on the Johnson administration's irresponsibility in inaugurating community programs "which, in the light of the tremendous (but not admitted) Vietnam War costs, could not be properly funded in ensuing years."[45]

Whalen came to be defined as a liberal mainly because of his opposition to the Vietnam war and what Dwight Eisenhower had called "the military-industrial complex." He began to have doubts about the war in 1967, when he stopped in at a funeral home to pay his respects to a University of Dayton graduate who had been killed in Vietnam. When the bereaved parents asked him for what purpose their son had died, he found that he could not answer them.[46] Later that year, Whalen would join with a group of forty-eight Republicans and four Democrats in the House in calling for a review of Vietnam policy to determine whether the war was worth the price, but he would not enter into open rebellion on the subject for some time to come.[47] Whalen came to oppose the war primarily on economic rather than moral grounds. His efforts reached beyond the war itself to what might be thought of as the militaristic assumptions of the American political process. As a member of the House Armed Services Committee, he was well placed to stir the pot.

One major defense contracting scandal of the time involved the Lockheed Corporation, which had revealed in late 1968 that its production of the mammoth C-5A aircraft could exceed its targeted cost of $2 billion by as much as 100 percent. When the Armed Services Committee met in the spring of 1969 to investigate, chairman Mendel Rivers of South Carolina discounted most of the cost expansion. He chalked up the $2 billion overrun to inflation caused by American prosperity, among other factors. But the hearings revealed that the Air Force had failed to exercise proper oversight of its contractors and had been less than candid in its dealings with Congress. Whalen came to realize that Congress was wholly dependent on the military services for information about deficiencies in weapons systems programs. Hearings on the Nixon administration's proposed Safeguard ABM system led Whalen and four other members of the Armed Services Committee—Vermont Republican Robert Stafford, and Democrats Robert Leggett, Lucien Nedzi, and Otis Pike—to develop doubts about the relevance and cost of Safeguard and other weapons systems. When the group went public with its criticisms of the American military establishment, they became known as "the Fearless Five."

Whalen observed numerous problems with the Armed Services Committee as it had operated under the control of Rivers and other militaristic Southern Democrats. The assumption that there was no room for partisanship in national security affairs meant that the Committee was one of only two whose minority members had no separate staff—the other being the House Internal Security Committee. More than two-thirds of the Committee's meetings in 1968 were closed to press and public, and nearly all those testifying before the Committee were Pentagon employees, who as Whalen pointed out were revealing only those facts "which the Pentagon wanted us to hear." Adversary proceedings were therefore virtually nonexistent: "In dealing with matters affecting not only billions of dollars, but, more important, life and death, I felt that I was hearing only one version of what may be a two-sided story."

Whalen and the other members of the "Fearless Five" met to discuss not only what weapons systems might be unnecessary, but also to scrutinize and challenge the assumptions underlying the nation's defense posture. They discovered that the design of the U.S. military was based on the "two and one-half war" theory, which called for a force capable of simultaneously fighting wars in Europe and Asia as well as a "brushfire" conflict in the Western hemisphere. This theory, which Whalen called "a principle with which few Congressmen are familiar," meant that the military was spending perhaps $5 billion annually to maintain a force to meet a potential Chinese attack, a matter about which there was no public comment or debate. The Armed Services Committee also failed to deliberate whether weapons systems met demonstrated strategic needs, the relative merits of one system over another, the likelihood of weapons systems actually being used, or the impact of proposed weapons systems on other Defense Department programs. In the Congress as a whole, the Defense budget had hitherto been "sacrosanct," according to Whalen. "Pentagon figures were accepted without question," although occasionally one of the Southern Democrats might complain to a military representative, "Why didn't you ask for more?" In failing to challenge the Pentagon, Congress had failed to achieve what Whalen called "a rational, effective, economically sound defensive posture," and its members "simply have not fulfilled our own responsibilities."

Junior members of the Armed Services Committee typically saw the annual Military Procurement Bill for the first time when they took their seats on mark-up day, giving them no more than two or three hours to consider the multibillion dollar proposal before casting their votes. This was part of the Committee's mode of operation that Whalen characterized as "democracy by stealth." In the fall of 1969, when the junior members requested more time to study the bill, they received their copies at 5:00 P.M. on the day before the meetings. The Fearless Five criticized the $21.3 billion authorization for being inflationary, diverting money from needed domestic programs, and funding weapons systems that were unnecessary for national security. Whalen and his colleagues prepared nine amendments, one of which was a proposal by Pennsylvania Republican Senator Richard Schweiker that the secretary of defense be required to make quarterly reports to Congress on the financial status of major projects, which would be subject to independent audits by the Comptroller General in case of deviation from original cost, quality, or delivery estimates. All of the amendments were defeated in Committee, with a maximum of thirty seconds devoted to each. When Whalen submitted the Schweiker amendment, Rivers rejected it out of hand with the remark: "We're not going to let the GAO [General Accounting Office] run this Committee."[48]

The Fearless Five voted against the authorization bill in committee, filed a sharp minority report, then decided to take their fight to the House floor. It was the House's first dissension on a Pentagon authorization bill since the end of World War II. One history of the debate recounted that "On the House floor, the Fearless Five and their followers offered specific, documented criticisms while advocates of military spending countered with personal attacks or absurd arguments."[49] The debate over the amendments extended to three days. The House rejected the Schweiker amendment by only a single vote.

Though the Fearless Five failed to win House approval of eight of their nine amendments, Whalen considered their effort to have been worthwhile, and indeed saw it as the forerunner of a new Congressional movement. By subjecting Pentagon authorizations to the same scrutiny applied to other departmental requests, Congress was finally reasserting its control of the military establishment, informing the public, and responding to a populace grown highly skeptical of military spending.[50]

Where the Vietnam war was concerned, Whalen believed that the costs outweighed whatever benefits the conflict might once have conveyed. As he said in one speech, his opposition to the war "reflects, perhaps, my background as an economist. I deplore the squandering of scarce resources."[51] He denied that his position against the war was necessarily a liberal one: "I have always been amused when pundits refer to a Congressman as 'liberal' for voting against $150 billion of waste in Vietnam and another Congressman as 'conservative' when he voted for it."[52] Ultimately, Whalen believed that the country's overall defense posture and grandiose international ambitions were unaffordable and unsustainable. In this respect, he was in a measured way upholding some of the old Midwestern anti-interventionism of the late Senator Robert Taft.

Like most other members of the moderate House Wednesday Group, Whalen consistently supported Nixon's domestic initiatives. In April 1970, he voted for the Family Assistance Plan for welfare reform, which passed the House by a 243–155 margin.[53] Of those votes in the first session of the 91st Congress where Nixon had taken a position, Whalen voted with the President 72.2 percent of the time. Within the Ohio House delegation, that was somewhat less than Robert Taft Jr. (81.8 percent), but considerably more than Donald "Buz" Lukens (55.2 percent).[54] Hard-edged ideological conservatives like Lukens were more out of step with Nixon than Republican progressives. While the conservative group Americans for Constitutional Action gave Lukens a nearly perfect rating and Whalen a rating of only 19 percent, Nixon's rating of 22 percent was much closer to Whalen than Lukens.[55]

That overlap of views between Nixon and the moderates was easy to miss, however, when it came to foreign affairs, particularly with regard to the Vietnam conflict. On the evening of April 30, Nixon appeared on national television to announce that he had widened the seemingly endless Indochina conflict by sending U.S. troops to invade Cambodia in an attempt to destroy North Vietnamese sanctuaries. Nixon knew that the Cambodian incursion would throw gasoline on the flames of the antiwar movement, but intentionally shaped his message, with the help of conservative speechwriter Pat Buchanan, in such a way as to violently polarize public opinion. The President cast his address in apocalyptic terms, warning Americans that "we live in an age of anarchy, both abroad and at home." He equated all student and antiwar protests with the violent actions of a handful of self-styled revolutionaries, describing the protests as "mindless attacks on all the great institutions which have been created by free civilizations in the last 500 years." Portraying the Cambodian action as a test of American will and character, he strongly implied that his opponents were willing to see the nation suffer humiliation and defeat and be reduced to acting "like a pitiful, helpless giant."[56]

In Lee Huebner's recollection, the April 30 address was the only foreign policy speech Buchanan ever wrote, and for that reason it was "an abnormal Nixon speech, because in his Vietnam speeches he usually was very careful to mollify public opinion and show hope. The Cambodia speech was just an angry speech." Nixon knew that national security advisor Henry Kissinger would not agree with his use of the incursion to inflame public opinion, and Buchanan worked on the speech without Kissinger's knowledge or approval. But both the Cambodian invasion and the speech provoked such an enormous public upheaval that Nixon's attempt to rally the silent majority backfired. In Huebner's opinion, the speech "surely turned out to be a real setback for Nixon. I think it started the whole period of trouble that never really ended."[57]

In the short term, Nixon did persuade at least a plurality of Americans of the rightness of his Cambodian policy; a Gallup poll in May found that 50 percent approved, and only 35 percent disapproved.[58] But while Nixon had anticipated that demonstrations would erupt on campuses across the country after his speech, he seems to have been surprised by the depth and intensity of the reaction against Cambodia, as some five hundred colleges and universities shut down in May and nearly two million students went on strike.[59] He also had not expected the extent to which the protest and counter-protest would make moderates fear for the stability of the country. Neither did he foresee that he would encounter significant opposition in Congress, particularly from antiwar moderates in his own party. Charles Whalen was one of the first Republicans to criticize the Cambodian invasion, calling it "a mistake of tragic proportions" as well as another administrative attempt to usurp the war powers of Congress.[60] Whalen was one of nine Wednesday Group Republicans and nine Democratic congressmen who offered a bipartisan resolution to cut off Congressional support for further spending for U.S. military involvement in Cambodia, Laos, and Vietnam.[61] In the Senate, Kentucky moderate John Sherman Cooper and Democrat Frank Church proposed a similar amendment to the Foreign Military Sales Act.[62] The debate over Cooper-Church was a significant signal of Congressional reassertion of its warmaking powers.

On the morning of May 4, Whalen spoke against the incursion on the House floor. Colleagues and onlookers in the gallery applauded when he charged that Nixon's supposed secret plan to end the war "repeats the mistakes of the previous administration and incorporates new errors of its own."[63] A few hours later, in Whalen's home state of Ohio, national guardsmen shot and killed four young people at Kent State University while attempting to quell student riots there. When Whalen heard the news, "I immediately expressed the opinion that the murders were cold-blooded and completely unjustified."[64] Many campuses that had resisted going on strike after the Cambodian invasion now did so, inflamed not only by the killing but also by the White House's callous comment on Kent State that "when dissent turns to violence it invites tragedy," and Nixon's offhand reference to students as "these bums . . . blowing up the campuses."[65]

"Apparently, the world has gone exceedingly mad," Bruce Chapman wrote to Ripon Society president Lee Auspitz, "and rather suddenly too. I've stopped defending Nixon." He urged moderates to refrain from making rash, polarizing statements, and instead to try to "preserve some middle political ground in the country."[66] The problem for the moderate movement, however, was that as extremists of right and left became more inflammatory, moderates failed to close ranks and oppose them. Instead, as former HEW secretary John Gardner diagnosed the situation in May 1970, "The moderates take sides against one another. We all become a little readier to grow angry, a little readier to identify villains, a little readier to resort to violence ourselves." He observed that the moderates' lack of unity meant that they were in a sense complicit in the actions of the extremists: "The moderate conservative does not explicitly approve of police brutality, but something in him is not unpleased when the billy club comes down on the head of a long-haired student. The liberal does not endorse violence by the extreme left, but he may take secret pleasure in such action when it discomfits those in authority."[67]

Still, the instinct of many moderates was to reach out to the disaffected students and try to persuade them that change through the system was still possible. New York Senator Charles Goodell, whose credibility with students was enhanced by Nixon's criticism of his antiwar stance, told students at Colgate University that he understood "the bitterness and hostility, exasperation and frustration and the futility of those who try to change the course of this country." He emphasized that the antiwar movement had already achieved significant accomplishments in bringing about Lyndon Johnson's resignation and changing the terms of the debate on Vietnam and American military intervention abroad. But he warned that if the antiwar movement turned to violence, the antiwar cause would suffer: "The issue then will be violence versus order, not the merits or demerits of the war in Vietnam. And on that issue the American people rightly come down on the side of order. Wrongly they will even come down on the side of repressive order."[68]

Lee Huebner and some of the other young and moderate White House staffers met in the aftermath of Kent State to discuss whether they could do something to bridge the gap between the administration and the campuses. Huebner remembered that "In May 1970, there was a feeling in the White House of being completely cut off from the rest of the country. Those of us in that group wanted to prove in some way that we were doing our little part to communicate, and that we were listening to the younger generation."[69] As the Brock-Steiger group of House Republicans had done the previous year, the junior staffers traveled to campuses throughout the country to meet with protesters.

Huebner and the other staffers found that at nearly all of the thirty or so colleges and universities they visited, most protests were not led by radicals but by moderates who had become newly active in politics after Cambodia and Kent State. The staffers' report to Nixon emphasized that the protesters were the "sons and daughters of the silent majority."[70] These moderate students eschewed violence and seemed willing to work through legitimate processes to accomplish their objectives. However, the group warned the President that "the definition of 'moderate' is changing." Most students strongly disapproved of the Cambodian invasion, wanted a rapid withdrawal of all U.S. troops from Indochina, and shared "the widespread belief that students are an oppressed minority that has been written off by this administration." Students were particularly upset by Agnew's attempts to discredit moderate students by lumping them with violent radicals and Nixon's announcement that he had watched football rather than pay attention to the antiwar demonstrations of the previous November. Many contrasted Nixon's campaign pledge to "Bring us together" with an administration that seemed to encourage polarization and even violence.[71] Huebner and the other staffers cautioned that Nixon risked alienating the nation's future leaders and, perhaps more importantly, offending adult moderates with "a strategy which seems to produce or even tolerate continuing conflict between students and the administration." If Nixon did not make a good faith effort at being president of all the people, then "when push comes to shove, the silent majority may vote against both the pushers and the shovers and go for the person they sense can cure the conflict."[72]

Nixon met with Huebner and the other staffers, thanked them for their report, and accepted one of their key recommendations by creating the President's Commission on Campus Unrest, headed by William Scranton, the former Pennsylvania governor and moderate Republican leader.[73] But Nixon was far more interested in attracting the backlash voters who opposed the protests than he was in reconciling with the students. On May 8, hundreds of helmeted construction workers on Wall Street spontaneously attacked an antiwar demonstration and marauded around lower Manhattan beating up anyone who looked like a hippie. The hardhats then marched on City Hall, where Mayor John Lindsay had ordered the American flag lowered to half-mast in memory of the Kent State dead, forced their way into the building, and returned the flag to full-staff. Police stood by while the workers assaulted students at a nearby college. Flag-waving hardhats continued to return to the streets in the following days for rallies to cheer Nixon and his Vietnam policies while denouncing Lindsay for what they saw as his indulgence of blacks and antiwar protesters.[74]

The surge in blue-collar, union support for the administration and its policies presented the Nixon administration with what White House aide Michael Balzano called "an explosive moment in the creation of the New Majority."[75] Embracing the hardhat violence was likely to alienate moderates and Nixon's remaining sources of establishment support. The media depicted the riots as the sort of street brawling that had preceded the Nazi takeover in Germany. Large numbers of prominent Wall Street bankers and lawyers responded to the threat from "labor fascists" by urging legislators and government officials to end the war.[76] Garry Wills, a former conservative who broke with his mentor Bill Buckley after Cambodia and Kent State, noted the racial edge of the hardhat counter-protests: "Blacks looked on with startled uncomprehending eyes, like Jews early in nineteen-thirties Germany, not able to trust their own senses."[77]

But Nixon could not resist the opportunity to steal away what had been a key group in the Democratic coalition and to associate himself with what he saw as a spontaneous expression of nationalism. Days after the initial riot, Nixon invited leaders of the New York unions to the White House. They presented the President with an honorary hardhat, which Nixon praised as a "symbol, along with our great flag, for freedom and patriotism to our beloved country."[78] Nixon anticipated that he could use "the social issue" to appeal to white labor workers in much the same terms that he was trying to win over Wallace supporters in the South. Further, he believed that any appeals to blacks, students, intellectuals, or the establishment would cost him the support of the Silent Majority, including Southerners, white ethnics, blue collar workers, and "middle Americans." Nixon decided that taking a liberal stance on matters of race relations, welfare, the environment, and troop withdrawal would not win him Silent Majority votes, and resolved to pin the "race-liberal-student tag" on the Democrats. He spurned the recommendations that Huebner and the moderate staff group had made about reconciling with his opponents. He warned his advisors about his "concern that our Administration team—including the White House staff—has been affected too much by the unreal atmosphere of the D.C. press, social and intellectual set. Perhaps Cambodia and Kent State led to an overreaction by our own people to prove that we were pro students, blacks, left. We must get turned around on this before it is too late— emphasize anti-crime, anti-demonstration, anti-drugs, anti-obscenity. We must get with the mood of the country which is fed up with the liberals."[79] Nixon's eighteen-month flirtation with the moderate movement was over. The administration increasingly tended toward the view that, as Agnew allegedly declared, "the only good Republican is a conservative Republican."[80]

One other violent action in the summer of 1970 would have long-lasting political repercussions, though it was little recognized at the time. On the afternoon of June 6, police arrived at George Washington University in the nation's capital to break up a demonstration that had spun out of control. Around two hundred angry protestors had surrounded a building on the campus. One of the police on the scene later told reporters that the crowd "appeared no different to me than any other mob. It had the same appearance, the same hysterical rhetoric, the same reactions."[81] The protesters were waving banners, wearing strange clothing, and chanting furiously in a foreign language—Spanish, as it happened—that the police didn't recognize: "I don't know what it was," another officer recalled, "but it didn't sound good."[82] Several of the most committed radicals smashed the glass door of a locked campus building and overwhelmed the security guard who tried to stop them. They meant to occupy the building and put an end to business as usual. When the police burst in, the leader of the group struggled with them and, the police claimed, attacked them with a heavy wooden club. The officers subdued him and dragged him from the building, bleeding and in handcuffs, along with four of his followers. "The police acted, yes, brutally," the leader's wife wrote to her brother, "clubbing and beating up the group with absolutely no provocation. . . . The treatment the five got in jail was close to sadistic."[83]

Reporters soon discovered that the leader of this action fit the pattern of many other would-be revolutionaries around the country. He had begun as an idealist in a more mainstream political movement, but frustration over his inability to achieve his goals had led him into extremism over the course of the '60s. He was the editor of a small, anti-capitalist publication that had become increasingly apocalyptic and millenarian. The magazine was influenced by what most Americans considered to be the alien doctrine of a foreign regime, and depicted the United States as a hellish, immoral state, with the blood of murdered innocents on its hands. The radical leader slammed his former movement colleagues as sellouts. He was prepared to move beyond what he considered their armchair idealism and naïve trust in America, which the magazine often spelled as "Amerika" to emphasize its similarity to Nazi Germany. He warned the government that he would take direct action, putting his body on the line in the name of "the poorest of the poor."[84] He was willing to break laws and even commit violence against what he considered to be an illegitimate state in the name of a higher, revolutionary morality. If this meant turning against his country and the political movement he had helped to establish, so be it.

But this charismatic radical leader was L. Brent Bozell Jr., a forty-four year-old father of ten children and the brother-in-law of the prominent conservative journalist William F. Buckley Jr. The mainstream movement they had created was not the New Left but the New Right, and Bozell had been one of the founders of *National Review*, the magazine that was the leading organ of the new conservatism. The cause for which he advocated breaking the law was abortion, and the ideology for which he was willing to fight and die was extreme, theocratic Catholicism. His small, radical magazine was *Triumph*, which opposed the Vatican II reforms in the name of Catholic orthodoxy. His principal enemies were not liberals but those conservatives like Buckley who, as he saw it, had failed to take conservatism to its logical and proper conclusion and were too cowardly to take direct action to halt the slaughter of the unborn to which the U.S. government was a willing accomplice. The campus building he had occupied with his group, Los Hijos de Tormenta (The Sons of Thunder), was not the administration center but a hospital clinic where Bozell believed abortions were being performed. The strange uniform that they wore included the khaki slacks and red beret of the pro-monarchist Spanish Carlist movement, and the alien regime that influenced them was not Mao's China but Franco's Spain. The demonstration's Spanish chant was not "Castro si!" but "Viva Christo Rey!" ("Long live Christ the King!"), and the "weapon" that Bozell had used to break down the clinic's doors and assault the police was a five-foot tall, homemade wooden cross.[85]

New Right and New Left had come full circle. The sense of martyrdom, moral superiority, unwillingness to compromise, and exaltation of direct action that had characterized Students for a Democratic Society was now present on the right as well as the left. Bozell's erstwhile colleagues at *National Review* were appalled by his actions, and he attracted few converts to his quasi-fascist Catholic movement. But abortion would give the conservative movement the passionate, all-involving cause that civil rights had been for moderates and opposition to the war for the New Left. As the pro-life issue came to be embraced by evangelical Protestants, it would win new converts to the conservative movement and provide a new generation of activists at the grassroots. This revived movement would throw its forces on the side of a conservative Republican Party and would oppose any accommodation with pro-choice moderates. Anti-abortion activists would adopt the New Left's black-and-white worldview that saw their fellow citizens only in terms of being part of the problem or part of the solution.

Not long before Bozell's demonstration, the conservative group Young Americans for Freedom had published an article blasting Congressman George H. W. Bush, the head of the House Republican Task Force on Earth Resources and Population, as "the leading life-prevention henchman for the Administration in the House." The article took Bush to task not only for his support of abortion but birth control as well. The article's author, Bradley Warren Evans, emphasized that conservatives ought to support even a liberal Democrat like Ralph Yarborough over Bush in the Texas Senate race, so long as the liberal Democrat was pro-life. It made no difference that Bush stood for many other positions that conservatives liked: "if a man advocates government trammeling of the most sacred of human prerogatives, what does it matter what else he stands for?"[86]

At the same time that Bozell was breaking down clinic doors in Washington, his brother-in-law James L. Buckley was running against New York

Republican Senator Charles Goodell in the 1970 election as a candidate on the third-party Conservative line. Jim Buckley was the fourth of the ten Buckley children—William Jr. was number six—and as reserved as his younger brother was flamboyant. He was the manager of the Buckley family's oil company holdings overseas, and had little involvement with politics until he was persuaded to become the New York Conservative Party's challenger to progressive Republican Senator Jacob Javits in the 1968 election. Buckley received 1,139,402 votes, or 17.4 percent of the total. This was by far the Conservative Party's best showing to that point—although, as Bill had predicted, his campaign actually helped Javits by drawing off conservative Democrats, giving the Republican a triumphant million-vote margin.[87]

In 1970, however, Jim Buckley's prospects against Goodell were more promising. Goodell had incurred nationwide fame, and lasting Nixon enmity, for being the first senator to propose a Congressional cutoff of funds for the Vietnam war. The New York Liberal Party endorsed Goodell over his Democratic opponent Richard Ottinger in the 1970 race, and during the previous two decades no Republican with Liberal support had ever lost a statewide race.[88] But longtime conservative strategist Clif White, Buckley's campaign manager, realized that the Conservative could "squeak by" with a plurality if he could split the state's heavy liberal majority by portraying Goodell and Ottinger as "birds of the same feather despite their party allegiances."[89] An increasing number of voters also shared Buckley's conservative positions on the social issue, not just with regard to student and antiwar protests, but also with the emerging pro-life cause; in the summer of 1970, many New Yorkers were outraged when the state passed one of the nation's most permissive abortion laws.

When Charles Goodell entered politics in 1959 as a representative from largely rural Chautauqua County in western New York, four hundred miles away from Manhattan, it would have been difficult to have portrayed him as a liberal. He was a Phi Beta Kappa graduate of Williams College, turned down a professional baseball contract to attend Yale Law School, fought in both World War II and the Korean war, and was the father of five sons—one of whom, Roger, later became the long-serving commissioner of the National Football League. In Congress, he gained an early reputation as a conservative opponent of Kennedy's New Frontier and Johnson's Great Society programs. But "I was never as conservative as most make me out to have been," he felt.[90] He was an integral member of the Young Turks rebellion in 1965 that installed Gerald Ford as minority leader and pushed for reform of the House. As chairman of the newly created Republican Committee on Planning and Research, he was part of the House GOP leadership and a spur to the creation of constructive Republican alternatives to Democratic programs.

When Nelson Rockefeller appointed him to fill the unexpired Senate term of the slain Robert F. Kennedy in 1968, Goodell acquired a massively different constituency and responsibilities. Conservatives charged that Goodell turned left to ingratiate himself with the liberal majority of New York state, and that "this chameleon-like ability to change political coloration to suit the political environment" was evidence of his expediency and lack of principles.[91] Goodell denied this claim and emphasized that his change in ideological perspective had taken place while he was still in the House. At the start of the Johnson administration, he had proclaimed the objective of stopping Communist aggression in Vietnam to be "the duty of all responsible people," but by the end of Johnson's presidency he had come to believe that opposition to the war was more consistent with conservative than liberal philosophy.[92] Although he came from an area where urban poverty was nonexistent, during his time in the House he quietly visited nearly every large ghetto area in the country to educate himself about the problems their residents faced. His discoveries hardened his resolve against crime but made him skeptical of conservative law-and-order rhetoric. "Law enforcement is the last answer, the least productive resource after everything else has failed," he insisted to his fellow Republicans. "We have got to talk about the causes of crime and how we solve the crime that has been sweeping this country."[93]

As Senator, Goodell supported much of Nixon's domestic agenda, particularly those issues like welfare reform and revenue sharing that he had helped devise while a member of the House GOP leadership. But he recalled that he "gradually became concerned with many of the things that were going on in the Nixon administration: the general air of arrogance, the insensitivity to civil liberties, the wiretapping, the approach to dissent."[94] He introduced his legislation calling for military disengagement from Vietnam, and also became one of what conservatives in the White House referred to as the "Traitorous Eight" Republican senators who voted against the ABM and confirmation of Haynsworth and Carswell; the others were Brooke, Case, Hatfield, Javits, Mathias, Percy, and Schweiker.[95]

Goodell felt that the division between the progressive Republicans and the White House was "not so much along ideological lines as over the question of whether they were with the White House a hundred percent or not."[96] Nixon clearly tolerated some dissidents more than others. The independent *Congressional Quarterly* found that on crucial Senate votes concerning which Nixon had taken a definite stand over the previous year, Goodell more consistently supported the President than did most conservative senators, including Strom Thurmond and Barry Goldwater.[97] Clif White scoffed that Goodell's claim that he was a more regular Republican than Goldwater was as realistic as "Joe Namath comparing himself to

Cardinal Cooke because they both work on Sunday," but conservatives felt few compunctions about opposing high-profile presidential initiatives like the Family Assistance Plan or revenue sharing.[98] White was correct, however, that Nixon considered support for his Vietnam policies to be of primary importance. Goodell's dissent made it impossible for the President to portray the war as a partisan issue, or antiwar dissenters as a lunatic fringe, and therefore Nixon decided that the New York senator had to be purged. "The President's rule of endorsing all Republican candidates is being revoked in this case," Nixon told his staff. "We are dropping Goodell over the side. Everyone knows it."[99]

Fearing that an open endorsement of a non-Republican would split the party, Nixon resorted to indirect measures to bring down Goodell. Nixon flew into Westchester Airport outside New York City and stepped out onto the tarmac to pose with a crowd of YAFers, assembled by secret prearrangement, carrying "Nixon and Buckley" signs. Photographs of the seemingly spontaneous event allowed Nixon to endorse Buckley without a word being spoken. "It was a typically devious Nixon ploy," Clif White marveled.[100] Goodell later told an interviewer that he learned that Chuck Colson and other presidential aides sent letters to state party leaders in New York and Wall Street donors warning them against supporting his campaign, "which basically dried up all the normal campaign contributions that a Republican candidate in New York could have expected."[101] Nixon ensured that Goodell received none of the campaign funds that he had collected clandestinely since taking office, in what came to be known as "Operation Townhouse." Nixon also denied funds to other candidates whose support of the President was suspect, including Lenore Romney, wife of George, who was the GOP Senate nominee from Michigan. "She's not one of us," Nixon declared.[102] Nixon gave Agnew the green light to attack Goodell as well as the forces of progressive reform that he represented.

The Vice President denied that he was dividing the country, except in the most positive sense. The scourge of the Eastern media elite used the *New York Times* op-ed page to lecture his critics on the need "to differentiate between the kind of division that embitters and negates, and the division that encourages intelligent debate."[103] But Agnew egregiously failed to heed his own counsel. His speeches represented his opponents not as rational critics and fellow citizens with whom one might agree to differ, but as liars, clowns, homosexuals, traitors, and enemies of the American people. Former Vice President Hubert Humphrey thought that no politician since Joe McCarthy had made "such a calculated appeal to our nastier instincts."[104] Agnew lacked the manner of a demagogue, delivering his remarks with what journalist Mary McGrory called "a stunning absence of passion" that made him sound more like "a cranky village philosopher" than Nixon in his vindictive prime.[105] Nonetheless, his aim was to poison the wells of discourse, in Cardinal Newman's phrase, by imputing such malignant motives to his opponents that it was pointless to listen to their arguments.

Agnew first went after Goodell by calling him a "radiclib," the silly portmanteau word his speechwriters William Safire and Pat Buchanan had invented to describe a "radical liberal." Goodell took the bait and accused Agnew of McCarthyism and attempting to use federal power to coerce the media. "Mr. Agnew has not been a very good spokesman for the enlightened moderation in this country which is what I think we need," he told a news conference.[106] Agnew then upped the ante by terming Goodell "the Christine Jorgensen of the party," referring to a then-notorious young man who had undergone a sex-change operation in Denmark.[107] His crack implied that Goodell had surrendered not only his principles but his manhood.

Agnew's insult provoked an outpouring of disgust from moderate Republicans. "There is a limit which decent opinion draws to vilification in national politics," Nelson Rockefeller's advisor George Hinman admonished the Vice President. He regretted that the GOP's standard had been "dipped in filth" by the attack upon "another Republican whose only offense is an independent view of the issues of life and death in our time."[108] One national committeewoman threatened to resign, while angry moderates flooded RNC chairman Rogers Morton with mail criticizing Agnew's attempt to purge Goodell.[109] An unknowable but considerable number of moderate and progressive Republicans began to defect to the Democrats. "[W]hat kind of a future, if any, can I as a liberal expect as a functioning member of the Republican Party?" one longtime GOP voter asked.[110]

Morton stoutly defended Goodell, arguing that the minority party needed to broaden rather than narrow its base. "I was not elected chairman of the Republican Party to preside over its liquidation," he snapped.[111] Agnew loftily dismissed his fellow Maryland Republican as a "mere party functionary," but Goodell had other advocates in the party as well.[112] Several senators wearing "Charlie Goodell Is a Good Egg" buttons held a press conference at LaGuardia Airport to stump for their colleague. Nineteen of the Senate's forty-three Republicans signed a letter endorsing Goodell as "a man of conscience, courage and conviction," implicitly defying the White House's effort to read him out of the party. Most were members of the Wednesday Club, but conservatives like Norris Cotton of New Hampshire and Peter Dominick of Colorado also sent letters of support. Most of the senators emphasized that they were upholding the importance of the party structure and the big-tent concept rather than endorsing Goodell's views. Ohio Senator William Saxbe said that he didn't agree with the New Yorker on all issues, but felt that the GOP had to "reflect the diversity that springs from local differences."[113]

Garry Wills, who was well acquainted with the Machiavellian mind of Clif White, speculated that Agnew's over-the-top attack on Goodell back-fired—as it was intended to. One of White's key beliefs was that people vote against, not for. The insult to Goodell meant that many liberals would abandon the Democratic candidate in order to vote against Agnew by proxy, thus splitting the liberal vote.[114] The Ripon Society saw Agnew's intervention in Goodell's race as further evidence of Nixon's continued pursuit of the Scammon-Wattenberg thesis. They concluded that Nixon hoped to attract white Southerners and Northern white ethnics by encouraging the permanent defection to the Democrats of progressive Republicans, independents, Jews, African-Americans, New England Yankees and their offshoots, and "those in the knowledge-based industries, regardless of ethnic origin."[115]

Agnew backed off from attacking Goodell, but Jim Buckley quickly took up the slack. Using Agnew-style logic, Buckley claimed that Goodell's concern about the causes of crime amounted to tacit support of criminals. Both Republican Goodell and Democrat Ottinger, in Buckley's reading, were "conscientious objectors in the war against crime and disorder."[116] Buckley donned a hardhat to tell cheering construction workers that Goodell's ally John Lindsay was "a liability to the police in their fight against crime."[117] Goodell's efforts to get disaffected students to reject violence and participate in the political process became, in Buckley's interpretation, encouragement of "arson and intimidation."[118] The Conservative nominee in some ways campaigned as a Nixon-style centrist, balancing his inflammatory rhetoric against dissent with general support for labor and federal programs such as Medicare and Social Security. Unlike Nixon, Buckley was a genuine conservationist, who believed that federal intervention to protect the environment was necessary "for the simple reason that the states alone are not competent to handle this problem. Air, water and wild life don't observe state lines."[119] It was difficult, however, for moderates to appreciate these mitigating factors in light of Buckley's provocations.

Goodell's campaign had other problems besides the opposition of the White House and the Conservative Party. One major obstacle was New York Governor Nelson Rockefeller's belief in the patriotic necessity of his reelection to an unprecedented fourth term. In 1970, Rockefeller faced a formidable Democratic opponent in former Supreme Court justice and United Nations ambassador Arthur Goldberg, whose running mate for lieutenant governor was Basil Paterson, an African-American state senator from Harlem. Rockefeller had received about a third of the Jewish and black vote in New York City in 1966, but likely would lose many of those voters against a Jewish-black ticket. The governor also feared that Goldberg, as a former secretary of labor under Kennedy, would swipe Rockefeller's prized union endorsements. Playing defense, Rockefeller made a special effort to court the predominantly Catholic, blue-collar, outer-borough constituency that had voted for conservative Democrat Mario Procaccino in the previous year's mayoral race. He played to the social issue by criticizing welfare chiselers and calling for stiffer sentences for criminals, and bid for Catholic support by attempting to get around the Supreme Court ruling forbidding public assistance to parochial schools. He charged that the Goldberg campaign was infested with left-wing "extremists."[120]

Rockefeller even sought the endorsement of the Conservative Party that had been created specifically to oppose him, using Henry Kissinger as his intermediary with Bill Buckley. Buckley was noncommittal about the likelihood of the Conservatives reconciling with their major enemy, but—perhaps seeking to boost his brother's chances in the Senate race—declared to Kissinger that "I stand ready to help him [Rockefeller] in any way."[121] While courting conservatives, Rockefeller cut off his donations to the moderate activists in the Ripon Society. Ripon president Lee Auspitz complained that while those contributions had never made up a significant amount of the organization's budget, they were "important to us as an indication that Governor Rockefeller was grateful for work done for him by members of the Ripon Society and was willing, despite occasional disagreements with its positions, to support the only group in American politics recruiting progressive young people into the Republican party."[122]

Rockefeller did endorse Goodell, whom he had after all appointed as senator, but tepidly.[123] Anxious not to alienate Jim Buckley's followers, the governor failed to give the antiwar senator significant financial backing or to exercise his full political clout on his ticket-mate's behalf, as he might have by denying state committee funds to Republican candidates who refused to support Goodell. A group calling itself the Silent Majority Mobilization Committee distributed campaign materials touting "Rockefeller-Buckley," although both candidates denied any involvement.[124] Still as ardent a Vietnam hawk as ever, the governor denounced Goodell's troop withdrawal plan as a move that "can only undermine the effectiveness of the president's bargaining position."[125] Rockefeller also throttled the reelection bid of antiwar Representative Daniel E. Button, the first Republican congressman from boss-ridden, Democrat-controlled Albany County in half a century. At Rockefeller's behest, the state GOP denied Button campaign funds, and the Republican-controlled legislature redistricted him into a voting precinct, dominated by a solidly established Democratic member of the House Armed Services Committee, that he was destined to lose.[126]

If the 1970 elections had taken place during the spring, when public reaction against the war was at its peak, Goodell might have won handily. The Cooper-Church amendment prohibiting the funding of American military operations in Cambodia passed the Senate in June, with 16 of 42 Republicans voting in favor. The bill failed on a 237–153 vote in the House nine days later, however, after the last American troops had left Cambodia. During the summer, the Hatfield-McGovern amendment to cut off funds for the Vietnam war by July 1971 if it was not authorized by Congress—a proposal that no senator except Charles Goodell had supported the year before—broke the Senate record for the greatest volume of supportive mail received for a legislative proposal. But Nixon, working through the conservative Democratic chairmen in the Senate, succeeded in delaying the vote until September. By that time the antiwar fervor around the country had subsided. The nation's colleges and universities, which had braced for a renewed outbreak of protest, instead experienced an "eerie tranquility," in the phrase of Yale University president (and moderate Republican) Kingman Brewster.[127] Students had become disenchanted with the failures of mass protest, and Nixon's Vietnamization policies and the institution of the draft lottery meant that Vietnam was no longer a direct threat to most young men. Nixon credited the sputtering economy for the absence of campus protest: "Probably more than anything else what has helped to cool the campuses was the fact that these little jackasses couldn't get out and get a job."[128] As inflation and unemployment rose, intense public sympathies for the antiwar and civil rights movements waned. In this more conservative environment, the Hatfield-McGovern amendment received 39 votes but still went down to defeat.

Perhaps the most significant problem that Goodell faced, however, was his own failure to offer a convincing alternative to Ottinger on his left as well as Buckley on his right. Like a number of other progressive Republicans in the fevered atmosphere of the late '60s and early '70s, he lost sight of the need to assemble a moderate majority by dominating the center rather than trying to outbid the liberal Democrat for support from the left. Along similar lines, Francis Hatch, a state representative and a progressive Republican in Massachusetts, abandoned a contest with Democratic liberal Michael Harrington for a Congressional seat because there were not "enough really clear points of disagreement" between them, he admitted. He thought that "an Agnew-type might have a reasonably good chance" in the election, "but I just can't change my proverbial spots."[129]

Ripon president Lee Auspitz and several other members of the Society met with New York Mayor John Lindsay to discuss the problems he had with voters from the blue-collar, largely Catholic working class. By his own admission, Lindsay had become a polarizing figure to these people in the same way that Nixon appeared as a polarizer to students. Auspitz believed that, much like students, the northern white ethnics wanted their unique experiences to be appreciated by those in power, but progressive Republicans like Lindsay and Goodell had done little to "take positive steps to identify with their gut experiences" and "avoid affronting their deeper sensibilities." In particular, Auspitz felt that the Lindsay-loathing hardhats, many of whom had served in the military, were "sensitive to any glorification of 'draft dodgers' and any sentimentalizing of student casualties at Kent State which does not also recognize the loss of life in Vietnam." In Auspitz's view, Lindsay shouldn't have taken sides on whether the experience of military service or student dissent was more valid.[130] Lindsay and Goodell also tended to lose sight of a political truism that Richard Nixon never forgot, which was that the American people were willing to support progressive social policies only if they believed them to be consistent with American moral values such as patriotism and the work ethic. Nixon felt that Americans had become "turned off on welfare," as he put it, "not because they don't want to be generous—basically, I think most people are generous—but mainly because they just don't think the country should be built that way. [And] they consider that there are elitists in their country who want to take their money and take care of a lot of lazy bastards that won't work."[131]

The Conservative Party of New York had a significant following because large numbers of socially conservative working-class and lower middle-class whites genuinely felt unrepresented by both parties. This explained the effectiveness of Jim Buckley's campaign slogan: "Isn't It Time We Had a Senator?" Goodell's small-town personal values were more conservative than most people knew; when he was a House member, he had formed a weekly prayer group with fellow Young Turks Gerald Ford, Melvin Laird, and Al Quie, at a time when such groups were quite unusual in Congress.[132] Goodell kept this side of himself private, however, rather than trying to communicate with voters who were worried about the erosion of traditional morality.

The Ripon Society alumni who worked in the White House worried that their former colleagues were being swept up in the revolutionary enthusiasms of the time and losing their sense for the vital center. The moderates in the administration conceded that Nixon's sense of the center was not the same as theirs, but believed that Ripon's members should accept that he was the most electable moderate candidate, to paraphrase Bill Buckley's pragmatic formulation for conservatives. One Ripon alumnus at HEW felt that the moderates should "stop bitching" at the administration and pay more attention to the threat from the right: "they don't know what it's like here slugging it out with the [Strom] Thurmonds of the world." William

Matuzeski, at the new Council on Environmental Quality, fretted that Ripon's members had "bought [John] Lindsay lock, stock and barrel, and I don't quite understand why. As he moves away from the Republican party, I think he's pulling them with him."[133]

As Auspitz's exchange with Lindsay suggested, however, at least some of Ripon's members were thinking about the identity problems of moderates in the Nixon era. Auspitz, in the spring of 1970, while he was a graduate student at Harvard, wrote one of the era's most incisive philosophical explorations of moderate Republicanism, in an article entitled "For a Moderate Majority." It has been overlooked by political scientists mainly because it appeared in *Playboy* magazine, best known as a purveyor of cheesecake photos and Hugh Hefner's cheeseball pseudo-sophistication. The fact that Auspitz's article is little remembered by academics, however, did not mean that it was ignored. "I used to write for a lot of different publications at that time," Auspitz recalled, "but the only time I ever wrote something and people stopped me on the street in Cambridge to say that they'd read my article was the *Playboy* article, which says something about what Cambridge people really read."[134]

Auspitz began with the proposition that the existing ideologies of liberalism, conservatism, and radicalism were poorly suited to the realities of American life. New Deal liberalism had outlived its usefulness as a vision of what government should do. Its view of the centrality of the battle of haves versus have-nots was outdated "now that the majority of Americans no longer consider themselves have-nots." Instead, politics was moving in the direction of "asking which sectors of the economy and what styles of life deserve favored treatment by Government." However appropriate the big-government approach may have been to the prostrate economy of the 1930s, it was poorly suited to an era in which American prosperity would be driven by demands for new services and the growth of new industries based on technological breakthroughs. Conservatives were correct to criticize the shortcomings of liberalism, but were straitjacketed by ideology and their wish to return to the past. "What is needed," Auspitz believed, "is a radical's analysis of the forces at work in society, a liberal's sense of tolerance and his generous impulses toward the disadvantaged, and a conservative's respect for traditional values and his skepticism about bureaucracy."[135]

Neither liberalism nor conservatism spoke to the needs and wants of the emerging class at the center of American political life. Auspitz believed that this new class resembled a "mass aristocracy," not because its members were necessarily from privileged backgrounds but rather because they were politically engaged, independent-minded people seeking meaningful public roles of the sort that previously had been restricted principally to the upper class. They believed in public service and participation, individual freedom and responsibility. They were tolerant of dissent and put a high value on privacy. They were reform-minded and uncomfortable with rigid, hierarchical organizations and structures. In the past, these attitudes had mostly been associated with the "liberal establishment," the well-bred, progressively inclined gentlemen of the Northeastern upper class who dedicated much of their lives to public service, from Theodore Roosevelt and Henry Stimson through William Scranton and John Lindsay. Now they had spread through much of the baby boom generation. The new class was made up not only of the educated young but included professionals, white-collar workers, and some of the younger men and women in business, labor, and the armed forces.[136] Some of them would become leaders at the national level, but the vast majority would seek engagement and pursue innovation in their communities and workplaces, or through local politics and private associations. In order for the members of this large class to have a say in the decision-making process, it would be necessary to reverse the concentration of power in the federal government and bureaucracies that had grown since the Depression and accelerated with the Cold War. Only the moderates could arrest the trend toward liberal statism while effectively addressing present-day realities.

Auspitz conceived of the moderate position in terms of a number of dualities. The moderates preferred internationalism to interventionism. They viewed the ideal U.S. foreign policy as an attempt to influence other nations without imposing outcomes on them. They rejected nation-building and the interventionist mindset that preferred "unilateral to multilateral action, confrontation to negotiation, and military force to just about anything else." In the domestic sphere, moderates similarly favored a modest and limited view of government. They called for a devolution of power to reverse the centralization that had accrued over the previous four decades and had made government "flabby, overextended, and riddled with patronage."[137] Government, in the moderate view, worked better when it offered incentives for outside institutions—such as businesses, voluntary associations, universities, foundations, and semi-public corporations—to take on problems rather than trying to solve them through direct bureaucratic means. Market mechanisms were preferable to subsidies and controls. Transparency and a dispersal of decision-making authority were superior to secrecy and the concentration of power in the hands of a small group of experts. Nixon's New Federalism programs, including revenue sharing and the negative income tax, offered the promise of smaller yet more effective government, as did proposals for school voucher schemes and a free market in farming. As part of the decentralizing process, moderates wanted privatization rather than bureaucratization. They proposed to spin off certain government functions, for example by contracting out mail delivery to a private corporation, rather than have government agencies try to deal with every conceivable problem. Auspitz's thinking about privatization was strongly influenced by management guru Peter Drucker, with whom he was in regular correspondence.[138]

Auspitz admitted that certain values the moderates held dear sometimes conflicted; liberty and stability, for example, were often in tension. He believed that, in general, the imperatives of freedom and progress outweighed the desirability of domestic tranquility. "Free choice always disturbs the balance of things," he declared, "and the presence of it always forces one to ask whether he is devoted to preserving the *status quo* or to seeking new balances that will widen the scope for individual choice."[139] Here was a key contrast between the libertarianism of the moderate movement and the authoritarianism of Nixon's status quo centrism. Auspitz was careful to draw a further distinction between a bias in favor of freedom and liberation and the unholy union of libertinism and laissez-faire doctrine that characterized many libertarians; the pot-smoking right-winger in a three-piece suit was by this time a familiar character on many college campuses. Moderates, in Auspitz's view, should not seek to undermine old customs without giving thought to what should replace them, nor should they celebrate the unfettered operation of forces in America's past that had denied many people basic liberties because of race, sex, or poverty.

The Nixon-Agnew goal of creating a permanent majority struck Auspitz as extremely dangerous. He pointed out that the Founding Fathers had warned that a permanent majority inevitably would lead to polarization: "Those who are left out of such a majority become alienated and radicalized; they feel that they have no legitimate access to power, so they resort to illegitimate means. The permanent majority reacts by repressing the minority; but to do so effectively, it must adopt measures that restrict the liberty of all citizens." Auspitz believed that a progressively oriented Republican Party therefore needed to pursue a moderating rather than a polarizing political strategy. He also argued that Agnew could not have made either African-Americans or young people into targets if those groups had not been overcommitted to the Democrats. If they demonstrated a willingness to switch parties, "neither party will dare use them as a focus for polarizing the electorate." He hoped that a more responsive political system would have a maturing effect on groups whose extreme rhetoric was a product of their perceived isolation and powerlessness: "The best way to get Americans to lower their voices is to give them access to the quiet corridors of power."[140]

Auspitz naturally felt that the moderate wing of the GOP, led by men such as Lindsay, Percy, Hatfield, and Goodell, best deserved the allegiance of politically engaged people who shared his preferences. But he was well aware that organizing this group for concerted action would be difficult to achieve, for all the reasons that had plagued the moderate movement throughout the 1960s. Moderates failed to recognize that they had a common cause, and tended to be "so nonideological, so aware of the importance of objective facts that they often fail to see that a disposition to look at the facts in a hardheaded way is itself a unifying ideology." Assuming themselves to be in the mainstream of American life, moderates rarely bothered to define their positions or engage in the petty squabbles and struggles of party infighting. "Even more rarely do they unite with other moderates into a national movement," Auspitz lamented. "Their favored candidates are usually decent, intelligent, pragmatic men who so pride themselves on their independence that they are often unable to team up with others."[141] Moderates lacked the political infrastructure of the conservative movement or the network of party regulars around Nixon, and after a decade of turmoil and disappointment, many moderates had become disillusioned with the political process.

Still, Auspitz was optimistic that the new class whose outlines he described would become the dominant force in American politics, and the moderate wing of the Republican Party would be its vehicle. The shortage of leadership at the top of the GOP offered young people a historic opportunity to build a movement from the ground up, a movement based around intelligent discussion, persuasion, and the effort to develop workable proposals. Moderates would excite people with their ideas and ability to achieve results. They would revolutionize the political system, not through mass demonstration but through "reason, competence, persistence and tough-minded idealism."[142]

It didn't happen. For one thing, Auspitz made faulty predictions about the social conditions that might foster the growth of a huge, politically engaged, moderate class. He posited that the baby boomers "have not known want, so they are not preoccupied with material security." But 1970 ushered in a period of economic volatility and decline that lasted until the 1980s. While most Americans didn't experience hardship comparable to the Great Depression, they did become extremely preoccupied with their own material security and accordingly less interested in political reform. Auspitz also thought that the boomers, not having experienced a depression or world war, "think of social problems as manageable." In fact, the lesson most Americans seem to have drawn from the traumas of the late '60s and '70s was that social problems were terribly difficult to manage and that visionary, ambitious attempts to solve them only made them worse. The chastened tone of John Lindsay's second inaugural address in 1970 ("We are all human, we are all fallible. The test is whether we have learned from the mistakes we have made") suggested that the era of exciting innovation in social policy had already come to an end.[143]

The Ripon Society had never seen itself as the spearhead of a mass movement, but Auspitz hoped that Ripon might coordinate a moderate attempt to begin to retake the party machinery at the grassroots level in the 1970 elections. He went so far as to copy the relevant sections of Clif White's Goldwater campaign memoir and distribute them to those who might try to emulate the Syndicate's 1962–64 success.[144] It proved impossible, however, to raise funds for the effort or find sufficient numbers of moderate conspirators: "our part of the Party in general just doesn't have enough people across the country who are in sufficient contact with each other to be effective," one Ripon member sighed.[145]

Moderates had once united around the civil rights movement, but by the early 1970s the struggle for racial equality no longer held the same moral clarity that it had when the debate was over segregation and the denial of African-Americans' constitutional right to vote. As the movement devolved into quarrels over messy issues like busing and affirmative action, it no longer provided a rallying point for moderates. The Nixon administration, which might have provided a focus for moderate organizational efforts, alienated many moderates through its war policies, its sporadic attempts to pursue a Southern strategy, and its antagonism to Goodell's candidacy and the progressive wing of the party in general.

Moderates failed to agree on a number of strategic issues, of which the most critical was their posture regarding the Nixon administration. Some were willing to overlook Nixon's rhetorical conservatism because of his substantive accomplishments, but progressive leaders like John Lindsay began distancing themselves from the Republican Party and many rank-and-file Republicans threatened to switch parties. At a Ripon-sponsored conference in 1970, Auspitz pleaded with the dissidents to stay in the GOP at least until the November elections: "Don't leave the Republican Party before then. If we go, we all go together."[146] This earned Auspitz a rebuke from Ripon affiliate Mitch McConnell, an aide to moderate Kentucky Senator Marlow Cook. McConnell was a budding politician who later would become the conservative leader of the GOP in the Senate. Then still in his moderate and reformist incarnation, McConnell scolded Auspitz that "the quickest way to completely eliminate our effectiveness within the GOP is to even suggest the possibility of withdrawing from our party. The Nixon Administration, to this point, has been at worst completely reactionary and at best totally indecisive. No one is more frustrated with this state of affairs than I. However, for all the reasons you stated in your *Playboy* article, this is the logical home for us and we must not give up."[147]

Unfortunately for the moderates, the movement they sought to lead was inescapably an elite movement. The moderate political class whose dimensions Auspitz described was the product of a meritocratic social order. Its development had been shaped by a progressively minded establishment as well as the liberationist movements of the 1960s.[148] Most of the young men and women who participated in the moderate Republican movement had been educated at selective universities and worked in big business, academia, and the professions. They lived in the cities and affluent suburbs. Their political efforts were funded by East Coast multimillionaires like John Hay Whitney and David Rockefeller and publicized by the *New York Times* and *Washington Post*. They participated in and sympathized with the civil rights movement, the student and antiwar movements, and the nascent feminist movement. They campaigned for thoughtful, independent-minded candidates and aimed their appeals and proposals at intellectuals and "informed opinion."

To Richard Nixon, this made the moderates inseparable from the establishment that he intended to crush. One of his principal goals was to "build a new establishment," as he put it.[149] His secret tapes abound with his populist hatred for intellectuals, cosmopolitans, free-thinkers, activists, media elites, business leaders ("those farts"), and university presidents ("those assholes").[150] He professed that he was "ashamed of the people I come from. What I mean is, I'm from that group: lawyers, business people, so-called superior educations. Well, I'll tell you, they aren't fit to govern anymore—not fit to do it." He believed that "The American upper class now has become like the British upper class, or much worse, I should say like the French upper class was before World War II: decadent, incestuous, homosexual."[151] Within his administration and the society at large, he wanted to see loyalty and right-thinking replace the meritocratic emphasis on intelligence and ability as principal criteria for advancement. He complained that "there are too many Jews in this government, and basically their loyalties are not deep enough to what we believe in."[152] He anticipated that the Republican Party would build a new majority with the support of the people "that the elitists look down their nose at: these Southerners that they despise, these ethnics, the dese and dose guys, the labor guys, those farmers, those cattlemen, those people down around San Diego in Orange County."[153] Nixon's reordering of American society, if he had been able to realize it, would have resulted in a much different country from the one that exists today. But in the long term, Nixon did succeed in making populist conservatism the default condition of Republican politics. Nixon thereby helped undermine the moderates in his party, even though his policies were generally attuned to their aspirations.

As Clif White had predicted, Jim Buckley eked out a narrow plurality victory in the 1970 New York Senate race, while Charles Goodell came in a distant third. With Ronald Reagan's star seemingly on the decline—in his reelection bid, the California governor ran behind the moderates on his ticket and the Republicans lost control of both houses of the state legislature—Buckley for a time became the conservative's bright hope. Nelson Rockefeller won a fourth term as New York governor, thanks to a campaign that set a record for spending in a nonpresidential election. Still panting after the presidency, Rockefeller clearly intended to pursue a more conservative course, for all the good that would do him with the conservative movement.

The election episode that best epitomized Nixonian politics for many moderates involved White House staffer Donald Rumsfeld, who was not running for anything in 1970. Rumsfeld's best friend in Congress had been Allard Lowenstein, a leader in the antiwar movement and one of the most liberal Democrats in Congress, whom he had met when they both worked as Congressional aides in the late 1950s. The two ambitious, gifted men bonded across party and ideological lines, wrestling in the House gym and debating political philosophy late into the night. The Republican had stood with the Democrat on the victory platform when Lowenstein defeated a conservative Republican opponent in the 1968 elections, and the two discussed buying a country newspaper together.[154] In 1970, Rumsfeld defended his friend against scurrilous attacks from his Republican challenger, who charged that Lowenstein incited students to riot and worked toward American defeat in Vietnam. Rumsfeld gave Lowenstein important political cover, in a district where Republicans outnumbered Democrats, by telling reporters that his friend was a patriot who had always insisted that his college audiences forego violence and work within the system. Rumsfeld even emphasized that there was nothing subversive about the Democrat's criticism of Nixon's Vietnam policies.

The Long Island Republican organization complained to the White House, which forced Rumsfeld to recant and endorse Lowenstein's opponent. Lowenstein lost by a narrow margin and never held public office again.[155] Reporter Robert Novak, who knew both men well, thought that Lowenstein was more affected by Rumsfeld's betrayal, which shattered their friendship, than he was by losing the election. "I knew Rumsfeld well enough to ask whether ditching Lowenstein bothered him," Novak recalled. "'Sure,' he replied, 'but that's politics.' It was the first time that I fully appreciated Rumsfeld's genuine hardness."[156] Rumsfeld would go on to be one of the most durable and accomplished Republicans of his generation, but at the price of becoming one of Nixon's tough men of the center, unencumbered by excessive human sentiment.

The White House tried to hail the 1970 election results as an ideological triumph, largely because of Goodell's defeat, the replacement of Tennessee's liberal Democratic Senator Albert Gore Sr. by Republican William Brock, the victory of conservative Democrats in several key races, and the net gain of two Senate seats for the GOP. But the Republicans lost eleven gubernatorial seats, nine house seats, and more than two hundred seats in the state legislatures, making 1970 the worst election for the party since 1964. The Nixon-Agnew attempt to capitalize on the social issue had failed, even in the South where it presumably had the greatest resonance; the Republicans lost four of five Senate races in the South, along with six of seven contested governor's races.[157] Democrats enjoyed majorities of 55–45 in the Senate and 255–180 in the House.

The administration had also alienated Republican moderates and allowed the Democrats to steal the political center. Symbolically, the difference in the party stances seemed to be summed up by the national campaign broadcasts of Nixon confronting rock-throwing demonstrators in California—RNC finance chair Jeremiah Milbank observed that the poor audio quality of the tape "made the President sound like Donald Duck"— followed by Maine's Democratic Senator Edmund Muskie calmly rebutting charges that his party was soft on crime and urging voters to reject the Republican "politics of fear."[158] The Democrats successfully presented themselves as the party of the New South, electing a crop of moderate, integrationist governors such as Jimmy Carter in Georgia, Dale Bumpers in Arkansas, and Reuben Askew in Florida. The administration, in contrast, had supported the racist gubernatorial campaign of Republican Albert Watson Jr. in South Carolina, who lost to a racially moderate Democrat. The administration also helped to shatter Governor Linwood Holton's moderate Republican coalition in Virginia by backing the Senate candidacy of conservative independent Harry Byrd Jr. instead of the Republican candidate.[159] Across the South, the GOP drove away blacks, moderate independents, city residents and suburbanites, and young voters, who would have provided the margin of victory for losing moderate candidates like George H. W. Bush in the Texas Senate race.[160]

The moderate movement essentially was finished. There would be no more wide-scale efforts to reach those constituencies that moderates sought to draw into the party. After Elly Peterson retired as RNC vice-chair in the fall 1970, the Action Now program was quietly shelved. In vain, Lee Auspitz protested to RNC officials that Action Now had been "the only program that one can use to argue against the conclusion of many well-intentioned people, otherwise sympathetic to Republicans, that the GOP has written off the black vote."[161] The Ripon Society glumly predicted that Goodell's loss would "undermine progressive Republicanism nationally for the remainder of the decade." The Conservative Party's victory positioned them to dictate the composition of New York's delegation to the 1972 and 1976 conventions, and "without this delegation, progressive Republicanism will be a shadow of its former self." The Society also anticipated that Goodell's defeat would discourage other progressive Republican senators from "speak[ing] their consciences as Senator Goodell has done so courageously."[162] Ripon regretted that moderate Republicans had to "live with the fact that the White House can be expected to undermine them systematically and even to attack them directly, regardless of previous service performed for the Party or even for Nixon" himself.[163] Nixon effectively divided the moderates, who would never again experience the relative unity they had enjoyed in the late 1960s. Some resigned themselves to going along with Nixon's populist conservatism, some rebelled, and others left the party. The Ripon Society, which might have provided a base for a broader national movement, had peaked in terms of membership strength, intellectual production, financial support, press attention, and influence in the party.

Despite the exhaustion of the movement, moderates would remain an important part of the Republican coalition for some time to come. Indeed, the 1970 elections brought to the Senate two moderates, Robert Taft Jr. of Ohio and Glenn Beall of Maryland, and progressive Lowell Weicker of Connecticut. A number of moderates also won election to the House, including Stewart McKinney of Connecticut, Pierre S. DuPont of Delaware, and William Frenzel of Minnesota, as did Jack Kemp of New York, who would prove to be an idiosyncratic bridge between the moderate and conservative camps. Alarmed by the results of the elections, Nixon once again would pivot and become more accommodating to the moderates. The moderates would also be relatively advantaged by the weakness and disaffection of the conservatives. But the Congressional moderates would miss the support of the Republican governors, whose numbers had been greatly reduced by the elections. Lacking a thriving intellectual or political infrastructure, moderate leaders would have great difficulty establishing any kind of direction or coordination.

Nixon had believed that by getting tough on "the social issue," the Republicans could win the vote of the hypothetical average voter, the forty-seven year-old Dayton housewife. But in the 1970 elections, the voters of Dayton reelected progressive Republican Charles Whalen with a whopping 74 percent of the vote. Whalen's example implied that voters were not as susceptible to ideological appeals as many people involved in politics believed. When a conservative colleague asked him his formula for success, Whalen replied, "I don't think it has much to do with ideology. It is more a question of does he work hard, does he communicate, does he speak his own mind and do the people have the impression that nobody tells him what to do."[164] However, it passed almost unnoticed that Whalen, a devout Roman Catholic, was one of the most consistent adversaries of abortion in Congress. His personal conservatism, rather than his positions on the war and civil rights, may well have been a key factor in retaining the vote of the proverbial Dayton housewife. As one of his political opponents was overheard to complain, "He doesn't smoke, he doesn't drink, he doesn't womanize. So what the hell good is he?"[165] Whalen's example suggested that the successful moderate might be one who combined progressive and conservative impulses rather than simply aping liberalism or hewing to the middle of the road.

Whalen believed it was in the best interests of the GOP to leave room for moderates and progressives. He thought that ideological diversity within Republican ranks was "beneficial in that it provides the Party not only with the vitality necessary to keep astride of current political tides, but also the restraint that is helpful in making far-reaching decisions."[166] He opposed too much uniformity, whether within parties or in government as a whole. When one party had total control of government, he thought, there was a loss of balance and perspective. In the decades to come, however, both the GOP and the nation as a whole would become increasingly unbalanced.

CHAPTER 11

༄

Darkness Drops

Moderate Republican Decline from Nixon to Ford

to Reagan, 1971–80

The 1960s still loom large in the American public imagination. The 1970s do not. If historical eras can be compared to theatre, the '70s seem to lack the dramatic structure, exciting plot points, compelling characters, and serious moral content of the preceding decade. Most Americans' memories of the era revolve around images of economic stagnation, energy shortages, foreign policy failures, political scandals, vapid fads, and garish clothing augmented with a variety of bad haircuts. In recent years, however, a growing number of commentators have advanced revisionist claims about the political importance of the 1970s. Conservatives have denounced the period as one in which the incipient developments of the 1960s reached full and foul flower, a time when the toxic waste of the counterculture vomited into the mainstream.[1] Historians, on the other hand, have pointed to the gathering strength of the conservative movement during those years, including the rise of neoconservatism and the religious right, culminating in the election of the most conservative president since the 1920s.[2] The political developments of the 1970s were fraught with contradiction and confusion, and Republican moderates succeeded and suffered in about equal measure. They remained an important component of the GOP coalition throughout the 1970s, and by no means all moderates viewed Ronald Reagan's 1980 triumph as a defeat for moderation. But the developments of the period contributed to the rot and rust of the moderates' position, and they would end the decade in worse shape than they began.

Richard Nixon realized that his attempt to polarize the electorate along liberal-conservative lines during the 1970 elections had backfired, and so in typical Nixonian fashion he swung back toward the center. He dictated a postmortem memo in which he resolved to aid the remaining Senate Republican progressives in their reelection bids. He regretted the White House's tendency not to recognize that the progressives were to some extent beholden to their constituencies "but try to be with us when they can, and when they are against us do not try to make a virtue out of being against us. . . . Don't read people out of the Party at this point when we're going to need every one of them with us in 1972."[3] In early 1971, at the dedication of the new Republican National Committee building, Nixon extended an olive branch to the moderates by declaring that the GOP should be "a party with its doors open to all people of all races," and should resist the impulse to organize "fewer and fewer better and better" rather than create "something bigger than itself."[4] In keeping with moderate recommendations, the RNC initiated a "Project Open Door" to reach out to young voters, under the direction of University of Utah sophomore Karl Rove.[5]

The President also resumed his efforts to present himself as a reformer. The period leading up to the 1972 elections saw the passage of revenue sharing, major environmental legislation such as the Clean Air Act of 1970, the creation of new regulatory agencies such as the Environmental Protection Agency (EPA) and the Occupational Health and Safety Administration (OSHA), continuing desegregation of Southern schools, expanded rights for women and Native Americans, and substantial increases in support for education, cancer research, and drug abuse prevention efforts.[6] The recommendations of the President's Advisory Council on Executive Organization (better known as the Ash Council) pointed toward a reorganization of government by function that would result in smaller yet more effective government.

To be sure, many of these initiatives reflected pragmatism, opportunism, or even cynicism on Nixon's part. His environmental proposals, for example, did not spring from real convictions but from his political need to respond to rising public concern about pollution. Nixon also advanced his legislation with the intention of forestalling more aggressive alternatives from the liberal, Democratic-dominated Congress, and particularly from his potential rival in the 1972 presidential election, Senator Edmund Muskie.[7]

Still, Nixon saw many of his achievements as in the national interest and consistent with Republican philosophy. OSHA, for example, though bitterly resented by conservatives was largely a Republican creation, whose moving force was moderate Representative William Steiger. The Wisconsin

Republican was rated among the most business-friendly members of Congress, but he believed that business and industry were not adequately protecting their workers; by the early '70s, some 14,000 Americans were killed annually in on-the-job accidents, over 2 million were injured, and another 400,000 succumbed to work-incurred illnesses.[8] He insisted that OSHA was not intended to harass employers and small business owners, as the John Birch Society claimed, but to save them money by ending the carnage.[9]

Moderates praised Nixon's visionary opening to China, which he announced in July 1971, and which culminated in his visit to Peking six months later, bridging what Chinese premier Chou en-Lai called "the vastest ocean in the world, 25 years of no communication" between Communist China and the United States and indeed most of the rest of the world.[10] As with much of his domestic program, Nixon's conservative reputation gave him political cover to act in ways that liberals could not. His anti-Communist credentials meant that he was the only president of his era who dared to establish diplomatic contact with China and take steps to bring it back into the international community. The globalized world in which China now plays such a large role is to some extent Nixon's creation. Moderates also saluted Nixon's diplomatic summitry with the Soviet Union, his engagement with the SALT talks on arms limitations, and his general effort to move from an "era of confrontation" to an "era of negotiation." Significant numbers of moderate and progressive Republicans continued to challenge Nixon's war policies in Southeast Asia, however. GOP members contributed to the passage of the Cooper-Church amendment (prohibiting U.S. military involvement in Cambodia) and the repeal of the Gulf of Tonkin resolution. Some Republicans also voted for unsuccessful efforts to cut funds for U.S. military operations in Indochina and set a date for troop withdrawal.

In August 1971, New York Mayor John Lindsay defected to the Democrats, accusing the Nixon administration of indifference to domestic needs, repression of civil liberties, and delay in ending the Vietnam war. He told reporters that he had thrown over his lifetime allegiance to the GOP because it had become "a closed institution" that had "stifled dissent and driven progressives from its ranks."[11] Lindsay resisted entreaties from his heaviest contributors—moderate Republicans like John Hay Whitney, Walter Thayer, and David Rockefeller—and activists in the Ripon Society, who warned their hero that his departure from the GOP would "contribute directly" to the creation of a "monolithic conservative party."[12]

Lindsay changed parties partly because he believed that it was impossible for him to run for president as a Republican, but he proved to be a poor fit for the Democratic Party. His positions on urban issues and Vietnam seemed to position him on the left wing of the Democrats, but he had always spoken the language of moderate Republican communitarianism and New Federalism, not the patois of big-government, interest-group liberalism or the racial/ethnic/gender/sexual rights revolution. He had made enemies of some black and Puerto Rican groups when he insisted on making appointments based on merit rather than the traditional ethnic spoils system, and continued to have antagonistic relations with labor unions.[13] Many Democrats also distrusted what they saw as the opportunism of his party switch. Lindsay's bid to win the presidency as a Democrat in the 1972 primaries was embarrassing and short-lived. He served out the remainder of his mayoralty with some distinction; crime rates fell and the economic picture brightened in his last years before the city slid into catastrophe under Lindsay's Democratic successor, Abe Beame. But when Lindsay left office in 1973, he was a man without a party, and spent the rest of his life in political exile.

Ogden Reid, a progressive Republican representative from Westchester County outside of New York City, switched parties a few months after Lindsay. Before his election to Congress in 1962, Reid had been the president of the *New York Herald Tribune*, the leading organ of moderate Eastern Republicanism. The paper, in different inceptions, had been in his family's possession for nearly ninety years, and he was heir to an even longer family Republican tradition. His forebears had helped to found the GOP, and his grandfather, Whitelaw Reid, had been the party's vice-presidential nominee in 1892. It was a matter of national significance, then, when Reid went over to the Democrats, and his abandonment of his ancestral party raised questions about the viability of Republican progressivism.

Reid had joined the family paper in 1950, after completing college and paratrooper service in World War II. After a few years of writing a crudely anti-Communist column spiced with unverifiable inside dope direct from J. Edgar Hoover, he moved to Paris to head up the paper's European edition, then returned to New York as president and editor. After the Reid family was forced to sell the *Herald Tribune* to John Hay Whitney, Eisenhower appointed Reid the U.S. ambassador to Israel, an appropriate assignment given the Zionist leanings of the *Herald Tribune* and Reid's WASPy philo-Semitism. Reid returned to the United States in 1961 to chair the New York State Commission for Human Rights on behalf of Governor Nelson Rockefeller, then was elected to Congress.

Reid began office as a *Herald Tribune*-style Republican, slamming Kennedy for weakness against Communism and listlessness in support of civil rights. He approved the education and health components of Lyndon Johnson's War on Poverty, but not its public works spending on marginal enterprises: "Federal subsidies do not create new markets," he insisted.[14] He decried Johnson's inflationary policies and demanded a return to pay-as-you-go financing and balanced budgets. Reid didn't believe that ideology was important to most voters: "they just want a government that works. They're uptight when they see they can't make ends meet, when they can't send their children to college or pay the doctor bills. All they want is a little stability in their lives."[15]

The events of the '60s began to move Reid leftward. A visit to Vietnam shook his previously resolute defense of the American war effort there, as he realized that Johnson had not leveled with the American people about the scale of U.S. military involvement required or the weakness of the South Vietnamese government. From 1966 on, he faced primary challenges from the Conservative Party of New York. By the early 1970s, Reid was in open rebellion against the Nixon administration and what he perceived as its divisiveness, disrespect for Congress, indifference to civil liberties, antagonism toward the media, ambivalent racial attitudes as reflected in the Southern strategy, and the intolerably slow pace of withdrawal from Vietnam. "Finally, I woke up one morning and just couldn't swallow it all any longer," he told a reporter. "Just as in World War II, there came a time when some of us simply couldn't eat another can of Spam."[16] He was also driven out of the GOP by a determined conservative effort to defeat him in the primary elections; he had barely fended off one such challenge in 1970 and was unlikely to survive another.[17] Reid was reelected as a Democrat in the 1972 elections, overcoming a furious challenge from a Rockefeller-financed Republican, but declined to seek office in 1974 and never won office to any other post in several attempts.

Representative Pete McCloskey, a progressive from northern California, deemed Reid's party switch "a dismaying reminder that the present party leadership is deviating sharply from traditional Republican principles of individualism, openness and truth in government, and in human rights and dignity."[18] McCloskey decided to fight rather than switch, and launched an insurgent challenge to Nixon's renomination in the 1972 presidential primaries. McCloskey had become a national figure in the years following his election to Congress in 1967, partly because the House Republican leadership denied him a place on the committees he wanted, such as Armed Services or Ways and Means. Instead he became the ranking Republican on what was then the little-regarded Fish and Wildlife Subcommittee, which over the next few years originated nearly all of the significant environmental legislation that passed through the House, including the Clean Water Act, the Clean Air amendments, the Endangered Species Act, the Marine Mammal Protection Act, the Estuary Protection Act, and the Coastal Zone Act. McCloskey's status as the leading Republican in the environmental movement was ratified when he served as co-chair of the first Earth Day in

April 1970. In the fall elections, the movement targeted the twelve worst environmental offenders in Congress for defeat, and seven of the "Dirty Dozen" lost their seats. When Congress reconvened in 1971, McCloskey recalled, "everybody was now an environmentalist; they had seen the writing on the wall, and they were all worried that the kids were going to knock them off like they had knocked off most of the Dirty Dozen. So you had the golden age of environmentalism: 1971, '72, and '73."[19]

McCloskey bristled at accusations that his environmentalism and outspoken antiwar stance unfitted him for the Republican Party. "I've voted the Republican line 77 percent of the time," he told reporters in early 1971, "which is the third highest of all California congressmen. So I think it's unjustified when it's inferred I'm not a loyal Republican."[20] But McCloskey had come to believe that Nixon's Vietnam policies were immoral, impractical, unconstitutional, and damaging to the Republican Party as well as the country as a whole. He felt that Nixon would change his stance only if Congress impeached him—at that time an unlikely prospect—or if someone from the moderate Republican ranks challenged him in the 1972 primaries, as Eugene McCarthy had upended Lyndon Johnson in 1968. McCloskey and another moderate congressman, Donald Riegle of Michigan, tried to talk John Lindsay into staying in the GOP and leading the opposition to Nixon. When Lindsay refused the gauntlet, as did other leading moderates including John Gardner, Charles Percy, Mark Hatfield, and "Mac" Mathias, McCloskey decided to enter the New Hampshire primary himself.[21]

McCloskey's insurgency tapped some of the idealism of the McCarthy movement, as young volunteers from around the country flocked to New Hampshire to sleep in church basements and subsist on peanut butter while canvassing voters. Most antiwar liberals dismissed the significance of Vietnam dissent in the GOP, however, and supported George McGovern in the Democratic primary instead. Even those liberals who did support McCloskey often listened in puzzled silence as he lectured them on the evils of deficit spending.[22] Moderate and progressive Republican members of Congress kept their distance from the campaign, which was beset by organizational difficulties and lack of funds. McCloskey received 20 percent of the vote, a substantial total but only half the percentage McCarthy had received in 1968, and he closed down the campaign.

At the same time that McCloskey was challenging Nixon from the left, Ohio Representative John Ashbrook was attacking the President from the right. A dozen prominent conservatives including William F. Buckley Jr. and *National Review* publisher William Rusher had declared a "suspension of support" for Nixon in August 1971, incensed by his welfare reform proposal, his advocacy of Keynesian economic policies, his early overtures toward China, and his pursuit of détente with the Soviet Union. Most of these conservatives broke outright with the administration when Nixon established relations with China and acceded to the expulsion of Taiwan from the United Nations. Ashbrook complained that Nixon had "greatly expanded almost every wasteful giveaway program started by the liberal Democrats."[23] Conservative journalist M. Stanton Evans judged that "Nixon has made impressive strides toward the political liquidation of American conservatism. . . . Nixon has taken the country further left than Humphrey, given the realities of American party politics, could ever have managed to do."[24]

Ashbrook's campaign against the President in the 1972 GOP primaries, like McCloskey's, aimed to send Nixon a message; as Rusher put it, Ashbrook didn't expect to beat Nixon, but intended his candidacy "simply as a demonstration of the depth of conservative dissatisfaction."[25] The campaign also hoped to show that Nixon faced a greater threat from his right than his left. Ashbrook received only 10 percent of the vote in the New Hampshire primary, however, and his campaign folded after another ineffectual showing in the California primary. The overwhelming majority of Republican conservatives were as wary of Ashbrook's challenge as Republican moderates were of McCloskey's. Both campaigns ultimately seemed to confirm Nixon's claim to speak for the broad center of both the Republican Party and the American populace.

When George McGovern won the Democrats' presidential nomination, the leaders of the Ripon Society uneasily concluded that Nixon, despite his war policies and Southern strategy, was the better representative of the moderate position. The *Ripon Forum* editorialized that while the Nixon administration "could have fashioned a more positive record over the last four years," the President's statesmanship abroad and his domestic achievements merited his reelection.[26] McGovern had gone out of his way to turn off moderates with his attack on "the establishment center" and his prediction that the winner of the presidential election would "not be the one who clings most tightly to the center."[27] McGovern also stood for an isolationism that was opposed to moderate Republican internationalism, and his domestic agenda was improvident and unrealistic. For example, McGovern's proposal for a "demogrant" that would have paid every man, woman, and child in the United States $1,000 a year encouraged liberal Democrats to oppose Nixon's Family Assistance Plan as insufficiently generous; the end result was no welfare reform at all. Ripon president Howard Gillette remembered that endorsing Nixon "seemed to be on balance the only choice, after long debate, that we could take, even though some of us had supported McCloskey."[28] The endorsement created a schism within Ripon. Many members rebuked Ripon for supporting Nixon, who "stands for everything the Society has fought against since its beginning," as one put it.[29] Several officers resigned, one charging that "Ripon should have been the rallying focus for disaffected Republicans instead of a rubber stamp for the party organization."[30] The national organization never endorsed candidates again.

Republican moderates were becoming increasingly divided, not only over the Nixon administration but also over emerging social and cultural issues. A case in point was George Gilder, the editor of the *Ripon Forum* and author of the editorial endorsing Nixon's reelection. Gilder had written an editorial in January 1972 in support of Nixon's veto of the Mondale-Javits bill to increase federal support for day care centers for children. Nixon had turned down the bill because of reservations about cost, which would start at $2.1 billion but according to some projections could rise to a possible $20 billion. Gilder objected to what he saw as the classism and anti-family animus behind the proposal. The women's liberation movement advocated federally funded day care in order to free mothers from the burdens of child care and allow them to hold full-time jobs. Gilder conceded that upper- and middle-class educated women would benefit from the bill, but argued that it would devastate poorer families by pushing women to compete with men in the already crowded low-skilled labor market. Gilder believed it "quite possible that the new federal program, by making families less dependent on a male provider, would contribute to the familial disintegration already promoted for years under federal welfare laws."[31] Inner-city children had already lost their fathers to the perverse anti-family incentives of welfare; now they would lose their mothers as well.

Ripon president Gillette remembered that Gilder's editorial, with its implicit message that a woman's place was in the home, "blew everybody's minds."[32] Support for the women's movement had to that point been uncontroversial for most moderates and progressives. Several of Ripon's women members had lobbied for the day care bill, including Bobbie Greene Kilberg at the White House and Patricia Goldman as liaison for the House Wednesday Group. The editorial stirred widespread media coverage and provoked a significant portion of Ripon's National Governing Board to dissent, along with the leadership of Ripon's New York chapter.[33] Much of the next issue of the *Ripon Forum* was given over to furious denunciation of Gilder. He responded defiantly that for working- and middle-class men, "the psychic wounds inflicted by a pervasive restriction of relative male earning capability are likely to have dire social and political consequences. The daycare subsidies, in fact, will tend to extend to the lower middle class the kind of familial catastrophe currently endemic to the ghetto."[34]

A later profile of Gilder claimed that as a result of his editorial, "he was fired from his position almost immediately" and was expelled from the

Ripon Society.[35] In fact, Gilder remained a member in good standing of Ripon and stayed on as the *Forum* editor until September 1972, when he decided to leave to work on a book inspired by the controversy.[36] He moved to New Orleans to help a friend who was running for the Senate and to write *Sexual Suicide,* the first of several anti-feminist books that made him a *cause célèbre.* Gilder's friends suspected that he struck increasingly provocative positions against feminism because he enjoyed the attention it brought him, especially from women. Gilder himself commented that "All these years I'd been looking for a way to arouse the passionate interest of women, and it was clear I had reached pay dirt."[37]

Nonetheless, the controversy was an ominous development for the Ripon Society for several reasons. It provided further confirmation of the power of emerging social issues to polarize political opinions. Gilder found that his opposition to feminism increasingly led him toward other conservative positions; other moderates made similar discoveries as they responded to subsequent battles over issues such as the Equal Rights Amendment and the *Roe v. Wade* Supreme Court decision legalizing abortion. At the same time, feminists in the moderate ranks became less willing to agree to disagree with their fellow Republicans where women's issues were concerned. Gilder's argument against day care was entirely consistent with the position he had maintained since the mid-1960s, influenced by thinkers like Daniel Patrick Moynihan whom the moderate Republicans had regarded as allies. For moderate Republican feminists, however, Gilder's arguments against women's opportunities came as a betrayal. "It was one thing to hear Strom Thurmond opposed to child care," Ripon member Tanya Melich growled. "It was another to learn that not only the president [Nixon] but members of the leading moderate Republican organization thought child care would 'destroy' the family."[38] Former Ripon president Lee Auspitz lamented that the day care controversy introduced an ideological rigidity that proved fatal to the Society. "The question was raised: how could one be represented by something one didn't agree with on every point? And this just led to the stifling of the intellectual role of this group."[39]

The Ripon Society itself became the subject of considerable controversy when it filed a lawsuit challenging the Republican Party's convention delegate apportionment formula. Moderate and progressive Republicans had long been dissatisfied with the way GOP national convention delegates were selected and the methods by which the numbers of delegates were allocated to the states. In fact, the overrepresentation of Southern states at the 1908 Republican national convention, and Theodore Roosevelt's narrow failure to pass a convention measure reforming the situation, had impelled TR to bolt the GOP and run as the presidential candidate of the "Bull

Moose" Party in 1912. In the modern era, moderates' dissatisfaction with delegate allocation increased considerably after the 1968 Miami convention, at which the Southern states reaped rewards for having been virtually the only part of the country to have voted for Barry Goldwater in 1964. Ripon attendees at the convention were struck by the disproportionate strength of the state delegations from the South and small states in the Plains and Southwest. The delegate apportionment formula gave a structural advantage to conservatives from the "Sunbelt," in strategist Kevin Phillips' terminology, in their bid to take over the Republican Party. Moderates were further disadvantaged by the underrepresentation of women, minorities, and young people in convention delegations. Ripon and other moderate allies mounted a two-pronged effort to open up the party through the courts and internal party committees.

Independently of the Ripon effort, New York lawyer Robert M. Pennoyer had begun to research the effect of the Republican rules on apportionment of delegates. He found that a particular problem was the bonus provision that awarded six delegates to each state, no matter how large or small, which elected Republican candidates for president, governor, senator, or a majority of House seats. The bonus provision, in combination with rules that weighted representation heavily according to the Electoral College, meant that larger states received delegate assignments well below their proportionate contribution to the national vote for Republican candidates.[40] At the 1972 convention, the nation's eight most populous states, which had half the nation's population and had cast 52 percent of Nixon's popular votes in 1968, would only have 37 percent of the delegates. Or, to put it differently, 37 states which cast only 34 percent of Nixon's popular vote would have over 50 percent of the delegates. Analysis revealed enormous discrepancies in relative delegate strength. Alaska had 12 delegates to New York's 88, although New York had sixty times as many people.[41] The six-delegate bonus provision was also disproportionately generous to small-population states, amounting to a 100 percent increase for states like Alaska, Delaware, Nevada, North Dakota, and Wyoming.[42]

Ripon member Tanya Melich felt that by testing the constitutionality of the delegation apportionment formula, moderates aimed "to break the ideological slant of the formulas, to attract more participants from urban areas, and to establish a starting place after each election that would open the process more fairly to all ideologies, interests, and regions. In other words, the suit aimed to level the playing field for each new set of Republican presidential contenders." Potential moderate candidates for the 1976 presidential elections, including Nelson Rockefeller, George Romney, and Charles Percy, came from large, northern industrial states that were discriminated against under the existing arrangements. Ripon's suit, if successful, would boost their chances by "counting in the formulas more people from urban areas who were new to the party, were not necessarily conservatives, and had demonstrated that they would vote for GOP moderates" despite living in heavily Democratic-registered cities.[43]

Ripon filed suit against the Republican National Committee, charging that apportionment based on a victory bonus system was contrary to the one-man, one-vote principle. The RNC countered that delegate apportionment was an "internal" matter of a private association, not subject to constitutional prescriptions. In April 1972, the U.S. District Court for the District of Columbia declared the bonus delegate provision to be in violation of the Equal Protection Clause of the 14th Amendment.[44] While the RNC appealed the decision, reformers took the battle to the 1972 GOP convention. A floor fight over Representative William Steiger's proposal to change the delegate allocation formula provided the convention's only real drama. Steiger's alternative formula lost by a 434–910 vote, but reformers managed to pass a resolution calling for a committee to study the delegate selection process for the 1976 convention with the goal of opening it up to greater participation by women, minorities, youth, and the elderly.[45] Steiger was appointed chairman of the committee, much to the discomfiture of conservatives who viewed him as a Ripon fellow traveler.[46] Eventually the RNC squashed the committee's recommendations for broadening the party base.

The Ripon lawsuit churned through the courts for the next several years, failing at last when the Supreme Court declined to review an appeals court ruling in favor of the RNC. Initially, most of Ripon's leaders believed that the organization's venture into direct political action had enhanced its reputation. According to one longtime member, "For years, others criticized Ripon members by saying they didn't have calluses. At the convention, we got into a good fight and got our hands dirty for the first time."[47] An amicus brief filed in the Supreme Court case by three Republican senators and a dozen Republican representatives argued that the lawsuit was the only way to break the self-perpetuating party dominance of conservative forces from the small Southern and Western states.

In the long run, however, the lawsuit allowed Ripon's conservative enemies to persuade many rank-and-file Republicans that the progressives were not loyal critics but a subversive element in the party. As Mississippi Republican chairman Clarke Reed put it, one does not sue members of one's own family.[48] Conservatives portrayed Ripon's lawsuit as the moderates' attempt to gain through the courts what they could not achieve through grassroots participation or the democratic process. The right compared moderate efforts to open the GOP to broader participation to the affirmative action requirement that George McGovern had forced on the Democratic Party after the 1968 elections, which overthrew traditional bosses like Chicago Mayor Richard Daley and enabled McGovern's nomination at the 1972 party convention. The lawsuit consumed most of Ripon's energies and its meager treasury. Ripon member Steve Livengood felt that the delegate suit was the wrong tactic, since it represented an attempt at "using judicial power to work out what are basically political issues. It offended the whole Republican establishment and gave us a bad name." It also allowed the moderates' conservative critics to caricature them as "people from Harvard looking down on America."[49] Dan Swillinger, who was one of the leaders in persuading Ripon to file the suit and move its headquarters to Washington, D.C. in order to play a more direct role in national politics, admitted that "the policy of political activism for the Society has been a disaster."[50]

Nixon demolished McGovern in the 1972 presidential elections, winning more than 60 percent of the vote and carrying every state except Massachusetts and the District of Columbia. No Republican had ever won the White House by so large a margin; no president had ever won so many popular votes or carried so many states. With George Wallace out of the race after an assassination attempt that left him paralyzed, Nixon swept up the votes of millions of Southerners and blue-collar Democrats in the North. The election was more of a victory for Nixon and the Committee to Reelect the President (inevitably known as CREEP), which operated independently of the Republican Party, than it was for the GOP as a whole. Republicans gained twelve House seats but lost two Senate seats, leaving the Democrats comfortably in control of Congress. Most moderate and progressive Republican incumbents won reelection, and moderates could take comfort in Christopher "Kit" Bond's victory in the Missouri governor's race, and the House victories of moderates such as William Cohen in Maine, Joel Pritchard in Washington, and Alan Steelman, the former director of the President's Advisory Council on Minority Business Enterprise, in Texas. But overall, the election results confirmed the trend of the Republican Party toward conservatives in the South and West. Nixon received his largest state margin of victory—78 percent—in Mississippi, which also elected future conservative Republican standouts Thad Cochran and Trent Lott to the House. Lott had been a legislative aide to retiring Democratic Congressman William Colmer, but Colmer endorsed his protégé despite Lott's decision to run as a Republican, agreeing that McGovern's presence atop the Democratic ticket would be a liability for any Mississippi politician in 1972.[51] The Senate Republican contingent shifted perceptibly to the right with the defeats of several moderates, including Maine's long-serving Margaret Chase Smith, and the victories of conservative hardliners such as Jesse Helms of North Carolina.

Worse still, from the moderates' standpoint, were losses that didn't necessarily appear in the election tallies. Senator John Sherman Cooper of Kentucky retired, depriving the GOP antiwar forces of one of their most respected and influential spokesmen. In the Colorado Senate race, the Democratic winner Floyd Haskell, who defeated Republican conservative incumbent Gordon Allott, had been a Republican and served as Colorado's manager of Nelson Rockefeller's 1968 presidential campaign. Haskell had switched parties, he said, because "I objected to the attempt to put Harrold Carswell, a known racist, on the Supreme Court."[52] Representative Brad Morse, the founder of the moderate House Wednesday Group, left Congress to become Under Secretary General of the United Nations, replacing the late Ralph Bunche. The appointment released Morse from the frustrations of doing battle with both the Republican right and the Democratic majority, but no one ever took his place as a political dealmaker and organizer of the moderate forces in Congress.

One person who might have played such a role, Representative Donald Riegle of Michigan, switched to the Democrats not long after Nixon's re-election. Riegle had been the only House Republican to give open support to Pete McCloskey's primary challenge to Richard Nixon, and he had not endeared himself to his colleagues by publishing a candid account of McCloskey's campaign and the shortcomings of Congress. But as columnists Evans and Novak reported, presidential aides regarded the thirty-five year-old Riegle as "a tough, young political comer," and regretted his loss to the Democrats. House Republican leader Gerald Ford was personally fond of Riegle, whom he saw as the "golden boy" of his home state's GOP, and believed that his departure sent a bad signal about the Republicans' tolerance for ideological diversity. Ford repeatedly tried to talk Riegle out of his decision, arguing that progressives would have an easier time in the party after the end of the Vietnam war.[53] Riegle responded that he could not support Nixon's positions on human rights and national spending priorities, or his unseemly campaign tactics, including the emerging scandal over the break-in at the Democratic headquarters at the Watergate office complex in Washington, D.C. "There are roughly 190 Republicans in Congress," Riegle told the press, "and maybe 10 of them see things as I do. There are about 240 Democrats in Congress, of whom 160 see things as I do and vote as I would vote."[54] Riegle's defection turned out to be a good political move on his part, as he won election to the Senate as a Democrat in 1976 and remained there for three terms. But his inference that there was little difference between a progressive Republican and a liberal Democrat denied the distinctiveness of the Republican position, and contributed to the growing perception that moderate Republicans were in the wrong party.

The high-profile party switches of Republicans-turned-Democrats like Reid and Riegle, and of Democrats-turned-Republicans like Texas Governor John Connally and former Virginia Governor Mills Godwin, were far outnumbered by less prominent switches by state and local officeholders and individual voters. The long-anticipated realignment of politics into liberal and conservative parties, which would continue over the next several decades but was identifiably under way by the early '70s, provoked a spate of editorial comments. David Broder, who viewed ticket-splitting and anti-party sentiment as harmful to effective government, felt that party realignment would produce greater party responsibility and a coherent governing strategy for Republicans and Democrats alike. For those who feared that realignment would lead to extremist ideological warfare, he offered the soothing message that "This is a practical country, not an ideological one, and all that the present sorting-out is accomplishing is to get more of the politicians with similar *tendencies* to view political issues alike into the same camp."[55] Most observers were not so sanguine about the potential collapse of the traditional American political system. The *New York Times* editorialized that "Heterogeneous national parties are confusing and untidy but they lend stability to a diverse society which always needs a stabilizing influence." When the parties spanned a broad ideological spectrum, each was forced to appeal to independents and moderates in the opposing party, which softened the sharpness of partisan battles.[56]

Moderate Republicans had particular reason to fear the impact of realignment on their party. Every defection from the moderate ranks had the effect of pushing the Republican center to the right, leaving the remaining moderates and progressives more exposed and less influential. The influx of Southerners and Westerners threatened to make the GOP not only more conservative, but fundamentally a different kind of party. George Gilder, for one, was extremely uncomfortable with Nixon's attempt to make John Connally his political heir because he considered the Texan to be "ideologically alien to the deepest traditions of Republicanism." Gilder pointed out that both the Republican left and right shared "an instinctive aversion to federal power and a strong commitment to the private enterprise system. These values join James Buckley with Charles Percy, and the Ripon Society with the American Enterprise Institute." All Republicans were suspicious of state subsidies that would allow politically connected companies to socialize their risks while privatizing their gains: "The very legitimacy of the profit system—both in moral and functional terms—depends on the existence of a competitive economy in which the entrepreneur risks reward or penalty for the quality of his judgment and initiative." Both moderate and conservative Republicans were uneasy about the wage and price controls that Nixon and treasury secretary Connally had imposed on the economy in an effort to combat inflation. Gilder emphasized that while the operation of market forces would necessarily be subject to some degree of regulation and social programs, "the free market ideal is the lodestar of Republican ideology."

Connally, despite his hawkish stand on military issues and the Vietnam war, was a statist in economic matters, like the vast majority of Southern conservatives. He was the political product of the South's postwar industries—such as aerospace, defense, agribusiness, mining, and oil and natural gas extraction—that depended on government protection and subsidy, and what Gilder called "the overwhelming maldistribution of federal wealth, supervised by Southern Congressional satraps, in favor of the South and Southwest." As a nationalist and mercantilist, Connally opposed international free trade where his region's favored industries were concerned. As treasury secretary he attempted to create a federal fund that would bail out corporations such as Lockheed, whose failure allegedly would jeopardize the nation's economy or security. The inclusion of crony-corporatist Southerners in the Republican Party, Gilder concluded, "attacks the very core meaning of our party."[57]

Nixon's attempt to realign the political system, and perhaps even to create a New Majority party as an alternative to the Republican Party, ground to a halt as the Watergate scandal devoured his presidency. Disclosures of White House malfeasance and convictions of former administration officials, starting with G. Gordon Liddy and James McCord Jr. in January 1973, roiled the GOP. One moderate activist noted with bitter satisfaction that "Republicans of all shades are displaying a bewilderment usually found only among our allies."[58] Moderates realized early on that public anger at Watergate was directed mainly at the Republican right, with which Nixon was most associated despite conservative opposition to his generally centrist record. The Ripon Society believed Watergate offered moderates an opening: "Only progressive Republicans, unscathed by the scandal, can restore to the party an image of integrity and objective government. The combination of independence, intelligence and integrity makes them ideal for party leadership."[59]

The scandal did in fact make national heroes of several moderate Republicans, beginning with Tennessee Senator Howard Baker, who as vice-chairman of the Senate committee investigating Watergate asked the question that defined the crisis: "What did the President know and when did he know it?"[60] Watergate forced Nixon to appoint Secretary of Defense Elliot Lee Richardson, a Massachusetts moderate who had also served as head of HEW, as attorney general. Richardson was widely regarded as one of the cleanest and ablest administrators in government, and Nixon needed someone of stainless integrity to restore public confidence in Justice. Barely a month into office, Richardson received evidence that Spiro Agnew had taken bribes and kickbacks as Maryland governor and continued to do so as Vice President. He initiated the process that led to Agnew's resignation in October 1973 on a plea of no contest to one count of tax evasion.

Conservatives, who had lost their front-runner for the 1976 presidential race, beseeched Nixon to appoint Ronald Reagan in Agnew's place, while moderates and progressives pushed for Nelson Rockefeller. Nixon favored Connally or George H. W. Bush but decided that House minority leader Gerald Ford, a Midwestern stalwart and Nixon loyalist, would be likelier to receive Congressional confirmation. Ford's nomination met with approval from members of Congress in both parties, who saw him as a steadying influence, and from all factions in the Republican Party. At that point, few anticipated that Nixon would not serve out the remainder of his term. Moderates excitedly discussed the 1976 possibilities of Charles Percy or the inevitable Rockefeller, who resigned from the New York governorship to prepare for a presidential campaign and to become chairman of his own creation, the Commission on Critical Choices for America. As many wits observed, Rockefeller doubtless believed that the most critical choice America faced was whether it would elect him president in 1976.

As the Watergate morass deepened, however, the chances of Nixon's remaining in office steadily decreased. Special prosecutor Archibald Cox issued a subpoena demanding copies of the taped conversations the President had clandestinely recorded over the previous two years, and refused to be put off by Nixon's claim of executive privilege. On October 20, ten days after Agnew's resignation, Nixon ordered his attorney general to fire Cox. Richardson refused and resigned in protest, as did Deputy Assistant Attorney General William Ruckelshaus, a moderate from Indiana. Solicitor General Robert Bork then fired Cox. The "Saturday Night Massacre" shocked and angered the public and provoked eighty-four members of Congress to introduce resolutions for impeachment. From that point on, Nixon's days were numbered. The tug-of-war between Nixon and Cox's replacement, Leon Jaworski, continued until July 1974, when a unanimous Supreme Court ruling compelled Nixon to hand over the tapes. The revelation in the "smoking gun" tape that Nixon had committed obstruction of justice demolished his remaining support in Congress. He resigned in August, and Gerald Ford became President.

Richard Nixon had been simultaneously the moderates' greatest ally and enemy. No other president implemented as much of the moderate agenda as Nixon. Nixon's speechwriter Lee Huebner recalled that when he went from the Ripon Society to the White House, he brought with him a list of major policy proposals that the Society had helped to develop and promote.

Virtually all became part of the Nixon program, including revenue sharing, welfare reform, government reorganization, an end to the military draft, and normalization of relations with China.[61] Nixon had de-escalated American participation in the Vietnam war and effected a ceasefire in January 1973. He had implemented affirmative action programs, desegregated the Southern schools, given federal support to minority businesses, and taken significant steps to protect the environment. The *New York Times* recognized that by 1972 Nixon had "moved the G.O.P. closer to a party of government rather than a chronic opposition which occasionally holds office by accident. This administration thus has narrowed the gap between the two major parties. . . . The grand, stark alternatives no longer exist."[62]

In so doing, Nixon had "effectively paralyzed the whole conservative movement," William Rusher raged, since "only a Republican president could have carried the day for liberal policies as successfully as Mr. Nixon has."[63] But Nixon's rhetorical conservatism, his willingness to polarize the country around controversial social issues, and his abuse of his office and the rule of law made moderates turn against him. Watergate depressed the faith that Americans had in government generally, which ultimately damaged moderate Republicans as well as liberal Democrats. The percentage of Americans expressing "a great deal of confidence" in the executive branch of government declined from 41 percent in 1966 to 19 percent in 1973; for Congress the drop was from 42 percent to 29 percent. Apathy and cynicism toward government were also reflected in declining voter turnouts, which meant that the most ideologically committed partisans of both parties made up a larger share of voters. This development, too, would prove detrimental to moderates.

Moderates and conservatives accused each other of responsibility for the Nixon administration's descent into criminality. Moderates saw Watergate as the ultimate expression of the conservative political approach in which the ends justified the means, while conservatives claimed that the Nixon administration reflected moderate expediency and lack of principle. There could be no definitive answer to this argument, but Pete McCloskey gained some insight into the administration's downfall when he visited John Ehrlichman at the federal prison in Safford, Arizona, following the former White House assistant's conviction on charges of conspiracy, perjury, and obstruction of justice. McCloskey and Ehrlichman had been Stanford Law School classmates and close friends. They had also generally agreed about the need for moderation in the Republican Party, but their friendship and political alliance had disintegrated when McCloskey had called for Nixon's impeachment and challenged the President in the 1972 GOP primaries. Now Ehrlichman was housed in a prison barracks that he shared with sixty-nine Mexican inmates, in double rows of cots one foot apart. The two men sat in the desert watching the Mexicans play baseball while, several hundred yards away, a group of white-collar criminals played tennis. When their talk turned to Watergate, McCloskey recalled, "I asked him, 'What happened to you?' John was no coward. He had flown fifty missions over Germany in the nose of a B-17, which was like committing suicide. So how did he end up trying to bribe judges and lying to Congress? He looked out across the desert for at least half a minute. I thought he wasn't going to answer. Then he said, 'Pete, it took us three and a half years to be corrupted by the power of the White House. We came to think that reelecting Nixon was essential to the security of the United States.'"[64]

Gerald Ford's elevation to the presidency in August 1974, and his selection of Nelson Rockefeller as Vice President, seemed to indicate that moderate Republicans were back in command of their party. In the words of one *New York Times* account, the Ford-Rockefeller team "reunited venerable symbols of Main Street and Wall Street in a balmy revival of Dwight D. Eisenhower's inclusive, middle-ground politics."[65] The fall 1974 elections, following economic slump and public outrage against Ford's pardon of his predecessor, were disastrous for Republicans, as the party lost forty-nine seats in the House and five in the Senate, as well as four governorships. But the punishment fell more heavily on conservatives, whom the public identified with Nixon, than on moderates and progressives who were seen to have taken an independent stand during the Watergate crisis. All of the GOP's progressive senators up for election were returned to office, including Javits in New York, Mathias in Maryland, Packwood in Oregon, and Schweiker in Pennsylvania. Of the thirty-six House Republican incumbents who were defeated in the elections, twenty-five were members of the conservative House Steering Committee (later renamed the Republican Study Committee), including the organization's chairman, hardliner Lamar Baker of Tennessee, and three of the group's four vice presidents. The losses, combined with retirements, cut the Steering Committee's membership in half, from seventy to thirty-five, and significantly reduced conservatives' representation in the party caucus. The Steering Committee had been created as a right-wing rival to the moderate Wednesday Group which, by contrast, only lost one of its members in the 1974 elections. Columnists Evans and Novak concluded that the Republican losers "tended to be those with starkly negative, rigidly conservative voting records."[66] The Southern strategy appeared to be in decline, as ten Republican House incumbents went down to defeat in the region, while the party picked up only one new representative from Florida and another from Louisiana. In the Ripon Society's reckoning, moderates and progressives made up more than half of the Senate and House Republican delegations.[67]

But in fact, nearly all of the events and trends of the period were working against the moderates. Party workers at the grassroots tended to view the moderates who had broken with Nixon over Watergate as disloyal. Thomas Railsback, a moderate member of the House Judiciary Committee who had voted to impeach Nixon, remembered that after his vote, "Some people left the room or turned their backs on me when I went back to Illinois. I got picketed by a Republican precinct committeeman. There were some Nixon people who didn't like what I had done, voting to impeach a Republican president."[68] Ford's appointment of Rockefeller, the bête noire of the right, infuriated conservatives without greatly exciting moderates. Dan Swillinger, the former executive director of the Ripon Society, told David Broder that "I gave up on Rockefeller being one of us four or five years ago, even though you in the press still think he is. Maybe he is, symbolically, but he operates so selfishly that he's not likely to risk anything to help us as a movement."[69]

Conservatives battled the GOP establishment, rallied against the ERA, and built up their organizational infrastructure with renewed vigor, while moderates, disgusted by Watergate, withdrew from political activity. Wealthy conservative businessmen including Joseph Coors, Richard Scaife, John Olin, and the Koch brothers created grassroots organizations like the Conservative Caucus and think tanks such as the Heritage Foundation to promote their cause. Moderate donors, by contrast, closed their pocketbooks or directed their money to allegedly nonpartisan organizations like Common Cause that increasingly came under the sway of liberal Democrats. The moderate-oriented Republican Workshops, a grassroots organizational effort centered in the upper Midwest, lost steam. Minnesota Congressman Bill Frenzel felt that the Workshops were "a casualty of the faster pace of American life and the growing number of women in the workplace. People didn't have coffee parties in their neighborhoods any more. Politics became less of interest except to the pure of heart on the right and the left."[70]

The Ripon Society had once operated almost two dozen chapters and study groups around the country, but as the organization's funds dried up, these dwindled to a handful. The *Ripon Forum* was reduced from a substantial monthly magazine to a newsletter, and by November 1974 the Society could no longer afford even to have the newsletter typeset. Ripon officer Patricia Goldman admitted that Ripon had not been as effective in the early 1970s as it had been in the late '60s, "but it is the *only* organized effort that the Republican Party has going for it as a moderating influence. . . . I wish that there was a large organized force of moderate Republican Party members out there working to make the party in their image. Unfortunately, there is not. Ripon is all there is."[71] With moderate activism moribund and broke, conservatives dominated party activities.

The media dismissed the Republican minority in Congress as irrelevant, focusing instead on the Democrats, who led the Senate by 61 to 39 and the House by 291 to 144, and who were prepared to implement widespread reforms. Many of the seventy-one new Democratic House members, known collectively as the "Watergate babies," were strongly liberal, iconoclastic, and had run outside the regular party structure. Often Democrat-led reforms ended up hurting moderates. The 1974 Campaign Reform Act, combined with the Supreme Court's decision in *Buckley v. Valeo* that limitations on campaign spending limits were a violation of freedom of speech, opened the door to soft-money campaign spending and political action committees (or PACs). The reforms ended the large donations from Wall Street and wealthy Northeasterners that once had formidably advantaged the moderates, yet proved a godsend for conservatives. Conservative PACs made extensive use of direct mail solicitations for small contributions, a field pioneered by activists like Richard Viguerie. Moderate activists had no luck attempting similar efforts for their causes, candidates, and campaigns. They lacked the extensive mailing lists that conservatives possessed, and the potential donors they approached proved unresponsive to their appeals. The Ripon Society lost money on its direct mail campaigns.[72]

The House Democrats' attack on the rule of seniority, which led to the overthrow of several of the conservative Southern committee chairmen, did not necessarily result in better treatment for the Republican minority. Barber Conable, a New York moderate, felt that one of the toppled Southerners, Wilbur Mills of Ways and Means, had "practiced the kind of bipartisan, consensus politics" that allowed Republican members to play a significant cooperative role. Mills also consulted extensively with the minority party to ensure that the bills he reported out of committee would pass the full House.[73] After Mills was removed as chairman, Democrats packed the committee with liberals and excluded the Republicans from committee deliberations. The era of bipartisan consensus in Ways and Means was over.[74]

The Republican Congressional leadership began to tighten discipline within their ranks in response to the upsurge in Democratic partisanship, but still permitted members considerable latitude. Representative Thomas Railsback, listening to testimony in the House Judiciary Committee hearings on firearms regulation in the mid-1970s, gradually concluded that handgun violence was driven by small, concealable weapons: "The talk in the papers was about 'Saturday Night Specials,' cheap handguns, but the real issue wasn't cost but size." He favored a ban on guns in this category. Railsback observed that Henry Hyde, a stalwart Illinois Republican, also was persuaded by the evidence to support gun control, and later broke with the party on the issue of banning semi-automatic weapons. "In those days," he believed, "there was less pressure on you to take a particular ideological position if the evidence convinced you otherwise."[75]

Ideological pressures were in the ascent, however, driven by the skyrocketing cost of television campaign advertising and the growth of issue groups and lobbying organizations. Ohio Senator William B. Saxbe, elected in 1968, recalled that "I found out that if you're going to ask people for big money . . . that they damn well want their money's worth." He declined to run for reelection, figuring that if he had to raise what at that time seemed the outlandish sum of $10 million, "I'd be a captive of special interests."[76] Oregon Senator Robert Packwood, extrapolating from the trends of the mid-1970s, predicted the rise of "narrowly targeted massive spending of organizations dedicated to the defeat of a candidate whose sole sin was to vote his conscience, and in so doing crossed the passions of a particularly massive and wealthy special interest group." When that development came to full fruition, "Woe be to the candidate who votes for gun registration and earns the wrath of the National Rifle Association. Say good-bye to the candidate who votes for legal abortion and draws the wrath of Right-to-Life."[77]

Moderates felt much more comfortable with Ford than they had with Nixon, even though Ford was somewhat to the right of his predecessor. Ford "didn't have a vigorous ideology," one of his assistants felt, since "he had been through too many arguments and too many fights in Congress to believe that he had an answer for every issue. He had a keen sense of what was practical."[78] Ford's integrity, openness, and emphasis on unity and pragmatism helped restore public trust in the presidency. Ford adopted a big-tent stance toward his party's moderates and progressives. His focus, however, was on reducing inflation and fending off budget-busting proposals from the liberal Democratic Congress through extensive use of his veto pen. As Nelson Rockefeller quickly discovered, the President had little interest in fulfilling Nixon's unfinished attempts at welfare reform or national health insurance, or backing any of the Vice President's ambitious plans for domestic social reform. White House chief of staff Donald Rumsfeld stymied Rockefeller at every turn, although Rumsfeld emphasized that his principal aim was to defend the President's sphere of authority.[79]

Conservative activists made little secret of their distaste for Ford's moderation and their desire to see a conservative replace him as President. Some conservatives thought the time was ripe for a conservative third party, which would be free of the taint of Watergate and the need to accommodate moderates. "There is not the slightest chance, in my view, that the GOP can 'win' in 1976, or for that matter, ever again," Clare Boothe Luce wrote in 1975. A new party was needed, she thought, since both parties were "dominated today by a small band of Liberals, whose domestic and foreign policies are bringing the nation to ruin."[80] William Rusher believed that a forthrightly conservative party, ideally led by Ronald Reagan, would win by appealing to the majority of Americans who described themselves as conservative. It would fulfill Rusher's old dream of uniting Republican conservatives with George Wallace's social-conservative followers in the Democratic Party. The Democrats would become the party of unadulterated liberalism, and the Republicans would wither away.[81] Rusher's view that it would be impossible to expel the moderates from the GOP was unduly pessimistic. But the conservative drive for a third party "made the 1970s a hopeful period for moderates," one activist remembered. "I would have left the [Republican] Party sooner if it hadn't been for the hope that the conservatives would leave instead of taking over."[82]

Reagan was too canny to be captured by the conservatives. He toured the country touting the "hidden conservative majority" thesis that voters had stayed away from the polls in 1974 out of a belief that there was not enough difference between the parties. "Our people look for a cause to believe in," he told conservative audiences. What was needed was not a third party but a revitalized GOP, "raising a banner of no pale pastels, but bold colors which make it unmistakably clear where we stand."[83] In November 1975, Reagan declared that he would run against Ford for the presidential nomination.

The conservative challenge drove Ford to the right. For many moderates, his rhetoric on school prayer, busing, government spending, and abortion began to sound uncomfortably like Reagan's. "We are going to forget the use of the word détente," Ford told Americans.[84] He dumped Rockefeller, the most obvious symbol of the administration's progressivism, from the 1976 ticket. Some moderates protested against this rude treatment of their former hero, but others shed few tears for his political passing. Dick Behn, the editor of the *Ripon Forum*, felt that "For too long, Rockefeller has held tenaciously onto his position as pastor emeritus of the progressive flock, preventing more committed, less divisive politicians from rallying progressive enthusiasm. For a decade and a half, Rockefeller has told the progressive congregation that they needed him, while doing little to organize the congregation, preach new homilies, or attract new converts."[85] Maryland's progressive Senator "Mac" Mathias considered entering the presidential primaries as a way of pressuring Ford from the left to counter the pressure from the right. Ford persuaded him that this would only strengthen the Reagan insurgency. Fearing that any further erosion of Ford's already weak position would hand victory to the conservatives, "progressive Republicans were largely paralyzed," Mathias recalled.[86]

Reagan's campaign stumbled coming out of the gate, as the candidate proposed to cut $90 billion from the federal budget and slash income taxes while simultaneously balancing the budget, all of this to be achieved by transferring spending authority to the states. This would also transfer a massive taxation burden to the states, which New Hampshire residents quickly realized would end their freedom from state income and sales taxes. Ford pulled out a narrow victory in the state's January 1976 GOP primary election. Reagan lost the next four primaries until, in North Carolina, he started running against the treaties Ford was negotiating to transfer owner-ship of the Panama Canal to Panama. "[W]e built it, we paid for it, it's ours and . . . we are going to keep it," Reagan told cheering crowds.[87]

Reagan's nationalistic slogan buoyed him to victory in North Carolina and kept him in the running until the GOP convention in August in Kan-sas City, where Ford won the nomination by only 117 votes out of 2,257. Reagan's campaign illustrated both the gathering strength of the conserva-tive movement within the Republican Party and its ability to stir the blood of voters with emotional appeals that moderates conspicuously lacked. Reagan's success further revealed that the growing number of binding state presidential primaries—85 percent of convention delegates had been "bound" to candidates in primary elections or conventions in 1976, versus 48 percent in 1968—was an unfavorable development for moderates, even though it was one that most had supported in the name of greater openness and democratic participation. The right wing was able to dominate low-turnout primaries and open caucuses through its organizational muscle and the ideological zeal of its followers. In such elections, 80 percent of success is showing up, to paraphrase Woody Allen, and the conservatives were simply far more likely to turn out and vote than the half-hearted, dis-organized moderates.[88]

The 1976 election results proved dismaying to moderates and conserva-tives alike. Ford narrowly lost the presidential race to Jimmy Carter, who was able to reunite the Democratic coalition of traditional party loyalists, liberals, labor, minorities, and Southerners that seemingly had been shat-tered in 1972. Moderates were discouraged that Carter, who had been a ra-cially progressive governor of Georgia, defeated George Wallace in the Southern primaries with the help of those "New South" forces that mod-erate Republicans had coveted—African-Americans, racially moderate business elites, and suburbanites—as well as the white working class. Ford's defeat removed the moderates' last defense against a conservative takeover of the GOP.

Conservatives did not yet appreciate that possibility, since much of the New Right was implacably hostile to the party establishment and the compromise that party politics entailed. Paul Weyrich, an influential con-servative activist, claimed that "The Republican Party is not built on prin-ciples, it's a tradition maintained by effete gentlemen of the northeastern

Establishment who play games with other effete gentlemen who call themselves Democrats."[89] But the attempt by William Rusher and other right-wingers to establish a new, conservative party to replace the GOP met with disaster: the American Independence Party fell under the control of unredeemed George Wallace followers, who nominated the infamously racist Lester Maddox as their presidential candidate. "The whole situation sounds to me awfully close to the kooks," Bill Buckley admonished Rusher. "In the last analysis, if you have to deal with people of that sort, a) you're not going to get anywhere; b) you are simply going to besmirch yourself."[90] The AIP received only two-tenths of one percent of the popular vote in the 1976 election, ending realistic consideration of a right-wing alternative to the Republican Party.[91]

Conservatives saw little grounds for optimism about the fate of the GOP in the wake of Ford's defeat, however. An internal party survey suggested that only 18 percent of Americans described themselves as Republicans, compared to 42 percent who regarded themselves as Democrats and 40 percent as independents.[92] Carter won all of the states in the former Confederacy except Virginia, which threatened the longstanding dream of a conservative Republican Party based in the South. New York Senator James Buckley, described by conservative columnist James J. Kilpatrick as the right's "best and brightest prospect for 1980," failed to win reelection.[93] Buckley's fiscal conservatism played poorly with voters, especially in New York City, which he had been conspicuously unwilling to defend when it was threatened with bankruptcy. "Whatever the defects of the present federal system, it exists," one New York paper lectured Buckley. "And a senator has a duty to see to it that his constituents share fully in whatever benefits it has to offer—from government contracts to aid to the jobless."[94] Conservatism seemed even less popular than the Republican Party.

The GOP's dire situation did not bring a truce to the internecine warfare within the party. The progressive Representative Charles Whalen had long been one of Ohio's most respected politicians; a *Cleveland Plain Dealer* survey of journalists and congressional staff aides found that he was rated Ohio's best congressman, while columnist Jack Anderson rated him among the ten best members of the House.[95] He was also one of the GOP's most popular officeholders, regularly winning elections with margins of 70 percent and more. In 1974, one of the least favorable years for Republican candidates in decades, the Democratic Party had declined to put up a challenger against Whalen. Although Whalen represented a predominantly Democratic district in Dayton, local Democratic leaders informed the *New York Times* that they saw no point in throwing money away on the "lost cause" of trying to defeat Whalen. "Let's say you find a reasonably attractive candidate and put on a credible campaign," a Democratic state legislator told the *Times*. "What happens? Chuck wins with only 60 percent of the vote instead of 75."[96]

But the independence of Republican progressives became increasingly unbearable to the GOP political establishments in their home states and districts, and representatives like Whalen and senators like Lowell Weicker and "Mac" Mathias found themselves at war with their party organizations. Republican leaders in Dayton made it clear to Whalen that they would support primary challenges against him unless he went along with the increasingly conservative drift of the party. Representative Donald Riegle of Michigan recalled Whalen telling him that "He can accept the prospect of losing his seat in a hard-fought general election, but he can't tolerate the thought of being defeated in 'a narrow little primary by a bunch of nuts.'"[97] Whalen protested that his support of civil rights, education, conservation, and fiscal responsibility was well within the Republican tradition reaching back to Theodore Roosevelt, but his protests fell on deaf ears. His chief tormentor was H. K. "Bud" Crowl, a local radio station owner and state GOP committeeman, who insisted that "There is a strong wave of conservatism hitting this country and they might as well bury the elephant and the donkey because the two parties are dead. There should be two new parties, the conservatives and the socialist liberals."[98] Party professionals knew that there was a high probability that Whalen's seat would be turned over to the Democrats if he was forced out, but Crowl found such practical considerations contemptible: "we could lose a seat but keep our honor and integrity."[99] Outside conservative organizations, including Paul Weyrich's Committee for the Survival of a Free Congress, devoted time and money to hounding Whalen from political life.[100] Finally in 1977, he announced that he was retiring from Congress, at the relatively young age of fifty-eight. At the next election, Democrat Tony P. Hall handily won election to succeed Whalen. Hall kept his seat for the next twenty years, while the district's Republican leaders presumably kept their honor and integrity.

The two principal developments that revived the Republican Party's fortunes in the late 1970s emerged from contradictory sources. The first was a resurgence of grassroots conservative activism fuelled principally by the growth of the religious right. Slade Gorton, a moderate Republican in the Washington State legislature, noticed a trend in the state's party elections after 1976 that would hold important implications for the future. In 1964, moderates had lost to Goldwater supporters in the intra-party contests of that critical year, and the local and state organizations remained in the hands of conservatives even after Goldwater's electoral wipeout. But across the 1960s and 1970s, "the Goldwater people who were in the party organization became more pragmatic," as a consequence of governing and attempting to appeal to a broader constituency. This led conservative supporters of Reagan, who were energized by his presidential bids, to run against the Goldwaterites and turn them out of office. The newly elected Reaganites in their turn were to become more pragmatic by the very act of attempting to govern and win reelection, until a dozen or so years later they would be deposed by people to their right in the 1994 elections, and the same cycle would repeat itself with the Tea Party movement. "The people who are in party organizations and want to win elections have to make certain compromises in order to win," Gorton concluded, "and then they get thrown out by true believers."[101] This logic implied that the Republican Party's ability to govern would always be undercut by the demands of its most fervent supporters. The same dynamic also implied that in some ways, each successive wave of grassroots activism would move the definition of movement conservatism further to the right, like a ratchet. A 1964 conservative activist would seem like a comparative moderate by the late '70s. Each wave of conservatism would move the Republican Party further away from moderation and its own heritage.

The other development that sparked a Republican renewal, however, did not emerge from strife between moderates and conservatives but rather from collaboration between them. Supply-side economics is still an explosively controversial subject. Proponents claim that the doctrine restored American prosperity after a decade of economic stagnation, while detractors charge that it gave rise to massive income inequality and the ballooning fiscal deficits that continue to imperil the country's standing as a great power.[102] Whatever the truth of these claims, supply-side economics indubitably did emerge from the efforts of some moderate as well as conservative Republicans, while also meeting with severe criticism from all sides. In strictly political terms, supply-side thinking and proposals provided a positive and even inspiring message that allowed the GOP to seize the initiative from the Democrats.

Richard Rahn, one of the leaders in the development of the supply-side message, was a moderate Republican who became involved with the Ripon Society while he was a graduate student in economics at Columbia University in the late 1960s. In the early 1970s, he worked for Nelson Rockefeller's campaign organization and served as Ripon's director of finance and chairman of its Washington, D.C. chapter, while heading the American Council for Capital Formation. In 1976, at a Ripon meeting in Chicago, he met Arthur Laffer, another young economist who shared his interest in the problems of economic growth. Laffer had taught economics at the University of Chicago, and had followed the dean of the faculty, George Shultz, to Washington when Nixon appointed Shultz director of

the Office of Management and Budget. Laffer served as OMB's chief economist. In 1974, at a lunch meeting with Ford's deputy chief of staff Dick
Cheney, Laffer used a napkin to sketch his famous curve, which suggested
that if taxes were so high as to discourage work, then lowering the tax rate
might actually encourage people to work more and thereby increase tax
revenues.[103] The more important thrust of Laffer's approach, which he
shared with distinguished economists such as Robert Mundell and Paul
Craig Roberts, was that lowering tax rates at the margin would provide
people with incentives to work, save, and invest.

This message resonated with Rahn and other members of the Ripon Society because they had spent the previous decade advocating incentives to
achieve desired social outcomes, as opposed to direct government intervention, and had generally worried about production more than consumption. Rahn had also become dissatisfied with the inability of Keynesian
economics to account for stagflation, the combination of stagnant growth
and high inflation that afflicted the U.S. economy during the 1970s. "The
Keynesian model never really fit together for me," Rahn recalled, "and
Laffer's approach made much more intuitive sense."[104] Rahn and Laffer,
together with two other young economists, created the first supply-side
econometric model.

Rahn and Laffer became informal advisers to New York Congressman
Jack Kemp, who was one of the most prominent cheerleaders for the
supply-side doctrine within the Republican Party. Laffer, who by the late
1970s had become a professor at the University of Southern California,
frequently would take the red-eye flight to Washington's Dulles Airport,
where Rahn would pick him up and drive him to Kemp's home in Bethesda,
Maryland. Rahn remembered that "Jack, dressed in his bathrobe, would
cook breakfast for us while peppering Art with questions and challenging
his assertions."[105] In 1977, Kemp and Delaware Senator William Roth
introduced legislation to cut individual taxes by 30 percent across the
board. Kemp-Roth, as the bill became known, did not pass Congress
during Carter's administration but attracted increasing Republican support. By 1978, Representative John B. Anderson was one of the many
GOP moderates who believed it was "a very healthy sign with respect to
the vitality of the party that we do have this broad consensus [behind
Kemp-Roth] that includes progressives, moderates, conservatives."[106]
Conservative activist Randall Teague agreed, in a metaphorically mixed
way, that "The senators and congressmen that I'd consider Ripon types
have not only been behind us on Kemp-Roth and the whole tax cut issue,
they've been way out in front on it."[107]

Kemp typically was identified as a conservative, but his experiences of
playing alongside African-American teammates for the Buffalo Bills football

team and representing the Rust Belt city of Buffalo made him a passionate advocate of a more inclusive Republican Party that was sensitive to the needs of minorities and the working class. The self-described "bleeding-heart conservative" believed that the Republican Party's traditional focus on balanced budgets and fiscal austerity forced it to play the essentially negative role of Scrooge to the Democrats' Santa Claus. Supply-side economics would allow the GOP to go on the offensive with a positive program for economic growth that Americans would embrace. Kemp supported many of the government programs that assisted disadvantaged minorities, but he also believed that economic policies that allowed inner-city entrepreneurs and small business owners to keep more of their earnings would enable more people to lift themselves out of poverty. As reporter Jason DeParle observed, Kemp "brought more zeal to America's poverty problems than any national politician since Robert Kennedy" and likely was "the only official to have won standing ovations in black ghettos by calling for a capital gains tax cut."[108]

The Republican who became most closely identified with proposals to cut the capital gains tax was not Kemp but William Steiger, a representative from Wisconsin and one of the leaders of the GOP's moderate bloc. Steiger was deeply disturbed by the economic misery America endured during the Carter years. By the late '70s, the prosperity of the broad middle class was being eroded by inflation, which not only raised prices but pushed more people from middling incomes into higher tax brackets, as well as by unemployment. Americans also suffered from rising Social Security payroll taxes and property taxes, and a stagnant stock market. Democratic tax relief programs tended to benefit the very poor or special groups such as the elderly, while only the rich could take advantage of tax loopholes. Businesses were subjected to capital gains tax rates that, combined with inflation, could amount to a hundred percent or more in real terms. Investment capital dried up, and with it the innovation that drove business creation. In early 1978, Ed Zschau, a Southern California small businessman, contacted Richard Rahn, hoping to alert members of Congress to the plight of would-be entrepreneurs. Rahn put him in touch with Steiger, who invited Zschau to testify before hearings of the Ways and Means Committee. Steiger was shocked to learn that venture capital was so hard to come by in California that Zschau had been forced to seek funding in Japan.

In April 1978, Steiger introduced an amendment to Carter's tax bill proposing to cut the capital gains tax nearly in half, from 49 to 28 percent, in the hopes of encouraging widespread stock ownership, unfreezing capital for investment, and facilitating the growth of new companies and the jobs they would produce. He emphasized that there was nothing magic about tax-cutting in and of itself, and that Congress would need to account for how much of the increase in positive outcomes such as business startups could be attributed to the tax cut and how much to other factors. He hoped to ensure that as much of the benefits as possible accrued to the middle class, and particularly to minority-owned businesses. Steiger's proposal was conceived in a much different spirit from the populist tax revolt in California, where residents reacted furiously against the combination of a $5 billion state revenue surplus and skyrocketing property value assessments. In June 1978, voters passed Proposition 13, which rolled back property values to 1975 levels and essentially froze them there, and prevented the legislature from raising taxes without a two-thirds vote in each house.[109] Steiger lacked the angry, anti-government animus that motivated tax rebellions around the country and made tax-cutting under any and all circumstances a conservative fetish.

Nonetheless, Steiger's tax reduction proposal was well suited to the moment, and somewhat to his surprise he managed to gain enough Democratic support that Carter was forced to sign his measure into law. The passage of the Steiger Amendment, in the view of *Wall Street Journal* editor Robert Bartley, marked the moment when "a decade of envy came to its close, and the search for a growth formula started in earnest."[110] Supply-side economists credited the amendment with inspiring a venture capital boom that launched companies like Apple, Sun Microsystems, and FedEx. At the very least, Steiger's tax proposal offered common ground for moderates and conservatives. A 1978 conference of Republican officials, ranging from conservatives like Utah Senator Orrin Hatch to progressives like Representative Pete McCloskey and Senator Jacob Javis, achieved surprising unanimity in support of the tax reform proposals of Kemp and Steiger, as well as in opposition to Carter's energy legislation and foreign policy. Skeptics could point out that the emerging consensus did not prevent conservative supply-side crusader Jeffrey Bell from knocking off long-serving progressive Clifford Case in the 1978 New Jersey GOP senatorial primary, with the net result that the seat was lost to a Democrat in the November elections. Conservatives eventually would take the cautious insights of the early growth advocates to extremes, transforming supply-side into an essentially theological commitment against tax increases of any kind. Nonetheless, Republican National Committee chairman Bill Brock pointed to the agreement between moderates and conservatives on economic matters as evidence that "there's an awful lot more that unifies people in this party than divides us."[111]

Steiger did not live to see his bill take effect. He died from a heart attack in December 1978, at age forty. Of all of the moderate might-have-beens, Steiger was one of the greatest. Columnist George Will spoke for many when he lamented that Steiger's death cut short "what would have been one of the most distinguished careers Congress has known." Steiger's sudden decease was widely mourned, not just on account of his youth but also because his dozen years of service in Congress seemed to promise that politics could be improved. He was a solid party man, but had worked to make the GOP more open, particularly to women and minorities and young people. He was skeptical of liberals' grandiose claims for government, but never pretended that government was unnecessary, and he fought hard to get Republicans to modernize government at all levels and to enlist the brainpower of the academic community. He brought a youthful exuberance to even the unglamorous, everyday operations of public service, and his willingness to work with Democrats allowed him to amass a significant record of achievement. As the *Washington Post* editorialized, "His death was untimely, a blow to his party and a loss to civility and seriousness of purpose in the House."[112] The Republicans also lost Steiger's intangible but real moderating influence on many people who eventually would play a leading role in the party, such as George H. W. Bush, who was the godfather of Steiger's only child.[113] Steiger had helped elect his protégé Dick Cheney as Wyoming's sole House representative in the 1978 elections; Cheney might not have pursued such an obdurately conservative course in Congress and the White House if his mentor had still been alive.

The likelihood of a Republican unseating Jimmy Carter as president increased along with the steady drumbeat of bad news that cast a pall over 1979 and 1980: double-digit inflation, oil shortages, soaring interest rates, the Soviet invasion of Afghanistan, and the takeover of the U.S. embassy in Iran by Islamic Shiite radicals. As usual, however, moderate Republicans could not decide on a presidential candidate. Many believed that their best possibility was Howard Baker, the Tennessean who had been elected Senate minority leader after Hugh Scott's retirement in 1977. Baker had earned the nickname "the Great Conciliator" on account of his trustworthiness, civility, and effectiveness in negotiating closed-door, bipartisan compromise. One Democratic senator told *Newsweek* that if there were a secret ballot in the Senate for President, Baker would win a majority, even among Democrats.[114] But Baker had destroyed his standing with conservatives by supporting the Panama Canal treaties, which he more than anyone else could have stopped. As one of his advisers had pointed out to him when the treaties first came under consideration, Baker could either choose to be hailed as a statesman by the media by supporting the treaties, or he could play to the GOP's increasingly conservative base by opposing them. "The people who make media judgments," his adviser warned, "are not the same people as those who attend Republican National conventions." A vote in favor of the treaties "could well foreclose the possibility of nomination."[115] Baker believed that the treaties were in the United States' best interests, and like his senatorial predecessor Henry Clay, decided that he would rather be right than president. When the treaties were approved by the Senate in 1978, conservatives denounced Baker as a traitor, and his presidential campaign never really got off the ground.

The moderates' remaining candidates included Gerald Ford (if he could be enticed into running again), George H. W. Bush and his weighty résumé of service in various government and party positions, and Representative John B. Anderson, who hewed closest to the progressive position but was little known to the public. Moderates briefly hoped that candidates such as Philip Crane, John Connally, and Bob Dole would split the right-wing vote, but Ronald Reagan inexorably came to the fore as the conservative choice. Some moderates vowed to resist Reagan to the last, while others gloomily resigned themselves to his nomination; moderate Pennsylvania Governor Richard Thornburgh predicted that "If the Reagan candidacy has the appearance of being inevitable, you're not going to see anyone on a kamikaze mission [to stop him]."[116]

Some members of the Ripon Society, however, had begun to feel that there were good reasons for moderates to positively prefer Reagan as the nominee. No one was under any illusions that the conservative movement behind Reagan had become less hostile to moderates. When several Ripon members attended the Young Republicans' national leadership conference in 1979, their suite was invaded by conservative members of "the Team," the successor generation to the Syndicate, who disrupted Ripon's recruiting attempts by singing hostile songs. "It was stupid, junior high stuff," Ripon member Steve Livengood remembered. "It was kind of doggerel that they had made up about us, with puns. Essentially the message was, 'You're all commie pinkos and we're the wave of the future.' . . . It was a little scary. That was the first time that I really saw the kind of hostility that I'd heard about from the Goldwater convention and things like that. Those people needed enemies. And we set ourselves up as the enemy that they could confront, because they couldn't confront the Democrats."[117]

Even so, both the conservative leadership and the Republican Party had changed over time, and some of the changes reflected moderate victories. As George Gilder wrote to other alumni of the Ripon Society in April 1980, "The central themes of early Ripon—civil rights, free markets, a balanced internationalism in foreign affairs, a new generation of excellence in party leadership, an openness to new ideas—have largely prevailed." The new breed of Republicans in Congress were not uninformed Neanderthals like the Roman Hruskas of old. There were no influential Republican politicians who still condoned the denial of civil rights to

African-Americans, openly supported extremist groups such as the John Birch Society, or advocated protectionist restrictions on free trade. Even Ripon's old enemies at *National Review* had evolved in some ways, with Bill Buckley supporting the Panama Canal treaties and his brother Jim becoming one of the nation's leading conservationists. "We must realize, as strange as it may seem at this difficult moment in our history, that we have mostly won," Gilder concluded. He argued that moderates for their part should change by seeking common ground with conservatives on supply-side economic policies. "Ripon statements of the early years," he pointed out, "rang with appeals for 'fiscal integrity,' which in general meant raising taxes to pay for the new social programs of the Democrats."[118] Gilder encouraged moderates to work with Reagan and their former opponents to embrace new conservative means of achieving the longstanding goals of the progressives.

By the spring of 1980, Gilder was staying with his old friend Bruce Chapman in Seattle and working on his book, *Wealth and Poverty*, which was destined to become an international bestseller and one of the most influential statements of supply-side doctrine. Gilder's manuscript was in large part a reworking of the never-published book he had ghostwritten for George Romney's 1967-68 presidential campaign, which pointed to the continuity between the moderate movement and supply-side economics.[119] Reagan embraced this essentially moderate vision of entrepreneurship working in tandem with traditional values, and Gilder would become Reagan's most-quoted living author.

Chapman had won a seat on Seattle's City Council in 1971, and spent the next several years working to revive the urban core with innovative ideas for new parks, arts programs, political term limits, a more transparent and effective city government, and the preservation of landmarks like Pike Place Market and Pioneer Square. "By the mid-'70s, Seattle was America's hottest city," in the verdict of one profile of Chapman. "[T]he turnaround was based in part on Chapman and other young leaders who had good ideas and plenty of federal dollars to spend on them."[120] Chapman won election as Washington's secretary of state in 1975. In that office, he worked with moderate Republican Governor Dan Evans on various progressive programs, including the decision after the fall of Saigon to welcome Vietnamese refugees while California's Democratic Governor Jerry Brown was refusing to accept them. When Gilder became electrified by supply-side economics, he converted Chapman and other moderates in his circle. "George had a lot of impact on me," Chapman recalled. "I was out here [in Washington] doing local politics and focusing on issues that didn't really pertain to the national picture. . . . George led me toward thinking about the national issues again in a different way."[121]

After Reagan won the 1980 New Hampshire primary and it became increasingly probable that he would win the GOP presidential nomination, Chapman worked with other Ripon members to determine where the Society stood with respect to Reagan's positions. Chapman categorized dozens of issues and confirmed that Reagan and the moderates still did not see eye to eye on the social controversies that had divided Republicans over the previous decade, including capital punishment, handgun restrictions, ratification of the Equal Rights Amendment, and a Constitutional amendment to ban abortion. But he found significant overlap on economic issues, particularly with respect to tax incentives for savings and investment, curbs on excessive government regulation, accelerated depreciation schedules for business equipment, deregulation of key industries, and a lowering of trade restrictions and tariffs. Reagan also agreed with moderates on the desirability of inner-city enterprise zones, inducements for neighborhood rehabilitation, sunset laws to curb bureaucracy, and the promotion of human rights and capitalism abroad, as well as the undesirability of reinstituting the draft, establishing fixed quotas for minority employment, or creating a program of guaranteed federal jobs.[122] For many moderates, there was enough common ground with Reagan to support his nomination.

Peter Wallison, the former head of Ripon's New York chapter, convinced several of his friends in the Society that Reagan would be a superior President. When Wallison had been counsel to the Vice President during the Ford years, he had seen Rockefeller and Reagan work together on a blue-ribbon commission to investigate allegations that the Central Intelligence Agency had overstepped its authority. The experience changed Wallison from being a Reagan skeptic to an admirer. While it became evident that Rockefeller was not a critical or analytical thinker, Reagan showed an impressive ability to quickly summarize complex issues and propose the adjustments that would enable compromises. Although Wallison had supported Rockefeller in his repeated pursuit of the presidency, he wrote that he "eventually concluded that, as between Reagan and Rockefeller, Reagan would make the better president."[123] Ripon was also in touch with some former Reagan foes in California who had become admirers. William Bagley, a leader of the progressive forces in the California Assembly, attested that Reagan "became a pretty darn good governor because he learned to compromise, which is a bad word to conservatives. He became in some senses a liberal."[124] Alphonzo Bell, a member of the House Wednesday Group, was another strong Reagan advocate in moderate circles; Reagan lived in the Los Angeles district Bell represented, and had been chairman of "Democrats for Bell" in the late 1950s.[125]

Many other moderates, however, could not accept the possibility of Ronald Reagan and the New Right in command of the GOP. The primary defeat of venerable progressive New York Senator Jacob Javits by conservative Alphonse D'Amato, and the wounding right-wing primary challenge mounted against Massachusetts progressive Senator Ed Brooke, put them in a fighting mood. During the presidential primaries, they had pinned their hopes on John Anderson's candidacy. The white-haired, rugged-featured Illinoisan was widely considered to be one of the most intelligent and effective members of Congress and one of the few real orators on Capitol Hill. Anderson had been counted in the conservative ranks when he first entered the House in 1961. A deeply religious man, he had been "born again" at an evangelical tent meeting at age nine. In 1964, when he was an enthusiastic Goldwater supporter, he was named Outstanding Layman of the Year by the National Association of Evangelicals. In 1969, he was elected chairman of the House Republican Conference, the third-ranking position in the House GOP leadership. He remained a hardheaded, balance-the-budget fiscal conservative, opposed to protectionism, waste in government programs, and wage and price controls. As a co-sponsor of the Steiger Amendment, he was sympathetic to the cause of tax reduction, though he maintained that tax cuts had to be offset by spending cuts.

The traumas of the 1960s convinced Anderson that Republicans had to combine fiscal conservatism with what he called "a humane approach to the issues."[126] He became one of the GOP's most prominent advocates of civil rights and urban strategies to achieve equal opportunity for disadvantaged minorities. Anderson came under increasing fire from the right for becoming the first House Republican to call for Nixon's resignation, and for his support of the Equal Rights Amendment and opposition to increased defense spending on what he considered wasteful and unnecessary programs such as the B-1 bomber and the MX mobile missile system. Conservatives repeatedly attempted to unseat him from his party leadership position. Right-wing groups around the country contributed lavishly to the primary challenge against him in 1978 by an evangelical minister who attacked his endorsement of the Panama Canal treaties and SALT II strategic arms limitations negotiations, and his votes against constitutional amendments instituting school prayer and banning abortion. The campaign also previewed future culture-war strategies by castigating Anderson for voting against legislation denying government-funded legal aid to homosexuals.[127] He found himself "increasingly harassed and isolated," as he put it, unlikely to ever advance further in the Republican leadership, and convinced that "the party was going down the wrong road . . . hopelessly wedded to policies that were appropriate to the past but not the future."[128]

Anderson despaired of resisting the conservative tide in the House, and announced that he would not run for reelection to Congress. His presidential campaign was conceived as a means of recentering the GOP, as he wrote to one potential donor: "[I]t seems to me that the center of gravity of the party has shifted too far to the right. Virtually all of the candidates, with the exception of myself, are basically courting the right wing of the Republican Party." He believed that his campaign represented "perhaps the last remaining effort on the part of moderates and progressives to have a voice in the nomination."[129] When he announced his candidacy, he quoted William Butler Yeats' oft-cited lines—"Things fall apart, the center cannot hold"— and declared his intention to "restore that vital center that can bind our nation and society together."[130] The Anderson campaign staff was made up largely of Ripon Society members, and drew particular support from Republican feminists. Anderson received only some 10 percent of the vote in the New Hampshire primary, but fell merely a few hundred votes short in Massachusetts and Vermont, which he lost to Bush and Reagan, respectively. Moderate excitement over Anderson's prospects in the GOP race dissipated after disappointing showings followed in Wisconsin and his home state of Illinois, where moderate Senator Charles Percy endorsed Reagan.

In the campaign's early stages, Anderson had presented himself as a genuine Republican moderate, highlighting his fiscal responsibility and winning the grudging respect of *National Review* for being the only GOP candidate in the Iowa debates with sufficient courage to support the grain embargo against the Soviet Union, which Carter had imposed in response to the Afghan invasion.[131] Although Anderson was sympathetic to some aspects of supply-side economics, he spoke for many fiscal conservatives when he said that Reagan's plan to balance the budget while also cutting taxes and increasing defense spending could only be achieved "with mirrors."[132] What drew media attention, however, was not Anderson's attempt to find common ground among Republicans but his attacks on social conservatives and members of the newly formed Moral Majority as "extremists" and "zealots." Anderson had formerly deplored the ascendancy of social over economic issues, telling reporters that "I feel very strongly that those emotional, hot-button type of social issues are not the basis on which you really build a political credo."[133] Under the influence of media advisors and political consultants like David Garth, however, Anderson increasingly made liberal social positions the basis of his candidacy, appealing to left-wing Democratic supporters of Ted Kennedy rather than to moderate Republicans. This was helpful in the New England states that allowed independents and Democrats to vote in Republican primaries, but doomed his candidacy in states dominated by the local Republican leaders Anderson had never bothered to cultivate.

Anderson abandoned the Republican race in order to run for president as an independent, a decision that splintered the already fractured moderates. Some Ripon activists left the GOP to work with the campaign, while most of the group's founding members begged Anderson to "reject an independent candidacy and to fight for his ideals and beliefs within the Republican party."[134] Anderson's withdrawal gave conservatives the run of the July 1980 GOP national convention in Detroit, at which the right wing finally had the opportunity to rewrite the party platform to their liking. They removed the plank in support of the Equal Rights Amendment that had been included in previous platforms since 1940, and inserted a call for a constitutional ban on abortion and a right-to-life litmus test for judicial appointments. Republican National Committee co-chair Mary Dent Crisp, who was sympathetic to the feminist cause, was forced to resign.

Reagan might have had a difficult time maintaining the façade of party unity if Anderson had remained in the GOP and had addressed the convention. In the event, Reagan appeased most of the moderates by appointing George H. W. Bush as his running mate, and mollified some of the feminists by meeting with them and promising to name a woman to the Supreme Court—as indeed he would with his nomination of Sandra Day O'Connor.[135] Reagan did not repeat the errors of Goldwater in 1964 by reading moderates out of the party, and most of the convention's prime speaking spots went to moderates including Ford, Rumsfeld, and Representative Margaret Heckler. It was clear nonetheless to most observers that conservatives had finally triumphed within the party, as evidenced by Bush's renouncing his previous moderate position on abortion as well as his primary campaign charge that supply-side was "voodoo economics."

Reagan's ascension meant that the Southern strategy was fully in the saddle. The GOP's limited outreach efforts toward minorities, particularly African-Americans, ground to a halt. This struck longtime Republican and civil rights activist John McClaughry as a terrible missed opportunity because much of the Reagan message could have appealed to black audiences. While attending the GOP convention as part of Reagan's speechwriting team, McClaughry visited a neighborhood committee meeting in a struggling, predominantly minority section of Detroit. He talked with the residents at the meeting, and "When I got around to busing, I asked them, 'Do you believe that students should be bused to achieve racial balance in the schools?' A black man looked at me and said, 'Stupidest idea ever conceived by the mind of man.' The next question I asked was about gun control, and a little black lady in a lavender dress and gloves said, 'Better police get you with it than mugger get you without it.' They were right down the line with Reagan on every issue . . . I recognized a lot of common ground there."[136] But few conservative politicians other than

Jack Kemp had any real interest in cultivating the black vote. Reagan proceeded to alienate African-Americans immediately after the national convention by evoking states' rights before a nearly all-white audience in Philadelphia, Mississippi, where three civil rights workers had been murdered by Klansmen in 1964.

For many moderates such as former Ripon president Howard Gillette, Reagan's nomination propelled them out of the Republican Party. When Gillette went to work for Anderson, he became increasingly unhappy with the leftward drift of the campaign under the direction of David Garth and other liberal advisors. "Garth continues to talk about attracting liberal Democrats to our ticket," Gillette complained in August 1980. "No one in the campaign has been quoted about the interest in attracting moderate Republicans disaffected with the platform."[137] But while moderates like Gillette remained uncomfortable with many aspects of the Democratic Party, the prospect of the Republican Party under New Right control was too much to bear. "For me, 1980 was really the end of the line for liberal and moderate Republicanism," Gillette remembered. "The thought that the Republican Party would swallow Reagan . . . that ended any prospect of being a moderate Republican."[138]

The progressives' departure in 1980 wasn't as dramatic as the Bull Moose bolt in 1912, but the net effect in both cases was to shift the GOP center of gravity to the right. Donald Hodel, a Syndicate protégé of William Rusher, crowed that "when John Anderson left the Republican Party he took with him most of the liberal wing of the Republican Party—not its elected liberals, but the party activists who were liberal and finally felt that this wasn't the party for them."[139] The remaining Republican moderates blamed Anderson for being a sort of pied piper leading the progressives out of the GOP. Tanya Melich called Anderson's independent candidacy "a death knell for any leverage that moderate Republicans would have in the national party throughout the Reagan-Bush years."[140] The departure of Anderson and his followers enabled the polarization of Republicans and Democrats into conservative and liberal parties, an outcome that conservatives had sought for decades. The fate of moderates within the GOP now rested in Reagan's hands.

CHAPTER 12

✿

Slouching Toward Bethlehem

The Collapse of the Moderate Republicans, 1980–2010

A well-known chart produced after Napoleon's Russian invasion of 1812 tracks the annihilation of the French army across its disastrous winter campaign. What begins as a wide band on the left side of the chart, representing the French forces as they set out in seemingly irresistible strength from Paris, narrows by fits and starts as it moves toward Moscow on the right, paying graphic testimony to the dreadful toll of diversionary splits, battles, cold, hunger, disease, defections, and desertions. By the time the band has doubled back to its starting point, it has been reduced to a thin, shaky line. It's a useful metaphor for considering the fate of the moderate movement in Republican politics since 1960. A broad and apparently formidable group suffered progressive decimation until it consisted only of a handful of stunned survivors stumbling into the second decade of the twenty-first century. A period in which the moderates enjoyed significant advancements, from 1960 to 1970, was followed by years of miserable retreat. Historians have overestimated the impact of the conservative movement during the 1960s and 1970s, but from 1980 onward the trajectory of the Republican Party increasingly was determined by the right, not the center. The decline of the moderates owed something to structural factors that already were evident during their final period of efflorescence, but also to events and setbacks over the three decades after 1980 too numerous to describe in the space of a concluding chapter. Still, a brief recounting of the moderates' long recessional offers some insights into the Republican

Party's modern development and the increasingly polarized condition of American politics.

Ronald Reagan decisively defeated Jimmy Carter in the 1980 elections, winning 51 percent of the vote to Carter's 41 percent, with John Anderson accounting for 7 percent, or some seven million votes. The Republicans shocked most political analysts by gaining twelve seats in the Senate, taking control of that body for the first time since January 1955. The Democrats retained a 243–192 majority of the House, but Republicans were able to make common cause with many of the "Boll Weevil" conservative Southern Democrats, who were fully aware that white Southerners had voted for Reagan by wide margins.

Reagan's inaugural address revealed his skill at rousing conservatives while retaining moderates. The address is best known for his pronouncement that "government is not the solution to our problems; government is the problem." But Reagan quickly reassured the nation that he was no right-wing anarchist: "[I]t's not my intention to do away with government. It is rather to make it work—work with us, not over us; to stand by our side, not ride on our back. Government can and must provide opportunity, not smother it; foster productivity, not stifle it."[1] Throughout his presidency, Reagan would demonstrate his almost unique ability to stir the blood of the faithful while also mollifying moderates and framing conservativism in a way that made it appealing to a majority of Americans.

The Republican delegation in Congress enjoyed an unusual degree of cohesion during Reagan's first year in office, in large part because the White House decided to prioritize the economic issues that most moderates agreed with over the social issues they did not. Virtually all Republicans supported Reagan's tax reduction proposals, and the House Republican party unity score in 1981 was higher than in any year of the 1970s. Moderates moved toward rebellion, however, when Reagan cultivated Southern Democratic votes for his budgetary measures by cutting funding for programs—including Medicaid, mass transit, low-income heating fuel assistance, food stamps, guaranteed student loans, and vocational training—that disproportionately affected the Northeast and Midwest, while sparing large public works in the South and West. This Southern favoritism sparked an insurgency of about twenty moderate House Republicans from the Frostbelt, who organized a "Gypsy Moth" coalition to counter the Boll Weevils, both groups being named for agricultural pests distinct to their regions. The Moths for the most part presented themselves as a regional coalition voting to protect the interests of their districts rather than as a moderate ideological faction. They argued that leaning too far South would cost the support of the Northeast, and convinced the administration to restore $4 billion to the affected programs.[2]

Third-term Representative Jim Leach of Iowa attempted to turn the Gypsy Moth group into a moderate power bloc to compete with the conservative Republican Steering Committee, which by 1981 included a majority of House GOP members. A former Foreign Service officer who had resigned on principle to protest Nixon's "Saturday Night Massacre," Leach was a moderate in temperament as well as political outlook; David Broder described him as "characteristic of the breed in his combination of brains, good manners and innocuousness."[3] In September 1981, Leach became chairman of the Ripon Society, which was attempting to reinvent itself as a lobbying group. He used the occasion to issue "A Moderate Manifesto," which turned out to be the last substantive articulation of the moderate Republican position. Leach praised Reagan for giving the nation a new sense of direction, and emphasized that Republican moderates had more in common with Republican conservatives than with Democrats. He called for radical decentralization, a breakup of the federal bureaucracy, and significant cuts in federal employment and spending. But Leach differed from conservatives in favoring environmentalism, civil rights, and deficit reduction, and in opposing corporate subsidy, military bloat, and what he considered to be Reagan's excessively bellicose foreign policy.[4]

Leach's manifesto stirred mild media interest, but he failed in his goal of making the Gypsy Moths into a rallying point for moderate principles and programs. To the extent that the Moths enjoyed influence as a swing group during the early '80s, it was as contestants for regional pork-barrel funding. The 1982 midterm elections, coinciding with a severe recession and high unemployment, took a particular toll on the moderates. Of the twenty-six Republican incumbents who lost reelection, sixteen were from Frostbelt-districts. As the GOP increasingly became identified with Reagan's conservatism, moderate Republicans in those predominantly Democratic districts in the Northeast and Midwest came under increasing attack from the left, while continuing to contend with primary challenges from the right.[5] Even when prosperity returned after 1983 and continued for the remainder of the decade, those districts tended to remain under Democratic control.

The Gypsy Moths' limited ambitions represented another missed opportunity for moderation, because it was becoming evident that Reagan and the New Right were abandoning a central tenet of Republican belief: fiscal responsibility. Moderates, in that sense, remained more conservative than the conservatives. Representative Bill Gradison, an Ohio moderate who was a member of the House Budget Committee, remembered that "Democrats wanted to increase domestic spending more than Republicans; Republicans wanted to increase defense spending more than Democrats. So they came up with a compromise and they did both! And Ronald Reagan went along with it."[6] In real terms, defense spending increased by over one-third between 1981 and 1985, and totaled $2 trillion over Reagan's eight years in office.[7] The federal deficit tripled under Reagan, while the federal debt jumped from $900 billion to close to $3 trillion dollars. The United States went from being the world's largest creditor to the world's largest debtor. Interest payments on the national debt more than doubled, accompanying a sharp drop in national savings and severe neglect of the national infrastructure. The fiscal imbalance offered Republican moderates a chance to regain some of their lost influence and standing in the party.

Their failure to do so was epitomized by the travails of Representative William Frenzel, who had represented suburban Minneapolis since 1971. Frenzel was the Ripon Society's ideal member of Congress, with a 97 percent average in the Society's ratings during the 1970s. A Dartmouth graduate, Korean War veteran, and successful businessman, Frenzel fit the once-familiar profile of the socially moderate, fiscally conservative Republican. He arrived in Congress as an opponent of the Vietnam war and a reformer willing to tilt with old Democratic dragons of the status quo such as the tyrannical House Administration Committee chairman Wayne Hays, who was known to retaliate against his critics by depriving them of parking spaces and shutting off the air conditioning in their offices during the broiling Washington summers. Frenzel joined the House Wednesday Group and established himself as the point man in compromise agreements with his Democratic counterparts on the Ways and Means and Budget committees. But he was also an ardent fiscal conservative, who was described as "the only real free-trader in Congress."[8]

Frenzel typically found himself in political no-man's land, strafed by all sides. Liberals objected to his tight-fisted approach to social spending, his skepticism towards welfare, and his unwillingness to bail out unsound financial entities such as New York City circa 1975 and the Chrysler Corporation circa 1979. Labor and consumer interest groups awarded him failing grades year after year. At the same time, his moderately pro-choice position earned him the enmity of evangelical Christian groups. His opposition to agricultural subsidies and import quotas on textiles was anathema to Southerners like Jesse Helms and Strom Thurmond, while his criticism of cheap, federally subsidized electric power put him on the opposite side of Westerners like Dick Cheney.[9] His votes against bloated defense appropriations annoyed conservatives who considered it unpatriotic to apply economic rationality to military spending. Frenzel did not share the New Right's fetishization of tax-cutting. Realism compelled him to admit that some level of government spending was necessary and would have to be paid for. But he was impolite enough to observe that some of the most avid tax-cutting conservatives outdid even liberal Democrats as earmarkers and free-spenders, and curmudgeonly enough to dwell on the deficits that supply-siders dismissed as irrelevant.

Ultimately, Frenzel was punished for refusing to go along with his colleagues' appropriations requests, and his fiscal conservatism likely cost him a significant leadership role in the House. He took a resigned view of the devolution of Republican conservatives into big spenders, knowing that they worried about reelection just like the Democrats. And, he observed, "Once you become an appropriator, you get used to spreading the goodies around. You've been in Santa's workshop for a long time, and you know how to send out the electric trains and the sleds and the dolls. And you learn how to go along to get along." The back-scratching struck him as one of the worst aspects of Congress, and he regretted that "If you're a moderate Republican, you get the worst of both worlds, because you get punished both for being socially liberal and for being fiscally conservative. You're doubly handicapped."[10]

Moderate Republicans continued to play a pivotal role in achieving bipartisan compromises, as with the 1983 reform of Social Security, which became unavoidable when the program essentially ran out of money and had to borrow funds from the Heath Insurance Trust Fund. Bill Gradison was a member of the House subcommittee chaired by Democrat Jake Pickle that recommended measures to put Social Security on a sounder financial basis. Republicans acceded to increased payroll taxes, while Democrats went along with reducing the annual cost-of-living adjustments and raising the age at which seniors could receive full benefits from 65 to 67. Reagan then appointed a bipartisan commission chaired by Alan Greenspan that essentially followed the recommendations of Pickle's subcommittee, and Congress voted the reforms into law.[11] Gradison felt that the episode was "a very good example of where moderates had an impact." He emphasized, however, that moderate Republicans and Democrats were able to take the lead mainly because of the pressing need to rescue Social Security from insolvency.[12] Members of both parties increasingly would find it impossible to compromise unless they were confronted with imminent crisis and catastrophe.

The *Congressional Quarterly* determined that by 1984, the ranks of Republican moderates and progressives had been drastically thinned. The House Republicans who scored less than 81 percent in the journal's annual Conservative Coalition scores shrank from half of the delegation in 1982 to one-third in 1984; only one Senator, Lowell Weicker, had a voting record that CQ judged to be progressive.[13] As moderates exerted less impact in Congress and the GOP, the increasingly conservative Republican leadership became—for a time—generally more tolerant of them. "There's still a place for the moderates, liberals and progressives," House Republican Policy Committee chairman Dick Cheney said in 1984. "I don't want to drum anybody out of the party. One of the Democrats' greatest strengths is their ability to encompass a broad range of views within the party. We can't become the majority party by trying to read people out."[14] Toleration for moderates did not extend to actual respect for their views. The conservatives who wrote the platform at the 1984 GOP national convention slapped down the Republican Mainstream Committee, which moderates formed to lobby for women's and civil rights, arms control, and environmental policies.[15] Nonetheless, moderates stuck with Reagan rather than embrace the Democratic nominee, Walter Mondale, who seemed to embody that party's continuing subservience to interest groups and big-government liberalism.

Reagan's landslide win in the 1984 elections, in which he carried 49 states and 525 electoral votes, paradoxically gave rise to some serious problems for the Republicans. Reagan's managers ran an idea-free campaign, based on the President's sunny personality and the fuzzy theme of "Morning in America," while burying conservative proposals such as privatizing Medicare, restricting abortion, and abolishing the departments of Energy and Education. These proposals likely would have proven divisive and unpopular, but a public debate over them might have strengthened the moderate position within the GOP. Reagan's electoral triumph, like Nixon's in 1972, was a personal rather than a party victory, as Republicans lost two Senate seats and gained only a few seats in the House. Mondale's wipeout proved to be beneficial for Democrats in the long run, since it stimulated moderate Democrats' efforts to reposition their party in the mainstream of public opinion, demonstrate that it shared broadly held American values, and restore its competitiveness in the South. In 1985, a group of Democratic moderates—made up largely of "Blue Dog" Southern conservative Democrats and the fiscally conservative but socially liberal "New Democrats" who represented suburban districts—formed the Democratic Leadership Council, which became an effective generator of new political ideas. Many "third way" proposals that had once been debated in moderate Republican circles—welfare reform, charter schools, community policing, ombudsmen—now acquired a Democratic coloration.[16] Moderates gravitated toward this exciting new centrist program, and the DLC became the power base for Arkansas Governor Bill Clinton.

At the same time that Republican moderates were drawn towards the DLC, many were repelled by the growing influence of the religious right within the GOP. In Minnesota, conservative Christian evangelicals seized the Republican Party machinery in Representative Bill Frenzel's district and trounced his allies on the state central committee. "The evangelicals had these powerful telephone trees," Frenzel remembered, "where one church member would be given ten names to call, and they in turn would call ten other church members."[17] His political director was impressed by the conservatives' rigid discipline at the district GOP election. The evangelicals delegated a young man in a straw boater hat to stand in the aisles, she recalled, and "When he had his hat on, everybody would vote yes, when he took his hat off, everybody would vote no. It was an amazing thing to watch. The votes went exactly the way his hat went. We had less than 100 votes out of more than 300. They were in total control."[18] Frenzel conceded that "We just got out-organized, outsmarted, and out-worked by those people." While conservative forces in the GOP benefited from the grassroots strength of the religious right, however, the party lost the support of moderates and independents who did not share the evangelicals' doctrinaire view of abortion, homosexuality, school prayer, the threat of "secular humanism," and a host of other moral issues. As Frenzel put it, the takeover by the religious right deprived the party of "potential Republican voters who would vote in a primary but who wouldn't come to a caucus and sit through hours of talk about killing babies."[19]

The GOP's embrace of polarizing figures like Rev. Jerry Falwell, with his blasphemous certainties about God's intentions with regard to U.S. foreign and domestic policies, also led some moderates to switch parties. John Yarmuth had been a rising star in Louisville, Kentucky's moderate-dominated Republican organization. He succeeded Mitch McConnell as legislative assistant to Senator Marlow Cook, and ran on the Republican ticket headed by McConnell in the 1981 Jefferson County elections. He was described by one of McConnell's operatives as "a good, progressive, pro-choice Republican."[20] But Yarmuth was angered by the rising influence of the religious right in the GOP and upset by McConnell's opportunistic shift toward conservatism. Republican leaders' failure to repudiate Falwell in 1985, when he defended the apartheid system of South Africa's racist white government, proved to be "the final straw" for Yarmuth.[21] He won election to Congress as a Democrat in 2006, and was reelected to a third term in 2010.

In the wake of the 1986 Iran-Contra scandal, which revealed that the administration had sold arms to Iran in order to fund the Nicaraguan Contras in their guerrilla war against the socialist Sandinista government, Reagan's popularity sagged and the Republicans lost six Senate seats and control of the upper house. During his last two years in office, Reagan focused much of his energies on negotiating an end to the Cold War in partnership with Soviet leader Mikhail Gorbachev. Many hard-line conservatives were outraged at Reagan's success in lessening tensions between the superpowers and reaching significant arms limitations agreements with the Soviets, but Reagan was never seriously threatened by conservative disaffection. As Nixon had demonstrated with his opening to China, a leader with a right-wing reputation had sufficient cover to achieve what liberals could not.

As Reagan's departure from office neared, the struggle to succeed him intensified. The leading candidate was George H. W. Bush, who had Reagan's endorsement. Moderates were wary of the Vice President for having repudiated his earlier support for gun and birth control, but many still considered him one of their own. "He can't really dissociate himself from his Connecticut heritage," Vermont Senator Robert Stafford thought. "A lot of the Eastern moderates will believe that essentially. He's been born and bred to be at least a moderate kind of guy."[22] By the same token, conservatives did not consider Bush to be a true heir to Reagan no matter how often he proclaimed his undying loyalty to every feature of right-wing dogma. In the 1988 Iowa presidential caucus, Bush shockingly came in third behind television evangelist Pat Robertson and the winner, Kansas Senator Bob Dole. Bush recovered to beat Dole by nine points in the New Hampshire primary, but Robertson's well-organized legions of Christian Right activists appeared poised to deliver victory to the televangelist in South Carolina.

Bush was rescued by the unlikely figure of Pete McCloskey, the former progressive Congressman who had left politics in 1982 after running for the Senate in California and losing in the primary. A Bush supporter, McCloskey became suspicious when he noticed that Robertson had described himself in his autobiography as a "Marine combat officer in Korea." As a highly decorated Marine veteran of that war, McCloskey knew that "Marines who have been in combat do not commonly refer to themselves as 'combat' veterans. The word is too respected, if not revered, in the Corps to permit its acceptable use by way of self-characterization. . . . It just wasn't done." After some investigation, McCloskey and Congressman Andrew Jacobs of Indiana told the press that Robertson had asked his father, Virginia Senator A. Willis Robertson, to keep him out of combat and had been a "liquor officer" rather than a combatant in Korea. Robertson denied everything and filed a $35 million lawsuit against the two former Marines, which led to court testimony that supported McCloskey's charges and proved highly embarrassing to Robertson. A week before the South Carolina primary, Robertson asked to dismiss the suit, thereby conceding the truth of the charges.[23] He dropped from an expected first-place finish to third in South Carolina and scored poorly in other Southern races, which effectively ended his campaign. McCloskey wryly observed that "A lot of people still say, 'That's the only good thing you did in politics, McCloskey, taking Robertson out of the presidency.'"[24]

Bush disappointed moderates with his decision to make the young, lightweight, and gaffe-prone J. Danforth Quayle, a conservative second-term senator from Indiana, his vice-presidential running mate, and to reassure the right by pledging, "Read my lips: no new taxes." Moderates also generally disapproved of the nasty campaign masterminded by Lee Atwater that cast Bush's centrist Democratic opponent, former Massachusetts governor Michael Dukakis, as a raving liberal. Atwater, who had cut his political teeth with the Young Republicans and as a strategist for Strom Thurmond, updated and institutionalized a populist, Southern strategy for the GOP. The central motif of the campaign was William J. Horton Jr., an African-American convict serving a life sentence for murder who had committed rape and assault while on an unsupervised weekend furlough from a Massachusetts prison during Dukakis' governorship. The fact that the furlough program had been initiated by Dukakis' Republican predecessor was irrelevant to Atwater; the point was to use "Willie" Horton's menacing mug shot to play upon white fear of black crime, and pin the responsibility for social disorder on permissive liberal elites. The episode effectively Southernized the Republican stance on race relations, much to the moderates' dismay. Bush also called his Democratic opponent a "card-carrying member of the ACLU," McCarthyite rhetoric that demonized the cause of civil liberties that moderates held dear. Bush defeated Dukakis by seven percentage points in the 1988 election, but the ugly campaign further alienated moderates from the GOP.

Oddly enough, one of the last occasions when moderates were able to have a decisive impact on the internal politics of the Republican Party came when they helped elect Representative Newt Gingrich of Georgia as House Republican whip in 1989. Although Gingrich would lead what was considered to be a conservative "revolution," he himself was anything but a conventional conservative. In fact, when he became involved with politics in the late 1960s, as a Ph.D. student in history at Tulane University, he was a moderate or even progressive Republican with connections to the Ripon Society. At the 1968 Republican national convention, Gingrich was one of New York Governor Nelson Rockefeller's strongest Southern supporters. After becoming a history professor at West Georgia State University, he narrowly missed election to Congress in 1974 and 1976, running as a moderate against a segregationist Democrat. Most of Gingrich's biographers have assumed that he gained election to Congress in 1978 by abandoning his former positions and converting to Southern-fried conservatism, but there's considerable evidence that Gingrich himself did not share that view. As he told an interviewer in 1989, his goal was to build the GOP as "a caring, humanitarian reform party." He believed that "one of the gravest mistakes the Reagan administration made was its failure to lead aggressively in civil rights." He identified with "the classic moderate wing of the party, where, as a former Rockefeller state chairman, I've spent most of my life."[25]

Gingrich also spent a good deal of time with the conservative wing of the GOP, of course, helping to found the Conservative Opportunity Society (COS) in the House and mobilizing the shock troops of the Moral Majority. But he consistently proclaimed himself a "big tent" Republican who served as a bridge between conservatives in the COS and moderates in the counterpart 92 Group and the so-called Tuesday Lunch Bunch. His view of himself as a "Theodore Roosevelt Republican" described his preference for progressive, pragmatic reform and a more active role for government than many of his erstwhile right-wing allies were willing to contemplate. His enthusiasm for greater government involvement in technological innovation and space exploration, including much higher spending on NASA as well as the "Star Wars" antimissile program, earned him the nickname "Newt Skywalker." Gingrich's idea-driven, eclectic, heterodox conservatism was attractive to many moderates, as were many of the specific programs he advocated such as tax cuts, welfare reform, spending reductions, decentralization, urban renewal, and improved government accountability.

Stylistically, Gingrich's scorched-earth attacks on Democrats, and on Congress as an institution, stunned moderates and some conservatives too, as when he succeeded in ousting House Speaker Jim Wright on ethics charges in 1989. However, the House Democrats' worsening abuse of their majority power—in matters including denying adequate staff to the minority party, excluding Republicans from committee deliberations, and even what Republicans considered to be stealing elections—convinced many moderates that Gingrich's strategy of no-holds-barred confrontation was the only way to overturn an entrenched and corrupt Democratic majority. Gingrich alone had "the vision to build a majority party," according to Connecticut moderate Congresswoman Nancy Johnson, as well as "the strength and charisma to do it."[26] Minnesota moderate Bill Frenzel nominated Gingrich for House Republican whip in 1989, and Maine's Olympia Snowe seconded the nomination.[27] Moderates supported Gingrich over the more conciliatory candidate of the older conservatives, Illinois' Ed Madigan, and Gingrich carried the New England delegation by a 7–3 vote. "There's no question that I would not be House Republican whip if activists in the moderate wing had not supported me," Gingrich said afterwards. "I regard my election as a coalition victory for activists of all the ideological views of the Republican Party."[28]

George H. W. Bush was not comfortable with the right wing of his party or the Reaganite ideology. He called for a "kinder, gentler America," which was widely interpreted to mean a less hard-edged and grasping America, and a more moderate and bipartisan politics. Bush talked about AIDS (as Reagan never had), expressed sympathy for the homeless, and aspired to be known as the education president. He secured passage of an updated and expanded version of the Clean Air Act, defied the National Rifle Association by supporting a ban on AK-47 assault rifles, and supported the 1990 Americans with Disabilities Act. Conservatives accused him of conducting a purge of the Reagan staff and refusing to appoint anyone from the Goldwater-Nixon-Reagan wing of the party. Many of Bush's appointments were decidedly moderate, including James Baker as secretary of state and Colin Powell as the first African-American chairman of the Joint Chiefs of Staff. Many on the right were particularly enraged by Bush's appointment of Richard Darman as director of the Office of Management and Budget. They viewed Darman, a moderate protégé of Baker and Elliot Richardson, as an unprincipled cynic. "If the cavalry is winning, he's for Custer," one former colleague said of Darman. "And if the Indians are winning, he's for Sitting Bull."[29]

Darman became Bush's chief economic advisor, and in ever more forceful terms alerted the President to the need for a tax increase to combat the growing deficit, address the collapse of the savings and loan industry that had occurred on his predecessor's watch, and meet the spending reduction requirements of the Gramm-Rudman-Hollings Act that Reagan had signed into law in 1981. After a year of resistance, Bush agreed to go along with a tax increase in 1990 as part of a $492 billion deficit-reduction package put together by the Democratic-controlled Congress. Bush acceded to an increase in the top marginal tax rate, from 28 to 31 percent, in exchange for a package of spending cuts. Darman argued that as a share of GDP, the 1990 tax increases were less than half of those Reagan had accepted in 1982, and that Reagan had in any case raised taxes eleven times during his presidency.[30] But Bush lacked Reagan's ability to convince the right that he was really a tax-cutter at heart, no matter what increases Reagan signed off on. Conservatives gnashed their teeth over what they perceived as Bush's betrayal of his sacred lip-reading oath, and predicted that the budget deal would wreck the economy and fail to cut the deficit. Both predictions proved faulty, as federal spending fell from 22 percent of the GDP to 18 percent across the remainder of the decade, while revenues rose to bring the budget into surplus for the first time since the 1960s. Bruce Bartlett, who participated in the negotiations as a Republican economics adviser, further observed that the 1990 budget talks took place against the backdrop of Iraq's invasion of Kuwait, and speculated that "a key reason why Bush supported the budget negotiations is because he knew we were almost certainly going to war shortly and believed that it ought to be paid for."[31]

Bush's skillful diplomacy in leading an international coalition to victory in the Persian Gulf in 1991, as well as in assisting the peaceful dissolution of the Soviet Union in the same year, raised his poll ratings to astronomical heights and seemingly made his apostasy on tax-cutting irrelevant. But Bush's popularity leaked away as Americans confronted a brief but painful economic recession and the polarizing events of 1991–92, including the sexual harassment controversy that dominated hearings for Bush's Supreme Court nominee Clarence Thomas, the Los Angeles riots, and the ongoing "culture wars" over issues including political correctness in the universities and the National Endowment for the Arts' support for obscene and sacrilegious art. Within the GOP, neoconservative thinkers criticized Bush for ending the Gulf War too soon, leaving Saddam Hussein in control of Iraq and much of his elite Republican Guard intact, while America-First paleo-conservatives protested Bush's talk of a "New World Order." Patrick Buchanan, the former Nixon speechwriter turned paleocon journalist and TV talking head, challenged Bush's moderate policies and nearly pulled off an upset in the 1992 New Hampshire primary, running on a position of social conservatism, immigration reduction, and economic nationalism.

Buchanan's showing in New Hampshire highlighted Bush's weakness with conservatives, and forced the President to try to win them back by giving the right the leading role at the Republican national convention in Houston. Although strategist Lee Atwater, before he died of a brain tumor in 1991, had called for the GOP to be a "big tent" on the subject of abortion, pro-lifers dominated the party platform committees and gave no quarter to pro-choice Republicans. A pro-choice member of the California Young Republicans told a reporter at the convention that "People of sensibility tend to understand that other people would have different points of view. . . . It's not hard for me to understand how someone who is pro-life could be that way."[32] No such consideration was forthcoming from the right, who crushed their opponents unmercifully. Buchanan spoke on the first night of the convention and declared a religious and cultural war against Democrats, feminists, and homosexuals. The convention was a public relations disaster, as most voters had little interest in the religious right's jihad or the message of spokesmen like Buchanan that their opponents were not real Americans.

In the 1992 elections, Bush faced Democratic opponent Bill Clinton, whose "third way" proposals were more attractive to many moderate Republicans than the hard right platform of their own party. Third-party candidate Ross Perot also leached votes away from the Republicans with his populist appeal against out-of-touch, big-spending government, despite the political sacrifices Bush had made to reduce the deficit. Clinton won with a plurality of 43 percent of the popular vote, against Bush's 37 percent and almost 19 percent for Perot. Bush lost principally because he seemed unresponsive to public anger over the economic slowdown and because his campaign veered too far to the right for the liking of an overall moderate electorate. The lesson that most Republicans drew from the election, however, was that Bush had committed political suicide by raising taxes in 1990 and alienating the conservatives who arguably comprised the party's base. Bush's defeat ensured that across the next two decades, Republicans would make no serious effort to reduce the deficit.

Clinton's policies were popular with most Americans. When he left office, he enjoyed an approval rating of over 60 percent despite the scandals that plagued his second term. The 1990s witnessed significant although unevenly shared prosperity. Clinton balanced the budget for the first time in nearly three decades, while increasing spending on liberal priorities such as education and health care. He made possible the conservative goal of ending federal welfare for the poor, but at the same time presided over the largest reductions in poverty that had been achieved since the 1960s. He never did quite manage to bring into being the "third way" politics that he had promised, synthesizing the best of liberalism and conservatism. But through policies such as welfare reform, he advanced liberal goals—like expanding opportunity and rewarding work—through conservative means, such as encouraging fiscal discipline and personal responsibility. Crime rates dropped throughout his presidency, drug use declined, and even teen pregnancies decreased, all of which might have been expected to have mollified conservatives. Instead, both Clinton and his wife, Hillary Rodham Clinton, proved to be intensely polarizing figures, and the culture wars that had already begun under his predecessor intensified during Clinton's first term. Political polarization resulted not only from Clinton's well-publicized ethical and moral lapses but also from the luxuriant growth of the conservative infrastructure throughout the 1990s, including the rise of conservative talk radio hosts like Rush Limbaugh.

Polarization also became enshrined as the strategy of the Republican Party thanks to Newt Gingrich and the conservatives who swept to victory in the House GOP leadership elections at the end of 1992. Robert Michel won reelection as House Republican leader, which left him as the only remaining moderate in the leadership, but his retirement was imminent. Gingrich retained his number-two position as whip. Richard Armey defeated California moderate Jerry Lewis to become head of the House Republican Conference, while Armey's fellow Texan conservative Tom DeLay became secretary of the Conference. In practical terms, this meant that Southern conservatives for the first time controlled the Committee on Committees, which allowed them to enforce party discipline by determining committee assignments and the ranking order of Republicans within those committees. They would use this power to demand fealty to their breed of conservatism. "In the past," the newly elected DeLay announced, "we fell into the same trap as the Democrats, accommodating ourselves to every viewpoint in the party. But we are not the Democratic Party and don't have to reflect every view . . . and we won't, from now on."[33] Bill Gradison, who lost to DeLay and had lost a previous election to Mississippi's Trent Lott, pinpointed the moderates' reluctance at fundraising as the cause of their downfall. "I wasn't very good at fundraising for myself," he admitted, let alone raising money for other candidates as Republican leaders were now expected to do. "I was always uneasy about PAC money, for example, and Trent and Tom had no such inhibitions."[34] The conservatives' victory was a defeat for "good government" forces, particularly after the Republicans became the majority party in Congress.

Gingrich led Republicans to victory in the 1994 elections, and the party regained control of both houses of Congress for the first time since January 1955. Gingrich succeeded in nationalizing the election, making each local contest a referendum on Bill Clinton and the perceived leftish Democratic excesses of his first two years in office, particularly his 1993 tax increase, anti-gun legislation, and the cumbersome health care proposal advanced under the direction of Hillary Clinton. However, Gingrich was careful to keep divisive social issues out of the Republican campaign platform, the "Contract with America," and aimed its provisions at the angry independents who had supported Ross Perot two years earlier. Gingrich also supplied money, guidance, and logistical assistance to moderate and conservative candidates alike, in all regions of the country. Despite later claims, the "Contract" did not much influence the election; 71 percent of voters polled during election week had never even heard of it.[35] But it was a clever move on Gingrich's part, because it symbolized the public's desire for action-oriented, accountable government, allowed him to keep Republican candidates on-message, and would give him an unusual degree of discipline over his party (at least for a while) when he became Speaker of the House.

The 1994 election is most notable for marking the Republican breakthrough in the South. While Southern states had already been voting for Republican presidential candidates, this was the first election since Reconstruction in which Democrats lost their Southern majority. The South would become the nation's most reliably Republican region, and its distinctive form of conservatism increasingly would dominate the GOP. The new Southern complexion of the Republican Party was reflected in the House GOP leadership after the 1994 elections, with Gingrich becoming Speaker, Armey majority leader, and DeLay majority whip. Lott's election as Senate majority leader two years later would provide further confirmation of this trend.

The "freshman class" of seventy-three Republican representatives who swept into office included a core of deep-dyed conservatives, many of whom would go on to have long political careers, including later senators Sam Brownback, Tom Coburn, and John Ensign, along with future South Carolina governor Mark Sanford. "You won't believe what a bunch of ideologues you are going to have to deal with," Gingrich's advisor told him on the '94 election night. "They are going to kill you."[36] That prediction would prove substantially correct, as the two dozen or so "True Believers" in the freshman class harassed Gingrich constantly on his right flank, pressured him into some of his worst errors, and eventually led to his undoing as Speaker. But the Class of '94 also included more than a dozen moderates, and the GOP still held almost half of the House seats in the Northeast; moderates provided the margins that had allowed the Republicans to retake control.

Although Republican moderates had given Gingrich their enthusiastic support in his drive to make the GOP the majority party, they quickly discovered that there are few things in life more dangerous than getting what you wish for. New York moderate Representative Amory "Amo" Houghton Jr. remembered that when he was first elected to Congress in 1986, "There was something about being in the minority that tended to pull us Republicans together. Conservatives and moderates used to talk to each other a lot, and we got along wonderfully well."[37] After the 1994 victories, GOP Congressional leaders implemented a series of measures to institutionalize partisan warfare, punish wayward moderates within the Republican ranks, and turn the party into a sort of mechanism for delivering big-government benefits to its conservative base and backers. Gingrich's abolition of seniority rules deprived moderates of the committee chairmanships and assignments to which they previously would have been entitled. Moderate hopes that Republican rule would restore good government were dashed immediately after the elections when DeLay and conservative activists like Grover Norquist instituted the K Street Project, which essentially allowed business lobbies to write legislation to their liking but required that they stop giving money to Democrats and even purge their Democratic employees.[38]

Gingrich and the conservative leadership quickly succumbed to ideological overreach, particularly in 1995 when Gingrich tried to get Clinton to sign a budget that included a trillion dollars in spending cuts and would have eliminated close to three hundred programs, including the Departments of Energy, Education, and Commerce. When Clinton refused, the GOP leadership forced two government shutdowns, the second of which lasted three weeks. The American public, which did not share the conservative hatred of government, turned against Gingrich and his allies, effectively ending his "revolution" before it was a year old. But the conservatives had succeeded in shattering bipartisanship and cooperation in Congress, to the extent that unprecedented numbers of moderates retired before the

1996 elections. In the eyes of many moderates, the new crop of young, ideologically driven Republicans lacked civility and respect for Congress as an institution. One retiring Republican described them as "rogue elephants . . . who don't listen to their fellow members or understand them." Mark Hatfield announced his decision to leave Congress not long after Rick Santorum, a religious rightist from Pennsylvania and the youngest member of the Senate, attempted to oust him from the chairmanship of the Appropriations Committee. Conservatives did succeed in forcing out moderate Wyoming Senator Alan Simpson as deputy leader of the Senate; Simpson announced his retirement with a blast against the "bug-eyed zealots" in his party.[39]

Clinton responded to the conservative upsurge with a strategy of "triangulation," which amounted to trying to steal the GOP's thunder by adapting some Republican ideas, including welfare reform, tax cuts for the middle class, and balanced budgets. Triangulation found concrete expression in Clinton's statement in his 1996 State of the Union message that "The era of big government is over," and passage of the Personal Responsibility and Work Opportunity Reconciliation Act of 1996, which ended the Aid to Families with Dependent Children welfare program. Although liberals denounced AFDC's termination as heartless, the Earned Income Tax Credit, adapted from Nixon-era moderate Republican proposals for a negative income tax, mitigated its effect on the working poor. Clinton's willingness to defy his critics on the Democratic left, combined with the booming economy, increased his appeal to moderate voters.

There was one potential Republican candidate who might have defeated Clinton in the 1996 election: retired general Colin Powell, the former chairman of the Joint Chiefs of Staff. As a longtime moderate Republican and hero of the Gulf War, Powell had Eisenhower-like popular appeal. His nomination as the first African-American presidential candidate would have made history, radically altered the GOP's standing with minorities, and restored moderates to prominence within the party. Unfortunately for the moderates, Powell didn't want to be President. "I'm going into political seclusion to try and end the speculation," Powell wrote to Amo Houghton, "which continues notwithstanding my one-syllable, two-letter answer."[40]

Instead, Clinton faced Republican presidential nominee Robert Dole, the Senate majority leader. Dole, a Gerald Ford-style Midwestern stalwart, had been forced to tack right to secure the GOP nomination, particularly after paleocon Patrick Buchanan surprised even himself by winning the New Hampshire primary. Most of the public doubted the feasibility of Dole's proposal to balance the budget while cutting tax rates by 15 percent across the board. Dole's vice-presidential nominee, supply-side crusader

Jack Kemp, turned out to be a lackluster campaigner. Clinton handily won a second term, becoming the first Democratic president to do so since Franklin D. Roosevelt, while Republicans retained Congress for a successive election for the first time since 1928. The continuing trend toward regional polarization was confirmed by Dole's failure to carry a single Congressional district in New England and New York, although he did well in the South and Rocky Mountain states.

Clinton interpreted his reelection as a vindication of "New Democrat" moderation, and evidence that "the vital center is alive and well," as he said on election night. Privately, Gingrich drew much the same conclusion. The Speaker had been chastened by the failed budget showdown and weakened by an ethics investigation. A coup attempt mounted against him by more conservative members of the House Republican leadership, including DeLay and Armey, increased his distrust of the right wing and made him more willing to seek bipartisan compromise. In August 1997, Gingrich made what he called "a conscious decision . . . to prove that we could govern," and gave his blessing to a balanced budget bill crafted mostly by moderate Republicans and conservative Democrats. The bill provided for a balanced budget and the largest tax cut since Reagan's 1981 measure, along with increased spending on education and children's health. Gingrich subsequently entered secret talks with Clinton to find common ground on reform of the Social Security and Medicare programs, whose financial stability was threatened by the aging of the baby boomers. The two leaders inched toward a tentative compromise in which Republicans would agree to use the budget surplus to strengthen the programs rather than diverting it into tax cuts, while Democrats would accept the incorporation of privately managed accounts into Social Security. As Gingrich described his negotiations with Clinton to historian Steven Gillon, "We were trying to think through the necessary reforms to modernize America to move into the twenty-first century."[41] The deal would have required Gingrich to do battle with his party's conservatives and form a coalition based around moderates of both parties, which in all likelihood would have changed the political landscape.

This potentially historic realignment was derailed by the revelation of Clinton's sexual encounters with White House intern Monica Lewinsky. Clinton was forced back into the embrace of his strongest defenders on the Democratic Party's left, and Gingrich had to go along with the GOP conservatives who were calling for the President to resign or be impeached. Although polls showed that the majority of Americans wanted Clinton to be censured rather than removed from office, Republicans pushed ahead with the sordid and embarrassing impeachment proceedings nonetheless. While the GOP had the numbers to pass articles of impeachment in the

House, where a simple majority was needed, Senate rules required a two-thirds majority. But the Republican leadership showed no interest in reaching across the aisle to secure the votes of the dozen Democrats they would need in the Senate, which ultimately made the impeachment proceedings an empty exercise in symbolism.

Further, the GOP was not even assured of all the votes of the remaining two dozen or so moderate Republicans in the House. "Godammit, that whole impeachment thing was wrong," moderate Representative Amo Houghton fumed. "It was obvious that it wasn't going to go anyplace. The Senate wasn't going to approve it, the public didn't want it, and it was bound to reflect badly on the Republican Party, so why waste everyone's time?"[42] In late 1998, Houghton was one of five House Republicans to break party ranks in the critical first vote of impeachment charging Clinton with lying to a federal grand jury.[43] DeLay kept most of the other moderates in line by stirring up Christian rightists in their districts and threatening them with primary opposition in the 2000 elections.[44] The Senate eventually acquitted Clinton on both charges of impeachment that passed the House. Public anger against conservative hubris was manifest in the 1998 elections, in which the Democrats gained five seats in the House, narrowing the GOP majority to 221–211. Reporters dug up the fact that this was the first time that a president's party had added seats in his sixth year in office since 1822. The election results tipped the balance of Republican support against Gingrich, and he stepped down as Speaker.[45]

Houghton was a former chairman of Corning Glass Works and the only member of the House during his time in office who had been a CEO. When he first joined Congress, he complained of being "buffeted around by a lot of lawyers who'd rather argue & gesture than act."[46] Houghton noticed that fundraising pressures and the growing convenience of jet travel were leading more members of Congress to leave their families back in their districts and spend only three days a week in Washington. The result was fewer cross-party friendships, accordingly less bipartisanship, and more distrust of the moderates who inclined toward compromise. Distressed by these developments, Houghton instituted a yearly bipartisan retreat, at which members could get to know each other as human beings. The retreats restored a measure of civility to Congress's proceedings until the impeachment crisis brought back partisanship with a vengeance.[47] Houghton also founded an organization to promote contact between Republican lawmakers and corporate executives, in the hope that this might persuade the former to adopt more of the latter's pragmatic worldview. Houghton initially called it the Reasonable Group, and then, after other colleagues grumbled that nothing succeeded on Capitol Hill unless it was extreme, renamed it the Extremely Reasonable Group.[48] Eventually it became a bipartisan organization under the more respectable moniker of the John Quincy Adams Society. The Adams Society gave birth to a moderate fundraising organization, the Main Street Coalition (later renamed the Republican Main Street Partnership), which Houghton envisaged as a counterweight to the Christian right and a GOP counterpart to the Democratic Leadership Coalition.[49]

The Main Streeters' favored candidate in the 2000 presidential election was Arizona Senator John McCain, a former Navy pilot who spent five-and-a-half years as a prisoner of war in North Vietnam. McCain, who succeeded Barry Goldwater in the Senate, was not really a moderate but rather a conservative with a maverick reputation who dared to cross the Republican leadership on select issues including campaign finance reform. By this point, however, strongly libertarian conservatives like Goldwater and McCain were practical allies of moderates in their struggles against the religious right; Goldwater had famously declared that "Every good Christian ought to kick [Moral Majority leader Jerry] Falwell right in the ass."[50]

Opposing McCain in the primaries was Texas Governor George W. Bush, the eldest son of the former president, who was the consensus choice of grassroots conservatives as well as the GOP establishment and had amassed a seemingly bottomless campaign chest. McCain routed Bush in New Hampshire, buoyed by a huge independent turnout. In the South Carolina primary, however, conservatives bombarded McCain with a barrage of foul tactics that harkened back to the dirty warfare within the Young Republican National Federation in the early 1960s—unsurprisingly so since Bush's campaign manager, Karl Rove, got his start in politics doing black ops with the YRs and College Republicans.[51] False charges that McCain wanted to remove the anti-abortion plank from the Republican platform appeared in South Carolinians' mailboxes, and anonymous callers insinuated that McCain had fathered an illegitimate black child (when in fact he and his wife had adopted an East Asian girl). Bush swung far to the right by speaking at fundamentalist Bob Jones University, which banned interracial dating, and siding with conservatives who wanted to keep the Confederate flag flying over the state capitol, where it had first appeared during the Massive Resistance against integration during the 1950s. McCain was disgusted by the performance of Bush and his operatives— "They know no depths, do they?" he groaned in front of reporters—but the right-wing mud bath was quite effective.[52] McCain lost badly in South Carolina and never regained momentum.

Bush nonetheless was able to convince a number of moderates that he had at least some of their interests at heart. As Texas governor, he had been conservative on issues like tax cuts and capital punishment, executing a record 152 prisoners on death row and granting clemency in only a single case. Still, he had shown an ability to work harmoniously with Democratic state legislators, an affinity for issues that moderates cared about (such as education), and considerable success in attracting Hispanic and African-American voters. Bush sought to combine traditional principles of individual responsibility, free enterprise, low taxes, and resistance to government spending with an acceptance of the important role that government had come to play in American life. The doctrine of "compassionate conservatism" that Bush proclaimed had grown up more or less independently from the moderate movement, but shared some of the same emphases on the need for Republicans to confront issues of racism and poverty, which suggested a degree of convergence between moderate and conservative ideas.[53] As the GOP presidential nominee, Bush ran as "a uniter, not a divider," a results-oriented reformer, and an environmentalist who pledged to regulate carbon dioxide emissions and other greenhouse gases that caused global warming. In his debates with the Democratic nominee, Vice President Al Gore, Bush vowed to conduct a "humble," non-interventionist foreign policy. And after the conflict and scandal of the Clinton years, many moderates looked back nostalgically to the presidency of Bush's father.

Bush won a narrow and contested election and the Republicans retained control of Congress, giving the party control of both executive and legislative branches for the first time in forty-five years. The election hardly offered a mandate for conservatism, and even Bush's legitimacy was in question. Bush had lost the popular vote, and Republicans shed five incumbent Senators to throw the upper chamber into a 50–50 balance, although since ties would be decided by the new Vice President, Dick Cheney, Republicans retained the majority.

The small group of moderate senators in the Wednesday Club saw the election results as an indication that Bush would have to govern from the center. The Club once had consisted of nearly two dozen senators at its height, but now was reduced to five members: Arlen Specter of Pennsylvania, James Jeffords of Vermont, Susan Collins and Olympia Snowe of Maine, and Lincoln Chafee of Rhode Island. Since his appointment to the Senate to fill the vacancy left by the death of his father in 1999, Chafee had dreaded the moderate meetings, he recalled, "because we never seemed to get past complaining about the insignificant role the Republican caucus allowed us to play in shaping legislation." In an evenly divided Senate, however, he anticipated that the moderate group would play a pivotal role in passing the unifying program Bush had spoken of on the campaign trail. Cheney dashed Chafee's optimism when he met with the moderates shortly after the election. The Vice President-elect laid out what Chafee called "a shockingly divisive political agenda for the new Bush administration." It included renouncing international agreements such as the Anti-Ballistic Missile Treaty and the United Nations' Kyoto Protocols on global climate change, wiping out the budget surplus with a gargantuan $1.6 trillion tax cut, and emphasizing confrontation with foreign and domestic enemies. Instead of protesting, the moderates meekly acquiesced. "It was the most demoralizing moment of my seven-year tenure in the Senate," Chafee wrote.[54]

As Cheney had predicted, Bush presided over a highly divisive administration and aggravated the partisan intensity of Congress and the nation. Bush and his principal advisors, Cheney and political strategist Karl Rove, subordinated policy to politics across the board. Bush did not govern consistently as an ideological conservative. At times, he made sporadic gestures in the direction of compassionate conservatism. He set up the White House Office of Faith-Based and Community Initiatives to use activist government for conservative ends by allowing faith-based charitable organizations to provide social services to the poor. He called for greater Republican outreach to Hispanics, along with liberalized immigration policies. He worked with Democrats, notably Ted Kennedy, to make public schools more accountable by linking federal aid to national standards through the program known as No Child Left Behind. He appointed moderates, including Colin Powell as Secretary of State, Paul O'Neill as Secretary of the Treasury, and Christine Todd Whitman as head of the Environmental Protection Agency. At other times, political considerations dictated that he pursue opportunistic policies that pleased neither moderates nor conservatives; in his first year, these included massive subsidies for corporate farming and steel tariffs that sparked an international trade war.

The overall direction of the Bush presidency, however, was unquestionably toward the right. Bush displayed little interest in compromise or bipartisanship, and moderates in the administration were humiliated at every turn. In March 2001, at Cheney's behest, Bush abandoned his campaign stance on climate change and declared that, contrary to the preponderant judgment of the world's scientists, there was no evidence that global warming was occurring or that carbon emissions contributed to it. Bush's reversal infuriated America's allies and was undertaken without even consulting the administration moderates who were most affected by his decision, notably Whitman, Powell, and national security advisor Condoleezza Rice.[55] Cheney dismissed O'Neill's concerns about the fiscal irresponsibility of massive, regressive tax cuts on the grounds that "Reagan proved deficits don't matter."[56] John DiIulio, head of the Office for Faith-Based and Community Initiatives, complained that White House staff at all levels "consistently talked and acted as if the height of political sophistication consisted in reducing every issue to its simplest, black-and-white terms for public consumption, then steering legislative initiatives or policy proposals as far right as possible."[57]

In May 2001, White House indifference to Republican moderates cost the party control of the Senate when Vermont Senator Jim Jeffords became an independent and caucused with the Democrats. Jeffords was upset that the entire budget surplus, and more, was to be spent down in the form of a record $1.6 trillion income tax cut over ten years. He insisted that $450 million be diverted to help states pay for the federal government's unfunded mandate on special education for the disabled. Bush refused, Jeffords resigned from the GOP, and control of the Senate reverted to the Democrats. Jeffords' request was trivial in comparison to the political price of losing control of the Senate, but the administration set a higher value on demonstrating that there would be no compromises with moderates.[58]

The terrorist attacks of September 11, 2001 only reinforced Bush's inflexible approach. The administration squandered the goodwill of potential allies at home and abroad, politicizing the War on Terror and attacking dissent against its policies as unpatriotic, even treasonous. Congressional moderates overwhelmingly voted in favor of war against the Taliban government of Afghanistan, which had harbored Osama Bin Laden and other members of Al-Qaeda's leadership. Increasingly, however, they opposed the administration's curtailment of civil liberties in the name of national security, the exclusion of moderates from policymaking, the use of torture by the military, and the abandonment of human rights and the Geneva Convention. Only a handful of the remaining Republican moderates in Congress voted against the 2002 resolution authorizing the administration's unilateral use of force against Iraq, although the likes of Lincoln Chafee, Jim Leach, and Amo Houghton were prescient in their skepticism over claims about Iraq's possession of weapons of mass destruction and worries that the war could "undercut core American values and leadership around the world," as Leach put it.[59] The war that followed in 2003 proved to be based on a false premise. Political considerations corrupted its planning and execution, from the insufficient numbers of troops allocated to restore order after the invasion to the appointment of ideologically driven incompetents to staff the Coalition Provisional Authority.[60]

The makeup of the GOP grew ever more conservative during the first decade of the twenty-first century, particularly with the spread of partisan redistricting. The 2001–02 reapportionment in California, for example, used sophisticated computer programs to gerrymander district boundaries, "packing" each district with the most partisan supporters of one party or another in order to make them safe seats for that party. For the rest of the decade, California predictably elected far-left Democrats and far-right Republicans, with only a handful of seats changing parties out of several hundred district contests.[61] Party officials also enforced conservative discipline by giving tacit approval to organizations like Americans for Tax

Reform, which demanded that Republican candidates sign its pledge never to raise taxes, and the Club for Growth, a deep-pocketed right-wing pressure group founded in 1999 with the principal aim of electing anti-tax conservatives and forcing moderate Republicans out of office. The Club made an impact soon after its founding by backing a primary challenger to New Jersey moderate Representative Marge Roukema in 2000. Roukema survived the challenge and won reelection, but was sufficiently discouraged to announce her retirement in 2002, after which she was succeeded by a conservative.

By 2002, the Club had become the largest source of campaign funds for Republicans outside of the party itself. In 2004, the group poured millions of dollars into Pat Toomey's right-wing primary challenge to Pennsylvania Senator Arlen Specter. The purge attempt failed, but the Club counted it a victory that Specter's voting patterns became more conservative over the next six years, until the threat of another challenge from Toomey forced him to switch to the Democrats. Club president Stephen Moore boasted that when his organization threatened to "primary" moderate Republicans, "they start wetting their pants."[62] The Club's efforts bolstered the Congressional GOP leadership's efforts to keep moderates in line, and accelerated the departure of moderates from the party.

The Bush years demonstrated anew that conservatives were skilled at politics but deficient at governing, and that a Republican Party without moderates was like a heavily muscled body without a head. Bush gained reelection in 2004 and the Republicans won majority control of Congress for the fifth straight election, but conservatives proved unable to achieve their goals, largely because they lacked the ideas the moderates had once provided and the skill at reaching compromise with the opposition at which moderates had excelled. In the wake of the 2004 elections, Bush's top priority was to privatize Social Security and Medicare, in effect rolling back much of the New Deal. He failed because conservatives lacked the credibility necessary to reform those troubled programs while assuring Americans that the public welfare would not suffer. The administration's buffoonish response to Hurricane Katrina in 2005 reinforced the perception that conservatives undervalued competence in government and didn't care about poor and minority Americans.

The Bush administration's politics of polarization damaged moderate as well as conservative Republicans. When the GOP lost control of both houses of Congress in the 2006 mid-term elections, one of the casualties was Lincoln Chafee, one of the six Republican senators who failed to regain office; if any of them had succeeded, the GOP would have retained the Senate. By the unwritten laws of electoral politics, Chafee should have won his race hands down. He was a popular senator, with a 63 percent approval rating. He had cast the lone Republican vote in the Senate against the Iraq war authorization in 2003, an act of conscience that should have paid dividends by 2006, when the Iraq intervention had turned into a quagmire that had lost the support of most Americans. Chafee also had the editorial endorsement of nearly every newspaper in the state, and the powers of incumbency. But still he lost, in part because he had not been able to make a convincing case for why moderate voters should, in supporting him, allow the continuation in power of a deeply conservative and mainly Southern Republican leadership that had conceded nothing at all to moderates like Chafee on issues such as Iraq, the environment, abortion, taxation, and deficit spending. Angry centrists and independents voted down even moderate Republicans that they agreed with on most issues in order to send a message to the national Republican Party.[63]

The 2008 elections were even worse for the Republicans, as GOP nominee John McCain lost the presidential election to Barack Obama and the Democrats strengthened their hold on Congress. The results were no more encouraging for moderates. Connecticut Representative Christopher Shays, a moderate who was the sole remaining House Republican from New England, lost his reelection bid. A hundred years earlier, New England had been the most solidly Republican section of the country; now the party had been all but eliminated from its historic home. In many of the New England states, the Republican Party in effect ceased to exist on the local level. In Massachusetts, for example, Republicans held no statewide constitutional offices, were outnumbered seven-to-one in the state legislature and twelve-to-zero in the state's Congressional delegation.[64] In one of his last interviews as president, Bush called for a "compassionate" Republican Party and warned that the GOP must not become too rigidly and ideologically conservative: "It's very important for our party not to narrow its focus, not to become so inward-looking that we drive people away," the President told Fox News. "We shouldn't have litmus tests as to whether or not you can be a Republican."[65] This message, however, carried little weight since it came from a party leader who had spent most of the previous eight years failing to take his own advice.

The Republican leadership did not respond to the setbacks of 2006 and 2008 by engaging in agonizing reappraisals or reaching out to moderates. Instead, the party hunkered down, waited for the bad memories of the Bush era to fade, and pursued an unrelentingly negative program of opposition to Obama and the Democrats. The strategy paid off, at least in the sense that Republicans, buoyed by the populist grassroots activism of the "Tea Parties," achieved significant political gains in 2010 by retaking the House and narrowing the Democratic margin in the Senate.

Conservative politicians and media outlets hailed the Tea Party movement as a glorious and historically unprecedented people's revolt. Moderates, however, had a distinct feeling of déjà vu. The Tea Party movement
was only the latest in a cycle of insurgencies on the Republican right that
had shaken the GOP since the McCarthy movement of the 1950s and the
Goldwater revolt in the early 1960s. Even the name of the movement was
a throwback to the "T Parties" of the early '60s, part of the right-wing, anti-
tax crusade of that era.[66] Like earlier waves of the conservative movement,
the Tea Party mostly was made up of financially secure members of the
middle and upper-middle classes, predominantly male and middle-aged
and overwhelmingly white and Republican, who feared that the country
was being taken away from them. The activists' push to seize power in the
GOP from the ground up, not only by flooding into electoral campaigns
but by signing up to be Republican precinct leaders and occupying other
low-level party positions, mimicked the Goldwater takeover masterminded by Clif White in the early 1960s.[67] The Tea Partiers' hyperbolic
claim that Democrats and moderate Republicans were out-and-out
socialists called to mind *Advance* magazine's observation almost a half-
century earlier that conservatives were "unable to make even the most ele-
mentary distinctions."[68]

The upset victory of Scott Brown in the Massachusetts race to succeed
the late Senator Ted Kennedy in early 2010 gave the deceptive impression
that the movement might benefit moderate as well as conservative Republicans, since the Tea Partiers' alarm over swelling government and rising
deficits historically had been a primary concern of the moderates. Outside
of Massachusetts, however, the movement supported few fiscally conservative candidates who were not also rigid social and cultural conservatives,
and none who could be described as moderate. In Utah, the movement
knocked off incumbent Senator Robert Bennett, a Republican who had
always taken pains to maintain his conservative bona fides, largely
because he was perceived as being insufficiently angry and partisan. Tea
Party activists also viewed his experience and policy expertise as deficiencies, and charged him with failing to curb the growing deficit.[69] But
the movement-affiliated candidates who claimed the mantle of fiscal conservatism had no real plans for reducing government expenditures
beyond the standard conservative pursuit of politics-as-warfare: cutting
programs that benefited Democratic constituencies while preserving
programs that benefited Republican constituencies and avoiding any serious reform of defense spending or middle-class entitlement programs.

Far from benefiting moderates, the Tea Party movement brought far-
right ideas that even conservatives had once resisted into the Republican
mainstream. In previous decades, conservative gatekeepers like William F.

Buckley Jr., pressured by moderates and the mainstream media, had marginalized the paranoid conspiracy-mongers of the John Birch Society and "kook" books like *None Dare Call It Treason*. Now tea-tinged conservative entertainers like Glenn Beck peddled the crackpot theories of Birch theoreticians like W. Cleon Skousen to a television audience of millions, and books of the sort that once had been viewed as the political equivalent of hardcore pornography soared brazenly up the bestseller lists. While conservative politicians like Reagan had kept the Birch Society at arm's length, now members of the Republican leadership sponsored and spoke at Tea Party rallies at which demonstrators equated Democrats with Nazis and charged that Obama was a foreign-born dictator ravaging the Constitution.[70] GOP politicians were unable to resist the rightward pressures from their base, even if they had wanted to, and echoed the extreme charges of the movement. As Obama complained to a gathering of Congressional Republicans, "You've given yourselves very little room to work in a bipartisan fashion because what you've been telling your constituents is, 'This guy's doing all kinds of crazy stuff that is going to destroy America.'"[71]

One of the likeliest ways America might in fact be destroyed would be if one of its two major parties were rendered dysfunctional, and yet this seemed to be the direction in which the GOP was heading as the 2012 elections approached. The version of the Republican Party that greeted the second decade of the twenty-first century was one that apparently was in the process of shucking off most of its own history and heritage. Its leaders showed little interest in appealing to moderates, repudiating extremism, reaching out to new constituencies, or upholding the party's legacy of civil rights and civil liberties. There seemed little likelihood that the GOP would take the lead in working toward bipartisan solutions to the economic crisis or present itself as an effective governing party. The half century–long struggle of moderates and conservatives within the Republican Party had finally ended in the conservatives' complete domination, but the fruits of this victory were proving to be bitter.

Conclusion

ↄᴍᴼ

A philosopher not widely read by Republicans once observed that history repeats itself: the first time as tragedy, the second time as farce.[1] The story of the moderate Republicans' collapse reached a farcical conclusion of sorts with the GOP senatorial primary in Delaware in 2010. Mike Castle, the favored nominee, was perhaps the most prominent remaining moderate Republican in the House and the most popular Republican politician in an increasingly Democratic state. He had been twice elected as governor as well as serving nine terms as Delaware's at-large representative in the House. He was considered unbeatable, and the strongest potential Democratic candidates had essentially conceded the Senate race, leaving their party's nomination to a virtual unknown. Castle was popular because he was a thoughtful, practical, intelligent man, who was estimated to have had personal conversations with a majority of the state's voters. His business-friendly but socially moderate political positions held wide appeal. He had stood with the GOP in voting against President Barack Obama's economic stimulus plan and calling for all of George Bush's 2001 tax cuts to be made permanent. He had opposed Obama's health care proposal as well, believing that it would be "too costly and unmanageable," though he tried to come up with a Republican alternative that would retain what he considered to be the attractive features of the Democratic plan.[2] At the same time, he had angered conservatives by supporting abortion rights and campaign finance reform, and by opposing oil drilling in the Alaskan National Wildlife Refuge and the use of torture in the "War on Terror." He had also been one of the eight GOP representatives—the "Traitorous Eight," in conservative parlance—who voted for the Democrats' cap-and-trade legislation to reduce global warming.[3] Castle was one of the last House Republicans to openly proclaim the virtue and necessity of bipartisan compromise, insisting that "There are issues on which, as Republicans and Democrats, we should sit down and work out our differences."[4] Despite his moderation, the conservative Republican leadership supported Castle's 2010 election bid, and indeed needed his victory if the party was to retake the Senate.

Their calculations, and Castle's campaign, were derailed by the rise of the Tea Party movement. Many Americans first became aware that conservative forces were brewing inside the GOP with the broadcast of a video of Castle's town hall–style meeting with his constituents in June 2009. One woman, brandishing a copy of her birth certificate, insisted that Obama had been born in Kenya and was ineligible for the presidency. When Castle calmly replied that the President was an American citizen, he was roundly booed. Others in attendance retailed Birch-flavored conspiracy theories that they had mostly learned from the internet and the Fox News Channel, including the notion that global warming was a hoax and that the AIDS virus was engineered at Fort Dix.[5] Not long after the town hall confrontation, activists in the nascent Tea Party movement mounted a primary challenge to Castle's nomination.

The movement took several forms and backed a variety of candidates, but in Delaware the Tea Party's preferred candidate was Christine O'Donnell, a religio-political activist who was unqualified for the nomination by any conventional measure. She had become a minor television curiosity over the previous decade by crusading against masturbation, abortion, and Darwinism. She had a troubled financial history, had engaged in questionable use of campaign donations for personal expenses, and had lied about her education and payment of student loans and taxes. As far as many Tea Partiers were concerned, however, O'Donnell's unrelenting hard-right postures absolved all her sins. O'Donnell hammered Castle as a free-spending liberal, mainly for his ventures into bipartisanship and his support of the Troubled Asset Relief Program (TARP), George W. Bush's measure to keep the U.S. economy from melting down during the 2008 credit crisis. TARP was widely reviled but succeeded in stabilizing the banking sector at minimal cost to the government.[6]

O'Donnell offered no alternative view of how she would have saved the economy, nor did she seriously attempt to match Castle's problem-solving approach to complex fiscal issues such as the rising federal budget deficit. It was enough for her to insult Castle's manhood and to proclaim that he was a Republican in Name Only who "doesn't stand for anything that the party stands for."[7] Her supporters seemed to view the contest through the Troll's Eye of old legends, in which all that is fair appears gross and vice versa.[8] For them, O'Donnell's financial woes were evidence of her "realness," her most bizarre outbursts proof of her passion. The fact that no less a Republican leader than Karl Rove had called her unfit for office only reinforced her followers' belief that her victory would provide a stinging and necessary rebuke to the party elite. By contrast, Castle's experience, competence, reasonableness, and moderation all made him seem like an emotionless drone of the status quo—"an establishment android," in one sneering description.[9]

Moderate Republicans like Castle could not escape the "establishment" label despite the fact that they had long ceased to exercise power in the GOP. Indeed, most of the advantages in the Delaware contest were on the conservative side. O'Donnell received the endorsement of celebrity conservatives like Sarah Palin, South Carolina Senator Jim DeMint, and radio talk show host Mark Levin. While O'Donnell had trouble raising money in-state, the California-based Tea Party Express spent more than $200,000 on campaign advertisements and mailings on her behalf. The group also demonstrated the national reach of movement conservatism by mobilizing volunteers in other states to telephone Delaware voters.[10] Although Delaware had about 182,000 registered Republicans, only 55,000 could bestir themselves to get to the polls on the September 14 primary election. O'Donnell won the election by a margin of just over 3,000 votes.[11] What had been a certain Republican pickup in the Senate race instantly became a guaranteed Democratic win. O'Donnell ran a hapless campaign, which included one memorable television ad in which she was forced to deny that she was a witch, and lost by a substantial margin. Nonetheless, conservatives proclaimed victory in pushing the state and national GOP further to the right. Media eulogies for Castle saluted his decency and the near-vanished tradition of bipartisanship that he had upheld, but few seemed to recall that there was anything to moderation besides compromise, and none suggested that the Tea Party might have undercut its professed goal of fiscal conservatism by removing Castle.

The verging-on-ridiculous circumstances of Castle's defeat seemed to signal an end to moderation within the Republican Party. Even the word "moderate" had become a term of abuse. A presidential candidate like Mitt Romney, who had built his reputation as a moderate governor of Massachusetts, had to run as far to the right as possible to have any chance of succeeding in the 2012 GOP primaries. Romney thereby turned his back not only on his own accomplishments, but on the moderate Republican tradition of which his father, Michigan Governor George Romney, had been a shining example. Much of the current conservative movement is characterized by this sort of historical amnesia and symbolic parricide, which seeks to undo key aspects of the Republican legacy such as Reagan's elimination of corporate tax loopholes, Nixon's environmental and labor safety programs, and a variety of GOP achievements in civil rights, civil liberties, and good-government reforms.[12] In the long view of history, it is really today's conservatives who are "Republicans in name only."

The moderate Republican heritage has faded from the public memory largely because the moderates themselves have passed from the political scene. Indeed, the moderates' defeat now seems to define them. Moderate Republicanism has crumbled as a political force in Congress, although some Republican governors and big-city mayors have continued to stand for pragmatism and varying degrees of fiscal responsibility and social tolerance. Moderate Republicans have not vanished from the earth; a *Washington Post*/ABC 2008 election exit poll found that fully 10 percent of the electorate described themselves as moderate Republicans.[13] Combined with the 18 percent of voters who were moderate Democrats and the 16 percent who were moderate independents, moderates made up a plurality of the American electorate. And yet, following the 2010 elections there were only a handful of moderate Republicans remaining in Congress. In today's Republican Party, moderates—and indeed entire regions of the country where moderates predominate—are essentially unrepresented.

In keeping with the trend toward political polarization, the left wing of the Democratic Party also enjoys disproportionate influence relative to that party's moderates.[14] Still, most observers agree with Mike Castle that the domination of one ideological wing is "a more extensive problem right now in the Republican Party than in the Democratic Party."[15] The conversion of one of America's two major parties into an ideological vehicle, against the preferences of many of the party's own voters, is a phenomenon without precedent in American history. Once upon a time, conservatives feared far-reaching and untried innovations in social and political organization; now it is only conservatives who welcome this radical departure from the American political tradition.

To some extent, the moderates' downfall was caused by forces beyond their control. These included the shift of population and power from the North and Midwest to the South and West, the declining cultural sway of the Eastern WASP establishment and its ethos, and the waning public memory of the Depression and World War II. Political developments after 1960 also tended to favor the conservatives. The disappearance of Democratic liabilities, such as the solid, segregated South and the corrupt ethnic machines of the North, made the Democrats less objectionable to many Republican moderates, while those moderates were turned off by their party's open-armed welcome of racist former Southern Democrats such as Strom Thurmond. The Civil Rights Act of 1964, that signal achievement of the moderates, benefited the Republican right by allowing them to pick up the votes of conservative white Southerners without having to defend the radioactive issue of segregation. When the New Deal coalition crumbled, the conservatives' populism and stark opposition to liberalism proved more attractive to the white ethnic working class than the measured and often elitist approach of the moderates. Even technological developments advantaged the conservatives. The advent of computer-driven redistricting, for example, often resulted in tacit gerrymandering deals between conservative Republicans and liberal Democrats to marginalize moderates.

Within the GOP itself, the national convention's delegate-allocation formula disproportionately rewarded smaller states, helping to Southernize and conservatize the party; the allocation of seats on the Republican National Committee also disproportionately favored conservatives. The more widespread use of binding presidential primaries and caucuses advantaged the right, whose better-mobilized troops tended to dominate those lower-turnout elections, while state party organizations exercised less control over the nominating procedures. Although moderate politicians often had considerably more general-election appeal than their conservative challengers, they found it much more difficult to survive primary challenges, especially when extra-party forces such as the Club for Growth entered into the equation. The growing importance of grassroots participation and fundraising also worked against the moderates, whose top-down approach had traditionally relied on party leaders and financiers. The entry of evangelical religion into Republican politics helped the party win elections, notably in the South, but the evangelicals' fiery espousal of social and cultural causes alienated many moderates and eroded their common ground with conservatives. Fiscally conservative but socially moderate Republicans in particular were increasingly disadvantaged in Congressional politics: Democrats opposed them for their tight-fisted approach to social spending while their conservative GOP colleagues, whose fiscal conservatism was more honored in the breach than the observance, frequently punished them for not going along with appropriations requests and for cooperating with Democrats on social issues.

At the level of strategy, moderate activists were badly outplayed by their conservative opponents. Moderate vehicles for party influence, such as the All-Republican Conference and National Republican Citizens Committee, were undermined by conservatives and inadequately defended by moderates. Conservative activists had access to funds beyond the wildest dreams of moderates, who were left to wonder what might have been if only, say, a plutocrat like Paul Mellon had supported moderates as ardently as his cousin Richard Mellon Scaife supported conservatives. It was the moderates' great misfortune that Nelson Rockefeller devoted his storied wealth to his fruitless and counterproductive quest for the White House rather than building up the moderate movement.

The Goldwater campaign highlighted the growing importance of cultivating a wide base of dedicated grassroots donors, which moderates struggled to match. Conservatives proved better institution-builders, creating an infrastructure of think tanks, publishing houses, media outlets, PACs, and pressure groups in imitation of an establishment that proved unable to exert itself for moderates in the same way. Moderates lacked organizational entrepreneurs such as Richard Viguerie or Paul Weyrich, partly because they didn't share the conservatives' aggrieved sense of marginalization and didn't view the world through a similar ideological lens.

Conservatives opened their wallets for grassroots efforts such as the takeover of the Young Republican National Federation in the early 1960s, and also had the advantage of large numbers of zealous, movement-driven supporters. Rockefeller, by contrast, actually sabotaged moderate Republican activism on his behalf out of a delusional belief that his money and charisma eventually would win over the conservatives. Moderate activists failed to develop effective grassroots organizations or to prevent the ones they had, such as the California Republican Assembly, from being taken over by conservatives. Moderates too often proved incapable of coordinating their activities or even seeing a need to cooperate, an inability that partly stemmed from their diverse origins as stalwarts, moderates, and progressives. All three groups found themselves on the moderate side of intraparty battles with the conservatives, and were defined as moderates by the conservatives regardless of how they perceived themselves. Most came to realize, usually too late, that this gave them a common identity.

Moderates had seen their lack of a rigid ideology as an advantage, since they were free to examine each issue as it came up, dispassionately and on the merits, in keeping with the dictates of the Founding Fathers. But while this pragmatism often served moderates well in the task of governance, it unsuited them for political competition. And, as many moderate activists observed about the ranks they sought to rally, moderates are by nature— moderate. Except on the rare occasions when they felt threatened or alarmed or unusually inspired, it was difficult to rouse them to the level of effort and commitment that was routine for the more ideologically driven conservatives.

Some of the Republican politicians who called themselves moderates were merely opportunists who shifted to the conservative ranks after the right became dominant within the party. Some moderates, particularly from the progressive ranks, shifted to the left and became indistinguishable from liberal Democrats. Other prominent moderates lived down to the conservative claim that they were "me-too" Republicans, whose lack of fixed ideology implied absence of principle and a finger-in-the-wind approach that merely split the difference between the two parties. This made moderates increasingly vulnerable to the gibe by conservatives and liberals alike that they were really political bisexuals, transsexuals, transvestites, and hermaphrodites.

Moderate politicians, not seeing themselves as participants in a common movement with other similarly embattled moderates, were prone to make operational errors as well. Unable to commit to one presidential candidate in 1964, and unable to prevent Rockefeller and his matchless resources from driving other progressive candidates out of contention during the primaries, moderates were powerless to block Goldwater from gaining the nomination. Although moderates had potentially dominant forces in the Senate and the ranks of Republican governors during the '60s and '70s, they were unable to coordinate their efforts. Congressional moderates failed to mobilize themselves through organizations such as the House Wednesday Group along the lines of their opponents in the Conservative Opportunity Society. In some cases, the good-government idealism and gentlemanly behavior of moderates inhibited them from adapting to a political era in which money and the power of vested interests became vastly more important to the electoral and governing processes.

While the moderates' strength likely would have deteriorated over time in any case, their near-complete disappearance during the first decade of the twenty-first century was due to conscious political decisions by conservative leaders in the George W. Bush era. The dynamic of ideological conservatism has tended toward an ever-narrower definition of political acceptability, to the point that by the end of his career, even Barry Goldwater was accused of being a RINO. Bush and his allies were not consistent ideologues by any means, but they accelerated the process of ideologically driven political polarization.

Even former moderate Republican activists could not agree on what value and meaning moderation retained in the twenty-first century. An informal poll of Ripon Society veterans, conducted at the organization's fortieth anniversary reunion in 2002, revealed that some three-quarters had become independents or Democrats. Progressives in particular had found the growing conservative domination of the GOP to be intolerable, and most had left the party along with progressive leaders like John Lindsay and John Anderson. Many of them were still mistrustful of the Democratic Party, but saw Bill Clinton's moderation as something close to what they had hoped for the GOP.[16] Other Ripon alumni remained moderate Republicans, with varying degrees of discomfort. Ripon co-founder Emil Frankel felt that he was too old and contrarian to leave the Republican Party, and further that "my views, for good or ill, remain much what they were thirty and forty years ago: centrist, moderate, pragmatic, reform-oriented."[17] He found it incongruous that he had been an assistant secretary of transportation under George W. Bush, "the most conservative administration on all issues—social, economic, national security—since the late nineteenth century . . . and yet I was a part of it." His experience was that moderates who

stayed in the party and served in the Bush administration "made concessions and gritted our teeth" when the administration pursued disagreeable
policies outside their areas of responsibility.[18] Thomas E. Petri, Ripon's first
executive director, was elected to Congress in 1979 to fill the Wisconsin
seat of the late Representative William Steiger. Petri continued Steiger's tradition of fiscal conservatism and social moderation, which proved popular
with his constituents; he ran unopposed in several elections and won a
fourteenth term in 2010. But while Steiger's moderation had not prevented
him from being a leader in the GOP, Petri's made him an outsider. After the
1994 elections, Congressional moderates who deviated from an increasingly rigid conservative line were punished with undesirable committee
assignments, loss of position within committees (with resultant loss of publicity opportunities), lack of campaign support, and official party indifference when incumbents were challenged by outside conservative enforcers
like the Club for Growth. Petri repeatedly was passed over for committee
chairmanships to which he was entitled by seniority, although he felt that
this owed more to the growing power of the Florida-Texas-California bloc
than to explicit ideological discrimination.[19]

Some Ripon alumni, however, became active conservatives. Christopher
DeMuth had been a Ripon officer and one of its leading civil rights advocates. After graduating from Harvard, he worked on the 1968 campaign of
James Farmer, a black Republican who had co-founded the Congress of
Racial Equality (CORE). Farmer lost, but joined the Nixon administration,
as did DeMuth, who impressed the President with his work on environmental issues; Nixon wrote on one of DeMuth's memos, "Where can we
find more men like that?"[20] DeMuth's government experience brought him
"face-to-face with programs that were meant to help the poor or the environment and which often did the opposite," he recalled. "This close encounter sealed the deal with my becoming a conservative."[21] Law school at
Chicago exposed him to the emerging law-and-economics movement and
lured him further to the right. He became the so-called deregulation czar
during the Reagan administration, and in 1986 was hired as president of the
American Enterprise Institute, a conservative think tank which had then
fallen on hard times. DeMuth built AEI into the most influential conservative policy organization of the early twenty-first century; twenty AEI
scholars had served in George W. Bush's administration by 2003, and the
organization's work shaped policies ranging from Bush's 2001 tax cut to the
military surge in Iraq.[22]

Bruce Chapman, who had helped initiate the moderate Republican
movement of the early '60s, also wound up on the right. Like DeMuth,
Chapman served in the Reagan administration, joining as director of the
Census Bureau and later becoming domestic policy advisor to the President

and ambassador to the United Nations Organization in Vienna. An Evans and Novak column noted that Chapman as census director "became attuned to what the government has done to the family" and "emerged inside the administration as a champion of the family."[23] A reporter who had known Chapman as a moderate Republican in Seattle spoke with him during the Reagan years, and remembered him saying that his politics had changed along with the Reagan Revolution: "I have grown more conservative on social issues as I have become more disillusioned with any aspect of the Great Society, the welfare state, or the endless parade of liberation movements as solutions to any problems."[24] Chapman's general stance within the Reagan administration could fairly be characterized as "compassionate conservatism." In an evaluation of policy and political objectives for Reagan's second term, Chapman insisted that although the administration had to hold its traditional conservative base, Republicans also needed to be "reaching out to 'populist' liberals and moderates and the poor and the blacks."[25]

Chapman returned to Seattle and founded the Discovery Institute think tank in 1991. Discovery covered many issues of longstanding interest to Washington State Republicans, such as regional, cross-boundary solutions to transportation and environmental problems. These were issues that William Gates Sr. had been involved with as early as the 1950s when he was ringing doorbells for progressive Republican candidates like Dan Evans, so it was no great surprise when the foundation he headed pledged over $10 million to a Discovery project focusing on transportation.[26] But Discovery became best known for its controversial Center for Science and Culture, which promoted "intelligent design" as an alternative to Darwinism. While Discovery's activities in this field were not explicitly religious, Chapman's attacks on "scientific materialism"—a worldview that, he argued, underlay evolutionary theory, the physical and social sciences, and much of American culture—made him an effective ally of the religious right.

The rightward progression of former moderates like DeMuth and Chapman suggested something about the limitations of moderation. DeMuth considered the moderate Republican movement to have been an appropriate response to the specific political conditions of the early 1960s: "Ripon's members were civil rights libertarians," he emphasized. In his view, when Southern segregation was overcome and the Republican Party distanced itself from Birch Society extremists, moderation's mission was accomplished, and the differences between moderate and conservative Republicans ceased to be significant.[27] Chapman generally agreed, but pointed out that moderation was more a temperament than a policy. He believed that moderates tended to define themselves as occupying a midpoint between liberals and conservatives, "and that takes it out of one's control, because that leaves it up to the left and right to decide what those terms mean. . . . You're at the mercy of either end, when you really ought to have your own position and stick to it."[28] Of course, the meanings of liberalism and conservatism have also shifted over time, but moderation did appear to be a more elastic and relativistic outlook, which made it seem less of a faith worth fighting and dying for. One of Chapman's longtime friends commented that "Everybody's always wondering how Bruce could change from a liberal to a conservative. Well, Bruce has always been a believer, and that has informed all his activities."[29] Chapman's conversion from the Episcopal Church to Roman Catholicism in 2002 could be seen as part of his search for a more rooted and absolute creed.[30]

With all of its flaws and failures, why should anyone lament the passing of moderate Republicanism? The most important reason is that the moderates upheld values and positions that are no longer adequately represented in American politics. The political obituaries for the likes of Mike Castle identified moderation with a bygone culture of compromise, but it would be a serious mistake to equate moderation with mere difference-splitting or compromise for its own sake. Nor should anyone take at face value the judgment of Rush Limbaugh, who sniggered that "By definition, moderates can't be brave—they don't have opinions! . . . I mean, brave moderates? 'Great Moderates in American History'? Show me that book."[31]

In fact, moderate Republicanism *was* bravely defended as a distinctive political philosophy, different from both Democratic liberalism and Republican conservatism. Moderate Republicans helped shape many of what are typically thought of as Democratic achievements, from certain Progressive era and New Deal reforms to the architecture of the post-World War II global order and civil rights legislation. Particularly during the critical decade of the 1960s, moderates defended civil rights and civil liberties, often in the face of Democratic and Republican opposition. Neither the Civil Rights Act of 1964 nor the Voting Rights Act of 1965, for example, would have passed without Republican backing, and the bipartisan support those measures received facilitated their acceptance by the American public.

Many of the moderates' most significant contributions revolved around issues that did not fit neatly into a liberal-conservative dichotomy. Historically, the moderates were the strongest advocates of good government. While they were skeptical of the Democrats' impulse toward centralization and bureaucratization, they didn't pretend to hate government as many conservatives did. As a result, the moderates were better able than both liberal Democrats and conservative Republicans to exercise fiscal responsibility and to seek both effectiveness and efficiency in government. Because they believed in disinterested consideration of the issues, they were able to work with Democrats to solve problems, and to maintain a level of balance and civility in politics that has long since vanished. But because they were not beholden to the Democrats' coalition of special-interest constituencies, they could take a broader and longer-term viewpoint and uphold values such as civil liberties and meritocracy that commanded only weak support from both Democrats and conservative Republicans. In some states, such as California, the waning of moderate Republican influence spelled the end of effective government.

If, as many observers believe, the American political system proves unable to make necessary reforms to meet the long-term challenges posed by energy dependence, environmental degradation, Social Security's shaky economic foundation, and the rising tide of government deficits and pension liabilities, the absence of the moderate Republicans may be the single greatest explanatory factor. If American politics can be compared to an ecosystem, then the disappearance of the moderate Republicans represents a catastrophic loss of species diversity.

The moderate die-off also harmed the Republican Party itself. Many of the party's proudest achievements were typically the result of negotiations among the GOP's factions as well as maneuver and compromise with Democrats. Internal dispute, for the Republican Party, was often an indication of its vitality as a national force. Some key moderate assumptions came to permeate the party, and moderates paradoxically helped reshape and strengthen conservatism as well. Moderates' views on civil rights, free markets, globalization, balanced internationalism in foreign affairs, and party modernization largely prevailed within the GOP—often, obviously, with an assist from Democratic pressures. By the 1980s, few reputable conservative spokespersons still advocated protectionism, isolationism, or the denial of civil rights to African-Americans, or were calling for preemptive nuclear strikes against China and the Soviet Union. At times, the conflict between moderates and conservatives didn't allow for compromise, particularly at the level of grassroots activism. Moderates battled to the death against segregationists, Birchers, Rat Fink neo-fascists in the Young Republican National Federation, and purge-minded exclusionists in the Club for Growth. But moderates engaged in productive dialogue and debate with thoughtful conservatives like William F. Buckley Jr., and worked with President Reagan, who restrained the furies of movement conservatism while offering enough leeway to moderates to keep them in the GOP tent. The most successful Republican presidents of modern times tended to be those like Nixon and Reagan, who understood that they had to mediate between a conservative party base and a moderate public, and who reserved a role within the party for moderates rather than expelling them for ideological heresy.

Moderates also found common ground with pragmatic conservatives on many issues such as budgetary restraint, decentralization, revenue sharing, and market-based alternatives to federal programs. In many cases, conservatives eventually adopted policies that had been pioneered by moderates, and moderates made an outsized contribution in generating new research and ideas. Moderate Republicans allied themselves with the first generation of neoconservatives and shaped the domestic policy approaches and interpretations that still determine many GOP positions. Moderates were among the original champions of supply-side economics. Moderates supplied not only the ideas but many of the individuals who later became prominent leaders on the conservative side, including Bruce Chapman, George Gilder, Newt Gingrich, Dick Cheney, Donald Rumsfeld, and Mitch McConnell. In this respect, the moderate wing of the GOP performed much the same role that Britain's Liberal Party once did; in 1926 Maynard Keynes observed that "The brains and character of the Conservative Party have always been recruited from the Liberals, and we must not grudge them the excellent material with which, in accordance with our historic mission, we are now preserving them from intellectual starvation."[32]

In an ideal world, moderates might once again form an integral part of the Republican coalition. A reinvigorated moderate Republican faction modeled after the 1960s movement would continue to promote civil rights and civil liberties, and to broaden the party's outreach to constituencies such as minorities, intellectuals, professionals, feminists, and urbanites who are increasingly estranged from the conservative-dominated GOP. Moderates could build on the preferences that Ripon Society theorist Lee Auspitz laid out in 1970: internationalism rather than interventionism, devolution of power to states and localities rather than increasing federal government centralization, the use of market incentives in preference to bureaucratic controls, and transparency and dispersed decision-making authority instead of secrecy and the concentration of power in the hands of a few unaccountable experts.

The current furor over spiraling deficits also would seem to demand a moderate, pragmatic, and commonsensical approach. As various bipartisan commissions have pointed out, an effective debt- and deficit-reduction effort will require both revenue increases and spending cuts. Surely a new movement for fiscal responsibility should look to Dwight Eisenhower as its model. Ike understood that the nation's financial credibility and national security demanded progressive taxation, restraint of middle-class entitlements, and restrictions on military budgets and operations. At the same time, he believed that the budget could not be balanced at the expense of the most vulnerable and disadvantaged citizens, and that far-sighted policy required wise public investments as well as lean government.

In reality, however, moderates are unlikely to play a significant role in the Republican Party in the near future. Conservatives dominate every aspect of the party and its political infrastructure, and moderates would be hard put to mount a serious challenge in any area. Neither does peaceful coexistence seem to be much of an option. Movement conservatives have, if anything, become increasingly intolerant of Republican moderates as their numbers have shrunk. The movement has proved unrelentingly hostile even to those thinkers, including David Brooks, Ross Douthat, David Frum, Reihan Salam, Andrew Sullivan, and Sam Tanenhaus, who are the real heirs of William F. Buckley's struggle to make the GOP a party of responsible, effective, and constructive conservatism.[33]

As the Republican Party continues to reject its own heritage and forgets the hard lessons of the 1960s, it seems increasingly likely that right-wing activists may prevail over the party professionals and nominate an extreme presidential candidate. Such a candidate might so alienate the American majority, as Goldwater did in 1964, that Republican candidates would be wiped out across the board. Indeed, the carnage might be worse than in 1964, since the GOP is no longer an ideologically diverse party and would be less able to survive a widespread public rejection of the conservative brand.[34] In that event, moderates might help to reconstruct the Republican Party along more moderate and electable lines, much as happened with the Conservative Party in Britain under David Cameron. For obvious reasons, however, this is not a scenario that many moderate Republicans will discuss openly. Proposals for a moderate third party surface at regular intervals, but the entire course of American political history suggests that such efforts are foredoomed to failure.[35] Reforms to curb partisan redistricting, such as the one passed in California in 2010, may revive the fortunes of moderates in both parties, but this will be a slow process.

A nation as large and complex as the United States, with its world-spanning obligations and interconnections, requires both the Republicans and Democrats to be serious and responsible governing parties. If moderation remains long absent from one party, let alone both, the consequences are likely to be dire. As many commentators have warned, the growth of ideologically polarized politics may prove toxic to government effectiveness and perhaps even to America's social stability. The research of numerous political scientists and sociologists confirms that while the media exaggerates the extent to which the public is split into Red and Blue nations, the division of the parties by ideology increasingly threatens to divide Americans by geography, race, ethnicity, religion, and class as well.[36] Political movements based on dogmatic, unthinking certitude may be fatal to treasured

American values. As Judge Learned Hand famously observed, the spirit of liberty is the spirit which is not too sure that it is right.

The Founding Fathers, steeped in classical history and morality, feared that America might fall as the Roman Republic had if it failed to guard against the corrosive forces of corruption, petty interests, and the unrestrained zeal of faction. George Washington called upon his fellow citizens to show "mutual forbearance" and follow "a middle course."[37] America's very survival as a republic may depend on its ability to maintain a political system that can balance the nation's massive needs and its great but finite resources, represent all of its people, and reflect what the first Republican president called "the better angels of our nature."

NOTES

PREFACE

1. These include John A. Andrew III, *The Other Side of the Sixties: Young Americans for Freedom and the Rise of Conservative Politics* (New Brunswick, NJ: Rutgers University Press, 1997); Mary C. Brennan, *Turning Right in the Sixties: The Conservative Capture of the GOP* (Chapel Hill, NC: University of North Carolina Press, 1995); Dan T. Carter, *The Politics of Rage: George Wallace, the Origins of the New Conservatism, and the Transformation of American Politics* (Baton Rouge, LA: Louisiana State University Press, 1995); Donald T. Critchlow, *The Conservative Ascendancy: How the GOP Right Made Political History* (Cambridge, MA: Harvard University Press, 2007); Matthew Dallek, *The Right Moment: Ronald Reagan's First Victory and the Decisive Turning Point in American Politics* (New York: Free Press, 2000); Laura Jane Gifford, *The Center Cannot Hold: The 1960 Presidential Election and the Rise of Modern Conservatism* (DeKalb, IL: Northern Illinois University Press, 2009); Jerome Himmelstein, *To the Right: The Transformation of American Conservatism* (Berkeley, CA: University of California Press, 1990); Godfrey Hodgson, *The World Turned Right Side Up: A History of the Conservative Ascendancy* (Boston: Houghton Mifflin, 1996); Matthew D. Lassiter, *The Silent Majority: Suburban Politics in the Sunbelt South* (Princeton, NJ: Princeton University Press, 2006); Allan J. Lichtman, *White Protestant Nation: The Rise of the American Conservative Movement* (New York: Atlantic Monthly Press, 2008); Lisa McGirr, *Suburban Warriors: The Origins of the New American Right* (Princeton, NJ: Princeton University Press, 2001); Bethany Moreton, *To Serve God and Wal-Mart: The Making of Christian Free Enterprise* (Cambridge, MA: Harvard University Press, 2009); Rick Perlstein, *Before the Storm: Barry Goldwater and the Unmaking of the American Consensus* (New York: Hill and Wang, 2001); Kim Phillips-Fein, *Invisible Hands: The Making of the Conservative Movement from the New Deal to Ronald Reagan* (New York: W. W. Norton, 2009); Jonathan M. Schoenwald, *A Time for Choosing: The Rise of Modern American Conservatism* (New York: Oxford University Press, 2001); and Steven M. Teles, *The Rise of the Conservative Legal Movement: The Battle for Control of the Law* (Princeton, NJ: Princeton University Press, 2008).

2. Political scientists have paid more attention to the role of moderate Republicans than have historians. The best analysis of this kind is Nicol C. Rae, *The Decline and Fall of the Liberal Republicans from 1952 to the Present* (New York: Oxford University Press, 1989). Other helpful sources include William F. Connelly Jr. and John J. Pitney Jr., *Congress' Permanent Minority?: Republicans in the U.S. House* (Lanham, MD: Littlefield Adams, 1994); Daniel J. Galvin, *Presidential Party Building: Dwight D. Eisenhower to George W. Bush* (Princeton, NJ: Princeton University Press, 2010); Jacob S. Hacker and Paul Pierson, *Off Center: The Republican Revolution and the Erosion of American Democracy*

(New Haven, CT: Yale University Press, 2005); Tanya Melich, *The Republican War Against Women: An Insider's Report from Behind the Lines* (rev. ed.) (New York: Bantam, 1998); A. James Reichley, *Conservatives in an Age of Change: The Nixon and Ford Administrations* (Washington, DC: Brookings Institution, 1981); and Barbara Sinclair, *Party Wars: Polarization and the Politics of National Policy Making* (Norman, OK: University of Oklahoma Press, 2006).

3. Theodore H. White, *The Making of the President 1960* (New York: Atheneum, 1961), p. 64.

4. This book does not seek to explain the intellectual origins and development of modern conservatism. The best source on that subject remains George Nash, *The Conservative Intellectual Movement in America Since 1945* (New York: Basic Books, 1976). See also Patrick Allitt, *Catholic Intellectuals and Conservative Politics in America, 1950–1985* (Ithaca, NY: Cornell University Press, 1993) and E. J. Dionne Jr., *Why Americans Hate Politics* (New York: Simon & Schuster, 1991).

CHAPTER 1

1. David Wise, "Lodge Cites Struggle to Save World," *NYHT* July 29, 1960, p. 1.

2. Clinton Rossiter, *Parties and Politics in America* (Ithaca, NY: Cornell University Press, 1960), p. 1.

3. As it turned out, 1960 was the last time the Republicans would hold their national convention in Chicago. After the fall elections, the party would vow never again to return to the Windy City, as a protest against what they believed to be Democratic mayor Richard Daley's vote-stealing.

4. A useful overview of the GOP's development is Lewis L. Gould, *Grand Old Party: A History of the Republicans* (New York: Random House, 2003).

5. An insightful analysis of Roosevelt's and Wilson's contrasting varieties of progressivism is John Milton Cooper Jr., *The Warrior and the Priest: Woodrow Wilson and Theodore Roosevelt* (Cambridge, MA: Belknap, 1983).

6. Warren Rogers Jr., "Nixon Balks at Occupying 'Smoke-Filled Room' of '20," *NYHT* July 24, 1960, p. 17.

7. Nelson Polsby, *How Congress Evolves: Social Bases of Institutional Change* (New York: Oxford University Press, 2004), p. 33.

8. Joan Hoff Wilson, *Herbert Hoover: Forgotten Progressive* (Boston: Little, Brown, 1975).

9. James T. Patterson, *Mr. Republican: A Biography of Robert A. Taft* (Boston: Houghton Mifflin, 1972), p. 157.

10. Quoted in Ronald Brownstein, *The Second Civil War: How Extreme Partisanship Has Paralyzed Washington and Polarized America* (New York: Penguin, 2007), p. 63.

11. William F. Buckley Jr., "Politics Hides Genuine Qualities" [ns, 1991]. Robert Taft Jr. Papers (Library of Congress) 1:1.

12. Charles P. Taft to Jack Miller, April 11, 1966. Charles P. Taft Papers (Library of Congress) 217: "Republicans for Progress (February-April 1966)."

13. Patterson, p. 437.

14. Richard Norton Smith, *Thomas E. Dewey and His Times* (New York: Simon & Schuster, 1982), p. 361.

15. David M. Oshinsky, *A Conspiracy So Immense: The World of Joe McCarthy* (New York: Oxford University Press, 2005), p. 108.

16. Peter Viereck, "Conserving Is Not Conforming," address to the American Historical Association, December 28, 1954. Source courtesy of Peter Viereck.

17. Janann Sherman, *No Place for a Woman: A Life of Margaret Chase Smith* (New Brunswick, NJ: Rutgers University Press, 1999).

18. Walter Kohler quoted in Oshinsky, p. 232.

19. Smith, p. 586.
20. *Ibid.*, p. 594.
21. *Ibid.*, p. 584.
22. John W. Sloan, *Eisenhower and the Management of Prosperity* (Lawrence, KS: University Press of Kansas, 1991), p. 54.
23. Michael Korda, "Being More Like Ike," *LAT* August 20, 2007.
24. Patterson, p. 312.
25. Fred I. Greenstein, *The Hidden-Hand Presidency: Eisenhower as Leader* (New York: Basic Books, 1982), p. 52.
26. Oshinsky, p. 442.
27. William Graham to Charles T. Percy, July 10, 1959. Charles T. Percy Papers (CTPP) (Chicago Historical Society) 12:84.
28. William A. Rusher to William F. Buckley Jr., March 9, 1972. William F. Buckley Jr. Papers (Yale University) I-166:1093.
29. Greenstein, p. 50.
30. Steven Wagner, *Eisenhower Republicanism: Pursuing the Middle Way* (DeKalb, IL: Northern Illinois Press, 2006).
31. Arthur Schlesinger Jr., *The Vital Center: The Politics of Freedom* (orig. pub. 1949; rev. ed. New York: Da Capo, 1988), pp. 26–28.
32. Arthur Schlesinger Jr., *A Life in the 20th Century: Innocent Beginnings, 1917–1950* (Boston and New York: Houghton Mifflin, 2000), p. 516.
33. Arthur Larson, *A Republican Looks at His Party* (New York: Harper & Brothers, 1956), p. 18; David Stebenne, *Modern Republican: Arthur Larson and the Eisenhower Years* (Bloomington, IN: Indiana University Press, 2006), p. 161.
34. Sloan, p. 71.
35. Dwight D. Eisenhower, "The Chance for Peace," address delivered before the American Society of Newspaper Editors, April 16, 1953. Available at http://www.presidency.ucsb.edu.
36. Matthew Dallek, "Eisenhower Interstate Highways Offer a Road Map for Obama Stimulus," *Politico* February 5, 2009.
37. Larson, p. 19.
38. Barry Goldwater to William A. Steiger, May 16, 1957. William A. Steiger Papers (Wisconsin State Historical Society) 60:6.
39. William F. Buckley Jr., *Up From Liberalism* (New Rochelle, NY: Arlington House, 1959), p. 189.
40. For example, Buckley charged that Kingman Brewster Jr., the reformist president of Yale University in the 1960s, had by sympathizing with student demonstrations become "a Kerensky . . . wooing the cheers of the mob." William F. Buckley Jr., "Capitulation of Kingman Brewster," *New York Journal-American* May 1, 1970.
41. John B. Judis, *William F. Buckley, Jr.: Patron Saint of the Conservatives* (New York: Touchstone, 1990), p. 162.
42. See Russell Wheeler Davenport Papers (Library of Congress) boxes 29 and 30.
43. Kevin Mattson, *When America Was Great: The Fighting Faith of Postwar Liberalism* (New York: Routledge), pp. 42–43.
44. Jennifer Burns, "Liberalism and the Conservative Imagination," in Neil Jumonville and Kevin Mattson (eds.), *Liberalism for a New Century* (Berkeley, CA: University of California Press, 2007).
45. John B. Judis, "The Conservatism of Henry Kissinger," 1986, available at http://aliciapatterson.org/stories/conservatism-henry-kissinger.
46. August Heckscher, "Where are the American Conservatives?," *Confluence* 2:3 (September 1953), pp. 60–61.

47. Paul G. Hoffman, "How Eisenhower Saved the Republican Party," *Collier's* October 26, 1956, p. 47.
48. Daniel J. Galvin, *Presidential Party Building: Dwight D. Eisenhower to George W. Bush* (Princeton, NJ: Princeton University Press, 2010), p. 57.
49. "Publisher's Statement," *NR* November 19, 1955, p. 5.
50. Gould, p. 339.
51. Louis Harris, *Is There a Republican Majority?: Political Trends, 1952–1956* (New York: Harper and Brothers, 1954), p. 201.
52. Thomas E. Dewey, *Thomas E. Dewey on the Two-Party System* (Garden City, NY: Doubleday, 1966), p. 9.
53. Interview with Willis D. Gradison Jr., April 7, 2009.
54. Sloan, p. 62.
55. The names of these factions depended on who was doing the naming. The moderate Republican *Advance* magazine, for example, in 1962 called them "radical rightists" (conservatives), "Old Guard Republicans" or "Standpatters" (stalwarts), "constructive conservatives" (moderates), and "Me-Tooers" (progressives). See "The Republican Dilemma on Capitol Hill: In the House," *Advance* 1:5 (March 1962), pp. 12–13. The best taxonomy of the Republican factions is in A. James Reichley, *Conservatives in an Age of Change: The Nixon and Ford Administrations* (Washington, DC: Brookings Institution, 1981), pp. 22–34. Reichley denominates the right-wing group as "fundamentalists," a term that is potentially confusing since it suggests a religious influence that for the most part was absent until the 1970s. I have otherwise adapted my description of the factions from Reichley's account.
56. Interview with Daniel J. Evans, December 12, 2005.
57. In Keith Poole and Howard Rosenthal's ordering of members of Congress on a liberal-conservative axis, Javits was the most liberal Republican member of Congress from 1937 to 2002. Even so, his DW-nominate score (0.234) was still to the right of the median Senate Democratic score over that period (0.243). See http://pooleandrosenthal.com/Is_John_Kerry_A_Liberal.htm.
58. Reichley, p. 33.
59. Jacob Riis, *How the Other Half Lives: Studies Among the Tenements of New York* (orig. pub. 1890; New York: Bedford Books, 1996), p. 233.
60. Alan R. Raucher, *Paul G. Hoffman: Architect of Foreign Aid* (Lexington, KY: University Press of Kentucky, 1985).
61. John B. Judis, *The Paradox of American Democracy: Elites, Special Interests, and the Betrayal of Public Trust* (New York: Pantheon, 2000), pp. 66–69.
62. Oshinsky, p. 357.
63. Interview with Jonathan Moore, November 6, 2006.
64. Interview with John R. Price, July 20, 2007. See also Fred Schwengel, *The Republican Party: Its Heritage and History* (Washington, DC: Acropolis, 1987).
65. Hoffman, p. 47.
66. *Ibid.*
67. William F. Buckley Jr., "Why the South Must Prevail," *NR* August 24, 1957.
68. For a discussion of the "fusionism" that linked the disparate strands of conservatism, see George H. Nash, *The Conservative Intellectual Movement in America* (2nd ed.) (Wilmington, DE: Intercollegiate Studies Institute, 1998), pp. 161–171.
69. Theodore H. White, *The Making of the President 1960* (New York: Atheneum, 1961), p. 199.
70. Garry Wills, *Nixon Agonistes: The Crisis of the Self-Made Man* (orig. pub. 1969; Boston, MA: Mariner, 2002), p. 32.
71. Michael Kramer and Sam Roberts, *"I Never Wanted To Be Vice-President of Anything!": An Investigative Biography of Nelson Rockefeller* (New York: Basic Books, 1976), p. 3.

72. Interview with Howard Gillette Jr., November 2, 2006.
73. White, pp. 203–205.
74. Roscoe Drummond, "Rockefeller Liberal Views Seen Vital to Nixon Victory," *NYHT* July 22, 1960, p. 11.
75. Richard M. Nixon, *Six Crises* (Garden City, NY: Doubleday, 1962), p. 313.
76. Karl A. Lamb, "Civil Rights and the Republican Platform: Nixon Achieves Control," in Paul Tillett (ed.), *Inside Politics: The National Conventions, 1960* (Dobbs Ferry, NY: Occana, 1962), p. 65.
77. Ivan Hinderaker, "The 1960 Republican Convention: Chicago and Before," in Tillett (op cit.), p. 23.
78. Barry M. Goldwater remarks to the Republican Party National Convention, July 27, 1960. F. Clifton White Papers (Cornell University) 7: "Statement/BG Withdrawing Nomination—1960."
79. Roscoe Drummond, "A Virtual Capitulation by Conservatives Is Seen," *NYHT* July 29, 1960, p. 13.
80. John J. Womey to Kenneth Keating, November 16, 1960. Kenneth Keating Papers (University of Rochester) 2–139:9.
81. Laura Jane Gifford, *The Center Cannot Hold: The 1960 Presidential Election and the Rise of Modern Conservatism* (DeKalb, IL: Northern Illinois University Press, 2009), p. 20.

CHAPTER 2

1. William J. Miller, *Henry Cabot Lodge: A Biography* (New York: Heinman, 1967), p. 134.
2. "Republicans: The Great Surprise," *Time* September 26, 1960.
3. Henry Cabot Lodge Jr. address to Westchester County [NY] Republican Committee Dinner, January 26, 1961. George L. Hinman Papers (GLHP) (Rockefeller Archives) IV-J2-1–34:207.
4. See for example Conservative Society of America, "Where Henry Cabot Lodge Really Stands," March? 1964. William F. Buckley Jr. Papers (WFBP) (Yale University) I-29: "Coudert-Courtney (1964)."
5. Thomas Hayden, "Who Are the Student Boat-Rockers?," *Mademoiselle* August 1961, p. 236. The piece was Hayden's first work of paid journalism. He neglected to mention it in his autobiography, possibly because of the incongruity of the future SDS leader's analysis appearing alongside ads touting control-top panties and warning of the dangers of "emotional perspiration." Tom Hayden, *Reunion: A Memoir* (New York: Random House, 1988).
6. James Miller, *"Democracy Is in the Streets"* (Cambridge, MA: Harvard University Press, 1987), p. 65.
7. John A. Andrew, *The Other Side of the Sixties: Young Americans for Freedom and the Rise of Conservative Politics* (New Brunswick, NJ: Rutgers University Press, 1997).
8. Bruce K. Chapman, "Private Reflections on a Public Life" (unpublished memoir, 1994), p. 289.
9. *Ibid.*, p. 293.
10. Bruce K. Chapman, "George's Journey," in Frank Gregorsky (ed.), *Speaking of George Gilder* (Seattle, WA: Discovery Institute Press, 1998), p. 24.
11. Bruce K. Chapman, "A 'Progressive's' Progress," *NR* April 17, 1981, p. 412.
12. Larissa MacFarquhar, "The Gilder Effect," *New Yorker* May 29, 2000.
13. Hayden, p. 236.
14. Todd Gitlin, *The Sixties: Years of Hope, Days of Rage* (New York: Bantam, 1993).
15. Interview with Bruce K. Chapman, December 8, 2009.
16. Charles Lucey, "Conservatism Takes Moderate Tinge," *Pittsburgh Press* May 1, 1961.
17. Dan Flynn interview with Howard Phillips, August 17, 2005, available at http://www. flynnfiles.com/blog/phillips/phillips3.htm.

18. "Education: Campus Conservatives," *Time* February 10, 1961; interview with Christopher Bayley, July 2, 2007.
19. Hayden, p. 333.
20. Bruce K. Chapman, "Young Republicans: The Amateur Pros," *Harvard Crimson* May 1, 1963.
21. Occasionally the editors referred to themselves as the Republican Advance organization. The name had no apparent connection to the identically-named group of moderates that had been active in the late 1940s and early 1950s.
22. Bruce K. Chapman to "Dear Sir," November 15, 1960. GLHP IV-J2-1–9:46.
23. Chapman, unpublished memoir, p. 309.
24. Elliot L. Richardson to Richard M. Nixon, January 19, 1961. Kingman Brewster Jr. Personal Papers (Yale University) 74: "Brewster, Kingman—Personal."
25. See Daniel J. Galvin, *Presidential Party Building: Dwight D. Eisenhower to George W. Bush* (Princeton, NJ: Princeton University Press, 2010), pp. 41–69.
26. Dwight D. Eisenhower, "Farewell Radio and Television Address to the American People," January 17, 1961, available at http://www.presidency.ucsb.edu; Stephen A. Ambrose, *Eisenhower: Soldier and President* (New York: Simon & Schuster, 1990), p. 537.
27. Rick Perlstein, *Before the Storm: Barry Goldwater and the Unmaking of the American Consensus* (New York: Hill and Wang, 2001), p. 20.
28. Stephen Hess, "Ike's Second Army," *Weekly Standard* February 26, 2007, pp. 38–39.
29. Dwight D. Eisenhower to William W. Flenniken, December 3, 1953, in Alfred D. Chandler Jr. (ed.), *The Papers of Dwight D. Eisenhower* (21 vols.) (Baltimore, MD: Johns Hopkins University Press, 1970–2001) 15:727–728.
30. William Rentschler to Charles T. Percy, July 22, 1959. Charles T. Percy Papers (Chicago Historical Society) 12:86.
31. Galvin, p. 61.
32. Walter N. Thayer to Richard M. Nixon, December 5, 1960. Walter N. Thayer Papers (WNTP) (Hoover Presidential Library) II-7:5.
33. "House Republican Challenges Halleck on Coalition with South," *CQ* December 15, 1960.
34. National Committee for an Effective Congress, "Congressional Report," July 10, 1961; Charles P. Taft to George Hecht, March 24, 1961. Charles P. Taft Papers (CPTP) (Library of Congress) 209: "National Committee for an Effective Congress."
35. Robert C. Albright, "House GOP Liberals Hold Power Balance," *WP* February 13, 1961, p. A2. See also "House Enlarges Rules Committee," *CQ Almanac 1961*, pp. 402–406; Robert Remini, *The House: The History of the House of Representatives* (New York: HarperCollins, 2006), pp. 366–387; Julian Zelizer, *On Capitol Hill: The Struggle to Reform Congress and Its Consequences* (New York: Cambridge University Press, 2004), pp. 56–60; Ronald Brownstein, *The Second Civil War: How Extreme Partisanship Has Paralyzed Washington and Polarized America* (New York: Penguin, 2007), pp. 66–69.
36. "Advance Notice," *Advance* 1:2 (April 1961), p. 2.
37. Walter Lippmann, "Today and Tomorrow," *NYHT* December 20, 1960.
38. Bruce K. Chapman to Alan E. Povey, January 6, 1964. Ripon Society Papers (RSP) (Cornell University) 3:16.
39. "Advance Notice," *Advance* 1:1 (February 1961), p. 2.
40. *Advance* brochure [nd]. RSP 3:160.
41. "You Have to Play to Win," *Advance* 1:5 (March 1962), p. 3.
42. "Ideas and Images," *Advance* 1:5 (March 1962), p. 19.
43. "Civil Rights: A Republican Imperative," *Advance* 1:3 (July 1961), p. 7.
44. "Toward a Republican Advance," *Advance* 1:1 (February 1961), p. 6.
45. Bruce K. Chapman to Alan E. Povey, January 6, 1964. RSP 3:16.

46. Moderates contrasted Republican intellectual inactivity with the Democratic Advisory Council, formed in 1956 to develop new ideas and approaches. Its work shaped the 1960 Democratic platform and most of Kennedy's campaign issues.

47. Ray C. Bliss et al., "Report of the Committee on Big City Politics" (Republican National Committee), January 2, 1962. Thomas H. Kuchel Papers (University of California) 79B:4 "Republican Fact Sheets."

48. "The Charge Up Capitol Hill," *Advance* 1:5 (March 1962), p. 29.

49. "Ideology and the Party Split," *Advance* 1:5 (March 1962), p. 26.

50. Clifford Case, "Course for the GOP," *Advance* 1:1 (February 1961), p. 12.

51. "Ideology and the Party Split," *Advance* 1:5 (March 1962), p. 23.

52. Richard Norton Smith, *Thomas E. Dewey and His Times* (New York: Simon & Schuster, 1982), p. 218.

53. Frederick C. Groshens, "Old Friends" [nd—1967.] Hope C. Kading Papers (Idaho State Historical Society) 2.

54. William A. Rusher to William F. Buckley Jr., March 9, 1972. WFBP I–166:1093; David M. Oshinsky, *A Conspiracy So Immense: The World of Joe McCarthy* (New York: Oxford University Press, 2005), pp. 393–394.

55. William A. Rusher, *The Rise of the Right* (New York: William Morrow, 1984), p. 26.

56. William A. Rusher to William F. Buckley Jr., March 23, 1960. WFBP I-10: "Milbank, Jeremiah J. (1960)."

57. Interview with Christopher Bayley, July 2, 2007.

58. Interview with Bruce K. Chapman, December 8, 2009.

59. Tanya M. Melich, "Youth Politics: A Study of Cliques within the Association of New York State Young Republican Clubs, 1932 to 1959" (unpublished master's thesis in political science, Columbia University, 1961), p. 184. Source courtesy of Tanya Melich.

60. F. Clifton White with Jerome Tuccille, *Politics as a Noble Calling: The Memoirs of F. Clifton White* (Ottawa, IL: Jameson, 1994), p. 57.

61. See for example Cord Meyer, *Facing Reality: From World Federalism to the CIA* (New York: Harper & Row, 1980), pp. 51–55.

62. Marvin Liebman, *Coming Out Conservative* (San Francisco, CA: Chronicle, 1992), p. 149.

63. Hayden, p. 334.

64. Liebman, p. 146.

65. Arthur M. Richardson to L. Judson Morhouse, March 16, 1961. GLHP IV-J2-1–9:46.

66. Interview with Steven Livengood, March 1, 2009.

67. George L. Hinman to Nelson A. Rockefeller, March 15, 1961. GLHP IV-J2-1–42:255.

68. Michael N. Scelsi to Robert R. Douglass, March 14, 1963. GLHP IV-J2-1–51:321.

69. Bruce K. Chapman to Alexander Halpern and L. Judson Morhouse, July 8, 1961. GLHP IV-J2-1–9:46.

70. Bruce K. Chapman to L. Judson Morhouse, July 8, 1961. GLHP IV-J2-1–9:46.

71. Rusher, pp. 98–101; F. Clifton White with William Gill, *Suite 3505: The Story of the Draft Goldwater Movement* (New Rochelle, NY: Arlington House, 1967), pp. 31–32.

72. Robert R. Douglass to George L. Hinman, October 10, 1961. GLHP IV-J2-1–9:46.

73. George L. Hinman handwritten note on Robert R. Douglass to George L. Hinman, October 10, 1961. GLHP IV-J2-1–9:46.

74. Bruce K. Chapman to Robert R. Douglass, February 19, 1962. GLHP IV-J2-1–9:46.

75. Nelson A. Rockefeller to George E. Agree, April 10, 1962. GLHP IV-J2-1–9:46.

76. Robert R. Douglass to George L. Hinman, June 26, 1961. GLHP IV-J2-1–14:77.

77. George L. Hinman to Nelson A. Rockefeller, August 29, 1962. GLHP IV-J2-1–20:118.

78. George L. Hinman to Oscar M. Ruebenhausen, July 7, 1961. GLHP IV-J2-1–62:395.

79. George L. Hinman to Irene Slater, August 25, 1961. GLHP IV-J2-1–26:153.

80. John D. Deardourff to Robert R. Douglass, December 17, 1962. GLHP IV-J2-1–13:71.

81. Robert R. Douglass to George L. Hinman, July 17, 1962. GLHP IV-J2-1-9:46.
82. George L. Hinman to Roswell B. Perkins, January 17, 1963. GLHP IV-J2-1-9:46.
83. Interview with Thomas B. Curtis, October 23, 1972 (Columbia University Oral History Archives) (CUOHA).
84. Thomas B. Curtis to Raymond R. Tucker, January 3, 1958. Thomas B. Curtis Papers (TBCP) (University of Missouri) 24183.
85. Thomas B. Curtis, "A Report from Your Congressman," October 15, 1952. TBCP 24180.
86. Bruce K. Chapman to John S. Saloma III et al., February 21, 1967. RSP 11:5.
87. Remini, pp. 403–404.
88. Interview with Thomas B. Curtis, October 23, 1972 (CUOHA); Thomas B. Curtis and Donald L. Westerfield, *Congressional Intent* (Westport, CT: Praeger, 1992), p. 50.
89. Roscoe Drummond, "Republicans Default," *NYHT* February 19, 1961.
90. "The Republican Dilemma on Capitol Hill: In the House," *Advance* 1:5 (March 1962), p. 14.
91. "Ideas and Images," *Advance* 1:5 (March 1962), p. 20.
92. "You Have to Play to Win," *Advance* 1:5 (March 1962), p. 3.
93. "The Republican Dilemma on Capitol Hill: In the House," *Advance* 1:5 (March 1962), p. 13.
94. "The Political Notebook," *Advance* 2:1 (June 1962), p. 10.
95. *Advance* 2:1 (June 1962), pp. 25, 27.
96. "An Open Letter to the Members of the Republican National Committee," *Advance* supp. December 1962. GLHP IV-J2-1-9:47.
97. Walter N. Thayer to Bruce K. Chapman, March 5, 1962. WNTP III–2:12.
98. "Ike Likes Us," *Advance Notice* 1 (July 1962), p. 8. GLHP IV-J2-1-9:47; Dwight D. Eisenhower, remarks at All-Republican Conference in Gettysburg, Pennsylvania, June 30, 1962. Available at www.eisenhowermemorial.org.
99. Kenneth B. Keating press release, June 29, 1962. Dwight D. Eisenhower Post-Presidential Papers (DDEPPP) (Eisenhower Presidential Library) PA-19: "National Republican Citizens Committee (2)."
100. George F. Gilder and Bruce K. Chapman, *The Party That Lost Its Head* (New York: Alfred A. Knopf, 1966), p. 97.
101. The NRCC was later renamed the Republican Citizens Committee of the U.S.A. to avoid confusion with the Republican National Committee.
102. National Republican Citizens Committee memo, June 30, 1962. DDEPPP PA-19: "National Republican Citizens Committee (2)." See also interview with Walter N. Thayer, April 28, 1967 (CUOHA).
103. Dwight D. Eisenhower to Bryce N. Harlow, June 5, 1962. DDEPPP SNF-7: "Harlow, Bryce (1962) (4)."
104. Dwight D. Eisenhower to William E. Miller, July 3, 1962. DDEPPP PA-19: "National Republican Citizens Committee (3)."
105. Gilder and Chapman, p. 97.
106. Bruce K. Chapman, "The State of the Republican Party," December 2, 1963. GLHP IV-J2-1-9:46.
107. Robert C. Albright, "Goldwater Blasts GOP Plan to Use Old Guard Chiefs," *WP* July 3, 1962.
108. Barry Goldwater to *Washington Star* July 10, 1962.
109. Bruce K. Chapman, "The State of the Republican Party," December 2, 1963. GLHP IV-J2-1-9:46.
110. Dwight D. Eisenhower to Charles S. Jones, July 3, 1962. DDEPPP SNF-10: "Jones, Charles S. (1962)."
111. Arthur M. Schlesinger Jr., *Robert Kennedy and His Times* (New York: Houghton Mifflin, 1978), p. 557.

112. "The Political Notebook," *Advance* 2:2 (November 1962), p. 39; George Gilder, "Why Kennedy Has Failed," *Advance* supplement October? 1962. GLHP IV-J2-1-9:47.

113. Edwin A. Lahey, "Richard Nixon: An Obituary of a Career," *BG* November 8, 1962, p. 10; Mary McGrory, "Mr. Nixon's Last Stand," *BG* November 9, 1962.

114. "Statistics Show Nixon Victory," *Advance Notice* 2.

115. Arthur M. Richardson, "Report on California," March 5, 1962. GLHP IV-J2-1-32:189.

116. "The Republican Dilemma on Capitol Hill: In the Senate," *Advance* 1:5 (March 1962), p. 17.

117. "An Open Letter to the Members of the Republican National Committee," *Advance* supplement December 1962. GLHP IV-J2-1-9:47.

118. "The Charge Up Capitol Hill," *Advance* 1:5 (March 1962), p. 29.

119. "Re-opening the Open Letter," *Advance* 2:3 (spring 1963), pp. 45–46.

120. William A. Rusher, "Crossroads for the GOP," *NR* February 12, 1963, pp. 109–112.

121. "The Ford in the GOP Future," *Advance Notice* 5 (January 29, 1963), pp. 1–2.

122. George F. Hobart, "Inside the Goldwater 'Draft,'" *Advance* 2:3 (spring 1963).

123. F. Clifton White to Barry Goldwater, April 16, 1963. F. Clifton White Papers (FCWP) (Cornell University) 18: "Goldwater Correspondence."

124. F. Clifton White to Charles R. Barr, September 25, 1962. FCWP 18: "Young Republicans."

125. Bruce K. Chapman, "Young Republicans: The Amateur Pros," *Harvard Crimson* May 1, 1963.

126. Arthur M. Richardson to George L. Hinman, February 19, 1963. GLHP IV-J2-1-51:321.

127. Robert R. Douglass to George L. Hinman, March 20, 1963. GLHP IV-J2-1-9:46.

128. Novak, pp. 199–200.

129. Bruce K. Chapman, "The State of the Republican Party," December 2, 1963. GLHP IV-J2-1-9:46.

130. Interview with Leonard Nadasdy, June 26, 2007.

131. Novak, pp. 196–197.

132. Edward D. Failor to Donald E. Lukens, August 12, 1963. FCWP 18: "Young Republicans."

133. Mercer Cross, "Mob-Style Tactics Cited," *Minneapolis Tribune*, July 7, 1963.

134. See for example John M. Ashbrook speech of August 23, 1963 and attachments in CR September 24, 1963.

135. Novak, p. 207.

136. James Desmond, *Nelson Rockefeller: A Political Biography* (New York: Macmillan, 1964), p. 305.

137. Stanley Meisler, "View of Rockefeller Remarriage Here Reported: 'Political Suicide,'" *WP* May 2, 1963, p. A8.

138. John Deardourff to Nelson A. Rockefeller, May 24, 1963. GLHP IV-J2-1-14:77.

139. Robert R. Douglass to George L. Hinman, May 8, 1963. GLHP IV-J2-1-1:2.

140. Bruce K. Chapman to George L. Hinman, October 28, 1963. GLHP IV-J2-1-9:46.

141. Meg Greenfield, *Washington* (New York: PublicAffairs, 2001), pp. 184, 186–188.

142. "Who's Playing Politics on Civil Rights?," *Advance Notice* 7 (July 25, 1963), pp. 8–12.

143. Martin Luther King Jr., "Letter from a Birmingham Jail," in Paul F. Boller Jr. and Ronald Story, *A More Perfect Union: Documents in U.S. History*, vol. 2 (Boston, MA: Houghton Mifflin, 1996), p. 247.

144. Howard Hubbard, "Five Long Hot Summers and How They Grew," *Public Interest* Sep. 1968.

145. "The Birds and the Beasts Were There," *NR* June 18, 1963, pp. 485–486.

146. Bruce K. Chapman memo, August 13?, 1963. GLHP IV-J2-1-1:2.

147. George L. Hinman to Nelson A. Rockefeller, August 20, 1963. GLHP IV-J2-1-1:2.

148. Bruce K. Chapman to Alvin Dozeman, December 18, 1963. RSP 3:160.

149. Bruce K. Chapman and George F. Gilder to Charles P. Taft II, December 12, 1963. CPTP 199: "Committee to Support Moderate Republicans."
150. Bruce K. Chapman to Alan E. Povey, January 6, 1964. RSP 3:161.
151. "The Unprepared Meets the Unforeseen," *Advance* 2:5 (fall 1963), p. 5.
152. "Can Goldwater Win? No," *Advance* 2:5 (fall 1963), p. 16.
153. Bruce K. Chapman, "The State of the Republican Party," December 2, 1963. GLHP IV-J2-1–9:46.
154. *Advance* Staff to Friends of *Advance*, April 1964. Tanya Melich Papers (SUNY Albany) V–6:14.
155. See for example Nicol Rae, *The Decline and Fall of Liberal Republicanism* (New York; Oxford University Press, 1989), p. 119.
156. Bruce K. Chapman to George L. Hinman, August 3, 1964. GLHP IV-J2-1–9:46.

CHAPTER 3

1. Interview with John R. Price, July 20, 2007.
2. Walter N. Thayer notes on meeting with Dwight D. Eisenhower, March 9, 1964. Walter N. Thayer Papers (Hoover Presidential Library) III-2:13.
3. John S. Saloma III to William W. Scranton, January 3, 1964. Ripon Society Papers (RSP) (Cornell University) 1:2.
4. Geoffrey Barr, *The Bow Group: A History* (London: Politico's, 2001).
5. Emil Frankel, "A Republican Looks at the Tories: Conservatives Who Win," *Advance* 1:5 (March 1962), pp. 27–28.
6. John S. Saloma III, "The New Political Order: A History of the Conservative Infrastructure" (unpublished manuscript), December 1982, pp. 16–17. Tanya M. Melich Papers (TMMP) (SUNY Albany) V-8:15.
7. "Editorial," *RF* 5:8 (August 1969), p. 3. Many of Ripon's members had also been inspired by Theodore H. White's bestseller *The Making of the President 1960* and particularly by his assertion that until the 1920s, "the natural home party of the American intellectual, writer, savant and artist was the Republican Party." Theodore H. White, *The Making of the President 1960* (New York: Atheneum, 1961), p. 65.
8. Emil Frankel and John S. Saloma III, "A Proposal for an American Bow Group" (nd–December? 1962). RSP 1:24.
9. Ripon Society minutes, December 12, 1962. RSP 1:24.
10. Donald Gibby Paige, "The Ripon Society" (unpublished Harvard undergraduate honors thesis), March 1968, pp. 52–53.
11. Saloma, "The New Political Order," p. iv.
12. Ripon Society, "A Call to Excellence in Leadership: An Open Letter to the New Generation of Republicans," January 1964. RSP 3:175.
13. Robert J. Samuelson, "Ripon Society Owes Its Success to the Enemy, Sen. Goldwater," *Harvard Crimson* February 12, 1965.
14. Ripon Society, "A Call to Excellence."
15. Saloma, "The New Political Order," p. 115.
16. Thomas E. Petri and J. Eugene Marans, "Ripon at Twenty-Five," *RF* February 1988, p. 21.
17. Ripon Society, "A Call to Excellence." Senator Hugh Scott commented on the manifesto: "I like your last line . . . The story of my life!" Hugh N. Scott to John S. Saloma III, September 12, 1966. RSP 11:29.
18. Lee W. Huebner and Thomas E. Petri (eds.), *The Ripon Papers 1963–1968* (Washington, DC: National Press, 1968), p. 3.
19. Neal Gregory, "The Ripon Society," *National Journal* June 6, 1970, p. 1213.
20. Ken Cascone to Emil Frankel, January? 1964. RSP 2:83.
21. Dwight D. Eisenhower to Walter N. Thayer, January 23, 1964. RSP 3:177.

22. John S. Saloma III to Lee W. Huebner and John R. Price, May 17, 1965. RSP 7: "Behn corr."
23. "Ike," *RF* 5:5 (May 1969), p. 3.
24. Interview with Lee W. Huebner, April 11, 2007.
25. Stewart D. Davis, "Ripon's History," *Harvard Law School Bulletin* January 1965, p. 7.
26. Interview with Jonathan Moore, November 6, 2006.
27. Interview with George Cabot Lodge, March 23, 2007.
28. Nelson A. Rockefeller to Henry Cabot Lodge Jr., January 7, 1964. George L. Hinman Papers (GLHP) (Rockefeller Archives) 1–34:207.
29. Robert R. Mullen, National Draft Lodge Headquarters press release, February 29, 1964. GLHP 1–34:207.
30. National Draft Lodge Headquarters, press release, February 11, 1964. GLHP 1–34:207.
31. William F. Buckley Jr. to A. H. Barton, May 23, 1962. William F. Buckley Jr. Papers (WFBP) (Yale University) I–19, "Buckley, William F. Jr.—Personal (Connecticut Bank and Trust Co.) (1962)."
32. Liebman, pp. 143–144.
33. Charles McC. Mathias news release, April 29, 1964. Charles McC. Mathias Papers (CMMP) (Johns Hopkins University) IX-2: "Primary Campaign Press Releases (1964)."
34. Interview with Charles McC. Mathias, June 24, 2005.
35. "You 'Backed Mac' . . . But Did Mac Back YOU?," Bozell campaign flyer May 15, 1964 (r); Mathias fact sheet, April? 1964. CMMP IX:2, "Brent Bozell—Primary Campaign (1964)."
36. Interview with Lee W. Huebner, April 11, 2007.
37. Patricia Buckley Bozell to William F. Buckley Jr., February 25, 1964. WFBP I-29: "Bozell, L. Brent (1964)."
38. L. Brent Bozell Jr., "Freedom or Virtue?," *NR* September 11, 1962.
39. Lee Huebner, Ripon Society dossier on L. Brent Bozell Jr. prepared for Charles McC. Mathias, April 1964. CMMP IX-2: "Brent Bozell—Primary Campaign (1964)."
40. Garry Wills to William F. Buckley Jr. [nd—1964]. WFBP I-33: "Wills, Garry (1964)."
41. Charles McC. Mathias news release, April 30, 1964. CMMP IX-2: "Primary Campaign Press Releases (1964)."
42. William Chapman, "Mathias Sees Threat to Party from Far Right," *WP* April 29, 1964.
43. Charles McC. Mathias to *Baltimore Sun*, May 13, 1964. CMMP IX-2: "Brent Bozell— Primary Campaign (1964)."
44. L. Brent Bozell Jr., "The Challenge to Conservatives, II," *NR* January 14, 1961, p. 12.
45. Charles McC. Mathias news release, April 29, 1964. CMMP IX-2: "Primary Campaign Press Releases (1964)."
46. Drew Pearson, "Barry's Disciples Aid Rights Tieup," *WP* May 16, 1964.
47. Charles McC. Mathias to Louis A. Gravelle, May 6, 1964. CMMP I-1:26.
48. "The Primary," *Suburban Record* [Montgomery County, MD] May 7, 1964.
49. Robert Novak, *The Agony of the G.O.P. 1964* (New York: Macmillan, 1965), p. 332.
50. Kramer and Roberts, p. 235.
51. *Ibid.*, p. 5.
52. Cary Reich, *The Life of Nelson A. Rockefeller: Worlds to Conquer 1908–1958* (New York: Doubleday, 1996), pp. xv–xvi.
53. Theodore H. White, *The Making of the President 1964* (New York: Atheneum, 1965), pp. 119–121.
54. George E. Mowry, *The California Progressives* (Berkeley, CA: University of California Press, 1951), especially pp. 86–104. A useful overview of historical scholarship on progressivism is Glenda Elizabeth Gilmore, *Who Were the Progressives?* (Boston, MA: Bedford/St. Martin's, 2002).

55. Jackson K. Putnam, "The Progressive Legacy in California," in William Deverell and Tom Sitton (eds.), *California Progressivism Revisited* (Berkeley, CA: University of California Press, 1994), pp. 248–250.

56. See Lisa McGirr, *Suburban Warriors: The Origins of the New American Right* (Princeton, NJ: Princeton University Press, 2001).

57. California Republican Assembly Board of Directors minutes, June 9, 1963. California Republican Assembly Papers (CRAP) (UCLA) 1: "1959–65"; Rus Walton interview May 10, 1983. Bancroft Library Reagan Gubernatorial Oral History Project (BLRGOHP) (University of California).

58. UPI report March 17, 1964. CRAP 32:19.

59. Memo RLN-PAR, March 1964. William A. Rusher Papers (WARP) (Library of Congress) 155:8.

60. Paul Beck, "How the Ultra-Conservatives Could Take Over State GOP," *LAT* May 25, 1964, p. A1.

61. William A. Rusher to *National Review* editors, May? 1964. WFBP I-30: "Inter-Office Memos (August-December 1964)."

62. Paul Beck, "Is the Militant Right Trying to Seize Control of the GOP?," *LAT* May 24, 1964, p. B2.

63. Paul Beck, "How the Ultra-Conservatives Could Take Over State GOP," *LAT* May 25, 1964, p. A1.

64. Caspar Weinberger interview March 6, 1979 (BLRGOHP).

65. Kurt Schuparra, *Triumph of the Right: The Rise of the California Conservative Movement, 1945–66* (Armonk, NY: M. E. Sharpe, 1998), p. 85.

66. Phyllis Schlafly, *A Choice Not an Echo* (3rd ed.) (Alton, IL: Pere Marquette Press, 1964), p. 110.

67. *Ibid.*, pp. 5, 108.

68. *Ibid.*, p. 102.

69. *Ibid.*, p. 116.

70. *John Birch Society Bulletin*, March 1, 1961, pp. 6–7. WFBP I-14: "John Birch Society (2 of 2) (1961)."

71. Donald T. Critchlow, *Phyllis Schlafly and Grassroots Conservatism: A Woman's Crusade* (Princeton, NJ: Princeton University Press, 2005), pp. 98, 121.

72. T. J. Toma to "Our Governors and Editors," May? 1964. William W. Scranton Papers— James Reichley Files (WWSP-JRF) (Pennsylvania State Historical Library) Campaign Material 2:40.

73. "What the People Should Know About Rockefeller," January 1960. Charles P. Taft Papers (CPTP) (Library of Congress) 215: "Republican Party—Presidential Candidates (1955–59)."

74. Dick Darling interview June 23, 1981 (BLRGOHP).

75. Paul L. Adams, address to New York County Conservative Party dinner, February 22, 1972. WARP 56:5.

76. Interview with Douglas L. Bailey, March 22, 2007.

77. Novak, p. 391.

78. Stuart K. Spencer interview, February 23, 1979 (BLRGOHP).

79. *Ibid.*

80. Jacquelin Hume interview January 26, 1982 (BLRGOHP).

81. William T. Bagley, *California's Golden Years: When Government Worked and Why* (Berkeley, CA: Berkeley Public Policy Press, 2009), p. 109.

82. Donald K. White, "Young Executives Get Into Politics," *San Francisco Examiner* May 2, 1961.

83. Interview with Douglas L. Bailey, March 22, 2007.

84. William E. Roberts interview, June 26, 1979 (BLRGOHP).

85. Stuart K. Spencer interview, February 23, 1979 (BLRGOHP).
86. "A-Arms Could Aid Viet Fight, Goldwater Says," *LAT* May 25, 1964, p. A1.
87. Rockefeller for President Committee, "Whom Do You Want in the Room with the H-BOMB Button?," April? 1964. WFBP I-30: "Goldwater, Barry—Printed Matter (1964)."
88. Stephen Horn, memo to California newspapers, radio, and television stations, May? 1964. WWSP-JRF Campaign Material 2:40; George F. Gilder and Bruce K. Chapman, *The Party That Lost Its Head* (New York: Alfred A. Knopf, 1966), pp. 136–137.
89. Novak, pp. 399–400, 411.
90. Barry Goldwater to William F. Buckley Jr., May 15, 1964. WFBP I-30: "Goldwater, Barry—Correspondence (1964)."
91. Gilder and Chapman, p. 141.
92. "Waiting for California," *NYHT* June 1, 1964, p. 18.
93. Gilder and Chapman, pp. 142–143; White, *The Making of the President 1964*, p. 130.
94. Novak, p. 408.
95. Samuel Lubell, "Goldwater Victory Hinges on Southland," *LAT* May 26, 1964, p. A2.
96. William E. Roberts interview, June 26, 1979 (BLRGOHP).
97. Novak, p. 415.

CHAPTER 4

1. Interview with Daniel J. Evans, December 12, 2005.
2. Ripon Society, "After Cleveland: A Report and Proposal to Republican Moderates," June 12, 1964. Tanya M. Melich Papers (TMMP) (SUNY Albany) I-2:10.
3. *CQ Almanac 1964*, pp. 678, 696.
4. Thomas B. Curtis interview October 23, 1972. Columbia University Oral History Archives (CUOHA).
5. William M. McCulloch statement May 8, 1963. William M. McCulloch Papers (WMMP) (Northern Ohio University) 43: "Statement—Civil Rights."
6. Thomas B. Curtis interview October 23, 1972 (CUOHA).
7. William M. McCulloch to John McCarroll Keefe, October 1, 1963. WMMP 11: "Newspapers."
8. David Shribman, "Ohio's Unlikely Warrior," *Pittsburgh Post-Gazette* March 28, 2010; "Facing Responsibility," *Akron Beacon-Journal* February 11, 1964.
9. "The Evolution of the Civil Rights Bill from the Administration Proposal to the Bill Ordered Reported by the House Judiciary Committee," January 29, 1964. WMMP 43: "Civil Rights of House and Senate."
10. Frank van der Linden, "GOP Leader Misses Message of Praise," *Dayton Journal Herald* February 12, 1964.
11. William M. McCulloch statement to the House of Representatives, January 31, 1964. WMMP 43: "Statement—Civil Rights—Support of H.R. 7152."
12. Meg Greenfield, *Washington* (New York: PublicAffairs, 2001), p. 188.
13. Neil MacNeil, *Dirksen: Portrait of a Public Man* (Cleveland, OH: World, 1970), pp. 233–235.
14. Charles Whalen and Barbara Whalen, *The Longest Debate: A Legislative History of the 1964 Civil Rights Act* (New York: Mentor, 1985), pp. 187–188.
15. Byron C. Hulsey, *Everett Dirksen and His Presidents* (Lawrence, KS: University of Kansas Press, 2000), p. 201.
16. Republicans voted for the bill by 27–6 versus the Democrats' margin of 46–21. *CQ Almanac 1964*, p. 96.
17. Barry Goldwater, *The Conscience of a Conservative* (orig. pub. 1960; Princeton, NJ: Princeton University Press, 2007), p. 30.

18. *Ibid.,* p. 31.
19. Quoted in F. Clifton White with William Gill, *Suite 3505: The Story of the Draft Goldwater Movement* (New Rochelle, NY: Arlington House, 1967), pp. 429–431.
20. Roy Wilkins statement to the Resolutions Committee of the Republican National Convention, July 7, 1964. William W. Scranton Papers—James Reichley Files (WWSP-JRF) (Pennsylvania State Historical Library) Campaign Material 2:41.
21. Betty Farris to U.S. Senate and Americans, March 12, 1964. WWSP-JRF Campaign Material 2:40.
22. Andrew J. Glass, "Goldwater's 'No!' on Rights Bill," *NYHT* June 19, 1964, p. 4.
23. Dan T. Carter, *The Politics of Rage: George Wallace, The Origins of the New Conservatism, and the Transformation of American Politics* (2nd ed.) (Baton Rouge, LA: Louisiana State University Press, 2000), pp. 204–215.
24. "NAACP Breaks a Rule, Denounces Goldwater," *NYHT* June 28, 1964, p. 14.
25. William M. McCulloch statement to the House of Representatives, January 31, 1964. WMMP 43: "Statement—Civil Rights—Support of H.R. 7152."
26. See Rick Perlstein, *Before the Storm: Barry Goldwater and the Unmaking of the American Consensus* (New York: Hill and Wang, 2001), pp. 360–361.
27. Clarence Mitchell speech to Ohio State Conference of NAACP Branches, September 19, 1964. WMMP 11: "NAACP."
28. A. James Reichley, *Conservatives in an Age of Change: The Nixon and Ford Administrations* (Washington, DC: Brookings Institution, 1981), p. 24.
29. Clarence Mitchell speech to Ohio State Conference of NAACP Branches, September 19, 1964. WMMP 11: "NAACP."
30. Brian Feinstein and Eric Schickler, "Platforms and Partners: The Civil Rights Realignment Reconsidered," *Studies in American Political Development* 22:1 (March 2008), p. 1. The authors claim there is "scholarly consensus" on this position.
31. "Don't Water Down Rights Bill—GOP," *Dayton Daily News* February 16, 1964.
32. William S. Beinecke with Geoffrey M. Kabaservice, *Through Mem'ry's Haze: A Personal Memoir* (New York: Prospect Hill Press, 2000), pp. 418–419.
33. "William Warren Scranton," *Current Biography 1964* (Bronx, NY: H. W. Wilson, 1964), p. 398.
34. "The Boomlet for Bill Scranton: How to Succeed Without Trying," *Newsweek* January 27, 1964, p. 26.
35. George D. Wolf, *William Warren Scranton: Pennsylvania Statesman* (University Park, PA: Keystone, 1981), p. 109.
36. Theodore H. White, "Landslide 1964: Jubilant Winners, Republican Wreckage—Now What?," *Life* November 13, 1964.
37. Bailey Laird, "A Political Fiction," *New Yorker* September 16, 1967.
38. Background interview.
39. Jimmy Breslin, "The Newest Candidate's Busy Day," *NYHT* June 14, 1964, p. 8.
40. "What the Governor Told the Press About His Future," *NYHT* June 13, 1964, p. 4; Richard Dougherty, "2nd Ike-Scranton Summit; Anti-Goldwater Balloon?," *NYHT* June 7, 1964, p. 1.
41. Ripon Society, "After Cleveland: A Report and Proposal to Republican Moderates," June 12, 1964. TMMP I-2:10.
42. Roscoe Drummond, "Republicans Cast an Eye on Possible Seat Losses," *NYHT* June 10, 1964, p. 23.
43. A. James Reichley to William W. Scranton, July 2, 2007. Source courtesy of A. James Reichley.
44. "Scranton's Call for 20th Century Republicanism," *NYHT* June 13, 1964, p. 4. Scranton announced his candidacy at the Maryland State Republican Convention, which led to

the original text of his statement ending up in Charles Mathias's papers: Charles McC. Mathias Papers (CMMP) (Johns Hopkins University) I-2:2.

45. John Sherman Cooper statement, June 7, 1964. John Sherman Cooper Papers (University of Kentucky) 300: "Republican Party—Barry Goldwater (1961–67)."

46. J. Eugene Marans to John S. Saloma III, June 25, 1964. Ripon Society Papers (RSP) (Cornell University) 1:1.

47. Ripon Society, "A Declaration of Conscience," July 4, 1964. RSP 3:176.

48. Quoted in John S. Saloma III to "Dear fellow Riponer," July 29, 1964. RSP 1:33.

49. Background interview.

50. Nelson A. Rockefeller to Charles McC. Mathias, June 15, 1964. CMMP I-2:2.

51. Richard Dougherty, "Lodge 'Duty' to GOP," *NYHT* June 30, 1964, p. 1.

52. Michael F. Keating and Earl G. Talbott, "Scranton Whirlwind," *NYHT* June 14, 1964, p. 1.

53. Richard L. Madden, "Scranton: Let's Debate—Goldwater: Why Should I?," *NYHT* June 30, 1964, p. 6.

54. Cincinnati Republicans for Scranton, "Scranton vs. Goldwater," *Cincinnati Enquirer* July 8, 1964, p. 21.

55. National Scranton for President Committee, "In the Great Tradition," June? 1964. WWSP-JRF Campaign Material 2:45.

56. Peter E. Rentschler to Ray C. Bliss, July 9, 1964. Ray C. Bliss Papers (Ohio Historical Society) 17:50.

57. Conservative Society of America, "Where Scranton Really Stands," June? 1964. William F. Buckley Jr. Papers (WFBP) (Yale University) I-29: "Coudert-Courtney (1964)."

58. "The Myth of Moderation," *Cincinnati Enquirer* June 14, 1964.

59. George Gallup, "Gallup Poll: Scranton Tops Goldwater," *NYHT* June 28, 1964, p. 1.

60. Interview with A. James Reichley, October 7, 2008.

61. George F. Gilder and Bruce K. Chapman, *The Party That Lost Its Head* (New York: Alfred A. Knopf, 1966), p. 198.

62. Sherwin Goldwin to Hugh Scott, June 30, 1964. WWSP-JRF Campaign Material 2:41.

63. Richard Dougherty, "Goldwater Shuns Platform Fight," *NYHT* July 6, 1964, p. 1.

64. Memo [ns], June 26?, 1964. Thomas H. Kuchel Papers (University of California Berkeley) 79B: "Republican Fact Sheets (2)."

65. Hugh Scott, *Come to the Party* (Englewood Cliffs, NJ: Prentice-Hall, 1968), p. 210.

66. Robert Novak, *The Agony of the G.O.P. 1964* (New York: Macmillan, 1965), p. 451.

67. Hugh Scott interview March 17, 1978. United States Capitol Historical Society Oral History Collection (Library of Congress).

68. Scott, *Come to the Party*, p. 210.

69. "Here Is the Scranton Letter That Raised All the Fuss," *NYHT* July 15, 1964, p. 8.

70. Novak, pp. 456–457.

71. Interview with A. James Reichley, October 7, 2008.

72. David Wise, "Rights Change Rollcall Loses by 897–409," *NYHT* July 15, 1964, p. 1.

73. Nelson A. Rockefeller remarks to the Republican National Convention, July 14, 1964. TMMP III-2:6.

74. Interview with Douglas L. Bailey, March 22, 2007.

75. Interview with Tanya M. Melich, February 13, 2007.

76. Victor Wilson, "Eisenhower Raps Conduct at Republican Convention," *NYHT* June 20, 1966, p. 3.

77. "Niece Chased at GOP Meet: Ike," *Washington Daily News* June 29, 1965.

78. Murray Kempton, "They Got Him," *New Republic* July 25, 1964, p. 9.

79. Quoted in Carey McWilliams, "Goldwaterism: The New Ideology," *Nation* August 24, 1964, p. 71.

80. Kirkpatrick Sale, *Power Shift: The Rise of the Southern Rim and Its Challenge to the Eastern Establishment* (New York: Random House, 1975), pp. 12–13.

81. Republican national convention wall poster, nd [July 1964]. WFBP I-30: "Frawley, Patrick J. (1964)."

82. Richard Dougherty, "Goldwater Invites All Blocs in GOP to Join 'Our Crusade,'" *NYHT* June 4, 1964, p. 6.

83. Novak, pp. 28–33.

84. Robert Alan Goldberg, *Barry Goldwater* (New Haven, CT: Yale University Press, 1995).

85. Gerhart Niemeyer to William F. Buckley Jr., July 22, 1964. WFBP I-31: "Niemeyer, Gerhart (1964)."

86. David Wise, "Goldwater Nominated," *NYHT* July 16, 1964, p. 1.

87. Lewis L. Gould, *Grand Old Party: A History of the Republicans* (New York: Random House, 2003), p. 365.

88. "Rockefeller's Words About 'Extremism,'" *NYHT* July 18, 1964, p. 4.

89. "Goldwater's Off-Key Keynote," *NYHT* July 18, 1964, p. 10.

90. John S. Saloma III to "Dear fellow Riponer," July 29, 1964. RSP 1:33.

91. Interview with William T. Bagley, May 28, 2009.

92. Rowland Evans and Robert Novak, "In Burch's Wake," *NYHT* January 14, 1965, p. 18.

93. John C. Nunn, "Notes on GOP National Convention," July 16, 1964. Clarence L. Townes Papers (CLTP) (Virginia Commonwealth University) 7: "National Negro Republican Assembly (1964)."

94. Michael F. Keating, "State GOP, Once the Top, Near Chaos," *NYHT* July 17, 1964, p. 6.

95. Jackie Robinson, "Hitlerism Is Reborn," *NYHT* July 19, 1964, p. 11.

96. Grant Reynolds to "Dear Fellow Republican," October 15, 1964. CLTP 7: "National Negro Republican Assembly (1964)."

97. George G. Fleming speech at National Negro Republican Convention, August 22, 1964. CLTP 7: "National Negro Republican Assembly (1964)."

98. Negro Republican Convention, "Statement of Principles and Policies," August 22–23, 1964. CLTP 7: "National Negro Republican Assembly (1964)." See also Leah M. Wright, "Conscience of a Black Conservative: The 1964 Election and the Rise of the National Negro Republican Assembly," *Federal History* 2009.

99. Goldberg, p. 140.

100. William T. Bagley, *California's Golden Years: When Government Worked and Why* (Berkeley, CA: Berkeley Public Policy Press, 2009), p. 49. Bagley pointed out that the existing California statutes allowed all GOP candidates for congressional and state offices to write the party platform. As a result, in 1964 the nominees—many of them conservatives from heavily Democratic districts where moderates declined to run—outnumbered the predominantly moderate incumbents by approximately a 2-to-1 ratio at the California GOP state convention. Afterwards, the Young Turks in the state legislature amended the state government code in order to bolster the influence of incumbents and their appointees on the California Republican State Committee.

101. George Wallace, *Face the Nation* transcript, July 19, 1964. TMMP I-2:9.

102. Irvin J. Smith and Iris Smith to Charles McC. Mathias, July 17, 1964. CMMP I-1:24.

103. W. H. Goss to Charles McC. Mathias, August 4, 1964. CMMP I-1:24.

104. Brent Bozell to "Dear Fellow Republican," July 25, 1964. CMMP IX:2, "Brent Bozell—Primary Campaign (1964)."

105. Kenneth Keating, "Comment on Senator Javits' Statement with Regard to Republican Ticket and Platform," July 21, 1964. Kenneth Keating Papers (University of Rochester) 2-227:7.

106. Rowland Evans and Robert Novak, "The Scott Surrender," *WP* August 14, 1964.

107. Howard Baker, *No Margin for Error: America in the Eighties* (New York: Times Books, 1980), p. 7.
108. Interview with Slade Gorton, December 12, 2005.
109. Republicans & Independents for Johnson, "About 'Goldwaterism'" [nd—Sep.? 1964]. Charles P. Taft Papers (Library of Congress) 214: "Presidential Election 1964."
110. "We Choose Johnson," *NYHT* October 4, 1964, p. 22.
111. Ripon Society Executive Committee to "The members and friends of the Ripon Society," September 21, 1964. RSP 1:33.
112. Turnout had, however, been heavier in the 1960 election.
113. Ripon Society, *From Disaster to Distinction: The Rebirth of the Republican Party* (New York: Pocket Books, 1966), pp. 46–48.
114. Rowland Evans and Robert Novak, "Burch's Firing Is Virtually Certain," *Cleveland Plain Dealer* December 14, 1964.
115. Robert J. Samuelson, "Ripon Society Owes Its Success to the Enemy, Sen. Goldwater," *Harvard Crimson* February 12, 1965.
116. Ripon Society, "A New Republican Mandate: A Ripon Society Report and Preliminary Analysis of the 1964 Elections," November 5, 1964. RSP 3:185.
117. George F. Will, Foreword to Barry Goldwater, *The Conscience of a Conservative* (orig. pub. 1960) (Princeton, NJ: Princeton University Press, 2007), p. xix.
118. George Wallace's populist campaign efforts in the North also presaged future Republican strategies.

CHAPTER 5

1. The Ripon Society calculated that the conservative Americans for Constitutional Action had given the thirty-six incumbent Republican members of Congress who were defeated an average rating of 80.6 percent. Ripon Society, *From Disaster to Distinction: The Rebirth of the Republican Party* (New York: Pocket Books, 1965), p. 47.
2. Classifying the ideological position of members of Congress is a tricky business, but I have derived my numbers from the 1964 election endorsements of the Committee to Support Moderate Republicans and the Ripon Society, along with the conservative *National Review*'s listing of the House Republicans who had most often provided the margin of victory on "crucial Administration measures of an anti-conservative nature," beginning with the vote to enlarge the Rules Committee in 1961. For the entering 89th Congress, these lists yield a total of 51 progressive and moderate Republicans in the House and a dozen in the Senate. See Committee to Support Moderate Republicans press release, October? 1964. Ripon Society Papers (RSP) (Cornell University) 1:58; Ripon Society press release, October 28, 1964. RSP 3:185; "The Democrat Margin of Victory," *NR* November 3, 1964, pp. 960–964.
3. John G. Rogers, "Javits—Let's Go, GOP," *NYHT* November 7, 1964, pp. 1, 4.
4. John Sherman Cooper to George J. Long, November 10, 1964. John Sherman Cooper Papers (JSCP) (University of Kentucky) 300: "Republican Party—Correspondence (1961–72)."
5. John Sherman Cooper to Morgan B. Eversole, September 2, 1965. JSCP 300: "Republican Party—Barry Goldwater (1961–67)."
6. Quoted in Ripon Society, *From Disaster to Distinction*, p. 35.
7. Charles Daugherty, "Percy's GOP Formula: A 'Progressive' Party," *NYHT* February 19, 1965, p. 3.
8. Ripon Society, *From Disaster to Distinction*, p. 35.
9. Michael Beschloss, *Reaching for Glory: Lyndon Johnson's Secret White House Tapes, 1964–1965* (New York: Simon & Schuster, 2001), p. 162.

10. Rowland Evans and Robert Novak, "No Win Republicanism," *NYHT* October 25, 1964, p. 26.
11. Patricia Reilly Hitt interview, May 18, 1977 (Bancroft Library Women in Politics Oral History Project).
12. Thruston B. Morton remarks to Republican National Committee, January 22, 1965. Rogers C. B. Morton Papers (RCBMP) (University of Kentucky) 97: "Morton, Sen. Thruston."
13. Newton I. Steers, "The 1964 Presidential Election" [nd]. Charles McC. Mathias Papers (CMMP) (Johns Hopkins University) I-1–36: "Republican Party Maryland—Republican Party misc. (1965)."
14. Ripon Society, *From Disaster to Distinction*, p. 48.
15. David Wise, "'Sad, Sorry Mess' of 4th Estate," *NYHT* November 5, 1964, p. 12.
16. Richard Dougherty, "Goldwater Bows Out Humbly and Bitterly," *NYHT* January 23, 1965, p. 1.
17. Dom Bonafede, "Goldwater—Aims to Keep Party Reins," *NYHT* November 5, 1964, p. 12.
18. Dean Burch, "Chairman's Report," February 1965. Ray C. Bliss Papers (RCBP) (Ohio State Historical Society) 1:15.
19. Dave Gater, "Tentative Plan for Permanent Precinct Organization," January 1965. California Republican Assembly Papers (UCLA) 3:1.
20. Richard Bergholz, "Young GOP Affirms Support of Goldwater," *LAT* November 11, 1964.
21. Gerald A. Smith to Barry Goldwater, November 28, 1964. RCBP 1:14.
22. Charles McC. Mathias to Walter Lippmann, February 16, 1962. CMMP III-1: "Personal (1962)."
23. David B. Goldberg and Douglas L. Bailey to Charles P. Taft, November 8, 1964. Charles P. Taft Papers (CPTP) (Library of Congress) 219: "Republicans for Progress— Miscellany."
24. Interview with Douglas L. Bailey, March 22, 2007.
25. Minutes of Ripon Society meeting, November 17, 1964. RSP 1:61.
26. "Taft Heads Group to Help Moderates," *Cincinnati Enquirer* September 27, 1964.
27. The CRO members included the leading moderate and progressive Republican organizations, but there were many other such organizations in the mid-'60s. California was home to the California Republican Forum, the California Republican League, the Fremont Society, and the Republican Alliance. Other groups included the Lincoln Republicans in Connecticut, the Associated Republicans for Educated Action in Philadelphia, the Compass Society in central New York, the Haven Society in Michigan, the Lincoln Research Center in Washington, D.C., and the Oregon Council for Constructive Republicanism, in which the key figure was state senator Robert Packwood. A number of other moderate Republican study groups existed on college and university campuses, including the Trumbull Society at Columbia and Republican Advance at Yale, both of which eventually were folded into the Ripon Society.
28. "GOP Moderates Form Group to Rebuild Party," *Washington Star* November 22, 1964.
29. Roscoe Drummond, "New GOP Action Centers Called Life of the Party," *NYHT* April 23, 1965, p. 23.
30. William W. Scranton to Elmer Andersen, November 6, 1964. William W. Scranton Papers (WWSP) (Pennsylvania State Historical Library) II-74:18.
31. Ripon Society, "The Republican Governors' Association: The Case for a Third Force," December 1, 1964. RSP 3:187.
32. Ripon Society, "A History and Prospectus," January 1966. RSP 1:31.
33. *U.S. News & World Report* November 16, 1964.

34. Proposals by Republican Governors Association, December 3–5, 1964. WWSP II-74:17.
35. Barry Goldwater to George Romney, December 6, 1964. George Romney Papers (GRP) (University of Michigan) RA 45: "Goldwater, Barry."
36. George Romney to Barry Goldwater, December 21, 1964. GRP RA 45: "Goldwater, Barry."
37. "Opinion in the Capital" interview with Barry Goldwater, October 30, 1966. GRP RA 45: "Evans, Mark."
38. John D. Morris, "House G.O.P. Bloc Seeking Alliance," *NYT* December 2, 1964.
39. Charles McC. Mathias to *New York Herald Tribune. NYHT* January 31, 1966, p. 18.
40. Brad Morse interview with Robert L. Peabody, January 26, 1965. Peabody interview transcripts (Ford Presidential Library) 1: "Morse, Brad."
41. List of House Wednesday Group members, 1963–83. Brad Morse Papers (Boston University) 242.
42. Robert G. Smith, "Destiny's Tot," *NR* October 6, 1964, p. 861.
43. Tristam Coffin, "Yankee on Olympus," *Vista* July/August 1973.
44. Robert Ellsworth, Brad Morse, Charles McC. Mathias, and Stanley Tupper to Charles P. Taft, November 22, 1965. CMMP I-1–36: "Republican 'Bailey File'—Republican Task Force Comte. (1965)."
45. Interview with Douglas L. Bailey, March 22, 2007.
46. Rowland Evans and Robert Novak, "The December Caucus," *WP* November 20, 1964, p. A17.
47. Donald Rumsfeld interview with Robert L. Peabody, December 30, 1964. Peabody interview transcripts (Ford Presidential Library) 1: "Rumsfeld, Donald."
48. Donald Rumsfeld to John Mitchell, November 29, 1968. Bryce Harlow Files (Nixon Presidential Library) I-3:5. See also Donald Rumsfeld, *Known and Unknown: A Memoir* (New York: Sentinel, 2011), pp. 91–93.
49. Donald Rumsfeld interview with Robert L. Peabody, January 26, 1965. Peabody interview transcripts (Ford Presidential Library) 1: "Rumsfeld, Donald."
50. These problems, which had festered for years, included the unaddressed scandal of inadequate minority staff, Republicans' poor public relations, the shortcomings of the Republican Policy Committee, the procedures for committee assignments, Democratic abuse of the majority power, and the tendency of GOP leaders to cut side deals with the administration and Democratic leadership. Younger members were particularly frustrated by rigid adherence to seniority rules. Thomas B. Curtis to "Dear Colleague," November 18, 1964. Peabody interview transcripts (Ford Presidential Library) 1: "Curtis, Thomas."
51. Gerald R. Ford, "What Can Save the G.O.P.?," *Fortune* January 1965, p. 140.
52. Charles Nicodemus, "The Sacking of Halleck Was a Cold, Bitter Fight," Chicago Daily News Service January 6, 1965. CPTP 199: "Committee to Support Moderate Republicans."
53. Robert Remini, *The House: The History of the House of Representatives* (New York: HarperCollins, 2006), p. 405. Some members of the House Wednesday Group, including Lindsay and Morse, voted for Halleck over Ford. This was not for ideological reasons, but because they had made a deal to back Halleck in return for his support of Wednesday Group member Peter Frelinghuysen of New Jersey as chairman of the House Republican Conference. Frelinghuysen lost to Laird, but Lindsay was satisfied that Halleck had lived up to his side of the bargain. Members of the Wednesday Group then secured Ford's support for a campaign to get Frelinghuysen elected as whip to replace Les Arends; Lindsay recalled that "We wanted to see an Eastern liberal as part of the leadership." Frelinghuysen lost again, but Lindsay said that Ford's work for his election made a positive impression on the moderates as an "expression of good intent." Moderates also viewed Rep. Charles Goodell's appointment as head of a new Committee on Planning and Research as a positive outcome. John Lindsay interview with Robert

L. Peabody, January 14, 1965. Peabody interview transcripts (Ford Presidential Library) 1: "Lindsay, John."

54. John B. Anderson interview with Robert L. Peabody, January 11, 1965. Peabody interview transcripts (Ford Presidential Library) 1: "Anderson, John B."

55. William F. Arbogast, "GOP's New Image Maker: Ford on Dixie," *NYHT* January 10, 1965, p. 11.

56. Gerald R. Ford to "Dear Colleague," January 28, 1965. CMMP I-1–36: "Republican Conference—H. o. Reps (1965)."

57. "Text of Dean Burch's Letter to GOP," *NYHT* January 3, 1965, p. 15.

58. Earl Mazo, "Goldwater Fears Harm to the G.O.P. If Burch Is Ousted," *NYT* December 29, 1964.

59. Barry Goldwater to William F. Buckley Jr., December 19, 1964. William F. Buckley Jr. Papers (WFBP) (Yale University) I-30: "Goldwater, Barry—correspondence (1964)."

60. George Romney to Dwight D. Eisenhower, December 28, 1964. Dwight D. Eisenhower Post-Presidential Papers (DDEPPP) (Eisenhower Presidential Library) SNF-17: "Romney, George (1963–66)."

61. Rowland Evans and Robert Novak, "Burch's Firing Is Virtually Certain," *Cleveland Plain Dealer* December.14, 1964.

62. Rowland Evans and Robert Novak, "Soul Searching in Texas," *NYHT* January 5, 1965, p. 22.

63. George F. Jenks, "Reorganize, Hell—I'm Going to Organize It," *New Republic* February 6, 1965.

64. Joseph Alsop, "A Fantasy Called 'Right to Work,'" *WP* November 9, 1958.

65. Transcript of executive session of the Executive Committee of the Republican National Committee, January 21, 1965. Republican National Committee Papers (RNCP) (Library of Congress) I-B:4.

66. Transcript of executive session of the Executive Committee of the Republican National Committee, January 21, 1965. RNCP I-B:4; John S. Saloma III, "The New Political Order: A History of the Conservative Infrastructure" (unpublished manuscript), December 1982, p. v, 117. Tanya M. Melich Papers (SUNY Albany) V-8:15.

67. Dean Burch, "Chairman's Report," February 1965. RCBP 1:15.

68. Roscoe Drummond, "Extreme Conservatism: The GOP Says Farewell," *NYHT* January 15, 1965, p. 33.

69. Richard M. Nixon, address to the Republican Women's Conference, April 1, 1965. RCBP 95:14.

70. Frank S. Meyer, "What Next for Conservatism?," *NR* December 1, 1964, p. 1057.

71. James Burnham, "Must Conservatives Be Republicans?," *NR* December 1, 1964, p. 1052.

72. "The Republican Party and the Conservative Movement," *NR* December 1, 1964, pp. 1053–1055.

73. Elizabeth Morony to William F. Buckley Jr., November 30, 1964; William F. Buckley Jr. to Elizabeth Morony, January 6, 1965. WFBP I-36: "Moran-Morony (1965)."

74. William F. Buckley Jr. to Walter N. Thayer, June 5, 1964. Walter N. Thayer Papers (Hoover Presidential Library) 1:1.

75. William F. Buckley Jr. to John M. Olin, April 1, 1965. WFBP I-36: "Olin, John M. (1965)."

76. Sibner's rating by the liberal Americans for Democratic Action was only 47 percent compared to his opponent's rating of 88 percent.

77. Rowland Evans and Robert Novak, "Fifty Bucks from Buckley," *NYHT* June 4, 1965.

78. Kuchel shares this record with Alan Simpson, who won successive elections as whip from 1984 to 1992.

79. Panetta was a registered Republican throughout the 1960s, although he voted for Hubert Humphrey in 1968. Leon Panetta interview with A. James Reichley, September 19, 1977. A. James Reichley interview transcripts (Ford Presidential Library) 2: "Panetta, Leon."

80. Robert D. Fagaly Jr. to Ted Curtis, July 30, 1965. RSP 1:48.

81. Thomas Kuchel address to United States Senate, *CR* March 30, 1961, p. 5003; Lionel Van Deerlin, "Kuchel, A Courageous Public Servant," *San Diego Union-Tribune* November 29, 1994. See also Anthony Lewis, "Kuchel Scores Birch Society as 'Fright Peddlers,'" *NYT* May 3, 1963, p. A9.

82. Ewing Hass to William D. Russell, July 2, 1965. Thomas Kuchel Papers (TKP) (University of California Berkeley) 147:7.

83. "Christopher Governor Bid Faces Right Wing Clash," *Sacramento Bee* February 11, 1965; William W. Turner, "Pat Frawley: Right-wing Money Bag," *Progressive* Sep. 1970, pp. 14–19; Bryan W. Stevens, *The John Birch Society and California Politics* (West Covina, CA: Publius Society, 1966).

84. Andrew J. Glass, "The Man Who Defied His Defamers," *NYHT* February 21, 1965, p. 10; "Triumph Over Radical Right," *Detroit News* March 3, 1965; Mary McGrory, "Kuchel K.O.'s Smear Bid," *BG* March 7, 1965; "Mr. Kuchel's Vindication," *NYT* May 10, 1965, p. 32; "Sen. Kuchel's Victory," *Chicago Daily News* July 1, 1965.

85. Thomas Kuchel statement, March 15, 1965. TKP 79C:6.

86. James M. Coram, "Negro Law Vote Predicted," *Washington Star* February 6, 1965; Roy Reed, "Dr. King to Seek New Voting Law," *NYT* February 6, 1965; "GOP Unit Charts Stand on Rights," *NYHT* February 8, 1965.

87. Rowland Evans and Robert Novak, "Dirksen and Katzenbach, Inc.," *NYHT* March 14, 1965, p. 22.

88. "GOP Offers Registration Speedup Bill," *WP* February 9, 1965; Offices of Charles McC. Mathias and Thomas Kuchel statement, February 24, 1965. CMMP I-1-36: "Republican Conference—H. o. Reps (1965)"; John V. Lindsay to William McCulloch, March 4, 1965. William M. McCulloch Papers (WMMP) (Northern Ohio University) 16: "Judiciary Subcommittee #5 (Civil Rights)."

89. Byron C. Hulsey, *Everett Dirksen and His Presidents* (Lawrence, KS: University of Kansas Press, 2000), p. 211.

90. Harold Achor to Ralph Harvey, April 14, 1965. WMMP 16: "Judiciary Subcommittee #5 (Civil Rights)."

91. Wirt Yerger Jr. to William M. McCulloch, April 16, 1965. WMMP 16: "Judiciary Subcommittee #5 (Civil Rights)."

92. Richard Dougherty, "Alabama: GOP Outrage," *NYHT* March 11, 1965, p. 4.

93. Elliot Lee Richardson, "Lt. Gov. Richardson at Selma: 'A Sense of Unity,'" *Boston Herald* March 21, 1965.

94. Thruston B. Morton remarks to Republican National Committee, January 22, 1965. RCBMP 97: "Morton, Sen. Thruston."

95. William M. McCulloch statement to the U.S. House of Representatives, July 6, 1965. WMMP 38: "Voting Rights Act."

96. Dick Gale, "Ford Proposal May Aid GOP Rights Bill; Reid Opposes It," *Reporter Dispatch* [White Plains, NY] July 9, 1965.

97. Beschloss, p. 387.

98. The Voting Rights Act passed the Senate on May 26, 1965 by 77–19, with 30 Republicans voting for it and 2 (Strom Thurmond and John Tower) against; the Democrats' vote was 47–17. The bill passed the House on 9 July, with a GOP vote of 112–124 versus the Democrats' 221–261. The conference report passed the House on 3 August, with a 111–120 Republican vote as compared to a 217–254 Democratic vote, and passed the Senate the next day with a GOP vote of 30–31 and a Democratic vote of 49–17; Thurmond was the only Republican senator to oppose it. *CQ Almanac 1965*, pp. 976, 984, 1042, 1063.

99. Clarence Mitchell to William M. McCulloch, August 5, 1965. WMMP 16: "Judiciary Subcommittee #5 (Civil Rights)."

100. Frank T. Bow to "Dear Republican Colleague," January 5, 1965. CMMP I-1–36: "Republican Conference—H. o. Reps (1965)."

101. Frank T. Bow, "The Alternative—Free, Voluntary, Private," *Advance* 2:1 (June 1962), pp. 15–17.

102. Kitsy Beck to Charles McC. Mathias, August 23, 1965. CMMP I-1–36: "Republican Party Maryland—Republican Party misc. (1965)."

103. Kenneth Reich, "O.C. Politician and Ex-Senator Kuchel, 84, Dies," reprinted in *CR* October 11, 2002, p. E1856. GOP vote tallies on the Medicare legislation from *CQ Almanac 1965*, pp. 950, 982, 1057, 1062.

104. Andrew J. Glass, "Who Built America? A Senatorial Clash," *NYHT* February 25, 1965, p. 1.

105. Republican National Committee, "Republican Record" May 1965. TKP 79B:4.

106. Joseph W. Sullivan, "GOP Turnabout: Republicans in Congress Try to Outdo Democrats with Broad New Plans," *WSJ* March 9, 1965.

107. Ripon Society, "Government for Tomorrow: Opportunity and Crisis," July 13, 1965. RSP 3:185.

108. "Progress on Tax Sharing," *RF* 1:7 (November 1965), pp. 4–5.

109. A concise history of American involvement in Vietnam is George C. Herring, *America's Longest War: The United States and Vietnam, 1950–1975* (2nd ed.) (New York: Alfred A. Knopf, 1986). A good study focusing on the escalation of the conflict in 1965 is Larry Berman, *Planning a Tragedy: The Americanization of the War in Vietnam* (New York: W. W. Norton, 1982).

110. Charles Goodell statement August 25, 1964. TKP 79B:3 "Republican Fact Sheets."

111. Ripon Society minutes, January 13, 1965. RSP 1:24.

112. Gary Spiess to John R. Price, 1966? RSP 7: "Behn corr."

113. Tom Lambert, "GOP Rallies to Johnson in Viet War," *NYHT* February 19, 1965, p. 1.

114. William F. Buckley Jr. to Ross Mackenzie, February 2, 1965. WFBP I-36: "Mackenzie, Ross and Wallace (1965)."

115. Hamilton Fish Jr. to *NYHT* March 12, 1965, p. 22.

116. Siler was not present and was paired against the bill with another member who favored the bill, so his opposition was not counted and the bill passed the House 416–0. David T. Beito and Linda Royster Beito, "The Christian Conservative Who Opposed the Vietnam War," *History News Network* August 21, 2006. Available at http://hnn.us/articles/28879. html.

117. House Wednesday Group to Dean Rusk, March 31, 1965. CMMP I-1–36: "Republican 'Bailey File'–Republican Task Force Comte. (1965)."

118. *CR* 111, p. 2155.

119. The 1971 film *The French Connection* includes a snippet of dialogue in which a French movie director visiting New York agrees that Lindsay is "the sexiest man in the world."

120. Interview with Charles R. Morris, February 26, 2009.

121. James Lynn, "N.Y.'s Second-Best-Known Republican," *NYHT* November 1, 1964, p. 34.

122. Sidney Zion, "A Nightmare and a Prayer," *New York Post* December 27, 2000, p. 35.

123. Erwin Savelson, "Keating Suspected Office Was Bugged Under Kennedy," *NYHT EE* January 6, 1967, p. 3.

124. Nat Hentoff, "The Man Who Stood Up to Bobby Kennedy," *Village Voice* January 23, 2001.

125. Jo-Ann Price, "Door Left Open on Race for Mayor, Lindsay Says," *NYHT* February 17, 1965, p. 19.

126. "New York's Three Wise Men," *NYHT* February 24, 1965, p. 24.

127. Hentoff, "The Man Who Stood Up to Bobby Kennedy."

128. Murray Kempton, "Nice Place to Visit," *New York Telegram & Sun* June 25, 1965.

129. John B. Judis, *William F. Buckley, Jr.: Patron Saint of the Conservatives* (New York: Touchstone, 1990), pp. 240–241.

130. Barry Goldwater to J. William Middendorf II, June 9, 1965. WFBP I-35: "Goldwater, Barry (1965)."

131. William F. Buckley Jr., *The Unmaking of a Mayor* (New Rochelle, NY: Arlington House, 1966), p. 96.

132. George Stigler, "The Problem of the Negro," *New Guard* December 1965.

133. Roy Wilkins to William F. Buckley Jr., April 19, 1965. WFBP I-36: "New York City Police Department Communion Breakfast Speech (corr.) (1965)."

134. Marquis Childs, "Division and Dollars in N.Y. Campaign," *Des Moines Tribune* October 14, 1965.

135. David Lawrence, "War Against Crime: America's Biggest Defeat," *NYHT* April 21, 1965, p. 29.

136. See also Michael Flamm, *Law and Order: Street Crime, Civil Unrest, and the Crisis of Liberalism in the 1960s* (New York: Columbia University Press, 2005).

137. Theodore H. White, *The Making of the President 1960* (New York: Atheneum, 1961), p. 257.

138. Matthew Dallek, *The Right Moment: Ronald Reagan's First Victory and the Decisive Turning Point in American Politics* (New York: Free Press, 2000), p. 165.

139. Timothy N. Thurber, "Goldwaterism Triumphant?: Race and the Debate Among Republicans Over the Direction of the GOP, 1964–68." Unpublished paper delivered at The Historical Society Conference, June 3, 2006. Available at http://www.bu.edu/historic/06conf_papers/Thurber.pdf.

140. "Republicans and the Negro Revolution—1965: A Special Year-end Ripon Editorial Report," *RF* 1:8 (December 1965), p. 6.

141. Paul Hope, "Washington Close Up," *Washington Star* November 21, 1965.

142. "NAACP Asks Voters Reject Buckley Bid," *Amsterdam News* October 23, 1965.

143. "Mayor John Lindsay: New GOP Hope?," *Newsweek* November 15, 1965.

144. Barry Goldwater on *Face the Nation*, November 14, 1965. RCBP 95:14.

145. "Mayor John Lindsay: New GOP Hope?," *Newsweek* November 15, 1965.

146. Kenneth Crawford, "Buckleyism Forever?," *Newsweek* November 15, 1965.

147. Jules to Charles Percy, November 21, 1965. WNTP III-1:12.

148. William F. Buckley Jr. to Ferdinand Lothrop Mayer, December 2, 1965. WFBP I-36: "Mayer, Ferdinand Lothrop (1965)."

149. William F. Buckley Jr. to Russell Kirk, November 11, 1965. WFBP I-35: "Educational Reviewer (1965)."

150. Theodore H. White to William F. Buckley Jr., December 2, 1965. WFBP I-36: "Mayoralty Campaign (1965)."

151. Peter Wallison to William F. Buckley Jr., October 19, 1966. WFBP I-40: "Rimanoczy–Rippowam High School Debating Society (1966)."

152. "Parallel Pattern," *Newsweek* November 15, 1965, p. 36.

153. Ripon Society, "A Second Mandate to Republicans: A Ripon Society Report and Analysis of the 1965 Elections," November 1965. RSP 3:187.

154. Arlen Specter campaign address, January 25, 1966. George L. Hinman Papers (Rockefeller Archives) IV-J2-1–62:398.

155. Joseph R. Daughen and Peter Binzen, *The Cop Who Would Be King: The Honorable Frank Rizzo* (Boston: Little, Brown, 1977), p. 102.

156. William Cowger address to Republican National Committee, June 28, 1965. RNCP I-B:4.

157. "Cities: The Negro's New Force," *Time* November 12, 1965, p. 34.

158. "Virginia: The Goldwater Thing," *Time* November 12, 1965, p. 34.

159. Ripon Society, "A Second Mandate to Republicans." RSP 3:187.
160. "New Look in Virginia," *Washington Star* November 5, 1965, p. A12.
161. Linwood Holton, *Opportunity Time* (Charlottesville, VA: University of Virginia Press, 2008), pp. 55–64.
162. Angelo Baglivo, "GOP Project Started," *Newark Evening News,* June 8, 1965.
163. Ronald Sullivan, "Rutgers Professor is Called 'Left' of U.S. Reds," *NYT* August 12, 1965.
164. Richard M. Nixon statement, October 24, 1965. DDEPPP SNF-14: "Nixon, Richard M. (1963–66) (3)."
165. "New Jersey Nonsense," *NYT* August 9, 1965.
166. Albert E. Abrahams to Eleanor and Webster Todd, August 4, 1965. CPTP 219: "Republicans for Progress—Dumont, Wayne Jr."
167. "New Jersey: Getting the Garden Growing," *Time* November 12, 1965, p. 33.
168. William F. Buckley Jr. remarks at *National Review* tenth anniversary dinner, November 11, 1965. WFBP I-36: "*National Review*—Tenth Anniversary Dinner—correspondence (1965)."
169. "Lindsay's Victory Formula and the Future," *Washington Star* November 7, 1965, p. C2.

CHAPTER 6

1. The song concluded with a line referring to the growth of the minority population in a poor city near Newark: "Where have all the niggers gone? Gone to Plainfield." Jeffrey Paley, "GOP's Radical Right: Trouble in New Jersey," *NYHT* January 28, 1966, p. 4; Jeffrey Paley, "The Rat Finks: Just Who Sang THOSE Songs?," *NYHT* March 20, 1966, p. 5.
2. Transcript of executive session of the Republican National Committee, January 31, 1966. Republican National Committee Papers (RNCP) (Library of Congress) I-B:5.
3. Rowland Evans and Robert Novak, "The Ordeal of Ray Bliss," *Saturday Evening Post* November 6, 1965, p. 35.
4. Charles S. Mack to Ray C. Bliss, July 10, 1965. Ray C. Bliss Papers (RCBP) (Ohio Historical Society) 77:8; Boisfeuillet Jones, "The Young Republican Plight," *Harvard Crimson* July 11, 1967.
5. Rowland Evans and Robert Novak, "Ellender Loses Out," *WP* August 29, 1965, p. E7.
6. Hugh Scott address to Washington D.C. Young Republicans, April 25, 1966. CR May 10, 1966, p. 9661.
7. "Republicans Riot in Washington," *RF* 2:4 (June 1966), p. 4.
8. *LAT* November 25, 1965; David Broder, "Christopher Matches Reagan Before Coast G.O.P. Committee," *NYT* February 28, 1966.
9. Christine Todd Whitman, *It's My Party Too: The Battle for the Heart of the GOP and the Future of America* (New York: Penguin, 2006), pp. 48–49.
10. Bruce K. Chapman, "Behind and Beyond the Rat Finks," *NYHT* February 19, 1966, p. 10; "Rat Finks and Fink-Baiters," *New Guard* September 1966, p. 13.
11. "The Party, Too, Has Rights," *NYHT* January 31, 1966, p. 18.
12. Transcript of executive session of the Republican National Committee, June 19, 1966. RNCP I-B:5.
13. Chapman, "Behind and Beyond the Rat Finks."
14. George L. Hinman to Ray C. Bliss, May 27, 1966. George L. Hinman Papers (GLHP) (Rockefeller Archives) 1-5:23.
15. Hugh Scott address to Washington D.C. Young Republicans, April 25, 1966. CR May 10, 1966, pp. 9661–9962.
16. Los Angeles County Young Republicans resolution, September 7, 1965. Ronald Reagan Gubernatorial Papers (RRGP) (Reagan Presidential Library) C32: "Kuchel, Sen. T."
17. Excerpt from WRC-Radio NBC broadcast, July 9, 1965. RCBP 77:8.

18. William A. Rusher, *The Rise of the Right* (New York: William Morrow, 1984), p. 183.
19. Transcript of executive session of the Republican National Committee, June 19, 1966. RNCP I-B:5.
20. Rowland Evans and Robert Novak, "Republican Surgery," *NYHT EE* June 25, 1966, p. 4.
21. The survivors after 1967 were the *Times*, the *Post*, and the *Daily News*. Susan E. Tifft and Alex S. Jones, *The Trust: The Private and Powerful Family Behind the New York Times* (Boston, MA: Little, Brown, 1999), pp. 392–393.
22. Richard Kluger, *The Paper: The Life and Death of the New York Herald Tribune* (New York: Alfred A. Knopf, 1986), p. 714.
23. John Hay Whitney to Dwight D. Eisenhower, August 22, 1966. Dwight D. Eisenhower Post-Presidential Papers (DDEPPP) (Eisenhower Presidential Library) SNF-20: "Whitney, John Hay (1966)."
24. Raymond Price, *With Nixon* (New York: Viking, 1977), p. 83.
25. Interview with Raymond Price, February 25, 2009.
26. "Ad Nauseum," *NYHT* June 25, 1966, p. 18.
27. Interview with Raymond Price, February 25, 2009.
28. "Peace and Human Rights," *NYHT* April 25, 1965, p. 22.
29. "Building on the Urban Frontier," *NYHT* March 6, 1966, p. 18.
30. "A Repeat Performance," *RF* 1:4 (June 1965), p. 4.
31. Stephen Horn to Thomas Kuchel, June 11, 1964. Thomas Kuchel Papers (TKP) (University of California at Berkeley) 79B:4.
32. Thomas Kuchel statement September 22, 1965, UPI. RRGP C32: "Kuchel, Sen. T."
33. Rowland Evans and Robert Novak, "VIPs in Vietnam," *NYHT* January 16, 1966, p. 22; Richard Rodda, "Democratic Hopes Soar in State," *Sacramento Bee* September 21, 1965.
34. "George Christopher's Positive Program for California," May? 1966. RRGP C31: "Christopher, George (2)."
35. George Christopher speech transcript, June 1, 1966. RRGP C31: "Christopher, George (2)."
36. Richard Bergholz, "Young GOP Affirms Support of Goldwater," *LAT* November 11, 1964.
37. Stuart K. Spencer interview, February 23, 1979 (Bancroft Library Reagan Gubernatorial Oral History Project) (BLRGOHP).
38. Ronald Reagan statement, September 24, 1965. RRGP C31: "Birch Society (1)."
39. Paul R. Haerle interview, March 26, 1982 (BLRGOHP).
40. Nancy Reagan to William F. Buckley Jr., January 26, 1966 [r]. William F. Buckley Jr. Papers (WFBP) (Yale University) I-40: "Reagan, Ronald and Nancy (1966)."
41. Mary McGrory, "Real World Intrudes at GOP Parley," *Washington Star* February 28, 1966.
42. Sometimes the Commandment was rendered as: "Thou shalt not speak ill of any other Republican," or similar variations.
43. William E. Roberts interview, June 26, 1979 (BLRGOHP).
44. Franklin C. Nofziger interview, October 10, 1978 (BLRGOHP). It was later revealed that Parkinson had received a $33,000 retainer from the Reagan campaign. Joseph Lewis, *What Makes Reagan Run? A Political Profile* (New York: McGraw-Hill, 1968), p. 113.
45. Gaylord C. Parkinson interview, November 21, 1978 (BLRGOHP).
46. "The Twelfth Commandment," *RF* 2:4 (June 1966), pp. 3–4.
47. Aime G. Michaud to Thomas Kuchel, February 24, 1966. TKP 270:7 "Camp. others 1966"; Albert E. Abrahams to Carl J. Gilbert, May 6, 1966. Charles P. Taft Papers (CPTP) (Library of Congress) 217: "Republicans for Progress (May-June 1966)."
48. Aime G. Michaud to Charles P. Taft, August 12, 1965. CPTP 216: "Republicans for Progress (June-August 1965).")

49. The "big tent" metaphor was already in the air by this time; Bliss had told the RNC that the diversity of views within the Republican Party argued for "the idea of a big tent accommodating many points of view." Transcript of executive session of the Republican National Committee, January 22, 1965. RNCP I-B:4.

50. Albert E. Abrahams to Republicans for Progress Executive Committee, May 13, 1966. CPTP 217: "Republicans for Progress (May-June 1966)."

51. William T. Bagley, George W. Milias, and Alan G. Pattee to Ronald Reagan, April 15, 1966. RRGP C29: "'66 Campaign—Gov. Personal corr.–Letters of Particular Interest [A-L]."

52. Christopher for Governor news release, April 25, 1966. TKP 270:2 "Camp. 1966-Christopher."

53. Matthew Dallek, The Right Moment: Ronald Reagan's First Victory and the Decisive Turning Point in American Politics (New York: Free Press, 2000), p. 203.

54. Interview with Michael Chabot Smith, February 12, 2007.

55. Franklin C. Nofziger interview, October 10, 1978 (BLRGOHP).

56. Dallek, pp. 212–213.

57. William T. Bagley interview, December 21, 1981 (BLRGOHP).

58. "He's Almost Certain," [Palm Springs CA] Desert Sun October 15, 1965; Ron Kenney, "No Doubt in His Mind: Christopher's in Race," [Escondido CA] Daily Times-Advocate September 8, 1965.

59. John A. McCone to Marian Hancock, April 26, 1966. DDEPPP SNF-12: "McCone, John (1963–66) (1)."

60. Ronald W. Reagan to Harry Feyer, July 21, 1966. RRGP C35: "Republican Party."

61. John S. Saloma III to Barry Goldwater, April 6, 1966. Ripon Society Papers (RSP) (Cornell University) 11:11.

62. "Ripon Society Hits Y.A.F.," BG May 9, 1966.

63. Rowland Evans and Robert Novak, "GOP Death Wish," NYHT EE May 16, 1966, p. 4. The Washington Post reported that the far right also accused Schweiker of being a "coddler of criminals" because "he was upset when an Alabama bondsman dragged a Negro youth out of his Pennsylvania home just before Christmas for a minor offense." "Shafer Leads in Pa. Primary," WP May 18, 1966.

64. "Goldwater Conservatives Showing Powers of Recovery," NYHT EE July 16–17, 1966, p. 3.

65. "Moderates Miss the Mark," RF 2:5 (July 1966), p. 5.

66. "Who Needs Kingmakers?," NYHT EE September 17–18, 1966, p. 3.

67. "China Today—Containment and Contact," in Thomas E. Petri and Lee W. Huebner (eds.), The Ripon Papers 1963–1968 (Washington, DC: National Press, 1968), pp. 176–181. Rep. Paul Findley read the paper into the Congressional Record shortly after its release on April 7, 1966. See also Richard Dougherty, "GOP Liberal Faction for New China Policy," NYHT April 7, 1966, p. 6.

68. "Beyond the Absurd," RF 2:4 (June 1966), p. 6.

69. American Conservative Union, "The Ripon Society: A Study by the Staff of the American Conservative Union on the Influence of Liberals within the Republican Party," October? 1966, p. 7. RSP 1:52.

70. Interview with Josiah Lee Auspitz, October 21, 2006.

71. Richard M. Nixon to D. R. Starrett, September 26, 1966. RCBP 95:14.

72. Richard H. Amberg, "Nixon: GOP's Big Winner in '66," St. Louis Globe-Democrat December 3–4, 1966.

73. David S. Broder, "Nixon Consults Leaders of Conservative Groups," NYHT EE August 25, 1966, p. 1.

74. See for example Samuel G. Freedman, The Inheritance: How Three Families and the American Political Majority Moved from Left to Right (New York: Touchstone, 1998).

75. Grant Reynolds address to Harris County Young Republicans, July 6, 1965. RSP 11:23.
76. Transcript of executive session of the Republican National Committee, June 20, 1966. RNCP I-B:5.
77. David Murray, *Charles Percy of Illinois* (New York: Harper & Row, 1968), pp. 67–70.
78. Interview with John McClaughry, November 15, 2009.
79. Interview with Michael Chabot Smith, February 12, 2007.
80. Quoted in Nathan Wright Jr., *Let's Work Together* (New York: Hawthorn, 1968), pp. 212–213.
81. Interview with John McClaughry, November 15, 2009.
82. John McClaughry, "The Troubled Dream: The Life and Times of Section 235 of the National Housing Act," *Loyola University Law Journal* 6:1 (winter 1975).
83. Charles Nicodemus, "Why Dawson Shuns the Spotlight," *Chicago Daily News* October 14, 1966.
84. "David R. Reed Letter Appeals to 1st District Voters," *Chicago Gazette* August 11, 1966.
85. "The New Breed" (1966). John McClaughry Papers (JMP) (author's possession) 1: "Dave Reed (1966)."
86. "Battle in the Ghetto," *Newsweek* June 13, 1966.
87. "Report: First Congressional District, Illinois 1966," July 1966. JMP 1: "Dave Reed (1966)."
88. David R. Reed to Ray Bliss, July 21, 1966. JMP 1: "Dave Reed (1966)."
89. David R. Reed speech to Republican Luncheon Group of Capitol Hill, October 6, 1966. JMP 1: "Dave Reed (1966)."
90. Roscoe Drummond, "Black Power at Its Best in 1st District," *Chicago Sun-Times* October 27, 1966.
91. "Candidate Reed and Force Investigate War on Poverty," *South Suburban News* [Harvey, IL] August 27, 1966.
92. Tom Roeser, "Flashback: Strategizing Two City Congressional Campaigns," December 20, 2006. Available at http://blog.tomroeser.com/2006/12/flashback-strategizing-two-city.html.
93. Elliot Richardson was one of the many Republicans at the time emphasizing that "today we want to see government operate as close to the people as possible." "Panel at Yale Agrees on Need for Federal Decentralization," *New Haven Register* March 7, 1967.
94. Public Housing Mothers for Reed & Percy, "Here's What Charles Percy and Dave Reed Say About Public Housing," October 1966. JMP 1: "Dave Reed (1966)."
95. Lois Wille, "Inside 'Ranger' Street Gangs," *Chicago Daily News* August 1, 1966.
96. Jesse W. Woods Jr., "Reed Is Ready Campaign," August 12, 1966. JMP 1: "Dave Reed (1966)."
97. John McClaughry to Dave Reed, July 21, 1966. JMP 1: "Dave Reed (1966)."
98. Interview with John McClaughry, November 29, 2009.
99. "Five Draw Long Sentences for Terrorism Scheme," *NYT* December 31, 1987; Don Terry, "In Chicago Courtroom, Nation's First Super Gang Fights for Life," *NYT* May 18, 1991.
100. Rowland Evans and Robert Novak, "A Rare Chance for GOP Here," *Chicago Sun-Times* September 6, 1966.
101. Percy campaign leaflet, "Had Enough?," Sep.? 1966. JMP 1: "Dave Reed (1966)."
102. "For Reed and Rumsfeld," *Chicago Sun-Times* October 11, 1966.
103. Edward W. Brooke, *Bridging the Divide: My Life* (New Brunswick, NJ: Rutgers University Press, 2007), p. 55.
104. John Henry Cutler, *Ed Brooke: Biography of a Senator* (Indianapolis, IN: Bobbs-Merrill, 1972), p. 89.
105. John P. Avlon, *Independent Nation: How the Vital Center Is Changing American Politics* (New York: Harmony, 2004), p. 262.

106. Brooke, *Bridging the Divide*, p. 109.
107. Edward W. Brooke news release, February 19, 1964. Edward W. Brooke Papers (EWBP) (Library of Congress) 40: "Press Releases (January-February 1964)."
108. *Greenfield [MA] Recorder-Gazette*, January 31, 1964. EWBP 40: "Press Clippings."
109. Brooke, *Bridging the Divide*, p. 148.
110. *Ibid.*, p. 67.
111. W. Stuart Parsons to Stephen Jones, November 20, 1966. RSP 1:43. Saloma had to bow out of the research director's job after breaking his leg on a skiing vacation.
112. "U.S. Senator Edward Brooke: An Individual Who Happens to Be a Negro," *Time* February 17, 1967, p. 21.
113. Milton Friedman, *Capitalism and Freedom* (Chicago: University of Chicago Press, 1962), p. 191.
114. "The Negative Income Tax: A Republican Proposal to Help the Poor," *RF* 3:4 (April 1967).
115. Edward W. Brooke news release, May 31, 1966. EWBP 42: "Press Releases (May 1966)."
116. Wallace Turner, "Hatfield Defeats Duncan in Oregon," *NYT* November 9, 1966.
117. Mark O. Hatfield, *Against the Grain: Reflections of a Rebel Republican* (Ashland, OR: White Cloud Press, 2001), pp. 102, 104.
118. "Mark O. Hatfield," *Current Biography Yearbook 1984*, p. 154.
119. David Broder and Stephen Hess, *The Republican Establishment: The Present and Future of the G.O.P.* (New York: Harper & Row, 1967), p. 387.
120. Tom Roeser, "Flashback: Strategizing Two City Congressional Campaigns—Republican Hoellen vs. Democrat Pucinski on the Northwest Side and Republican Reed vs. Democrat Dawson on the South Side," December 20, 2006. Available at http://www.tomroeser.com/blogview.asp?blogID=23307.
121. Interview with John McClaughry, November 29, 2009.
122. Rowland Evans and Robert Novak, "Negro Eagle Eye," *WP* December 8, 1966.
123. Nicholas von Hoffman, "Black Tuesday for Daley's 'Tribe,'" *NYHT EE* November 12–13, 1966, p. 3.
124. Richard C. Wade, "Backlash in the Percy Campaign," *Reporter* January 1967, pp. 37–40.
125. Walter Larke Sorg, "Comparative Study of the Negro Vote in Chicago," 1969. JMP 1: "Dave Reed (1966)."
126. Broder and Hess, p. 222.
127. David S. Broder, "Negro Candidate Tries to Avoid Issue," *NYHT EE* October 20, 1966, p. 3.
128. Ronald W. Reagan to Edward W. Brooke, November 17, 1966. RRGP C29: "'66 Campaign—Gov. Personal corr.–Letters of Congratulations (1)."
129. J. Lee Annis Jr., *Howard Baker: Conciliator in an Age of Crisis* (Lanham, MD: Madison, 1995), p. 35.
130. *Ibid.*, pp. 36–39.
131. "The Potential to Govern," *RF* 2:8 (November 1966), p. 5.
132. Dallek, p. xi.
133. Dwight D. Eisenhower to Charles S. Jones, August 19, 1966. DDEPPP SNF-11: "Jones, Charles S. (1966)."
134. "Meet the Press," September 11, 1966. RRGP C31: "'66 Campaign Debate—Issues and Answers/Meet the Press Transcripts."
135. Ronald W. Reagan to John A. McCone, October 3, 1966. RRGP C32: "Kuchel, Sen. T."
136. John A. McCone to Dwight D. Eisenhower, October 28, 1966. DDEPPP SNF-12: "McCone, John (1963–66) (1)."
137. Ronald W. Reagan to Paul A. French, July 19, 1966. RRGP C8: "Correspondence—Frasier–Freshman."

138. Labor for Reagan Committee, "Can a Union Man Be Elected Governor?" [nd—1966]. WFBP I-41: "Stoltenberg-Stillman (1966)."

139. "Plans to Beat Reagan Unveiled by AFL-CIO," *LAT* July 15, 1966.

140. Caspar Weinberger interview March 29, 1979 (BLRGOHP).

141. Patricia Reilly Hitt and John G. Veneman to "Dear Friend," June 1, 1966. TKP 270:5 "Campaign others 1966."

142. Alan L. Otten, "Unity Candidate," *WSJ* May 25, 1966.

143. Paul R. Haerle interview, March 26, 1982 (BLRGOHP).

144. Spiro Agnew to W. Stuart Parsons, November 4, 1966. RSP 11:1.

145. Spiro Agnew to Jay T. Cloud, May 14, 1964. Spiro T. Agnew Papers (University of Maryland) I-SS1.1–1: "Personal correspondence (1964)."

146. "Rightists Claim Major Vote Gain," *NYT* November 20, 1966.

147. Ray C. Bliss to Charles McC. Mathias, November 22, 1966. Charles McC. Mathias Papers (Johns Hopkins University) I-1–41: "Republican Party miscellaneous— Republican Conference H. o. Representatives (1966)."

148. John H. Chafee address to Pennsylvania Council of Republican Women, November 14, 1966. RSP 11:7.

149. Warren Weaver, "Nixon 'Bats'. 686 for 1966 Season," *NYT* November 13, 1966. Quoted in Broder and Hess, p. 174.

150. Richard M. Nixon, "Dixie Democrats' Fatal Error" (unamended column for North American Newspaper Alliance), October 30, 1966. RCBP 95:17.

151. Mahout, "The View from Here," *RF* 2:8 (November 1966), p. 1.

152. "The Potential to Govern," *RF* 2:8 (November 1966), p. 5.

CHAPTER 7

1. Larissa MacFarquhar, "The Gilder Effect," *New Yorker* May 29, 2000.

2. Interview with Bruce K. Chapman, December 8, 2009.

3. George F. Gilder and Bruce K. Chapman, *The Party That Lost Its Head* (New York: Alfred A. Knopf, 1966), pp. vi, 269–270.

4. William F. Buckley Jr., *Flying High: Remembering Barry Goldwater* (New York: Basic, 2008), pp. 71–72.

5. William F. Buckley Jr. to George F. Gilder, November 29, 1966. William F. Buckley Jr. Papers (WFBP) (Yale University) I-39: "Gilbert-Giordano (1966)."

6. Buckley, *Flying High*, p. 71.

7. "Political Notes," *RF* 4:1 (January 1968), p. 4.

8. Barry Goldwater to William F. Buckley Jr., July 5, 1967. WFBP I-43: "Goldwater, Barry (1967)."

9. See Bruce K. Chapman to Thomas E. Petri, September 29, 1967. Ripon Society Papers (RSP) (Cornell University) 11:5.

10. John B. Judis, *William F. Buckley, Jr.: Patron Saint of the Conservatives* (New York: Touchstone, 1990), pp. 246–247.

11. Interview with Bruce K. Chapman, December 8, 2009.

12. James Carney, "10 Questions for William F. Buckley," *Time* April 12, 2004.

13. William F. Buckley Jr. to Neil McCaffrey, February 1968. WFBP I-52: "McCaffrey, Neil (January-July) (1968)."

14. William F. Buckley Jr. to Neil McCaffrey, May 1968. WFBP I-52: "McCaffrey, Neil (January-July) (1968)."

15. Bruce K. Chapman, "A 'Progressive's' Progress," *NR* April 17, 1981, p. 412.

16. Bruce K. Chapman to Thomas E. Petri, September 29, 1967. RSP 11:5.

17. Bruce K. Chapman to Roswell B. Perkins, June 15, 1964. George L. Hinman Papers (GLHP) (Rockefeller Archives) IV-J2-1–14:78.

18. Interview with Bruce K. Chapman, December 8, 2009.
19. Bruce K. Chapman, "Private Reflections on a Public Life" (unpublished memoir, 1994), p. 320.
20. Thomas B. Curtis, "Youth and the Military," *Advance* 2:4 (summer 1963), pp. 23–26.
21. Richard Rovere, "Letter from Washington," *New Yorker* December 17, 1966, pp. 200–201.
22. Bruce K. Chapman to Robert D. Behn, May 22, 1967. RSP 7: "Behn corr."
23. Interview with Bruce K. Chapman, December 8, 2009.
24. Bruce Chapman to John S. Saloma III et al., February 21, 1967. RSP 11:5.
25. Charles W. Whalen Jr. address to Ohio State University Council of Graduate Students, April 5, 1967. Charles W. Whalen Jr. Papers (CWWP) (University of Dayton) L205: "Speeches, articles, and background papers (1965–67)."
26. "Can We Bridge the Ideological Gap?," *RF* 3:6 (June 1967).
27. Lou Cannon, *Governor Reagan: His Rise to Power* (New York: PublicAffairs, 2003), p. 212.
28. "Can We Bridge the Ideological Gap?," *RF* 3:6 (June 1967).
29. Bruce K. Chapman to John S. Saloma III et al., February 21, 1967. RSP 11:5.
30. Lee W. Huebner, "'The Fierce Urgency of Now,'" *RF* 4:5 (May 1968), p. 4.
31. These included House Republicans Gerald Ford and Robert Taft Jr., governors John Love, John Chafee, and Dan Evans (of Colorado, Rhode Island, and Washington), and senators Thruston B. Morton of Kentucky and Edward Brooke of Massachusetts.
32. Stephen Hess and David S. Broder, *The Condition of Republicanism* (New York: Harper & Row, 1967), p. 5.
33. "Political Notes," *RF* 3:2 (February 1967), p. 9. Cowger had made notable efforts to win black votes for Republicans in Louisville. See William O. Cowger to John McClaughry, May 17, 1966. RSP 11:6.
34. Republican Governors Association news release, April 28, 1967. RSP 2:82.
35. "Presidential Politics," *RF* 3:5 (May 1967), p. 2. Percy introduced the bill on April 20 with Rep. William B. Widnall of New Jersey. The bill (S. 1592) would have chartered a National Home Ownership Foundation to supply mortgage funds and technical assistance to community-based sponsors of home ownership programs for low-income families. A subsidy in the form of a "coupon mortgage" would have assisted families in meeting monthly payments, with the net amount of subsidy phased down as family income increased. The plan was savaged by HUD Secretary Robert C. Weaver on April 21. See John McClaughry, "GOP Initiatives," *RF* 4:2 (February 1968), p. 17.
36. Rowland Evans and Robert Novak, "The Consular Fight," *IHT* February 3, 1967, p. 4.
37. Thruston B. Morton speech to the Senate, January 31, 1967. Thruston B. Morton Papers (University of Kentucky) 1: "Consular Treaty."
38. Hess and Broder, pp. 87–88.
39. "A Conservative Speaks Out about China," *RF* 3:5 (May 1967), p. 7.
40. John W. Kole, "Gadfly of GOP: Ripon Society's Success Story," *Milwaukee Journal* May 21, 1967.
41. "Birchite Domination Seriously Damages GOP," *Nashville Tennessean* March 29, 1966.
42. Craig Guthrie, "Far Right Rally Fetes Anderson," *Nashville Tennessean* July 5, 1966.
43. William F. Buckley Jr. to Sarah Tyrell, November 27, 1963. WPBP I-26: "John Birch Society (1963)."
44. Jane Hardaway to Charles P. Taft, September 2, 1966. Charles P. Taft Papers (CPTP) (Library of Congress) 207: "John Birch Society."
45. "Taft and the Radicals," *Atlanta Journal* September 17, 1966.
46. Charles P. Taft to "Dear Robins," October 1, 1966. CPTP 15:6. Schlafly biographer Donald Critchlow presents the Robert Taft Club as an example of how Schlafly's supporters were victimized by the NFRW establishment, without mentioning its Birch Society

connections or failed efforts to take over the regular Nashville chapter. Donald T. Critchlow, *Phyllis Schlafly and Grassroots Conservatism: A Woman's Crusade* (Princeton, NJ: Princeton University Press, 2005), p. 153.

47. Patricia Reilly Hitt interview, May 18, 1977 (Bancroft Library Women in Politics Oral History Project).

48. Elly M. Peterson, "Elly!: Confessions of a Woman Who Walked the Streets" (unpublished manuscript, 1997), p. 118. Elly M. Peterson Papers (University of Michigan). Source courtesy of David Hamstra.

49. "GOP Women Lead the Way," [Long Beach, CA] *Independent Press-Telegram* May 16, 1965.

50. "GOP Women Herald Rift?," *Cincinnati Enquirer* March 9, 1967.

51. Phyllis Schlafly, *Safe—Not Sorry* (Alton, IL: Pere Marquette Press, 1967), p. 149.

52. Critchlow, p. 151.

53. Charles P. Taft to Fowler McCormick, May 2, 1967. CPTP 218: "Republicans for Progress (May-September 1967)."

54. Critchlow, p. 156.

55. Patricia Reilly Hitt interview, May 18, 1977 (Bancroft Library Women in Politics Oral History Project).

56. Transcript of Republican National Committee meeting, February 23, 1968. Republican National Committee Papers (RNCP) (Library of Congress) I-B:5.

57. Schlafly, *Safe—Not Sorry*, p. 169.

58. Critchlow, p. 160.

59. *Phyllis Schlafly Report* 1:1 (August 1967).

60. David S. Broder, "Who Really Runs the Republicans?," *WP* May 9, 1967.

61. Don Bruce, "Inside Out," *Success* June 1967. WFBP I-42: "Bruce–Bruner (1967)."

62. Bruce Chapman to Terry Barnett, May 9, 1967. RSP 11:5.

63. J. Eugene Marans, "Republican Governors Talk 1968," *RF* 3:8 (August 1967), p. 11.

64. "Overkill at Omaha," *RF* 3:7 (July 1967), p. 8.

65. Interview with Jonathan Moore, November 6, 2006.

66. Alf Landon to George W. Romney, February 1, 1967. GRP RA 45: "Landon, Alf."

67. "The Action Team for the Action State," 1966. CWWP M2: "Campaign 1966: Position Papers, Lindsay Material."

68. David Hamstra, "'Lonesome George' Romney and the Perils of Independence" (unpublished senior essay in history, Yale University, April 5, 2010).

69. Glen L. Bachelder, Walter D. De Vries, and Travis Cross to George W. Romney, June 26, 1967. GRP RA 45: "Romney Associates."

70. William A. Rusher to *National Review* editors, January 3, 1967. WFBP I-43: "Inter-Office Memos (January-June 1967)." A characteristic example of Romney's stubbornness occurred on the campaign trail in 1967, when he was taken to a bowling alley for the first time. Romney insisted on rolling dozens of gutterballs, much to the amusement of the press and the chagrin of his handlers. "Time Out for Bowling," *Chicago Daily News* September 15, 1967.

71. Leonard Hall to George Romney, January 10, 1967. GRP RA 45: "Hall, Leonard." White claimed in his autobiography that his talks with Hall were subterfuge and that his loyalties always were to Reagan. However, he seems to have negotiated not only with the Romney campaign but with the Nixon and Rockefeller campaigns as well. In June 1968, Peter Flanigan of the Nixon campaign reported that White had met with Walter Thayer and had considered offering his services to the Rockefeller campaign. According to Flanigan, White was being paid $150,000 by Reagan backer Henry Salvatori for being a consultant to the California delegation, but "White apparently was sufficiently interested in Thayer's proposal to have had the gall to ask Salvatori if his consulting obligations prohib-

ited him from working with the NR [Rockefeller] people. The answer was a flat 'yes.' (Thank the Lord we didn't get White.)" F. Clifton White with Jerome Tuccille, *Politics as a Noble Calling: The Memoirs of F. Clifton White* (Ottawa, IL: Jameson Books, 1994), p. 175; Peter Flanigan to Dwight Chapin and John Mitchell, June 6, 1968. White House Special Files (Nixon Presidential Library) 35.

72. Louis Harris, "Romney Leads Johnson in Nationwide Survey," *NYHT EE* November 21, 1966, p. 1.

73. Al Applegate report on conversations with Henry Kissinger, March 3, 1967. GRP RA 45: "Kissinger, Henry."

74. Glen L. Bachelder, unpublished memoir, 2010. Glen L. Bachelder Papers (University of Western Michigan). My thanks to David Hamstra for bringing this source to my attention.

75. Rowland Evans and Robert Novak, "The Romney Muddle," *IHT* February 15, 1967, p. 4. A comprehensive catalogue of the Romney campaign's flaws appears in Richard Melvin Eyre, "George Romney in 1968, From Front-Runner to Drop-Out, An Analysis of Cause" (unpublished M.A. thesis in political science, Brigham Young University, August 1969). My thanks again to David Hamstra for supplying me with this source.

76. Thomas E. Petri, "A Note on the Press," *RF* 3:11 (November 1967), p. 4.

77. Dwight D. Eisenhower to Barry Leithead, March 24, 1967. Dwight D. Eisenhower Post-Presidential Papers (DDEPPP) (Eisenhower Presidential Library) SNF 11: "Leithead, Barry (1967) (3)."

78. Nelson A. Rockefeller to Tom McCall, April 11, 1967. GRP RA 45: "Misc."

79. Saul Friedman, "GOP's Eastern Eggheads Are Cool Toward Romney," *Detroit Free Press* June 11, 1967.

80. Rowland Evans and Robert Novak, "Relaying an SOS: Morton to Scranton to Romney," *New York World Journal Tribune*, February 5, 1967.

81. J. Eugene Marans, "Republican Governors Talk 1968," *RF* 3:8 (August 1967), p. 11.

82. Charles P. Taft to Members of Republicans for Progress, November 2, 1967. Walter N. Thayer Papers (Hoover Presidential Library) III-2:11.

83. Lee W. Huebner, "The Conservative Battle Plan," *New Leader* July 17, 1967, p. 5.

84. John S. Saloma III, "The New Political Order: A History of the Conservative Infrastructure" (unpublished manuscript), December 1982, pp. 115–116. Tanya M. Melich Papers (SUNY Albany) V-8:15.

85. Hess and Broder, p. 95.

86. T. George Harris, *Romney's Way: A Man and an Idea* (Englewood Cliffs, NJ: Prentice-Hall, 1967), pp. 30–31.

87. Nick Thimmesch, *The Condition of Republicanism* (New York: W. W. Norton, 1968), p. 121.

88. Associated Press report, April 4, 1967. Robert T. Hartmann Papers (Ford Presidential Library) 98: "Romney, George."

89. Delbert L. Stapley to George W. Romney, January 23, 1964. Available at http://www.boston.com/news/daily/24/delbert_stapley.pdf.

90. George Romney statement 1967. GRP RA 45: "Misc."

91. Interview with John McClaughry, November 29, 2009. One of Romney's campaign managers, John Deardourff, also felt that "it is very hard for working political reporters to believe that guys like George Romney are really for real. . . . these are, by and large, not people who have very religious convictions." John Deardourff interview, February 18, 1995. Howard H. Baker Jr. Oral History Project (University of Tennessee).

92. Hess and Broder, p. 96.

93. Dan T. Carter, *The Politics of Rage: George Wallace, the Origins of the New Conservatism, and the Transformation of American Politics* (Baton Rouge, LA: Louisiana State Press, 2000), p. 298.

94. Joyce Braithwaite-Brickley, "Peterson Paved the Way," *Traverse City* [Michigan] *Record-Eagle* June 14, 2008.

95. Peterson, "Elly!," pp. 113–118.

96. Otto Kerner et al., *Report of the National Advisory Commission on Civil Disorders* (New York: Bantam Books, 1968), p. 92.

97. Interview with Joseph A. Califano Jr., January 16, 2003; "After Detroit," *Time* August 4, 1967.

98. Peterson, "Elly!," p. 117.

99. Harris, *Romney's Way*, p. 45.

100. Lawrence E. Davies, "Reagan Brands Those in Riots 'Mad Dogs Against the People,'" *NYT* July 26, 1967, p. 19.

101. Schlafly, *Safe—Not Sorry*, pp. 23–24.

102. George W. Romney address to the National Advisory Commission on Civil Disorders, September 12, 1967. DDEPPP SNF 17: "Romney, George (1967) (1)."

103. George W. Romney address to the National Association of County Officials, July 31, 1967. GRP RA 53: "Re 'Urban Speech.'"

104. George W. Romney news release, August 28, 1967. GRP RA 57: "Urban Tour—Miscellaneous."

105. H. C. McKinney to William Prendergast, August 31, 1967. GRP RA 57: "Urban Tour—Miscellaneous."

106. "The Second Day of Governor Romney's Urban Tour," September 12, 1967. GRP RA 57: "Urban Tour—General."

107. Tom Shawver, "Romney Trades Advice with Negroes in Rochester," *Detroit Free Press* September 14, 1967.

108. Jon Lowell, "Negro Militants Applaud Romney," *Detroit News* September 14, 1967.

109. George Romney Urban Tour schedule September 11–29, 1967. GRP RA 57: "Urban Tour—Miscellaneous"; Charles Orlebeke to George W. Romney, September 26, 1967; William Whitbeck to George W. Romney, September 26, 1967; John Martin to William Prendergast, September 28, 1967. GRP RA 57: "Suggested Approaches to Urban Report."

110. Warren Weaver Jr., "Urban Rebellion Feared by Romney," *NYT* October 1, 1967, p. 1.

111. Anthony Ripley, "Romney Censures 'Violence' of Protest Groups," *NYT* October 31, 1967, p. 30.

112. *CQ* September 8, 1967.

113. "Whalen Against Surtax Plan," *Dayton Daily News* December 4, 1967.

114. Charles W. Whalen Jr., "Washington Report," Sep. 1967. CWWP L205: "Speeches, articles, press clippings—Vietnam (1967–71)."

115. Charles W. Whalen Jr., "Washington Report," December 1967. CWWP L205: "Speeches, articles, press clippings—Vietnam (1967–71)."

116. *WHIO Reports* interview with Charles Percy and Charles W. Whalen Jr., April 23, 1967. CWWP L205: "Speeches, articles, and background papers (1965–67)."

117. Interview with Paul N. McCloskey Jr., December 7, 2005.

118. Paul N. McCloskey Jr. statement, September 12, 1967. Paul N. McCloskey Jr. Papers (Hoover Institution) 65.

119. Interview with John McClaughry, November 29, 2009.

120. Interview with Jonathan Moore, November 6, 2006.

121. Jonathan Moore to George W. Romney, July 10, 1967. GRP RA 55: "Memos to and from J. Moore." Ultimately Romney envisaged a "guaranteed neutralization" of Vietnam.

122. John M. Taylor, "Romney Bids U.S. Encourage China," *NYT* August 19, 1967, p. 2.

123. "Romney Deplores Vietnam Buildup," *NYT* August 16, 1967, p. 8.

124. Warren Weaver Jr., "Peace Called Key in '68 by Romney," *NYT* August 17, 1968, p. 1; Warren Weaver Jr., "Romney Says G.O.P. President Would Be Better at Settling War," *NYT* August 21, 1967, p. 6.

125. "Romney Starts to Emerge From the Vietnam Tangle," *Detroit Free Press* August 28, 1967, p. A6.

126. "Republicans: The Brainwashed Candidate," *Time* September 15, 1967; Theodore H. White, *The Making of the President 1968* (New York: Atheneum, 1969), p. 59.

127. Joshua Zeitz, "The Brainwashing of George Romney," *American Heritage* September 4, 2007.

128. "He Should Bow Out!," *Detroit News* September 10, 1967.

129. Robert Sandoz, "Romney's Amateur Hour," *New Leader* September 25, 1967, p. 3.

130. George W. Romney news conference, September 9, 1967. DDEPPP SNF-17: "Romney, George (1967) (1)."

131. Interview with Paul N. McCloskey Jr., April 19, 2007.

132. Bruce K. Chapman to Thomas E. Petri, October 29, 1967. RSP 11:5. Chapman reported that Gilder felt the two of them should hold a press conference to expose the Romney campaign's deterioration and try to run Mark Hatfield in New Hampshire instead.

133. George W. Romney to Jack Severson, February 29, 1968. GRP RA 55: "Misc. (2)."

134. Ripon Society Executive Board minutes, February 27, 1968. RSP 11: "February 1968."

135. Stephen E. Ambrose, *Nixon: The Triumph of a Politician, 1969–72* (New York: Simon and Schuster, 1989), p. 89.

CHAPTER 8

1. Mark Kurlansky, *1968: The Year That Rocked the World* (New York: Random House, 2005).

2. Donald Rumsfeld to Working Group for Percy, July 24, 1967. Alphonzo Bell Papers (ABP) (University of Southern California) 11:25.

3. Thomas Houser to Working Group for Percy, August 7, 1967. ABP 11:25.

4. Donald Rumsfeld to Working Group for Percy, July 17, 1967. ABP 11:25.

5. Working Group for Percy memo, August 21, 1967. ABP 11:25.

6. Donald Rumsfeld to Working Group for Percy, July 17, 1967. ABP 11:25.

7. Working Group for Percy memo, August 21, 1967. ABP 11:25.

8. Stewart Alsop, "Goldwater Will Have His Say," *Saturday Evening Post* March 1967.

9. William F. Buckley Jr. to Evan G. Galbraith, December 8, 1966. William F. Buckley Jr. Papers (WFBP) (Yale University) I-39: "Galbraith (Evan–John Kenneth) (1966)."

10. Thomas Houser to Working Group for Percy, November 13, 1967. ABP 11:26.

11. WGP to Charles H. Percy, November? 1967. ABP 11:26.

12. Interview with John McClaughry, November 15, 2009.

13. Richard Blades to Donald Rumsfeld, October 2, 1967. ABP 11:26.

14. Richard Blades to Donald Rumsfeld, November 21, 1967. ABP 11:26.

15. Joseph E. Persico, *The Imperial Rockefeller: A Biography of Nelson A. Rockefeller* (Thorndike, ME: Thorndike Press, 1982), p. 97.

16. Interview with John R. Price, July 20, 2007.

17. Interview with Lee W. Huebner, April 11, 2007. Some of the dinners also took place at Whitney's Manhattan townhouse.

18. Interview with Josiah Lee Auspitz, October 21, 2006.

19. Interview with John R. Price, July 20, 2007.

20. Persico, p. 21.

21. Interview with John R. Price, July 20, 2007.

22. Peter J. Wallison interview, October 28–29, 2003 (Ronald Reagan Oral History Project, Miller Center for Public Affairs, University of Virginia).

23. Interview with John R. Price, July 20, 2007.

24. Persico, pp. 94–95.

25. Interview with Jonathan Moore, November 6, 2006.

26. James Reston, "The Calmest Voice in the Capitol," *IHT* February 10–11, 1968, p. 4.

27. Thomas E. Petri to George L. Hinman, February 26, 1968. Ripon Society Papers (RSP) (Cornell University) 9:8.

28. "Republican Arithmetic," *RF* 4:8 (August 1968), p. 9; Howard Gillette Jr. to Robert D. Behn, October 16, 1968. RSP 13.

29. William K. Woods to Josiah Lee Auspitz, April 1, 1968. RSP 9: "Auspitz corr."

30. William W. Cobbs Jr. to Thomas E. Petri, April 22, 1968. RSP 9:3.

31. Charles Pillsbury to Josiah Lee Auspitz, April 20, 1968. RSP 9:21.

32. James Reston, "New Haven: God and War at Yale," *NYT* April 26, 1967, p. 46.

33. E. J. Dionne Jr., *Why Americans Hate Politics* (New York: Simon & Schuster, 1991), p. 189.

34. Eugene J. Dionne Jr. to Ripon Society, April 15, 1968. RSP 9:4.

35. Interview with Steven Livengood, March 1, 2009.

36. Lee W. Huebner, "'The Fierce Urgency of Now,'" *RF* 4:5 (May 1968), p. 4.

37. Charles R. Morris, *The Cost of Good Intentions: New York City and the Liberal Experiment, 1960–1975* (New York: W. W. Norton, 1980), p. 77.

38. Vincent J. Cannato, *The Ungovernable City: John Lindsay and His Struggle to Save New York* (New York: Basic Books, 2001), pp. 211–212.

39. Barry Goldwater *Face the Nation* transcript, February 26, 1967. GRP RA 45: "Goldwater, Barry."

40. Otto Kerner et al., *Report of the National Advisory Commission on Civil Disorders* (New York: Bantam Books, 1968), pp. 1-2.

41. Robert W. Gordon, "Repression Is Not the Answer," *RF* 4:4 (April 1968), pp. 7–8.

42. J. Eugene Marans and Peter J. Wallison, "What Republicans Should Do," *RF* 4:4 (April 1968), pp. 9–10.

43. Ripon Society of New York Executive Board, "New York Group Objects," *RF* 4:7 (July 1968), pp. 22–23.

44. Christopher DeMuth, "Georgia: At the King Funeral," *RF* 4:5 (May 1968), p. 17.

45. "Editorial Points," *RF* 4:5 (May 1968), p. 3.

46. The group hoped to put down Minority Leader Gerald Ford's request for a House-Senate conference to consider the bill, which might result in editing out clauses pertaining to open housing. "Ohio: Three Congressmen Who Cared," *RF* 4:5 (May 1968), p. 18.

47. "Community Self-Determination Act," *RF* 4:9 (Sep. 1968), pp. 13–14.

48. Huebner, "'The Fierce Urgency of Now,'" p. 4.

49. Interview with John McClaughry, November 15, 2009; John McClaughry to John Conyers, October 29, 1968. Clarence L. Townes Papers (Virginia Commonwealth University) 8: "RNC (1968)."

50. John McClaughry, "Black Power Progress Report," *RF* 4:6 (June 1968), p. 10. See also Dean J. Kotlowski, *Nixon's Civil Rights: Politics, Principle, and Policy* (Cambridge, MA: Harvard University Press, 2001), p. 126.

51. "Editorial Points," *RF* 4:6 (June 1968), p. 5.

52. Ripon Society, *The Lessons of Victory* (New York: Dial Press, 1969), p. 17.

53. Interview with Howard Gillette Jr., November 2, 2006.

54. John E. Lawrence to Thaddeus Beal, March 27, 1968. RSP 9:2.

55. Interview with Tanya Melich, February 13, 2007.

56. Persico, p. 109.

57. "Editorial Points," *RF* 4:7 (July 1968), p. 3.

58. James Reston, "The Final Irony of Death," *NYT* June 10, 1968.

59. William A. Rusher to James Lewis Kirby Jr., January 31, 1969. William A. Rusher Papers (WARP) (Library of Congress) 48:8.
60. Bryan W. Stevens, *The John Birch Society in California Politics* (West Covina, CA: Publius Society, 1966), p. 68.
61. Lance Gilmore, "Rafferty Fires Broadside at UC's 'Odd Birds,'" *Berkeley Gazette* March 2, 1967. Ronald Reagan Gubernatorial Papers (RRGP) (Reagan Presidential Library) RS104: "Personalities: Rafferty (1)."
62. "Rafferty Critical of Kuchel," *Oakland Tribune* March 8, 1967.
63. Thomas Kuchel to Mary Landis, March 8, 1968. Thomas Kuchel Papers (University of California at Berkeley) 564:41 "Civil Rights Misc. '68."
64. Lou Cannon, *Governor Reagan: His Rise to Power* (New York: PublicAffairs, 2003), p. 536.
65. Thomas Kuchel farewell address to Senate, CR October 14, 1968.
66. Lionel Van Deerlin, "Kuchel, A Courageous Public Servant," *San Diego Union-Tribune* November 29, 1994.
67. Eleanor Fowle, *Cranston: The Senator from California* (San Rafael, CA: Presidio, 1980), p. 200.
68. Dick Darling to "Dear Friend of Max Rafferty," September 7, 1968. RRGP RS104: "Personalities: Rafferty (1)"; Michael Djordjevich to William A. Rusher, October 8, 1968. WARP 26:1.
69. Fowle, pp. 210–211.
70. Interview with Alan Cranston, August 4, 1999.
71. Interview with Michael C. Smith, February 12, 2007.
72. Michael C. Smith, "Ronald Reagan: Here's the Rest of Him," *RF* 4:6 (June 1968), pp. 13–32.
73. "Reagan Looks Toward the Presidency," *IHT* February 21, 1967, p. 3.
74. Smith, "Ronald Reagan," pp. 13–32.
75. "Editorial Points," *RF* 4:6 (June 1968), p. 4.
76. Cannon, p. 199.
77. Interview with Daniel J. Evans, December 12, 2005.
78. "Wise Words from Reagan," *LAT* April 4, 1967.
79. Josiah Lee Auspitz to John R. Price, April 1968. RSP 9:16.
80. Interview with Josiah Lee Auspitz, October 21, 2006.
81. "Notes from Miami Beach," *RF* 4:9 (Sep. 1968), p. 4.
82. Tanya Melich to Newt Gingrich, August 12, 1968. Tanya M. Melich Papers (TMMP) (SUNY Albany) II-3:17.
83. F. Clifton White with Jerome Tuccille, *Politics As a Noble Calling* (Ottawa, IL: Jameson Books, 1994), p. 177.
84. Interview with Tanya Melich, February 13, 2007.
85. Tanya Melich to Mike O'Neill, August 12, 1968. TMMP II-3:17.
86. Tanya Melich to Frank Newman, August 12, 1968. TMMP II-3:17.
87. "Notes from Miami Beach," *RF* 4:9 (September 1968), p. 4.
88. Tanya Melich to Hope Kading, August 12, 1968. TMMP II-3:17.
89. Interview with Josiah Lee Auspitz, October 21, 2006.
90. Fred L. Zimmerman, "GOP Microcosm," *WSJ* August 6, 1968.
91. Ripon Society, *The Lessons of Victory*, p. 69.
92. *Ibid.*, p. 88.
93. Spiro T. Agnew press release, July 29, 1963. Spiro T. Agnew Papers (University of Maryland) I-SS1.1-1: "Personal correspondence (1963)."
94. "Notes from Miami Beach," *RF* 4:9 (Sep. 1968), p. 5.
95. Interview with William W. Scranton, July 16, 1992.

96. Spiro T. Agnew press conference, April 11, 1968. Rogers C. B. Morton Papers (University of Kentucky) 112: "General (1968)–Agnew, Gov. Spiro T."

97. John H. Hauberg to Lee W. Huebner, November 20, 1968. RSP 9:8.

98. Richard A. Zimmer to Lee W. Huebner, August 12, 1968. RSP 13.

99. "The Ripon Poll," *RF* 4:10 (October 1968), pp. 16–19.

100. Dwight D. Eisenhower to Milton G. Baker, March 2, 1968. Dwight D. Eisenhower Post-Presidential Papers (Eisenhower Presidential Library) SNF-1: "Baker, Milton (1967–68)."

101. William J. Kilberg letter, *RF* 4:11 (November 1968), pp. 21–22.

102. Thomas S. Winter to Thomas E. Petri, October 16, 1968. RSP 9:23.

103. "Editorial Points," *RF* 4:10 (October 1968), p. 3.

104. "Notes from Washington," *RF* 4:8 (August 1968), p. 8.

105. Robert D. Behn to Ripon research staff, November 1968. RSP 11: "November 1968."

106. Robert Crangle to Robert D. Behn, October 14, 1968. RSP 13.

107. Robert D. Behn to Ripon Society state correspondents, national associate members, and Ripon research staff, October 21, 1968. RSP 11: "October 1968."

108. "Editorial," *RF* 4:9 (Sep. 1968), pp. 1, 3.

109. Josiah Lee Auspitz to Glenn Olds, September 12, 1968. RSP 9:20.

110. Interview with Lee W. Huebner, April 11, 2007.

111. "Editorial," *RF* 4:12 (December 1968), pp. 3–5.

112. Christopher W. Beal, "Election '68: What Did and *Didn't* Happen," *RF* 4:12 (December 1968), pp. 8–9.

113. Christopher W. Beal, "The Collapsing Coalitions," *RF* 4:11 (November 1968), p. 8.

114. "Editorial," *RF* 4:12 (December 1968), pp. 10–11.

115. Walter N. Thayer to Dwight D. Eisenhower, November 19, 1968. Walter N. Thayer Papers (Hoover Presidential Library) III-2:14.

116. Interview with Michael C. Smith, February 12, 2007.

117. "Can a VISTA Find Happiness Attacking Elephants with a Pea Shooter?," *RF* 5:7 (July 1969), p. 12.

118. Interview with Michael C. Smith, February 12, 2007.

119. *Yale Reports* January 14, 1968. WFBP I-50: "Herberg, Will (1968)."

120. Interview with Michael C. Smith, February 12, 2007.

121. William A. Rusher notes on the Ripon Society dinner, December 15, 1968. WARP 169:14.

122. John V. Lindsay, "An Era of Greatness?," *RF* 5:1 (January 1969), pp. 22–24.

CHAPTER 9

1. "Editorial," *RF* 5:1 (January 1969), p. 3.

2. Robert and Donna Simms to Rogers C. B. Morton, December 31, 1968. Rogers C. B. Morton Papers (RCBMP) (University of Kentucky) 97: "Hickel, Walter." Moderate suspicions of Hickel seemed to be confirmed when he appointed anti-conservationist James G. Watt, later a controversial secretary of the Interior under Ronald Reagan, to a position in his office. E. L. Smith to Charles McC. Mathias, February 11, 1969. RCBMP 120: "General (1969)–Hickel, Walter."

3. "Editorial," *RF* 5:1 (January 1969), p. 3.

4. "Nixon at the Crossroads: Presidential Action for Human Rights," *RF* 5:2 (February 1969), p. 3.

5. Ray C. Bliss to Richard M. Nixon, February 17, 1969. Ray C. Bliss Papers (Ohio Historical Society) 77:10.

6. Rogers C. B. Morton address to Republican Party Victory Dinner in Louisville, Kentucky, May 15, 1969. RCBMP 210: "Speeches (1)."

7. Interview with Lee W. Huebner, April 11, 2007.
8. "Nixon Names Seattle Lawyer as Counsel," *Seattle Times* November 26, 1968; interview with Paul N. McCloskey, December 7, 2005.
9. Interview with Lee W. Huebner, April 11, 2007.
10. Howard L. Reiter, "Ripon: Left Spur to the GOP," *Nation* February 17, 1969.
11. Thomas E. Petri to Charles S. Rhyne, November 14, 1968. Ripon Society Papers (RSP) (Cornell University) 9:18; Thomas E. Petri to Peter Flanigan, November 13, 1968. RSP 9:6.
12. Reiter, "Ripon: Left Spur to the GOP."
13. David S. Broder, "Two Major Talent Factories Struggle to Dominate the GOP," *WP* February 17, 1970. Two other Syndicate alumni later became governors: Robert List in Nevada and Charles Thone in Nebraska.
14. Leonard Garment, *Crazy Rhythm: From Brooklyn and Jazz to Nixon's White House, Watergate, and Beyond* (New York: Da Capo, 2001), p. 156.
15. William Safire, *Before the Fall: An Inside View of the Pre-Watergate White House* (Garden City, NY: Doubleday, 1975).
16. Garry Wills, *Nixon Agonistes: The Crisis of the Self-Made Man* (Boston, MA: Houghton Mifflin, 1969), p. 581.
17. Ripon Society, *The Lessons of Victory* (New York: Dial Press, 1969), pp. 390–391.
18. Raymond Price, *With Nixon* (New York: Viking, 1977), pp. 30, 34.
19. Interview with Lee W. Huebner, April 11, 2007.
20. Reiter, "Ripon: Left Spur to the GOP."
21. Nick Thimmesch, "Nixon and the New York Republicans," *New York* April 7, 1969, p. 39.
22. Price, pp. 77–78.
23. Ripon Society press release, April 29? 1969. RSP 17:4.
24. "Delay Tactics Hit House Over Reforms, Debate Bills," *CQ Almanac 1968*, pp. 647–650; Donald Rumsfeld, *Known and Unknown: A Memoir* (New York: Sentinel, 2011), p. 95.
25. Eugene Methvin, "Is Congress Destroying Itself?," *Reader's Digest* April 1969.
26. David S. Broder, *Behind the Front Page: A Candid Look at How the News Is Made* (New York: Simon & Schuster, 1987), pp. 214–216.
27. Donald R. Rumsfeld, "Thoughts on the 91st Congress and the House Minority," December 18, 1968. Bryce Harlow Papers (Nixon Presidential Library) I-3:5.
28. Robert D. Behn to Ripon Society National Governing Board, October 10, 1968. RSP 11: "October 1968."
29. Fred Pillsbury, "Big Doings in Only 2 Small Rooms," *BG* June 25, 1967.
30. *Firing Line* 137, February 24, 1969 (Hoover Institution).
31. John B. Judis, *William F. Buckley, Jr.: Patron Saint of the Conservatives* (New York: Touchstone, 1988), p. 280.
32. *Firing Line* 137, February 24, 1969 (Hoover Institution).
33. Petri wrote to Buckley afterwards that "I think you may have mellowed a bit since you and I were at Harvard's Quincy House when I was an undergraduate." Thomas E. Petri to William F. Buckley Jr., February 27, 1969. RSP 13.
34. *Firing Line* 137, February 24, 1969 (Hoover Institution).
35. William A. Steiger to Robert Finch, April 17, 1969. William A. Steiger Papers (WASP) (Wisconsin Historical Society) 1:8.
36. "Urban Problem Causes Ignored, Says Steiger," *Wisconsin State Journal* January 15, 1967. WASP 61A:5.
37. William Brock, "Proposed: A Republican Initiative on Campus," May 15, 1969. WASP 1:11.
38. "Questions and Answers on the Proposed Task Force on Academic Reform," May? 1969. WASP 1:12.

39. Richard B. Cheney, "University of Wisconsin (Madison)," May 20, 1969. WASP 1:11.
40. Richard B. Cheney, "Interviews," May? 1969. WASP 1:12.
41. Interview with Thomas Railsback, April 16, 2009.
42. Richard B. Cheney, "Interviews," May? 1969. WASP 1:12. Hampton would be killed in his bed in a Chicago police raid in December 1969.
43. Richard B. Cheney to William A. Steiger, June 5, 1969. WASP 1:12.
44. Tom Railsback, "Student Unrest: Discussions with Students, Faculty and Administrators," May? 1969. WASP 1:12.
45. John C. Danforth to Earl Pelster, June 16, 1969. John C. Danforth Papers (University of Missouri) 69: "Black Militants Action."
46. William A. Steiger to House Committee on Education and Labor, June 16, 1969. WASP 1:12.
47. William Brock et al. to Richard M. Nixon, June 17, 1969; William Brock et al. to "Dear Colleague," July 28, 1969. WASP 1:8.
48. Richard B. Cheney to William A. Steiger, June 16? 1969. WASP 1:11.
49. John R. Coyne Jr., *The Impudent Snobs: Agnew vs. the Intellectual Establishment* (New Rochelle, NY: Arlington House, 1972), p. 37.
50. Edward W. Brooke, *Bridging the Divide: My Life* (New Brunswick, NJ: Rutgers University Press, 2007), pp. 182–183. See also Miriam Horn, *Rebels in White Gloves: Coming of Age with Hillary's Class—Wellesley '69* (New York: Times Books, 1999), pp. 45–47.
51. Christopher W. Beal (ed.), *The Realities of Vietnam: A Ripon Society Appraisal* (Washington, DC: Public Affairs Press, 1968), p. 4.
52. Melvin Small, *The Presidency of Richard Nixon* (Lawrence, KS: University Press of Kansas, 1999), p. 162.
53. Clair Warren Rodgers Jr. and Christopher W. Beal to *New York Times*, September 16, 1969. RSP 13.
54. Tom Wicker, *One of Us: Richard Nixon and the American Dream* (New York: Random House, 1991), p. 522.
55. Hugh Davis Graham, *Civil Rights Era: Origins and Development of National Policy, 1960–1972* (New York: Oxford University Press, 1990), p. 325.
56. Paul Frymer and John David Skrentny, "Coalition-Building and the Politics of Electoral Capture During the Nixon Administration: African Americans, Labor, Latinos," *Studies in American Political Development* 12 (spring 1998), p. 146.
57. Dean J. Kotlowski, *Nixon's Civil Rights: Politics, Principle, and Policy* (Cambridge, MA: Harvard University Press, 2001), p. 125.
58. Maurice H. Stans, "Nixon's Economic Policy Toward Minorities," in Leon Friedman and William F. Levantrosser (eds.), *Nixon: Politician, President, Administrator* (New York: Greenwood Press, 1991), pp. 239–246.
59. Interview with John McClaughry, November 15, 2009.
60. David I. Bruck, "The Ripon Forum," *Harvard Crimson* October 11, 1968.
61. Wicker, p. 489.
62. *Ibid.*, p. 493.
63. Charles H. Percy to Edward W. Brooke, August 12, 1969. Edward W. Brooke Papers (Library of Congress) 188: "Percy, Charles H."
64. "New York: If at First . . .," *RF* 5:2 (February 1969), p. 4.
65. William A. Rusher to Charles B. Goldberg, July 15, 1969. William A. Rusher Papers (WARP) (Library of Congress) 34:8.
66. "Editorial," *RF* 5:4 (April 1969), p. 3.
67. Clair Warren Rodgers Jr. to Josiah Lee Auspitz, June 6, 1969. RSP 13.
68. Vincent J. Cannato, *The Ungovernable City: John Lindsay and His Struggle to Save New York* (New York: Basic Books, 2001), p. 402.

69. Charles E. Goodell to Clair Warren Rodgers Jr., May 28, 1969. RSP 13.
70. William A. Rusher to Charles B. Goldberg, June 18, 1969. WARP 34:8.
71. "Lindsay's Non-Future," *NR* July 15, 1969, pp. 681–682.
72. Patrick J. Buchanan to Richard M. Nixon, June 20, 1969. Nixon Presidential Materials (National Archives II) POF—President's Handwriting, Box 2: "1969."
73. "Editorial," *RF* 5:6 (June 1969), p. 3.
74. "New York: Marchi Beats Lindsay, Buffalo Version," *RF* 5:6 (June 1969), p. 4.
75. Interview with Lee W. Huebner, November 24, 2009.
76. Richard M. Nixon, "Address to the Nation on Domestic Programs," August 8, 1969. Available at http://www.presidency.ucsb.edu.
77. "Editorial," *RF* 5:8 (August 1969), p. 3.
78. Ripon Society and Clifford W. Brown Jr., *Jaws of Victory: The Game Plan Politics of 1972, the Crisis of the Republican Party, and the Future of the Constitution* (Boston, MA: Little, Brown, 1974), p. 31.
79. Theodore Rosenof, *Realignment: The Theory That Changed the Way We Think About American Politics* (Lanham, MD: Rowman & Littlefield, 2003), pp. 113–114.
80. Christopher W. Beal, Robert D. Behn, Clair W. Rodgers Jr., and Michael S. Lottman, "It's Not That Simple," *RF* 5:10 (October 1969), p. 10.
81. Wills, *Nixon Agonistes*, pp. 265, 267.
82. Kevin Phillips, *The Emerging Republican Majority* (New Rochelle, NY: Arlington House, 1969), pp. 465–466.
83. Wills, *Nixon Agonistes*, p. 266.
84. William A. Rusher to Kevin Phillips, August 18, 1969. WARP 71:10.
85. Howard L. Reiter, "Mr. Evans Builds His Dream House," *RF* 5:3 (March 1969), pp. 29–30.
86. "It's Not That Simple," p. 9.
87. *Ibid.*, p. 17.
88. Christopher W. Beal and Clair Warren Rodgers Jr. to *New York Times*, September 17, 1969. RSP 22: "1969–70."
89. "It's Not That Simple," p. 16.
90. *Ibid.*, p. 15.
91. *Ibid.*, p. 20.
92. *Ibid.*, p. 18.
93. *Ibid.*, p. 13.
94. *Ibid.*, p. 11.
95. Andrew Hacker, "Is There a New Republican Majority?," *Commentary* November 1969, p. 66.
96. Josiah Lee Auspitz to Norman Podhoretz, November 18, 1969; Andrew Hacker to Clair W. Rodgers Jr., December 5, 1969. RSP 13.
97. A. James Reichley interview with Charles E. Goodell, August 30, 1977. Reichley interview transcripts (Ford Presidential Library) 2: "Goodell, Charles.
98. Harvard Negotiation Project website, http://www.pon.harvard.edu/hnp/theory/tools/yesable.shtml.
99. Michael Chabot Smith to Geoffrey Kabaservice, January 4, 2009.
100. Interview with Michael Chabot Smith, February 12, 2007.
101. Michael Chabot Smith to Geoffrey Kabaservice, January 4, 2009.
102. Ripon Society press release, October 11, 1969. RSP 8.
103. Richard M. Nixon, "Address to the Nation on the War in Vietnam," November 3, 1969. Available at www.presidency.ucsb.edu.
104. Ripon Society newsletter to *Ripon Forum* subscribers, November 13, 1969. Tanya M. Melich Papers (TMMP) (SUNY Albany) V-5:4.

105. Interview with Michael Chabot Smith, February 12, 2007.

106. Michael Chabot Smith to Geoffrey Kabaservice, January 4, 2009.

107. Ripon Society press release, November 1969. RSP 8.

108. Michael Chabot Smith to Geoffrey Kabaservice, January 4, 2009.

109. Interview with Howard Gillette Jr., November 2, 2006.

110. "14a Eliot Street," *RF* 5:12 (December 1969), p. 27.

111. Interview with Howard Gillette Jr., November 2, 2006.

112. Rick Perlstein, *Nixonland: The Rise of a President and the Fracturing of America* (New York: Scribner, 2008), pp. 435–436.

113. "Virginia: Second Shot," *RF* 5:2 (February 1969), p. 4.

114. Linwood Holton, inaugural address, January 17, 1970. Reprinted in Linwood Holton, *Opportunity Time: A Memoir* (Charlottesville, VA: University of Virginia Press, 2008), pp. 224–225.

115. "Cahill Leads GOP Resurgence," *RF* 5:6 (June 1969), p. 13. Kevin Phillips, while working in John Mitchell's office, described Cahill as "a middle-road Republican" with strong middle America and Silent Majority appeal. Kevin Phillips, "New Jersey 1969— An Analysis of the Causes and Constituency of the Cahill Victory," December? 1969. WARP 71:10.

116. "New Jersey: Cahill's Sweep and the Consequences," *RF* 5:11 (November 1969), p. 5.

117. Republican National Committee news release, November 6, 1969. RSP 13.

118. "D.C.: RNC Action Program Invades Democratic Turf," *RF* 5:6 (June 1969), p. 5.

119. Richard A. Zimmer, "New Haven: GOP Moderates Unite Behind Capra to Wrest Mayoralty After 16 Years of Lee," *RF* 5:8 (August 1969), pp. 4–5.

120. "New Haven: The Ninth, But a Narrow Loss," *RF* 5:11 (November 1969), p. 4.

121. Josiah Lee Auspitz to Norman Podhoretz, November 18, 1969. RSP 13.

122. Ripon Society newsletter to *Ripon Forum* subscribers, November 13, 1969. TMMP V-5:4.

123. "14a Eliot Street," *RF* 5:12 (December 1969), p. 27.

124. "Illinois: Too Many Moderates," *RF* 5:10 (October 1969), p. 5; "Illinois: The Meteoric Mr. Crane," *RF* 5:12 (December 1969), p. 4.

125. Donald E. Fraher Jr. to A. Douglas Matthews, June 3, 1969. RSP 13.

126. John W. Finney, "G.O.P. Names Scott as Senate Leader, Griffin as Whip," *NYT* September 25, 1969, p. 1. See also Dean Kotlowski, "Unhappily Yoked? Hugh Scott and Richard Nixon," *Pennsylvania Magazine of History and Biography* July 2001.

127. Ripon Society press release, December 1969. RSP 17:12.

128. Bruce K. Chapman, "A Visit with President Nixon," *Seattle Times* April 5, 1970.

129. "14a Eliot Street," *RF* 6:1 (January 1970), p. 23.

130. *Ibid.*

131. Chapman, "A Visit with President Nixon."

132. Ripon Society to Richard M. Nixon, November 26, 1969. RSP 14.

133. Allan H. Ryskind to Harry Dent, December 19, 1969. RSP 13.

134. Interview with Howard Gillette Jr., November 2, 2006.

CHAPTER 10

1. Richard M. Nixon conversation, October 14, 1972. Nixon Tapes (National Archives II) 798–15.

2. "Mitchell Depicts Ripon Society as Little Juvenile Delinquents," *NYT* January 18, 1970.

3. Mary McGrory, "Riponers, Mitchell en Riposte," *Washington Evening Star*, January 20, 1970, p. A3; "14a Eliot Street," *RF* 6:2 (February 1970), p. 23.

4. "A Message from the President," *RF* 6:2 (February 1970), p. 1.

5. Mary McGrory, "Riponers, Mitchell en Riposte," *Washington Evening Star*, January 20, 1970, p. A3

6. Don Oberdorfer, "Youthful Team Drew Environment Plan," *Denver Post* February 15, 1970.

7. "Nixon Names Head of Urban Council," *WP* December 6, 1969.

8. Statement of Black Elected Officials, March 20, 1970. Rogers C. B. Morton Papers (RCBMP) (University of Kentucky) 219: "Civil Rights/Minorities (Conference—Black Elected Officials)."

9. "Editorial," *RF* 6:1 (January 1970), p. 3.

10. Josiah Lee Auspitz to Richard M. Nixon, January 14, 1970. Ripon Society Papers (RSP) (Cornell University) 13.

11. "John Mitchell as Attorney General: A Political Approach to Justice," *RF* 6:1 (January 1970), pp. 5, 12.

12. "Editorial," *RF* 6:1 (January 1970), p. 3.

13. James A. Wechsler, "The Making of . . .," *New York Post* January 20, 1970.

14. Stanley R. Tupper to Josiah Lee Auspitz, February 10, 1970. RSP 13.

15. R. C. Morris to Rogers C. B. Morton, January 16, 1970. RCBMP 219: "Civil Rights/ Minorities (McCarty-White)."

16. William A. Rusher to Spiro Agnew, February 16, 1970. William A. Rusher Papers (WARP) (Library of Congress) 6:6.

17. "Nixon Names Head of Urban Council," *WP* December 6, 1969.

18. Interview with Lee W. Huebner, April 11, 2007.

19. William F. Buckley Jr. to William A. Rusher, March 3, 1970. William F. Buckley Jr. Papers (WFBP) (Yale University) I-165:1081.

20. Bryce Harlow address to the Washington, D.C. chapter of Sigma Delta Chi, January 13, 1970. Paul N. McCloskey Papers (PNMP) (Hoover Institution) 5: "Nixon on Haynsworth, Calley, Mason and Watson—Supreme Court."

21. Howard L. Reiter, "How Nixon Plays His Hand," *Nation* February 2, 1970, pp. 106–107.

22. "Nixon Has Alternatives to Carswell," *Denver Post* January 28, 1970.

23. Frank Samuel remarks at press conference, March 5, 1970. RSP 22: "1969–70."

24. Barry Goldwater, "New Political Alignments," *Houston Tribune* April 2, 1970.

25. Ripon Society, "The Case Against Carswell," March 1970. RSP 17:15.

26. John W. Ehrlichman, *Witness to Power* (New York: Simon & Schuster, 1982), p. 126.

27. Spencer Rich, "Hruska Calls Foes of Carswell Unfair," *NYT* March 17, 1970, p. A2.

28. "Four Crucial Nays: Why They Did It," *Time* April 20, 1970.

29. "Oust Ripon," *Indianapolis News* March 30, 1970.

30. Interview with Howard Gillette Jr., November 2, 2006.

31. Interview with Lee W. Huebner, November 24, 2009.

32. Daniel J. Galvin, *Presidential Party Building: Dwight D. Eisenhower to George W. Bush* (Princeton, NJ: Princeton University Press, 2010), p. 77.

33. Dan Lufkin news release, February 10, 1970. RCBMP 231: "Political Education."

34. Elly M. Peterson, "Elly!: Confessions of a Woman Who Walked the Streets" (unpublished manuscript, 1997), p. 132. Elly M. Peterson Papers (EMPP) (University of Michigan). Source courtesy of David Hamstra. See also Elly M. Peterson to Rogers C. B. Morton, Jim Allison Jr., and Bob Hitt, June 4, 1970. EMPP 14: "RNC Files—Inter-Office Correspondence (April-June 1970)."

35. In her first year in the RNC co-chairmanship, Peterson enlarged the scope of the Women's Division by creating the Women's Advisory Council on Black Involvement and similar groups for Jewish women and white ethnic women (predominantly from Eastern European backgrounds). Her efforts to recruit new voters through these organizations met with sluggish responses from GOP state chairs. In April 1970, she wrote to Morton and other RNC leaders that the states should "get off their duffs and decide if they . . . want these people in the party or not." Elly M. Peterson to Rogers C. B. Morton, Jim

Allison Jr., and Bob Hitt, April 27, 1970. EMPP 14: "RNC Files—Inter-Office Correspondence (April-June 1970)."

36. Peterson, "Elly!," p. 131.

37. Christie Todd, "Listening Program," March 1970. RCBMP 231: "Political Education—Listening Programs."

38. Paul Frymer and John David Skrentny, "Coalition-Building and the Politics of Electoral Capture During the Nixon Administration: African Americans, Labor, Latinos," *Studies in American Political Development* 12 (spring 1998), p. 141.

39. Richard M. Scammon and Ben J. Wattenberg, *The Real Majority: An Extraordinary Examination of the American Electorate* (New York: Coward-McCann, 1970), p. 46.

40. Richard M. Nixon, *RN: The Memoirs of Richard Nixon* (New York: Simon and Schuster, 1990), p. 491.

41. Charles W. Whalen Jr., "Rural Congressmen Learn Urban Problems," ns [1968?]. Source courtesy of Charles W. Whalen, Jr.

42. Charles W. Whalen Jr. to Robert J. Gargrave, October 9, 1975. Charles W. Whalen Jr. Papers (CWWP) (University of Dayton) G53: "General, State of Ohio; Political Philosophy, CWW."

43. Doug Walker, "Last Hurrah Fades, Whalen Faces Vows," *Dayton Daily News* November 27, 1966.

44. James N. Talbert, "Free Trade: The Whalen Plan," *Dayton Journal Herald* April 4, 1967.

45. Charles W. Whalen Jr. position paper, June? 1967. CWWP L205: "Speeches, articles, and background papers (1965–67)."

46. Charles W. Whalen Jr., statement on H.R. 15090 (Fiscal 1970 Department of Defense Appropriations Bill), December 8, 1969. CWWP L205: "Speeches, articles, background papers (1968–70)."

47. Richard L. Lyons, "Review of Viet Policy Asked by 52 in House," *WP* September 26, 1967.

48. Charles W. Whalen Jr. memo, December? 1969. CWWP L205: "Speeches, articles, background papers (1968–70)."

49. Robert David Johnson, *Congress and the Cold War* (London: Cambridge University Press, 2005), p. 160.

50. Charles W. Whalen Jr. memo, December? 1969. CWWP L205: "Speeches, articles, background papers (1968–70)."

51. Charles W. Whalen Jr., Congressional address on the introduction of Vietnam War Disengagement Act of 1973, January 15, 1973. CWWP L206: "Speeches, articles, background papers (1973)."

52. Charles W. Whalen Jr. to Robert W. Booher, October 14, 1972. CWWP L213: "Voting Record Summary (1970–73)."

53. A. James Reichley, *Conservatives in an Age of Change* (Washington, DC: Brookings Institution, 1978), p. 145.

54. Statistics compiled from *Congressional Quarterly Weekly Reports* 1969. CWWP L213: Voting Record Summary (1970–73)."

55. Charles W. Whalen Jr. to Norma McKeehen, February 24, 1970. CWWP L213: "Voting Record Summary (1970–73)."

56. Richard M. Nixon, "Address to the Nation on the Situation in Southeast Asia," April 30, 1970. Available at http://www.presidency.ucsb.edu.

57. Interview with Lee W. Huebner, November 24, 2009.

58. Reichley, p. 118.

59. Richard E. Peterson and John A. Bilorusky, *May 1970: The Campus Aftermath of Cambodia and Kent State* (Berkeley, CA: Carnegie Foundation for the Advancement of Teaching, 1971), p. 7.

60. Charles W. Whalen Jr. statement, May 1, 1970. CWWP L205: "Speeches, articles, press clippings—Vietnam (1967–71)."

61. Daniel Button et al., "Bi-Partisan Resolution to Limit FY 1971 Defense Appropriations," May 7, 1970. CWWP L205: "Speeches, articles, press clippings—Vietnam (1967–71)."

62. John Sherman Cooper statement, May 7, 1970. John Sherman Cooper Papers (University of Kentucky) 496: "Indochina—Cooper-Church Amendment (1970)."

63. Charles W. Whalen Jr., statement on House floor, May 4, 1970. CWWP L205: "Speeches, articles, background papers (1968–70)."

64. Charles W. Whalen Jr., unpublished memoir, p. 134. Source courtesy of Charles W. Whalen Jr.

65. Charles DeBenedetti, *An American Ordeal: The Antiwar Movement of the Vietnam Era* (Syracuse, NY: Syracuse University Press, 1990), p. 279.

66. Bruce K. Chapman to Josiah Lee Auspitz, May 4, 1970. RSP 13.

67. John W. Gardner, "The Crisis in Authority," *RF* 6:6 (June 1970), p. 17.

68. Charles E. Goodell speech at Colgate University, May 8, 1970. Charles E. Goodell Papers (CEGP) (New York Public Library) 175: "Transcripts: Press Conferences."

69. Interview with Lee W. Huebner, November 24, 2009.

70. John L. Campbell et al. to Richard M. Nixon, June 6, 1970. Robert H. Finch Collection (RHFC) (National Archives II) WHCF-SF 27:5.

71. John L. Campbell et al. to Richard M. Nixon, June 5, 1970. RHFC WHCF-SF 27:5.

72. John L. Campbell et al. to Richard M. Nixon, June 6, 1970. RHFC WHCF-SF 27:5.

73. The group originally was called the President's Commission on Campus Violence; Huebner changed the title since "I figured that 'unrest' was a little less provocative, and the issue went deeper than the more violent episodes." Interview with Lee W. Huebner, November 24, 2009.

74. Vincent J. Cannato, *The Ungovernable City: John Lindsay and His Struggle to Save New York* (New York: Basic, 2001), p. 452.

75. Michael P. Balzano Jr., "The Silent v. the New Majority," in Leon Friedman and William F. Levantrosser (eds.), *Politician, President, Administrator* (New York: Greenwood Press, 1991), p. 264.

76. Thomas F. Brady, "1,000 'Establishment' Lawyers Join War Protest," *NYT* May 15, 1970, p. 21.

77. Garry Wills, "USA All the Way," UPI column May 10, 1970. WFBP I-279:2442.

78. James T. Patterson, *Great Expectations: The United States, 1945–1974* (New York: Oxford University Press, 1996), p. 756.

79. Frymer and Skrentny, pp. 152–153.

80. Josiah Lee Auspitz, "The Senate: Excuses, Excuses," *RF* 6:12 (December 1970), p. 8.

81. "'Life Day' Participants Charge Police Brutality," NC News Service June 9, 1970. WFBP I-101:353.

82. David R. Boldt and Anne Hebald, "Police, Abortion Opponents Clash in March on GW Hospital Clinic," *WP* June 7, 1970.

83. Patricia Buckley Bozell to William F. Buckley Jr., June 8, 1970. WFBP I-101:353.

84. L. Brent Bozell Jr. to John Mitchell, May 6, 1970. WFBP I-101:353.

85. My thanks to my former student Kevin Michel for helping me to work out this sequence and for the insights in his Yale senior essay in the history major, "A Struggle Between Brothers: A Reexamination of the Idea of a Cohesive Conservative Movement Through the Intellectual Life and Personal Conflict Surrounding L. Brent Bozell," April 6, 2009. See also Patrick Allitt, *Catholic Intellectuals and Conservative Politics in America, 1950–1985* (Ithaca, NY: Cornell University Press, 1993).

86. Bradley Warren Evans, "The Great Patriotic Health Movement," *New Guard* April 1970.

87. William F. Buckley Jr. to James L. Buckley, March 13, 1968. WFBP I-48: "Buckley Family—Buckley, James L. (1968)"; John B. Judis, *William F. Buckley, Jr.: Patron Saint of the Conservatives* (New York: Touchstone, 1988), p. 311.
88. "Why Goodell Wins," 1970. CEGP 178: "Polling Data."
89. F. Clifton White with Jerome Tuccille, *Politics as a Noble Calling: The Memoirs of F. Clifton White* (Ottawa, IL: Jameson), p. 193.
90. "Will They Love Him in Gotham as They Did in Chatauqua?," *RF* 5:8 (August 1969), p. 9.
91. James D. Griffin address to Syracuse Rotary Club, March 14, 1969. WFBP I-59: "Conservative Party of New York (1969)."
92. Charles E. Goodell press release, August 25, 1964. Thomas Kuchel Papers (University of California) 79B:3.
93. Charles E. Goodell address to New York State Republican Party Convention, April 7, 1970. CEGP 175: "Acceptance Speech."
94. A. James Reichley interview with Charles E. Goodell, August 30, 1977. Reichley interview transcripts (Ford Presidential Library) 2: "Goodell, Charles."
95. Josiah Lee Auspitz to Larry K. Martin, October 30, 1970. RSP 14.
96. A. James Reichley interview with Charles E. Goodell, August 30, 1977. Reichley interview transcripts (Ford Presidential Library) 2: "Goodell, Charles."
97. Charles Robb, "Party Record Beats Barry's, Goodell Says," *New York Daily News* August 20, 1970.
98. "Goodell Under Fire," *Long Island Press* August 24, 1970.
99. William Safire, *Before the Fall: An Inside View of the Pre-Watergate White House* (Garden City, NY: Doubleday, 1975), p. 318.
100. White with Tuccille, p. 193.
101. Nicol C. Rae, *The Decline and Fall of the Liberal Republicans From 1952 to the Present* (New York: Oxford University Press, 1989), p. 104.
102. Richard Reeves, *President Nixon: Alone in the White House* (New York: Simon & Schuster, 2001), pp. 244–245.
103. Spiro T. Agnew, "Topics: On Dividing the Country," *NYT* July 11, 1970.
104. Rick Perlstein, *Nixonland: The Rise of a President and the Fracturing of America* (New York: Scribner, 2008), p. 506.
105. Mary McGrory, "Agnew: Grimness and Affability," *Washington Star* October 25, 1970.
106. Charles E. Goodell WABC-TV Eyewitness News conference, August 2, 1970. CEGP 175: "Transcripts: Press Conferences."
107. Reeves, p. 268.
108. George L. Hinman to Spiro T. Agnew, October 8, 1970. George L. Hinman Papers (Rockefeller Archives) IV-J2-1–1:2.
109. Tina Harrower to Rogers C. B. Morton, October 9, 1970. RCBMP 242: "Chairman Correspondence (1970)—States—New York—Senator Goodell."
110. Brenda E. Rupli to Rogers C. B. Morton, October 2, 1970. RCBMP 219: "Chairman Statements Regarding Senator Goodell."
111. Rogers C. B. Morton to Reginald Everett, October 13, 1970. RCBMP 219: "Chairman Statements Regarding Senator Goodell."
112. Ripon Society and Clifford W. Brown Jr., *Jaws of Victory: The Game-Plan Politics of 1972, the Crisis of the Republican Party, and the Future of the Constitution* (Boston, MA: Little, Brown, 1974), p. 40.
113. Karl E. Meyer, "GOP Senators Stump New York for Goodell," *WP* October 27, 1970; William B. Saxbe with Peter D. Franklin, *I've Seen the Elephant: An Autobiography* (Kent, OH: Kent State University Press, 2000), pp. 90–91.
114. Garry Wills, "The Making of a Senator," November 11, 1970. WFBP I-279:2442.

115. "Agnew Equals Nixon," *RF* 6:11 (November 1970), p. 3.

116. James L. Buckley news release, September 17, 1970. CEGP 175: "Buckley Bible."

117. *New York Daily News,* September 3, 1970. CEGP 175: "Buckley Bible."

118. James L. Buckley news conference on WINS, September 6, 1970. CEGP 175: "Buckley Bible."

119. James L. Buckley address to New York State Conservation Council, September 27, 1968. WFBP I-48: "Buckley Family—Buckley, James L.—Senate Race (1968)."

120. Michael Kramer and Sam Roberts, *I Never Wanted To Be Vice-President of Anything!: An Investigative Biography of Nelson Rockefeller* (New York: Basic Books, 1976), pp. 344–345.

121. William F. Buckley Jr. to Henry Kissinger, March? 1970. WFBP I-274:2399.

122. Josiah Lee Auspitz to George L. Hinman, February 5, 1971. RSP 13.

123. It didn't help Goodell's standing with Rockefeller that he had tied himself so closely to John Lindsay. His endorsement of Lindsay after the mayor lost the 1969 Republican primary angered the New York Republican organization. Lindsay's endorsement of Goldberg in the 1970 gubernatorial race caused further friction between the rival Lindsay and Rockefeller camps.

124. "Charles Goodell, Outcast and Underdog, Fights Agnew and the Conservatives," *RF* 6:11 (November 1970), pp. 10–14.

125. Kramer and Roberts, p. 346.

126. Joseph E. Persico, *The Imperial Rockefeller: A Biography of Nelson A. Rockefeller* (Thorndike, ME: Thorndike Press, 1982), pp. 134–135; interview with Daniel E. Button, June 15, 2005.

127. Kingman Brewster Jr., address to the American Jewish Committee Human Relations Dinner, November 10, 1970. Kingman Brewster Jr. Personal Papers (Yale University) I-25:1.

128. Richard M. Nixon conversation, October 14, 1972. Nixon Tapes (National Archives II) 798–15.

129. Francis W. Hatch to Edward W. Brooke, March 31, 1970. Edward W. Brooke Papers (Library of Congress) 182: "Hatch, Francis W."

130. Josiah Lee Auspitz to John V. Lindsay, June 2, 1970. Steven Livengood Papers (SLP) (Cornell University) 2: "Auspitz—Chron file."

131. Richard M. Nixon conversation, October 14, 1972. Nixon Tapes (National Archives II) 798–15.

132. Dale Van Atta, *With Honor: Melvin Laird in War, Peace, and Politics* (Madison, WI: University of Wisconsin Press, 2008), pp. 114–115.

133. Julius Duscha, "Ripon Unit Young Turks 'Infiltrating' White House," *Duluth News Tribune* July 5, 1970. SLP 3: "Press Clippings (July-Sep. 1970)."

134. Interview with Josiah Lee Auspitz, October 21, 2006.

135. Josiah Lee Auspitz, "For a Moderate Majority," *Playboy* April 1970, p. 94.

136. This was a broader constituency than the young, upwardly-mobile professionals who have typically been seen as the Ripon audience, although E. J. Dionne has a point when he argues that "Ripon could lay legitimate claim to having discovered the yuppies before anyone knew they existed." E. J. Dionne Jr., *Why Americans Hate Politics* (New York: Simon & Schuster, 1991), p. 189.

137. Auspitz, "For a Moderate Majority," p. 186.

138. See for example Peter Drucker to Josiah Lee Auspitz, January 5, 1970; Josiah Lee Auspitz to Peter Drucker, January 14, 1970. RSP 13.

139. Auspitz, "For a Moderate Majority," p. 187.

140. *Ibid.,* pp. 188–189.

141. *Ibid.,* p. 186.

142. *Ibid.,* p. 190.

143. Charles R. Morris, *The Cost of Good Intentions: New York City and the Liberal Experiment, 1960–1975* (New York: W. W. Norton, 1980), p. 147.

144. Josiah Lee Auspitz to Robert Dehlendorf II, March 24, 1970. RSP 13.

145. Robert Behn to Thomas Kuchel, June 10, 1971. RSP 13.

146. "A Call for Republican Disaster," *Republican Battle Line* March 1970, p. 1.

147. Mitch McConnell to Josiah Lee Auspitz, March 21, 1970. RSP 13.

148. For much, much more on this subject see Geoffrey Kabaservice, *The Guardians: Kingman Brewster, His Circle, and the Rise of the Liberal Establishment* (New York: Henry Holt, 2004).

149. Richard M. Nixon conversation, October 17, 1972. Nixon Tapes (National Archives II) 801–24.

150. Richard M. Nixon conversation, October 14, 1972. Nixon Tapes (National Archives II) 798–15.

151. Richard M. Nixon conversation, October 17, 1972. Nixon Tapes (National Archives II) 801–4.

152. Richard M. Nixon conversation, October 17, 1972. Nixon Tapes (National Archives II) 801–24.

153. Richard M. Nixon conversation, October 14, 1972. Nixon Tapes (National Archives II) 798–15.

154. James Mann, *Rise of the Vulcans: The History of Bush's War Cabinet* (New York: Penguin, 2004), p. 8.

155. William H. Chafe, *Never Stop Running: Allard Lowenstein and the Struggle to Save American Liberalism* (New York: Basic Books, 1993), pp. 350–351.

156. Robert D. Novak, *The Prince of Darkness: 50 Years of Reporting in Washington* (New York: Three Rivers Press, 2007), p. 204.

157. "The State Legislatures: A Democratic Lever," *RF* 6:12 (December 1970), p. 11.

158. "The Nation: A Campaign Retrospective," *RF* 6:12 (December 1970), p. 4.

159. Linwood Holton, *Opportunity Time: A Memoir* (Charlottesville, VA: University of Virginia Press, 2008), pp. 169–171.

160. Michael S. Lottman, "The South: Southern Strategy Flops," *RF* 6:12 (December 1970), p. 24.

161. Josiah Lee Auspitz to Richard Curry, November 20, 1970. RSP 13.

162. "Charles Goodell, Outcast and Underdog, Fights Agnew and the Conservatives," *RF* 6:11 (November 1970), p. 10.

163. "Agnew Equals Nixon," *RF* 6:11 (November 1958), p. 4.

164. Richard L. Madden, "House Candidate Runs with No Foe," *NYT* June 24, 1974.

165. Andrew Alexander, "His Allies Were the Voters," *Dayton Journal Herald* July 6, 1977.

166. Charles W. Whalen Jr. to Michael B. Mills, October 25, 1975. CWWP G53: "General, State of Ohio; Political Philosophy, CWW."

CHAPTER 11

1. David Frum, *How We Got Here—The 70's: The Decade That Brought You Modern Life (For Better or Worse)* (New York: Basic Books, 2000).

2. Laura Kalman, *Right Star Rising: A New Politics, 1974–1980* (New York: W. W. Norton, 2010); Bruce J. Schulman and Julian E. Zelizer (eds.), *Rightward Bound: Making America Conservative in the 1970s* (Cambridge, MA: Harvard University Press, 2008).

3. Richard Reeves, *President Nixon: Alone in the White House* (New York: Simon & Schuster, 2001), p. 279.

4. Richard M. Nixon, "Remarks at the Dedication of the Dwight D. Eisenhower National Republican Center," January 15, 1971. Available at www.presidency.ucsb.edu.

5. Joe Abate to Wallace Bennett et al., January 28, 1971. College Republican National Committee Papers (Hoover Institution) 24: "Chairman 1971."

6. A useful discussion of the historical debate over the liberal aspects of Nixon's presidency appears in Chapter 8 of David Greenberg, *Nixon's Shadow: The History of an Image* (New York: W. W. Norton, 2003).

7. Elizabeth Drew, "Nostalgia for Nixon?," *WP* June 9, 2007, p. A17.

8. National Associated Businessmen Inc. news release, October 10, 1968. William A. Steiger Papers (Wisconsin Historical Society) 61:2; "Safety Disagreement," *Washington Evening Star* November 28, 1970.

9. William A. Steiger, "More Fiction Than Fact about OSHA," *CR* March 21, 1973.

10. Reeves, p. 437.

11. David S. Broder, "Lindsay Shifts to Democrats, Pledges '72 Role," *WP* August 12, 1971, p. A4.

12. Martin Tolchin, "City G.O.P. Group Bids Lindsay Stay," *NYT* August 11, 1971, p. 1.

13. Garry Wills, *Nixon Agonistes: The Crisis of the Self-Made Man* (orig. pub. 1969; Boston, MA: Mariner, 2002), pp. 200–201.

14. "House OKs $3.25 Billion Works Bill," *Reporter Dispatch* [White Plains, NY] August 14, 1965. Ogden R. Reid Papers (Yale University) 346:7.

15. Judith Michaelson, "The Man Who Beat Rocky," *New York Post* November 11, 1972.

16. Alan L. Otten, "Switch Hitter," *WSJ* October 26, 1972.

17. Linda Greenhouse, "Two Challengers Planning to Face Reid in Republican Primary," *NYT* February 27, 1972.

18. Paul N. McCloskey Jr. statement, March 22, 1972. Paul N. McCloskey Jr. Papers (PNMP) (Hoover Institution) 428: "Republican or Democrat."

19. Interview with Paul N. McCloskey Jr., December 7, 2005.

20. Patrick McNulty, "They Shrugged When Pete McCloskey Challenged the President," *West* May 23, 1971.

21. Donald Riegle with Trevor Arbrister, *O Congress* (Garden City, NY: Doubleday, 1972), pp. 38–40.

22. Paul N. McCloskey Jr. news release, February 13, 1971. William F. Buckley Jr. Papers (WFBP) (Yale University) I-165:1087.

23. John M. Ashbrook to "Dear Fellow Conservative," January? 1972. Robert T. Hartmann Papers (Ford Presidential Library) 37: "Ashbrook, John—Presidential Campaign (1972)."

24. M. Stanton Evans, "Submerging the Republican Majority: The First 1,000 Days of Richard Nixon." William A. Rusher Papers (WASP) (Library of Congress) 30:2.

25. William A. Rusher, *The Rise of the Right* (New York: William Morrow, 1984), p. 244.

26. "Progressives and the President," *RF* 8:18 (September 1972), p. 3.

27. "McGovern Lashes Out at 'Establishment Center,'" *WP* April 21, 1972.

28. Interview with Howard Gillette Jr., November 2, 2006.

29. Steven D. Berkshire to Editor, *RF* 8:19 (October 1972), p. 18.

30. Ken Kaiserman to George Gilder, September 19, 1972. Ripon Society Papers (RSP) (Cornell University) 24:13.

31. "The Daycare Veto," *RF* 8:1 (January 1972), pp. 3–4.

32. Interview with Howard Gillette Jr., November 2, 2006.

33. "Daycare Edit Stirs Dispute," *RF* 8:2 (January 15, 1972), p. 4.

34. George F. Gilder, "Nixon's Breakthrough in Social Policy," *RF* 8:3 (February 1972), p. 12.

35. Larissa MacFarquhar, "The Gilder Effect," *New Yorker* May 29, 2000.

36. Howard Gillette Jr. to Ripon Society Steering Committee, August 2, 1972. Steven Livengood Papers (SLP) (Cornell University) 5: "*Forum* articles (1971–73)"; Mark C. Frazier, "Former Ripon Editor Asserts Feminism Jeopardizes Society," *Harvard Crimson* April 2, 1973.

37. Susan Faludi, *Backlash: The Undeclared War Against American Women* (New York: Crown, 1991), p. 285.
38. Tanya M. Melich, *The Republican War Against Women: An Insider's Report from Behind the Lines* (New York: Bantam, 1996), p. 32.
39. Interview with Josiah Lee Auspitz, October 21, 2006.
40. Interview with Robert M. Pennoyer, March 12, 2007. There was precedent for an investigation of delegate selection procedures in *Georgia v. National Democratic Party* (1971) and *Bode v. National Democratic Party* (1972).
41. Howard F. Gillette Jr. to Hugh Scott, October 23, 1971. RSP 24:12.
42. Ripon Society, "Delegates Discrimination and the Constitution," 1971. Tanya Melich Papers (SUNY Albany) V-7:6. While the "incentive program" dated back to 1924, the six-delegate bonus scheme apparently was created in 1952. Jim Mann, "GOP Division of Delegates Held Invalid," *WP* April 29, 1972. Moderates also complained that the seemingly democratic practice of having the Republican National Committee be made up of a committeeman and committeewoman from each state also gave disproportionate weight to the small states.
43. Melich, pp. 23–24.
44. "Ripon Wins Suit on Delegate Formula," *RF* 8:9 (May 1972), p. 3.
45. Robert J. Huckshorn and John F. Bibby, "National Party Rules and Delegate Selection in the Republican Party," *American Political Science Association* 16:4 (Autumn 1983), p. 658.
46. Alan L. Otten, "Opening Up the GOP," *WSJ* March 1, 1973.
47. Robert Walters, "Ripon Moves to Activism to Revitalize GOP," *Washington Star* December 3, 1973.
48. "Party Life in Washington, D.C.," *RF* 9:4 (February 15, 1973), p. 1.
49. Interview with Steven Livengood, March 1, 2009.
50. Daniel J. Swillinger to Ripon Reunioners, April 3, 1980. SLP 13: "Reunion (1980)."
51. "Politics: Reports," *RF* 8:22 (November 1972), p. 13.
52. Robert D. Behn, "Needed: A Successor for the Southern Strategy," *RF* 8:22 (November 1972), p. 6.
53. Rowland Evans and Robert Novak, "GOP Chief Sought to Sway Defector," *Hartford Courant* March 2, 1973, p. 16.
54. Robert Pisor, "Mich. GOP Loses Its Golden Boy," *WP* February 28, 1973, p. A8.
55. David S. Broder, "Realignment of Politicians and Parties," *WP* March 6, 1973, p. A20.
56. "Choosing Up Sides," *NYT* March 13, 1973.
57. George Gilder, "Connally's Phase III," *RF* 8:13 (July 1972), pp. 6–8.
58. Michael MacLeod to Ripon Society National Governing Board, April 25, 1973. SLP 5: "April 1973."
59. "Editorial," *RF* 9:11 (June 1973), p. 4.
60. Lloyd Shearer, "A Senate Star is Born," *Parade* July 29, 1973; J. Lee Annis Jr., *Howard Baker: Conciliator in an Age of Crisis* (Lanham, MD: Madison, 1995), p. 72.
61. Lee W. Huebner, "A Word on Ripon Past and Future," *RF* 8:23 (December 1972), p. 4.
62. "Are There Any Issues?," *NYT* January 31, 1972.
63. Rusher, pp. 248–249.
64. Interview with Paul N. McCloskey Jr., December 7, 2005.
65. Christopher Lydon, "G.O.P. Still Faces the Realities of Decay and Minority Status," *NYT* September 1, 1974.
66. Rowland Evans and Robert Novak, " . . . With a Weakened Republican Right," *WP* November 13, 1974. For background on the House Steering Committee, see Allan J. Lichtman, *White Protestant Nation: The Rise of the American Conservative Movement* (New York: Atlantic Monthly Press, 2008), p. 310.

67. The Ripon Society's tallies of House Republicans scoring between 76 and 100 (on Ripon's 0-to-100-point scale, with 100 representing the Society's beau ideal) in 1974, and who returned to Congress in 1975, dropped only slightly from 35 to 34 (with the defeat of John Dellenback of Oregon), while the number of those Republicans scoring between 51 and 75 fell from 60 to 46, and those scoring between 0 and 50 fell from 88 to 61. Calculations based on Ripon Society ratings for the 1974 and 1975 Congresses in *RF* 11:5 (March 15, 1975) and 12:19 (October 1, 1976). These figures differ considerably from those of most historians and political scientists, who have been influenced by the estimates of ideological group distributions in Congress produced by the *Congressional Quarterly*. A. James Reichley, basing his totals on the CQ ratings, judged that the number of Republican moderates and progressives in the House decreased from 48 in the 93rd Congress (1973–74) to 26 in the 94th Congress (1975–76), along with a drop in the number of stalwarts from 75 to 48, but that the number of fundamentalist conservatives increased from 64 to 71. This conclusion is at odds with the estimates of most contemporary political observers. The CQ figures also indicate that the increase in House Democratic strength over the same period was almost entirely due to a jump in the numbers of Democratic "regulars" rather than "liberals," which contradicts nearly every contemporary account of the "Watergate babies" and their impact on the Democratic establishment. Congressional rating systems are notoriously inexact, but Ripon's ratings seem to better reflect the perceptions of 1974–75 than CQ's. See A. James Reichley, *Conservatives in an Age of Change: The Nixon and Ford Administrations* (Washington, DC: Brookings Institution, 1978), p. 319.
68. Interview with Thomas Railsback, April 16, 2009.
69. David S. Broder, "Parties Shifting from Old Alignments," *WP* October 27, 1974.
70. Interview with William E. Frenzel, January 29, 2009.
71. Patricia A. Goldman to Charles W. Whalen Jr., July 22, 1974. Charles W. Whalen Jr. Papers (University of Dayton) G42: "Wednesday Group."
72. Michael MacLeod to Ripon Society National Executive Committee, February 26, 1976. SLP 2: "NLF—Founding Historical File."
73. Robert V. Remini, *House: The History of the House of Representatives* (Washington, DC: Smithsonian Books, 2007), p. 443.
74. James S. Fleming, *Window on Congress: A Congressional Biography of Barber B. Conable* (Rochester, NY: University of Rochester Press, 2004), p. 213.
75. Interview with Thomas Railsback, April 16, 2009.
76. Nixon Staff oral history interview with William B. Saxbe, September 27, 2002. Nixon Presidential Materials (National Archives II) Staff—Oral Histories/Oral History Interviews 2.
77. Quoted in Chris R. Brewster to John C. Danforth, July 13, 1977. John C. Danforth Papers (University of Missouri) 7:10.
78. Philip Buchen interview in Kenneth W. Thompson (ed.), *The Ford Presidency: 22 Intimate Perspectives of Gerald R. Ford* (Lanham, MD: University Press of America, 1988), p. 28.
79. Donald Rumsfeld interview with A. James Reichley, January 25, 1978. Reichley interview transcripts (Ford Presidential Library) 1: "Rumsfeld, Donald." See also Donald Rumsfeld, *Known and Unknown: A Memoir* (New York: Sentinel, 2011), pp. 185–187.
80. Clare Boothe Luce to O. C. Carmichael Jr., May 15, 1975. WASP 53:8.
81. William A. Rusher, *The Making of the New Majority Party* (New York: Sheed & Ward, 1975).
82. Interview with Steven Livengood, March 29, 2009.
83. Ronald Reagan address to American Conservative Union and Young Americans for Freedom, February 15, 1975. WFBP I-101:359.
84. Sean Wilentz, *The Age of Reagan: A History, 1974–2008* (New York: Harper, 2008), p. 64.

85. Dick Behn, "The Presidential Pulpit," *RF* 12:4 (January 15, 1976), p. 4.
86. A. James Reichley interview with Charles McC. Mathias, September 22, 1977. Reichley interview transcripts (Ford Presidential Library) 2: "Mathias, Charles."
87. John Robert Greene, *The Presidency of Gerald R. Ford* (Lawrence, KS: University of Kansas Press, 1995), p. 165.
88. Nicol C. Rae, *The Decline and Fall of the Liberal Republicans From 1952 to the Present* (New York: Oxford University Press, 1989), p. 124.
89. Kevin P. Phillips, *Post-Conservative America: People, Politics, and Ideology in a Time of Crisis* (New York: Random House, 1982), p. 48.
90. William F. Buckley Jr. to William A. Rusher, March 4, 1976. WFBP I–167:1106.
91. Rusher, pp. 258–259.
92. James M. Naughton, "Some Republicans Fearful That Party Is On Its Last Legs," *NYT* May 31, 1976, p. 1.
93. James J. Kilpatrick, "The GOP: A Time for Licking Wounds," November 9, 1976. WFBP I-101:360.
94. "For Senator Moynihan," *New York Sunday News* October 31, 1976. WFBP I-101:360.
95. Richard G. Zimmerman, "How Your Congressmen Rate," *Cleveland Plain Dealer* March 23, 1975; Andrew Alexander, "Whalen Makes List of Top 10 House Members," *Dayton Journal Herald* September 27, 1976.
96. Richard L. Madden, "House Candidate Runs with No Foe," *NYT* June 24, 1974.
97. Riegle, p. 145.
98. Richard G. Thomas, "Trouble in the 'Gimpy Old Party,'" *Mansfield* [OH] *News Journal* November 23, 1975.
99. Pat Ordovensky, "Whalen Says Foes Hurt GOP," *Dayton Journal Herald* September 4 1975.
100. Interview with Charles W. Whalen Jr., January 30, 2009.
101. Interview with Slade Gorton, December 12, 2005.
102. Two recent books that make diametrically opposed claims about supply-side economics are Jonathan Chait, *The Big Con: The True Story of How Washington Got Hoodwinked and Hijacked by Crackpot Economics* (Boston, MA: Houghton Mifflin, 2007) and Brian Domitrovic, *Econoclasts: The Rebels Who Sparked the Supply-Side Revolution and Restored American Prosperity* (Wilmington, DE: ISI Books, 2009).
103. Arthur Laffer, "The Laffer Curve: Past, Present, and Future," June 1, 2004. Available at http://www.heritage.org/Research/Reports/2004/06/The-Laffer-Curve-Past-Present-and-Future.
104. Interview with Richard Rahn, May 3, 2010.
105. Richard W. Rahn, "The Jack Kemp I Knew," *Washington Times* May 4, 2009.
106. *Issues and Answers* transcript, ABC-TV September 17, 1978. John B. Anderson Papers (JBAP) (Illinois State Historical Library) 115: "Issues and Answers."
107. Alan Crawford, "A Mid-Life Crisis," *NR* September 14, 1979, p. 1155.
108. Jason DeParle, "How Jack Kemp Lost the War on Poverty," *NYTM* February 28, 1993.
109. Peter Schrag, *Paradise Lost: California's Experience, America's Future* (Berkeley, CA: University of California Press, 2004), pp. 151–155; Robert Kuttner, *Revolt of the Haves* (New York: Simon & Schuster, 1980).
110. Quoted in Charles R. Morris, *The Two Trillion Dollar Meltdown: Easy Money, High Rollers, and the Great Credit Crash* (New York: Public Affairs, 2009), p. 20
111. David S. Broder, "GOP Leaders Heartened by Unity at Issues Session," *WP* May 1, 1978, p. A9.
112. "William Albert Steiger," *WP* December 6, 1978, p. A22.
113. William R. Steiger, who served in the administration of George W. Bush.
114. George F. Will, "The Professional," *Newsweek* November 12, 1979, p. 136.

115. Don Kellerman to Howard H. Baker Jr., September? 1977. Howard H. Baker Jr. Papers (University of Tennessee) 14:6.

116. Thomas W. Ottenad, "GOP Moderates Wait on Reagan," *St. Louis Post Dispatch* November 20, 1979.

117. Interview with Steven Livengood, March 29, 2009.

118. George Gilder, "The Problematical Ripon Triumph," April 1, 1980. SLP 13: "Reunion (1980)."

119. Interview with George Gilder, May 27, 2011.

120. Ross Anderson, "Evolution of a Think Tank," April 29, 2008. Available at http://crosscut. com/2008/04/29/religion/13794/.

121. Interview with Bruce K. Chapman, December 8, 2009.

122. Bruce K. Chapman to Steven Livengood, September 10, 1980. SLP 5: "Misc. correspondence (1980)."

123. Peter J. Wallison, *Ronald Reagan: The Power of Conviction and the Success of His Presidency* (Boulder, CO: Westview, 2004), p. 88.

124. "Bagley Says Reagan a Liberal," *Independent Journal* [San Rafael, CA] August 21, 1975. Alphonzo Bell Papers (ABP) (University of Southern California) 148:35.

125. "Interview with Alphonzo Bell," *Independent Journal* [San Rafael, CA] April 3, 1975. ABP 148:35.

126. NBC-TV, "Meet the Press" December 10, 1978. JBAP 115: "Meet the Press, NBC."

127. John B. Anderson to Edward H. Sebesta, September 4, 1979. JBAP 147: "P. Chron. (September)."

128. Rae, p. 139.

129. John B. Anderson to J. Irwin Miller, July 6, 1979. JBAP 147: "P. Chron. (July)."

130. John B. Anderson statement, June 8, 1979. JBAP 115: "Announcement (June 8, 1979)."

131. "GOP Disgrace in Des Moines," *NR* January 25, 1980, pp. 79–80.

132. Edward F. Coyle, "A Message from the Executive Director," *Independent Action News* September 1981. SLP 13: "Ripon misc. (2) (1981)."

133. NBC-TV, *Meet the Press* December 10, 1978. JBAP 115: "Meet the Press, NBC."

134. Ripon Society news release, April 21, 1980. SLP 13: "Reunion Papers (1980)."

135. Melich, pp. 132, 144–145.

136. Interview with John McClaughry, November 29, 2009.

137. Howard Gillette Jr. to Michael MacLeod, August 1, 1980. RSP 26:10.

138. Interview with Howard Gillette, November 2, 2006.

139. Donald Hodel interview, *World* October 10, 1987. WARP 40:5.

140. Melich, p. 131.

CHAPTER 12

1. Ronald W. Reagan, Inaugural Address, January 20, 1981. Available at http://www. presidency.ucsb.edu.

2. Nicol C. Rae, *The Decline and Fall of the Liberal Republicans From 1952 to the Present* (New York: Oxford University Press, 1989), p. 188.

3. David S. Broder, "'Gypsy Moths' Come Out of Their Cocoons," *WP* September 27, 1981.

4. Jim Leach, "A Moderate Manifesto," September 21, 1981. Paul N. McCloskey Papers (Hoover Institution) 188: "Republican Leadership."

5. Thomas B. Edsall, "'Gypsy Moths' Split Over Voters' Message," *WP* November 21, 1982, p. A4.

6. Interview with Willis D. Gradison Jr., April 7, 2009.

7. James T. Patterson, *Restless Giant: The United States from Watergate to Bush v. Gore* (New York: Oxford University Press, 2005), p. 200.

8. "The Power Brokers," *Toronto Globe and Mail* June 6, 1987.

9. Martin Tolchin, "House, After Stiff Debate, Backs Cheap Power for 3 Western States," *NYT* May 4, 1984, p. A1.
10. Interview with William E. Frenzel, January 29, 2009.
11. Lou Cannon, *President Reagan: The Role of a Lifetime* (New York: Simon & Schuster, 1991), p. 252.
12. Interview with Willis D. Gradison Jr., April 7, 2009.
13. *CQ Almanac 1984*, pp. 38–39C.
14. Rae, pp. 182–183.
15. "Republicans Establish Panel of Moderates," *NYT* June 21, 1984, p. B10.
16. Jules Witcover, *Party of the People: A History of the Democrats* (New York: Random House, 2003), p. 643.
17. Interview with William E. Frenzel, January 29, 2009.
18. Thomas Edsall, "Onward, GOP Christians, Marching to '88," *WP* January 20, 1985, p. C1.
19. Interview with William E. Frenzel, January 29, 2009. An important Republican critique of the role of the religious right in politics is John Danforth, *Faith and Politics: How the "Moral Values" Debate Divides America and How to Move Forward Together* (rev. ed.) (New York: Penguin, 2006).
20. New Leadership Fund candidate profile of John Yarmuth, October 1981. SLP 2: "John Yarmuth."
21. Interview with John Yarmuth, June 5, 2009.
22. Sidney Blumenthal, "For the GOP's Moderates, A Time of Hope," *WP* October 12, 1988, p. D1.
23. Paul N. McCloskey Jr., *The Taking of Hill 610* (Woodside, CA: Eaglet, 1992), pp. 106–116. See also Robert Boston, *The Most Dangerous Man in America: Pat Robertson and the Rise of the Christian Coalition* (Amherst, NY: Prometheus, 1996), pp. 40–42.
24. Interview with Paul N. McCloskey Jr., April 19, 2007.
25. Bill McKenzie, "A Conversation with Newt Gingrich," *RF* May 1989, p. 3.
26. Dan Balz and Ronald Brownstein, *Storming the Gates: Protest Politics and the Republican Revival* (Boston: Little, Brown, 1996), p. 133.
27. Mel Steely, *The Gentleman from Georgia: The Biography of Newt Gingrich* (Macon, GA: Mercer University Press, 2000), p. 204.
28. McKenzie, p. 3.
29. Marjorie Williams, *The Woman at the Washington Zoo* (New York: PublicAffairs, 2005), p. 31.
30. Richard Darman, *Who's In Charge?: Polar Politics and the Stable Center* (New York: Simon & Schuster, 1996), p. 272.
31. Bruce Bartlett, "A Budget Deal That Did Reduce the Deficit," *Fiscal Times* June 25, 2010. Available at http://www.thefiscaltimes.com/Issues/Budget-Impact/2010/06/25/A-Budget-Deal-That-Did-Reduce-the-Deficit.aspx.
32. Judy Gallagher quoted in NPR "Morning Edition," August 19, 1992.
33. Ralph Z. Hallow, "Conservatives Rule GOP Roost in House," *Washington Times* December 9, 1992, p. A4.
34. Interview with Willis D. Gradison Jr., April 7, 2009.
35. Linda Killian, *The Freshmen: What Happened to the Republican Revolution?* (Boulder, CO: Westview, 1998), p. 6.
36. Steven M. Gillon, *The Pact: Bill Clinton, Newt Gingrich, and the Rivalry That Defined a Generation* (New York: Oxford University Press, 2008), p. 129.
37. Interview with Amory Houghton Jr., March 21, 2009.
38. Thomas B. Edsall, *Building Red America: The New Conservative Coalition and the Drive for Permanent Power* (New York: Basic, 2006), pp. 132–137.

39. Michael Shanahan and Miles Benson, "Moderates Can't Stand Heat, Leave Kitchen," *Cleveland Plain Dealer* December 14, 1995, p. 22A.

40. Colin Powell to Amory Houghton Jr., April 20, 1996. Amory Houghton Jr. Papers (AHP) (Houghton family) 28: "VIP Notes and Letters." Source courtesy of Amory Houghton Jr.

41. Gillon, p. 213.

42. Interview with Amory Houghton Jr., March 20, 2009.

43. "Impeachment: The Mavericks," *NYT* December 20, 1998.

44. Sean Wilentz, *The Age of Reagan: A History 1974–2008* (New York: HarperCollins, 2008), p. 398.

45. Sidney Blumenthal, *The Clinton Wars* (New York: Farrar, Straus and Giroux, 2003), pp. 494–495.

46. Amory Houghton Jr. to George Parker, November 25, 1991. AHP 7: "Correspondence (A-Z) (1991)."

47. Wendy Koch, "'People Were Crying' at Second Retreat for Lawmakers," *USA Today* March 12, 1999, p. 11A.

48. Amo Houghton Jr., "Let Us Praise Reasonable Middle America," *CSM* October 6, 1992, p. 19.

49. Frank Rich, "Power of the Purse," *NYT* March 2, 1997, p. 4:15.

50. Ed Magnuson, Evan Thomas, and Joseph J. Kane, "The Brethren's First Sister: Sandra Day O'Connor," *Time* July 20, 1981.

51. James Moore and Wayne Slater, *Bush's Brain: How Karl Rove Made George W. Bush Presidential* (New York: Wiley, 2006), pp. 129–135.

52. Wilentz, p. 414.

53. Steven M. Teles, "The Eternal Return of Compassionate Conservatism," *National Affairs* September 2009. Available at http://www.nationalaffairs.com/publications/detail/the-eternal-return-of-compassionate-conservatism.

54. Lincoln Chafee, *Against the Tide: How a Compliant Congress Empowered a Reckless President* (New York: Thomas Dunne, 2008), pp. 6–10.

55. Barton Gellman, *Angler: The Cheney Vice Presidency* (New York: Penguin, 2008), p. 85.

56. Ron Suskind, *The Price of Loyalty: George W. Bush, the White House, and the Education of Paul O'Neill* (New York: Simon & Schuster, 2004), p. 291.

57. Jacob S. Hacker and Paul Pierson, *Off Center: The Republican Revolution & the Erosion of American Democracy* (New Haven, CT: Yale University Press, 2005), p. 4.

58. John Lancaster and Helen Dewar, "GOP Makes Pitch To Keep Jeffords; Republicans Offer Senator a Leadership Post," *WP* May 24, 2001, p. A1; Gellman, pp. 77–80.

59. "2 Wars, 2 Votes in Congress, Only 10 Who Got Both Right," *USA Today* October 30, 2006, p. 12A.

60. Rajiv Chandrasekaran, *Imperial Life in the Emerald City: Inside Iraq's Green Zone* (New York: Vintage, 2006), pp. 103–106.

61. William T. Bagley, *California's Golden Years: When Government Worked and Why* (Berkeley, CA: Berkeley Public Policy Press, 2009), p. 79.

62. Hacker and Pierson, pp. 53–54.

63. Stephanie Grace, "The Messenger," *Brown Alumni Monthly* March/April 2007.

64. Easha Anand, "House Republicans Bid Farewell to New England," *NYT* November 5, 2008.

65. Perry Bacon Jr., "Bush Tells His Party to Be 'Open-Minded,'" *WP* January 12, 2009, p. A4.

66. The "T" stood for tax. Wesley McCune (Group Research Inc.), "Activity of the American Right Wing, January 1962 to March 1963" [nd–1963]. William F. Buckley Jr. Papers (Yale University) I-29: "Grindle–Group Research, Inc. (1963)."

67. Kate Zernicke, "In Power Push, Movement Sees Base in G.O.P.," *NYT* January 15, 2010.

68. "Ideology and the Party Split: Myth and Reality," *Advance* 1:5 (March 1962), p. 25.

69. Amy Gardner, "Utah Conservatives Sing Chorus of 'Bye Bye Bennett' with Glee," *WP* April 30, 2010.

70. Sean Wilentz, "Confounding Fathers: The Tea Party's Cold War Roots," *New Yorker* October 18, 2010.

71. David Barstow, "Tea Party Movement Lights Fuse for Rebellion on Right," *NYT* February 16, 2010.

CONCLUSION

1. Karl Marx, *The Eighteenth Brumaire of Louis Napoleon* (orig. pub. 1852).

2. David S. Broder, "Delaware's Battle," *WP* October 18, 2009.

3. Michael Gerson, "Cap and Traitors," *WP* July 1, 2009.

4. E. J. Dionne Jr., "Mike Castle's Defeat—and the End of Moderate Republicanism," *WP* September 16, 2010.

5. Video of the June 30, 2009 town hall event is widely available on youtube.com. See also Ed Brayton, "Mike Castle Plays Poker with Crazy People," July 23, 2009, available at http://scienceblogs.com/dispatches/2009/07/mike_castle_plays_poker_with_c.php.

6. As of March 2011, the Treasury Department had recovered $244 billion of the $245 billion it had invested in the banks under TARP. Robert Samuelson, "Why TARP Has Been a Success Story," *WP* March 27, 2011.

7. Michael D. Shear, "O'Donnell Says Rove Is Eating 'Humble Pie,'" *NYT* September 15, 2010.

8. Or, as the philosopher Friedrich Nietzsche observed, "Moderation sees itself as beautiful; it is unaware that in the eye of the immoderate it appears black and sober, and consequently ugly-looking." Friedrich Nietzsche, *Daybreak: Thoughts on the Prejudices of Morality* (tr. R. J. Hollingdale) (New York: Cambridge University Press, 1997), p. 167.

9. Charles P. Pierce, "Can We Calm Down About Delaware's Tea Party Already?," September 15, 2010. http://www.esquire.com/blogs/politics/christine-o-donnell-delaware-091510#ixzz0zoIoOoWG.

10. Amy Gardner and Sandhya Somashekhar, "In Delaware, Frustration with Republican Party Led to Christine O'Donnell's Win," *WP* September 15, 2010.

11. Michael D. Shear, "The Morning After: Whose Party Is It?," *NYT* September 15, 2010.

12. The Republican contribution to Wisconsin's collective bargaining agreements with public and private unions was invoked in William Cronon, "Wisconsin's Radical Break," *NYT* March 21, 2011.

13. This was about half of the 21 percent that identified as conservative Republicans; one percent of voters still characterized themselves as liberal Republicans.

14. The same 2008 exit poll revealed that there were more moderate Democrats (18 percent) than liberal Democrats (15 percent), with another 5 percent of the electorate describing themselves as conservative Democrats. Washington Post/ABC 2008 exit poll data supplied courtesy of Jonathan Cohen and the *Washington Post,* January 9, 2009.

15. Dionne, "Mike Castle's Defeat."

16. Interview with Howard Gillette Jr., November 2, 2006.

17. Emil Frankel to Geoffrey Kabaservice, June 30, 2007.

18. Interview with Emil H. Frankel, June 23, 2007.

19. Interview with Thomas E. Petri, November 22, 2010.

20. Julius Duscha, "Ripon Unit Young Turks 'Infiltrating' White House," *Duluth News Tribune* July 5, 1970. Steven Livengood Papers (Cornell University) 3: "Press Clippings (July-September 1970)."

21. John J. Miller, "The Man Who Saved AEI," *NR* January 26, 2009.

22. Timothy Noah, "Chris DeMuth, Hack Extraordinaire," *Slate* October 11, 2007.

23. Rowland Evans and Robert Novak, "Reagan's Break for the Family," *WP* April 18, 1984.

24. Ross Anderson, "Evolution of a Think Tank," April 29, 2008. Available at http://crosscut.com/2008/04/29/religion/13794/.

25. Bruce K. Chapman, "Policy and Political Objectives in 1985" [nd—1984?]. Bruce K. Chapman Papers (Reagan Presidential Library) OA 11689: "Tax Reform."

26. Interview with William Gates Sr., December 16, 2005.

27. Interview with Christopher J. DeMuth, March 3, 2009.

28. Interview with Bruce K. Chapman, December 8, 2009.

29. Interview with Christopher Bayley, July 2, 2007.

30. Roger Downey, "Discovery's Creation," *Seattle Weekly* February 1, 2006.

31. Transcript of *The Rush Limbaugh Show*, July 21, 2009.

32. John Maynard Keynes, address to the Manchester Reform Club, February 1926, in *Essays in Persuasion* (London: Macmillan, 1931), p. 343.

33. Ross Douthat and Reihan Salam, *Grand New Party: How Republicans Can Win the Working Class and Save the American Dream* (New York: Anchor, 2009); David Frum, *Comeback: Conservatism That Can Win Again* (New York: Broadway, 2009); Andrew Sullivan, *The Conservative Soul: How We Lost It, How to Get It Back* (New York: HarperCollins, 2006); Sam Tanenhaus, *The Death of Conservatism* (New York: Random House, 2009).

34. Democratic strategists also argue that the GOP is also handicapped by a lack of geographic and demographic diversity. See John B. Judis and Roy Teixeira, *The Emerging Democratic Majority* (New York: Lisa Drew, 2002).

35. Thomas Friedman, "Third Party Rising," *NYT* October 2, 2010.

36. Thomas B. Edsall, *Building Red America: The New Conservative Coalition and the Drive for Permanent Power* (New York: Basic Books, 2006); Morris P. Fiorina, *Culture War?: The Myth of a Polarized America* (2nd ed.) (New York: Pearson Longman, 2006); Morris P. Fiorina and Matthew Levendusky, "Disconnected: The Political Class versus the People," in Pietro S. Nivola and David W. Brady (eds.), *Red and Blue Nation?* (vol. 1) (Palo Alto, CA and Washington, DC: Hoover and Brookings, 2006); Jacob S. Hacker and Paul Pierson, *Off Center: The Republican Revolution and the Erosion of American Democracy* (New Haven, CT: Yale University Press, 2005); Thomas E. Mann and Norman J. Ornstein, *The Broken Branch: How Congress is Failing America and How to Get It Back on Track* (New York: Oxford University Press, 2006); Theda Skocpol and Morris P. Fiorina (eds.), *Civic Engagement in American Democracy* (Washington, DC: Brookings, 1999); Alan Wolfe, *One Nation After All* (New York: Viking, 1998).

37. Quoted in Gil Troy, *Leading from the Center: Why Moderates Make the Best Presidents* (New York: Basic, 2008), p. 31.

SELECT BIBLIOGRAPHY

MANUSCRIPT COLLECTIONS

Gottlieb Archival Research Center, Boston University, Boston, Massachusetts
    F. Bradford Morse Papers
Chicago Historical Society Library, Chicago, Illinois
    Charles T. Percy Papers
Carl A. Kroch Library, Cornell University, Ithaca, New York
    Barber B. Conable Papers
    Barry Goldwater Post-Presidential Papers
    Steven Livengood Papers
    Ripon Society Papers
    F. Clifton White Papers
Dwight David Eisenhower Presidential Library, Abilene, Kansas
    Dwight D. Eisenhower Post-Presidential Papers
Ford Foundation Archives, New York, New York
    Ford Foundation Records
    Ford Foundation Office of the President: Records of McGeorge Bundy
Gerald R. Ford Presidential Library, Ann Arbor, Michigan
    Gwen A. Anderson Papers
    James M. Cannon Papers
    Richard Cheney Papers
    Gerald R. Ford Congressional Records
    Gerald R. Ford Special Files
    Gerald R. Ford Vice Presidential Papers
    David Gergen Papers
    Robert A. Goldwin Papers
    Robert T. Hartmann Papers
    Bobbie Greene Kilberg Papers
    Melvin R. Laird Papers
    Patricia Lindh and Jeanne Holm Papers
    Charles McCall Papers
    Michael Raoul-Duval Papers
    Robert P. Visser Papers
Harvard Law School Library, Harvard University, Cambridge, Massachusetts
    W. Barton Leach Papers
Hoover Institution on War, Revolution, and Peace, Stanford, California
    College Republican National Committee Papers
    Patrick Dowd Papers
    Firing Line Collection

Denison Kitchel Papers
Paul N. McCloskey Papers
Raymond Moley Papers
Henry Regnery Papers
Herbert Hoover Presidential Library, West Branch, Iowa
    Walter N. Thayer Papers
Idaho State Historical Library, Boise, Idaho
    Hope C. Kading Papers
Illinois State Historical Library, Springfield, Illinois
    John B. Anderson Papers
    James D. Nowlan Papers
University of Iowa Libraries, Iowa City, Iowa
    Frederick Schwengel Papers
Milton S. Eisenhower Library, Johns Hopkins University, Baltimore, Maryland
    Charles McC. Mathias Papers
Manuscripts Division, Library of Congress, Washington, D.C.
    Edward W. Brooke Papers
    Russell Wheeler Davenport Papers
    August Heckscher II Papers
    Republican National Committee Papers
    Elliott Lee Richardson Papers
    William A. Rusher Papers
    Charles P. Taft II Papers
    Robert A. Taft Papers
    Robert A. Taft Jr. Papers
New York Public Library, New York, New York
    Charles E. Goodell Papers
National Archives and Records Administration (Archives II), College Park, Maryland
    Roy Ash Papers–President's Advisory Committee on Executive Reorganization
    Patrick J. Buchanan Papers
    Charles W. Colson Papers
    Council for Urban Affairs Files
    Robert H. Finch Papers
    Nixon Presidential Materials
    Nixon Presidential Tapes Collection
    White House Central Files
Richard M. Nixon Presidential Library, Yorba Linda, California
    Robert H. Finch Collection
    H.R. Haldeman Collection
    Bryce Harlow Papers
    White House Special Files
Ohio Historical Society, Columbus Ohio
    Ray C. Bliss Papers
    Clarence J. Brown Papers
    James Rhodes Papers
    William B. Saxbe Papers
Pennsylvania State Historical Library, Harrisonburg, Pennsylvania
    William W. Scranton Papers
    A. James Reichley Campaign Files
Seeley G. Mudd Manuscript Library, Princeton University, Princeton, New Jersey
    James A. Baker III Papers

Ronald Reagan Presidential Library, Simi Valley, California
   Lee Atwater Files
   Howard Baker Files
   Bruce K. Chapman Papers
   Ronald Reagan Gubernatorial Papers
Rockefeller Archives, Sleepy Hollow, New York
   George L. Hinman Papers
   Nelson A. Rockefeller Papers
Hugh and Jane Ferguson Seattle Room, Seattle Public Library, Seattle, Washington
   The Seattle Collection
Green Library, Stanford University, Palo Alto, California
   John W. Gardner Papers
Department of Special Collections and Archives, SUNY Albany, Albany New York
   Tanya M. Melich Papers
Melville Library, SUNY Stony Brook, Stony Brook, New York
   Jacob Javits Papers
Bancroft Library, University of California, Berkeley, California
   Thomas H. Kuchel Papers
Charles E. Young Research Library, University of California, Los Angeles, California
   California Republican Assembly Papers
Roesch Library, University of Dayton, Dayton, Ohio
   Charles W. Whalen Jr. Papers
Margaret I. King Library, University of Kentucky, Lexington, Kentucky
   John Sherman Cooper Papers
   Rogers C.B. Morton Papers
   Thruston Ballard Morton Papers
Hornbake Library, University of Maryland, College Park, Maryland
   Spiro T. Agnew Papers
   Constance A. Morella Papers
Bentley Historical Library, University of Michigan, Ann Arbor, Michigan
   Elly M. Peterson Papers
   George W. Romney Papers
Western Historical Manuscript Collection, University of Missouri, Columbia, Missouri
   Thomas B. Curtis Papers
   John C. Danforth Papers
Taggart Library, University of Northern Ohio, Ada, Ohio
   William M. McCulloch Papers
Rush Rhees Library, University of Rochester, Rochester, New York
   Kenneth Keating Papers
Doheny Memorial Library, University of Southern California, Los Angeles, California
   Alphonzo Bell Papers
John C. Hodges Library, University of Tennessee, Knoxville, Tennessee
   Howard H. Baker Jr. Papers
Alderman Library, University of Virginia, Charlottesville, Virginia
   Hugh N. Scott Papers
Waldo Library, University of Western Michigan, Kalamazoo, Michigan
   Glen L. Bachelder Papers
James Branch Cabell Library, Virginia Commonwealth University, Richmond, Virginia
   Clarence L. Townes Jr. Papers
Wisconsin Historical Society, Madison, Wisconsin
   William A. Steiger Papers

Sterling Memorial Library, Yale University, New Haven, Connecticut
  Kingman Brewster Jr. Personal Papers
  Kingman Brewster Jr. Presidential Papers
  William F. Buckley Jr. Papers
  John Vliet Lindsay Papers
  Ogden R. Reid Papers

INTERVIEWS AND ORAL HISTORIES

Author's Interviews
Richard Aurelio: January 28, 2009
Josiah Lee Auspitz: October 21, 2006
Douglas L. Bailey: March 22, 2007
Christopher Bayley: July 2, 2007
Donald Bliss: April 3, 2009
Ronald Boster: April 7, 2009
Michael Brewer: May 7, 2010
William F. Buckley Jr.: March 25, 1991
McGeorge Bundy: April 29, 1991, May 22, 1991
Daniel E. Button: June 15, 2005
Joseph A. Califano Jr.: January 16, 2003
Bruce K. Chapman: December 18, 2009
Alan Cranston: August 4, 1999
Christopher J. DeMuth: March 3, 2009
James Ellis: February 27, 2001, October 29, 2004
Daniel J. Evans: December 12, 2005
Emil Frankel: June 23, 2007
William E. Frenzel: January 21, 2009, June 19, 2009
John W. Gardner: July 8, 1994
William Gates Sr.: December 15, 2005
George Gilder: May 27, 2011
Howard Gillette, Jr.: November 29, 2005, November 2, 2006
Andrew J. Glass: September 24, 2008
Slade Gorton: December 12, 2005
Willis D. Gradison Jr.: April 7, 2009
Stephen Hess: May 4, 2007
Amo Houghton Jr.: March 20, 2009
Lee Huebner: April 11, 2007, November 24, 2009
Steve Isenberg: February 27, 2009
Vernon Jordan: January 9, 2001
Nicholas DeB. Katzenbach: June 4, 2003
Bobbie Greene Kilberg: April 10, 2010
Joseph Lieberman: July 7, 1992
Martin Linsky: March 13, 2007
Steven Livengood: March 1, 2009, March 29, 2009
George Cabot Lodge: March 23, 2007
Charles McC. Mathias: June 24, 2005
John McClaughry: November 15, 2009, November 29, 2009
Paul N. McCloskey: December 7, 2005, April 19, 2007
Jean McKee: June 1, 2007
Tanya M. Melich: February 12, 2007
J. Irwin Miller: December 18, 1991, February 17, 2001

Jonathan Moore: December 2, 2002, November 6, 2006
Constance A. Morella: August 21, 2009
Charles R. Morris: February 26, 2009
Leonard Nadasdy: June 26, 2007
Robert Pennoyer: March 12, 2007
Thomas E. Petri: November 22, 2010
John R. Price Jr.: July 20, 2009
Raymond K. Price Jr.: February 25, 2009
Richard W. Rahn: May 3, 2010
Thomas Railsback: April 16, 2009
A. James Reichley: October 7, 2008
Arthur Schlesinger, Jr.: July 8, 2002
William W. Scranton: July 16, 1992
Michael C. Smith: February 11, 2007
Peter J. Wallison: July 2, 2002
Charles W. Whalen Jr.: January 30, 2009
John Yarmuth: June 5, 2009

Columbia University Oral History Archive, Oral History Research Office, Butler Library, Columbia University, New York
George Aiken: April 27, 1967
Thomas B. Curtis: October 23, 1972
Robert H. Finch: June 19, 1967
Stephen Hess: June 14, 1972
Kenneth Keating: February 2, 1968
Ogden R. Reid: June 14, 1967
Walter N. Thayer: April 28, 1967
Webster B. Todd: October 26, 1972

Robert L. Peabody Interview Transcripts, Gerald R. Ford Presidential Library, Ann Arbor, Michigan
John B. Anderson: January 11, 1965
Alphonzo Bell: January 11, 1965
John V. Lindsay: January 14, 1965
Charles McC. Mathias: January 12, 1965
Brad Morse: January 26, 1965
Donald Rumsfeld: December 30, 1964

A. James Reichley Interview Transcripts, Gerald R. Ford Presidential Library, Ann Arbor, Michigan
John B. Anderson: September 21, 1977
Pat Buchanan: September 13, 1977
William Coleman: December 19, 1977
John C. Danforth: January 7, 1981
Harry Dent: April 3, 1978
William Frenzel: October 14, 1977
Leonard Garment: October 19, 1977
David Gergen: February 21, 1978
Charles Goodell: August 30, 1977
Bryce Harlow: November 3, 1977
Stephen Hess: October 21, 1977
Lee W. Huebner: December 9, 1977
Charles McC. Mathias: September 22, 1977

John McClaughry: December 22, 1980
Daniel Patrick Moynihan: July 13, 1978
Leon Panetta: September 19, 1977
John R. Price: March 24, 1978
Ray Price: March 2, 1978
Thomas Railsback: September 15, 1977
Ronald Reagan: January 4, 1978
Elliot L. Richardson: January 9, 1978
Donald Rumsfeld: January 25, 1978
Richard Schweiker: January 17, 1978
Hugh Scott: December 6, 1978
William W. Scranton: June 30, 1978
William A. Steiger: November 22, 1977
Caspar Weinberger: January 4, 1978

Oral History Collection of Former Members of Congress, Manuscript Division, Library of Congress, Washington, D.C.
Hugh Scott: March 17, 1978

Nixon Presidential Materials Staff Oral Histories/Oral History Interviews, National Archives II, College Park, Maryland
Roy L. Ash: January 13, 1988
Charles W. Colson: June 15, 1988
Elliot L. Richardson: May 31, 1988
William B. Saxbe: September 27, 2002
John C. Whitaker: May 4, 1973, December 30, 1987

Reagan Gubernatorial Oral History Project, Bancroft Library, University of California, Berkeley, California
William Bagley: December 21, 1981
George Christopher: May 2, 1977, August 31, 1978
Dick Darling: June 23, 1981
Paul A. Haerle: March 26, 1982
Jaquelin Hume: January 26, 1982
Robert T. Monagan: June 22, 1981, July 13, 1981
Franklin C. Nofziger: October 10, 1978
Gaylord B. Parkinson: November 21, 1978
William E. Roberts: June 26, 1979
Albert S. Rodda: January 13, 1981
Stuart K. Spencer: February 23, 1979
Robert C. Walker: August 30, 1982, May 5, 1983
Russel S. Walton: May 10, 1983
Caspar Weinberger: December 13, 1978, December 20, 1978, March 6, 1979, March 29, 1979

Women in Politics Oral History Project, Bancroft Library, University of California, Berkeley, California
Patricia Reilly Hitt: May 18–19, July 27, 1977

John Sherman Cooper Oral History Project, Louis B. Nunn Center for Oral History, University of Kentucky, Lexington, Kentucky
John Sherman Cooper: October 2, 1974

Thruston B. Morton: October 2, 1974

Howard H. Baker Jr. Oral History Project, Howard H. Baker Jr. Center for Public Policy, University of Tennessee, Knoxville, Tennessee
John Chafee: July 23, 1993, November 14, 1995
John C. Danforth: July 20, 1993
John Deardourff: February 18, 1995
Mark Hatfield: February 21, 1997
Charles McC. Mathias: July 8, 1993, September 23, 1993
Robert Michel: April 19, 1995

Ronald Reagan Oral History Project, Miller Center for Public Affairs, University of Virginia
Peter J. Wallison: October 28–29, 2003

Washington State Oral History Program, Office of the Secretary of State, Olympia, Washington
Joel M. Pritchard: September 1996 to October 1997

INDEX